W. B. YEATS
AND
GEORGE YEATS

The Letters

W. B. YEATS

AND

GEORGE YEATS

The Letters

Edited by
ANN SADDLEMYER

OXFORD
UNIVERSITY PRESS

OXFORD

UNIVERSITY PRESS

Great Clarendon Street, Oxford OX2 6DP

Oxford University Press is a department of the University of Oxford.
It furthers the University's objective of excellence in research, scholarship,
and education by publishing worldwide in

Oxford New York

Auckland Cape Town Dar es Salaam Hong Kong Karachi
Kuala Lumpur Madrid Melbourne Mexico City Nairobi
New Delhi Shanghai Taipei Toronto

With offices in

Argentina Austria Brazil Chile Czech Republic France Greece
Guatemala Hungary Italy Japan Poland Portugal Singapore
South Korea Switzerland Thailand Turkey Ukraine Vietnam

Oxford is a registered trade mark of Oxford University Press
in the UK and in certain other countries

Published in the United States
by Oxford University Press Inc., New York

British Library Cataloguing in Publication Data

Data available

Library of Congress Cataloging in Publication Data

Library of Congress Control Number: 2010943333

Typeset by SPI Publisher Services, Pondicherry, India
Printed in Great Britain on acid-free paper by
Clays Ltd, St Ives plc

ISBN 978-0-19-818438-6

1 3 5 7 9 10 8 6 4 2

For Kevin B. Nowlan, friend,
adviser and colleague,
and in memory of Anne and
Michael Yeats

PREFACE

As she did with all her husband's manuscripts and papers (at least, those she could lay her hands on), George Yeats preserved their correspondence, scrupulously storing it in large brown envelopes. At the same time, while generously opening her home to scholars or 'seekers', she tried to protect her own privacy. As far as she was concerned, biography was not as important as the work—and wives and children had no place in that narrative. But she did preserve her letters, writing to her son in 1958, after suffering a demanding summer scholars' season, 'will think about my own letters to WBY, but do not think I shall change my mind. His to me will be handed over to you in a sealed package "do not open until after my death" (!)'.

Ten years later, after reading both sides of the correspondence, Michael and his sister Anne were determined that their parents' story should be told in their own words. But it was not until after the contract was signed for *The Collected Letters of William Butler Yeats* that Michael began to campaign for a separate edition of what became known as 'the marital correspondence', and asked me to be the editor. With the permission of John Kelly, general editor of *The Collected Letters*, and after the publication of biographies of W. B. Yeats by Roy Foster and mine of George Yeats, I began the slow work of transcription and annotation. I regret that neither Anne nor Michael is alive to see the completion, but as always I am grateful to them and to Gráinne Yeats and her children for the support and encouragement I have always enjoyed.

The delay in completing this edition has been in part because of circumstances beyond my control, but also because of the need for annotation in letters that covered not just the Irish world of family, arts, letters, theatre, politics, and society, but the wider arena in which the couple operated.

Included here are 149 letters from George, 436 from WBY, and 29 written to their children. Anne, who lived at home, preserved most cards and letters: 22 from her father and many important ones from her mother, of which some of the most significant are printed here; when both her parents were away, she became their link with Dublin, and it is revealing that WBY's final four letters in this collection are requests to her. Michael, who was a school boarder, appears to have saved only three messages from his father, probably rescued by George, and none from his mother. Some of George's letters were doubtless carelessly scattered by WBY during his travels, but only one has turned up elsewhere, in the Edith Shackleton Heald papers now at Harvard. But George, aware of their significance and in spite of the revelations concerning their private lives, loyally preserved all of his.

Why are these letters important? In some cases they offer biographical and historical corrections to the popular narrative of WBY's life, offering subtle indications of intention and commitments. There are drafts of poetry, statements of belief, unbuttoned descriptions of people and events, discussions of family and friends. Why did they write so many letters? Even during his later post-Steinach amorous adventures, WBY worked at sustaining a relationship, to continue a friendship with George. On her part, there was a clear determination to promote their partnership beyond her secretarial and administrative roles, to remind him of his family life, and to contribute to his creative work; through their letters and the occasional telegram or telephone call, both maintained a presence during absence. Despite the gradual change in mode and manner from endearment to familiarity, there was an acknowledgement that they needed each other. And always, beyond the free give and take of ideas, there was the added enjoyment of a good story to be told and appreciated. Like Oscar Wilde, WBY frequently practised a phrase or an anecdote to provide the best effect in his correspondence. And not for nothing would he write to his wife, 'you are much the best letter writer I know, or have known'.

ACKNOWLEDGEMENTS

Nothing can adequately convey my appreciation to the Yeats family, who have been generous and encouraging ever since Michael Yeats read the correspondence left by his mother and determined to have his parents' story told in their own words. My search for biographical details and appeals for information have been willingly helped by many friends and scholars, with a special debt of gratitude for the research already made available by John Kelly and Roy Foster, and Yeats scholars throughout the world. James McGuire and James Quinn and their colleagues of the Royal Irish Academy generously gave me advance access to the files for the *Dictionary of National Biography*; Chris Murray explored various routes to unearth difficult details; Colin Smythe as always generously made available his treasures and knowledge and on behalf of the Gregory estate granted permission to quote from Lady Gregory's papers; Lisa Bernadette Coen pursued details in Dublin and the west of Ireland; Warwick Gould and Deirdre Toomey continue to be a generous resource. Margaret Burwell, Kathleen Yeats McCawley, and Chris Yeats helped unravel the story of the Canadian branches of the Yeats family. I was assisted in my search by John D. Barrett, William Benzie, Eric Binnie, Nicola Gordon Bowe, Alan Browne, Deirdre Carroll, Yoko Chiba, Jared Curtis, Sister Mary de Lourdes Fahy, Alan Denson, Fiorenzo Fantaccini, Declan Foley, Elizabeth Grove-White, Margaret Mills Harper, Elizabeth Heine, Gordon Hickson, Jocelyn Hillgarth, Lloyd Howard, Denise Iredell, Robin Jeffrey, Anne Kelly, Tom Kenny, Clodagh Kingston, Catherine Leeney, Joseph McBrinn, James McConica, Sinead McCoole, Ciarán MacGonigal, Philip L. Marcus, Cameron Milliken, Maureen Murphy, the late William M. Murphy, Brendan O'Donoghue, Peadar O'Dowd, Edward O'Shea, Pádraig Ó Siadhail, Lois Overbeck, James Pethica, Maureen Russell, Michael J. Sidnell, Kate Slattery, Alexis Somarakis, Thomas Staley, Madeleine Stoops, Henry Summerfield, Donald J. West, and Barbara Wright. I am grateful to William Stoneman and the Houghton Library, Harvard University, for permission to publish a letter in their possession from George to WBY, and to the National Gallery of Ireland for permission to reproduce a letter and sketch by John Butler Yeats. The following representatives of institutions willingly answered my queries: Pauline Adams, Librarian and Archivist, Somerville College, Oxford; The Archivist, Garda Síochána Museum/Archives, Dublin Castle;

Alumni Office, Trinity College Dublin; Michelle Ashmore, National Museums Northern Ireland; Harold Averill, University of Toronto Archives; Leah Benson, Marie McFeely, and Louise Morgan, National Gallery of Ireland; Rita Boswell, Archivist, Harrow School; Janice Braun, Special Collections Curator, F. W. Olin Library, Mills College; Helen Carvalho, Queen's University Belfast; Francis Christie, Sothebys; Diane Clements, Freemasons Hall; Nancy Crisp, St Columba's College; Graham Davies, Lyme Regis Museum; Mairéad Delaney, Abbey Theatre Archivist, and her assistant Mairéad Lynch; June Ellner, Special Libraries and Archives, King's College University of Aberdeen; L. Garratt, Dorset History Centre; Society of Genealogists; Rachel Hart, University of St Andrews Library; Trish Hayes, BBC Written Archives Centre, Reading; David Horn and Justine Hyland, Boston College Library; Peter Horton, Reference Librarian, Royal College of Music; Adrian James and Sophy Jubb, St Paul's Church, Knightsbridge; Peter Keelan, Special Collections Library, Cardiff University; Norah Kelso and Evelyn McGovern of administration offices, and Aisling Lockhart, Trinity College Dublin; Elizabeth King, Royal Academy Library; Lambeth Palace Library; David Land, editor of the *Royal Photographic Society Journal*; Terese Lundin, National Archive of Sweden; Gavin McGuffie, *Guardian* and *Observer* archivist; Carrie Marsh, Special Collections, Honnold/Mudd Library, The Libraries of the Claremont Colleges; Lesley Martin, Chicago History Museum; Francis Maunze, Royal College of Psychiatrists; Robert W. Mills, Librarian, Royal College of Physicians of Ireland; National Portrait Gallery; Oxford University Archives; Sarah Phillips, Librarian and Archivist, Cardiff University; Prints and Drawings Department, British Museum; Tom Ruffles, Librarian, Society of Psychical Research; Hannah Sandford, The London Library; Nicholas Scheetz, Special Collections, Georgetown University Library; Molly Schwartzburg, Harry Ransom Center, University of Texas at Austin; Stephen Sendall, The Maddermarket Theatre, Norwich; David Smith, Librarian and Archivist, St Anne's College, Oxford; Diane Spaul, Victoria and Albert Museum; Claes Tellvid, National Archive of Sweden; Trinity College, Cambridge; University College of South Wales; Amelia Walker and Petr Hons, Wellcome Library, London; Janet Waudby, University of Hull; Westminster Cathedral. The staff in Special Collections and Interlibrary Loan at the University of Victoria have been helpful and accommodating as always.

I owe a special debt of gratitude to Hilary Thomas, who painstakingly and faithfully pursued an ongoing barrage of queries through endless newspaper files and local libraries; this edition, already long in the making, would not have appeared without her able assistance. As always Colin Smythe, Kevin B. Nowlan, Faith White, and Joan Coldwell have been supportive and illuminating.

As always too I have benefited from the assistance and encouragement of Linda Shaughnessy of A. P. Watt, who continue to serve as literary agents to the Yeats estate. And to the officers and editors of Oxford University Press, especially Ariane Petit and Kathleen Kerr, who steered this through to final publication, my thanks for your patience. Finally, my admiration and thanks to Jackie Pritchard for her scrupulous copy-editing, and to Ann Broughton for her care with the proofs.

CONTENTS

LIST OF PLATES

Unless indicated otherwise, all illustrations are reproduced by permission of Gráinne Yeats.

in occultism & has read the books. A Surprise to me & to the others.' [courtesy of the National Gallery of Ireland]

15. George Yeats with baby Michael, one month old, and Lily Yeats, taken by Lolly Yeats at Dundrum, September 1921

16. George Yeats's horary for 18 July 1923 before deciding to take charge of the embroidery section of Cuala during Lily Yeats's illness

17. The Yeatses in Algeciras, early November 1927, with Mrs Jean Hall (centre), a still from a film by John Hall [courtesy of Ann Saddlemyer]

18. Anne and Michael on the beach in Cannes, December 1927

19. 'L'Alpe Fleurie' in Villars sur Bex, Switzerland, where Anne and Michael went to school for three years from 1928

20. Michael at Villars sur Bex, photograph by George Yeats

21. Anne and Michael at Villars sur Bex, photograph by George Yeats

22. Anne and Michael on the beach in Rapallo

23. Anne in Dundrum, photograph by Lolly Yeats

24. W. B. Yeats and Joseph Hone at 'Sorrento', home of Lennox Robinson in Dalkey, during a Dublin Drama League performance of Euripides' *Ulysses*, summer of 1926

25. George with Michael and his godfather Lennox Robinson

26. Anne at Gurteen Dhas with Aunt Lily in the doorway, Easter Saturday 1928, photograph by Lolly Yeats

27. W. B. Yeats to 'Dobbs' (George Yeats), 26 August 1928

28. Michael at Gurteen Dhas, photograph by Lolly Yeats

29. Three street photographs of George and W. B. Yeats

30. Studio portrait of Anne and Michael 1929 [photograph by Graphic Studio, Dublin]

31. W. B. Yeats and Jack B. Yeats leaving Gurteen Dhas after a tea party, photograph by Lolly Yeats

32. W. B. Yeats delivering his first BBC Belfast broadcast, September 1931 [photograph by A. R. Hogg, 81 High Street, Belfast]

33. W. B. Yeats and Shri Purohit Swami in Majorca, 1936

34. Anne Yeats's designs for the Abbey Theatre production of her father's play *On Baile's Strand*, 1938

35. George and Willy's last resting place in Drumcliffe churchyard [photograph © Keith Parsons]

EMBEDDED IMAGES

NOTES ON EDITORIAL PRINCIPLES

I have transcribed the letters as written, including WBY's eccentric spelling, spacing, and punctuation, editing as little as possible so that the speed of thought might be unhindered. Where the meaning would remain too obscure, editorial emendations are indicated by square brackets. When passages are struck out but can be deciphered, these are indicated by < >. I have however silently corrected obvious typing errors and erratic spacing in GY's typescripts, while retaining any unique spelling or punctuation such as the two points occasionally added for emphasis. Salutations and signatures ('yrs scly', 'yrs affly', 'yrs affecly', 'yrs', etc.) are as written. It is worth noting that WBY nearly always signed his name the same way, 'WB Yeats' with the WB closed together, while GY made use of 'George', 'G', 'GY', and her childhood pet name 'Dobbs'. All who have worked on Yeats's manuscripts will appreciate the difficulties in deciphering his hand; his wife was probably the most adept at grasping his meaning. Her writing, even when arthritis afflicted her, was always remarkably strong and clear.

CONCERNING ANNOTATIONS

Familiar and well-known individuals and places are given brief identification, emphasizing those details that apply in the context of the letter; the bulk of the annotations are devoted to identifying people and events essential to an understanding of the correspondence. Unfortunately, there are some people I was unable to trace.

MANUSCRIPT SOURCES

With the exception of one letter from GY to WBY, 6 November 1938, in the Houghton Library, bMS Eng 338.12 (3), and one telegram from WBY to GY, 21 June 1937, published in John Unterecker, *Yeats and Patrick McCartan: A Fenian Friendship* (Dublin, 1965), 402, all correspondence so far discovered between George and W. B. Yeats and with their children is in the hands of Gráinne Yeats, Dublin, and is published with her generous permission. Unless otherwise indicated, GY's letters to others are also in the hands of the family. Twenty-two letters from George when WBY was at Coole during Lady Gregory's final year (31 July, 15, 16, 26, 29, 30 or 31 October, 1, 3, 18, 24, 27 November, 15 or 20 and 22 December 1931, 2, 4, 21, 25 January, 1 and 29 February, 2 and 19 March, 12 April 1932) were previously edited by me and published as '"Yours Affly, Dobbs": George Yeats to her Husband, Winter 1931–32' in Susan Dick, Declan Kiberd, Dougald McMillan, and Joseph Ronsley (eds.), *Essays for Richard Ellmann: Omnium Gatherum* (Kingston, 1989), 280–303.

The following abbreviations are used in the description of each letter:

AL   unsigned autograph letter
ALCS   autograph lettercard signed
ALS   autograph letter signed
APS   autograph postcard signed
Dict   dictated
Encl   enclosure
Frag   fragment
MS   manuscript
Tel   telegram
TL   unsigned typed letter
TLS   typed letter signed

ABBREVIATIONS AND SHORT FORMS

ABY	Anne Butler Yeats
AE	George William Russell
AG	Augusta Gregory
DDL	Dublin Drama League
DP	Dorothy Shakespear Pound
DW	Dorothy Wellesley
ECY	Elizabeth Corbet Yeats (Lolly)
EET	Edith Ellen Tucker (Nelly, '17')
EP	Ezra Pound
GHL	Georgie Hyde Lees
GY	George Yeats
HTT	Henry Tudor Tucker (Bunk, Harry)
IG	Iseult Gonne Stuart (Maurice)
JackBY	Jack Butler Yeats
JBY	John Butler Yeats
LR	Lennox Robinson
MBY	Michael Butler Yeats
MG	Maud Gonne MacBride (Moura)
OS	Olivia Shakespear
SMY	Susan Mary Yeats (Lily)
TCD	Trinity College Dublin (University of Dublin)
TD	Teachta Dála, member of Dáil Éireann
WBY	W. B. Yeats

PRINCIPAL SOURCES CITED OR QUOTED

BG Ann Saddlemyer, *Becoming George: The Life of Mrs W. B. Yeats* (Oxford, 2002)

CL I, II, III, IV *The Collected Letters of W. B. Yeats*, gen. ed. John Kelly (Oxford, 1986–2005)

CL InteLex *The Collected Letters of W. B. Yeats*, gen. ed. John Kelly (Oxford University Press (InteLex Electronic Edition), 2002)

Foster i, ii R. F. Foster, *W. B. Yeats: A Life*, i: *The Apprentice Mage* (Oxford, 1997); ii: *The Arch-Poet* (Oxford, 2003)

G–YL *The Gonne–Yeats Letters 1893–1938*, ed. Anna MacBride White and A. Norman Jeffares (London, 1992)

Journals *Lady Gregory's Journals*, i, ii, ed. Daniel J. Murphy (Gerrards Cross, 1978)

LWBY 1, 2 *Letters to W. B. Yeats*, ed. Richard J. Finneran, George Mills Harper, and William M. Murphy (London, 1977)

LWBYEP *Letters to W. B. Yeats and Ezra Pound from Iseult Gonne*, ed. A. Norman Jeffares, Anna MacBride White, and Christina Bridgewater (New York, 2004)

Stonybrook W. B. Yeats microfilmed manuscripts collection at Stonybrook University Special Collections and Archives

Vision A W. B. Yeats, *A Critical Edition of Yeats's 'A Vision' (1925)*, ed. George Mills Harper and Walter Kelly Hood (London, 1978)

Wade *The Letters of W. B. Yeats*, ed. Allan Wade (London, 1954)

Yeats Library Edward O'Shea, *A Descriptive Catalog of W. B. Yeats's Library* (New York, 1985)

YVP i, ii, iii *Yeats's Vision Papers*, ed. George Mills Harper et al., 3 vols. (Iowa City, 1992)

YVP iv *Yeats's Vision Papers*, vol. iv, ed. George Mills Harper and Margaret Mills Harper, assisted by Richard W. Stoops, Jr. (Basingstoke, 2001)

GENERAL INTRODUCTION

Although they belonged to the same social circle, Georgie Hyde Lees (1892–1968), known as 'Dobbs' to her family and close friends, and William Butler Yeats (1865–1939), 'Willy' to his own family, were not introduced until May 1911. George Yeats was certain of the date, recalling the occasion many years later for Virginia Moore: 'one morning when her mother thought she was at art school, she went to the British Museum, where she saw Yeats rush past her like a meteor; and that very afternoon, taking tea with her mother at Olivia Shakespear's, was formally introduced.'[1] At the time Georgie was studying at Heatherley's School of Art in London, and enjoying occasional sketching adventures elsewhere with her close companion Dorothy Shakespear, Olivia's only child. Yeats was living in Woburn Buildings, but spending considerable time in Ireland between the Abbey Theatre in Dublin and Lady Gregory's demesne in Coole Park, while making periodic visits to Maud Gonne MacBride in France.

Their introduction was inevitable: in February 1911 Georgie's widowed mother had married Olivia Shakespear's beloved brother Harry Tucker, whom she had known for at least five years; Yeats and Olivia[2] were lovers in the 1890s, renewed their friendship in 1900, and very likely renewed their affair briefly in 1910. When Ezra Pound arrived in London in 1909, he soon became part of the Shakespear retinue, and captivated Dorothy whom he would marry five years later. By 1912 Yeats was staying with the Tuckers in Margate, then later that year and again the next joined them in Lynton, north Devon, with Olivia and Dorothy. Everybody was attending exhibitions by Jack B. Yeats and performances by the Abbey players in London; 'step-cousins' Georgie and Dorothy dutifully joined their mothers in the social round of afternoon teas and soirées where talented musicians performed and poets read; and Ezra and Dorothy brought their younger friend to Yeats's Monday evenings in Woburn Buildings.

Georgie and WBY were soon meeting in other more arcane circles also. Already familiar with the writings of the philosopher William James and of Madame Blavatsky, who had previously initiated Yeats in theosophical research, Georgie joined Rudolf Steiner's Anthroposophical Society after the

---

[1] Virginia Moore, *The Unicorn: W. B. Yeats' Search for Reality* (New York, 1954), 229.

[2] Olivia Shakespear, née Tucker (1863–1938), novelist and lifelong friend to both the Yeatses, whose marriage she encouraged, was referred to in WBY's autobiographies as 'Diana Vernon'.

London lodge was founded in 1912, and while on holiday in Italy with Olivia and Dorothy in 1913 she bought Latin works on the Cabbala; back in London she was studying Dante and Plotinus.[3] Then for two weeks in August 1913 WBY joined Georgie and the Tuckers at The Prelude, a house in Ashdown Forest. Full of excitement over the automatic script of Elizabeth Radcliffe, who had been introduced to him by a mutual friend, he sought advice from all on abstruse references in Bessie's script. The first tentative beginning to this correspondence therefore offers a picture of Georgie as eager researcher. We know from notes on horaries and horoscopes that WBY trusted her astrological skills, but for the next four years any further correspondence disappeared or is hidden among the welter of papers concerning his study of the occult, and the efforts of both to understand the relationship between the seen and unseen. From references in George's own automatic script we know that their paths crossed more and more frequently at séances; when she reached the requisite age of 21 she asked him to sponsor her membership in the Order of Golden Dawn, where they met more regularly. In 1914 her closest friend Dorothy Shakespear married Ezra Pound, and Georgie became more involved in Yeats's London circle. It was not long before she seems to have determined to marry WBY and take possession of Ballylee, the Norman tower Yeats was negotiating to purchase near Coole, Lady Gregory's home in the west of Ireland, sketches of which he flourished among his women friends.

But the well-worn story of his renewed courtship of Maud Gonne, then of her daughter Iseult, interrupted their friendship.[4] It was not until September 1917 that WBY turned back to Georgie (as she was still called) and the prospect of marriage. Records of their first years together are one-sided, for during their brief courtship Georgie remained silent, refusing to answer her lover's requests for replies, and although we know that she did eventually write to him, those early letters are missing. The first preserved here is from 1920, after their move to Oxford, the birth of their daughter, and WBY's hasty mission to Ireland to rescue Iseult from an unhappy marriage. No matter, for almost daily during those first three years of their marriage she was indeed writing to him, creating a dialogue through the medium of automatic writing.[5] Particularly illuminating are the discussions that followed the making of *A Vision*, for unlike the automatic script itself these reveal the logic of argument and elaboration of thought based on their many years of study and searching questions.

These letters cover their entire married life; whenever they were apart, for whatever reason, the conversation kept going. They offer in themselves a story of the marriage of two minds and the world they created.

---

[3] *BG*, ch. 4 discusses in detail GHL's early studies in the occult.

[4] See espec. Foster ii, chs. 1 and 2; *BG*, 87–92.

[5] See *BG*, Foster ii, *YVP* i, ii, iii, and *A Vision* for details of the automatic script, a method of trance writing, in the Yeatses' case evoked by a series of prepared questions.

Part One

Beginnings

1913–1917

In May 1913 Maud Gonne wrote to WBY, 'you are thinking dangerously much about a wife,' to which he replied gloomily, 'A mistress cannot give one a home & a home I shall never have.'[1] As if in answer to his fears, only a few months later Georgie Hyde Lees purchased WBY's volume of essays *The Celtic Twilight* and wrote inside the back cover the prophetic lines from the Book of Joel 2:28, 'your young men shall see visions; your old men shall dream dreams.'[2]

Appropriately, this edition begins with the report of Georgie Hyde Lees's first trip to the British Museum, having received her card for the purpose of 'reading all available literature on the religious history of the 1st 3 centuries A.D.' She put that extensive study to good use in preparation for her admission the following year into the Order of the Golden Dawn, choosing as her motto 'Nemo Sciat' ('Let Nobody Know'). Soon WBY was consulting her concerning horoscopes, and some time, perhaps as early as November 1915, that discussion included the possibility of marriage. But the next few years were ones of tumult both personally and nationally: Georgie joined the Red Cross as a voluntary aid; WBY careened back and forth between the Gonnes in France and various theatrical ventures including the production of *At the Hawk's Well* in London. In March 1917 he claimed possession of Ballylee; now he needed a wife.

His letters to Georgie (she is not yet George) begin with those arrangements.

[1] *G–YL*, 320.
[2] A few months earlier she had copied the same quotation (also in Acts 2:17) inside the cover of a recent purchase, Michael de Molinos, *The Spiritual Guide which Disentangles the Soul*, ed. Kathleen Lyttleton (London, 1911). Both books are in the Yeats Library, now in the National Library of Ireland.

1913

[ALS]   [16 Montpelier Square, London SW
                                                      *c.*18 Nov. 1913[1]]

                    Concerning Anna Luise Karschin.[2]

There is no evidence in any biography, biographical sketch or other source,
of Karschin's having belonged to any mysticall society. She seems to have
had no inner mysticale life, but to have been religious & a good church-
woman. Schlichtegroll says of her that she was very reserved, & that no one
knew much of her life, save the externals.[3]

Three letters from Goethe to K., none of particular interest.[4] He is writing
to her in 1775–6–7 & visits her in 1778 on which occasion she writes him a
poem.[5] (she was then 56, G:29)

Till she goes to Berlin in 1761 K. had but little education & few books.
There is no mention of Goethe's having met her <u>before</u> 1778 & her correspondance & acquaintance with him is not mentioned in any written matter
concerning her life.

If details of G's letters or other matters are of any use to you, or you want
anything else looked up, send me a post card.

                                                      <u>G. Hyde Lees</u>

   [1] GHL, whose application was sponsored by the novelist and playwright Richard Pryce
(1864–1942), a neighbour of her mother and stepfather, received her reader's ticket from the
British Museum on 18 November 1913.
   [2] Elizabeth Radcliffe's automatic script—which WBY was avidly studying while visiting the
Tuckers at The Prelude, Coleman's Hatch, Sussex in August 1913—had included the name of
the German poet Anna Louisa Karsch ('die Karschin') (1722–91); hailed in the critical fashion
of the period as 'the German Sappho', she first became famous for her celebration of the
exploits of Friedrich II. For Radcliffe see introduction and letter 29 Nov. 1925 below.
   [3] Adolf Heinrich Friedrich Schlichtegroll (1765–1822), a philologist, was editor of the annual
Nekrolog der Deutschen.
   [4] Johann Wolfgang von Goethe (1749–1832), German poet, playwright and philosopher
of the German Romantic period, at the time of his meetings with Karsch was chief political
adviser to the Duke of Saxe-Weimar and had recently completed *The Sorrows of Young Werther*
(1774); Radcliffe's automatic script had quoted lines from Goethe's poetry and a passage from
Faust.
   [5] Her poem dated 18 May 1778 begins 'Schön' guten Morgen, Herr Doktor Goeth!'

1917

[ALS]   STEPHEN'S GREEN CLUB, | DUBLIN.
                                              Oct 3 [1917]

My beloved: I forgot that wretched sugar card after all. I have now filled it
up.[1] Will you be very kind & ask a policeman what is the food office for the
neighbourhood of St Pancras & post it. Probably it is enough to write 'St
Pancras' on the blank space & put into the nearest pillar box to where you
live.[2] I cannot it seems post it here

I am sorry to give you this trouble & yet glad too. It makes me think of
the time when I shall find you, when my work is over, sitting at the gass fire
or dealing firmly with Mrs Old.[3] As the train passed through Wales I noticed
a little house at the road side & thought of Stone Cottage[4] & myself walking
home from the post to find you at the tea table.

I had a stormy passage. I shall dine in a few minuites & then go down to
the Abbey Theatre. I go to Galway at 7 to morrow morning.[5]

                                              Yours with love
                                              WB Yeats

[ALS]   Coole Park | Gort | Co Galway | Ireland
                                              Oct 4 [1917]

My beloved: I arrived an hour ago. The masons are at work at Ballylee.[1]
Lady Gregory[2] thinks that we should get married as soon as possible & that

---

[1] During the First World War ration cards were distributed by the local borough, in WBY's
case St Pancras, where his flat in Woburn Buildings was situated.

[2] To satisfy the fifteen days' residence requirements for their marriage to take place at Harrow Road Registry Office in Paddington, GHL had moved to 21 Kildare Gardens.

[3] Sarah Martha Old (1855–1939) was WBY's housekeeper in his rooms in 18 Woburn
Buildings, owned by her husband Thomas Old (1842–1921); see *CL II*, 725–32 for an excellent
description of WBY's years in his London residence.

[4] He and GHL planned to spend their honeymoon at Stone Cottage, the cottage in Sussex
which WBY had discovered while visiting the Tuckers at nearby Prelude, and which for three
winters he rented for himself and Ezra Pound.

[5] WBY was en route to Coole to seek Augusta Gregory's support for their marriage; he
may have realized that a letter from GHL's mother had already reached Coole, requesting
that Gregory persuade WBY to cancel the engagement; see *BG*, 92–5.

[1] Ballylee Castle, later renamed Thoor Ballylee, the old square Norman keep WBY had
purchased from the Gregory family in May 1917 after much negotiation with the Congested
Districts Board and which he was at last in the process of restoring.

[2] Isabella Augusta Gregory née Persse (1852–1932), playwright, essayist, and biographer,
who had provided WBY with a second home at Coole Park since the late 1890s, was not

I should bring you here before the weather grows very cold & gloomy that we may make our Ballylee plans to gether while the Castle looks well. She does not want us however till we are married—that one candle being I think the danger, or at least what the neighbours might say about the possible number of our candles. I was in the theatre last night, & I know that to day or to morrow Lady Gregory will show me a list of proposed plays with several [o]f mine. I shall cross mine off the list, for this winter at least I will have no rehersals to distract us. We shall be together in the country, here I hope & in Stone Cottage & then we shall be alone in France & Italy.³ You found me amid crowds but you will lead me to lonely places. Let us begin at once our life of study, of common interests & hopes. Lady Gregory is very pleased at the thought of our marriage, & thinks it the best thing that could have be fallen me. I grow more fond of you every time we meet, but never quite escape my dread of that old intreaguer Neptune.⁴ I shall have no ease of mind till he has been finally put to <the> rout. Lady Gregory is writing to your mother & I think her letter will compell him to take his trident out of our flesh.⁵ You will soon see me again—what day I cannot say till I have had another talk with Lady Gregory & learn what necessary business there is, if there is any. There are generally a few plays which I have to be read— and then I long to recieve from you one of [or] two letters. Remember you have never yet written to me. I think I must go down stairs as I am to row the children⁶ a cross the lake. I kiss your hands

Yours affectionly
WB Yeats

only a co-director of the Abbey Theatre but his closest friend and confidante, collaborator, frequently his typist, and sometimes his patron; she had long wished to find WBY a suitable wife, though GHL had apparently not been on her list of eligible young women.

³ GHL in particular was anxious to return to Florence, where she had been happy as a child; WBY had for some time been contemplating a lecture tour of France and Italy.

⁴ Both of them were concerned about a horary drawn up by WBY after a momentous meeting between them on 18 Mar. 1917 which suggested 'man and woman in full sympathy but deception pulls them apart', Neptune promising the deception.

⁵ Edith Ellen ('Nelly') Tucker (1868–1942), née Woodmass, had married as her second husband Olivia Shakespear's brother Henry Tudor ('Harry') Tucker (1866–1943) in 1911. On 30 September, four days after GHL accepted WBY's proposal, EET was sufficiently distressed by her daughter's unease that she wrote to AG asking that she discourage the marriage; AG's reply was apparently satisfactory (*BG*, 93–5).

⁶ AG's grandchildren Richard Graham Gregory (1909–81), Augusta Anne Gregory, later Mrs Robert William Michael de Winton (1911–2008), and Catherine Francis Gregory, later Mrs Robert Kennedy (1913–2000), who spent much of their childhood at Coole, a time vividly recalled by Anne Gregory de Winton in *Me and Nu* (Gerrards Cross, 1970).

[ALS]   COOLE PARK, | GORT, | CO. GALWAY.
                                                       Oct 5 [1917]

My beloved: My thoughts are always with you—at first you were but a plan &
a dream & then you became a real woman, & then all in a moment that real
woman became very dear. And now I watch every post for your first letter.
I keep wondering how you will begin it, what you will say. I cannot yet say
upon what date I shall return to you. I have to read eight plays & that seems
to be all there is to do.—that and to decide on the theatre programme. This
after noon I drive to Ballylee to give some directions to the workmen. Lady
Gregory comes with me. I have slipped into my old routine, writing from 11 to
2 & then again after five. Last night my first night here was difficult for dark
comes on early, & after a very little writing I must sit with my hands before
me grudging the passing hours to empty talk with a couple of not interesting
visitors. O my dear child if you can add your eyes to mine we will do to gether
fine & stirring things. Endless hours will be saved from shere non-being. I kiss
the tops of your fingers where they are marked by the acid[1]

                                                         Yrs affecly
                                                         WBY.

[ALS]   COOLE PARK, | GORT, | CO. GALWAY.
                                                       Oct 6 [1917]

My beloved: No letter yet from you. <&> I keep wondering how you will
begin the letter which seems full of mystery. A letter has come from Maud
Gonne praising you. She calls you 'charming'…graceful and beautiful'. and
adds 'I think she has an intense spiritual life of her own and on this side you
must be careful not to disappoint her…Iseult likes her very much & Iseult is
difficult & does not take to everybody'[1] She is sure that you & I will be very
happy. I have noticed that though she judges badly when she uses her intellect
she judges subtly & truly when as as now she uses her intuition & sympathy.

[1] Probably an accident occurred while GHL was nursing in a London hospital with the
Voluntary Aid Detachment Programme; she withdrew from active duties with the Red Cross
in August 1917.

[1] WBY's sometime lover Maud Gonne (1866–1953), whose marriage in 1903 to Major John
MacBride altered but did not diminish WBY's romantic obsession, had rejected his marriage
proposal once again in 1916 after her estranged husband's death; WBY then proposed marriage to her daughter Iseult (1894–1954), and when she too refused him in 1917, he turned
to GHL (*BG*, 85–92; A. Norman Jeffares, 'Iseult Gonne', in Warwick Gould (ed.), *Poems and
Contexts: Yeats Annual No. 16: A Special Number* (Basingstoke, 2005), 197–278). MG was in London
where she had taken a flat for six months in the King's Road while agitating to be allowed to
return to Ireland; WBY must have introduced GHL to MG and IG about 2 Oct. 1917, just
before he sailed for Ireland (*G-YL*, 392–3).

I went to Ballylee yesterday to see the men at work on the cottage—mudd & litter ever[y]where & thought it was a pity you would see it in no better weather. It looks so different in spring with the island full of daffadils—but then spring may find us in Italy. They think they may get the roof on the castle some time in November. I have tried to start an essay (the one for Per Amica Silentia Lunae[2]) & could not & then a poem & could not. I am therefore but reading plays. Ah dear you are in my blood & I must get back to you. Perhaps to morrow will bring a letter from your mother settling all.[3] To morrow at any rate I will decide what day we are to meet again—Tuesday perhaps. I shall be almost at peace when I see you though only the day when we begin to be to gether always shall give me full peace.

Yours with love
WBY

[ALS]   COOLE PARK, | GORT, | CO. GALWAY.
Oct 7 [1917]

My beloved: I am sad that there is no letter and perhaps I shall not get one at all for I go to Dublin to morrow. I have asked the architect[1] to wire if he can see me. If he can I shall not cross to England until Tuesday. If he cannot I shall go straight through & if you could hear the wind howling in the chimney you would know how great is my longing to see you. I shall have a damnable crossing. This seperation has made you dearer to me—& strangely disquieting. Years ago knowing that I had ♂ in my VII I feared your strong magnetism. I know now that the strong magnetism is not a thing to dread but a foundation for lasting love. Did you notice that ♀ ♂ ♂ and △ ♄ & ♀ [is] in mutual reception with ♃?[2] When I hear this howling wind

[2] The essay he was probably proof-reading when he went to Crowborough, East Sussex, to propose to GHL; it contained a prologue and epilogue addressed in easy, familiar terms to 'Maurice' (IG) and was published 18 Jan. 1918.

[3] EET's mollified reply to AG of 9 October asks that GHL not be informed of their correspondence.

[1] William Alphonsus Scott (1871–1921), Professor of Architecture at the National University and the acknowledged expert of the Arts and Crafts movement as it flourished in Ireland, had already completed commissions for the Gore-Booth family and Edward Martyn, who had introduced Scott to WBY (Nicola Gordon Bowe and Elizabeth Cumming, *The Arts & Crafts Movements in Dublin & Edinburgh* 1885–1925 (Dublin, 1998), 190–1). According to a letter from Gogarty to AG 1 May 1917, Scott's work on Ballylee was without charge (Berg).

[2] Astrological symbols for Mars in his seventh house; Venus conjoining Mars and trining Saturn and Venus in mutual reception with Jupiter. Both WBY and GHL were accomplished astrologers and this reading promised a union of good fortune: the Venus Mars conjunction with Venus and Jupiter, in signs which are each ruled by the other, harked back to horoscopes

I no longer wish you to come to Ireland. I think we will go straight to Stone Cottage & then when I have roofed & cleared the castle you can come & see it & add what you will & add nothing at all if it does not please you. When we come from Italy, if we return at all before the end of the war, it will be surrounded by green boughs & wild flowers. O my dearest I kiss your hands full of gratitude & affection—do not draw them away while my lips are still hungry. Am I not Sinbad thrown upon the rocks & weary of the seas?³ I will live for my work & your happiness & when we are dead our names shall be rem[em]bered—perhaps we shall become a part of the strange legendary life of this country. My work shall become yours and yours mine & do not think that because your body and your strong bones fill me with desire that I do not seek also the secret things of the soul That magnetic ♂ will not make me the less the student of your soul.

Yours always
WBY

PS. Probably—for Scott the architect will probably forget to send the wire I have asked for—I shall be in London when this reaches you. Unless I wire from Dublin I shall go to see you at the first possible moment—before noon certainly.

[ALS]   [London]
16 Oct [1917]¹

My beloved: I was so sorry not to have seen you to day. I wanted to tell you that I did not mean to chaff you last night about Maccheavele.² I got up all that discussion about books in youth to get you to explain your liking. But you were too modest—you had not our gay self-assertion. You are only confident I think in the service of others

Tomorrow at 3

Yours always
WBY.

cast for 18 and 20 March, when marriage had been discussed earlier that year (and Moon was in opposition to Neptune). Woman's Mars to man's Moon suggests a less passive role for her in the seventh house of partnership; while the fortunate trine of Venus with Saturn was a reminder of the grand trines they shared in their natal horoscopes.

³ Stories from *The Arabian Nights*, especially the tale of Sinbad the Sailor, became a leitmotif in WBY's letters and poems to his wife; see also 'A Prayer on Going into my House'.

¹ WBY may not have been aware that this was GHL's 25th birthday.

² As WBY would soon discover, GHL's reading was as extensive as his own, including the Renaissance political philosopher Niccolò Machiavelli (1469–1527); see *BG*, chs. 4, 5.

Part Two
Family Matters
1918–1921

Georgie and WBY were married on 20 October 1917 in the Harrow Road Registry Office, Paddington, with Ezra Pound and Georgie's mother as witnesses. Their honeymoon was spent in Sussex, first in the Ashdown Forest Hotel and then in Stone Cottage, just down the road from The Prelude where they had together pored over Bessie Radcliffe's automatic script in 1914. Almost immediately young Mrs W. B. Yeats was also involved in automatic writing, after some experiments producing 'a very profound, very exciting mystical philosophy' which her excited husband was hammering into dialogue form.[1] London was too busy, and the air raids dangerously close to Woburn Buildings, so they decided to rent a house in Oxford until Ballylee would be ready to inhabit. They had many visitors from London, and among their guests was Maud's daughter Iseult, whom Georgie had befriended; the Gonne family would remain a concern for many years, especially after Iseult's marriage.

It is now, close to the Bodleian Library, that their 'life of study' began in earnest. So did their travels, for after a summer in Ballylee where they began to collect the animals as part of their permanent household, they went to Dublin so that their first child could be born in Ireland. Almost immediately after their return to Oxford they embarked for the United States, leaving baby Anne in Ireland in the care of Lily Yeats. In New York, while WBY was engaged in a successful lecture tour, George met her father-in-law for the first and last time. Through all of their travels around America, the automatic writing and other enquiries into the supernatural continued.

[1] Wade, 643–4.

1918

Ballinamantan House | Gort | Co Galway[1]
May 28 [1918]

My dear George:[2] When I went to Coole yesterday I found Edmonds &
asked him about the bit of land & the wall. He put a knot on his handker-
chief to remind him about the land and promised the wall at once.[3] He says
'there was no plot' but Loydd George 'had to invent it to get the Shinn-
Feiners arrested' & so far from expecting, as Loydd George said, the man in
the collapsable boat 'one of my own coast-guards invited him to breakfast &
lent him money. He must be a half-lunatic to have landed where he did'[4]

I have had a long letter from poor Maurice which <explains itself> I have
not yet replied to. I imagine your money arrived in the nick of time. Moura[5]
is in Holloway and Shawn[6] is in the flat, as the family are in a great state

---

[1] While waiting for Ballylee to be made habitable, they had accepted AG's offer to rent
Ballinamantan, the dower house opposite the road into Coole, close enough to keep watch
over the builders.

[2] Christened Bertha Georgie Hyde Lees, by the time she was 21 GHL was occasionally
signing her name 'George Hyde Lees'. On 25 Nov. 1917 WBY wrote to Lady Gregory, 'We
have abolished Georgie—she is now George', but she continued to alternate her signature
between 'Georgie' and 'George' until well into the 1930s, and when necessary elsewhere for
legal purposes.

[3] Leslie Wynne Edmunds (1872–1922), chief inspector in Galway for the Congested Districts
Board, was responsible for deciding the boundary of the acre surrounding Ballylee; it was
agreed that a wall was to be built separating the Castle grounds from the public way through
the original castle yard over the bridge, and that the picturesque stepping stones on the other
side of the island be retained. Edmunds was killed when he ran into an ambush near Galway
in July 1922. I am indebted to Dr Christopher Murray for information concerning Edmunds.

[4] On 17 May MG, who had escaped to Ireland although forbidden to do so by the British
authorities, was arrested and sent with other Sinn Féin sympathizers back to England under
threat of a 'German plot' which had apparently been concocted to silence anti-conscription.
David Lloyd George (1863–1945; elevated to the peerage as Earl Lloyd-George of Dwyfor in
1945) was Liberal Prime Minister 1916–22. De Valera's biographers identify the supposed spy
as 'a brother-in-law of Mrs de Valera' (The Earl of Longford and Thomas P. O'Neill, Éamon
de Valera (Dublin, 1970), 77).

[5] IG's name for her mother (a transposition of 'Amour'), adopted by friends and family.

[6] MG's son Séan MacBride (1904–88), who became chief of staff of the IRA (1936–7) while
studying at the Bar, later founded Clann na Poblachta ('the party of the republic') and served
as Minister for External Affairs in the first Inter-Party Government (1948–51); a signatory
of the 1950 European Convention for the Protection of Human Rights, a founder member
of Amnesty International, member of the Irish Representative to the Council of Europe
Assembly, Secretary-General of the International Commission of Jurists (1963–70), and United
Nations Commissioner to Namibia; he was awarded the Nobel Peace Prize in 1976 and the
Lenin Peace Prize in 1977.

of excited politics. She cannot think of the 'little Review' or anything but the problem of the moment. She has taken a weeks holiday 'on grounds of fatigue' to attend to matters, & knew nothing but what she saw in papers until she got our wire & letters she says 'thank Georgie for her sweet letter to me.'[7] She wrote on May 25.

I have finished my medieval history & shall take to Spinoza[8] & letter writing until your return. I miss you beyond words & have carefully watered your seeds on the window sill as the only form of attention I can show you & am now going to the garden to water the rest. They do not require watering but I am doing it to satisfy my feelings so they must endure it. You will come in for 'a little bit of youth' at the Abbey an amusing play we passed at Glendalough I think.[9]

I <enclose> send on a letter which is I suppose from your mother— nothing else has come.

Yours with love
WB Yeats

[ALS]   Ballinamantan House | Gort | Co Galway
                                              May 28 [1918]

My dearest: here is Maurices letter which I have now answered.[1] I did not think I could do so before post. I think the Oxford project will not come off as Moura will refuse to leave London where she can see MPs

---

[7] WBY had secured a position for IG ('Maurice') at the School for Oriental Languages, but, worried that MG would not have made financial arrangements for her family, GY had sent £5 to IG 'for emergencies' and invited her to join them and her brother Séan in Galway; WBY meanwhile was discussing with EP the possibility of IG working as his secretary for the *Little Review*, of which he was foreign editor, he and GY offering to pay her salary.

[8] Evidently study in relation to the philosophy they were developing out of GY's automatic writing. WBY's library in the 1920s contained the 1916 edition of *Ethics and de Intellectus Emendatione* by the Rationalist philosopher Benedict de Spinoza (1632–77), a provocative and monumental work identifying God with Nature (see Edward O'Shea, 'The 1920s Catalogue of W. B. Yeats's Library', in Warwick Gould (ed.), *Yeats Annual No. 4* (Basingstoke, 1986), 279–90).

[9] Although suffering from a 'raging toothache', GY managed to attend Christian Callister's one-act comedy *A Little Bit of Youth*, produced by Fred O'Donovan (1889–1952) at the Abbey Theatre, entertain her two sisters-in-law, buy furniture for Ballylee, enquire of MG's friends about the MacBrides' welfare, and examine MSS in the National Library.

[1] IG's letter of 5 May 1918 from 54 Beaufort Mansions in Chelsea describes MG's incarceration in Holloway prison and her dislike of life in London with its 'uncompromising jingoism', but insists that she cannot think of leaving while MG is in Holloway and expresses a wish to take her mother to live in Oxford, 'a quiet safe place' (see *LWBYEP*, 102–3); WBY's reply has not survived.

& the like. However I am afraid her evading D.O.R.A may now delay her release.[2]

I am just sending Norah[3] to the post.

Yours with love
WB Yeats

[ALS]   Ballinamantan House | Gort | Co Galway
                                            Thursday [30 May 1918]

My dear: Your two letters dated Monday & Tuesday came this morning.[1] Both very good letters—vivid & wise. The worst of it is that your account of the acting of 'A little bit of youth' makes it the more desirable that I should stay for a while in Dublin while your absence from me now makes it seem quite impossible. I cannot bear the thought of being away from you again. I say to myself every day that is one day less of parting, she will be home in so many days. I have done nothing but tidy the table & read my books & discuss with Lady Gregory the new stanza that is to commend Robert's courage in the hunting field.[2] It has been a little thorny but we have settled a compromise. I have got from her a list of musical place-names where he has hunted & hope for a new representation of the place. I have firmly resisted all suggested eloquence about Aero planes '& the blue Italian sky'. It is pathetic for Lady Gregory constantly says 'it is his monument—all that remains' I see that she feels that his pictures are as it were his thought but not himself.

I wonder how Maurice will struggle with Mrs Old—I am afraid that she will never keep the book down Barry might have done so.[3] I wonder if they

---

[2] WBY and other friends were lobbying to have MG released from Holloway on the grounds of ill health, and GY and WBY had offered the house in Oxford that GY had recently rented; the Defence of the Realm Act (1915–21) gave sweeping powers of arrest to Dublin Castle authorities in an effort to prevent collaboration between Irish revolutionaries and Germany during the First World War but later used to suppress suspect Irish revolutionary organizations.

[3] Nora Dooley (1882–1979), daughter of AG's land steward Michael 'Mike' Dooley (1853–1923) who lived in the Gate Lodge at Coole, was the first housekeeper GY hired on her arrival at Ballinamantan. Nora later married Jack Quinn of the nearby township of Corker and emigrated.

[1] These letters are missing.

[2] To commemorate AG's only son William Robert Gregory (1881–1918), who had been killed in action 23 Jan. 1918 while flying over Italy, WBY was writing 'In Memory of Major Robert Gregory', the second of three elegies; his difficulties were exacerbated by the knowledge that AG's son was far from being 'our Sidney and our perfect man' (see James Pethica, 'Yeats's "Perfect Man"', *Dublin Review* (Summer 2009), 18–52).

[3] Mary Barry O'Delaney (or Delaney) (1862–1947), sometime journalist, friend, and helper in Paris to MG since the 1890s, had returned to Ireland with the family in 1918 and was attending to MG's business affairs in Dublin while she was in prison; IG, Séan, and their French cook Josephine Pillon (1865–1927) were meanwhile staying in Woburn Buildings, with IG in charge of the book of household expenses.

could do their own house-keeping. As things are Mrs Old will use all Maurices salery. I think Mrs Old a good-hearted woman but I do not know how to give her a hint. Which of us is to write to her? When is it to be?

I have opened the big parcel of books which has come address for you. One book will give me all I want for Thomas.[4] On looking over Mrs Fowlers copy of that old script I have found the form ⋈ surely the two cones.[5]

I think of spending the afternoon perch fishing. I feel always that I am just filling up an empty space in life waiting your return.

Yrs ever
WB Yeats

[ALCS]   [postmark Gort Co. Galway
15 July 1918]

No envelopes so only this card—sorry.[1] Macdonough has returned design to 'G Yeats Esq' & says he has no seasoned ash or oak.[2] I have asked what seasoned wood he has. We may have to use red larch or the like & perhaps paint door. We cannot move in without a front door. If you want me to order door or a door in what I can get from the nearest or quickest man I can find wire. I send on some letters. I suppose if [?Dan] starts with the beds that will be soon enough.[3] Sorry you have such wretched weather. No news here except an obscure message about Rafferty about sedge—'Steward had not time to go with him'—he is to come in to day.[4] WBY.

---

[4] WBY was already drafting the new philosophy dictated by 'Thomas of Dorlowicz', chief Instructor or Control for the first eighteen months of GY's automatic writing (see *YVP* i, ii).

[5] During the period 1912–14 Elizabeth Radcliffe's automatic writing (see letter 29 Nov. 1925) had also been eagerly studied by their London friend and fellow occultist Eva Fowler (1871–1921) of 26 Gilbert Street, American wife of the financier Alfred Fowler; the script contained a great many symbols, including what would become the cones, later renamed 'gyres', of *A Vision*.

[1] Addressed to 'Mrs Yeats | Aberdeen Arms Hotel | Lahinch | Co Clare'; GY had been sent by Scott to arrange with James Nestor (b. 1883), blacksmith at Liscannor, the making of wrought-iron hinges for the Castle doors and candelabra, and while there to examine old slate roofs in the village made from the light-green flags of the local quarries. Scott had met Nestor while designing a Round Tower in Liscannor.

[2] Máirtín Mór McDonogh (1863–1934), founder of a hardware, building supplies, and general merchant business in Galway city, who was also asked to seek out suitable slates. I am grateful to Dr Christopher Murray and Tom Kenny of Galway Art Gallery for this information; see also Mary de Lourdes Fahy, RSM, *Kiltartan: Many Leaves One Root* (Gort, 2004), 211.

[3] Scott provided designs for two beds made of wood from local elm trees; working at Ballylee at various times were Patrick Connolly, a craftsman joiner from Gort, John ('Jack') Hallinan of Ballinamantan (1878–1963), Thomas Brennan of Ballylee (1856–1924), and William O'Connor.

[4] Scott had instructed the local builder Michael Rafferty of Glenbrack (1877–1933) to cut sedge from Coole demesne and 'save as one would hay' for the thatched roofs of the two cottages adjoining the Castle.

[ALS]   STEPHEN'S GREEN CLUB, | DUBLIN.
                                            Sunday [18 Aug. 1918]

My dear George: I went to Ricketts's & showed him the designs.¹ He says we
should risk the wicker hoods & that at the worst they would smoulder but will
he thinks be safe. He thought the bed too like a bed for 'King Lears Wife' but
liked the big fire place said he 'had not seen it before'. He suggests our using
a mill stone as flagging for the castle floor. He re-touched the candlestick
design; & to demonstrate a point gave me a beautiful brass-candlestick.

I brought Maurice out to dine. She spoke of Eva Duckatt.² She had
thought her a 'successful woman of the world' when they first met & had
not liked her but met her again and thought 'there is great kindness in her'
& liked her greatly. I wonder of you could get them to meet.

Alas I forgot all about my fountain pen—perhaps you may be in that
direction before you return & can bring it. However I have made up my
mind to steal this excellent jay nib & its holder from the Club so I shall get
on all right & may even like the change.

It was very noisy all night at the Euston Hotel but the getting off in the
morning was very easy as the hall porter gets a seat for one in the train. I am
afraid, when you come you must sleep there as you have to be on platform at
least 40 minuets before the train starts to get a good seat. I saw however chalked
up on—a board that a train for Holy Head left at 6.40 at night. If that is a
regular train you might take it & sleep at Holy head where it would be quiet.

                                            Yours with all love
                                                    WB Yeats

Did you give new address to De Vere Hotel?³ I shall go to Ballylee on
Tuesday & tell you all about

---

¹ The designs were by Scott, their architect. The multi-talented artist Charles de Sousy
Ricketts (1866–1931) was for many, including Oscar Wilde and Bernard Shaw, the arbiter
of good taste and model of generosity; GY preserved a drawing, evidently by Ricketts, of a
mirror with the annotation 'Italian two lira piece Greek 2 Drachma piece', and in the upper
left-hand corner the word 'Wire'.

² Eva Ducat (1878–1975), a woman of independent character and a strong influence on the
young GHL (*BG*, 28–9), was at this time living in Earls Court, London; niece of Charles Baron
Clarke, botanist and sometime director of Kew Gardens, she was the author of *Another Way
of Music* (1928) and acted for some time as WBY's official musical agent, until GY took over.
She had visited the Yeatses in Oxford in February 1918.

³ The Yeatses had made a hasty trip to London to install IG with her maid, cat, birds, and
furniture once again in Woburn Buildings; she had been sharing lodgings in Chelsea with Iris
Barry (1895–1969), a co-worker in the Institute of Oriental Studies and disapproved of by both
Yeatses because of her love affair with Wyndham Lewis (by whom she was to have two children) and her inability to pay her share of the living expenses. Barry, a poet and novelist, later
became well known as a film historian, and was the first curator of the Museum of Modern
Art Film Library in New York. The De Vere Hotel was in Kensington W 8; GY had stayed
on in London for a week to visit friends and inform her mother of her pregnancy.

[ALS]   Ballinamantan House | Gort | Co Galway
August 18[?19] [1918]

My dear: All well except that Thomas is ill again & very thin. Norah gave him meat only 'sometimes' so liquid diet is the cause. She had sent him to her father to be cured so her conscience was arroused. Hares and Pangur[1] (he is very dirty but busy cleaning himself) are well and Seagan says bigger.[2] This afternoon I go to Ballylee unless the rain, which threatens, comes in earnest. Three aero-planes have just passed over flying low & causing much fright among the crows. That is all my news. When you cross Seagan says you should take the 6.40 from Euston going there 30 or 40 minutes before train starts. No dining car so bring food. Get out at first Hollyhead station—that I told you was for Hotel—& take the North Wall boat. You will reach Holyhead between 12 & 1. Go to bed & wake up in Dublin. Boat nominally starts at 3 but actually at 6 reaching Dublin about 10. In any case you need not get up till you arrive. Seagan says there is a slow goods train that takes a few passengers & should get connection at Athenry but you had better sleep in Dublin. You could of course sleep at Holyhead & get the afternoon boat to Dublin. At Euston you should go to enquiery office & wire for a berth.

I am now going upstairs to begin my work on Thomas.[3]

Yours with love
WB Yeats

[ALS]   STEPHEN'S GREEN CLUB, | DUBLIN.
Friday [27 Sept. 1918]

My dear George: We had a good evening—I think I made a good speech & Cruse O Brien[1] gave an amusing performance—two of my best George Moore[2]

[1] By now the Yeats menagerie included Pangur, the first of their many cats, renowned for having been smuggled into their bedroom at Coole on GY's first visit (see *BG*, 160–1), the angora cat Thomas, and five hares.

[2] MG's son Séan MacBride (who at that time spelled his name Seagan), known to the family as 'Bichon', was staying with them in Ballinamantan House.

[3] The Control 'Thomas of Dorlowicz' of GY's automatic script.

[1] Francis Cruise O'Brien (1885–1927), advocate of dominion self-government, freelance journalist, and librarian of the Co-operative Reference Library in Plunkett House, and soon to be deputy editor of the short-lived *Irish Statesman*, was a raconteur and mimic well known for his character imitations.

[2] George Augustus Moore (1852–1933), novelist, playwright, and essayist, and their collaborator during the early years of the Irish literary theatre, had alienated both WBY and AG with his wickedly amusing trilogy *Hail and Farewell* (1911–14).

stories as I am supposed to tell them. Jacky O Connell[3] amazed us all by proposing the Kings health. I was so angry—as I knew the difficulty it put all the Sinn Fein part of our audience in—that I did not stand up. O'Connell explained afterwards that he thought Chesterton would like it[4]

Write & tell me how you got home & how all the beasts are[5]

Yours affly
WB Yeats

[ALS]   STEPHEN'S GREEN CLUB, | DUBLIN.

Tuesday [1 Oct. 1918]

My dear George: I go over 73 to morrow with Lilly & probably get the furniture.[1] I think you have planned well at Ballylee.[2] I am working at the dialogue & dictating it in the evenings—at last it seems fairly complete & clear though I would like an answer to this question. 'Is there a form of excess that has for its harmonization sanctity?' I think there is but would like confirmation & a description. I hope Thomas will not mind my calling anti & primary the two Tinctures, to distinguish them from the Four Faculties, or ego, Mask Etc. I think too of calling Spirit, CB & PB the three Principles. Last night I think Thomas tried to communicate as I saw letters on stone but I could only read something about a lecture, but what I do not

---

³ Solicitor and later a priest, Sir John Robert O'Connell (1868–1943), prominent Irish Catholic nationalist and author of *The Problem of the Dublin Slums* (1914) and at this time chairman of the executive committee of the Arts and Crafts Society of Ireland, was responsible for the commissioning of Irish craftspeople and artists for the Honan Chapel in the university grounds in Cork.

⁴ A series of lectures held at the Abbey Theatre in aid of the United Arts Club included a debate on 'Private Property' between the prominent English critic and novelist G. K. Chesterton (1874–1936) and Thomas Ryder Johnson (1872–1963), founder member of the Labour party and treasurer of the Irish Transport and General Workers' Union, with Bernard Shaw (who would lecture the following month) in the audience; afterwards Chesterton was entertained at a dinner at the Club, whose members included many prominent members of the Sinn Féin party, dedicated to the establishment of an Irish Republic.

⁵ Having decided that their first child (expected in February 1919) should be born in Ireland, they had postponed returning to Oxford; now comfortably settled in Ballylee, both had spent a few days in Dublin looking for a house for the winter that would be suitable for GY's confinement.

¹ They arranged to rent MG's house at 73 St Stephen's Green for four months at £2.10 a week; GY and WBY were both especially fond of his eldest sister, Susan Mary ('Lily') Yeats (1866–1949), artist in charge of the embroidery division of Cuala, who was also a visionary and the family historian.

² GY had arranged for Michael Rafferty to continue work through the winter and to spend most of his nights in the Castle.

know.³ I am expecting a call from John Dillon in connection with the Lane pictures,⁴ & so am at a pause in my day. I have been correcting typed script of dialogue.⁵ There is no news—I have been working at lecture plays etc.⁶

Did you find shaving brush. Coat came yesterday!

Yrs affly
WB Yeats

Our health was proposed at the Arts Club dinner in very energetic speach.⁷

[ALS] STEPHEN'S GREEN CLUB, | DUBLIN.
Wednesday [2 Oct. 1918]

My dear George: I enclose a note from Mrs Old which wants attention.¹ In a few minuites Lilly comes to go to 73 with me. I have just found in my pocket I am sorry to say a card she sent me some days ago asking me to address it to 'The Kennedy Employment Bureau' she had been unable to find it in Telephone book or directory. It was there she was to interview servant for you. Is that name correct?² How are the beasts & are the carpenters on 'peice-work'. How is your own health?

Yours affly
WB Yeats

---

³ The vocabulary later used in *A Vision* was becoming established, but WBY was still dependent for clarification on GY's automatic script and the Instructor 'Thomas of Dorlowicz'; the script for 8 Oct. 1918 discusses this question (see *YVP* ii. 71 ff. and Margaret Mills Harper, *Wisdom of Two: The Spiritual and Literary Collaboration of George and W. B. Yeats* (Oxford, 2006)).

⁴ AG's nephew Sir Hugh Percy Lane (1875–1915), just before his death on the torpedoed *Lusitania*, had added an unwitnessed codicil to his original will, naming AG sole Trustee and stating that he wanted to leave his famous collection of 39 European paintings to the new gallery in Dublin rather than to the National Gallery in London, but a British commission deemed the codicil invalid. All available resources were being sought by AG and, with her encouragement, WBY; Dr John Dillon (1851–1927) was leader of the Irish parliamentary party and MP for Tipperary, soon to be defeated by Éamon de Valera.

⁵ Apparently WBY first intended to structure the explanation of their new philosophy by using a dialogue between Michael Robartes, 'a pious libertine', and Owen (or John) Aherne, 'a bad Catholic', two characters resuscitated from his stories 'Rosa Alchemica' (1896), 'The Tables of the Law (1896), 'The Adoration of the Magi' (1897), and returning again in later poems and *A Vision* (see *YVP* iv).

⁶ WBY did not give his promised lecture on their philosophical system until the following January.

⁷ GY would later be honorary secretary of the United Arts Club, which had been founded in 1907 by the nationalist Constance Georgina Markievicz, née Gore-Booth (1868–1927), her Polish artist husband Count Casimir Dunin-Markievicz (1874–1932), and Ellen Maria ('Ellie') Duncan, née Douglas (1850–1937), first curator of the Municipal Gallery of Modern Art from 1914 to 1922.

¹ Enclosure missing.

² Thom's Directory lists 'Kenny's Advertising Agency' at 65 Abbey Street.

[ALS]   STEPHEN'S GREEN CLUB, | DUBLIN.
                                                                    Oct 3 [1918]

My dear: We bought yesterday for £7.11.0 one chest of drawers (not bad)
two small tables (one mahogony & quite decent) two wash stands. I have
mislaid your letter & so went by the last you sent Lilly. Did you say in my
last something about kitchen arm-chairs? Lilly can lend one & I can get a
padded basket chair for 24/-. This furniture when we are done with it can
be sold at an auction room & should fetch a very good price all furniture
now is some much wanted. It will I think be cheaper than hiring & hiring
seems impossible now. Lilly will spend Oct 8 at 73 & on that day furniture
etc will be put in. Please send or wire coal-controllers address as I have
mislaid letter with it. Lilly will have wood & turf sent in. With luck house
should be clean & habitable on Oct 9.

   We failed to get into 73 yesterday as Delaney was out I am asking Friery
to say when I can have key.[1]

                                                               Yrs affecly
                                                               WB Yeats

♄[2] has been bad chiefly because cannot find anything to read but to day
I am in good spirits. I shall finish dictation of dialogue after lunch.

   Your description of our household has relieved my mind & I am grateful
to the crows & the sea gulls[3]

---

   [1] The rental was arranged with Barry Delaney; MG's solicitor was Christopher Friery
(1859–1926), coroner for North County Dublin with an office at 52 Rutland Square West, and
a keen sportsman who owned several racehorses. I am indebted to Dr Christopher Murray
for this information.
   [2] Astrological symbol for Saturn.
   [3] GY's letter is missing.

1919

[ALS[1]]   96 S. Stephens Green | Dublin[2]
                                      Wednesday [?12 Feb. 1919]

My dear George: I enclose a note from Rafferty. You had better wire about
roof of shed. We can talk over arch though I shall be content if you decide
that too.[3]

   I am just recovering from violent cold. I spent Tuesday either half asleep
in bed room or in sitting room quarelling with Pangur who was in a damnable mood. He howled at the door, & he filled the room with a smell of
singed hair by putting his tale in the candle & then nearly pulled the electric
lamp down by getting his tale lassoed in by the cord of his toy—further
more he eat a whole herring without gratitude.

                                                            Yrs a.
                                                            WB Yeats

[ALS]   STEPHEN'S GREEN CLUB, | DUBLIN.
                                                  May 7 [1919]

My dear George: I shall probably though not yet certainly have to shift
on Thursday. Geogurty was ready to take me so I shall ask him for a bed
on Thursday night.[1] If your afternoon solitude becomes less sweet wire or
phone to me but as I think, after having had so little of it, you will continue
to find it sweet I shall not come unless I hear.[2]

   [1] On the verso is a horoscope for 'Feb 23–Mch 10' in GY's hand.
   [2] GY was spending a few days with WBY's sisters in Dundrum while he remained in the
furnished rooms they had rented after MG returned to Dublin and GY had recovered sufficiently from influenza; they left 96 Stephen's Green on 22 February and ABY was born four
days later in Elpis Nursing Home (*LWBYEP*, 113; *BG*, 194–7).
   [3] Rafferty wrote on 9 Feb. 1919 asking for further instructions concerning GY's sketch for
the woodshed and restoration of the arch in the Castle (NLI MSS 30,663).

   [1] The accomplished surgeon specializing in ear and throat, Oliver St John Gogarty (1878–
1957), wit and raconteur, poet, essayist, and autobiographer, and later a fellow Senator, was
one of WBY's closest Dublin friends; the Yeatses stayed at 'Renvyle', the Gogartys' private
hotel in the west of Ireland, and saw them frequently at social events in Dublin. WBY persist-
ently misspelled his friend's name.
   [2] After renting a furnished house in Dundrum for six weeks, GY and baby Anne moved in
with her sisters-in-law while seeking a satisfactory nurse, and WBY went to his club.

Gogorty said one amusing thing. 'America the English press says, must not interfear because Ireland is a domestic question, but that is what Blue-Beard said to the detectives'[3]

I have taken the fur-coat to Mitchell, got my ticket, phoned to many people & generally done my duty.[4]

I dined last night with Gogorty

Yrs ev
WB Yeats

Did I leave my pen with you?

[ALS]   STEPHEN'S GREEN CLUB, DUBLIN.
                                        Thursday [8 May 1919]

My dear George: All right Friday 4 at D.B.C.[1] I have a room here for to-night & am very comfortable.

Maurice wants to see you to make plans about her visit to Ballylee.[2] I suggested her going to you on Saturday but I wonder if Lilly being free that day does not make it a bad day.

Sylvia Pankhurst is at 73 & is to speak at the Russian lecture on Sunday—she is all 'golden dreams' something wonderful just going to happen—'happy future of mankind' etc[3]

Yrs ev
WB Yeats

---

[3] The *Irish Times* for 5 and 6 May 1919 reported a demonstration in Dublin on the arrival at Sinn Féin headquarters of three Americans for the purpose of 'an unofficial political mission', the securing of international recognition for an Irish Republic at the Paris Peace Conference.

[4] John Mitchell's furrier shop was on Wicklow Street; WBY was travelling to London ahead of his wife.

[1] The Dublin Bread Company had restaurants in Dame Street and on Stephen's Green North.

[2] While the Yeatses were in England IG had been invited to spend a fortnight at Ballylee.

[3] The suffragette and pacifist Sylvia Pankhurst (1882–1960), who was staying with MG in her Stephen's Green house, defended the Bolshevist movement at the Abbey Theatre on Sunday 11 May at 8 p.m. as part of a debate on 'The Truth about Russia'; Pankhurst's pro-communist articles in the weekly journal *Women's Dreadnought* led to her five-month imprisonment for sedition.

[ALS]   27 Royal Crescent | Hollond Park | London. W. 11[1]
                                                     May 13. [1919]

My dear George: Your mother & I went to Woburn Buildings—all kinds of damage & dirt but nothing that will not be put reasonably right before you come.[2] A strange banjo in the study which suggests a loger of Mrs Old, & also a strange & very common hearth rug beside the bed in my bed room. I have ask[ed] Mrs Old to clean up & will ask Mrs Robinson (Ezra's[3] char) to finish up after. This was your mothers idea.

I saw Cyrano de Bergerac last night—a prosaic, half inaudible perform-ance & Dulacs decorations not as good as I had hoped, not broad enough in treatment for the stage.[4] He did not think of his players when he made his background—they were lost in complexity of detail. However everybody seems to praise his work. I dine with him to night & remind my self every five minutes to keep off that subject

                                                              Yrs ev
                                                              WB Yeats

[1] WBY was staying with the Tuckers, who had moved from Montpelier Square where GHL had lived with them before her marriage.

[2] GY was still at Ballylee. After MG and her family left, the journalist and novelist Douglas Goldring (1887–1960) and his first wife Betty, Eleanor Amorette Duncan (1893–1977), daughter of Ellen and James Duncan and MacGreevy's goddaughter, had rented the flat at 18 Woburn Buildings for 30 shillings a week; Goldring later recalled, 'We were not only desperately poor, we were both of us hopelessly incompetent and inexperienced in the business of housekeep-ing....It was a strange, ghost-haunted flat, heavy with Celtic twilight and magical influences. The hall, from the bottom of the stairs to the front door, was so thickly charged with unseen presences that Betty, who was to some extent psychic, used to send me on ahead to open the door for her, so that she could run straight out. I remember one morning when I descended to the study to write a letter and found the desk covered all over with chalk marks shaped like a hen's claws' (see *Odd Man Out* (London, 1935), 232).

[3] Ezra Loomis Pound (1885–1972), American poet, essayist, and influential modernist; friend to Eliot, Joyce, and many other writers and artists. He first met GY in 1909 through the Shakespears and, although differing in temperament, later became an essential part of the WBY circle, for a brief time serving as his secretary and later contributing to a change in literary style; having married GY's closest friend, Dorothy Shakespear (1886–1973), EP's relationship with the Yeatses was lifelong if sometimes turbulent.

[4] A man of astounding versatility and zest, French by birth though by now a confirmed Anglophile, Edmund Dulac (1882–1953) was one of WBY's closest friends in London from the time they met about 1913; he was chief musician and designer for the first production of *At the Hawk's Well* (1916), illustrator of *Four Plays for Dancers* (1921), *Plays and Controversies* (1923), and *A Vision* (1925), a designer of the ballet, posters, jewellery, stamps, bank notes, tapestries, carpets, furniture. He drew caricatures as well as portraits, including a significant portrait of GY shortly after her marriage; see pp 474ff. for the quarrel with WBY over the composition of musical settings to some of Yeats's later poems. He had designed the pro-duction at the Garrick Theatre of *Cyrano de Bergerac* adapted by Mary E. Guillemand and Gladys Thomas from the 1897 play by Edmond Rostand, but was not himself happy with the result (*LWBY* 2, 360–1).

[ALS]   27 Royal Crescent. London. W.11
                                                    May 13. [1919]

My dear George: I have income tax forms to fill up. It will do when you come¹ but let me know if you have my pass-book. It is not among my papers. I think it must have gone to Ballylee.

Bring with you when you come any copies of 'Two Plays for Dancers'² that went to Ballylee. I want one for Dulac. If there are none let me know that I may get one from Lolly before they are all sold.³

                                        Yrs ev
                                        WB Yeats

[ALS]   STEPHEN'S GREEN CLUB, | DUBLIN.
                                        Wednesday [?9 July 1919]

My dear George: I went on Monday morning to College Library to find it closed for two weeks.¹ I am now trying to get in as a special favour. As I had not you to take care of me I talk much, read in bed & smoked much— result two days headache. Fit for nothing else I spent yesterday evening wandering about Chapel-Izod looking for the ruins of the great house of the Ormonds—a tower was still left in 1830—but there is not a trace.² I have looked through all the histories of Dublin & of Christ Church but found nothing except that we should have gone into the crypt.³ One gets into the crypt for I think 1/-. There is no use my going, as it is clearly a job for

¹ Leaving her infant daughter with WBY's sister Lily, GY joined her husband from 21 May to mid-June, during which time she arranged for the furnishings from Woburn Buildings (where the lease expired on 25 June) to be moved to Oxford.

² *Two Plays for Dancers* (*The Dreaming of the Bones* and *The Only Jealousy of Emer*) had been published by the Cuala Press in January 1919.

³ Elizabeth Corbet Yeats, 'Lolly' (1868–1940), was a painter, gifted teacher, and founder of the Cuala Press, of which WBY was editor, an arrangement which caused considerable tension between the two siblings who were temperamentally similar.

¹ WBY was in Dublin while Rafferty did some plastering in Ballylee. Trinity College Library (TCD) houses Ireland's greatest collection of books, manuscripts, and other historical papers.

² Encouraged by the mysterious 'Anne Hyde' who for a time had monopolized GY's automatic script (see *YVP* i, ii), WBY was still seeking evidence that he was descended from James Butler, 1st Duke of Ormonde (1610–88). Chapelizod, a village on the Liffey 3 miles west of the Dublin General Post Office on the road to Lucan and adjoining Phoenix Park, housed the vice-regal residence of the Duke of Ormonde, who established a linen factory in the area.

³ The groin-vaulted crypt of Christchurch Cathedral, dating to the 12th century and extending under the entire building, contains many gravestones and statues.

Amyntus.[4] Plunkett has just been in & has talked long on politics—would like to entice me into a speach.[5]

At Chapel-Izod hardly a trace even of Lefanu's world remaining.[6] I think the mills or [are] on the site of the Ormonds house.[7]

Yrs affectionately
WB Yeats

[ALS]   STEPHEN'S GREEN CLUB, DUBLIN.
                               July 10 [1919]

My dear: would you like to go to Japan? Last night I got a letter from a Japanese who is proffessor in the Keio Gijuku University, Tokyo.[1] I hold it in my hand a moment before I opened it & thought 'This is inviting me to lecture in a Japanese university' & when I opened it that is exactly what it contained. We would have to stay two years & I would lecture on

---

[4] 'Amyntus' does not appear in the preserved script; WBY may mean 'Ameritus', the Control most closely identified with GY, who was the principal Instructor of the script during the search for Anne Hyde.

[5] Sir Horace Curzon Plunkett (1854–1932), founder of the Co-operative Movement and its co-ordinating body the Irish Agricultural Organization Society whose slogan was 'Better Farming, Better Business, Better Living', had been a Commissioner on the Congested Districts' Board, and Unionist MP for south County Dublin, later a campaigner for Home Rule; he was attempting to gain support for his newly founded Irish Dominion League which sought self-government for Ireland within the British Empire. He was appointed a Senator in 1922 and continued his campaign for a programme for socio-economic reform, though when his home was destroyed by the Republicans in 1923 he settled in self-imposed exile in England.

[6] Joseph Thomas Sheridan Le Fanu (1814–73), Dublin journalist and novelist, serialized many of his Gothic novels in the *Dublin University Magazine*, of which he was editor and later proprietor; his novel *The House by the Churchyard* (1863) was set in Chapelizod and his introduction to *Ghost Stories of Chapelizod* (1851) describes the village: 'A broad street, with a well-paved foot-path, and houses as lofty as were at that time to be found in the fashionable streets of Dublin... [and] has... even in its decay, a sort of melancholy picturesqueness of its own.'

[7] WBY is probably referring to the Anna Liffey flour mills, built in 1820 on the site of an 18th-century mill; owned by the Shackleton family and in use till 1999, the mills are in the Strawberry Beds on the outskirts of Chapelizod on the way to Lucan.

[1] The invitation had been arranged by the Japanese poet, novelist, and critic Yone Noguchi (Noguchi Yonejirō; 1875–1947), Professor of English at Keiō Gijuku University, who met WBY on his first visit to England in 1903, and again during the winter of 1913–14 when invited to lecture at Oxford. In New York in 1919 they discussed the possibility of such an appointment, and the following year he dedicated his *Japanese Hokkus* to WBY. The first Japanese national to publish poetry in English, Noguchi had been swept up by the west's interest in Japonisme, but admiration for him declined during the 1930s. His long-term friendship with Tagore deepened when the Japanese government sent him on a tour of India in 1935–6, but this too ended a few years later over the Sino-Japanese war; during the Second World War he was a fervent propagandist for Japan. I am indebted to Professor Yoko Chiba for information on Noguchi.

English Literature. The writer of the letter says 'I am asked to find out if you would be inclined & able to come out a couple of yeres hence or even next year. I dont know yet the exact figure of fees... any how you would return home no poorer financially than you would ordinary be and richer in knowledge of a wonderful people & their literature and art' We should live I gather in a guest house provided by the university. Certainly I could not have known contents of letter had not my Daimon known all about it.² Think it over.

I am just off to College Library.

Yrs ev
WB Yeats

[ALS]   STEPHEN'S GREEN CLUB, | DUBLIN.
July 10 [1919]

My dear George: I have just come from Library. No ephemeris there of any kind.¹ Unless I can think of somebody better I shall write to Miss Jacobs to night & ask her to get data in Museum.² I am just off to Bank to pay in that money which I forgot so far.

---

² The automatic script variously described their individual daimons, which were always of the opposite sex, as a 'distinct spirit', 'the ghostly self or soul', or 'another mind or another part of our mind'.

¹ It would be unlikely that the TCD library would have such astrological resources as an almanac of the daily motions and stars.

² As early as 1913 WBY used the typing service of Miss Louise Jacobs (1868–1960), whose office advertising 'Shorthand Typewriting Translations' was, from 1920 to 1941, at 47 Great Russell Street opposite the British Museum and (briefly in 1930) at 30 Museum Street; I am grateful to Deirdre Toomey for assistance in identification. On 25 July 1919 Miss Jacobs sent the astrological details, and five days later in his acknowledgement, while avoiding identification of either GY or Anne Hyde, WBY explained, 'A year before my daughter was born a certain spirit told me through a friend, who is a writing medium, that this spirit had belonged to my wife's family in the 17th century and was seeking rebirth. We had never heard of her but found after some research that she existed and that various facts told us about her were correct. When our daughter was born the most marked feature in her horoscope was a strongly placed conjunction of Mars, & Mercury and Herschel. I then had another sitting with the spirit & told him that I did not consider that mere telling me of a certain obscure person of the past, & the claim that this person has now return, was proof. I said the horoscopes must show continuity of character. The spirit said if you can find the birth date you will find the conjunction of Mars. Venus. After research in the Record Office Dublin my wife found the birth date... The sceptics will of course say I invented the automatic script after my child birth & picked the 17th century date myself but evidence of research though not conclusive carries some weight' (Stonybrook).

I am well of my headache but languid & idle—I have just sent away an interviewer.[3] He is to come again on Saturday. I was too idle even to talk. I suppose you are fishing for trout & that you have set all your plants.

Please send me Billy Binns address[4]—the other things have gone.

Yrs affly
WB Yeats

struggling hard to get out of taking the chair for Plunkett who is to debate with Shinn Fein at the Abbey[5]

Yours
WB Yeats

[ALS]   STEPHEN'S GREEN CLUB, | DUBLIN.
[11 July 1919]

My dear: I am just starting of to dine with the O Neills.[1] I have got out of taking the chair for Plunkett, by doing an article instead. I dictated my first draft this morning.[2] I shall come down on Monday—one o'clock train.

I am wondering what you think of Japan—just time perhaps to finish the system away from all distraction.[3] I wonder what Amyntus thinks.[4]

Yrs ev
WB Yeats

---

[3] I have been unable to find an interview around this time.

[4] William Norman 'Billy' Binns (1865–1945), the Galway-born civil engineer who received his BE at Queen's University, Galway, and was responsible for the renovations to the Castle, had begun his career as resident engineer on the building of the Galway–Clifden railway, and was later borough surveyor and harbour engineer for Galway. I am grateful to Dr Brendan O'Donoghue and Lisa Coen for assistance in tracking him down.

[5] Under the auspices of the Abbey Theatre Lectures Committee, a debate on 'Dominion or Republic?' was announced for 27 July at the Abbey Theatre; Horace Plunkett and Mrs T. M. Kettle, née Mary Sheehy (1884–1967), model for 'Emma Clery' in Joyce's *Stephen Hero*, and soon to be elected to the Dublin Corporation, represented the Irish Dominion League; journalist and scholar Aodh de Blácam (see 5 Feb. 1932) was the only speaker on behalf of Sinn Féin.

[1] Joseph James 'Seosamh' O'Neill (1878–1953), playwright, novelist, and Irish scholar, had been a schools inspector since 1907 and 1923–44 was Permanent Secretary of the Department of Secondary Education; he and his wife Mary Devenport (1879–1967), poet and dramatist, had spent a day with WBY and GY at Ballinamantan House the previous year and become close friends. They regularly held a Thursday 'At Home' in Rathgar which WBY frequently attended, where he and Mrs O'Neill discussed the philosophy of *A Vision*.

[2] Possibly the first draft of 'If I were Four-and-Twenty', published in *The Irish Statesman*, 23 and 30 August 1919.

[3] With GY's encouragement, and in spite of grave doubts expressed by his father, EP, and John Quinn among others, WBY accepted the offer by 9 August 'subject to reasonable terms etc'; however, by the time the Yeatses had made plans for his lecture tour to North America they and the Controls were having second thoughts and the dream of Japan faded.

[4] Apparently a slip for the guide in GY's script named 'Ameritus'.

[ALS]   STEPHEN'S GREEN CLUB, | DUBLIN.
                                                     Oct 7 [1919]

My dear George: I read in the paper to day that some letters do reach England so I write this on chance.¹ I wrote three or four days a go but seeing
there was no chance I did not post it & now it does not seem worth sending.
Yesterday Gogorty took me in his car for a drive in the mountains & said
I might now 'do as I liked again'. He said I have been the worst case of
<u>tonsilitis</u> he has ever known but he is a lover of the picturesque so I may not
have been as bad as that. I was certainly very uncomfortable, especially at
night. I wonder when we shall meet again. I think if the strike looks like lasting a very long time I will try & get by tramp steamer or other wise to some
place like Southampton. From that I could get occassional jaunts on cart
or motor & walk when I could not. I have long thought of a walking tour
of this kind, & with you at the end it would be full of Romance. Perhaps it
is not now possibl I think in a week or so one will be able to get information. Others will have had the same thought—at the present moment I have
not even a map of England to find where the sea runs nearest to Broad
St Oxford, & have just heard that the usual boats to Southampton are not
running. I wonder if you are very uncomfortable & tired out, & if you find
it hard to get milk for Anne. I am afraid setting the house in order without
the two maids will be a great fateague for you. After you went both the
chamber maid & the man who came up with my meals at the Hibernian²
talked of Anne with delight. Lilly telephoned here this morning and asked
if I had news of Anne she too had thought of the milk. I told her that you
were practically in the country at Oxford and that comforted her.

   No news here except that MG, has presented Shawn Gonne with a seven
seater motor car, out of the proceeds of the sale of Iseults house in Normandy
& bought a little house in Glenmalure where they are to spend their summers.
I hear they have all been made happy by this new extravagence.³

                                                            Yrs ev
                                                         WB Yeats

---

   ¹ GY, ABY, and the nurse had sailed for England on 24 September and then moved on
to the house in Oxford which they had let furnished to tenants while in Ireland; WBY was
delayed first by tonsillitis and then by a general transport strike in England.
   ² The Royal Hibernian Hotel, 48 and 49 Dawson Street, Dublin.
   ³ Contrary to Francis Stuart's claim that MG's summer house at Colleville in Normandy
had been given to IG by her father, MG's lover the Boulangist activist Lucien Millevoye
(1850–1918), 'Les Mouettes' had been purchased by MG in 1903 with a legacy. Ballinagoneen,
the house in Glenmalure on the slopes of Baravore valley (the setting of Synge's *In the Shadow
of the Glen* (1903) and site of battles in the 1798 rebellion), was in a lonely area of Wicklow
about 30 miles from Dublin; it is now a youth hostel. See *LWBYEP*, 116–17 for IG's description of the house.

1920

[ALS]   27 Royal Crescent | Hollond Park [London]
                                      Saturday [12 June 1920]

My dear George: The parrot has just given his first screach for joy.¹ A true
Parrot screach, but not loud. His cage hangs by a cord on the balcony out
side the drawing room & he looks more gay than hither to.

   I enclose Binns' wire.²

   Macmillan is to bring out at once my 'four plays for Dancers' with the
Dulac designs.³

                                                      Yrs affecly
                                                      WB Yeats

PS.

Enclosed is Dulacs figure for that horary. It does not look to me radical.⁴
Otherwise
   ☽ △ ♃ ♆ ⁵ should be a good omen. There is no detrement except ☽ □ ☿⁶

[ALS]   STEPHEN'S GREEN CLUB, | DUBLIN.
                                      [30 July 1920]

My dear George: Dunsaney¹ was at the Euston Hotel & asked to have my
coffee at his table. He forgot the coffee but was violently out of temper

---

   ¹ The first of their 'caged birds', purchased on return from New York before GY went to
Dublin to collect ABY from SMY, leaving WBY with her parents in London.
   ² Billy Binns, responsible for installing the new slates on the Tower roof, had been authorized to spend up to £400 of the money WBY earned on his American tour.
   ³ In 1916 after some years of hesitation, The Macmillan & Company Limited of London
had added WBY to their list of authors; thanks to the urging of John Quinn, The Macmillan Company of New York had begun publishing his work in America in 1903. *Four Plays
for Dancers*, designed by T. Sturge Moore, was published by Macmillan on 28 Oct. 1921 with
frontispiece and illustrations by Dulac drawn from the masks and costumes used in the first
performance of *At the Hawk's Well* (April 1916); the music Dulac composed for the play was
also published, with a note on the instruments.
   ⁴ Enclosure missing. A horary posed a specific question to be answered astrologically; if
'radical', the figure is based on the most precise information and is therefore valid.
   ⁵ Astrological symbols for Moon trined with Jupiter and Neptune.
   ⁶ Astrological symbols for Moon square Mercury, an exceptionally fleeting aspect; my
thanks to Elizabeth Heine for this interpretation.

   ¹ Edward John Moreton Drax Plunkett, 18th Baron Dunsany (1878–1957), prolific short
story writer, international chess player, fantasist, and novelist, saw several of his plays produced at the Abbey Theatre but, a veteran of the Boer and First World Wars and loyal British
subject, always felt marginalized by his fellow Irishmen.

with his wife who did not know the time of the train had been changed from 8.10 to 8.40. The steamer was more crowded than I have ever seen, but I got a bed on the floor. When Lilly crosses she must wire for a berth three or four days before hand—I wired at 6 from Euston but that is too late.[2] This morning Robinson came, & smelt violet very strongly.[3] I think it means help in what I have to do.[4] I have been to bed for a couple of hours & lunched & am now writing till it is time to start—3.30. My address will be I conclude

> c/o Madame Gonne
> Baravore
> Glenmalure
> Near Rathdrum
> Co Wicklow.

Robinson told me that Francis Stuarts mother[5] is an untrustworthy romantic minded woman & that she was most anxious for the marriage.

> Yrs affectionately
> WB Yeats

When the scent of violets came I attained a much calmer view of the whole thing & felt very sorry for the young man.[6] He does not drink or smoke, & so it must be insanity.

---

[2] They had invited SMY, who had not been well and missed ABY, to Oxford for a holiday, her first visit to England since 1916.

[3] Esme Stuart Lennox Robinson (1886–1958), playwright, biographer, essayist, and fiction writer, and staunch admirer of WBY, was manager of the Abbey Theatre 1909–14 and 1919–23, and member of the Board of Abbey Directors from 1923; an unsuccessful suitor of IG, he was to become one of GY's closest friends and confidants, eventually marrying the designer Dorothy Travers Smith (see 17 May 1927). When the Yeatses were studying occult matters, the scent of violets was frequently noticed.

[4] The scent of violets, connected to the tower symbols and frequently occurring during the Yeatses' investigative sessions, was always a comforting signal. MG had asked WBY for help with IG whose marriage on 6 Apr. 1920 to the young poet Henry Francis Montgomery Stuart (1902–2000) was in trouble; see *LWBYEP*, 118–20 for the most detailed description of these weeks.

[5] Elizabeth Barbara Isabel ('Lily') Stuart, née Montgomery (1875–1960), married her alcoholic cousin Henry Clements in 1913, eleven years after her first husband Henry Irwin Stuart of Rockwood, Queensland, Australia, committed suicide; at this time, separated from her second husband, she was living with her sister Janet Montgomery in the family home, Ballybogey, Benvarden House, Dervock, Ballymoney, Co. Antrim.

[6] Francis Stuart was seven years IG's junior. After joining the Republicans during the Civil War, he was captured and imprisoned for fifteen months; after his release he published a volume of poems, *We Have Kept the Faith* (1923), which was awarded a gold medal by the Royal Irish Academy, and then turned to novels and plays. He eventually left Ireland for Germany in 1940, not to return until after the death of IG. In 1954 he married Madeleine Gertrude Meissner, a student he had taught in Germany; he was the author of more than thirty novels, possibly the best known being the autobiographical *Black List Section H* (1971).

Luggage was examined at Holy head & searched for concealed fire arms—
great delay & great crowding & general vexation.[7]

[ALS]   Baravore | Glenmalure | near Rathdrum | Co Wicklow
Sat [31 July 1920]

Dear George: Post leaves here every second day only but there is a grocers
cart at the door & I can send this by that.[1] All as bad as possible but have
got Iseult to consent to go to a nursing home & while she is there we will
try for a settle ment & conditions under threat of a final breach. Of course
she will not believe but her husband seems to me a criminal lunatic. She is
exausted from lack of sleep & lack of food. His object has been to get her to
leave Ireland as he dislikes her friends who he says dislike him. He adopts
forms of punishment or torture, not letting her sleep, keeping her without
food & so on. I have got at all this by questioning Iseult & for the lack of
food I have an independent witness. I shall probably be the one to negociate
with his family. Iseult is still in love with him & defends him always & always
gets back to his longing for power (by this she means power over her).

I feel it was right to come & I thank you for letting me do so—all that
happens but shows me some new side of your goodness. Perhaps I am writing stupidly but there is such a hurry.

Yours with love
WB Yeats

[ALS]   write to | Stephens Green Club | Dublin.
Glenmalure
Sunday [1 Aug. 1920]

My dear George: I wrote a few words incoherent with haste yesterday.
When I arrived here both told me the story, as MG did Iseult was backing
& excusing her husband. He has in order to get Iseult to leave Ireland where
he says she has friends who dislike him he has regularly punished her. He
has left her without food, & in this house turned her out on the road in her
night-gown & then made a heap of her clothes soaked them in kerosene &
burned them. He is mad & I think a Sadist. In one of his poems he pictures

---

[7] Following the recruitment of the Black and Tans earlier this year, the ports were closely
guarded. So-called because of the colour of their uniforms, they were hired to assist the Royal
Irish Constabulary in the suppression of anti-British violence.

[1] The letter, addressed to GY at 4 Broad Street, Oxford, is postmarked 1 Aug. 1920 from
Rathdrum.

himself as crusefying a woman. She looks very ill & worn. What has brought things to a crisis is that she is probably going to have a child. She says that for its sake she must not be starved & kept without sleep (another devise of his contriving or accident of his temper). She has consented to my suggestion to go for a few days to a nursing home & only see her husband there. She undertakes not to return to him till there is a settlement on the child, & guarentees against starvation & persecution. She will not give him up. Maud thinks I am the right person to negociate these things. I was to start for town this afternoon to interview the doctor at the nursing home but Maud has gone off to Mass & when she returns it will be too late to get a conveyance to take me to the train. I might arrange that myself perhaps—though I have no idea how—but I want an interview with certain neighbours who saw the burning of the clothes. I have already got a deposition from a young art student who once gave her food when she had not eaten all day. Whether Maude [Maurice] is still in love with him I dont know—she sometimes talks as if she was. 'If he is mad he but needs me the more'.

I cannot go to Gogorty for I shall not be master of my time.

Yours with love
WB Yeats

In addition to all the rest the banshee has been crying here[1]

[ALS]   STEPHEN'S GREEN CLUB, | DUBLIN.
August 1 [1920]

Dear George: I have just come up from Glenmalure & am going to Dr Solomon[1] to get Iseult into a nursing home for a few days. & after that I hope she will be able to stay in the country with no address for a time. She has been starved, kept without sleap, & several times knocked down, & only now when she is with child has she got to the point of asserting herself. Of course she has been extrordinarily foolish—with her fine brain for all literary & ethical subelty she is credulous in all practical things beyond belief. I got at MGs request a vivid account from the elderly peasant woman who drove me to the train, of Francis Stuart driving Iseult out of doors in Glenmalure & then burning her clothes in the middle of the bed-room floor. He burnt 10 or 11 pounds worth. On one occasion he kept Iseult without food all day

[1] In Irish mythology, a spirit whose crying presaged a death in the family.

[1] Bethel Albert Herbert Solomons (1885–1965), former rugby internationalist and now a Dublin obstetrician and gynaecologist, had delivered ABY; later when he was master of the Rotunda Maternity Hospital (1926–33) the Yeatses lived in the upper two floors of his house at 42 Fitzwilliam Square. A brother of the artist Estella Solomons and on the committee of the Dublin Drama League (the DDL), he was an active supporter of the artistic community, which he describes in his autobiography *One Doctor in his Time* (London, 1956).

because she did not like his prose. Iseult confirms all, when one insists, but never showed indignation but once & that was when she told me that he liked De La Meres[2] poetry which she considers second rate.

I learned from my elderly peasant woman that he used to lie in bed all day & make Iseult fetch wood for the fire down an uneven path a mile & a half long 'A strong mans job' as my peasant woman said & this every day. Iseult insists that he often has charm, a delightful fancy & that after he has carried a point they were often happy for some days.

His father died in a Lunatic Asylum & his mothers father died of drink[3] with the result, as I think, that he is a Sadist & cannot love without torturing. 'He always', Iseult says 'wants power' which I only gradually found out meant power over her. The greatest power over the object loved comes from torture.

This young man reads my poetry imitates it, & has, I am told, the greatest desire to make my acquaintance hence I am perhaps to carry on the negociations.[4] I have little hope but Iseult says she will not return to him until some money is so settled that the child at least cannot be starved. If she holds to that one may do a little but not much. One can only put off tragedy with a child tainted with madness at the end of it.

Yours affecly
WB Yeats

I have so much to do. I cannot write more

[ALS]   STEPHEN'S GREEN CLUB, | DUBLIN.
August 2 [1920]

Dear George: I am told that Darrell Figgis is the proper person to apply to in matter of threatening letter.[1] I have written for appointment.

---

[2] Walter de la Mare (1873–1956), English poet, novelist, and essayist, had in 1911 been awarded the Polignac Prize of the Royal Society of Literature; WBY would include six of his poems in *The Oxford Book of Modern Verse* (1936).

[3] Stuart's maternal grandfather had died of alcoholism; after his father Henry Irwin Stuart committed suicide in Sydney, Australia, in 1902, he and his mother returned to Ireland; see *LWBYEP*, 221 for details.

[4] On 17 Nov. 1919, before her marriage, IG had written of her new 'great friend', 'He has an adoration which amounts to religion for you, but he is very shy and I cannot get him to send you any of his work' (*LWBYEP*, 117).

[1] Their servants, the Molloy sisters, had received a threatening letter because some time the previous winter they had gone to mass in a cart drawn by a mule owned by a neighbour disapproved of by the Republicans. Edward Darrell Figgis (1882–1925), journalist and novelist whose pen name was 'Michael Ireland', had been a member of the Irish Volunteers and participant in the Howth gun-running of 1914, and was interned after the 1916 Easter Rising and again during the War of Independence; at this time he was secretary of Sinn Féin and in 1922 would serve as acting chairman of the committee which framed the Irish Constitution, and 1922–5 a member of the Dáil for County Dublin.

Scott is in North of Ireland but I have arranged an appointment for 11 on Thursday.

I have just seen Solomons about Iseult. She goes to Ivanhoe Nursing Home to-morrow & Solomons will she [see] her husband. After she comes out, & while the young man is deciding what he will do, I hope Lady Gregory will take charge of her. I am trying to get out of having to negociate with him; & Solomons agrees with me in this. Solomons thinks there is just a chance that he is not mad, but simply has never grown up. It is a small chance but if it is so, he thinks, I may be able to influence him. If Iseult is ordered a long rest without him in the country, after his decission has been made (if that decission is what it should be) I may ask you to let me bring him over (of course without Iseult). I would take his decission as a sign that there was hope.

I told Robinson all yesterday. He was greatly upset & would eat no dinner, but drank some brandy.[2] He is coming at 4.30 to hear my news. I am so busy that the sense of tragedy is lightened for me.

I hope to-morrow to get to the College of Arms[3] but may have to put it off till Thursday.

I am not at all sad at this moment but very tired & I think I will two & four.[4] Write to me at this address. I have written every day but no letter has come from you—they are all perhaps at Glenmalure or on the way there.

Yours affectionately
WB Yeats

[ALS[1]]

4 Broad St.
Tuesday—[3 Aug. 1920]

My dear Willy—

Three letters arrived all together. I think it is not possible that Iseult's child will live. From the horoscope it seems impossible, & it is to be hoped so I think.[2] No settlement can be very satisfactory that is made <u>after</u>

---

[2] LR had fallen in love with IG and, encouraged by GY and WBY, proposed to her in vain; despite this disappointment, he had invited Stuart to live with him while arrangements were being made about the marriage (*LWBYEP*, 118–20).

[3] In an effort to establish his own ancestral line, WBY was seeking information about the Butlers; a sheet of Kildare Street Club stationery includes notes from 'Peerages of Ireland' and describes the Butler family crest.

[4] GY's term for an afternoon nap.

[1] This letter, the first to her husband that was preserved, is written in pencil on a page torn from a lined notebook similar to those used for the automatic script.

[2] Both Yeatses drew up natal horoscopes for the baby once she was born but neither added any interpretations; IG's daughter Dolores, born in March 1921, lived for only four months.

marriage & you should be very careful to go to the best possible lawyer about it. I hope negociations will fall through & that she will not return to him. It would be far better. Sadism in so young a man is incurable. Is she in great despair about the child? My thought is so much more for you than for her, because the spectator suffers more poignantly than the victim; his suffering being wholly subjective. As for my 'goodness in letting you come'—that was really nothing but the foreseing that you would have found it difficult to forgive me had I dissuaded you. If you cannot do much, at least you can do something.

The Mead's are with us for the night.[3] I have found them rooms. They are to stay 2 or 3 weeks in Oxford. We have had visitors, & I do not know whether having to adjust one's thought to their needs is more a distraction or a worry. I can think of nothing but your trouble & Lilly's chatter is maddening.[4]

Remember that it is almost impossible to settle money <u>after</u> marriage so that the man cannot take it away or fail to pay. You must exhaust that point in all its possibilities.

Yours with all love
George

[ALS]   STEPHEN'S GREEN CLUB, | DUBLIN.

August 4 [1920]

Dear George: They missed the train this morning which has rather upset my plans as I had arranged that both Iseult & the young man should see Solomons before they met. I am now off to meet the later train by which they are to arrive. I have been reading Stuarts poetry it gives me a little hope. Curiously since the odour of violets the morning I arrived I have been able to work without anger, & endeed almost without emotion of any kind. I am glad of one thing which is that Maud Gonne & I are very good friends now.[1]

Gogorty has just wired urging me to go to him but I am more likely to bolt back to Oxford & you at the first possible moment. I long for our

---

[3] George Robert Stowe Mead (1863–1933), author of more than two dozen books on Gnosticism and related matters, had been secretary to the founder of theosophy Helena Petrovna Blavatsky (1831–91) and editor of the *Theosophical Review* before founding in 1909 the Quest Society, whose lectures GY had attended in London before her marriage; he and his wife and fellow theosophist Laura Cooper Mead (1856–1924) were also friends of OS.

[4] SMY wrote to her father on 2 August: 'Willy unluckily had to go to Dublin a few minutes after I got here—some Abbey business, I hope he will be back in a few days' (NLI MSS 30 112/47).

[1] WBY and MG had quarrelled when he refused to admit her to the house when GY was pregnant and seriously ill with influenza (*BG*, 194–7).

orderly & sane house & the days work. Lady Gregory has not yet written but the raiders got my first letter to her.[2]

Now [Not] a word from you my dear, not a word since I left but I suppose you have written to Glenmalure. No time for more. I have just awoke from sleep & am full of activity & am endeed that decisive person you have never seen & have been these last four days. I am shocked at my own serenity.

Yours
WB Yeats

<Stewart has not I believe indecipherable>

[ALS]   STEPHEN'S GREEN CLUB, | DUBLIN.
August 4 [1920]

My dear George: Iseult is now in Nursing Home (there was a rebellion crushed by MG on Tuesday) Solomons sees her this morning & if Lady Gregory wires or writes that she can take her my work is probably done, & certainly done if the young man, as Solomons will recommend, goes to a lawyer to settle, & not to me to negociate. I give you my word of honour that to my own surprize I have suffered little. I have had bad hours, but they are nothing compared to the even serenity that rather shocks me. The truth is that so much has happened since that time in Normandy[1] that though I admire Iseults subtle thought I have no contact with her mind. Lennox is in contact & is suffering horribly & I greatly wish I had told him nothing. I beleive that ever since my return from America I have had a need of action & that this activity has been very good for me. I am even gay as if I were hunting some beast. I remember how Francis Stuart, shortly after the marriage, sold Iseult's engagement ring; & then I think of him confronted with the necessity of losing her or consenting (he is a minor) to a substantial portion of his income being paid to her direct. It is precisely because I am not deeply moved that I am useful, & can banter both Iseult & M G till they put away subjectivity and see bare fact. I am more Ezra Pound, butting his head against the wall, & laughing, as M G is the enfuriated philosopher.

I called at Scott's to day but he had not arrived from home. I gave an account of things to his clerk, who says Scott finds it very hard to get answers from Binns and asked for a new appointment with Scott.

---

[2] Groups of armed men were raiding the post offices in search of money.

[1] Just months before his marriage to GY, WBY was still proposing marriage to IG while visiting the Gonnes in France.

I have not yet heard from Darrel Figgis, who must be away & I dont want to go to Smith Gordon,[2] the other Sinn Fein authority, if I can help it, as I put him out of the Irish Statesman.[3] I will go to him of course if I dont hear from Figgis soon.

I shall go to the College of Arms after lunch if nothing intervenes

Iseult shows me as never before the extreme antithesis between her subjective mind, which is that of an inspired Griselda,[4] and the mind she turns towards the world which is that of a child of 14—credulous beyond belief. I wonder if her husband is not a 14, whose vanished primary has left a hole which a wild beast has chosen for its lair. Then too I notice this. 14s, according to Dionertes commonly marry 14s, & according to a communication of a year ago a woman falls in love with a mans antithetical. As Anti of 14 is the Fool all 14s should be in danger of marriages with deranged or deficient persons. Iseults description of what attracted her suggests this. He asked a series of naive questions, and made a series of naive statements suggesting an extreme simplicity, till she at last said to herself 'he is a blessed angel',—plainly she was hoping for 'Gods Fool'. His poetry suggests 14.[5]

I thank you for your letter I was worried at not hearing. Write often. I want to know every thing.

Yours affly
WB Yeats

---

[2] F. Lionel Eldred Pottinger Smith-Gordon (1889–1976), an economist, was a librarian for the Co-operative Reference Library and would in 1926 be appointed to the Banking Commission of Dáil Éireann; he was author of *Co-operation for Farmers* (1918), with Laurence C. Staples, *Rural Reconstruction in Ireland: A Record of Co-operative Organisation* (1917), and two volumes with Cruise O'Brien, *Co-operation in Many Lands* (1919) and *Co-operation in Ireland* (1921).

[3] Horace Plunkett had established the weekly review the *Irish Statesman* in 1919 and appointed as editor Warre Bradley Wells (b. 1892), translator and author among other books of *An Irish Apologia: Some Thoughts on Anglo-Irish Relations and the War* (Dublin, 1917), *Irish Indiscretions* (London, 1923), and, with N. Marlowe (pseud. of Joseph Maunsell Hone, 1882–1959), *A History of the Irish Rebellion of* 1916 (Dublin, 1916). Because of the fighting, the *Irish Statesman* temporarily ceased publication in April 1920; in 1923 it merged with the *Irish Homestead* under the editorship of George Russell (AE) and in April 1930 ceased publication altogether.

[4] Griselda, heroine of the last tale in Boccaccio's *Decameron*, was noted for her patience and obedience in spite of her husband's extreme and irrational demands; Chaucer based his version in 'The Clerk's Tale' in the *Canterbury Tales* on Petrarch's translation of Boccaccio's Italian into Latin as *De obidentia ac fide uxoria mythologia*.

[5] 'Dionertes' was one of GY's Instructors in the automatic script; according to their work on the system as expressed in *A Vision*, GY and WBY saw those personalities belonging to Phase 14, 'the greatest human beauty', as tending to be obsessive and when 'out of phase' 'may even become mad' or 'use its conscious feebleness and its consequent terror as a magnet for the sympathy of others, as a means of domination' (*Vision A*, 66–7).

[ALS] 4 Broad St.
August 4. 1920

My dear Willy,

I think the baby may not be a reality. I did on <Saturday> Sunday night, a horary; I had not heard from you & I was very worried.[1] In Vth house ☿☉♆♀□♂ & ☍☽.[2] I wrote at the time—Not knowing about the child.— 'There seems deception & entanglement of all kinds, especially in Vth house matters'.[3] Is this possible? Her illhealth from lack of sleep & food might have given cause for the mistake? However, Solomons will decide that. I hope you told him that you didnt want it known you had been to him? I dont at all want Lilly to get wind of it.

I think if you are not back 2 weeks from now, I shall get you to write to me to come over. I am so afraid she wont go, she talks of waiting till you return. And as there is unfortunately a spare room, I cannot say I want hers! I find her so uninterested in all my interests, & so unwilling to talk with those people who come here, & talk with me—She says 'Do talk about simple things tonight. I cant follow'. She is very inquisitive about your doings.[4] I am going to the Bodleian in the mornings to get a time alone, but my eyes have been so sore I can scarcely read.

The Banshee perhaps, (if it was on Sunday or Monday) was calling out another 6 weeks mishap I have had.[5]

I have many interesting things to tell you that I extracted from Mead & from one 'McGovern', an extremely subjective young man who came in with his mother last night, at the Mead's request.[6] I am rather hoping you

[1] The Yeatses were accustomed to consulting astrology as much to clarify the question as to discover the answer.

[2] Astrological symbols for Mercury Sun <u>Neptune</u> Venus squared Mars & opposition to Moon.

[3] The horary by GY dated Wednesday 4 August reads: 'e infelice per amore d'ella, e come se finire questa dolore?' and annotated 'one side of the affair, i.e. "X" does not wish to separate but yet is willing to play with the idea and will in all probability lead the ambassador to believe that she is in agreement with him. There seems deception and entanglements of all kinds ♂ [Mars] VII [in seventh house] probably represents young man who appears to have control of situation..delusion and false idealism.. The person in question will make no definite decision but probably will return to husband' (SB#7).

[4] SMY had only been told that AG required her brother's attendance on Abbey Theatre matters.

[5] An early miscarriage (evidently not the first); they were hoping for a second child.

[6] William Montgomery McGovern (1897–1964), though born in New York City, spent much of his early life in the Orient, graduating with a degree of doctor of divinity from the Buddhist monastery of Nishi Hongwanji in Kyoto. He then studied at the Sorbonne and the University of Berlin before receiving his D.Phil. from Oxford in 1922, after which he travelled to Tibet, publishing his adventures in *To Lhasa in Disguise* (1924). From 1919 to 1927 he taught Oriental Studies at the University of London, publishing among other works *An Introduction to Mahavana Buddhism* (1922); he returned to the United States in 1927 and taught at Northwest-

will be here before they go, as I should like to meet McDougall & Schiller & scarcely like to ask them for myself!⁷

Write to me whether there is any possibility of the Child being a false alarm. It worries me day & night for I am always thinking of your trouble over it. You are very good to write so often. Do not do so when you are tired. Now I have heard most of the details I shall not worry if I do not hear.

                                                                    Yrs as ever George

[ALS]   STEPHEN'S GREEN CLUB, | DUBLIN.
                                                        August 6 [1920]

Dear George: Your note of August 1 has just reached me, sent on from Glenmalure.¹ If Lilly still asks questions say that I have been considering among other things the production of Noh plays in Dublin,² but that my work has mainly been in connection with new plays, engagement of actors etc. But that nothing can be decided till next week when Lady Gregory comes to Dublin. Say if you like that Kerrigan & Miss Allgood are both here so there is much to arrange.³

ern University until his death. According to the Yeatses' system, a 'subjective' or 'antithetical' personality was intuitive, under the influence of the Moon, and hence approved of.

⁷ William McDougall (1871–1938), student of eugenics and heredity and exponent of 'hormic' or 'drive' psychology, was president of the Society for Psychical Research 1920–1 and of the American Society for Psychical Research in 1921; by this time Reader in Mental Philosophy at Oxford, he had published *Physiological Psychology* (1905), the frequently reprinted *An Introduction to Social Psychology* (1908), *Body and Mind: A History and a Defense of Animism* (1911), *Psychology: The Study of Behaviour* (1912), *Anthropology and History* (1920), and *The Group Mind* (1920). In 1920 he succeeded William James as Professor of Psychology at Harvard University; in 1927 he moved to Duke University where he founded the *Journal of Parapsychology* in 1937. Copies of his books *Body and Mind*, *The Group Mind*, and *National Welfare and National Decay* (1921), the latter expounding the danger of race degeneration, are in the Yeats Library. Ferdinand Canning Scott Schiller (1864–1937) of Corpus Christi College, Oxford, self-styled humanistic pragmatist whose books *Riddles of the Sphinx: A Study in the Philosophy of Evolution* (1891), *Humanism: Philosophical Essays* (1903), and *Formal Logic* (1912) also owed much to the influence of William James, whose work GY greatly admired.

¹ WBY may be referring to the letter of 4 August above.

² WBY's hopes for performances of his Noh plays in Dublin would not materialize until the end of March 1924, when *At the Hawk's Well* and *The Dreaming of the Bones* were produced in his drawing room as an 'At Home' for the DDL.

³ After Synge's death in 1909 a series of managers, each short term, had struggled to keep the theatre going during increasingly difficult political times while various groups of players left for the music halls, films, or America; LR, who had twice before held the position of manager, returned in 1919 as did Sara Allgood (1879–1950), who had joined the company in 1903, left in 1913, and had been touring in Australia since 1916. J. M. Kerrigan (1884–1964), who joined the Abbey Theatre company in 1906, went to the United States in 1916, making a brief return

I will write to Watt myself.[4]

Darrel Figgis is away but I have seen Desmond Fitzgerald who undertakes to deal with the threatening letter.[5] Would you mind sending me a copy.

No further news. Solomons spoke to Francis Stuart yesterday & to day at 3 Francis Stuart sees Iseult who will send him, (if he will go) to the lawyer. Solomons says there is no doubt about the child coming and he also gives a rather serious account of Iseults health. He gave this to Iseult & this may have been in obedience to my advice to 'scare her' so that she may keep to her good intentions for the childs sake. Neither I nor Madam Gonne have seen him since the examination. Lady Gregory (Margeret being at Coole[6]) cannot take Iseult so we must think of some new plan.

Scott has not yet given me that appointment but in a few minuites I shall get his clerk on the phone.

I was too tired yesterday to go to the College of Arms.

Now my dear about yourself. I am greatly distressed that you should have had another 'mishap'. Would you like to come over and see Solomons? Lady Gregory comes up next week & if I see her here I shall not go to Coole. Mr & Mrs Stuart reconciled, or Iseult despatched into the country, my work here is over. To day <u>may</u>, though it is not probable finish it, at any rate a few days must see all finished. If you came (say) next Monday we could go back to gether. On August 10 horse show week begins so you should wire for rooms.

After this little time away, after this necessary service, I shall return to you more completely yours than ever before. Is it not enough to say that through this week of painful discoveries, but for a few hours, mainly at the start, I have been tranquil, even happy, even gay. That strange first morning, when Robinson smelt the violets, seemed to make me see all objectively. I think it came when I pitied Francis Stuart, though I do not know why that should be. That night I preyed to be given enough harshness to act strongly.

to the Theatre in January 1920, and performed with various theatre groups until September 1920, but did not permanently rejoin the company.

[4] Alexander Pollock Watt (1834–1914) of A. P. Watt & Son, claimed to be the world's first literary agency, became WBY's sole agent in 1901; his younger son John Hansard Strahan Watt (1877–1960) then continued the relationship until retiring in 1937 when the file reverted to AP's oldest son Alexander Strahan Watt (1868–1948). WBY was negotiating with Macmillan over the English and American editions of *Four Plays for Dancers*.

[5] Desmond FitzGerald (1889–1947), journalist and poet, who had been in the Post Office with Pearse in Easter 1916 and in 1918 elected to the first (outlawed) Dáil Éireann, was director of publicity for Sinn Féin; he became Minister for External Affairs 1922–7, Minister for Defence 1927–32, and a member of the Senate 1938–47. See note to 2 Aug. 1920 above.

[6] Lilly Margaret Graham Gregory, née Parry (1884–1979), AG's widowed daughter-in-law, who resented WBY's role at Coole, normally lived in England while her three children spent much time with their grandmother.

The Banshee was heard by Iseult, while she & her husband were alone at Glenmalure. She went to the window & heard the cry. The omen I suppose would be fulfilled by the death of any one near to Iseult, herself, her child, her husband or any near relation. Maude suggests that it was a neighbour trying to scare away Francis Stuart, who had taken to burning furze & so had scared the sheep; but Iseult says this is impossible because no joker would have enough self restraint to give only one cry.

Immense houses at Abbey for Kerrigan & Miss Allgood in 'Mixed Marriage' & 'Kathleen-ni-Houlihan'. Miss Allgood acts exactly as before—no change at all—but has acquired in private life a desire to slap old friends on the back which I find an embarresment. It is the effect of prosperity.[7]

There is a barking dog out side so I will stop.

Yours affecly
WB Yeats

[ALS]   4, BROAD STREET, | OXFORD.
                                              August 6. 1920

My dear Willy

Your last letter was so great a relief to me that I must have cried, though I did not know it, for my face was wet, as sometimes after the Dionertian sleep.[1] I have written you three letters before this one, so you may now have had all. I think I will meet you in London & we can dine together & come to Oxford by that 8.30 train. Remember to take your ticket to Paddington & label your box Paddington as otherwise it goes via Crewe & gets lost on the way.

When you know when you leave Dublin wire to me. Do you go to Coole?

By coming to meet you I will not have the exasperation of small talk before Lilly. I think she suspects. She has perhaps heard you were at Glenmalure.

---

[7] *Mixed Marriage* (1911) by St John Greer Ervine (1883–1971), and the popular *Kathleen ni Houlihan* (1902) by WBY and AG, were revived 2–7 Aug. 1920, just before Horse Show week. Few knew of Sara Allgood's personal losses, the deaths of her baby in 1917, her husband, fellow actor Gerald Henson, in 1918, and her two brothers while she was performing in Australia during the First World War. In December 1921 several newspapers reported that she was to become director of 'the Irish National Theatre'; the project was unsupported but in 1924 she gained international fame as Juno Boyle in O'Casey's *Juno and the Paycock*. After performing both on stage and in film, she settled permanently in the United States in 1940, and in 1942 was nominated for an Academy Award as Best Performing Actress in *How Green was my Valley*.

[1] After several years of automatic writing, a new method had been introduced by Dionertes, whereby WBY questioned his wife after putting her in a sleeping trance.

I am hungering for a mind that has 'bite'. She disliked the Mead's. There was no small talk or social amenities. They were indeed a little too oblivious to her! Mrs Mead spoke to her about the jam—& Mead about the house—2 remarks in 24 hours! For the rest all the usual—The Lamb—The Jews in Mithras—Tibet—Bolsevism & Theosophy.[2] (Some interesting things I have collected for you) etc etc. She said (Lilly) 'Do bring the conversation round to simple things tonight—I cant follow'. But it was impossible. I hate small talk. I am writing this at the Bodleian where I go every morning on pretext of looking out things for you!!

Howard came to tea. He heard you were away but came all the same. Sent up his name. He talked from 4 to 6.30 & then only went reluctantly. He has charm but also too much of that quality of 22. Abstraction.[3] I am too dependent on you—I am lost when you are away.

With all love
George

[ALS]   STEPHEN'S GREEN CLUB, | DUBLIN.
August 7 [1920]

My dear George: All I think is going well. Yesterday Iseult at the Nursing Home had a long interview with the young man & was quite firm. He said it was very 'unbeautiful to speak of money' but finally he offered to get his mother to remit £150 a year to Iseult provided there was nothing so 'unbeautiful' as a legal document. Iseult refused this & he went off saying he would never see her again. This morning Maude Gonne & I saw her and I wrote two letters, which Iseult copied out & posted (the most important at any rate was posted, for she gave it to us). One letter was to the young man saying that he must decide for himself whether he wished to meet her again or not but that her decission was final. She would not see him again till the documents were signed & never if they were not. The other letter was to a solicitor telling him to act for her & enclosing copy of

---

[2] Having recently published a pamphlet on H. P. B. Blavatsky and theosophy and revised his translation and edition of *A Gnostic Miscellany*, Mead was probably doing research towards his next book, *The Gnostic John the Baptizer: Selections from the Mandæan John-book, together with Studies on John and Christian Origins, the Slavonic Josephus' Account of John and Jesus, and John and the Fourth Gospel Proem* (1924).

[3] Probably Thomas Evelyn Scott-Ellis, 8th Baron Howard de Walden (1880–1946), of great wealth and estates, polymath, accomplished sportsman and traveller, poet, and lavish patron of the arts and music, whom WBY had known for many years; in association with Frederic Herbert Trench (1865–1923) he produced Maeterlinck's *The Blue Bird* in 1909 and Ibsen's *The Pretenders* in 1913. The Yeatses' Phase 22 represented balance between ambition and contemplation.

letter to husband (this we posted). The husband has gone north we beleive to see his mother. To night Maude Gonne is to show me, before posting it, a letter not to the mother, who is a fool, but to the mothers sister who looks after her affairs & lives with her.[1] This letter will tell all. The last incident is that Maude has found out that the young man has been selling jewels, & that Iseult says these must be some family jewels his mother promised her. He went to see his mother last week & must have got them then. Iseult's attitude is very curious. She sees all, & gave an amusing description of yesterdays interview, during which he wept much, but she has no indignation and describes her self as in love with him. There is nothing now but to wait. On Monday the solicitor will write to the young man. On Tuesday or Wednesday, after Solomons has seen her, Iseult will return to Glenmalure, MG mounting guard (Lady Gregory owing to Margeret being there could not take her as I hoped) but will not give the young man or any body else her address. I thought her looking very ill to day, very white & weak. I wonder if you would calculate the young mans horoscope. He was born at Sydney on April 29 between 4 and 8 AM. He was 18 on his last birthday.[2]

If Lady Gregory were not coming to Dublin I would return on Tuesday. I have an interview with Scott on Monday & unless something crops up during the day my work will be over. It has been pure drama, the creating of a situation calculated to impress the conscience of Francis Stuart. Solomons interview with him, the Nursing Home Iseults refusal to see him again, the letter from the solicitor, Iseults dissapearance. This last will not be as secure as I hoped, for Glenmalure is too near Dublin, but Coole has failed & Iseult dare not go to England as that would be a precidant. She has resisted his endevour to take her away from Ireland by saying she is not well enough to travel. She dare not be alone with him. Iseult would not have obeyed Maude, as she thinks her too hostile to the young man, but as I have never seen him she does not think I am prejudiced.

Of course it would be much better if she gave him up, but she will not do that, so one has to choose a second best.

To morrow I shall start writing as a sign that normal life has begun once more.

[1] Lily Stuart's older sister Janet Maude Montgomery (*c.*1872–*c.*1950) had a farm at Bridesbush, Duleek, in Co Meath; although censorious, she was generous to the Stuarts throughout her life and left her estate to IG's children.
[2] Two natal horoscopes drawn up by GY for Frances Stuart exist, one for 5 a.m. and one for 6 a.m.; the earlier one states that the progressed moon is square Neptune's position at birth, an unlucky sign; I am indebted to Elizabeth Heine for assistance.

I too feel lost without you, I do not take care of myself & I tire myself out & there is no order in the day or peace in my thoughts

Yrs affly
WB Yeats

[ALS]
4 Broad St.
Sunday Aug 8. 1920

My dear Willy, I will not come over now to Dr Solomons, for I expect I shall come in September when you have your throat seen to.[1]

We have wonderful weather, sun all day, & I wish you were here enjoying it. I wish Lady Gregory would bring Pangur!!! If you go to Coole do not forget to fetch him from Mrs Molloy.[2]

I have not told Lilly about the mishap & I do not want her to know. I laid it all down to 'Martha'[3] to excuse my lying down & not walking.

I wonder what Stuart has consented to?

Some strange things have happened here. Lilly feels a hand every night either pressing upon her pillow or even stroking her head & one night the hand pulled her hair over her face! Then nurse came to me last night (Saturday) & said she had found a bill dated 1865 to a Miss Bonham 'in the press' That is, in the lower part of my father's bureau. It was lying on top of Anne's clothes! I investigated this morning & found about a dozen more, dates 1855 to '65. All stuffed in a small space between the desk (which pulls out like a drawer) & the boards, a space of at the most 1¼ inches in height & about 3 feet in length. It is <u>inconceivable</u> how they got there & how, if there since those dates they were not found before. I have used that bureau ever since 1908 & my father had used it to my certain knowledge for 18 years before that & probably longer.[4] I remember him using it ever since <u>I can</u> remember. An apport?[5] <u>And why!</u> I enclose one of the envelopes, do not lose it!—No I will not, lest this letter be lost—but it is the crest either a unicorn's or a stag's head rising out of a stumpy tower & a long tail with <u>arrow</u> end issuing out of the door of the tower!

---

[1] Gogarty had diagnosed severe tonsillitis and advised WBY to have an operation, which was arranged for October 1920.

[2] Their cat Pangur had been left in the care of James Molloy (*c*.1860–1939) and his wife Winifred (*c*.1865–1946), who had a farm in the nearby townland of Glenbrack and whose daughters Mary Anne and Delia were GY's servants in Oxford.

[3] GY's word for menstruation.

[4] GY's father, William Gilbert Hyde Lees (1865–1909), had been living apart from his wife and family for a number of years, latterly as a patient in a private nursing home for alcoholics (see *BG*, 22–4).

[5] An object transported by some immaterial means.

Thus roughly[6]

The envelope has one of the old brown stamps & the post mark is 1864 addressed to

    Miss Bonham
      Great Warley
        Brentwood.[7]

———

I am going to look up the address etc to try & find out any light on the matter. You see the strange thing is that the letters <u>cannot</u> have slipped out of the desk part or got in to the crevasse in any normal way. I had great difficulty in getting them out as only one finger would go in—

The last two days, Saturday & Sunday I have had the strangest feeling of liberation & of all calamity passed. Last night a voice said in answer to another whose sentence I could not distinguish

'Let the 3rd element begin its operation, for now Jupiter has no antagonists'.[8]

At 6 pm yesterday nurse & I smelt incense very strongly just outside the nursery door (about 3/4 of an hour before she found the first mysterious paper) Then Lilly smelt it too, but in the nursery & <u>only</u> near the door (also near the bureau which is by the door—)

It was I that found the crest & it was the last paper to appear & the most difficult to get out.

I have slept well these two nights, but that is perhaps because of your two letters

---

[6] The tower and arrow had special significance in their work on the automatic script, but there is also a slight resemblance to GY's bookplate, designed by Sturge Moore in 1918.

[7] The bureau may have passed on to GY's father during his military days. The 1881 census lists Sarah Bonham (c.1807–1885), an independent gentlewoman with two servants living in Croydon; an officer's daughter born in Dominica, her father Brigadier General Pinson Bonham (1767–1855), 69th regiment, was Governor of Surinam (1811–16).

[8] Apparently a reference to the work they were doing on the automatic script, perhaps concerning the birth of their second child.

Well now I must put Anne to bed, so goodbye my dear.

Yours affly
George[9]

[ALS]   STEPHEN'S GREEN CLUB, | DUBLIN.
                                        August 8 [1920]

My dear George: No news—I saw MGs letter to the family last night &
I suppose there will be no news for some days. I have not yet heard the
date of Lady Gregory's arrival. If she put it off I shall probably return to
Oxford without waiting for it. This is a rambling, empty life that tires me
more than much work. To-day I am trying to write some verse but do not
know if I shall succeed.

Yrs affecly
WB Yeats

[ALS]   STEPHEN'S GREEN CLUB, | DUBLIN.
                                        Monday [9 Aug. 1920]

My dear George: Nothing new except that Lady Gregory arrives to night.
So unless you are coming to consult Solomons I may get back on Wednesday. However one never knows what change of plan may be necessary.
Lady Gregory says she will 'consult' with me 'what is to be done with Iseult.'
Yesterday Iseult told me that she does not want to go back to Glenmalure
because she told her husband she was not, & he will think she is telling lies
(she thought she was going to Coole when she saw him) & because the house
at Glenmalure is so uncomfortable when one is ill. I have just told this to
Maude who became indignant & unreasonable at once. The slight on the
house was what she could not forgive. (There is no easy chair, no carpets,
no sanitation what ever except the noble sanitation of the fields. I was very
glad to get away). She will now talk to Iseult (she was on her way to see her)

[9] At the bottom of this letter WBY has made the following notes: 'Mrs Bertie Clay The
Homestead, near Ringwood Hants | Dalkey Tram— | Derreen Burdett Avenue Sandy
Cove | Airon Crowley[Crossley?] 1729 Playfairs British Families' and on another page 'Mrs
Jamesons "Court Bea[u]ties"'. Mrs N. S. Bertie-Clay ('May', née Mary Kemble Gonne, 1862–
1929), who also had a villa in Florence, was MG's cousin and confidante; together they had
briefly been members of the Order of the Golden Dawn. According to Thom's Dublin direc-
tories, M. A. Kennedy lived at Derreen, 24 Burdett Ave, Kingston, from 1916. Anna Brownell
Jameson (1794–1860), travel writer and art historian well known for her study of Shakespeare's
heroines, first published *The Beauties of the Court of King Charles the Second* in 1833.

in a sort of 'stand no nonsense' strain, & Iseult will be in a state [of] gloom for twenty four hours. Iseult wants to go to a relation in England.[1] I may stay in London for a few hours to try & arrange this, if Lady Gregory cannot find an alternative

I am just off to Scott & will add result later.

3.30 PM

Scott says Binns is 'good but careless' & Flaherty good, but possibly in some political trouble.[2] He will go down on Wednesday week, & look at slates, enquire about immediate work. If slates not enough he will put stone slabs, or paving stones arround lower part of roof. This he thinks should have been done in any case as while walking round parapet, or sitting upon it, one is liable to break slates. Owing to parapet these slabs will not show. He says the slates are beutiful.[3] He says work men if they sleap at Ballylee should bring their own bedding etc & that we should be paid—or amount allowed from price—for housing them. He says Binns should have used Raferty. When he has seen Binns & Castle he will write a detailed report. He says main supports for roof & floor were already up when he saw castle. Our own timber he thinks has been used.[4] He was quite sober, & quite healthy looking & attributed this to salt-water (he is at the sea side) and nothing much beside salt-water. I think he had heard some rumour of either Binns or Flaherty being in some political trouble for he kept returning to the point incoherently & finally said he would ask a certain barristor but I could make nothing of it. It was as if he had heard something & forgotten what he had heard, & yet I was not sure he had not imagined it.[5] He did not remember what the estimate of £400 had been for, or if that was the amount, but read me a letter of his to Binns enquiring about windows which looks as if it was

---

[1] Probably May Bertie-Clay (see note to GY's letter of 8 Aug. 1920 above).

[2] See n. 5 below.

[3] It was finally decided that the slates, purchased at great price on the advice of Sir Edwin Landseer Lutyens (1869–1944), British architect whose greatest achievement was the city of New Delhi, and approved by Scott, would not withstand the winter storms.

[4] They had purchased 'great beams and three-inch planks and old paving stones', the contents of Lord Gough's nearby disused Kinincha mill.

[5] According to *The District of Loughrea*, ii: *Folklore* 1860–1960 (Galway, 2003), 128, the Flaherty family were herds at Roxborough, but the name is common in Galway: in the January 1920 Galway municipal election a Martin Flaherty won for Sinn Féin in the East Ward. Lady Gregory's play *Spreading the News* was not without foundation: the *Galway Observer* of 15 May 1920 reported that a Martin Flaherty was fined for drunk and disorderly conduct in public, while the *Galway Express*, 29 May 1920, reported that James Flaherty and others were charged with unlawful assembly at Kilcolgan.

for much more than roof & floor. He showed me peices of glass, with 'bottle ends' in it which he had been collecting for us.

Scotts proof that the wood work of roof & cross beams of floors are up is that he had to fetch down Binns little boy who was climbing on them in danger of his life—this may have been merely our stored timber after all. However Scotts report will settle all that I hope.

Yours affecly
WB Yeats.

[ALS]   STEPHEN'S GREEN CLUB, | DUBLIN.
August 10 [1920]

My dear George: I had intended to go home to morrow, but there are still one or two possible tasks & I have not been to the College of Arms so unless I wire to the contrary I shall start on Thursday morning, & stay that night at the Gwalia.[1] I shall see MG in half an hour & will know if she has taken a suggestion made by Lady Gregory, through me, this morning: i.e. that the facts be put before a doctor in lunacy for his opinion. MG was very reluctant, I could see that she felt, as if I had asked her to go to the police; but finally she agreed to ask Solomons advice & went off to see him. She & Iseult go back to Glenmalure to morrow, & if the lunacy doctor is decided upon she will make a written statement, which Lennox will lay before the doctor. If she has missed Solomons I am to see him to-morrow. Your copy of the threatening letter for Desmond Fitzgerald has not come but may in the morning.[2] Your letter is very exciting. I am longing to be back. It will be some days before we here from Stuart & Iseult thinks he will take at least a month to make up his mind.[3] I am still in strangely good spirits.

Yours affecly
WB Yeats

---

[1] The Gwalia Hotel was around the corner from and adjacent to 18 Woburn Buildings; GY met WBY in London on 12 August; SMY returned to Dublin on 20 August.

[2] See note to 6 Aug. 1920 above.

[3] The Stuarts were eventually reconciled, but their relationship continued to be troubled, until it ended when Francis went to Germany in 1939.

1921

My dear George: The lecture went off well, & at the lunch before it Horace Plunkett gave £100. At the lecture a Lady somebody or other offered £20 if 20 other people would give £20. I think we will get the money.[1]

A bundle of patterns is come. Do you think I should be in green or in brown. I cannot make up my mind. If I were a rich man I should be in both. I am the donkey between the two bundles of hay & may starve.

Yesterday Mrs Huth Jackson[2] described how Laurence Oliphant[3] died in his mothers house & how as he died the dogs moved about uneasily & and cowered into corners as before terrifying presences. She also told how an old Lady somebody, who died in the middle of the war, said to her 'Laurence Oliphant told me that an attack on the human race from out side was coming. He would not live to see it but I should & now I see it' She said this on her death bed. 22, as the phase of the utmost dispersal, would be the phase, one thinks, of Frustration in a primary civilization—the event 'before' the Master. In Rome it was after.[4]

I saw Miss Stoddart last night but there is nothing new. I am just off to see Hammond.[5]

[1] WBY, AG, Shaw, and St John Ervine were lecturing in London on behalf of the Abbey Theatre, which was suffering financially to such an extent because of the curfews imposed that in the spring of 1921 the company was temporarily dismissed; Lady Ardilaun contributed £500.

[2] Clara Annabel Caroline Grant Duff Jackson (1870–1944), poet and society hostess; her memoir *A Victorian Childhood* was published in 1932.

[3] Laurence Oliphant (1829–88), travel writer, novelist, journalist, and diplomat, friend of Garibaldi and at one time private secretary to Lord Elgin, Governor-General of Canada. For many years he was a follower of the spiritualist prophet Thomas Lake Harris (1823–1906), founder of the Brotherhood of the New Life, and with his first wife, Alice Le Strange Oliphant (1845–86), wrote *Sympneumata: Evolutionary Forces now Active in Man* (1884), inspired by Harris and supposedly dictated by a spirit. A man of idiosyncratic energies, among his many works was *Scientific Religion, or Higher Possibilities of Life and Practice through the Operation of Natural Forces* (1888). Towards the end of his life, disillusioned by Harris, he devoted his energies towards the settlement of Jews in the Holy Land.

[4] In the system they were establishing for what would become *A Vision*, historical cycles as well as personality types were given phases on the great wheel.

[5] As a result of her enquiries into the origins of the occult Order of the Golden Dawn, Christina Mary Stoddart (1870–1949), 'Soror Het-ta' or 'Il faut chercher', had been removed as one of the ruling chiefs of the Stella Matutina Temple, and, supported only by her co-chief Dr William Hammond, MRCS, LRCP, FSA (1848–1924), 'Pro Rege et Patria', librarian at the Freemasons' Hall to the Grand Lodge of England and holder of high masonic rank, refused

Mrs Fagan talks of playing my Countess Cathleen.[6] I never saw her play & so have no idea what she is like.

I give a reading at Mrs Johnsons on Wednesday next.[7]

It is a miserable day cold & wet but there is a good fire here. At my room, I have a penny in the slot fire & am quite comfortable.

Yrs affecly

WB Yeats

[ALS] 1 Trafalgar Square | Chelsea[1]
April [May] 8 [1921]

My dear George: I am going this afternoon to see Eva Fowler; and I have just been to St Pauls Knightsbridge with Mrs Huth Jackson to see if his

---

to give up the Temple properties 'until they paid me my dues' (*LWBY* 2, 378–9). The Yeatses, both teachers in the Temple, were attempting to seek some kind of solution and advised patience, but the Order soon dissolved in disorder. Convinced that there was a worldwide Jewish conspiracy, Miss Stoddart became more and more unstable, under the pseudonym 'Inquire Within' writing a fortnightly column for the pro-fascist, anti-communist journal *The Patriot*, selections from which were published as *Light-bearers of Darkness* (1930) and *The Trail of the Serpent* (1936). The only daughter of Dr John Stoddart of Kirkcaldy, by 1923 she had divested herself of her London home and Temple and was staying with her brother Lt.-Col. G. E. Stoddart OBE in Essex.

[6] *The Times*, 6 May 1921, reported that WBY's lecture ('some delightful reminiscences of the Abbey Theatre') on the afternoon of 5 May had been at 213 Kings Road, Chelsea, the home of James Bernard Fagan (1873–1933), playwright, actor, and producer, founder of the Oxford Playhouse and at this time manager of the Duke of York Theatre, lessee of the Royal Court Theatre where the Abbey Theatre frequently performed and where the London production of O'Casey's *Juno and the Paycock* would open in 1925. His wife, the actress Mary Grey, née Ada Baron ap Rees Bryant (1896–1974), played Hesione Hushabye in the first production of Shaw's *Heartbreak House* and later at the Abbey Theatre where GY disapproved of her performance, but there is no record of her performing in WBY's *The Countess Cathleen*.

[7] Violet Charlotte Johnson, née Fletcher (1868–1921), described by WBY to AG as 'a most kind impulsive woman', who married her first husband Captain Bertram Charles Meeking (1864–1900) in 1893 and the wealthy stockbroker, entrepreneur, and sportsman Herbert Johnson (1856–1949) in 1912. A personal friend of the royal family, she frequently held soirées in her town house at 38 Portman Square as well as in Marsh Court, Stockbridge, a manor house designed for Johnson by his friend Edwin Landseer Lutyens with gardens created by Lutyens's colleague Gertrude Jekyll. During the First World War Marsh Court was used as a sixty-bed convalescent home to treat injured troops, run by Mrs Johnson at the family's own expense.

[1] WBY's relationship to the residents at this address is unknown. The Lodge at No 1 Trafalgar Square, Chelsea, was the residence of Sir Albert Gray, KCB, KC (1850–1928), at this time counsel to the Chairman of Committees in the House of Lords responsible for the general supervision of Private Bill Legislation and in 1924–5 Mayor of Chelsea; his wife Dame Sophie Gray (1855–1938), widow of Hon. Thomas Grosvenor, son of Lord Ebury, was the daughter of the missionary and Chinese lexicographer and geographer S. Wells Williams. The other address for No. 1 seems to have been a block of flats with four tenants, none apparently known to WBY.

brand of Anglican faith would suit Anne.[2] That is all my really solid news. I find it was you who precipitated the whole row in the Order. You said to Miss Stoddart 'who is S.D.A?' (Sapiens Dominabitur Astris) & she thinking S.D.A was Fraulein Sprengul, but not sure, went to the safe to find out & did find the sun masters instead.[3] I think if we want to get rid of our followers—about four in all—in the order we can put them into Steiners care & they will do their ceremonies, with his motherly care in the background.[4] But that is all too complicated for a letter, for the moment we have nothing but our enquiry to think of. Hammond is full of a kind of stick in the mud, touch me who dare ferocity. Dixon he says wants to be head of the order, & is, Landrieux says, a medium.[5]

I am comfortable here & I have a penny in the slot gass-stove.

Loydd Georges brief reference to Ireland in his speech certainly means negociations to[o] serious for comment;[6] on the other hand the sec of

---

[2] Revd Francis Leith Boyd (1853–1927), Vicar of St Paul's, Wilton Place, from 1908 until his death, was a popular and powerful preacher with a strong practical bent; ABY was eventually christened in Dublin, by a family friend, Canon F. D. R. Wilson (d. 1957), Rector of St Mary's Donnybrook, later Dean of St Patrick's Cathedral.

[3] After the convenient 'death' of the mysterious Anna Sprengel of Nuremberg, 'Sapiens Dominabitur Astris', whose name was allegedly on the 'discovered' cipher manuscripts on which the Order of the Golden Dawn was based, Dr Robert William Felkin (1853–1926), 'Finem Respice', a specialist in tropical diseases, former medical missionary in Africa, and WBY's personal physician, who became chief of Amoun Temple of the reorganized Stella Matutina branch, claimed to have made his own contact with the higher or Third Order through communications by means of automatic writing with the discarnate Arab adept Ara Ben Shemesh and 'the hidden masters of a Sun Order'. WBY had been a member of the Order since 1890, GY since 1914.

[4] Rudolf Steiner (1861–1925), former theosophist and founder of the Anthroposophical Society of which GY had briefly been a member, by now universally known through his lectures and writings on social renewal in art, education, sciences, social life, medicine, pharmacology, therapies, agriculture, architecture, and theology; his headquarters were in Dornach, Switzerland, where the Felkins sought his support and advice. The 'four followers' were probably Miss Stoddart, Hammond, Jean Nicolas René Landrieux (1865–1933), 'Ad Augusta per Angusta', a director of West India Cold Storage Ltd., who joined the Stella Matutina on 12 Mar. 1910, and his wife, Désirée Marie Landrieux (1870–1962), 'Pax Dei', who had been a member since 7 July 1909.

[5] The London pathologist and bacteriologist Dr William Elliot Carnegie Dickson (1878–1954), 'Fortes Fortuna Juvat', was a Freemason and long-time member of the Stella Matutina who would later assist in reviving the Amoun Temple; from 1929 he was WBY's consulting specialist in London.

[6] On 7 May Prime Minister David Lloyd George spoke briefly of the meetings being held between Sir James Craig (later Viscount Craigavon) (1871–1940), about to take office as the first Prime Minister of Northern Ireland, and Éamon de Valera, President of Dáil Éireann: 'All I will say about Ireland is that I am very delighted to hear that the two national leaders...have met together to discuss all questions bearing on the future of the country to which they belong....I am glad that has begun. I will not say another word on that topic' (*Irish Times*, 9 May 1921); this attempt was a failure but, through the appeal of George V, led in July to an uneasy truce negotiated by Lloyd George. Lloyd George was ousted as Prime Minister in October 1922.

Plunkets league[7] writes to me, that owing to reports from the military that the Irish Republican Army is running short of amunition Loydd George is getting stiffer in his attitude

I have re-written some of my poems and so have not started a new one Tell me how you are, & how you sleep

Yrs affecly
W.B. Yeats

[ALS[1]]   1 Trafalgar Square, Chelsea.
May 9 [1921]

My dear George

I saw Eva Fowler yesterday. Rummell has fallen in love with a girl who has been a pupil of Esidora Duncan's for sixteen years but Esidora is fighting hard to keep him.[2] He went to Evas & asked her to put him up & said 'if you dont I shall have to stay with Esidora at Claridges.' The girl, who is on the eve of a dancing engagement in USA, wont have him unless he gives up Esidora & he is bound by some legal engagement to finish his present tour. Result despair & threats to bolt to Paris where the girl is. Eva has advised him (she did not put him up however) to finish the tour first on the ground that his finishing it after going to Paris would cause new uproar between him & Esidora. He says 'O why did I spend my life with pure American girls till I was twenty two. I might have got all this over & been able to attend to my work.'

I have no other news. I spent a dull evening at Ricketts (conversation very tecnical painters talk) & Ricketts has renewed his promise of a cover for my poems.[3] I dine with Dulac to night.

---

[7] Sir Horace Plunkett founded the Irish Dominion League in June 1919 to seek self-government for Ireland within the British Empire; the secretary of the League was the Parnellite journalist Henry Harrison (1867–1954).

[1] On Broad Street stationery.

[2] Walter Morse Rummel (1887–1953), pianist and composer, son of the British pianist Franz Rummel and grandson of Samuel F. B. Morse, inventor of the telegraph, although an American citizen, spent most of his life in Europe, where he was a friend of Debussy, premiering ten of his piano works, and of EP, three of whose poems he set to music. An anthroposophist and spiritualist, he was introduced to WBY as early as 1911 and was a close friend also of GY, EET, and OS. Although having written settings for a number of WBY's poems, a project to compose music to *The Countess Cathleen* did not materialize, but in 1917 at Dulac's request he composed music for *The Dreaming of the Bones*. After divorcing his first wife and musical partner, the accomplished French pianist Thérèse Chaigneau (1876–c.1935), whom he had married in 1912, he was the lover of the famous American interpretative dancer and choreographer Dora Angela 'Isadora' Duncan (1878–1927); their liaison, which was also a professional partnership, lasted from July 1918 until in July 1920 he met one of the 'Isadorables', Anna Duncan, neé Denzler (1894–1980); but that relationship soon ended also (see 29 July 1930).

[3] Charles Ricketts's cover design appears on WBY's *Later Poems* (1922), *Selected Poems* (1929), *Collected Poems* (1933), *Collected Plays* (1935).

If my work here were finished I would return to you & take a room at 'the new inn' for I am lonely without you & bored by many people⁴

Yrs affecly
WB Yeats

[ALS]   1 Trafalgar Square | Chelsea.
May 9 [1921]

My dear George: dont be surprized if I just wire 'get me a room at New Inn' & turn up soon after my wire. At present I find life utterly detestable & if Lady Gregory will let me have it in mind to bolt when I have tried on my green clothes on Friday next. I am lonely, bored, tired, be colded in the head, toothachy, out of temper, Saturnian, noise-distracted, examaish, bathless, Theatre-hating, woman-hating, but otherwise well & cheerful. To morrow I shall ask to be let off & will write or wire result. I have decided to let the brown clothes wait. The green will cost about 12 pounds which strikes me as quite enough for the present.

I enclose Mrs Johnsons circular for my lecture to-morrow, that you judge its fashion¹

Yrs scy
WB Yeats

[ALS]   SAVILE CLUB, | 107, PICCADILLY. W.1.
May 24 [1921]

My dear George
Please send me word c/o Grace¹ to say what hour Friday you expect me in Oxford. I forget.

⁴ GY, now pregnant with Michael who would be born 22 Aug. 1921, was nursing ABY who had whooping cough. Minchin's Cottage at Shillingford, which they had rented for the summer, was too small to accommodate WBY and the nurse. The New Inn, 27 Henley Road, Shillingford, Oxfordshire, still exists, now named the Kingfisher Inn; I am grateful to Alexis Somarakis, the current innkeeper, for information.

¹ Enclosure is missing; the reading and lecture at Mrs Violet Johnson's raised £39 for the Abbey Theatre.

¹ GY's cousin Grace Spurway (1897–1996), newly graduated from Oxford, had arranged for WBY to give two lectures at the Training College for Women in Lincoln where she was teaching before moving to Paris to work on her doctorate; under her married name Grace M. Jaffe she later wrote of GY in *Years of Grace* (Sunspot, NM, 1979).

Masks in 'League of Notions' very fine, especially two quite serious ones—two beautiful impassive faces. The rest of the entertainment very dull.²

Yrs sy
WB Yeats

[ALS]   4, BROAD STREET, | OXFORD.
Oct 27 1921

My dear George

No news¹ except that last night nurse² got into a panic because the whole where her tooth had been bled but was comforted on going to a doctor; & that the old father canary has just caught himself in the bit of hanging string & hurt his foot at which he keeps pecking. It is not broken in any main bone & he is eating all right.³

There are a number of unopened letters of yours but as they seem all dated about Oct 8 I conclude you do not want them. One is from Heal.⁴

---

² *The League of Notions* by John Murray Anderson and Augustus Barratt was produced by Charles B. Cochran at the New Oxford Theatre, London, a well-known music hall. Starring the Hungarian-American dancers the Dolly Sisters (Jenny and Rosie), the revue, billed as 'an inconsequential process of music, dance, and dramatic interlude', ran for almost a year. There is no reference to masks in the reviews, but one of the performers, Grace Cristie, was known for her 'bubble dance'. Cf. WBY to OS, 27 May 1921: 'I spent 19/- to see a woman dance in masks in imitation of Ito. She danced beautifully & looked very beautiful masked, though when she showed her own head it was plain & touselled. The rest of the performance, or what I saw of it, was dull & mechanical. I knew that a grotesque mask was immensely effective, but was not sure of the effectiveness of a beautiful one till I saw her' (Wade, 669).

¹ GY was in London with baby MBY, who was to be operated on by Harley Street surgeon Harry Tyrell-Gray, FRCS (1880–1935), a highly skilled surgeon at the Great Ormond Street Hospital for Sick Children; after accompanying his wife and son, WBY had returned to Oxford. See note to 30 Oct. 1921 below.

² Beatrice Marsh (1888–1931), chief maternity nurse to Bethel Solomons and a friend of WBY's sisters, attended GY at the births of both her children and remained with the family until Christmas. 'She was one of those people who always had to be busy. She got a cordon bleu for cooking, a gold medal for violin-cello and then she decided to take out her maternity diploma at the Rotunda...knowledgeable and sweet-tempered' (Bethel Solomons, *One Doctor in his Time* (London, 1956), 88–9). In 1928–32, when the Yeatses lived in the upper two floors of 42 Fitzwilliam Square, she was serving as receptionist for Dr Solomons in rooms in the lower part of the house.

³ The Yeatses had enthusiastically added canaries to their menagerie.

⁴ Heal's, the fashionable furnishings shop at 196 Tottenham Court Road in London.

Mrs Herbert Johnson has just died of 'sleeping sickness.' She was taken ill last July. She is a loss to me & to you as she would have been friendly & hospitable. I had wondered at not hearing.[5]

Yours affectionly
WB Yeats

Enemy on the stair last night. May have been a warning not to fight ♃[6] etc.

[ALS]   4, BROAD STREET, | OXFORD.

Oct 29 1921

My dear George: Thank you for telegram.[1] You will be very anxious till it is all over—I wish I were with you & yet perhaps I would only worry you.

Here nothing has happened. Anne is gay & well & has taken to occasional joyous yells in the manner of the parot.

I have spent most of the day typing & sending off 'The Kings Threshold' emendations[2]—the version you brought to London was a rough early version I had the final version here on my table I found on coming down.

I gave great pleasure to Ashe King, an excitable old man of 82 who looks sixty.[3] I saw him to the station & in his joy at our meeting again he left his bag behind. I have sent it him by parcel post. He gave a very fine lecture exactly like his lectures of 1891, full of amusing but entirely apropriate anecdote.

Both last night & too night daring Taby canary has slept on the lowest perch of all. No other canary has ever done the like.

Yours affecly
WB Yeats

    [5] The death from exhaustion of this 'woman of remarkable personality and charm of manner' was announced in *The Times*, 22 Oct. 1921; her grave was designed by Lutyens, who had designed the Johnsons' house in Hampshire.

    [6] Astrological symbol for Jupiter. After MBY's birth and ensuing complications, both GY and WBY, seeing apparitions, feared their son's life was threatened by witchcraft; as an additional precaution against these 'Frustrators' WBY composed 'A Prayer for my Son'.

    [1] This telegram has not survived.

    [2] His *Seven Poems and a Fragment*, published by Cuala in June 1922, included 'A New End for "The King's Threshold"'.

    [3] Richard Ashe King (pseudonyms 'Basil' and 'Desmond O'Brien'; 1839–1932), Irish-born former curate, novelist, and long-time literary editor of the weekly *Truth*, had been with WBY one of co-founders of the National Literary Society in 1892; WBY attended all three of his lectures in Oxford and entertained him to dinner on 18 Nov. 1921.

[ALCS¹]   Please open immediately (from G.Y)²
                                          Sunday. [30 Oct. 1921]

Michael stood the operation very well. Under chloroform for 1 hour 25 minutes. Both ruptures & the hydrocele done.³ The ruptures were <u>larger</u>. He has
slept a good deal today & not been as uncomfortable as I feared. Both doctors were in this evening & say he is in fine condition. I am wiring you early
tomorrow morning (Monday). I told you Monday as I knew I couldnt wire
results on Sunday & feared you might worry at not hearing <u>Unless</u> I wire
to the contrary I shall arrive at Oxford by the 4.45 (arriving at <u>5 to 6 pm</u>)
on Tuesday evening for the night & can pack you for Scotland⁴ & return on
Wed: I will get you a room at Club & failing that, here.⁵ G.

[ALS¹]   More's Hotel, India St, | Charing Cross, | Glasgow
                                               Nov 6 [1921]

My dear George: I have seen nobody. I spent yesterday in the hotel reading with the exception of one long walk through streets which were all like
George St Oxford at its worst—no single building you could hang your
hat on, nothing but a monotony of damp & smoky squalour. This morning
I have got out my papers & hope to do some work on the 'memoirs'² &
many letters at the worst. I have liked the Hall Caine Rossetti book; you
might get from London library or get them to send to Oxford Hoggs 'life of
Shelley'.³ The Mormon book⁴ suggests to me that you have there a literarel
old Testement Second-coming revival, being gradually modified about the

---

¹ Postmark London NW 1 12.15 a.m. 31 Oct. 1921.
² Above and below the address to WBY 4 Broad Street, Oxford.
³ A hydrocele was a collection of clear fluid in the testes.
⁴ WBY was embarking on a financially essential lecture tour.
⁵ Probably the Gwalia Hotel.

¹ On Broad Street stationery with address struck out.
² He had begun work on what would become *Early Memories*.
³ Probably *Recollections of Dante Gabriel Rossetti* (1882). Sir Thomas Henry Hall Caine (1853–
1931), the Manx novelist, lived with the poet and Pre-Raphaelite painter Rossetti (1828–82)
as secretary and companion during the last year of the artist's life. The Yeats Library contains Archibald Strong, *Three Studies in Shelley and an Essay on Nature in Wordsworth and Meredith*
(Oxford, 1921) and *The Life of Percy Bysshe Shelley as Comprised in 'The Life of Shelley' by Thomas
Jefferson Hogg, 'The Recollections of Shelley & Byron' by Edward John Trelawney, 'Memoirs of Shelley'
by Thomas Love Peacock*, ed. Humbert Wolfe, 2 vols. (London, 1933). The London Library, for
which both WBY and GY had subscriptions, was in 14 St James's Square.
⁴ On their visit to universities in Utah in March 1920 the Yeatses had been intrigued by
what they learned of the Mormon religion; their library contained James Talmage, *The Articles
of Faith: A Series of Lectures on the Principal Doctrines of The Church of Jesus Christ of Latter-Day Saints*
(Salt Lake City, 1917).

time of the foundation of spiritism in America—of which the Mormons seem to know nothing—by a religion of spiritism, which tries to break its old bottle. From Swed[en]borg on that seems to have been the coming influence in the life of the soul—one can see what looks like design behind its different breakings out.

I shall await with anxiety your next report about Michael; I know he is out of danger but I hope to hear that he begins to get back his colour.

I cannot forget 'The Sleeping Beauty'—of which there is a very stupid notice, as I think, in to days 'Observer'—I have never seen anything on the stage that had such prolonged beauty for the eye[5]

As I have seen nobody I do not feel my lecture tour has begun & till it does there is nothing to report except that I wish you were here too

Yrs affecly
WB Yeats

Rossetti letters constantly remind me of Ricketts—Ricketts must when a boy have founded his manner upon him.

[ALS]   MORE'S HOTEL. | 18, ALSO 14,16,20 & 22 INDIA
                 STREET, | CHARING CROSS, | GLASGOW.
                 [8 Nov. 1921]

My dear George: Gave a good lecture last night in a church where I spoke from reding desk. Church full.[1] After lecture a man & his wife introduced themselves, & I found he was a Middleton, a branch of the Sligo family. He is an artist, a successful portrait painter of about 60 & had with him a very charming & very young wife.[2] I went to his studio afterwards & we talked there till bed time. I dine with him to night. His portraits are solid work, seem good likeness but are not very exciting. He had been to Burmah his studio was full of Burmese pictures of gay coloured crowds & golden looking shrines. I had no memory of ever having heard of him till he reminded

---

[5] While in London WBY and GY went to the Alhambra Theatre in Leicester Square (demolished in 1936) where Diaghilev's production of *The Sleeping Princess*, with music by Tchaikovsky and decor and costumes by Leon Bakst, had opened on 2 Nov. 1921.

[1] The *Glasgow Herald* of 8 Nov. 1921 reported on WBY's lecture to the Literary Society of Trinity Church, Claremont Street, on the Abbey Theatre and the founding of a National Theatre, in which he advised those interested in establishing a Scottish national theatre to 'Be as Scotch as ever you can…Get rid of that supercilious attitude towards the servant, the workman, the farmer's boy, and so on.'

[2] James Raeburn Middleton (1855–1931), the son of WBY's maternal grandmother's brother, was a portrait and genre painter in oil who exhibited scenes of Mandalay and Burma in the Royal Academy in 1905 and 1906, and also at the Paris salon; WBY wrote to Quinn that he had recently married a woman 'younger than George' (Foster ii. 203 and 705 n. 101).

me of a visit he payed to my fathers studio in the eighties. He is a friend of Cunningham-Grahame's.[3] At the lecture I was handed a letter, which I forgot till this morning. It is from a Miss or Mrs Imrie a member of the order, who asks if she may call & learn what the Felkin trouble is about. She is the only member in Glasgow & evidently very puzzled.[4]

No letter from you & when I do not hear I start wondering how Michael is.[5]

I am writing in the 'Palette Club' which very kindly gives me a private room & a fire to work in.[6] I shall be here every morning & after noon & am working at Memoir & will perhaps work at Deirdre.[7]

Yrs affecly
WB Yeats

[ALS[1]]   [Glasgow Scotland]
                                                 Nov 9 [1921]

My dear George: I was glad to get your wire.[2] I have written you I think two letters but do not feel sure that I got the address of your club right.[3] I told you of an artist I have been meeting one of the Sligo Middletons of whose existence I had no memory, & I have met another artist, a woman, of the same family whose work I have not seen—a pleasant, handsome cultivated woman.[4] I dine with her to morrow night & my head is faintly aching after the strain of a dinner party the other Middleton gave in my honour—much bad conversation every body with streams of irrelevant anecdotes, collected through long lives as fly-papers collect flies. Five or six minutes ago, [?on the]

[3] Robert Bontine Cunninghame Graham of Gartmore and Ardoch, nicknamed 'Don Roberto' (1852–1936), Scottish nationalist and socialist who with Keir Hardie organized the Scottish Labour Party. Author, traveller, and noted horseman, in 1927 he became the first president of the Scottish PEN, the association of writers, and was a model for a number of fictional characters in books by his friend Joseph Conrad, and also by Bernard Shaw.

[4] Miss or Mrs Imrie has not been traced; for 'Felkin trouble' see letter of 9 Nov. 1921.

[5] MBY was not taken back from the hospital to Oxford until mid-November.

[6] The Palette Club Ltd. was situated at 27 Newton Place, Glasgow; the secretary at the time was J. Brownlee Young.

[7] Perhaps in preparation for *Plays in Prose and Verse* (London, 1922), the second volume of Macmillan's *Collected Edition of the Works*.

[1] On Broad Street stationery.

[2] The telegram is missing.

[3] GY was a member of the Three Arts Club in Marylebone High Street, but may also have belonged to the Ladies Lyceum Club, 128 Piccadilly.

[4] Agnes Middleton Raeburn (1872–1955), a painter in oil and watercolour of landscapes and flowers, exhibited in London, Scotland, and abroad. One of the 'Immortals', a group of artists who had studied together at the Glasgow School of Art under Newbery, she was elected to the Royal Scottish Society of Painters in Water-colours in 1904.

other [?hand], a Miss Imrie left who came to see me about the order. She had some new fact she had been to Switzerland with, or at the same time as Miss Felkin. She says the idea of passivity, as Felkin has been teaching it, has been spreading from Steiner, whose later teaching is full of it. His followers stand round a large wooden image of Christ—Adam—Lucifer, & adore it with carefully emptied minds. She came to see me because she had recieved from the enemy a typed announcement of Miss Stoddarts suspension by FR.⁵ She was at my 'Quest' lecture⁶ & was told as she came away by Miss Stoddart that I belonged to the order. So far as I could judge by a very short conversation she was intelligent & sensible.

Both this morning & yesterday morning I did good [work] on the memoirs.

Yours affly
WB Yeats

[ALS]¹

[Scotland]
Nov 10 [1921]

My dear George: You will see by the enclosed² that my Aberdeen lecture has broken down. I must leave matters to the local people—as they would feel very upset if I got what would seem to them an inhos[pi]table reception & would be blamed. Interruptions by an audience after my Dublin experience are rather pleasantly exciting. One cannot however prevail against the singing of the National Antheme in the middle of a lecture. I have felt here, under the very friendly surface, a current of political hostility though no hostility to my self.

I shall probably keep to my old arrangement & return to Oxford Monday. I will write if I make any change of plans.

Yrs ev
WB Yeats

⁵ Dr Felkin was arranging to suspend Stoddart through his daughter Nora Ethelwyn Mary Felkin (1883–1962), 'Quaero Altissima', who served as his representative when he and his second wife, Harriet (*c*.1873–1959), 'Quaero Lucem', moved permanently to New Zealand in 1916; Miss Imrie reported her discussion with WBY to Stoddart (*LWBY* 2, 400).

⁶ In 1919 WBY had lectured on 'the system' to Mead's Quest Society in London.

¹ On Broad Street stationery.

² Probably the item in the *Glasgow Herald*, 10 Nov. 1921, 8, headed: 'Aberdeen Students and W. B. Yeats': 'Mr. W. B. Yeats, the Irish poet, was to have delivered a lecture to the English Association of Aberdeen on Saturday evening. In yesterday's issue of "Alma Mater" the Aberdeen University magazine, a letter appeared calling attention to Mr Yeats' association with the Sinn Fein movement, and hoping that something would be done in the nature of a protest against the appearance on a platform in Aberdeen of a "self-avowed enemy". In consequence of this letter it has been decided to cancel the lecture.'

[ALS[1]]   [Glasgow, Scotland]
                                               Friday [11 Nov. 1921]

My dear George: one of the evening papers here—I meant to send it you
but forgot it behind me—had an account of the stopping of my Aberdeen
meeting.[2] There had been a letter of protest against the meeting of 'an
enemy of the Nation' Last night Miss Raeburn, artist, one of the Middleton
connections asked a number of people, including some city magnate whose
brother is married to her sister, to meet me at dinner. Afterwards most of
the guests came to my lecture, which was the best I have yet given here.
Miss Raeburn is a water-colour painter and I have seen at an exhibition
here her very skillful water colours. She has been a good deal in France.
I remember her, & her sister as too little girls dressed in black coming on a
visit to Sligo. (Continues on back page)[3]
    I have collected some information for Lilly about the original Middleton,
who came to Sligo in the eighteenth century or early nineteenth having
got into trouble with the revenue—an office in London & an office in the
Channel Islands having no doubt been a temptation to smuggle.[4] He often
sailed on one of his own ships called the Argo & lived a life of adventure.
He & his ship were taken prisoner in some South American port but he
cut his cables at night & escaped. Some old Sligo paper reports a trial in
which he gave evidence, or was involved in some way, & the judge said after
something he had said 'that is a strange thing to say for a man who had
faced mutiny on his own deck & beaten it' He was my grand mothers father
& her brother was the father of the artist I have been meeting here. I am
rather vague about the link with the Raeburns.[5] So there is quite a spirited
ancestor for Michael.

                                               Yours affecly
                                               WB Yeats

P S.
I lunched with some of the students at the university yesterday & spoke to
the Union on the theatre. A very rowdy but very good humoured audience.
Constant interruptions at first, but they all listened very well & at the end

---

[1] On Broad Street stationery, address crossed out.
[2] See note to previous letter.
[3] He has written the outline of his lecture on the other side of the sheet, which is folded
to make four small pages: 'Peoples Theatre/Emotion of Truth/Coffee Palace/Emigration/
Rising of Moon/Synge/Proletarian Drama'.
[4] William Middleton (*c*.1770–1832) married Elizabeth Pollexfen (1798–1853); their daughter
Elizabeth Middleton (1819–92) was WBY's maternal great-grandmother (Foster i. xxii).
[5] They were very distant Pollexfen cousins of WBY: Elizabeth Middleton's brother John
married Janet Raeburn of Glasgow, and her sister Agnes married John Raeburn of Glasgow
(Foster i. xxii).

I had a grip of them. I spoke about 20 minutes & then invited questions, answered the questions, & then somebody asked me to go on speaking so I made a wind up speech of a quarter of an hour or so. They were so rowdy that I saw what the Aberdeen people were afraid of. Had there been hostility the whole thing might have turned into a political meeting where different parties shouted one another down. I have made a real success here, & I shall be invited again next year I am told. I grudge very much however the loss of the Aberdeen 10 guineas.

Part Three

A Home in Ireland

1922–1924

In February 1922 George Yeats posed the horary question, 'Am I right to go to look at houses in Dublin at once? Moon going to sextile Jupiter which promises no unexpected obstacles. Comfortable journeys. Significator of houses is conjoined with Venus sun in the neighbourhood of mid heaven trine Jupiter square Mars. This promises that a satisfactory house will be obtained but...it will either not be the house expected or it will be acquired in some unexpected way.' Two weeks later she annotated it: 'Correct. Got different house & circumstances generally unexpected. G. Yeats Feb 26 1922.'

82 Merrion Square would be their home in Dublin throughout the period during which WBY was a Senator and both he and George were engulfed in the political, artistic, and social scene. George became deeply involved in the Dublin Drama League and—through comments from the sidelines—the Abbey Theatre. The matter of the Hugh Lane pictures weighed heavily on WBY, as did the increasing frailty of Lady Gregory; frequent visits were paid by WBY to Coole, in part to discuss theatre business, but as a refuge for WBY when his wife was away. Despite the pleasant surprise of the Nobel Prize, financial matters were always a concern for both of them, especially when Lily's illness made the situation of Cuala Industries even more precarious. WBY's literary output correspondingly increased; so did his fame, drawing him into wider political arenas and serious international debate, necessitating even more absences in London on the Hugh Lane controversy and Anglo-Irish relations. George meanwhile kept close watch on the children's and her husband's health, and during WBY's absences the ever revolving Dublin circles. All of this hectic activity was reflected in their correspondence, with Ballylee serving as a necessary haven for both.

1922

[ALS]   4 Broad St | Oxford.
                                                          Feb 14 [1922]

My dear George: I have got black edged paper because Mrs Jackson, who has
lost her husband wrote on blacked edged to me & I want to reply to her.[1]

I hope you do not think my not going over leaves you too much respon-
sibily.[2] If you do a wire to-morrow will bring me over on Friday—even a
wire on Friday will. I have not gone because as I trusted your judgement
I thought it would be an extravagence to go. Between lost days & money
spent I might go near spending the difference between our Oxford & our
Dublin rent & taxes. Your letters have been more undecided & despondent
than your telegrams led me to expect, & so perhaps you really want me
over. Wire if you do. If I cross now I shall, I hope, have got the two copies
of the new sections of the memories despatched to Watt. I have been very
busy dictating to a typist since you left—16 letters & all the new passages
typed.

Do you know if I have a receipt for my deposit at the Bank?—I am to
sign it but as I dont know where it is they say it does not matter for the
moment. In fact I have enough apart from the deposit I think to meet the
£50 for Raftery & they will let me over draw.[3]

Anne came up to day to show her toy & to ask for a chock. Both children
are well & so am I. To-night I go to 'The Pretenders' with a young man
from Balliol.[4]

                                                          Yrs affecly
                                                          WB Yeats

[1] The Rt. Hon. Frederick Huth Jackson (1863–1921) was a wealthy merchant banker, Privy
Counsellor (1911), Sheriff of the City of London, and Lord Lieutenant of Sussex; his liberal-
minded wife put on his tombstone 'a great merchant, a great squire and a great lover'. The
black edging might have also have been a distant acknowledgement of JBY's death in New
York on 3 Feb. 1922.
[2] The Dáil having ratified the Anglo-Irish Treaty on 7 January making provision for an
Irish Free State of twenty-six counties independent of the United Kingdom, WBY was determined to play a part in the new state; GY, who had been urging the move, went over to
Dublin to look for a house.
[3] Rafferty, whom WBY and AG frequently called 'Raftery' after the famous blind 19th-
century Irish poet, had once more begun work on Ballylee.
[4] Ibsen's *The Pretenders* was produced by the Oxford University Drama Society in the New
Theatre, directed by William Bridges-Adams and featuring a St John's undergraduate, Tyrone
Guthrie, who would become one of the foremost directors of the 20th century.

I dont know who Maccready is but if he is solvent I am satisfied. It seems to me that if we get £50 a year for the top floor & let the stables we would have a very cheap house. Hugh Law does something of that kind.⁵

[ALS]   4, BROAD STREET, | OXFORD.
                                                            March 19. 1922

My dear Willy
    I enclose a letter which shows up Martindale's perfidy to an even more horrible degree than before!!¹ I found it in the <u>one</u> unsorted 'drawer'. (He wrote to you, you remember, also about the French priest of Mirabeau.²) There were a quantity of letters from Synge in the same drawer.³ These I have duly filed. I have ordered an aditional layer to the file as it is now over-choked. This will go to Dublin.⁴

                                                            Yours ever
                                                            George
                                                            P. T. O.

---

⁵ Macready is unidentified. GY decided in the end on 82 Merrion Square, planning to rent the top floor for six months 'to two young men of our acquaintance', again unidentified; the agreement to purchase was not signed until 22 March and the Yeatses had moved into the entire house by 22 September (*BG*, 291 ff.). Hugh Alexander Law (1872–1943) of Ballymore, Co. Donegal, was a barrister, nationalist MP, and author of *Anglo-Irish Literature* (Dublin, 1926).

¹ Enclosure missing. The well-known Jesuit Father Cyril Charlie Martindale (1879–1963) of Campion Hall, Oxford, was adviser during this period to the Duke of Marlborough over the nullity granted, on the grounds of coercion, of his marriage to Consuelo Vanderbilt (they separated in 1906) and later acceptance into the Roman Catholic Church. The new Duchess of Marlborough (the former Boston heiress Gladys Deacon, 1882–1977) had invited the Yeatses, LR, and Ottoline Morrell to lunch at Blenheim Palace after MBY was christened in December 1921 (*BG*, 282).

² In May 1914 WBY, in the company of MG and Everard Feilding, honorary secretary of the Society for Psychical Research, had travelled to Mirebeau, France, to investigate the claims by Abbé Vachère that religious pictures in the sacristy of the local church had produced drops of liquid blood. Although he wrote a long report on the manifestation, WBY concluded there was no miracle (Foster i. 518). On 1 May 1917 Martindale wrote to WBY on the advice of Feilding wishing to hear about 'any phenomena which can be called "spiritualist" even in a wide sense' (*LWBY* 2, 333–4).

³ John Millington Synge (1871–1909), poet, essayist, and playwright and co-director with AG and WBY of the Abbey Theatre; Synge remained an iconic image for WBY.

⁴ While GY was packing for their move to Ireland, WBY was in London visiting friends.

Katharine Scott came last night at 8.15 pm and stayed till 12.20 talking about her very American love affairs—I felt so old.[5] Have I already arrived at the age when young women come for advice about their love-affairs?!![6]

[ALCS]   STEPHEN'S GREEN CLUB, | DUBLIN.
                                            [?20 Mar. 1922]

My dear George
         Here is a note which needs an answer?[1]
         I will write a letter later on to day or on Tuesday. I send this now for fear I forget it.
                              Yrs ev
                              WB Yeats

[ALS]   STEPHEN'S GREEN CLUB. | DUBLIN.
                                            March 21 [1922]

My dear George: I have moved here from the Hibernian & shall stay till Friday as my 'Hour Glass' is played on Thursday night.[1]
         I enclose a note to Beatrice Erskine from your grandmother.[2] Mrs Erskine had this phrase 'it is just as well that all the money should not be left away

---

[5] Katharine Bishop Scott (b. 1897) from Cleveland, Ohio, entered the Society of Oxford Home Students (later St Anne's College) with a BA from Wellesley College, and before she graduated with a B.Litt. in May 1923 had married her supervisor, the brilliant scholar and poet Maurice Roy Ridley (1890–1969), chaplain and fellow of Balliol College, said to be the model for detective Lord Peter Wimsey in the novels by his friend Dorothy L. Sayers and reputed to have celebrated mass while wearing a monocle. The Ridleys were later divorced and Katharine returned to the United States where her last known address was 420 Beacon Street Boston, which was the chapel of the Ramakrishna Vedanta Centre until 1941. I am indebted to David Smith, Librarian and Archivist of St Anne's College, for his assistance.

[6] GY was not quite 30, only a few years older than Katharine Scott.

[1] Enclosure missing, but possibly from Rafferty, who was having difficulty finding wood for the castle floors. After a few days in London together, GY returned to Oxford to collect the children and WBY went on ahead to Dublin.

[1] WBY's play *The Hour-Glass*, first produced in March 1903 and subsequently revised a number of times in both prose and verse, had recently been given a new ending.

[2] The note is missing. Mrs Robert Steuart Erskine, née Beatrice Caroline Strong (1860–1948), was a prolific travel writer, translator, biographer, novelist, dramatist, member of the Golden Dawn, and author of a series of articles on mysticism in the *Occult Review* (5 Apr. 1907, 7 Mar. 1908). Her husband was a distant cousin of GY's maternal grandfather Montagu Woodmass, and she herself remained on good terms with EET's mother Edith Alice Woodmass (1848–1927). Because of a quarrel between EET and Mrs Woodmass, GY had not yet met her grandmother.

from the family' which suggests a public spirited animosity one had not thought of I think, and the National Gallery for the pictures. The significance of the phrase only occured to me next day so I did not question her. It was said in a comment on a sentence of mine which was merely 'I think a grandmother has every write to see her grandchild & even if the grandmother were in jail for forgery.'

When I told Dulac about our new carpet, he was most vehement on the subject & wanted you to get a kind of carpet which Harreds sell which is a literal copy of a persian carpet.³ He has one in his studio & there are many patterns & sizes. He would choose one for us or go with you. I wish you had been with me. I am not sure that the broad patch of pure green will not be more effective but I really do not know; & I promised to tell you. He & Ricketts are enthusiastic about their carpets. He paid £40 for his which measures 13 feet 8 inches by 11 feet but there are cheaper. I think however our carpet is bigger is it not? He has given us two large Chinease pictures which I admire very much.⁴ I said we would probably ask him to keep them till the Autumn as Ballylee is damp. I have seen Gogorty & Lennox Robinson & some dull members of the club & find general optimism except about the trouble with Ulster.⁵

I miss you & long for you

Yrs affecly
WB Yeats

[ALCS] STEPHEN'S GREEN CLUB, | DUBLIN.
Tuesday [?21 Mar. 1922]

My dear George

I have got enclosed from Lady Gregory. Read last sentence. I have asked for confirmation if it is our servants parents house as I am not always sure of Lady G's hand writing.¹ I have asked if it is desirable to give some money. One does not want to check voluntary effort when only that can remedy the mischief.

---

³ Harrod's fashionable department store in Knightsbridge, London, was noted for its claim to supply 'anything from a packet of pins to an elephant'. Dulac was an authority on carpets and well known for his paintings in the Persian style.

⁴ One of the Chinese pictures was still in the possession of ABY before her death.

⁵ The six counties of Northern Ireland had rejected the Treaty offer to join the Republic. Meanwhile civil war had broken out when de Valera, leader of 'the Irreconcilables' or 'Irregulars', repudiated the Treaty over the wording of the oath of allegiance.

¹ 'the night before last J.M.'s [James Molloy] house was burned down in the night without warning (some quarrel about land), wife and children and all in bed. All escaped and saved most of the furniture' (*Journals*, i. 333).

I shall not do any of the speaking Lady G suggests.² I could do no good in this whirlpool of hatred; & doing no good would be doing harm. I at least can refuse to hate & stay at home & write.

Yrs ev
WB Yeats

[ALS]   Coole Park | Gort | Co Galway
March 28 [1922]

My dear George: I wired to-day 'Ballylee all right' but as there is no post out, since the war, later than 1.30 this will have to wait till to-morrow. Ground floor room and the rooms on first and second floors will be ready for you. There are letters for you here & one for Michael Yeats, which I shall keep till you arrive. Lady Gregory can keep me as long as you like.¹

There is no news except that I am lonely for lack of you.

Yrs scy
WB Yeats

[ALS]   SAVILE CLUB, | 107, PICCADILLY. W.1.
Dec [Nov.] 19 [1922]

My dear Dobbs:¹ All well so far except that letters seem to have gone astray in the most surprising way not only letters from Sheffield to Dublin but a big fat letter from Christy to me sent here & marked to wait arrival.² I had my first adventure yesterday. Gosse passed me on the stairs that lead to the washing basins & cut me. I shouted 'hello Gosse'; but dipping his hands into the basin he turned his face away & said 'You have not called.' This explains that bad review of some months ago—I have not called.³

---

² With the hope that he would be named Minister of Fine Arts in the new government, a position urged by among others Ellen Duncan, still curator of the Municipal Gallery of Modern Art, AG was advising WBY to write or speak about the political situation.

¹ GY, who was still in Dublin with the children, insisted that WBY stay at Coole until she had all settled at Ballylee; the family then settled in to Ballylee for the next six months until the move to Merrion Square was accomplished.

¹ GY's nickname since childhood, always used by her brother Harold and close family friends.

² Probably from Christy and Moore Ltd., literary agents 225–7 Strand WC, who arranged some of WBY's lecture tours.

³ Edmund William Gosse (1849–1928), poet, biographer, critic, and translator, who had been in part responsible for WBY's pension, had slated *Four Plays for Dancers* (London, 1921) as 'childish', 'arbitrary', and 'devoid of meaning' and the notes and appendices 'a little too self-complacent' (*Sunday Times*, 'Plays in Verse', 11 Dec. 1921, 6). From 1904 to 1914, among his other roles, he was librarian to the House of Lords and was knighted in 1925.

I have got a room here from Monday Nov 27 for a week & I come back here after Cardif for Tuesday night.[4]

I went to Ricketts on Friday night & saw Miss Stoddart last night & dine with Dulac to night. Miss Stoddart says that if Hammond consents we can have all the order properties.[5] She seemed to me much better than usual & gave me a long description of a tower vision she had in 1914. I had not questioned her & she started on it herself being in a muddle as to whether it was or was not from the evil powers.—A ruined Tower & the Phoenix born from the fire on the top—she seemed to think it must be a real place. It got very ruinous as you got up.

I have a poem in my head started by the brawl with MG but if ever done it cannot be till I get back[6]

Yours affection[ate]ly
WB Yeats

[ALS]   SAVILE CLUB, | 107, PICCADILLY. W.1.
                                    Monday Nov 20 [1922]

My dear Dobbs: I go to Garsington at week end & Lady Otolline writes wishing you were over, & saying how much she misses you.[1] Did I tell you I have got a room here from Nov 27.

Dulac has a new love, a tall goodlooking girl of 28 or so[2]—I dined with them last night—& poor Madam Dulac has fled to her mother in germany. The new young woman has 'rescued' him, has been a 'deliverer'—in other

---

[4] WBY left Dublin 16 November for a lecture tour of Cardiff, Sheffield, and Leeds.

[5] Although by now removed as a ruling chief of the Order, Stoddart was still in charge of the Amoun Temple, to which the Yeatses belonged. Finally convinced that the Order was evil, under the pseudonym 'Inquire within' she published *Light-Bearers of Darkness* in 1923. In August 1922 WBY wrote to an American enquirer, 'Lately I find myself somewhat detached. I consider myself simply as belonging to "The Second Order" but not connected with one temple more than other, as I do not care to make my self responsible for the teaching of any particular chief' (*CL InteLex*, acc. 4165).

[6] With WBY and MG on opposite sides over the Treaty, there were frequent quarrels, exacerbated by his acceptance of honorary degrees this year from 'the enemy', TCD and Queen's University, Belfast. The poem is unidentified.

[1] The Yeatses were regular visitors of Garsington Manor just outside Oxford, the country home of Lady Ottoline Violet Anne Morrell, née Cavendish-Bentinck (1873–1938), well-known hostess and patron of the arts, and her husband Philip Edward Morrell (1870–1943), a Liberal MP.

[2] In 1903 Dulac married Alice May de Marine and after that marriage was dissolved in 1911 married Elsa Analice Bignardi; by the time they separated in 1923 Helen de Vere Beauclerk (1892–1969), novelist, translator, and journalist, had become his companion and would remain so for the rest of his life; a number of her novels were illustrated by Dulac.

words got him out of the 'whirl pool'; & he has 'rescued' & 'delivered' her from a 'whirl pool,' very plainly shown forth in her horoscope.[3] I astonished her by speaking of her probably friendship with a drug taker—☿ in 11th[4]—which turns out to be true. I liked her—thought her clever & reasonably simple & not I think a whirl pool. It has been going on for some months. She has a flat in Fitzroy St—& is a journalist, writes a weekly column in some London paper & also psychological stories.

Yrs affectionately
WB Yeats

Just off to Cardif

[TLS[1]]   82, MERRION SQUARE, | DUBLIN.
November 23 1922

My dear Willy;

I enclose part of today's Freeman's Journal. It contains the account of the very mysterious Childers trial, and a reference—which I have marked—to your probable election to the Senate.[2]

I havent any news. There was a terrific explosion last night about 1–15, but I havent heard yet where or what it was. I havent been to the Gogartys[3] or anywhere else as Anne has had a bad attack of tonsilitis and cough, and she had to be separated from Michael, so I had to nurse her. She is much better, and up again, so I shall be free from now on.

The young cat discovered the canaries! I heard a yell from Anne 'Sacred Heart, the cat is eating a canary'. I tore downstairs only just in time. Anne was full of moral indignation, for she said the 'cat had his tea'. Then she asked 'Could a canary eat the cat?' And when I said no, 'Couldnt <u>all</u> the canaries together eat the cat?' And she still is puzzled over it. The canaries are back in the Return room.[4]

I am sending you two clean shirts to Garsington, the remainder of your wash to Savile Club. I cant send it all to Garsington as the wash hasnt come back yet, and I am afraid of missing you. Please be sure and give the maid

---

[3] 'Whirlpool' was the Yeatses' term for a dangerous emotional state.

[4] Astrological symbols for Mercury, the planet of communication, in the eleventh house, that of friendship and allies.

[1] From now on most of GY's letters are typed.

[2] 'The Irish Senate/Men Who May sit in the Upper House/President's List…Candidates favorably spoken of and likely to be asked to consent to nomination are Sir John Purser Griffiths, Mr Wm Butler Yeats, and Sir Maurice Dockrell' (*Freeman's Journal*, 22 Nov. 1922, p. 5 col. 5).

[3] The Gogartys held regular 'At Homes' on Wednesdays.

[4] A room off the stairs between storeys.

at Gars: 10/- and tell her it is because I forgot to leave her anything when we stayed there last. Her name is Minnie. She is the stout parlourmaid.

You must try and get the Order properties!!!!!! <u>We shall have to pay for them, but it will be well worth it</u>.

I am very dull in this letter, but I have hardly been out and it is wearing and rather exasperating looking after a sick child whose conversation is unlimited and vocabulary small!

Send me a line from Garsington, and give my love to Ottoline.

Sean has brought the new shelves for the study, they look very well, and the new paint is a brilliant affair.[5] I hope you will like it. I have only done a little. In fact I only began today.[6]

Tonight I dine and go to the 'Pictures' with Tom Macreevy.[7] Tomorrow with some youth whose name I forget—I am afraid that your name publicly associated with the Senate will bring Maud and her ilk down upon you with prayers for intercession. There has been no placard parading for the last few days, and that is I think ominous! Cruise O'Brien will turn Republican shortly. He is very vehement over the executions, and if Childers and the other eight are shot there will be a tremendous row.[8] No one minds Mary Macswiney,[9] but the executions horrified nearly everyone, especially the working classes

Love

Yours Dobbs

[5] I have been unable to identify the carpenter, Sean.

[6] GY always arranged and painted WBY's study and bedroom herself.

[7] A misspelling of Thomas McGreevy, from 1943 spelled MacGreevy (1893–1967), poet and art critic, who was to become a lifelong friend not only of GY and WBY, but of Samuel Beckett and Jack B. Yeats. After serving in the First World War he enrolled as a mature student at TCD and immediately became part of the Dublin arts scene. After considerable time away from Ireland as editor in London and teacher in Paris, he returned to Dublin and in 1950 achieved his ambition to become the director of the National Gallery of Ireland (*BG*, 364 ff.).

[8] British-born though raised in Ireland, Robert Erskine Childers (1870–1922), sailor and author of the political spy thriller *The Riddle of the Sands* (1903) who, after distinguished service in the Boer War, became a staunch advocate of Irish Home Rule and was involved in 1914 with gun-running for the Irish Volunteers. In 1919 he was made director of publicity for Sinn Féin and in 1921 was elected to the Dáil, but, as secretary-general of the Irish delegation that negotiated the Anglo-Irish Treaty, supported de Valera's disagreement over the final draft and the oath of allegiance. When captured he was court-martialled because he was carrying an automatic pistol (which had been given him by Michael Collins), and was sentenced to death under the Free State's emergency powers legislation. Four young men had already been shot on 17 November; see the following four letters.

[9] Mary ('Min', Maire) MacSwiney (1872–1942), founder with her sister Annie of the primary school for girls Scoil Íta in Cork, and militant Republican activist. Her brother Terence Joseph MacSwiney (1879–1920), who had been elected to the first Dáil in 1918, became Mayor of Cork after the assassination of his friend Tomás MacCurtain (1884–1920), first Republican Mayor of Cork, and when arrested on 12 Aug. 1920 for making a 'seditious speech', embarked on the longest hunger strike in Irish political history, dying after 74 days; his strike and death on 25 October gained worldwide attention. Violently opposed to the Treaty, after election to the Dáil Mary was imprisoned in July 1922 and released after her own hunger strike; after a further arrest on 4 Nov. 1922 she immediately again went on a hunger strike, but after 24 days was released when near death.

[ALS]   SAVILE CLUB | 107, PICCADILLY. W.1.
                                          [23 Nov. 1922]

My dear Dobbs: I sent you for Blythe (whose address I had'nt) a poor telegraph.[1] I tried my best & re-wrote it many times. This morning a strange
thing hapened I was awakened by a volley or rather by two volleys one close
on the other. As if two squads of men had been told to fire but had not fired
exactly together. I said 'Childers is dead.' I was all the more sure from waking out of a parrellel dream—Blakes 'lost child' safe in a wildernes among
lions.[2] I had gone to sleep thinking that Gogortys intervention had probably
saved him. I am sorry because he was an able man—and yet—& yet. One
wonders what will this new yeast do with our Irish dough.

   I have got through my lecture easily & well—I am lecturing more simply,
I think, & naturally.

   I go to Oxford to-morrow & shall I dare say find a letter from you at
Garsington.

                                                              Yrs snly
                                                              WB Yeats

[TLS]   82, MERRION SQUARE, | DUBLIN.
                                            November 24 [1922]

My dear Willy;
   I hope you wern't angry with me for wiring you about Childers? It
is not so much a question of Childers, as of the other men. If they dont
shoot Childers there is a better chance for the others, and any way it is a
good thing for the ministry to see that people <u>do</u> care. The four men they
shot last week were shot without the knowledge of the Teachtai, and the
wives and relatives were not informed until the men had been dead eleven
hours.[1] They were not allowed to see their relatives at all before being
shot. Tuohig's wife, a young girl, had no idea he had even been tried, and
the first intimation she got was a telephone message, at the draper's shop
where she works, to tell her to go up to Portobello at 6 o'c in the evening.

---

   [1] Ernest Blythe (Earnán de Blaghd) (1889–1975), politician, writer and dedicated Gaelic
Leaguer who was frequently imprisoned for his activities with the Irish Volunteers. Elected in
1918 and later a supporter of the Treaty, he was successively in charge of various Sinn Féin
ministries (Trade and Commerce, Local Government, Public Health, and finally, 1923–32,
Finance); a Senator until 1936, 1941–67 he was managing director of the Abbey Theatre.
   [2] A reference to 'The Little Girl Lost' and 'The Little Girl Found' in William Blake's *Songs
of Innocence*.

   [1] Executed were Peter Cassidy, James Fisher, John Gaffney, and Richard Twohig; the
Teachtai Dála (TDs) are members of Dáil Éireann.

At Portobello she was informed that her husband had been shot at seven o'clock that morning.[2] Gogarty didnt say anything about getting you to wire. All I know is that he said he was going to speak to Cosgrave about the Childers execution, and that he had some influence with Cosgrave.[3] They will probably have to shoot men, but if they do it in this way and before the Constitution is passed in England the country will turn as it did after the Maxwell executions.[4] No one cares a damn about the Macswineys but there is great feeling about these unauthorised shootings.[5]

There was tremendous firing last night. I went to the Pictures with Tom McGreevy. We came down the stairs at 10–30 to find bullets whizzing down Grafton Street.[6] The fight began all over Dublin at 9.30. Tremendous machine gun firing, and no one but ambulance men on the streets. After waiting about ten minutes we decided to run over to Anne Street and try and get home. So we bolted over without mishap, got into Dawson street, and found a red cross man there. We questioned him as to where it was safe to go, and he advised a tram—if there was one. Presently one did turn up, and we went as far as Fitzwilliam street; walked down towards Merrion Square and were greeted by blasts of machine-gun fire from Oriel House and the Government buildings.[7] Decided it was too unhealthy, and went to the Arts Club where we drank tea until about quarter to twelve. Then a lull came, and I decided to try and get home. McGreevy insisted on coming although I pointed out that young men in trench coats were undesireable companions! However I got in, and he got home without mishap. Just as I got upstairs I smelt a fearful smell of burning, and rushed up to find that the cook had left a lighted candle in front of her window and the curtains etc were on fire. I extinguished them. Then the whole house roared and shook with that damned gun in the Govt. Buildings which started off afresh, joined by Oriel

[2] Portobello, the military barracks, was in nearby Rathmines.

[3] William Thomas Cosgrave (1880–1965), who fought in the General Post Office in 1916, was a member of the Treaty delegation and after the deaths of Arthur Griffith and Michael Collins was elected President of the Executive Council and Minister of Finance; in 1923 he was founder of the pro-Treaty party, Cumann na nGaedheal, which he led until 1933, returning as leader of Fine Gael from 1935 until his retirement in 1945.

[4] Fifteen of the 1916 leaders were executed on the orders of British General Sir John Grenfell Maxwell (1859–1929), who had been sent over to crush the rebellion.

[5] Annie MacSwiney (Eithne Nic Shuibhne) (d. 1954), co-founder of St Ita's School for Girls in Cork with her sister Mary, went on hunger strike at the prison gates on 21 November when refused permission to see her sister.

[6] Probably the film *Wicklow Gold* at the Empire Theatre in Dame Street, advertised as 'the best Irish film yet produced...a riot of laughter from start to finish'; starring the variety artist and comedian Jimmy O'Dea, the film was one of three produced in 1921 by Irish Photoplays.

[7] The local division of government was based in Oriel House, just across Merrion Square from 82.

house, sundry bombs and rifle fire. Went down to the nursery to find nurse
and the maids weeping over the fire. By this time I was cross. So I told them
they were idiots and carried them off to the downstairs back rooms. They
had been sitting all evening without any light on—God knows why—weeping
and praying. They all had their Rosaries in their hands. Anne was sitting up
in bed saying 'Sacred Heart what's that' My advent brought a more pagan
spirit, and they all cheered up and ate caramels.

A stop press is just out. Childers executed this morning at seven. More
rows tonight. I shall not go out!! I have laid in sundry stocks in case an
attempt is made to cut off Dublin and have another Four Courts Week.[8] So
if there is one you neednt worry. A stirring life.

Michael smiled whenever a particularly loud explosion came!

I hear from an eye-witness of the last Sundays O'Connell street episode
(soldiers firing on the crowd and killing one) that a woman fired at the
military, and that some women in the crowd tore the widow's weeds from
Madam Gonne's hat—[9]

I hope you are not too tired after your strenuous week?

Yours ever
George.

Love to Ottoline[10]

[ALS]   at | Garsington | Oxford
Nov 27 [1922]

My dear Dobbs: I wonder if my telegram of Nov 23 reached you—you do
not say if it did—I judge from your letters that things were as I thought the
army going its own road. When I read of those four men shot I remembered
that the government had planned—Gogorty my authority—to try men for

[8] On 14 Apr. 1922 the Four Courts, centre of the Irish judiciary, and other buildings including the Kildare Street Club had been seized by the Irish Republican Army although without authority of the IRA executive; on 28 June the Provisional Government shelled the buildings, wounding many and destroying twenty-five buildings in all. At that time the Yeatses in Ballylee were without trains, post, or telegrams and fresh food supplies for seventeen days.

[9] The *Irish Times* of 20 Nov. 1922 reported that on the previous afternoon national soldiers shot into a large gathering, mostly of women, who were protesting against the treatment of Irish prisoners, and that seven people were seriously wounded; that same evening a deputation led a large crowd of women to the Roman Catholic Archbishop's residence to protest the continued detention of Mary MacSwiney, who was on hunger strike; both meetings were led by MG and Mrs Despard.

[10] On the back of this letter WBY has written 'Isabel Ostrander. | "midnight". | "Return of Club Foot"'; Isabel Egenton Ostrander (1883–1924), who also wrote under the pseudonyms 'Christopher B. Booth', 'Robert Orr Chipperfield', 'David Fox', and 'Douglas Grant', was a popular American writer of detective fiction, a genre GY and WBY read avidly.

arson & loot & such things & so evade the making of martyrs. I felt that
I knew too little of the details to telegraph effectively & so sent but that
one sentence. Childers 'apologia' as printed to day puzzles me—it does not
impress me—he describes himself as 'mislead' by what he thought 'a war
for small nations.'[1] It seems unreal but perhaps he did not know that he had
been sentenced or even that his sentence was likely. It makes one wonder
if his importance has not, as he himself says, been exaggerated; & yet one
remembers very able work of his.

I am staying here till Tuesday—both Lady Ottoline & her husband have
pressed me to so I do not think I am in the way. There have been a stream
of people—Bertram Russell & his wife, some Austrian woman, a certain
Miss Baker known as 'the shy bride' because she ran away twice from
the church door—we discussed 'whirl pools' whom she declared to be really
sincere—her impossible mother who quoted the bible & was very deaf &
then to day young Cecil & three other young men.[2] O I forgot—yesterday
there were several young men one of them Strong who has had a dream or
vision of a flash of lightening which is 'devine suffering' 'the supreme manifestation of gods power.'[3] He told me that young Graves was very hard up
some time ago & 'a five pound note suddenly fell on the table before him'—
I remember your silver coin at Shillingford—& 'something of the kind has
happened again on the aniversary of the day.'[4] Strong reminded me that
the same thing—a pound in gold in this case—fell once before Francis

---

[1] *The Times*, 27 Nov. 1922, quotes the account of his life Childers made before the military
court, concluding with the statement, 'I fought and worked for a sacred principle, the loyalty
of the nation to its declared independence, and repudiation of any voluntary surrender to
conquest and inclusion in the British Empire.' The words quoted by WBY are a summary by
the unnamed correspondent, 'Like thousands of Irish Nationalists he was misled by the idea
of a war for small nations.'

[2] Bertrand Arthur William Russell (1872–1970), philosopher, logician, peace activist, a
former lover and long-time confidante of Ottoline's; his second wife Dora Russell, née Black
(1894–1986), whom he married in 1921, had recently given birth to their son; the 'Austrian
woman' was probably the governess to Julian, the Morrells' daughter; 'the shy bride' is
unidentified; Ottoline's nephew Lord Francis Morven Dallas Cavendish-Bentinck (1900–50)
was usually accompanied by his Oxford friends Edward Sackville-West (1901–65), Ottoline's
cousin Robert Gathorne-Hardy (1902–73), who would become her memorialist and editor,
and Lord David Cecil (1902–86), who would become a fellow of Wadham College and later
a well-known scholar and biographer (Miranda Seymour, *Ottoline Morrell: Life on the Grand Scale*
(London, 1994), 445).

[3] The lightning flash was an important image in GY's automatic script. Leonard Alfred
George Strong (1896–1958), poet, novelist, and critic, was one of the Oxford undergraduates
who regularly attended the Yeatses' 'At Homes' and later recorded his impressions in *A Letter
to W. B. Yeats*, Hogarth Letters No. 6 (London, 1932) and *Personal Remarks* (London, 1953).

[4] Robert von Ranke Graves (1895–1985), already known as a war poet, later distinguished
as translator, writer of historical novels, and mythographer, was the son of Irish poet Alfred
Percival Graves (1846–1931) with whom WBY had worked in the Irish Literary Society of
London in the 1890s.

Thompson.[5] Yesterday Lady Ottoline asked me up to her little study & then asked me questions of philosophy & said I had been the only person who had ever been of any help to her. This morning she questioned me again & many of her comments were very acute. She had felt that Bertram Russell had gone back in thought, become dry & narrow through refusal to admit anything beyond his own mind. We must keep her in our thoughts. I used to think her interested but as not understanding but I see that I was mistaken.

Both parcels of clothes, that to the Savile and that sent here have arrived. Your letter about the firing & about Anne is very vivid but nobody should have encouraged you to go out that night—I think you should be very careful for some little time—there will be some other attack.

I shall be very glad to be back though I am having a pleasant time enough.

Yours affectionly

WB Yeats

[TLS/MS]   82, MERRION SQUARE, | DUBLIN.

November 28 1922

My dear Willy;

I had hoped for a letter from you today. Did you get mine, sent to Garsington?

I saw Gogarty last night. No news that I can tell you in a letter. Apparently one of the four men executed was the man who betrayed Collins into the ambush. He was in the Gov. Service and informed the republicans all the details of Collins visit to Cork. Another of the four was in the raid during which Cosgrove's uncle was killed. I hear there are to be more executions. They are not executing men for fighting but for fighting *and* looting or robbing.[1]

The Gogartys have bought another house!! In Queens County. A huge house with desmesne and polished mahogany doors and central heating. They go there for Christmas and are to invite us there for a week-end.[2]

---

[5] Francis Thompson (1859–1907), religious poet who, despite the assistance of Wilfred and Alice Meynell, returned to opium addiction and died destitute in London; during the 1890s Thompson, who at least once attended the Rhymers' Club, wrote a number of essays on WBY's work.

[1] On 30 Nov. 1922 IRA chief of staff William Flanagan 'Liam' Lynch (1893–1923) issued a general order authorizing IRA units to target members of the Free State regime who had voted for the Army Emergency Powers Bill; on 8 December four IRA Volunteers were executed in reprisal for the IRA's assassination of government member Sean Hales the previous day; a further execution of seven prisoners at the Curragh Camp was carried out 19 Dec. 1922.

[2] 'Mount Henry' near Portarlington in what is now Co. Laois was not purchased by the Gogartys but rented for a year from Major Randal Charles Skeffington-Smyth (b. 1863) who had left for London at the outbreak of the First World War leaving the house in the charge of a caretaker. It was sold the following year and is now renamed Mount St Anne.

Lady Gregory is up. She is at Russells hotel and is coming in to tea today

Miss Macswiney was released because Michael Collins sisters and Mrs Mulcahy asked for it.[3] The Gov. apparently said they couldnt hold out when they asked.

I hope both the parcels arrived safely?

Maud Gonne is publishing wide and broadcast your statement that you wouldnt do anything for Miss Macswiney. Also that you want the English government back—that you are not even a free stater. I was told this twice, both times by republican women who wanted to know was it true. I think the way they make hay, or try to make hay—of your reputation for the sake of propaganda is too disgusting. I have set in motion amongst the de valera feminine branch a contradiction of the second statement, although I find on roundabout investigation that it is not believed outside the Despard group.[4] I am not at all sure from the evidence that the second statement has its origin in M.G. It sounds to me more like Helena Maloney[5] It is a very poisonous thing to start just at the moment. Number one woman who came to me on the matter gave herself away most beautifully. She was saying that only three letters of protest about Childers were received by the Gov. So I said I knew of four for a fact that were sent to Blythe. And she said 'O but they wouldnt come under the heading of government letters if they were

---

[3] Michael Collins (1890–1922), who had fought in the General Post Office in 1916, later became adjutant-general of the Irish Volunteers and president of the Supreme Council of the IRA. On election to the first Dáil he became Minister for Home Affairs, and one of the Treaty delegates; chair of the Provisional Government, he was commander-in-chief of the National Army, in which uniform GY had met him at the Gogartys shortly before he was killed in ambush on 22 Aug. 1922. The sisters most actively involved in nationalist politics were Margaret Collins-O'Driscoll (1877–1954), a schoolteacher who was elected a Cumann na nGaedheal TD for Dublin North (1923–33), and Mary Collins-Powell (1881–1955), a member of the pro-Treaty party Cumann na nGaedheal; Collins's other sisters were Johanna 'Hannie' Collins (1879–1971), who worked in the Post Office Savings Bank in London and with whom he lived for a number of years, Katherine 'Katie' Collins-Sheridan (1887–1964), and Helena 'Sister Celestine' (1883–1972). Mary Josephine 'Min' Mulcahy, née Ryan (1885–1977), a founder member of Cumann mBan, along with her husband Richard Mulcahy (1886–1971), Minister of Defence in the Provisional Government, supported the Treaty although her sister Nell Ryan (who would later go on hunger strike in Kilmainham Jail with Annie MacSwiney) did not.

[4] Mrs Charlotte Despard, née French (1844–1939), elder sister of the last Lord Lieutenant of Ireland, socialist, suffragette, and supporter of the IRA, had moved to Dublin during the summer of 1921 and with her close friend MG had formed in August 1922 the Women's Prisoners' Defence League.

[5] Helena Mary Molony (1883–1967), socialist, militant Republican, and member of the Women's Prisoners' Defence League and People's Rights Association, was also an occasional actor at the Abbey Theatre 1909–19. As an officer of the Citizen Army she occupied the City Hall in Easter week 1916 and was released from imprisonment at the 1916 Christmas amnesty; in 1917 she was appointed general secretary of the Irish Women Workers' Union and in 1936 president of the Irish Congress Trade Unions.

personally addressed to him.' So I said 'You mean he would have opened them himself instead of their being opened by the officials who open government letters?' And she said 'yes' So I said 'And therefore the republicans wouldnt get told about it.' She got very red and said nothing more.

I hope you are not too tired? I have to type your letters because my pen finger got shut in a window and is too sore still to use.

love DOBBS

[MS] Two letters from you today thankyou

[ALS]   SAVILE CLUB, | 107, PICCADILLY. W.1.
Nov 29 [1922]

My dear Dobbs: I got back here yesterday & went in the evening to the 'Chenci'—Today I shall see 'Medea'.¹ Grierson writes to say that 'The Trembling of the Viel' has reached him—his letter is very scottish & taken up with complaints about Magic he is the argumentative Scotsman.² On the other hand the copy you sent your mother has never reached her. I have only just heard this. I wrote to ask her as I noticed that when I saw her the other day she did not speak of it.

I am just off to telephone to Dulac—he is making copies of the masks³—& then I go to Freemasons library about the order properties.⁴

I miss you constantly & am always wondering if I am as much missed. I feel that the day of my return is so far off.

Yours affecly
WB Yeats.

Give Anne my love if you think she is old enough to understand & will not cry out 'Sacred Heart whats that.'

I have so much gossip but it must keep.

---

¹ Euripides' *Medea* opened at the New Theatre on 16 October, followed by Shelley's *The Cenci* on 13 Nov. 1922, both under the management of Bronson Albery, Lady Wyndham, Lewis Casson, and Sybil Thorndike; the latter two played the Judge and Beatrice respectively in *The Cenci*.

² Herbert John Clifford Grierson (1866–1960), essayist, editor, and critic of seventeenth-century poetry, was from 1894 to 1915 Professor of English at the University of Aberdeen, at whose house WBY was a guest when the riots over Synge's *Playboy of the Western World* occurred in 1907; he held the chair of Rhetoric and English Literature at Edinburgh University 1915–35 and received his knighthood in 1936.

³ WBY's hope of producing the Noh plays in Dublin with masks designed by Dulac for *At the Hawk's Well* was not fulfilled until March 1924.

⁴ Dr Hammond's office was in the Masonic library and museum in the Freemasons' Hall at 60 Great Queen Street.

[ALS]   SAVILE CLUB, | 107, PICCADILLY. W.1.
                                        Nov 29 [1922]

My dear Dobbs: Your mother writes that the book[1] has just come & her
letter is one of those gracious kind letters she writes so well. It seems I have
given you 'a great & splendid life'—ah if I only had.

I have just seen 'Medea,' a very strange poignant terrible thing—it is long
since I have been so moved by anything in a theatre. I dine with Dulac
to-night.

I look at the papers morning & night with anxiety to get the news from
Dublin.

There may be one new lecture—Leicester on Monday—but it is not
finally settled.

                                        Yours affecly
                                        WB Yeats

[ALS]   SAVILE CLUB, | 107, PICCADILLY. W.1.
                                        Nov 30 [1922]

My dear Dobbs: No letter from you except one I got last Saturday or Friday.
I enclose the very strange horoscope of Dulacs new lady.[1] Write your judgement before you know any facts & put it away for future use. I have never
seen one of the type. I called on Dr Hammond but he was away ill & now
I have written. I dined last night with Dulac & his lady & dine with them
again on Saturday. I have one new lecture—Leicester £15 on Monday.

I miss you greatly & count the days for my return

                                        Yours affectionly
                                        WB Yeats

[ALS]   SAVILE CLUB, | 107, PICCADILLY. W.1.
                                        Nov 30 [1922]

My dear Dobbs: I have been wondering what I should bring you & I have
seen some very pretty black & gold evening shoes (also to be had black &
silver but gold best). To day I lunched with Olivia at her club & as the shop

---

[1] WBY's memoir *The Trembling of the Veil* was privately printed for subscribers only by
T. Werner Laurie and issued in October 1922; 1,000 copies were printed on hand-made paper
and signed by the author.

[1] Among the Yeatses' astrological papers are the horoscopes of Helen Beauclerk, 20 Sept.
1892, 1 a.m., and Edmond Dulac, 22 Oct. 1882, 1.45 a.m.

is near the Club got her to inspect.[1] There will not be time for you to send me the number so I want you to send it to her & she will get them sent. She thoroughly approves of the shoes. They have funny tops

Yours affly
WB Yeats

[TLS/MS]   82, MERRION SQUARE, | DUBLIN.
December 1 [1922]

My dear Willy;

Lady Gregory has been up. She came to tea on Tuesday and stayed till she went down to the theatre. I ordered a taxi to take her down to the Abbey; I was to have gone to the Corinthian, which is almost next door to the Abbey, to see Charlie Chaplin, but when I had left her and walked round to the door, I found that there was a crowd of about three hundred people waiting to get in!!![1] So I humbly returned to the Abbey. Lady G was a little triumphant I thought. She had been a little cold about Charlie!! I brought her home to her hotel in another taxi, and she was really rather pathetically grateful. She said she didnt like being on the streets alone these nights. She was very delighted when the taxi came to take her down to the theatre. I hadnt told her it was coming, and she just found it at the door. She had been rushing round from early morning on all sorts of business.

You will perhaps be home now in ten days. I shall be very glad. The house seems very empty and lonely.

I hear that Joseph Stamford of Gort has been arrested. I am very glad as he is a bad lot. He evolved the brilliant scheme about the abandonment of the barracks.[2]

[MS] Dec. 2
I am delighted at the idea of the shoes. They are just what I want. Indeed I had tried a couple of months ago to get some here but with no success.

---

[1] OS was a member of the Lyceum Club at 128 Piccadilly (now the Royal Air Force Club), founded in 1904 'to provide a welcome and intellectually stimulating environment for educated and energetic women'.

[1] Charlie Chaplin's film *Pay Day* was showing at the Corinthian Cinema on Eden Quay; *Paul Twyning* by George Shiels, first produced in October 1922, was being performed at the Abbey.

[2] Possibly Joseph Stanford, who was one of the witnesses to the May 1921 ambush at Ballyturin (see note to 10 Apr. 1924). The 28th Battalion had its headquarters in the Gort Military Barracks during the Civil War.

Gogarty came in tonight to say that you were 'Senator Yeats' He wrote it in the fog on the door plate! It is <u>very</u> private so far as the Dail hasnt seen Cosgrave's list of names yet.[3] Things very quiet here for a few nights & days. There has been great military activity—Searchings & armoured cars—Nassau St—Grafton St—Stephens Green all with military holding up every tram car & horse vehicle & searching thoroughly. I send this to Liverpool—a telegram I shall send early tomorrow morning to Savile. I hope you will get it before you start for Leicester. One of my letters must have gone astray. I wrote you at Garsington & *2* letters since. This is the *3rd* since Garsington. I am glad you enjoyed being there. You will have a great deal to tell me when you come home.

Much love
George.

10.30 pm.

Such an excitement! I heard knocking—Maids not in. All alone in the house. I looked out of the window & saw the maids looking scared and 3 men talking to them, with two more standing by a large & very dusty car. I proceeded down the stairs in dressing gown to demand what it all meant, but before I got down, Delia opened the door with her key & brought in 2 of the men & said 'Two gentlemen from the Provisional Govt to see you.'[4] I skedaddled upstairs & dressed & hurried down. Two young men immaculately dressed asked if I thought you would accept nomination to the Senate. So I said as far as <u>I</u> knew you would but I couldnt commit you. So I am to wire to you tomorrow early & get a reply which I am to send to Cosgrave. The young men said the maids looked very suspicious of them—I had looked at them out of the window in my dressinggown & one of them 'Secretary' to Cosgrave said he was glad they had passed the test.

[ALS] SAVILE CLUB, | 107, PICCADILLY. W.1.

Dec 1 [1922]

My dear Dobbs: No letter from you for a week. Write to me to Liverpool c/o J. G. Legge, 3 Grove Park Liverpool—I get there on Wednesday Dec 6 or c/o W. A. Cadbury, Bournville, Birmingham—I cannot find full address

---

[3] The 1922 Constitution provided for the Seanad Éireann (Senate), of which half of the members were nominated by the head of government.
[4] Delia Molloy, who had returned from Oxford with them.

but this should suffice—I get there Dec 5.¹ I am anxious about Ireland as I do not trust the short reports in the English press

If by any chance you have gold brocade shoes let me know & I [will] find you something in a Liverpool curiosity shop perhaps. The shoes are very pretty I think. I gave a very good reading last night but am tired partly because the god of dreams was unwisely bountiful for two nights running. I expect a Daily Graphic reporter every minuite.²

Yrs affecly
WB Yeats

[ALS]   SAVILE CLUB, | 107, PICCADILLY. W.1.

Saturday [2 Dec. 1922]

My dear Dobbs: I have had another encounter with Gosse¹ & I have scored. I was sitting reading at one side of the fire & I heard some men drawing up their chairs at the other side. Presently I heard Gosse's voice, raised for my benefit as follows. 'Have you seen that disgraceful obscene book Ulysses? The author is a Sinn Feiner & a spy.' I waited a moment or two & then got up & strayed over to Gosses side & said 'Mr James Joyce is very grateful to Mr Gosse, who got him quite a large sum from the Royal Bounty Fund'² Gosse then said 'The Portrait of the artist' was a very different book from Ulysses & I said 'It is hardly less obscene in places' after a word or two more of quite a mild nature I strayed to the far end of the room. I heard Gosse (who evidently thought I had left the room,) say 'was Yeats embarrassed' & another voice reply 'Yes but I think he got rather well out of it.' I did not like to over hear any more & went down stairs.

---

¹ James Granville Legge (1861–1940), civil servant, author of several studies of European poetry, and friend of WBY's since the 1880s, had recently retired to Liverpool but returned to Oxford in 1925. William Adlington Cadbury (1867–1957) of the chocolate family and his wife Emmeline Agatha, née Wilson (1883–1966), of Wast Hills, King's Norton, near Birmingham, were long-time supporters of the Cuala Press and frequent hosts to ECY and SMY.

² 'Wonderful London Yesterday' column of *The Daily Graphic*, 2 Dec. 1922, mentions WBY's lecture tour of London, Leicester, and Birmingham and quotes him on the Abbey Theatre, LR's *Crabbed Youth and Age* ('a masterpiece'), and the political situation in Ireland which 'has not yet produced a great poet....I think that four or five poems written of the Great War may become a permanent part of English literature; that is as much as anyone has got out of a war.'

¹ See letter of 19 Nov. 1922.

² James Joyce (1882–1941) had, on the recommendation of WBY and EP to Gosse, received an award in 1915 on the publication of *A Portrait of the Artist as a Young Man* from the Royal Literary Fund, which was established in 1790 'to provide relief for distressed authors of published works of approved literary merit and their families'; his *Ulysses*, published in Paris on 22 Feb. 1922, was far more controversial, and its censorship for obscenity in America and England was not lifted until the mid-1930s.

I am being very extravagant. I am giving £10 for the reproductions of Blakes 105 Dante designs. It is a great treasure & I am convinced that with very little trouble I can write an essay upon it to substitute for the rather poor essay on the designs at the end of my Blake essays in 'Ideas of Good & Evil' & get more than £10 for it. I have been thinking about buying the book for months & even this morning walked up & down for some time before I decided to go into Quaritch's.[3]

Stay at home in the evening for the present till this crisis is over. I read the papers always with anxiety. I shall be relieved when Dec 6 is passed.[4]

Yrs affecy
WB Yeats

I got your letter about Maud & her vindictive slander this morning.

[ALS] SAVILE CLUB, | 107, PICCADILLY. W.1.

Dec 3 [1922]

My dear Dobbs: Eliot[1] has just lunched with me, & we have talked Joyce, poetry & the parallel dream for 3 hours & I have arranged to write my essay on the Dante Designs for his 'Criterion'. We shall have to read Dante in the evenings & put each design, in turn, (when we come to its place) up in front of us on a chair. He is to allow me to simply finish well what I finished badly in 'The Savoy'.[2] So I am not extravagent however I am overdrawn, or shall be when I pay Quaritch to-morrow. I wonder if you could send a dozen pounds or so to my account. You will get a goodish sum from these lectures. I am charmed with Eliot & find that I have a reasonable liking for his 'Sacred Wood'.[3] He told me a strange thing. Joyce is related through his

[3] Bernard Quaritch Ltd., 5–8 Lower John Street, publisher and antiquarian booksellers.

[4] On 6 Dec. 1922 the Peace Treaty signed in London in December 1921 was passed, creating the Irish Free State.

[1] Thomas Stearns Eliot (1888–1965), poet, dramatist, critic, and friend of EP, founded the influential journal *The Criterion* in 1922, which he edited for the next seventeen years. As it had been five years since they met, Ottoline Morrell had facilitated the meeting between the two poets.

[2] In July, August, and September 1896 WBY published three articles in *The Savoy* under the general heading 'William Blake and his Illustrations to the Divine Comedy', only the last of which, 'The Illustrations of Dante', was reprinted in *Ideas of Good and Evil* (1903). Although other writings by WBY appeared in the *Criterion*, the promised essays on Blake did not; instead, WBY sent him 'A Biographical Fragment, with some Notes' (July 1923) and *The Cat and the Moon* (July 1924) and other essays and poems.

[3] Eliot's *The Sacred Wood: Essays on Poetry and Criticism* (1920) included chapters on poetic drama, Blake, and Dante.

mother to the Macsweenys family, the hunger striking, family, & was stirred
by the death of the Mayor of Cork to his first political interest or emotion.[4]
I am very home sick, & long for you always my dear.

Yrs

WB Yeats

---

[4] Though not related to Terence MacSwiney the Mayor of Cork who had died in a hunger
strike, James Joyce was distantly related through his grandmother Ellen O'Connell Joyce to
Peter Paul McSwiney (1810–84), Lord Mayor of Dublin in 1864 and 1875, nephew of Daniel
O'Connell, and chairman of 'Palatial Mart' or 'New Mart' (later known as Clery's), one of
Europe's first department stores.

1923

[ALS]   SAVILE CLUB, | 107, PICCADILLY. W.1.
                                                    Jan 17 [1923]

My dear Dobbs: I was glad to get your wire.[1] I have asked for interviews
with Lord Plymouth & Lord Peel, also with Robert Lynd, who is on the
New Statesman.[2] I have lunched with Dulac, who was very amiable—that
was all a mares nest of mine[3]—& I have two-and-foured.[4] So my day has
been reasonably occupied. I had a most pleasant easy journey but am sleepy
& will soon go to bed. My love to you

                                                         WB Yeats

[ALS]   SAVILE CLUB, | 107, PICCADILLY. W.1.
                                                    Jan 20 [1923]

My dear Dobs: I may be back for the first meeting of the Senate. I have
been advised to delay the resolution in Senate & that in the Dail.[1] I am not
quite so hopeful. If we can get an a greed bill all will be well. I am meeting

---

[1] WBY wrote to AG on 19 January, 'George has just wired for me to see Harvey Hall at
the museum as he promises his fathers Parnell Commission drawings to the gallery, but which
gallery I dont know' (*CL InteLex*, acc. 4259); Sydney Prior Hall (1842–1922) was a portrait
painter and illustrator whose drawings of the proceedings of the Parnell Commission (1888–9)
were especially admired as examples of graphic journalism.

[2] On 17 Jan. 1923 GY wrote to Desmond Fitzgerald, 'My husband crossed last night to
London for the purpose of seeing Lord Beaverbrook, Ribbesdale and others on the matter
of the return of the Lane Pictures. He had a letter yesterday suggesting that an agreed bill
was possible and even probable, and therefore thought it better to go over before the matter
was brought up in the Dáil and Seanad.' Robert George Windsor-Clive, 1st Lord Plymouth
(1857–1923) was a trustee of the National Gallery and William Robert Wellesley Peel, 2nd
Viscount Peel (1867–1937), was at this time Secretary of State for India and would soon
become First Commissioner of Public Works and Public Buildings. Robert Lynd (1879–1949),
socialist and member of Sinn Féin, was literary editor 1912–47 of the *Daily News* (later the *News
Chronicle*), also wrote for *The Nation*, and from 1913 to 1945, under the pseudonym of Y.Y., a
weekly literary essay for the *New Statesman*; with his wife, the poet and essayist Sylvia Dryhurst
(1888–1952), he had considerable influence in the literary circles of London.

[3] I have been unable to discover any quarrel with Dulac at this time; during their last visit
in December they had discussed two Chinese pictures Dulac was giving to the Yeatses.

[4] GY's term for an afternoon nap.

[1] WBY did not introduce the resolution until 9 May 1923: 'That the Seanad ask the Government to press upon the British Government the return to Dublin of the pictures mentioned
in the unwitnessed codicil to Sir Hugh Lane's will.'

all manner of people but find them vague. I must wait to see Lord Peel & perhaps Lord Plymouth. To day I met Lord Londonderry & Lord Buckmaster but Lord Buckmaster was not concerned on the topic & Lord Londonderry is too see me again.[2] I dont think I can get any further until I can find out what the Trustees propose to do. I saw the one really important person Leonard Curtis this morning & he is for us I think but explained to me the practical difficulties.[3] I have not yet seen Beaver brook.[4] I have had a dramatic idea put into my head. If we cannot get a greed bill then Tim Healy is to ask as Governor General to be heard at the bar of the house.[5] Keep this private till I have sounded him. I am hoping for a letter— telegrams lack atmosphere even when numerous. I have done nothing but agitate for pictures, which does not mean that I fit many people into the day not having like the heroes in the detective stories 'a long grey car'. I may be back by Wednesday but am not sure.

Yrs affectly
WB Yeats

[ALS]   SAVILE CLUB, | 107, PICCADILLY. W.1.
Jan 21 [1923]

My dear Dobbs: I dined with Dulac & his lady last night (he asks me to stop with him but I doubt if I shall). I shall try to see Lord Peele on Monday or Tuesday & Beaver brook but I cannot see Plymouth I am afraid till later in the week. I think therefore that I had best go to Dublin for the senate & return after a few sittings. I have to find out (& may from Lord Plymouth) if we can get an a greed bill.

---

[2] Charles Stewart Henry Vane-Tempest-Stewart, 7th Marquess of Londonderry (1878–1949), an active member of the Ulster Unionist Party, was Minister for Education and leader of the Senate in the state of Northern Ireland. Stanley Owen Buckmaster, 1st Viscount Buckmaster (1861–1934), a distinguished barrister of liberal opinions, had been Lord Chancellor in 1915 and would later be chairman of Imperial College; see note to 20 Jan. 1923.

[3] Probably Lionel George Curtis (1872–1955), Imperial activist and writer, founder of the Royal Institute of International Affairs (1919) and since 1921 fellow of All Souls College, who had been asked by the Cabinet to draw up a report on the Lane pictures; it has been suggested that his article 'Ireland', in the June 1921 issue of the *Round Table* journal he established, was instrumental in persuading the British government to accept the Anglo-Irish Treaty of 6 Dec. 1921.

[4] William Max Aitken, Lord Beaverbrook (1879–1964), Canadian-born proprietor of the influential *Daily Express* and the recently founded *Sunday Express* and a powerful Conservative voice.

[5] Timothy Michael Healy (1855–1931), who had been MP for Wexford, became first Governor-General of the Irish Free State (1922–7), leading Gogarty to call the vice-regal lodge 'Uncle Tim's Cabin'.

I am back in the world I knew here ten years ago, & for the moment it is amusing—beatiful ladies who are so gifted that they seem to know everything yet know nothing. One drew me out yesterday on the most profound subjects & then said 'You use the word aphorism—I do not know that word—what is an aphorism?' I returned to frivolity. I had a long talk with Lord Buckmaster, who is I think the liberal leader in the House of Lords He was full of admiration for Ireland, train wreckers, murderers & all. 'Ah if only the Germans were like that, they would soon get rid of the French but they have been too much drilled.' I said 'Yes: & I hear that the Egyptian nationalists have asked an Irish politician to hire them a few gunmen as they say there own people lack moral force'—he became a little grave. It struck me that the liberal party mind was shifting about to find out if it could not take up the republicans. However he & everybody else talks of Gogorty with wonder & admiration.[1] I have even met a man who wants to broad cast the story & would have done so at once if I had consented to do the speaking.

To night I dine with Robert Lynd[2] to get journalists support for the pictures, but otherwise this is a day of rest for which I have felt the need. I am writing letters & little system but alas my head is full of poetry which I long to write. Ah if only you & I had a chance of a couple of weeks any where out of reach of bombs and business. I have a fire in my room as a country member with a loud voice talked me out of the smoking room, his great topics seem to be the diet of rats & the length of time expended by the elephant in gestation. Which are not among the subjects I have studied. I lunch both Monday & Tuesday with Lady Cunard & would have dined there to night but I said if I did I would quarrell with Philson Young who was to be asked He edits the Saturday.[3] Yesterday the woman, who asked what a aphorism is said of George Moore 'O is'nt he a cross old maid'. Did I tell you that the Sidney Webbs say France is on the verse [verge] of a royalist coup-de-Etat, which will come off on the

---

[1] Gogarty, recently appointed a Senator, had been kidnapped by armed men and escaped by diving into the Liffey; aware that his life continued to be in danger, he had moved temporarily to London, uncertain where he should continue his medical practice.

[2] See n. 2 to 17 Jan. 1923.

[3] Society hostess Maud Alice, née Burke (later 'Emerald'), Lady Cunard (1872–1948), was an influential friend to many artists and politicians, arranging private meetings in her home at Carlton House Terrace; WBY's *At the Hawk's Well* had received its first performance in her drawing room in 1916. Alexander Bell Filson Young (1876–1938), journalist, musician, and biographer, was editor of the conservative *Saturday Review* 1921–4, in which in a series of articles over December 1921 and January 1922 he mocked and exposed as fraudulent a séance to which he had been invited by Arthur Conan Doyle; as an Ulster Loyalist he was not one of WBY's favourite journalists.

failure of the present German policy.⁴ My dear I hate all absence from you

Yrs affly
WB Yeats

I wonder if you could put a few pounds into my bank account. I have only I think £4 in it now. I have about £4.10 in my pocket but will have to pay for a ticket, or a return ticket to Dublin, for the Senate. If an a greed bill proves impossible I shall have no cause to stay here but [if]neither Lord Peel or Lord Plymouth gives what I hope I can not return till towards the end of week I think.⁵ I shall get the Senate sitting soon I suppose.

[ALS]   SAVILE CLUB, | 107, PICCADILLY. W.1.

Jan 27 [1923]

My dear Dobbs: Lucky I came over as Lady Gregory has wired 'strongly against delay.' I see Lord Peel to-morrow & will be guided by him as he is her friend. She would have thought me very slack if I had taken no advice but that of Curtiss. I go to a number of lunch parties & write system. Lady Ottoline is in town & I lunched there to day—there being Cavendish Benedicks beautiful house at Queen Annes Gate—but she was ill in bed with a cold.¹ I long for a letter.

Yrs ev
WB Yeats

P S. Is this bit of system correct.

8 to 15 development of Mask
15 to 22 development of C G.
22 to 28 development of P.F.
28 to 8 development of Ego.

---

⁴ Sidney James Webb (1859–1947), Labour MP from 1922 to 1929, and his wife Beatrice Potter Webb (1858–1943), economists and socialists, long-time members of the Fabian Society and with Bernard and Charlotte Shaw founders of the London School of Economics, influenced contemporary political theory and practice with their prolific writings on trade unionism, labour history, and local government; in January 1923 the French and Belgian forces occupied the Ruhr district and other areas right of the Rhine due to a delay in the payment of German reparations, thrusting inflation even further and triggering national outrage at France in all of Germany.

⁵ WBY returned to Dublin on 23 January, then went back to London the night of the 26th.

¹ William John Arthur Charles James Cavendish-Bentinck, 6th Duke of Portland (1857–1943), was Ottoline Morrell's half-brother.

As I am at p[hase] 23 I rather want to know. It seems to me that the subsidence of final objective phases must be subsidence into P. F. & the awaking of first objective phase development of Ego. Is not p 8 mere naked energy, or desire. Or is it the reverse. Is 23–28 development of Ego—freeing ego from Mask—& 28 to 8 its submission to Fate.[2]

[ALS]   SAVILE CLUB, | 107, PICCADILLY. W.1.

Jan 28 [1923] Sunday

My dear Dobbs: Gogorty has just been in—he is off to Manchester. He has not made up his mind whether to start as a specialist in London or Manchester—I dont know whether this is private or not—but he will not go into society until started, probably a sound instinct. I saw him yesterday & went to Lady Leslies with him for tea.[1] He is going to send two swans to the Dublin Corporation 'having vowed two swans to the Liffey if it saved his life.'[2] I have written to Lord Peel but can hardly here before late to-morrow at earliest as he is out of town. Gogorty commends as a cheap & pleasant place for a holiday—The Cliff Hotel, Treadder (or Treader hes only sure of the sound of the name) Treadder Bay, Holyhead. If you meet Mrs Gogorty you might ask her about it. Lady Ottoline is in London, Morrel is staying at the Club & we met at Breakfast. I go to tea with them this afternoon— no he has just called me up on Telephone to say I am to go with them to dine with Birrell.[3] Meanwhile I have to get out of an invitation to Gogorty & myself to dine with Lady Cunard to-night but it is not yet twelve & she

[2] WBY was drafting the geometric table of the Four Faculties as dictated by GY's Controls: CG = Creative Genius (later renamed Creative Mind), P.F. = Persona of Fate (later renamed the Body of Fate), Ego (later renamed the Will), and the Mask; all possible human types were classified under one or other of the twenty-eight lunar phases of a wheel: the Ego and Mask (always opposite to each other on the wheel) were predominately Lunar or antithetical, the Creative Genius and the Persona of Fate (always opposite each other) predominately Solar or primary.

[1] Either Lady Constance Leslie, née Damer (1836–1925) of Manchester Square in London, or her daughter-in-law Leonie Blanche Leslie, née Jerome (1857–1943), American wife of Sir John Leslie, 2nd Baronet (1857–1944), sister of Jennie, Lady Randolph Churchill (1854–1921), and close friend of Prince Arthur, Duke of Connaught and Strethearn.

[2] This was done with due ceremony on 26 Apr. 1924 with WBY in attendance; Gogarty's book of poems *An Offering of Swans* (Cuala, 1923) further commemorated the event.

[3] Augustine Birrell, KC (1850–1933), Chief Secretary for Ireland 1907–16 during which time he established the National University of Ireland and Queen's University, Belfast, by the Irish Universities Act, 1908, and the Land Purchase Act, 1909. An essayist and biographer, his sympathy for the Irish led to his failure to comprehend the power of Sinn Féin or to predict the 1916 Rising and his subsequent withdrawal from politics, though he supported the return of the Lane pictures to Ireland.

does not get up till twelve so I cannot yet telephone. I am going to work now on system.

Is Anne old enough to understand that I send her my love?

Yours affectionately
WBY.

[ALS] SAVILE CLUB, | 107, PICCADILLY. W.1.

Jan 30 [1923]

My dear Dobbs: I was awakened at 6.30 this morning, at what seemed a shot. I have been anxious about you all since, had you a very bad night. The papers tell me that there were fires etc.

Lady Gregory writes urgently about pressing the picture claim—I shall get what advice I can but feel rather helpless. She discounts Lord Peel whom I am to see to day & whom I looked upon as her special friend. Through counting on that I may have lost two days, at least if we are to go on.

I brought Gogorty to Dulacs last night & I think it was a success. He dines with me to night He has I think decided to take rooms near Bond St & start as a London specialist. (This is I think private for the moment). He is pessamistic about Ireland but is recovering his nerve.

Yrs ev
WB Yeats

[ALS] 82, MERRION SQUARE, S. | DUBLIN.

Jan 30. 1923

My dear Willy

I dont think I had better go away just now. Last night there was great burning of houses,[1] & apart from anything else I dont want Lily to come here & get a bad shock.[2]

I have asked 'Oriel' to let us have men at 6 every evening but they say they are <u>very short</u>.[3] However they say they will send tonight. You will have

---

[1] The Irregulars had embarked on a campaign to burn down houses of supporters of the Provisional Government, and the houses of thirty-seven Senators were burned during January and February 1923.

[2] WBY had suggested that his wife join him for a few days, leaving his sister SMY in charge of looking after the children.

[3] Ever since November 1922 when Liam Lynch, one of the division commanders of the Irregulars had included Senators amongst those to be shot on sight, the government had provided armed guards to senior officials. In April 1923 Lynch himself was mortally wounded and the IRA chief of staff who succeeded him declared a ceasefire on 30 April, and on 24 May ordered IRA Volunteers to dump their arms and return to their homes. The local division of government was based in Oriel House, just across Merrion Square from 82.

seen in the papers that Kilteragh was burnt to the ground last night—The night before, it was mined. I suppose the Irregulars thought the destruction caused on Monday night was insufficient.[4]

Anne is very much better, & her glands going down.[5]

The 'Countess' is a really good production & Miss Crowe quite good.[6] I am sorry in a way that you wont see it. I wish there was somebody in the country that you could go & stay with. But with the Morrells in London I am afraid there is no chance.

Would you like to go to Sidmouth to the Tuckers?[7] You wouldnt stay in their house, but you could go <u>next door</u> to the Woodlands Hotel, & spend your evenings with the Tuckers.

If you <u>like</u> the idea, wire to my mother to get you a room at Woodlands hotel.

Best love my dearest
G.

[ALS]   SAVILE CLUB | 107, PICCADILLY. W
Jan 31 [1923]

My dear Dobbs: Not a word from you except that one telegram—not a word since I left—& I am anxious. I read every edition of the evening papers for the Dublin news. I am anxious about Anne for Monday night must have been very noisy & alarming.

The Lane Pictures promising. The subject is down on the agenda for the Cabinet, & Cabinet is expected to decide in three or four weeks to form a Commission to take evidence on the subject. If the Near East however turns out as badly as is feared it will all probably be put off a gain.[1] I got

---

[4] Home of Senator Horace Plunkett in Foxrock; LR lived in a cottage on the grounds.

[5] 3-year-old ABY was recovering from scarlet fever, another reason WBY was banished to London.

[6] The week of 30 January, in a double bill with Shaw's *The Shewing-up of Blanco Posnet*, the Abbey Theatre revived WBY's *The Countess Cathleen*, with Eileen Crowe (1899–1978) as the Countess. Crowe began her career at the Abbey Theatre in 1921 after six weeks with the Abbey School of Acting; she married fellow actor F. J. McCormick (Peter Judge) in 1925, and remained a member of the company, acting also in films, until her death.

[7] GY's mother and stepfather had recently moved from their London home to a cottage in Sidmouth, Devon. The Woodlands Hotel, Station Road, is now a listed building and still exists as a hotel.

[1] In September 1922 in defiance of the terms of the 1920 Treaty of Sèvres and the League of Nations, the Turks had taken control of Smyrna and driven the Greeks out of Anatolia; meanwhile a military junta had deposed the monarchy in Greece. The dispute between the two countries was finally settled by the Treaty of Lausanne in July 1923, but until then England, concerned for the neutral area of the Dardanelles, feared imminent war.

all this from Eddie Marsh yesterday—the first detailed statement I have heard.[2]

Yours affectionately
WB Yeats
P.T.O.

Your wire has just come.[3] Could you not put Anne, or Ann & Micael, in nursing home for a few days for you are in great need of rest. It is very possible that you may have to move them to Wales having insured house & its contents against war risks for (say) three months. Gogorty has impressed upon me that nervous shock may be very bad for Annes kidneys. The boat from Holyhead to Dublin is I think 11/6. So I could do all I had to do without much expense. The fate of Bagwell will settle the kidnapping question one way or the other.[4] I wonder if you would like me to go to Wales [to] enquire about lodgings.

[ALS]   82, MERRION SQUARE, S. | DUBLIN.
Feb. 1. 1923

My dear Willy

I <u>do</u> feel that things now are at the Climax—and therefore that one should if it is in anyway possible, stick it out. If it is, in any way, any use being here at all—that is to say if it is to be of any use in the future—this is the decisive moment.

Mrs Humphreys—In her house Ernie O'Malley was taken[1]—came to Mrs Buck Mulligan[2] & said she wished her to know that DeValera & <u>his</u> H.Q.

---

[2] Edward Howard Marsh (1872–1953), art collector, editor of the *Georgian Poetry* series, classicist, and translator, was private secretary to Winston Churchill 1906–29.

[3] Both telegrams from GY, apparently rejecting WBY's advice to leave Dublin, are missing from the correspondence (see 30 Jan. 1923).

[4] The *Irish Times* of 31 Jan. 1923 reported the kidnapping from his home in Howth of Senator John Philip Bagwell (1874–1946), general manager of the Great Northern Railway Company 1911–26 and Senator between 1922 and 1936. The officer in command of the Dublin area issued a proclamation announcing that, unless Senator Bagwell was released unharmed within forty-eight hours, 'punitive action will be taken against several associates in this conspiracy now in custody and otherwise'. Bagwell's family home Marlfield, Clonmel, Tipperary, was burned down in 1923 but rebuilt in 1925.

[1] Ernest 'Ernie' Bernard O'Malley (Earnán O Máille; 1897–1957), first divisional commander to reject the Treaty and repudiate the authority of the Provisional Government and a participant in the burning of the Four Courts, had been severely wounded when recaptured in November 1922, and was now imprisoned at Mountjoy under sentence of death. O'Malley later became well known for his Irish revolutionary autobiographies, in particular *On Another Man's Wound* (London, 1936), which earned him nomination to the Irish Academy of Letters. The 'safe house' at 36 Ailesbury Road in which he was captured, and which with its secret room served as IRA Dublin headquarters, belonged to Ellen O'Rahilly Humphreys (1871–1939), member of a staunchly Republican family who with her daughter Sighle was twice imprisoned during the Civil War; the building now houses the French Embassy.

[2] Mrs Gogarty, whose husband was the model for Buck Mulligan in James Joyce's *Ulysses*.

had <u>not</u> given the orders for the kidnapping & that they were extremely sorry about it.[3] It is <u>just</u> possible that Dev. may at last have the courage to dissociate himself from the extreme element. Do not think that I for one moment do not realise the upset to you that all this is, or that I neglect the possibilities of danger to you. I am not suggesting that you should come back—except for the senate—but I do think that a general removal might be a bitter mistake. Anne has slept through <u>everything</u>. That she is a little deaf may be a godsend to her! She is sleeping as she has never slept before & curiously enough seems to have lost all sense of fear at strange noises.

It seems strange to me that I have no feeling of fear over the future, but this very lack of anxiety increases my belief that there is no need for fear, for if I do not fear for you when you are my whole world surely my instinct is right?

Yours ever   George

[ALS]   SAVILE CLUB | 107, PICCADILLY. W
                                  Feb 2 [1923]

My dear Dobbs: Your letter of Jan 30 arrived by the last post last night. I am sorry that you cannot get away. I think we will have to make some re-arrangement of our plans to meet the dire situation. I beleive a lodging somewhere near Holyhead would be best for you & the children perhaps for me also. I am afraid of things getting much worse.

I have arranged with Miss Jacob for daily dictation of the chapters on the system. I began to day but will not decide until I have done two days dictation the date of my return to Dublin. If I can finish it now I will, I mean if I can dictate up to p[hase] 23 which is the phase I have reached. I had wanted to go into the country & write poetry but the poem I had in my head has faded a little & can wait. I dont think that verse will prove possible amid the strain of Dublin however.

My friends think I am returning at once—as I want to escape invitations, which tire me out. Here has been my week—<u>Sunday</u>, theatre <u>Wednesday</u> Cunard, <u>Monday</u>, dinner Dulac, Tuesday lunch, Lady Cunard, Dinner—Gogarty, <u>Wednesday</u> lunch, Lady Londonderry, <u>Thursday</u> Lunch Lord Granard,[1]

---

[3] Éamon de Valera (1882–1975), leader of a group of Sinn Féin rebels during the uprising of Easter Week, 1916, escaped the death penalty because of his American birth and the following year was elected president of the Sinn Féin party; objecting to the terms of the Anglo-Irish Treaty, he precipitated the Civil War and refused to participate in the Dáil until 1927 after forming a new party, Fianna Fáil, later becoming Ireland's first Prime Minister (1937–48; also in 1951–4 and 1957–9) and its President (1959–73).

[1] Bernard Arthur William Patrick Hastings Forbes, 8th Earl of Granard (1874–1948), whose home Castleforbes, Co. Longford, was damaged by the Irregulars on 26 Jan. 1923; see 10 Nov. 1924 for Marchioness of Londonderry.

dinner Lady Cunard. In addition I have been to sundry teas. To night I have supper with your grandmother.² I had some talk with Churchill about Ireland last night—he has a pleasant enthusiasm which is very unexpected, something naive & happy.³

I wish you would write oftener—I have had only one letter—

Yours with love
WBY

[ALS]   SAVILE CLUB | 107, PICCADILLY. W
Feb 3 [1923]

My dear Dobbs: I realized how rarely you express emotion from the great pleasure that last sentence of your letter gave me. Years have past since you have written me, if endeed you ever did write me such a sentence. It has filled my heart full.

As long as I attend the senate we abandon nothing, except material things that can be replaced. Your grandmother is full of the idea of your taking a lodging for your self & the children at Chester. She says there are such good trains, & you would be in reach of music & there are pleasant people there whom she knows.

I am busy writing & dictating system. I am also through Lord Granard asking questions of the government to try & find a way to peace—or rather to bring it a little nearer. I lunch with him Monday. He telephoned last night. Certain things seem to me necessary to make the Irish-situation correspond to facts as those facts are altered by opinion here. I feel that in this I keep within my province for every search for reality is a kin to every other.

D. V[alera] has a very defiant interview in The Daily Mail & will never I think change. He is a theologian turned politician & could take for his

² GY's maternal grandmother Mrs Montagu Woodmass, née Edith Alice Andrew (1848–1927), whom GY would meet for the first time later this year. GY's mother had for long been banished by her iron-willed mother, now a widow living at 7 Southwell Gardens in Kensington; it appears that WBY engineered an introduction between GY and her grandmother, although EET was not admitted into favour until a few months before Mrs Woodmass's death; GY and her brother Harold were included in their grandmother's will, but their mother was not.

³ Although currently out of office, Winston Leonard Spencer Churchill (1874–1965), who as Liberal minister had campaigned for the Home Rule Bill of 1912 and in 1921 played an active role in the Treaty negotiations, remained supportive of the new government in Ireland.

motto a saying of I think Newmans, 'better that the human race should perish than that one sin be committed.'[1]

Yours affecly
WB Yeats

I am very sorry that Ann is deaf—is it the result of her scarlet-fever or is it permanent. What [does] the doctor say about it. If permanent it is very tragic.[2]

[ALS]   82, MERRION SQUARE, S. | DUBLIN.
Feb 4 [1923]. Sunday

My dear Willy

The Seanad meets—as you probably remember—on February 7. You lecture at the Arts Club on 9th.[1]

The guard began to come in at 6. Then 5–30—and now today it came in at 4! Soon it will be an all-day affair! I dont know why it comes earlier every day. Possibly the young men find it more pleasant sitting by the fire reading, than patrolling in the rain or doing some equally uncomfortable job.

When you get back we can discuss what you are going to do.

I sat on at the Club last night till nearly eleven talking to the Manchester Guardian correspondent.[2] A simple, rather pleasant young man who was interested in mystical things, mainly in the direction of 'orders' and rituals.

I suppose you will cross on Tuesday (6th) night?

Yours
G.

[1] The reporter of the *Daily Mail*, 3 Feb. 1923, quotes from an interview with de Valera in his hiding-place: 'Peace on the basis of acceptance of the so-called "treaty" of December 6, 1921, is impossible. Irish Republicans will never consent to surrender Ireland's national independence and sovereignty to any threats or in any circumstances. That's definite. They will fight to the last against recognising any foreign authority, direct or indirect, here.' In his *Apologia pro Vita Sua* (1865) John Henry Cardinal Newman (1801–90), one of the founders of the Oxford Movement and Rector of the Catholic University of Ireland (1854–58), repeated his statement that 'The Catholic Church holds it better for the sun and moon to drop from heaven, for the earth to fail, and for all the many millions on it to die of starvation in extremest agony, as far as temporal affliction goes, than that one soul, I will not say, should be lost, but should commit one single venial sin, should tell one wilful untruth, or should steal one poor farthing without excuse.'

[2] ABY's deafness was temporary.

[1] WBY returned to London on the 9th, cancelling his proposed lecture.

[2] Unidentified; the annual subject index of the paper for 1923 simply credits stories to 'our special correspondent'. I am grateful to Gavin McGuffie, *Guardian* Archivist, for assistance in the search.

[ALS]   SAVILE CLUB | 107, PICCADILLY. W
                                        Jan [Feb.] 5 [1923]

Private
My dear Dobbs
 I think the senate meets on Wednesday—I may wire you for confirmation—but there is a possibility that I may not get over. I am trying to get
a modification of the treaty a slight modification that might have a great
effect & bring peace much nearer.¹ I have just been with Grannard &
Southborough;² & Grannard is trying to make an appointment for me with
one (of two or three possible men) who might negociate both with the Irish
Government the Republicans, & the English Cabinet. Southborough was
hostile at first but I talked him over completely. If lucky I will get through
my interview to-morrow & you will see me on Wednesday morning. I may
not get it over so soon, (& Granard says the Senate business will be quite
formal.) However I will be there if possible.³

                                                              Yrs ev
                                                             WB Yeats

[ALS]   SAVILE CLUB, | 107, PICCADILLY. W.1.
                                        Feb 10 [1923]

My dear Dobbs: I am established here. I went last night to the College of
Psychic Science. May I arrange a sceance with their trumpet medium for
Wednesday or Thursday or Friday.¹ Please wire. They have an ecellent direct
voice & 'phisical medium' called Sloan giving a sceance there on Tuesday
Feb 20.² Can you stay as long as that? If so wire. If we return Tuesday night

---

¹ Probably a modification of the oath required, which might persuade the Republican
opposition to be less intransigent; the plan was not successful.
² Francis John Stephens Hopwood, 1st Baron Southborough (1860–1947), British civil servant who
had served as Secretary to the Irish Convention, 1917–18, had been suggested as intermediary.
³ WBY arrived in Dublin on 7 February, spoke against the new Enforcement of Law Bill
in Senate on the 8th, and returned to London on the 9th.

¹ Probably Mrs Blanche Cooper, who began training at the College of Psychic Science
shortly after it was founded by James Hewat and Barbara McKenzie in 1920, and used various
means in her séances including a 'musical box' and a cardboard cone ('trumpet') from which
whispering voices could be heard (see letters of 13 Feb. 1923 and 24 Oct. 1929).
² John Campbell Sloan (1869–1950) was a physical medium from Glasgow controlled by
'White Feather', an American Indian who spoke through Sloan's vocal organs and direct
through a trumpet; after a number of years of tests, J. Arthur Findlay (1883–1964), founder of
the Quest Club and member of The International Institute for Psychical Research, published
his findings on Sloan, whom he considered 'the best Trance, Direct Voice, Clairvoyant and
Clairaudient medium' he had ever met (*An Investigation of Psychic Phenomena* (1924) and *On the
Edge of the Etheric: or Survival after Death Scientifically Explained* (1931)).

I would be in time for Senate. However you may not want to stay so long &
there is still a chance of my having to blott [bolt] back for political reasons
through that is unlikely. Grannard will have seen C[hurchill] last night.
I lunch there to day to hear result.

Yours ever
WB Yeats

Had some talk with Hogan[3] on journey over. He is full of warlike spirit, &
represents the obstacle.

[ALS]   SAVILE CLUB, | 107, PICCADILLY. W.1.

Feb 10 [1923]

My dear Dobbs: I have just wired 'negociations going as well as possible.'[1]
G[rannard] saw C[hurchill] last night & says C enthusiastic about idea.
S[Southborough] is now to see authorities. I am too excited to work at sys-
tem as I intended, & will probably stray through the British Museum or the
National Gallery. If it succeeds I shall be able to do much for the National
Gallery in Dublin & for the theatre. C brought another with him—K[2]—which
gives as I think weight to his decission

Yours ever
WB Yeats

[ALS]   SAVILE CLUB, | 107, PICCADILLY. W.1.

Feb 11 [1923]

My dear Dobbs: to day a check to plans. G[ranard] has seen K[?Curtis] &
C[hurchill] again & after 'a long talk' thinks it 'quite plain' 'that it would
be highly dangerous to attempt anything at present' His note has just come.
I wont know what value to put on this until I hear what was said. I do not
of course know what measure of time is covered by 'at present.'
 From all which you will see what a tangle Hugh Lane left his affairs in.

---

[3] Patrick J. Hogan (1891–1936), powerful Minister for Agriculture in the Irish government
from 1922 to 1932, when he was responsible for introducing the 1923 Land Act which made
compulsory the sale and purchase of all the land not yet dealt with under the abolished Congested Districts Board and the Estates Commission and also dealt with the question of arrears
in rent; from 1923 until his death he was a member of Senate.

 [1] This appears to refer to both the earlier suggestions about modifying the treaty and the
ongoing attempt to get the Lane pictures for Ireland (Foster ii. 230–1).

 [2] Unidentified, but possibly Lionel Curtis, whom he saw about the Lane Pictures on 20
Jan. 1923.

You will notice that G's experience has been exactly mine first comes agreement & then comes the hesitations.

Yrs ev
WB Yeats

[ALCS]   SAVILE CLUB, | 107, PICCADILLY. W.1.
Feb 13 [1923]

My dear Dobbs: I am delighted that I shall see you so soon. 1.30 at Mont Blanck in Gerrard St as you suggest.¹ We then go to the sceance with Mrs Cooper at 3.² You will have had my second wire saying that it is on Wednesday not Thursday (your wire said you were engaged at 3 on Thursday)

Yrs ev
WB Yeats

[ALS¹]   Savile Club, 107 Piccadilly, London
May 20 [1923]

My dear Dobbs: Thank you so much for writing.² I shall stay for May [?June] 6 but will find out from O'Sullivan what comes on at the Senate &

---

¹ Mont Blanc, a London restaurant in Gerrard Street off Shaftesbury Avenue in Soho, was favoured by the literary circles of the period (Jonathan Cape's reader Edward Garnett held weekly luncheons there on Tuesday); GY was in London 14–17 February and WBY returned to Dublin on 20 February.

² Blanche Kate Cooper, née Hounsell (1883–1943), born in Bristol, was a well-known direct voice medium who had two controls, Nada and Afid; she was known for her 'book-tests', in which instructions were given by her guide to seek a message on a specific line of a page in a book on a certain shelf, and from 1921 to 1922 she had been the subject of a series of twenty-three experiments reported by S. G. Soal in the *Proceedings of the Society for Psychical Research*, 35 (1926), 471–591. It appears, however, that although spiritualists were impressed by her performance, most psychical researchers were not. An actress until, associated with the medium Gladys Osborne Leonard, whom she had known since her theatre days, she began working at the British College of Psychic Science at 15 Queens Gate; *c.*1926/7 the London photographer and spiritualist Dora Head (?1905–64) produced a studio portrait of this elegant, good-looking, soft-voiced woman, but by 1929 Blanche Cooper had semi-retired due to illness, when she and her husband Henry John Cooper (b. 1874), a former actor, lived at 32 The Downs, Wimbledon, a house owned by Charles Benjamin Collett (1871–1952), chief mechanical engineer with the Great Western Railway at Swindon and an eager spiritualist himself. I am grateful to Tom Ruffles, librarian at the Society of Psychical Research, and Professor Donald James West for assistance.

¹ On stationery for 20 Queen's Road, Aberdeen struck out.
² GY's letter is missing.

if they can put off my MSS committee or hold it without me.³ If not I shall run over for a day.

I have had very full audiences & met many friendly people, and talked a great deal, & talked myself tired, & drunk port wine & been paid compliments, & what else is fame.⁴ I shall return to obscurity at the Savile Club with a pleasant feeling, as if I put my head upon a pillow.

I hope by now there are several eggs, but you will tell me that in your next letter & also how Anne and Michael are.

Yours affecly
WB Yeats

[ALS]   SAVILE CLUB, | 107, PICCADILLY. W.1.
May 22 [1923]

My dear George: I have wired Lolly for final proofs of K. There is an absurd sentence of which one half is in K & one half in L about a proud man, who, as aparent sign of pride, could not read French literature. I must change it in K now that I see what it leads to.¹

Olivia writes that Hope² has been very ill for a month past. She cannot leave him except for a very short time. 'He comes down for a few hours every day now, but is fearfully weak & gets fever nearly every afternoon.' I think one half illegible sentence means that she has not left the house for four weeks. I shall call & see her on Thursday afternoon.

---

³ The next meeting of the Committee on Irish Manuscripts, which he was chairing, met on 31 May; the final report was presented to Senate on 4 June 1924; Donal Joseph O'Sullivan (1893–1973), author of the controversial *The Irish Free State and its Senate: A Study in Contemporary Politics* (1940) and a distinguished expert on Irish folk music, served as clerk of the Senate from 1922 to 1936.

⁴ WBY had been on a lecture tour of Scotland since 13 May.

¹ *Early Memories of John Butler Yeats*, a condensed version of JBY's autobiography, unfinished at his death though long in the making, was completed by Cuala Press in July and published in September 1923; the section ending gathering 'K' and beginning gathering 'L' now reads: 'Synge, spiritually the most fastidious man I ever knew and the proudest, who turned away from modern French literature, told me that he preferred their [the Irish peasants'] society to the comforts of the best hotel. They are so happy in themselves and in each other's conversation that they are conservative, as conservative / as the people behind the barriers of privilege' (80–1).

² Henry Hope Shakespear (1849–1923), solicitor and amateur painter and musician, whom OS married in 1885.

I had a curious sceance last night with Powell, the Welsh miner.[3] Violent phisical phenomena. Table lifted into middle of circle & many lights. My arm pinched till it was painful.

In the morning I sat with the Crewe medium[4] & got a very marked 'extra' but cannot expect to recognise it until it is printed which may be to day or to morrow.

I wonder if you would phone to O'Sullivan[5] & ask him when Senate meets & what the business will be.

Will you be over by June 4? Could I think arrange sceance for you with Powell on that date. At the sceance before last he was levitated.
PS.
I have just got your letter. I think I shall return next week—I can come back here with you later. Probably in any case I should be back for the Senate.

I have an idea of turning Lolly disaster to advantage by breaking off the book at the point reached & stating why in a preface. Do not tell Lolly this as I want her to make a perfectly genuine effort to get a printer or to get her girls out. If we break off the book we must have a good case. It would make the book a treasure to collectors, but it would be undignified if no real necessity. I should have to find something to say on the situation in my preface which I would have to get printed here or some press with type that would go with Lollys.[6] Emery Walker would advise, I think I will talk things over with Emery Walker before I speak to Lolly.[7] I can do so to-morrow. Lolly is a trained compositor & might set the preface.

Yrs ev

WB Yeats

[3] Welsh-born Evan J. Powell (*c.*1881–1958), who began life as a miner during which time he developed his mediumship, was now a coal merchant and JP in Paignton, south Devon. A trance and direct voice medium who insisted on being securely tied during his seances, which were known for the frequent transport of objects as well as luminous phenomena, he was instrumental in converting Arthur Conan Doyle to a belief in spiritualism through his spirit guide 'Black Hawk'. In 1925 he was publicly challenged by the magician Harry Houdini (1874–1926) to prove the authenticity of messages he claimed came from the late newspaper magnate Alfred Harmsworth, 1st Viscount Northcliffe (1865–1922).

[4] William Hope (1863–1933), a carpenter from Crewe well known for his spirit photography; in 1922 there had been considerable controversy over Hope's sittings, but a great number of signed testimonies spoke for the authenticity of the psychic images.

[5] Donal O'Sullivan, clerk of the Senate.

[6] The Cuala Press had just been raided and ECY's two printers, Maire ('Mollie') Gill (1891–1977) and Esther ('Essie') Ryan (*c.*1886–1961), members of Cumann nBan (the strongly anti-Treaty 'League of Women' which had been active in 1916 and now revitalized), were imprisoned for six weeks; WBY did not pursue his idea for the preface.

[7] Emery Walker (1851–1933), engraver and typographical expert, associate of William Morris in the Kelmscott Press and co-director of the Doves press, first encouraged ECY to run a printing press and continued to serve as an admiring unofficial adviser to Cuala.

[ALS]   SAVILE CLUB, | 107, PICCADILLY. W.1.
May 25 1923

My dear Dobbs: I will return on Tuesday night, unless the mood takes me
to start on Tuesday morning in which case I will wire. If I attend Senate
on May 30 I shall feel free not to attend the week after when we want to
be in London. I warn you however that you will feel moved to welcome me
for I shall bring you a large & striking Hungarian broach which will make
a sensation in the Arts Club. I think the broach you lost was Hungarian.
The jewellers of Budh Pesth are ruined & so there wares reach London.
The man at Chelsea did not know the value of what he sold & I only paid
a few shillings. The man in Savile Row who sold me the new broach knew
all about its beauty & value which does not mean however that I have really
paid much. If you think it too large you can I know doubt change it. I hesitated between it & two other broaches which were perhaps more delicate in
form though not so large. The big broach is like this & about this size

The stones are green, red & white. I got it at a place Mrs Hamilton Fox recommends.[1]

Yrs affly
WB Yeats

[1] Elizabeth Valentine Fox, née Ogilvy (1861–1931), wife of brewer Thomas Hamilton Fox,
JP (1852–1923), of Hollydale, Keston (near Farnborough Kent), and 39 Cheyne Walk, London

Better put off Ballylee till Lady Gregory gets back which [will] be some time next week I think.²

[ALS]   SAVILE CLUB, | 107, PICCADILLY. W.1.

July 27 [1923]

My dear Dobbs: Lilly is in a very pleasant Nursing Home.¹ An old country house & she looks out on trees & gardens. I found her cheerful but week; & of course I saw Doctor She may be well enough in five or six weeks to go to Switzerland with Miss Boston² but he will let us know. This might be the best thing for her; though afterwards she might have to go back for treatment, inoculations to create immunity. He is an able man & a specialist in consumption (I mean Dr Simpson).³ Her frame of mind is as reported by Ruth.⁴ She dictated that telegram & says Lolly must not try to see her though she would like Lolly to write her—as Hilda does—a post card every day. She will never go back to Lolly. She cannot read books yet but presently would like 'some books of letters' and some 'modern anthology' with 'the poems she knows'. She does not care for fiction. She approves of all we have done or plan to do.

I have been very active

(1) Have seen Orpen & Shannon who agree to act on committee⁵

SW. A close friend of OS, she served as sponsor during WBY's affair with OS in the 1890s and by this time was involved in a long-time liaison with a wealthy barrister who doubtless encouraged her well-known extravagance.

² AG was visiting Bernard and Charlotte Shaw in Ayot St Lawrence.

¹ While on holiday in London visiting her recently married cousin Hilda, Mrs Charles Lloyd Graham, née Pollexfen (b. 1894), SMY collapsed, and was sent to the Roseneath Nursing Home in Winchmore Hill, North London, where she was at first incorrectly diagnosed as tubercular; it was not until 1929 that her stentorous breathing and fatigue were discovered to be the result of pressure from an abnormally enlarged and deformed thyroid gland. An undated horary denoting an unhappy outcome exists in GY's hand.

² Annie Elizabeth Boston (later Mrs Berlyne), known to the sisters as 'Phillida', was a boarder at Gurteen Dhas, home of ECY and SMY, while a student at TCD, receiving her BA in 1925 and her MA in 1928; on her return to England she remained a close friend of SMY. Her generosity extended to TCD where she established a fund in 1926 for undergraduates of narrow means.

³ The 1922 Medical Directory includes Robert Simpson, LRCP, LRCSI, and Robert Gordon Simpson, MRCS, LRCP, both of 'Roseville', Winchmore Hill; the specialist in consumption who was consulted was R. A. Young, later to examine WBY in 1929.

⁴ Ruth Lane Poole, née Pollexfen (1885–1974), WBY's cousin and SMY's surrogate daughter, lived with the Yeatses until her marriage in 1911; she had returned from Australia, where her husband was a forester, to give birth to her second child in England while Charles Lane Poole was surveying the forests of Papua New Guinea.

⁵ WBY was hoping to establish a government committee to oversee all artistic design decisions; the Irish portrait artist Sir William Newenham Montague Orpen (1878–1931) and Charles Hazelwood Shannon (1863–1937), the English painter, lithographer, and long-time partner of Charles Ricketts, had both agreed to be advisers, as had the Ulster-Scots artist Sir John Lavery (1856–1941).

(2) Have seen Alex Martin who, if 'Christies' consent, will take National gallery (This is private)[6]

(3) Tell Lennox that I have an almost definite offer of a tour for Abbey Players from Leon of St James Theatre, but may see another manager as Leon cannot say for six weeks.[7]

I shall stay here to night as I am to dine with Lutchens, who is to stay with Curzon & I want to talk over the Lane pictures.[8]

Yours affecly
WB Yeats

Will bring the Chinease pictures. Have seen many people beside those I name. A very crowded time.

[6] In 1924 Alec Martin (1884–1971; knighted 1934, KBE 1958), a partner in 1931 and later managing director (1940–58) of Christie's the art auctioneers, was made a governor and guardian of the National Gallery of Ireland, though WBY had unsuccessfully campaigned to have him appointed the next director; a close friend of Hugh Lane and named co-executor with AG of Lane's unsigned codicil, he strongly supported the return of the collection to Ireland and in 1960 received an honorary LLD from TCD.

[7] St James's Theatre was not available in 1923, since the actor, director, and producer Leon M. Lion (1879–1947) had sublet it for a long-running production of Dorothy Brandon's *The Outsider*, soon followed by a year's run of William Archer's *The Green Goddess*. Instead the Abbey toured in Ireland, and then in the early 1930s went on several extended tours of the United States and Canada; they did not return to England until 1937.

[8] At Hugh Lane's request, Lutyens had made several designs for his Gallery of Modern Art, the most controversial on the site of the Ha'penny Bridge straddling the Liffey, all such plans conclusively foundering when Lane drowned. Baron George Nathaniel Curzon of Kedleston (1859–1925), former Viceroy of India, an expert on Indian art and at this time Foreign Secretary, was a trustee of the National Gallery and although keen to keep the Lane pictures in England was open to the possibility of lending them to Ireland should they be 'properly housed' (see *LWBY 2*, 440).

1924

[ALS]   COOLE PARK, GORT, CO. GALWAY.
                              Monday [?7 Apr. 1924]

My dear: I have just heard of your illness—Lennox has written—& I am
wiring Delia for news.¹ It is great ill-luck for you my poor child. You have
been working too hard & taking no care of yourself. I would like to return
(but stay at Club) to be near you but cannot yet decide I dont want you to
be thinking 'he is uncomfortable' or some thing of the kind. I go to Ballylee
in an hour so I shall have done all business.

                                        Yours affectionly
                                                Willy.

[ALS]   at | COOLE PARK, GORT, CO. GALWAY.
                                    [?8 Apr. 1924]

My poor child I am so sorry you are ill. Yes I shall go to the Club on Monday & vote next day if I can, lacking your assistance.¹ I shall probably appeal
to the Hall Porter at the Club.
    I have finished my poem—a long poem & I think fine.²

                                        Yours affectionly
                                                WB Yeats

[ALS]   COOLE PARK, GORT, CO. GALWAY.
                                     April 8 [1924]
                                        Tuesday

My dear Dobbs: I have just had a wire from Delia saying you are much
better—she sent it off last night but it only came at Breakfast to day. I shall
hear again in a couple of hours.

---

¹ WBY had gone to Coole for a week, accompanying AG back from Dublin. Meanwhile
GY was suffering from an especially painful bout of pleuritis pneumonia which the doctor
assured LR she would be over in about ten days. Delia Molloy of Glenbrack, whose father
looked after GY's garden in Ballylee, had been their housekeeper since 1920.

¹ Possibly referring to the directors' meeting at the Abbey on 15 April concerning a mort-
gage on the Abbey buildings (*Journals*, i. 521), or a meeting of one of his numerous arts committees.

² Unidentified but possibly 'Leda and the Swan', first published in *The Dial* (June 1924), but
which he continued to revise.

I have seen Ballylee—you will have the whole Castle ready to inhabit very soon. The new room Raftery has plastered is practically ready. The room above—the top room—is the great surprise. It is magnifiscent—very high & even with one window—Raftery has for the moment filled up the others— sufficiently light. It would be the better of some filling up of spaces between stones with mortar but could be inhabited this year & quite comfortable if a door were made in one window. A quite ordinary window frame but on the inner side of the window nich[e] & leaving the stone mullions as they are would be all that is wanted. It will make a wonderful sitting room or study. Five or six pounds will make it habitable. So you will have a spare room for a friend.

There has been no flood since the day we left & the house looks perfectly dry & habitable. The little enclosed garden seems all right. It looked a pleasant friendly house.

Yours affectionly
W. B. Y.

Raftery & Diveney—who drove me—enthusiastic about top room.[1]

[ALS]
COOLE PARK, GORT, CO. GALWAY.
Wednesday. [9 Apr. 1924]

My dear Dobbs: As Cahill[1] says I am not to return I will not do so until Saturday, & then I will dine & lunch at club.

No news—Baggot comes to lunch & Rita Daly to tea so we are in a whirl of society.[2] This morning Lady Gregory recieved a most violent anonimous letter from some unionist denouncing her for writing 'The Old Woman Remembers.'[3]

I cannot get that fine top room at Ballylee out of my head—fire-place & all magnifiscent.

Yours ever
WB Yeats

[1] John 'Blocker' Diviney (1864–1943), who lived in the Coole Gate house, was AG's coachman and general steward.

[1] Francis Kennedy Cahill (1877–1930), physician and surgeon and authority on stomach disorders, was a neighbour at 80 Merrion Square South with offices nearby at 115 Stephens Green West. A prominent member of the Arts Club, he was also a strong supporter of the DDL and the Abbey Theatre.

[2] John ('Jack') Christopher Bagot (1856–1935), JP, of Ballyturin house on Lough Cutra in Kilbeacanty, four miles from Gort (see letter of 10 Apr. 1924). Rita Daly of Castle Daly, Gort, a regular visitor to Coole, was one of the older daughters of the Rector of Gort and Archdeacon of Clonfert and Kilmacduagh, Henry Varian Daly (1838–1925); in 1931 WBY refers to her as 'Mrs Leach' [Lynch].

[3] AG's 'rosary of praise' to the heroes of Ireland, 'The Old Woman Remembers', was first recited by Sara Allgood at the Abbey Theatre on 31 Dec. 1923 and published in the *Irish Statesman* and *New Republic* (New York) on 22 Mar. 1924.

[ALS]   COOLE PARK, GORT, CO. GALWAY.
                                                            April 10. [1924]

My dear Dobbs: Lennox in his last letter said 'Lolly has behaved rather
badly but is behaving better today'—or some such words—this means I conclude that, having a professional nurse, you can now keep her out.[1] Yesterday he wired but did not write as he had his meeting. Baggot lunched here
yesterday—a good country visit arriving at 1.30 & leaving at 6. PM. He is
alone at Ballyturin & lonely & about to flit to England for a time. His family
are there basking in the sympathy of their neighbours as refugees 'driven out
& all their property taken'. In reality they were not driven out, have come
in for money, & their property here is reasonably secure. One daughter is
married. The worst Baggot suffered was that four men from Clare came
in broad daylight & shot over his land the day before his Xmas shoot—he
had a house-party.[2] The same four men had meant to come here but had
been turned back by the country-people. Friendship is still something, if
law is nothing west of the Shannon. Loughrea[3] has been reciting 'The Old
Woman Remembers' with enthusiasm.

I had meant to walk over to Ballylee to day & have another look at the
great room, where all the legends come alive, but the wind is icy cold so
I shall keep to the shelter of the woods.

                                                            Yrs ever
                                                            Affectionly
                                                            WB Yeats

[ALCS]   COOLE PARK, | GORT, | CO. GALWAY.
                                                            May 9 [1924]

My dear Dobbs: No news of any kind. I am working all day long at
the script, & have not yet been to Ballylee. Lady Gregory has written to
Raftery to know when he can go over with us but has not yet heard. As

---

[1] GY was well enough by 23 April to accompany WBY on a visit to the Dunsanys.

[2] Bagot had two daughters. In April 1920 the extreme element in Sinn Féin, who promoted
renewed agrarian agitation to obtain grazing lands, had persuaded him to sell land; in 1922 he
was issued instructions by a party of Irregulars to give up more land and stock to them. WBY
seems to have forgotten that on 15 May 1921 the IRA ambushed a motor car as it left Ballyturin House after a tennis party, killing four occupants including Captain Cecil Arthur Maurice
Blake (1885–1921), district inspector of the Royal Irish Constabulary, and his pregnant wife, and
Captain Cornwallis and Lieutenant W. McCreery of the 17th Lancers, the only survivor being
Margaret Gregory, AG's daughter-in-law, who regularly played tennis there on Sundays.

[3] The 13th-century cathedral town situated on the main road between Athlone and Galway,
five miles from Roxborough, AG's birthplace.

the Government has accepted the ultimatum from the Tailtean Games Committee I must return to town for a meeting of that body next week. So you will find me there probably on Wednesday night. I dont want to go but I cannot leave those wild men to their own wildness till they have been sobered by some new members.[1] Remember me to your mother & Harry & to Olivia.[2] I owe your mother & Olivia letters I think but—well I have no excuse, except, on general principles, one puts off & so—. Try & persuade Olivia to come over. Here it is raining constantly so I can do much work, & am solving a number of problems.

Yours with love
WB Yeats

[ALS]   COOLE PARK, GORT, CO. GALWAY.
May 11 [1924]

My dear Dobbs: I went to Ballylee yesterday with Lady Gregory & Raftery but we could not get in as the damaged door refused to open. However to day I went back there with Raftery. Nothing stollen but door upstairs as well as front door burst in. I asked Raftery what he thought the intruder was up to & he said 'Somebody who wants a job as caretaker.' I have put Young Kelly to some work digging & vegitable planting but I confess to a desire to see the last of that family.[1] There was a wonderful view from the roof & it looked a pleasant place. On the white-wash of the wall somebody has written with pencil 'Tom Keirnan,[2] civic-guard Gort, take proper care

---

[1] 'Aonach Tailteann', the Tailteann Games, initiated as a tri-annual athletic festival, were to open 2 Aug. 1924, accompanied by a series of cultural events; WBY was chairman of the invitations committee to 'Guests of the Nation', whose other members were Sir Henry McLaughlin (1876–1927), Director-General of Irish Demobilization, Sir Simon Maddock (d. 1948), and the historian Valentine Emmanuel Patrick MacSwiney of Mashanaglass (1871–1945), created Marquess MacSwiney by HH Pope Leo XIII and a strong nationalist since his first visit to Ireland in 1903.

[2] GY was in London from 5 May 1924 and then went on to visit the Tuckers in Sidmouth; WBY was at Coole from 6 to 15 May.

[1] WBY and GY suspected that members of the John Kelly family of Dromore, Peterswell, about one mile from Ballylee, who worked at times as gardeners at the castle, were guilty of trespassing when the castle was vacant. About this time members of the Kelly family were frequently mentioned in the local papers charged with misdemeanours such as sheep stealing and cattle driving: two brothers, Michael and Patrick Kelly, were among the men accused of shooting dead AG's nephew Frank Shawe-Taylor on 3 Mar. 1920 but discharged for lack of evidence; Michael Kelly was remanded over a cattle driving incident on March 1925; Michael and John Kelly, described as farmers, were charged with sheep stealing, 27 June 1925.

[2] There is no record of a Keirnan or Kiernan in the Garda archives, but a Tom P. Cummins (b. 1902), whose career in the Guards was brief (1922–7), was stationed in Gort from May 1924 to August 1925.

of this property' which makes me think that the civic guard made some enquire after getting my letter & that this inscription is irony. Tom Keirnan may have called on the Kelly's.[2] I shall go to Dublin for Senate if there is a Senate. I shall wire to-morrow to find out. If you are still away I can return here so do not hurry.

Yrs affecly
WB Yeats

[ALS]   Coole Park | Gort | Co Galway
                                         Monday [12 May 1924]

My dear Dobbs: I went to Ballylee yesterday. Nothing so far as I could see has been stollen, but the bed has been slept in & the place ransacked. A pane of glass in a window by the kitchen door (road side of house) was broken, & an arm thrust in to reach window latch. The window was opened & some slim person—small boy no doubt—got in. He then broke lock of kitchen door from within. All cupboards were prised open but nothing I think taken. There is even still some brandy in the decanter. The place looks very damp on the ground floor especially—from flood & because water pours in through the hall thatch. The thatch is in an impossible state & is sinking about the kitchen chimney. The place had been made dirty by flood & things have been thrown about. Diveneys verdict is 'nothing wrong but thatch & need of a good cleaning up.' The closed in garden seems all right except for weeds & that the climbing rose-tree has been blown down. The front garden is all great weeds & the roses have either been stollen or eaten by a dark coloured horse that has been browsing there aparently for some time (I wonder if the Millar extended his license to browse in the field over the river).[1] There are seven or eight window panes broken by stones in the first upper row of castle windows. The bridge has been roughly mended by the neighbours. That is I think all I have to report but you will have to come & see for your self. Diveney says the threatening letter was sent 'by the lads on the bridge who told him they thought old Kelly more in need of the money than Molloy They did not like to see Mollou coming', which tale may or may not be true but may be a good tale to believe & act on.[2] He

---

[2] The previous year Ballylee had been broken into and a number of mirrors stolen. In October, they heard from AG that Ballylee had again been broken into. Probably unwisely given the political tensions in the district, WBY had written on 24 Oct. 1923 to the local Guards asking that the Kelly family be interviewed; AG preferred to follow the people's motto 'its best say nothing whatever is known' (*Journals*, i. 541).

[1] The miller in Ballylee from about 1909 was Martin Linnane (1854–1934), also a builder.

[2] The 'threatening letter' may have been to the Molloy family, who had received similar threats in the past over quarrels with neighbouring farmers (*BG*, 255).

added 'somebody should go there three times a week & when you go away all things like blankets should be stored at the laundry in Gort.' (I gather there is no laundry) He seemed anxious to point out how well young Kelly had nailed up the window & door. The most depressing sight was the front garden all green with great flaunting weeds & full of horse dung.

I return to-morrow (Tuesday). On Wednesday I see the President's secretary about my artistic committee of which the Executive Council approve.[3] I will write when I have seen him

Yours affly
WB Yeats

Post is just going to Gort so I can write no more. Lady Gregory seems weak. She went to sleep after breakfast to day.[4]

[ALCS]   COOLE PARK, | GORT,| CO. GALWAY.
May 12 [1924]

My dear Dobbs: Your letter has come. I have wired to know if there is a Senate on Wednesday & if there is will go up. I forgot to tell you how carful the Ballylee house-breaker was not to break the wood of the door. He struck all his blows upon the brass knob of the door handle. He was born for public life. He was meant to create parliamentary scenes till he found himself in the Ministry. Am full of curiosity to see that green coat which looks so old fashioned & is yet upon the very top of the fashion.

Yrs affly
WB Yeats

[ALCS]   COOLE PARK, | GORT, | CO. GALWAY.
May 14 [1924]

My dear George: I shall come on Friday by the first train & so will be with [you] about 2.30 or so. I am longing to see you & get all your news. I have worked very hard, grudging a moment away from that work I have almost finished all I brought with me. Spring beautiful in the woods

Yrs affly
WB Yeats

---

[3] He was urging the government to appoint an Advisory Committee of Artists.
[4] AG had been operated on for breast cancer in June 1923.

[ALS]   COOLE PARK, GORT, CO. GALWAY.
                                              Friday [?16 May 1924]

My dear Dobbs: I arrive by first train—2.30 I think—I will lunch on train.

I have finished lecture[1] & read some detective stories & walked all parts of the woods where one is out of the icy wind. Rita Daly came to lunch yesterday & praised you 'Mrs Yeats is so busy & so joyous'. The wife, or sister or daughter of the Mayor of Cork[2] had stayed with them & was full of curiosity about Ballylee, had wanted to get the key.

                                                        Yrs ev
                                                        WBYeats

I fear my letter of yesterday will have reached you very late. It was left ready for the post & forgotten.

[ALS]   82, MERRION SQUARE, S. | DUBLIN.
                                                   June 16 [1924]

My dear Dobbs: I am active again.[1] Yesterday put 'Bounty of Sweden'[2] in order for Cuala Press' & gave it to the girls to day & to day I have annotated those memories of Synge which on a re-reading rather touch me. Their writer had evidently a gentle flirtation with him & now writes of her own youth so long past away.[3] On Saturday night I strayed by shere accident into that dinner to Barrett, between the meal & the speches & settled down opposite young Esmond.[4] He was full of the Army enquiery. One General

---

[1] *The Irish Dramatic Movement*, his lecture delivered to the Royal Academy of Sweden on the occasion of the granting of the 1923 Nobel Prize, was published in Stockholm in 1924.

[2] Until the dissolution of the Corporation in October 1924, Séan French (1889–1937) was Lord Mayor of Cork, retaining the title in an honorary capacity and re-elected when the Corporation returned in 1929, remaining in the position until his death in 1937; from 1927 to 1932 he was a TD representing Fianna Fáil.

[1] WBY had been ill with a cold and GY was in England on Cuala business, having taken responsibility for the embroidery section during SMY's illness; the visit to Birmingham was probably for a sale of work sponsored by Emmeline Cadbury.

[2] *The Bounty of Sweden: A Meditation, and a Lecture Delivered before the Royal Swedish Academy and Certain Notes by William Butler Yeats* was published by Cuala Press in July 1925, with the last of the sixth notes dated 15 June 1924.

[3] C.H.H., 'John Synge as I Knew Him', a brief memoir by Synge's first love, Cherie Marie Louise, née Matheson, Mrs C. H. Houghton (1870–1940), with a brief introduction by WBY, was published in the *Irish Statesman*, 5 July 1924, 533–4.

[4] Denis Barrett (1876–1968), assistant commissioner of the Dublin Metropolitan Police, and entertainments secretary (1922–3), then honorary secretary (1924–6), of the United Arts Club, was given a dinner in his honour on the occasion of his wedding. Osmond Thomas Grattan Esmonde (d. 1936), TD for Wexford, was the son of Sir Thomas Henry Esmonde (1862–1935), Senator and nationalist MP.

felt a desire for a motor & announced that his officers were going to present it. All who did not subscribe he demobolised. Gorey of the farmers' party drew out the facts in cross-examination. Esmond had also a tale of a certain man calling on his brother officers with a bottle of pure-alcohol in his pocket that he might substitute it for the more harmless bottle of whiskey he expected to find, that they, not noticing the substitution, might tell all. No wonder Portabello became a little disturbed.[5]

I meet Lady Gregory at the train to night—she will be passing through on her way to London.

I am expecting Smilie to take [me] out for golf [6] & so had better finish

Yours ev
WB Yeats

[ALS]   82, MERRION SQUARE, S. / DUBLIN.
                                          Wednesday [18 June 1924]

My dear Dobbs: I enclose a telegram that must be for you or Lolly for I know nothing about it.[1]

A fiery debate in Dail last night about The Army Report. Mulcahy very demonstrative, but I felt all the time that I heard a Milkman saying 'I admit there are sticklebacks in the can but indignantly deney that I put water in the milk'[2] I think the report very adroit. No evidence is to be published & even part of the report it self—notes of Chairman—is suppressed. O'Higgins was not in the house but Macgilligan spoke.[3]

---

[5] Denis John Gorey (1874–1940), TD for Carlow-Kilkenny, was leader of the Farmers' Party from 1923 to 1927. After mutinies in two barracks, an ultimatum by the army in March led to the resignation of two ministers, a number of high-ranking officers, and an inquiry appointed by the Minister for Justice, Kevin O'Higgins, when legitimate grievances were conceded.

[6] Robert ('Bertie') Maire Smyllie (1894–1954), journalist and later editor of the *Irish Times* and the first to inform WBY of his Nobel Prize, attempted without much success to teach WBY golf.

[1] The telegram is missing.

[2] This quotation reappears in an unsigned article (but annotated 'C.C.' (probably Con Curran) by GY) in the *Irish Statesman*, 28 June 1918, 485–6, where it is implied that on all sides the final Report was considered inadequate; Richard Mulcahy, chief-of-staff of the Republican Army who later supported the Treaty and became general officer commanding of the military forces of the Provisional Government and 1923–4 Minister for Defence, was occasional TD during the 1920s and a Senator in 1943–4, when he followed Cosgrave as leader of the Fine Gael Party until 1960; a fluent Irish speaker, he twice served as Minister for Education.

[3] Kevin Christopher O'Higgins (1892–1927), Minister for Justice and Vice-President of the Executive Council, associated with the unpopular Public Safety Acts designed to destroy the Irish Republican Army, whose assassination in 1927 devastated the Yeatses; Patrick MacGilligan (1889–1979), TD for the National University, was secretary to O'Higgins and recently named Minister for Industry and Commerce, a position he held until 1932.

I am well of my cold & audaciously writing this at my desk between a wide open window & a glowing fire, rather like the damned who may be seen in a long cloud between hot & cold, as they hop to & fro. However I am not sneezing where the damned fry & snieze without ceasing.⁴ Gogorty drove me up towards the mountains last night & that renewed the desire I feel so constantly to go with you somewhere into the mountains for a few days away from all our complications & preoccupations. I must not write any more for it [is] Dail day & I have little time

Yours affecly
WB Yeats

I have just got enclosed bewildering letter from Lilly; & have pointed out its contradictions to her & told her that she must be definite.⁵

[ALS]   SAVILE CLUB | 107, PICCADILLY. W
July 11 [1924]

My dear Dobbs: I had a pleasant time in Scotland, & was applauded by the students vigerously.¹ I enclose a letter of Sturge Moores as it may amuse you think out emblems for the bookplate.² Lady Gregory writes enclosing letter of Carsons to Healy marked private.³ There is to be a special committee to take evidence as to Lanes intentions.—this is the suggestion of the Colonial Office. This repeats the plan of the late government. She asks me

---

⁴ WBY is probably thinking of Canto 3, lines 86–7, where Charon announces, 'I come to lead you to the other shore; into the eternal darkness; into fire and into ice' (trans. John Aitken Carlyle (Temple Classics, 1912), 31), but he and GY may well have known Boccaccio's commentary on *The Inferno*, Canto 16, line 70, which quotes the nobleman Guglielmo Borsier, who claimed that he knew of nothing that has not yet been seen except sneezing.

⁵ The enclosure is missing but WBY's reply indicates that ECY had found a house she expected to share with SMY, who was recuperating in France and still adamant that she did not wish to return to her sister.

¹ WBY received an honorary degree from the University of Aberdeen on 10 July 1924.

² WBY and GY wanted to have a bookplate ready for ABY's 'first sign of interest in books'. Thomas Sturge Moore (1870–1944), poet, playwright, art critic, editor, engraver, stage designer, and long-time friend of WBY, designed the covers for twelve of WBY's books, GY's bookplate, and emblems for the Cuala Press; on 26 June WBY had asked him to design a bookplate for ABY—see *W. B. Yeats and T. Sturge Moore: Their Correspondence 1901–1937*, ed. Ursula Bridge (London, 1953), 53–5 for this letter and Moore's reply.

³ AG continued to lobby the Governor-General and other members of the government to take action over the Lane pictures. Edward Henry Carson, Baron Carson of Duncairn (1854–1935), also well known as the lawyer who successfully represented the Marquess of Queensbury in the trial of Oscar Wilde and one of the founders of the Ulster Volunteers, resigned as leader of the Unionist Party to become Lord of Appeal in London.

to see Lionel Curtis about it.⁴ Lady Ottoline asks me to go down to her on Monday for the night. I shall go I think.

I am setting out to see the Gaugan exhibition at the Leicester galleries.⁵

Yours affecly

WB Yeats. <u>L.L.D</u>⁶

[ALS]   SAVILE CLUB, | 107, PICCADILLY.W.1

July 13 [1924]

My dear Dobbs: I shall wire to you to morrow saying that I feel I must return. I have asked Mrs Green¹ to wire if any change of plans makes my return unnecessary.

I am living in Museums—National Gallery, South Kensington, Tate & last night I went to Joan.² I thought all the scenes with the ecclesiastic & the last scene of all very fine—Shaws genius is a dialectical genius—but hated Joan partly because I almost always hate that particular actress but not altogether because of that. I thought her clearly thought of but obscurely felt & so not beleivable. A woman who has spoken with God & has no dignity & no simplicity—but is half cockney slut, half nonconformist street preacher. Even the wind does not change for such as she. I was leaving the theatre when I caught sight of Wilson³ who was there with his lady & delayed to

⁴ In January 1924 a coalition government was formed in Britain with J. Ramsay Macdonald (1866–1937) as Labour Prime Minister; on 14 July the Under-Secretary for the Colonies announced the formation of a committee 'to consider certain questions relating to the thirty-nine pictures bequeathed under the will of the late Sir Hugh Lane'.

⁵ The Leicester Galleries, which until 1963 were in Leicester Square, exhibited a range of works by the French Post-Impressionist painter Paul Gauguin (1848–1903) in July and August 1924.

⁶ Underlined twice.

¹ Alice Stopford Green (1847–1929), Irish social historian and strong supporter of the Treaty, had like WBY been nominated to the Senate in December 1922. While still living in London she published *The Making of Ireland and its Undoing 1200 to 1600* (1908) and *Irish Nationality* (1911) and in 1918, having returned to Ireland, published *Ourselves Alone in Ulster*, attacking Carson and supporting Home Rule; her last major publication was *A History of the Irish State to 1014* (1925).

² Bernard Shaw's *Saint Joan* with designs by Charles Ricketts and Sybil Thorndike in the leading role opened at the New Theatre, 26 Mar. 1924.

³ Probably Andrew Patrick Wilson (1886–1950), Scottish playwright, journalist (pseud. 'Euchan'), and briefly manager of the Abbey Theatre 1914–15 until he disgraced himself by privately negotiating tours with some of the players. His own plays *The Cobbler* and *The Slough*, one of the first Irish plays to depict Dublin slum life, were produced there under his direction in 1914; in 1921 he was co-founder of the Scottish National Players, and later a director of silent films and a scriptwriter for the BBC.

talk with them in the interval, & so did see the ecclesiastical last half of play which is sincere & even noble.

I dine with Dulac on Friday & they dine with me at the Ivey resterant to night.[4] I lunch to day with Olivia & Dorothy & go to morrow to Garsington so I shall have had a crowded hour

Yrs affecly
WBY.

[ALS]   82, MERRION SQUARE, S. | DUBLIN.

July 27! [1924]

My dear Dobbs: I think the Senate will meet every day next week, so I shall certainly not get away till Saturday week if then. But do not trouble to send Chrissie.[1] After all I made my breakfast every day for years. I shall get Miss Dodd probably to receive the Drama League on Tuesday—I mean to be posted there as I shall be at Senate.[2]

The House Agency people rang up yesterday. I said I thought you had formed other plans & they asked me to ask you to let them know if this was the case. I did not like to be positive as you may be looking for a place for Lolly to live in.

I am having a tremendous day—10 to 11.30 verse, 11.30 to 1:30 upsetting Col Moores apple cart at a committee to start a new party,[3] 2 to 3 letters & 3 to about six Senate. I am in high spirits but miss you much when the shadows lengthen.

Yrs ev
WB Yeats.

[4] The Ivy Restaurant in Covent Garden opened in 1917 and rapidly became a favourite meeting place for people in the theatre world.

[1] Chrissie [surname unknown], the housemaid who remained with them until the 1930s, was with GY who was repainting Ballylee; despite WBY's assertion of independence, GY arranged for Chrissie to go to Merrion Square.

[2] The DDL, which revived Pirandello's *Henry IV* on 10 Aug. 1924, had been started in 1918 to produce plays 'not likely to be seen in the Abbey Theatre or in the other theatres in Dublin'; WBY was the first president but LR and GY effectively ran the programme. Edith Stuart Dodd (b. 1885) was the first secretary of the League and occasional part-time performer in the DDL and other local amateur productions, then in 1927 became secretary of The New Players (first known as 'The Dramick'), an offshoot of the DDL.

[3] Senator Colonel Maurice George Moore (1854–1939), younger brother of the novelist George Augustus Moore, supported the National League party (established in 1926) and was later a founder member of Fianna Fáil.

[ALS]   82, MERRION SQUARE, S. | DUBLIN.
                                                    July 28 [1924]

My dear Dobbs: I have just recieved enclosures which explain themselves.
Keep Lolly letter for the sake of the crystal vision.¹ No news except that
I went to see Clark's glass yesterday² & that I shall get Lennox to preside at
the Drama League meeting as I shall be at Senate³

                                                    Yrs affly
                                                    WB Yeats

[ALS]   82, MERRION SQUARE, S. | DUBLIN.
                                                    July 28 [1924]

My dear Dobbs: I left all these letters, including one of my own, on the hall
table thinking Chrissie would take them with her even if I did not see her.
I did not see her for the Senate lasted till 8.30 & then when I had dined
I went to Gogortys. Senate every day & all day next week. Yesterday there
was a very fine debate on the Lane Bill the first real eloquence we have had
'This' said Coffey whom I chanced on coming away, 'is like a day of the
old Irish Parliment.'¹

                                                    Yours affecly
                                                    WB Yeats

[TLS]   Ballylee | Gort | Co. Galway.
                                                    August 18 [1924]

My dear Willy: I wired to you today to ask you to let me know if you
changed your address.¹ I saw Lady Gregory today, and she said that she

---

¹ Possibly a vision by their cousin Lucy Davies, née Middleton, daughter of WBY's great-
uncle, whom WBY frequently consulted on psychic matters; several of her visions are described
in Ella Young, *Flowering Dusk: Things Remembered Accurately and Inaccurately* (New York, 1945),
97–8.
    ² As part of the first Tailteann festival in August 1924 the stained glass artist Henry Patrick
'Harry' Clarke (1889–1931) was exhibiting *The Eve of St Agnes*, a window in six sections consisting of twenty-two small leaded panels illustrating Keats's poem, commissioned by the biscuit
manufacturer Harold Jacob for the landing in his father's house.
    ³ Although WBY was nominal president of the DDL, LR as vice-president was one of the
prime movers on its foundation and he and GY as secretary actually did all the work.
    ¹ Denis Joseph Coffey (1865–1945), Professor of Anatomy and first president of University
College Dublin (1908–40), was an avid supporter of the Gaelic League.
    ¹ WBY had been in London since 15 August and was staying at the Savile Club.

would have to go to London the first week in September about the pictures (Lane) so I imagine you will have to be there then. She suggested that you stay on and that you come back with her to Coole then. I could send you down a small crate of books, or you could stay a night in Dublin on your way through and take them with you. You might perhaps do that in any case as I would like to see you to hear all your news.

Like an idiot I forgot to send you particulars of the file, but I wrote to McGreevy asking him to go to 82 and write to you as to size, make and etc.

All well here, bar a drowned sheep a few yards down the river, and a few yards too near us!! Apparently no one knows whose it was and so no one can remove it.... Meanwhile we hope for mild flood.

I have been going to bed at nine every night and getting up at ten in the morning, so you may imagine I am getting rested.

Yours George.

[ALS]   SAVILE CLUB, | 107, PICCADILLY.W.1
Sunday | August 18 [1924]

My dear Dobbs: I was at Chilham yesterday.[1] Shannon is very anxious to do the robes but thinks much research needed & that it will be hard to be ready for Autumn.[2] He has given us a stained-glass window by Burne Jones.[3] He & Ricketts bought a set of I think three & were only able to use two in their Castle. The window he has given us you will understand from enclosed sketch with measurements.[4] I think it might go in top room or top landing of

---

[1] Chilham Keep was Shannon and Ricketts's country home on the grounds of Chilham Castle near Canterbury in Kent, owned by the Australian-born philanthropist and mining magnate Sir Edmund Davis (1861–1939), whose magnificent art collection was purchased with the advice of Ricketts.

[2] WBY was anxious to have Shannon, with Ricketts's assistance, design the robes for the new judges of the Irish state; he was unsuccessful in persuading the government.

[3] The Burne-Jones window eventually found its home in the window into the greenhouse at Riversdale, the Yeatses' last home.

[4]

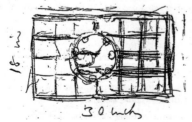

Castle, as I think we have no window in Dublin suitable. It commemorates St Cicilia & is rather charming.

I feel some doubt about putting it in Ballylee till the neighbourhood gets quiet though with a netting outside it would probably be safe enough. It might go in that little room outside the big room at top—the room we thought of for a chapel. You might measure that window. Of course we could put it in Dublin if we cared to lead a window—putting it in the middle.

I went to the place at corner of Chancery Lane to get the file boxes but found there were two sizes & do not know which I had got—they are trying [to] find my original order.[5]

Olivia must be away for I have had no answer to a wire I sent

Chilham is of course beautiful—they do no work there but run down for holidays & while there do nothing but garden. They seem to be friends with Dulac again & say that Madam Dulac brought things to some extent on herself. Dulac was friends with the present lady but friends only, for she 'hesitated for a long time' but Madam Dulac precipitated everything by her jealousey. I did not question & so know nothing but what I write. Madame Dulacs mother has some slight means & Dulac makes an allowance. That [&] a phrase of Ricketts—'the woman who lived opposite was very dangerous'—exausts my gossip.

I dined with Dulac & his lady on Friday night, but there was a queer plain little woman novelist there, a friend of his ladys, so conversation was not very interesting.[6]

I am putting off the moment when I must begin to work but must putt off no longer. O my dear I am beginning already to be lonely

Yours always
WBY.

Are you in the old bed room or have you moved up a floor?
The window is being sent to Dublin.

[TLS]   Ballylee | Gort | Co Galway
                                          August 19 [1924]

My dear Willy,

I was glad to get your letter, and I am glad that you have not been here this week, for I have never known it as wet. We had a few hours sunshine today almost for the first time. I am going to Dublin on Monday for the night, so write there <u>by return</u> if there are any papers or books that

[5] Partridge & Cooper, stationers in Fleet Street who supplied the boxes for GY's additional filing.
[6] GY has identified her on the letter as Edith Shackleton Heald (1884–1976), the journalist who would become WBY's last lover.

you want. The children are well, and I made the surprising discovery that
Michael can count up to six though he cant say the numbers! I asked him
to give me three sticks and to my amazement he carefully chose out three,
then four when I asked for them and so on. He has learnt it all by himself.
He is becoming very engaging, and much more active.

I am going to Dublin to collect some more padlocks and bolts for the winter.
We are so nearly quite secure that a little more and we may be boy-proof.

I have been reading some Italian plays that Walter Starkie lent me; none
very good, rather the bully-sentimental style, with people who must express
their temperament and so are without either moral or aesthetic code.[1]

I think we must keep the window in Dublin for a time at least

Yours with love
G.

[ALS]   SAVILE CLUB, | 107, PICCADILLY.W.1
Thursday [21 Aug. 1924]

My dear Dobbs—Savile Club says on last day in every May 'Summer is a
coming in' & on June first stops all fires. Result I got bad cold from which
I emerged yesterday & did a very good days work. Have seen nobody but
Dulac, Ricketts & Shannon & last night Mrs Mathers[1] & wont know my

---

[1] The DDL was interested in producing contemporary European plays. Walter Fitzwilliam
Starkie (1894–1976), romance scholar, translator of Spanish literature who was Professor of
Spanish and Italian at TCD, was the government appointee to the Abbey Theatre Board of
Directors from 1927 to 1933, when WBY made him an ordinary shareholding member of the
Board, a position he retained until 1942. A fluent speaker of Romany and authority on the
Romani people (known as Gypsies), during college vacations he travelled with his fiddle in
Hungary and Romania, first publishing accounts of his adventures in *Raggle Taggle* (1933). An
early apologist for Mussolini, in 1940 he was founder and first director of the British Institute
in Madrid and 1947–56 Professor of Comparative Literature at the University of Madrid, after
which he held various visiting positions in the United States.

[1] Mina 'Moina' MacGregor Mathers, née Bergson (1865–1928), 'Vestigia Nulla Retrorsum',
sister of the philosopher Henri Bergson and widow of Samuel Liddell (later MacGregor) Mathers
(1854–1918), 'Deo Duc Comite Fero', the magician who was primarily responsible for WBY's
introduction to the Order of the Golden Dawn; WBY's initiation took place in Moina's studio
and she contributed drawings for WBY's proposed Celtic Mystical Order, but her French translation of *The Land of Heart's Desire* was apparently never published. Like GY a medium and clairvoyant whose automatic writing provided occult materials for her husband, Moina returned to
London after MacGregor Mathers's death in Paris to establish a branch of the Alpha et Omega
Lodge, and remained a powerful force in preserving rituals of the Order and her husband's
memory. When WBY was writing the account of the origin of 'The Hermetic Students' for 'Four
Years: 1887–1891', Book I and 'The Tragic Generation', Book IV (*The Trembling of the Veil*, 1922),
he consulted Mrs Mathers, but was not prepared for her indignant rejection of the published
portrait of her husband (see *LWBY 2*, 446–9); in the 1926 edition WBY added a few mollifying
sentences, but did not alter his original description as Mrs Mathers had wished. However, in
belated tribute, he dedicated the 1925 edition of *A Vision* to 'Vestigia'.

plans for a couple of days So far I have found all needful books in Club Library except that I have bought a history of Byzantine Art. On about next Wednesday will arrive at 82 Merrion Square from Heal's a large cloth[es]-cupboard & washstand. You had better warn them & they can put them in strangers room² for the present. Please tell me if there is a basin jug etc or if I am to get these. They are not things to order without seeing them. I feel I have been a little extravagent but you will find the cup-board is charming & full of all kinds of contrivances to keep one tidy. It can be put in my present room till you re-arrange house after Cualas exit.³ It will be simpler however for the Maids to put all in strangers room till you or I get there. I had almost decided to start for Galway at once but yesterday I got your letter and did such good work that I have now no plan. I do not yet know whether I shall need books or not. I mean your letter about Lady Gregory of September 1—but for that I should probably have gone to Galway on Monday or Tuesday next. The one good thing in your letter is that you are getting rest & if I were with you or near you I fear it would not be as complete a rest. Do not persuade yourself out of that rest—you will always need long periods of it. Once I have this work finished I think I would be quiet companion for you but till that is through I cannot be myself at rest.

All blessings be upon you my beloved.

WBY.

[TLS]　　　　　　　　　　　　　　　　　Ballylee, | Gort. Co Galway
Thursday August 21 [1924]

My dear Willy.

Tom McGreevy sends me the measurements for the new file

Width 14 11/16 inches
Height 14 7/16'
Depth 27' (that is to say the <u>length</u> of each section.)

Will you order four new sections, that is to say four new middle pieces.

If you want any books or papers from 82 when I go up on Monday please write <u>at once to 82</u>.

I had a rather depressed letter from Lily, I suppose I shall see her on Monday but not alone unless a miracle supervenes.¹ She says 'Lolly I find

---

² The guest room.

³ After taking over ground floor rooms at Merrion Square for twenty months, Cuala Industries were moving to their own premises on the second floor of 133 Lower Baggot Street.

¹ SMY had recently returned to Ireland after having recuperated in Calvados, France, since June, and was once again living with her sister in Gurteen Dhas, Dundrum.

just the same, cross and full of venom. I have not yet found any topic we can talk on. Strange she should treat one for whom she describes herself as having an affection "so strong that it is the keynote of my life" so strangely. She says she will go in every second day, going in a little later than Lolly and coming out a little earlier, so as to get a calm journey.

I enclose a letter from the Society of Authors which I am afraid you will have to deal with and send on to Watt when you decide what you will do with it.[2] There are various other letters but I have answered them mostly saying you will attend to them later etc...nothing important, only requests for lectures or autographs etc.

Yours ever with love

G.[3]

[ALS]   82, MERRION SQUARE, S. | DUBLIN.

[*c*.22 Aug. 1924]

My dearest Willy.

You will want a jug & basin etc, & while you are at it get a <u>slop pail to match</u> and you might if you feel like it get a couple of bedroom chairs (for your own room.) as we are short of them. You know you are going to move into the large room at once, & my room will be a guest room for Lady G. when necessary (& I go into dressing room when she comes).

The weather is better & the green paint on Castle windows & shutters is fine. You ought to finish the Book on October 24th—Then it will be exactly 7 years since we started it.[1] I feel that if you dont finish then you will go on for another 7 years at the one book!

Yours ever

G.

[ALS]   SAVILE CLUB, | 107, PICCADILLY. W.1

August 22 [1924]

My dear Dobbs: No particular news—work goes well—Compton Mackenzie turned up last night & we talked through the evening partly of astrology—to

---

[2] This letter is missing, but evidently had to do with permissions, which WBY asked the Society to deal with.

[3] On the back of the letter WBY has written 'Hewat Mackenzie Park 4709 L.S.A. 5 Queen Square Southampton Row W.2 Museum 3160'; see letter of 24 Oct. 1929.

[1] GY began her automatic writing on 24 Oct. 1917 during their honeymoon (see *BG*, 102 ff.).

day he returns to his Island.¹ He wants a tower in Ireland & I told him of Dun-gorey Castle.² He has already, a flat in London, an island with a house upon it, & a house at Capri where I gather dwells a difficult or dissatisfied wife. He is very pleasant—all ☿ ♀ & ☽.³

Whaley came up to me in Piccadilly yesterday I let him walk beside me thinking he had some apology to make but no our conversation ran in this strain⁴

Whaley 'I am so sorry to hear that Dorothy Pound & her husband have finally parted'

WBY. 'I have heard nothing of the kind, & considering what I have heard it is exceedingly unlikely'

Whaley 'Well I do know that it was very seriously considered some time ago'

WBY 'strange that my wife who [is] such a friend of Dorothys should not have heard the news.'⁵

He then shifted to his own work &, through not knowing what to do, I let him talk but was not very cordial.

Yours affectly
WBY.

[ALS]   82, MERRION SQUARE, S. | DUBLIN.
                                      Saturday Aug. 23 [1924]

My dear Willy.

While you are in London <u>do</u>¹ go to see Laing about your eyes; it is three years since you saw him, so please dont forget.² I am sure you need a change of glasses—

---

¹ Edward Montague Compton Mackenzie (1883–1972), playwright, novelist, journalist, and Scottish nationalist, who after a distinguished career in intelligence during the First World War settled on Capri, later building a house on the island of Barra in the Outer Hebrides; he was knighted in 1952.

² Before WBY chose Thoor Ballylee, Edward Martyn (1859–1923), founding member of the Irish Literary Theatre who resigned because of differing dramatic allegiances, offered WBY the 16th-century Dungory Castle near Kinvarra, Co. Clare, on condition that he restore it and, should Martyn's heirs want it back, relinquish it.

³ The astrological symbols for Mercury, Venus, and Moon, that is communicative, pleasure-loving, and emotional.

⁴ Probably Arthur David Waley (né Schloss; 1889–1966), English orientalist and sinologist who 1913–29 worked with Binyon as Assistant Keeper of Oriental Prints and Manuscripts at the British Museum; his translations of Chinese poetry and Japanese Noh plays, though more scholarly than EP's, initiated an uneasy relationship with both WBY and EP.

⁵ By this time EP's amours were well known around London, but his wife remained with him.

¹ Underlined twice.

² Opthamologists William Lang FRCS (1853–1937) and Basil Thorn Lang, FRCS (1880–1928), consultant surgeons to the Royal London Ophthalmic Hospital, had their surgery at 22

If you can remember you might buy Michael a mechanical toy—He has got to the age for them and spent all yesterday (his birthday) with an \<inexpensive\> tin motor with a key that Mrs Reade (the Charwoman) sent him!³

In haste for post
G.

The shop will send it direct You neednt worry about the <u>parcel</u>!

[ALS]   SAVILE CLUB, | 107, PICCADILLY. W.1

August 23 [1924]

My dear Dobbs: There is no book necessary to me. If you find in the book shelf between the windows 'Apollo'—Octavo with green covers—you might post it to me.¹ I had meant to bring it. My work grows well I may have finished the history before we meet—or rather certainly will if no accident prevents. It is very tiring but very exciting work. If I were a rich man my dear I would go to Dublin just for that one day when you will be there but as it is I can only tell you that you are always in my thoughts.

I see people—Dulac once,—again however to night—Mrs Mathers once & that is all, apart from club members. People are out of town. I shall stay in the Club till Friday when it closes for its annual cleaning

Yrs ev
WB Yeats

[ALS]   SAVILE CLUB, | 107, PICCADILLY. W.1.

August 25 [1924]

My dear Dobbs

I have bought pail, jug & basin etc & two chairs & also the four sections for file. When do you return to Dublin for good.

Cavendish Sq. W 1; William Morris was Basil's godfather, and it is likely that Basil, known for his inventiveness and expertise, was WBY's ophthalmic surgeon. Later the spiritual healers George Chapman (1921–2006) and his son Michael (b. 1952) claimed William Lang and Basil Lang as their controls, practising 'spiritual surgery' under their direction.

³ MBY was 3 on 22 August. Mrs Reade, who served as caretaker when the house was empty, may have been mother of Florence Reade, the children's beloved nurse; one of Florence's younger sisters also worked at Merrion Square for some time as a housemaid.

¹ Lectures on art delivered at the École du Louvre in 1902–3 by Salomon Reinach (1858–1932) were published as *Apollo: An Illustrated Manual of the History of Art through the Ages*, trans. Florence Simmonds (new edn. 1907), a copy of which is in the Yeats Library.

I have got a letter from Senator Brown saying that he is sending me copy of the Hugh Lane case & asking to attend enquirey.[1]

I dine tonight with the Dulacs & some American at the Ivey Resterant. I have seen no one else except Mrs Mathers once. I shall however probably be going down to Garsington in a few days. Morrell wants to show me some book he is writing[2]

I envy your life at Ballylee, but I could not have worked without books though all I have wanted so far are in Club Library.

Yours always
WBY.

Olivia returns on Thursday & I dine with her on Friday. I shall not forget the mechanical toy.

[TLS] 82 Merrion Square | Dublin
Tuesday August 25 1924

My dear Willy.

The Corporation is very anxious that you shall be at the Commission on September 5 and that you shall 'consult' with Lady G. on Sept. 4. But I have sent you on their letter. They telephoned twice today to know would you stay on in London for this purpose and I said you would.

The wardrobe and washstand came this morning, but they are not unpacked yet as there was no one here to do it. Two nice young working men who were passing at the time helped get the crates into the house, and they promised to be back at 4.15 to unpack. Very fortunate as Owen is at Ballylee.[1] I have arranged the places for them in the spare room, the room to be yours in future.

The new canary has survived and looks large and lonely in the nest. His parents feed him but otherwise take no notice of him and dont even sleep on the nest with him at night. This is a typewriter borrowed from Carnegie for the day as I didnt bring mine up and I found a lot of letters here.[2]

[1] Samuel Lombard Brown, KC (1856–1939), of 68 Merrion Square, Regius Professor of Laws at Dublin University (1934), was a well-known barrister and Senator 1923–5 and 1926–36; he had been advising WBY and AG who were representatives of the Dublin Corporation, owners of the Municipal Gallery, on their response to the British government's establishment of a commission to examine the legality of Hugh Lane's codicil.

[2] Probably *Harriette Anne Morrell...A Description by Herself of Some of her Needlework and Painting*, edited by her son (Oxford, 1925).

[1] The general handyman employed at 82 Merrion Square.

[2] MacGreevy was at the time assistant secretary to the Irish Advisory Committee of the Carnegie United Kingdom Trust, of which AG was a member.

The Abbey made a profit of £170 for the week ending August 16. and £220 for last week.... [3]

Much love to you my dear
George.

[ALS]   SAVILE CLUB, | 107, PICCADILLY. W. 1.

August 26 [1924]

My dear Dobbs: I have had a letter from Senator Brown about my attendance at the Lane picture enquiery. I shall want for that the Observer article by myself which is in the cardboard box file in my study.[1] If you are not going up in time—Enquiery begins, I suppose first week in September—you might ask Lennox or MacGreevy to find it for me. It is no doubt under L for Lane.

I dined with Dulac last night & met an absurd American who represents the Hearst newspapers & is a person of importance.[2] Before dinner was served he crossed his hands in front of him & said, 'This is the most important evening of my life. I went to Harvard in such & such a year' & then proceed[ed]with his biography. Having finished with it he said 'Now I make only one request to you, that you speak to me out of your deepest thought & your deepest emotion' As you can imagine conversation languished.

Yrs affectionly
WB Yeats

---

[3] The Abbey Theatre prepared for the Tailteann Games with productions of *The Retrievers* by George Shiels, 'George Morshiel' (1881–1949), during the week of 21 July, *Ann Kavanagh* by Dorothy Macardle (1889–1958) and *The Country Dressmaker* by George Fitzmaurice (1877–1963) on 28–30 July, *Kathleen ni Houlihan* (WBY and AG), *Maurice Harte* by Thomas Cornelius Murray (1873–1959), and AG's *The Rising of the Moon* on 31 July–2 August, *The Grasshopper* by Padraic Colum (1881–1972) and AG's *The Workhouse Ward* on 4–6 August, followed on 8 August by a special performance for the delegates during which the literary awards were announced with productions of *Kathleen ni Houlihan*, *Riders to the Sea* (Synge), and *The Workhouse Ward*. LR's *Never the Time and the Place* and Sean O'Casey's *The Shadow of a Gunman* were performed 11–13 August, and Brinsley MacNamara's *The Glorious Uncertainty* 14–16 August; *The Shadow of a Gunman* and *The Shadow of the Glen* (Synge) followed the week of 18 August.

[1] During December 1916 and January 1917 WBY wrote a series of letters concerning the Lane pictures; passages from his article in *The Observer*, 21 Jan. 1917, were reprinted in AG, *Hugh Lane's Life and Achievement* (London, 1921) and the complete text in Wade, 616–23.

[2] Ray Long (1878–1935), one of the editors of the Hearst Corporation in New York, had commissioned Dulac to paint an annual series of watercolours for the covers of *American Weekly*, the Sunday supplement of the *New York Weekly American*. Once the highest paid magazine editor in the United States, he edited at various times *Red Book, Cosmopolitan, Ladies' Home Journal*, and *Photoplay*, and was for brief periods a publisher and Hollywood scriptwriter, finally committing suicide in 1935.

[ALS]   SAVILE CLUB, | 107, PICCADILLY. W.1.
                                                        August 28 [1924]

My dear Dobbs:¹ Yesterday I got at Harrods² three toys, a mechanical duck
with wings that wag, some sort of a cart that chimes when pulled again—
these for Michael not both at once. Then a top for Anne which changes
its note when banged on the head while spinning. I did not know where
to send them & as I thought you were perhaps on your way to Dublin got
them sent there. If you are staying on at Ballylee get Lennox to hunt out a
parcel from Harrods & send it.

Last night I dined with the Dulacs & Dulac told how that strange American I described to you was putting all his affairs right, ordering new pictures for publication & showing how to so simplify them that they would
take 3 days instead of 3 weeks. Then Mrs Dulac reminded me that when
last in London Dulac had complained of the low state of his fortunes &
I had said 'In six weeks a man will come from America & set all to the
rights.' I remember saying that & did not know why & then turning it off
as a joke.

I had a sceance yesterday with Mrs Cooper—it was very short but remarkable. Somebody came claiming to be my mother & spoke aparently of Lolly.
I asked if she meant 'Polly' & she said 'O no no no' & then I was told my
father would materialize. In a moment a hand came, quite distinct against
some vague luminous object—it was like my fathers hand but seemed smaller than life size. It touched me & was there for some time—very exciting
& strange. The sudden appearance of a sollid hand out of nothing—it
touched my head on the side opposite to the medium who remained perfectly motionless. I had hoped for a message for Lilly.

                                                        Yours ev
                                                        WBYeats
P. T. O
How long do you stay at Ballylee? I dine with Ricketts & Shannon to
night & hope to finally settle about the Robes. Shannon wants to make the
designs but wants more time. To night we shall I hope compose a letter to
Kennedy.³

¹ 'George' struck out and the familiar 'Dobbs' written in.
² Ever since the mid-19th century Harrods, 'the world's most luxurious department store'
advertising 'Everything for Everybody Everywhere', had been the ultimate source for shoppers.
³ Hugh Kennedy (1879–1936) had been legal adviser to the Irish delegation to the Anglo-
Irish Treaty negotiations and the most influential member of the committee that framed the
Free State Constitution; as first Attorney-General he oversaw the reform of the courts system
and was appointed Chief Justice in 1924, a position he held until his death.

[TLS]   Ballylee | Gort. | CO Galway
                                                    August 29 [1924]

My dear Willy.

   No particular news. I am going up to Dublin on Monday so write there
if you are writing. Owen is going to stay on at Ballylee to finish the painting and plastering. He will be there for about two weeks in September.
Macmillan (USA) writes that he is sending over 250 sheets to be signed
and numbered for the limited edition of 'Essays'[1] I have written to them
to say you will be away until September 10 and cannot do them before
that date at earliest. Otherwise there is nothing needing an immediate
answer.

   You cant think how well I am feeling, and my cough ever so much better.
I dont wake at all now in the night with it. Your wardrobe is exceedingly
nice and I like the washstand but it will have to go to Anderson and Ridgeway to have a leg mended.[2] It got broken on the way, but it is broken right
at the top so it can be mended invisibly.

   I have this instant seen for the first time the grey heron. There have been
no moorhens this year. Too wet and flooded I imagine.

                                                    Yours ever
                                                    George.

[ALS]   82, MERRION SQUARE, S. | DUBLIN.
                                                    [*c.*1 Sept. 1924]

My dear Willy.

   Judith Masefield is coming to stay on Tuesday Sept 9th until Thursday
Sept 11th.[1] Please will you be here. Do let me know (if you can) as soon as
possible. I told her I didnt know if you would be here or not.

                                                    Yours in haste
                                                    G.

----

   [1] 250 signed copies of *Essays* were published by Macmillan of New York on 26 Oct. 1924.
   [2] Anderson, Stanford & Ridgeway Ltd., furnishers, renewal, and storage contractors of
28–9 Grafton Street, Dublin.

   [1] Isabel Judith Masefield (1904–88), daughter of John and Constance Masefield; at this time
ambitious to be an actress but prevented by chronic asthma, she had already illustrated two of
her father's books, *King Cole* (1921) and *The Dream* (1922), and embarked on a career as writer
of children's books.

[ALS]   ARTS CLUB, | 40, DOVER STREET, W.1.
                                            Monday [1 Sept. 1924]

My dear George: I am in a new place as you see & will I think be very comfortable. I have seen Dorothy & on Wednesday next she goes back to Ezra
who is in Paris & a month or so later she, Olivia & Ezra all tour Italy. I wish
we could too but that will be too soon probably. My work is going well. I am
getting a good grasp of the history which you will find very interesting. The
Hugh Lane enquiery may put me off work—I cannot tell—but I may fear to
neglect that duty unless I wake myself out of my dream. I have had a pleasant letter of thanks from the Swedish Minister for our Dublin hospitality &
for a book I gave him.¹ He is in Sweden & has not yet had the bigger bundle
of books I sent a week ago. I see Dulac & his lady but that is about all & I go
to the theatre sometimes & that is about enough. I have paid your subscription at London Library—you had just been cut off their list—I hear they are
growing much sterner & they want Marmontel's autobiography which we
have it seems.² I work now in their Reading Room when I want books.

    This is a much more luxurious club than the Savile—pictures some rather
fine presented by artists all round the walls—most celebrities of the Victoria
era—Herkomer, Macbeth Etc.³ A huge portrait of Mrs Patrick Campbell in
her youth⁴—by whom I do not know—hangs in the entrance hall. Dined
last night with Dulac & a stranger came in, &, before I heard his name,
I thought, 'this is Dr Crippin but no that can't be right' & then Dulac said
may I introduce 'Dr Crimp'⁵

                                                            Yrs ev
                                                        WB Yeats

---

¹ Baron Erik Palmstierna (1877–1959), Swedish Minister for Foreign Affairs 1920–1, whom
they entertained at Merrion Square on 1 Aug. 1924, shared the Yeatses' interest in parapsychology and, with GY's friends the musicians Adila and Jelly d'Aranyi, was responsible for the
recovery of a manuscript by Robert Schumann; he would later publish memories of his intimate
conversations with GY in *Horizons of Immortality: A Quest for Reality* (London, 1937), 346–65.
    ² Jean François Marmontel (1723–99), French novelist, dramatist, and Academician, whose
autobiography *Mémoires d'un père* (1804) is a vividly drawn literary history of the period.
    ³ Sir Hubert von Herkomer (1849–1914), German-born popular social realist painter, exper-
imental film-maker, and dramatist-composer after his retirement as Slade Professor at Oxford,
was a strong influence on Edward Gordon Craig; he and the Scottish painter and photographer Norman Macbeth (1821–88), were both known for their portraits of eminent Victorians.
    ⁴ Mrs Patrick Campbell, née Beatrice Stella Tanner (1865–1940), the actress for whom
Bernard Shaw wrote the role of Eliza Doolittle in *Pygmalion*, performed in WBY's *Deirdre* in
Dublin and London in 1908; for many years she expressed interest in WBY's *The Player Queen*
but the plan came to nothing.
    ⁵ Dulac's physician and friend Dr George Lydstone Crimp (1876–1938) of 12 Bryanstown
Street was attached to the Ear, Nose, and Throat Division of Paddington Green Children's
Hospital and house surgeon of the Cancer Hospital; he frequently traded professional assist-
ance for works of art from Dulac.

No I think I would sooner be alone somewhere with you at least for a time than even with Ezra & Dorothy

[ALS]   ARTS CLUB, | 40, DOVER STREET, W.1.
                                              [*c*.2 Sept. 1924]

My dear Dobbs: Enclosed[1] has just come. Please send those pictures off but as the new address seems partly illegible better cut it out, stick it on & register. I have written to say my 'sec' had forgotten. I want you to get the washstand legge mended—I have a desire to find myself in full glory. Oh worst of all is the gass arrangement in middle of room. Would it be a great expense to get rid of it & to let a[n] electric light hang just over the bed?— one does read in bed you know, though it is quite plain our ancestors never did. However if all this is a great trouble leave it till I get back.

I too am much better endeed better than I have been for years. Do you know that I half think that finishing the philosophy getting all that abstraction put in concrete form makes one better. Perhaps I too am a medium & my force is used. I have now quite certainly mastered every abstract element & very surprizing some of them prove to be, in their ingenuity.

Tell me have you a good addres book or shall I get you one—either like mine from the Medici people or one in stamped leather from some Bond St shop? I was noticing them the other day.

Not having been flooded in all this wet must have restored your confidence in Ballylee a little.

                                              Yours affecly
                                              WB Yeats

I have seen the 'Green Goddess' and have read Bucans last book
                                              P.T.O

'The Three Hostages'.[2] I notice that the popular villain has changed his nationality. In 'The Green Goddess'—a play by William Archer[3]—an Indian is the Villan & in Bucan's book an Irish poet, who[se] verse is highly

---

[1] Enclosure missing.

[2] *The Three Hostages* (1924) was the third in the Richard Hannay adventure series by John Buchan, Lord Tweedsmuir (1875–1940), Scottish diplomat, historian, and novelist. It features the Irish villain Dominick Medina and his blind old mother whose beauty was 'devilish, and the soul within was on fire with all the hatred of Hell'. *The Thirty-Nine Steps*, the first of Buchan's series, has frequently been adapted for stage and film.

[3] *The Green Goddess*, a melodrama by the Scottish translator and drama critic William Archer (1856–1924), was first produced in 1923 at the St James's Theatre where it ran for a year and was immediately adapted for film.

finished & very melancholy. He is a hypnotist, a murderer, and an Anti English politician, & has a mother who looks like Maud Gonne as she is today but I am glad to say he has excellent manners. In the same book the German is a most sympathetic character, he lives but to do good.

[ALS]   ARTS CLUB, | 40, DOVER STREET, W.I.
                                        Thursday [4 Sept. 1924]

My dear Dobbs: I think I shall be back almost at once but I wont know till to-morrow at earliest. The Committee have decided to hear us now & to hear the Nat Gal in October. They may only want to hear us to morrow or they may want a second day.

I see Lady Gregory, & Mrs Shine & the Lane Agent from Dublin to day at 3 to arrange our procedure.[1]

Iseult writes that Madam Gonne is ill & they are to take her somewhere for complete rest 'worse than an ordinary nervous break down' They are going to 'a cottage in the hills' & then she goes to France. I wonder if Lennox has heard anything. Iseult asks us to dine with her & her husband at the Moira.[2]

If I can get another Fornights daily work I shal have finished system up to the point when I shall want you—probably however some accedent will delay me.

                                                Yrs ev
                                                WBYeats

[ALS]   ARTS CLUB, | 40, DOVER STREET, W.I.
                                        Friday [5 Sept. 1924]

My dear Dobbs: Enquiery to day, I have no doubt from attitude of judges that we have won on the facts but the doubt in there minds seems to be granting that the Codicil represented Lane['s] true mind is it desirable to make such an inovation or to make it legal by act of parliment. The delay

---

[1] Hugh Lane's sister Ruth (1880–1959) lived with him in Lindsay House, his London home, after the early death of her husband J. Hickman Shine in 1911, whom she married in 1905; as one of the chief beneficiaries of Hugh's will, she supported AG in the fight to honour the codicil and have the thirty-nine disputed pictures returned to Dublin; Mancini's portrait of her is in the Gallery in Dublin; in 1944 she married Thomas Heaven who died soon after.

[2] The Moira Hotel, 15 Trinity Street, close by the gates of TCD, was a favourite dining place; IG's letter with only the date '29th' has been given the provisional date '? Spring 1926' in *LWBYEP*, 127, but seems to belong here.

to October has been caused by Curzons desire to be heard in favour of the Nat Gall. I conclude he will press the point that it is not desirable.[1]

Now the sooner I get home the better but there is no Sunday night boat from Liverpool, & to-morrow at 4.30 (which would make it too great a rush to catch train) I have appointment with that woman who wrote about Japanese drama[2]—I had expected to be engaged to day—so I cannot cross till Monday night.

Yours affectionly
WBY

Just off to dine with Shannon.

[ALS]   Coole Park | Gort | Co Galway
                                              Friday [30 Oct. 1924]

My dear Dobbs.

Please make yet one more change in that poem. Stanza 5 should run thus

> I tore it from green boughs winds tore & tossed
> Until the sap of summer had grown weary,
> I tore it from the barren boughs of Eire
> That country where a man can be so crossed;[1]

I think that removes the last sentimentaly. If the copy has already gone to Russell send him this stanza. He can added it in proof.[2]

---

[1] The Committee found that Lane 'in signing the codicil of the 3rd February, 1915, thought he was making a legal disposition', but advised the British government against giving legal effect to it. The fight for the return of the pictures continued, with Ramsay MacDonald in 1932 suggesting a loan to the Dublin Corporation which was rejected, until finally in 1959 an agreement was reached to have groups of the pictures rotate every five years between the two cities; twenty years later it was negotiated that Dublin would be permitted to display thirty pictures to London's eight.

[2] Probably Zoe Kincaid Penlington (d. 1944), an authority on Kabuki theatre, on whose behalf WBY wrote to his publisher later that month; from 1912 she and her husband John N. Penlington, author of *The Mukden Mandate: Acts and Aims in Manchuria* (Tokyo, 1932), founded and published the weekly journal *Far East*. I am grateful for the assistance of Professor Yoko Chiba in identifying her.

[1] 'An Old Poem Re-Written', a new version with a prefatory note of WBY's 'The Dedication to a Book of Stories Selected from the Irish Novelists', was published in the *Irish Statesman*, 8 Nov. 1924.

[2] George William Russell (1867–1935), the poet, dramatist, theosophist, painter, and journalist known familiarly by his pseudonyms 'A.E.', 'O.L.S.', and 'Y.O.', and, less frequently, 'G.A.L.', 'Querist', 'L.M.E.', 'R.I.E.', was one of WBY's oldest friends, rivals, and fellow mystics. An authority on agricultural economy, he worked for Horace Plunkett's Co-operative Movement and its coordinating body the Irish Agricultural Organization Society in establishing cooperative banks and developing credit societies throughout the country. He then served as editor of the *Irish Homestead* (1905–23) and the *Irish Statesman* (1923–30), where he supported both young

I have just had some necessary Abbey business to do & want it be done before bigger work & so no more now.[3]

Yrs always
WBYeats

[ALS]   COOLE PARK, GORT, CO. GALWAY.
Oct [Nov.] 3 [1924]

My dear Dobbs: Am working well & keeping well, & the woods in their autumn colours at evening when I take my walk are magnificent. My only distress is absence from you & I miss you always, & when I see a lovely sight—evening light on the beeches or the light—long for you that I may talk of it. Is not love being idle together & happy in it. Working together & being happy in it is friendship. I wish you would write to me, but I know you are always busy <not that that would be busy also>

Nothing from Ashe King—I suppose he means to keep up the quarell & I shall have to rewrite that dedication.[1] I have re-written the song of 'the old Pensioner,' & [made] a good poem of it.[2] I must have worried you with all those em[end]ations of the poem for Russell.

Yrs affecly
WBYeats

[ALS]   Coole Park | Co Galway
Nov 6 [1924]

My dear Dobbs: I will send that dedication to Macmillan when I return to London.[1] Proofs are coming rather slowly so there is no hurry. Sally Allgood

and established writers. Despite many differences of opinion over the years, the bond between WBY and AE remained strong. Disillusioned with the political situation under de Valera, in 1932 he moved to England, made one final trip to America, and never returned to Ireland.

[3] WBY was at Coole from 29 October to 15 November during part of which time GY was in London.

[1] Despite WBY's attempt to explain the context of his remarks and apologize for their ambiguity, Richard Ashe King objected to the reference to him in *The Trembling of the Veil* (1922). In memory of his old friend WBY wrote on 26 Oct. 1924 asking permission to dedicate his *Early Poems and Stories* (1925) to him. See 29 Oct. 1921.

[2] 'The Lamentation of the Old Pensioner' was published in its revised form in 'The Rose' section of *Early Poems and Stories* (London, 1925).

[1] To Richard Ashe King, see previous letter. On 8 Nov. 1926 the Irish Literary Society of London, of which he was president, celebrated Ashe King's 87th birthday at a dinner in which WBY proposed the toast: he 'had helped to make Irish literature respected and worthy of respect by his books on Swift and Goldsmith' (*The Times*, 9 Nov. 1926).

is in a state of excitement because 'Playboy' is being put on & Miss Crowe is to play Pegeen Mike. She has been sending Lady Gregory wild letters.[2]

My work goes well & I am much better—I feel in ordinary good health, & that I am ill seems to me a dream. However Murhead's little aparatus will decide how many degrees of blood-pressure & I shall beleive.[3] However I certainly find tranquility a great delight. I have made a new poem of the 'Song of the Old Pensioner' & a good poem. I am doing a great deal of work.

Yours with all affection
WBY.

Get some tobaconist to send me 2 ozs of Turkish Cigarette to-bacco. Do not buy it your self & have the trouble of posting it. Get him to do that. If you were here I should be perfectly happy but I pine for you & rather dread the absence from you in England.

[TL/ALS]   [Merrion Square, Dublin
                             ?10 Nov. 1924]

Dear Willy.

I enclose a few letters.... Sturm's[1] because you will like to read it; Lady Londonderry's because you must...[2] Starkie's because you had better make an appointment with him for the week or ten days you will be here before

---

[2] Sara Allgood, who had always been one of AG's favourites, had for some time been agitating to return as director or manager of the Abbey Theatre; having performed in Synge's *Playboy of the Western World* a number of times, she was anxious to regain her status as one of the leading actors in the company, especially after her success as Juno Boyle in O'Casey's *Juno and the Paycock*, which had opened at the Abbey on 3 Mar. 1924. Meanwhile, Eileen Crowe had been given major roles. In May 1928 the theatre once again offered Allgood an engagement, but at half the salary she asked for.

[3] WBY was suffering from shortness of breath and his physician, the distinguished Professor of Medicine Thomas Gillman Moorhead (1878–1960), joint editor of *Dublin Journal of Medical Science*, had diagnosed severely high blood pressure and insisted on complete rest.

[1] Frank Pearce Sturm (1879–1942), a surgeon, poet, translator, and journalist deeply immersed in the occult and mysticism, who became a staunch supporter of and adviser on *A Vision*; described to OS as 'a very learned doctor in the North of England' (4 Mar. 1926), he and WBY had corresponded since 1902.

[2] Edith Helen Vane-Tempest-Stewart, Marchioness of Londonderry (1879–1959), known to her friends as 'Circe', influential society hostess and a close friend of Ramsay MacDonald; she had been actively engaged in the Women's Volunteer Reserve during the First World War and during the 1920s transformed the gardens of her husband's family estate of Mount Stewart, near Newtownards, Co. Down, into one of the finest in the United Kingdom; she had written to WBY for 'an authentic portrait of Cuchulain' in order to put up a statue of him in her garden, *Journals*, i. 603.

going away, and the Chief Justices for the same reason. There is also one from an enthusiast for your Banquet speech which may amuse you.[3] All others I have dealt with.... Your letter to the Evening Mail about the National Anthem has brought a flood of lyric effort. I have sent it all on firmly to Tivy,[4] and have sent a 'jelly'[5] letter to the various nuisances to say that you have now no connection with the competition and that I have sent on their verses to the Evening Mail.[6] One of them was a real gem.. It rhymed 'Spite' with 'State' So I gather the gentleman was a cockney.

[MS] I have dined with the MacSwineys—an amusing dinner with some talk. Hyde, O'Briens Gogarties & the Von Goertzs.[7]

Love G.

[ALS]   COOLE PARK, GORT, CO. GALWAY.
                                        Wednesday [12 Nov. 1924]

My dear Dobbs: I shall be up on Saturday by the evening train. I have been disturbed to see that you had to put off your Drama League performance.

---

[3] An unnamed Australian had written praising WBY's speech at the Tailteann banquet on 2 Aug. 1924, which had been printed in the *Irish Independent*, 4 August; proposing the health of 'our Guests' he acknowledged that the new nation finds itself 'in a very difficult and troubled world'.

[4] Henry Lawrence Tivy of Cork (b. 1848), principal proprietor and managing editor of the *Dublin Evening Mail* and several other Irish newspapers.

[5] Possibly a reference to the fulsome notes written by Jelly Eva d'Arányi de Hunyadvar (1895–1966), Hungarian-born violinist and grand-niece of the celebrated violinist Joseph Joachim, who was a lifelong friend of GY and her mother; Béla Bartók and Gustav Holst dedicated violin sonatas to her and Maurice Ravel wrote *Tzigane* for her.

[6] The *Dublin Evening Mail*, 13 June 1924, offered a prize of fifty guineas to the writer of the best lyrics for a new national anthem; LR, James Stephens, and WBY were appointed as adjudicators but decided that not one of the many entries was 'worthy of fifty guineas or any portion of it'. The *Evening Mail* editors reopened the competition, but when some 400 submissions appeared, WBY withdrew (WBY to LR, *CL InteLex*, acc. 4646). Eventually 'The Soldier's Song', composed in 1907 by Peadar É Cearnaigh and Patrick Heaney, a long revolutionary marching song, was considered the official anthem.

[7] Douglas Hyde (1860–1949), poet, playwright, historian, and folklorist who wrote in Irish as An Craoibhin Aoibhinn ('The Pleasant Little Branch'); in 1892 he helped found the National Literary Society in Dublin (where he spoke on 'The Necessity of De-Anglicising Ireland') and was first president of the Gaelic League (1893–1915), Professor of Modern Irish at the National University (1908–32), appointed a Senator in 1925, and first President of Ireland (1938–44). The Marquess MacSwiney, who had recently been unsuccessfully nominated by Gogarty to the Senate, was married to Anna Karoline von Görtz, Countess von Schlitz (1877–1938); they lived at 39 Upper Fitzwilliam Street. William Dermod O'Brien (1865–1945), landscape and portrait artist, was president of the Royal Hibernian Academy (1910–45) and of the Dublin United Arts Club; he and his wife Mabel (née Smyly; d. 1942) were present at WBY's death in France as described in Lennox Robinson, *Palette and Plough* (Dublin, 1948), 187–8.

I wonder if you had your Sunday night performance all right.[1] I am afraid it was a blow. I am very well except for eye strain from reading last night after Lady Gregory had gone to bed. I may have to get up with the birds & sleap when they do. It will increase my sympathy with the canaries. Otherwise I am exceedingly lively & have wholly rewritten 'The Death of Cuchullain' He does not now die at all.[2] To rewrite an old poem is like dressing up for a fancy dress ball. I am exceedingly glad that you have that sale in London that we may be together there.[3] May we not go to some hotel—as it is to be two days play—& not scatter our selves about London.

The book has been a little interrupted by proof sheets but if I have three good days I may finish this rough draft before we meet. One is delayed too by constant discoveries I have worked all day mostly & am none the worse.

The Miss Dalys of Caslte Daly came on Monday with their mother & brother.[4] The mother dominating, Gaelic Leagueish & clever & the two girls gentle & pretty, one more than pretty. I was surprized by them & charmed but they will not be our neighbours. The son, who has been in Free State army is getting married—some girl from Clifton probably from the shop counter—& is to live at Casle Daly & the girls are to be scatterd.[5] The son I had no talk with. He looked a rough type, & will probably sink into the squireen.

Yours affectionly

WB Yeats

The Daly girls get up plays in their barn. They do not act but teach the country people to do so. The next play is 'The Whiteheaded Boy'.[6] Mrs Daly wanted to know what its morel was.

[1] By this time GY was heavily involved in the DDL, which had advertised performances of Benavente's *The Passion Flower* at the Abbey Theatre on 9 and 10 November, but the second performance on Monday evening had to be cancelled due to the illness of Eileen Crowe who was playing a major role; the play was revived on 7 and 8 Dec. 1924.

[2] First titled 'The Death of Cuchulain' and published in *United Irishman*, 11 June 1892, the poem was considerably revised when published as 'Cuchulain's Fight with the Sea' in *Early Poems and Stories* (1925).

[3] Probably the Applied Arts and Crafts Exhibition at the Royal Horticultural Hall, opened on 4 Dec. 1924 by the writer Princess Elizabeth Bibesco (1897–1945), daughter of the former Prime Minister Herbert Henry Asquith (1852–1928) and his second wife Margot, née Emma Alice Margaret Tennant (1864–1945); at this time her husband Prince Antoine Bibesco was Romanian ambassador in Washington.

[4] The Venerable Henry Varian Daly had three sons and two daughters by his first wife and two sons and three daughters by his second wife Elizabeth Alice (b. 1849), whom he married in 1879; Rector of Gort since 1873 and Archdeacon of Clonfert since 1881, he had been in the reception committee when AG first came to Coole as mistress in 1880.

[5] On 12 Aug. 1925, doubtless spurred by AG, WBY wrote to Ernest Blythe, Minister of Finance, enquiring whether the Galway Council might let the old Gort Fever Hospital for £15 a year to Rita Daly, AG's friend, who must have been one of the older daughters; she seems to have remained in the Gort area and by 1931 was married to a Mr Leach or Lynch.

[6] *The Whiteheaded Boy* by LR was and continues to be a favourite comedy ever since its first production at the Abbey Theatre in 1916.

[ALS]   COOLE PARK, GORT, CO. GALWAY.
                                       Nov 13 [1924]

My dear George: Lady Gregory has just said that she has taken a lodging in Dublin this time as she means to stay some time. I thought I had better let you know at once.

I have worked very hard & I expect to finish the first draft of the philosophy tomorrow. I would have done so by this but lost three days with a cold. I have just turned an absurd old poem of mine called 'The Sorrow of Love' into a fine thing.¹

                                                       WBYeats

[ALS]   SAVILE CLUB, / 107, PICCADILLY.W.1
                                       Saturday [22 Nov. 1924]

My dear Dobbs:
    A pleasant easy journey despite a gale. I have spent the day reading Bell-Ami over the fire. Accomplished, accurately observed, cold—its subject matter a little faded like an old newspaper.¹ It is pleasing to know that in the seventies people played cup & ball & stuck transfer papers on their window panes, but it is not important.
    I forgot the golf sticks. Does it matter? Can your step-father supply me? or must you send them to Devonshire? I am afraid my dinner at the Duncans is spoilt.² I have nothing to right for nothing else has happened & the golf sticks will not bear dwelling on.
    I am afraid I have greatly added to your work, my dearest, by this sort of semi-illness of mine.³

                                                       Yrs
                                                  WB Yeats

¹ WBY continued to revise poems first published in *The Countess Kathleen and Various Legends and Lyrics* (1892); the new version of 'The Sorrow of Love' appeared for the first time in *Early Poems and Stories* (1925).

¹ *Bel-Ami or, The History of a Scoundrel* (1885), the realist novel by Henri René Albert Guy de Maupassant (1850–93); a copy of the 1903 French edition is in the Yeats Library.

² Ellen Duncan had left Ireland and her position as curator of the Municipal Gallery of Modern Art when her Unionist husband James Duncan lost his position as a British civil servant in charge of the Teachers' Pensions Office in January 1922; they first settled in London before moving to Paris, but eventually separated and Ellen returned to Dublin alone, only going back to Paris at the end of her life to be near her son Alan (see 5 Feb. 1931).

³ His doctor still considered WBY's blood pressure too high.

[ALS]   SAVILE CLUB, | 107, PICCADILLY.W.1
                                       Tuesday [25 Nov. 1924]

My dear Dobbs: I am off to-morrow to Sidmouth, & I have just been to
Watt. Would you mind sending that Dedication of 'Early Poems & Stories'
registered to me at Sidmouth. I will add an P.S. & send it to Watt.

   I feel very well & have worked steadily at the book.

   There is such a whirl of talk here at the moment that I cannot compose a letter—asking one another 'who is Mr A' & everybody with secret
information that [he] is a prince of Burma, or of Cashmeer—this Gosses
opinion—or of Egypt or of Pursia. 'A.D.C.' said to be a Capt Arthur & an
Irishman.[1]

                                       Yours affectionly
                                       W.B.Y.

Clothes came—trying to make up my mind if coat is tight under arms & till
I know will carry about two suits. It looks very well.

[ALS]   82, MERRION SQUARE, S. | DUBLIN.
                                       Thursday morning [?27 Nov. 1924]

My dear Dobbs: I send that poem re-written. 'Forhead on the breast' was
impossible—it was an over sight of course.[1] In amending that I amended
much more. It is my thought & experience of 1890 written [with] the skill of
today. Please put the old heading to it—'Poem Rewritten' etc—I forget it.

   No I do not breakfast in bed but shall be comfortable enough. Post
going[2]

                                       WBYeats

   [1] The daily Law Reports in *The Times* from 19 Nov. to 3 Dec. 1924 provide a detailed
discussion of the claim by Charles Ernest Robinson, a bookmaker from Sydney, Australia,
to recover £125,000 paid out by the Midland Bank to blackmailers of 'an Eastern potentate
referred to in Court as Mr. "A"', who was discovered...in compromising circumstances with
the plaintiff's wife in a Paris hotel'; the conspirators included the aide-de-camp, also unnamed
in Court, 'attached to the suite of the potentate on the occasion of his visit to this country'.
Judgment was entered for the defendants, although the Bank was never able to prove the
complicity of Mr and Mrs Robinson, and it was not until January 1925 that 'Mr A' was identified as Sir Hari Singh (1895–1961), who in September 1925 became the last ruling Maharaja
of Jammu and Kashmir.

   [1] Probably line 71 of 'Cuchulain's Fight with the Sea': 'with head bowed on his knees
Cuchulain stayed'—a necessary alteration originally suggested by GY.

   [2] Although written on Merrion Square stationery, this letter refers to his arrival in Sidmouth on 26 Nov. 1924, where he stayed in the hotel near Alkerton Cottage, home of the
Tuckers.

[ALS] Alkerton Cottage | Sidmouth | Devon
Nov 29 [1924]

My dear Dobbs: When do we meet—Remember I want to be some days
with you at the Garland Hotel in London & I want to write to one or two
people. Olivia told me that Dorothy wrote to you urging the charms of Sicily in January. Have you weighed them? The book is still in its difficult last
pages—shiftings—'state before birth' & so on—They expand in my despite.
Tomorrow I get to state before birth. Once that is finished it should be
but correction under your advice, & revision of style & arrangement. I am
well—I lie down in afternoons & will play golf when the weather clears.
Always when I [am] first away I get more or less des perate & I think
I cannot get any order or peace into my life without your help but after a
time—though I always want you—I get into some sort of pleasant existence
which serves for a season. Harry & your mother take great care of me & life
is pleasant, but I shall want you before long for all that.

Sidmouth is flooded every night at this time, by the sea which comes
higher up every year. For two or three nights it has put out the furnaces of
the Gass Works; & last night there was a tolerabl performance of 'The Dolls
House' by strolling players & the man at the door turned out to be an old
acquaintance of mine¹—that is all the local news. We talk of the Robinson
case² & little else.

Yours affly
WB Yeats

[ALS] ALKERTON COTTAGE, | SIDMOUTH, | DEVON.
Tuesday [2 Dec. 1924]

My dear Dobbs: Yes Sicily in January sounds delightful—if it does not upset
your plans. I am coming up for our week in London, & will probably go
back to Dublin with you < ... to know of Senate before Jan 3rd ... >. May
I come up next Saturday? I will consider that settled unless you pick some

---

¹ The *Sidmouth Herald*, 6 Dec. 1924, reviewed a production of Ibsen's play in the Manor
Hall, Sidmouth, on 29 November, noting that 'Mr WB Yeats the well-known Irish poet and
critic was present and expressed himself as delighted with the performance of this so unac-
countably neglected masterpiece.' The 'old acquaintance' was probably the actor-manager
and book collector Anmer Hall (Alderson Burrell Horne; 1863–1953), formerly associated
with managements of the Scala and Royalty Theatres in London and later with the Festival
Theatre at Cambridge and the Westminster Theatre in London.
² See note of 25 Nov. 1924.

other day. I say Saturday because your sales will be finished then.¹ Take a room for me at The Garland Hotel that I may go there from station.²

I have actually got to an end of the MSS; but I am re-doing the last pages again to get them simpler. I wont let you type anything but what I hope is the final text.³ There are long passages to be transposed & we can then send book as it is typed to Laurie.⁴ The hardest part & the most important is the last 50 pages but I think they have come right.

Yours ev

WB Yeats

[ALS]   ALKERTON COTTAGE, | SIDMOUTH, | DEVON.
Thursday [4 Dec. 1924]

My dear Dobbs: Take a room for me at Garlands Hotel. I shall come up Saturday. I will wire or write train when I know it. I shall go to Langⁱ while there—I am going to a dentist here. When I see you we will deccide on what to do up to Jan 3 & when I go. I shall know about Senate by then.

Yrs ev

WB Yeats

¹ See note to 12 Nov. 1924.
² Garland's Hotel, Suffolk Street, Pall Mall, was well known to writers and artists.
³ He was afraid that this would cause GY nightmares or other emotional trouble; as late as 23 Oct. 1930 when working on the second edition of *A Vision* he confided to OS, 'If I dictate to George it would almost certainly put her nerves all wrong. I dont want any more mediumship' (Wade, 776–7).
⁴ *A Vision* was to be published not by Macmillan but by T. Werner Laurie.

ⁱ See note to 23 Aug. 1924.

Part Four

Cuala and Theatre Business

1925–1927

In August 1924 WBY had apologized to a correspondent for his silence by explaining, 'I have a new book calle[d] A Vision to finish & as I am no historian & have to condense the worlds history & the spectacle of the contemporary world into a few pages, & interpret all by geometry am looking forward to a fearful two months labour & am unfit for human society.'[1] But it was not until the following April that the manuscript of *A Vision*, complete with drawings and diagrams by GY, was handed over to his publisher. Despite this, early in 1925 he and GY joined the Pounds in Sicily, then moving on to Naples and Rome where they enjoyed their first holiday together unencumbered by family concerns. By the time they returned to Dublin the Cuala Press, which had occupied rooms in 82 Merrion Square for twenty months, had moved out, but Cuala would continue to be a drain on their finances and George's energy. Meanwhile Merrion Square continued to be full of activity; Lady Gregory was a frequent guest while in town for theatre business, and Anne and Michael had more than the usual succession of childhood illnesses. Often, too, George sent her husband to Coole for rest and the peaceful regular environment that allowed him to write uninterrupted by Senate or theatre business.

[1] WBY to G. K. Chesterton, 24 Aug. 1924 (*CL InteLex*, acc. 4634).

1925

[ALS]   82, MERRION SQUARE, S. | DUBLIN.
                                    March 26. [1925]

My dear Dobbs: I enclose a wire which came last night. I have had letters
from Lilly & Lolly Lilly wanting me to call when Lolly is out, & Lolly rejoic-
ing I think a little too much in Lilly prospects of early recovery—on second
thoughts I enclose them as they give information about facts.[1]

Lennox & Tom last night & a pleasant evening & this afternoon I have
been to a rehersal of Lennoxs play which plays better than it reads.[2] Tomorrow may finish the philosophy—Saturday certainly I think.

Stay longer than Monday if you wish—it is a long time since you have
been away by yourself, & remember me to your mother.[3]

You are in my heart always

                                            Yrs ev
                                         WB Yeats

[ALS]   82, MERRION SQUARE, S. | DUBLIN.
                                    [?29 Mar. 1925]

My dear Dobbs: I thought you were not coming back till Monday & so
arranged to dine with O'Neill. I arranged it the day you left & when late last
night I found out the truth thought it too late to cry off. I have been upset
all day to think that you must return to an empty house.

                                            Yrs ev
                                         WB Yeats

---

    [1] Enclosures missing.
    [2] LR's latest play *Portrait: A Play in Two Sittings* opened at the Abbey on 31 Mar. 1925; influ-
enced by the Spanish dramatist Jacinto Benavente y Martínez (1866–1954) whose plays had
been produced by the DDL, it is a departure from his earlier works.
    [3] GY was spending the weekend of 26–9 March visiting her mother who had come up from
Sidmouth to London.

[ALS]   COOLE PARK, GORT, CO. GALWAY.
                                         May 16 [1925]

My dear Dobbs: All kind of misfortunes have decended upon the Mollou household. Poor Mary Ann has gone out of her mind—she was servant in a Mental Home in England & I suppose could not escape from suggestion She is now at home, & yesterday was screaming. Then old Mollou has been prosecuted by a man he, it seems, owed money to—some £20 pounds— Mollou produced a receipt & the man said the receipt was got from him by a trick. Mollou settled case out of court paying £20 & costs & the Judge spoke so sternly upon the matter the Mollou neighbours now say that he burned down his own house. Delia has gone to be a nurse in England & must feel well out of it all. I think that is all the local gossip. I [am] very sorry for Mary Ann who had charm & should have found a husband.[1]

It has rained all day but I have got on well with play.[2]

                                                        Yrs affecly
                                                        WB Yeats

[ALS]   COOLE PARK, GORT, CO. GALWAY.
                                       Tuesday [19 May 1925]

My dear Dobbs: Mary Ann Mollou has been sent to the Ballinasloe Asylum. She had not gone as servant but as nurse to the Mental Hospital in England. A sister—not Delia—one we never knew has come home to that luckless family with dropsy.

My play goes well but I am certain there will have to be a lyrical chorus— which could be detached if need be in performance. I think however the chorus with its barbaric gong & rattle will give the play an asiatic kind of solemnity & intensity. The chorus will be visable as in 'The Hawks Well'.

Amid this cold & wet I envy London the 80 in the shade recorded by 'The Times'. The Cunninghams—late of Ballylee—say that this winters

---

[1] Mary Anne Molloy and her sister Delia had worked for GY in Oxford and later in Dublin (see letter of 8 Aug. 1920); the townland of Glenbrack, where their father James Molloy farmed, lies between Gort and Coole Park.

[2] On 11 May 1925 WBY wrote to AG that he had started on his short play *The Resurrection*, 'a sort of overflow' from the just completed *A Vision*, with the working title *The Heart of the Phantom Beats*; published in the *Adelphi* (4 June 1927), the 'chaotic dialogue' underwent revisions from 1929 to early 1931, was finally seen at the Abbey on 30 July 1934, and in a further version was published in *Wheels and Butterflies*, November 1934. There exists what is apparently an early TS draft of a scenario for 'Resurrection. Dance Play', containing Christ, Dionysius, and Buddha, dated 21 and 22 January, with no year.

flood has been the worst since they married. Young Cunningham—who is still a model young man—has been beaten & half killed by certain ruffians called Hayes. Trial comes on on Saturday next. He ran away to Scotland to escape giving evidence though he had already sworn an affidavit. He was afraid of course of being beaten again or murdered.[1]

Yours affly
WBY

[ALS]   COOLE PARK, GORT, CO. GALWAY.

May 22 [1925]

My dear Dobbs.

We come up on Tuesday next, & I have asked Lady Gregory to stay with us. She has to be in Dublin for the Abbey Annual meeting, which must meet before end of month.

I think to day will finish the final version of play leaving out lyrics. It can be performed as an ordinary stage play without these lyrics & with drums & rattle off. I think however that it will gain in religeous intensity if played like a Noh play. Opening & closing curten & musicians in sight of audience, as this will give an element of ritual. If the play is good I may spend a part of the summer on the lyrics. We may however perform it before I do this—I can write the lyrics previsionally in a kind of free-verse to be spoken or sung, & put them into a elaborate form later, or leave them out of performance. I will not spend weeks on the lyrics till I am sure that the play is good. Its value to the reader must largely depend on the lyrics.

I have read the <u>Timaeus</u> very slowly & carefully. It seems the root of most mystical thought & Flinders Petrie thinks that it is Egyptian in oregen aparently.[1]

---

[1] Bernard Cunningham (1902–73) was the son of James and Elizabeth Cunningham of Ballylee; the three Hayes brothers charged with the beating lived nearby in Castletown. 'B.C., out of hospital, was to have appeared at the Gort Court yesterday to give his witness against the Hayes brothers. But he did not appear and there was a rumour he had been kidnapped' (*Journals*, ii. 10, 3 May 1925).

[1] Plato's lengthy monologue the *Timaeus* presents a carefully developed account of the divine origin of the universe as the handiwork of the 'demiurge', imposing mathematical order on chaos, and presenting a model for rational souls through the cooperation of Intellect and Necessity; the work provided WBY with, among other images, that of the gyres he employed in *A Vision* (see, among other studies, Brian Arkins, *Builders of my Soul: Greek and Roman Themes in Yeats* (Gerrards Cross, 1991)). Sir William Matthew Flinders Petrie (1853–1942), known as 'the Father of Archaeology' for his statistical analysis of Stonehenge and the Egyptian pyramids, was from 1892 Professor of Egyptology at University College London. Two copies of his *The Revolutions of Civilisation*, 3rd edn. (London, 1922) are in the Yeats Library.

I am buying <u>Hermetics</u> to have complete collection of Hermetic Books.[2] I write of these things because there is no news.

Yrs ev

WB Yeats.

[ALS]

Coole Park | Gort

May 23 [1925] Saturday

My dear Dobbs: I read my play to Lady Gregory yesterday—she approves very fully. Thinks it right as it is without lyrics. What I want to discover however is if the folding & unfolding of the curtain to music & without words sung will have the ritual quality I want—I want barbaric music certainly—I think the music used at the opening & close of 'The Hawks Well' would do. At least at our performance at 82.[1]

I hear that old Mollou (or Lady Gregory thinks his wife) offered 10/- to the man who prosecuted for something like £20 being his wages for work done. Lady Gregory thinks this a piece of Mrs Mollou's craziness, which restores ones sympathy—if true—to that luckless tribe.

I wonder if Lennox should see Gillespie?[2] If you have not Gillespies number Russell might know it or know if there is any hurry.

Yrs—

WB Yeats

[ALS]

COOLE PARK, GORT, CO. GALWAY.

Monday [25 May 1925]

My dear Dobbs:

Expect me to-morrow by the second train. Lady Gregory will come later—the day before theatre meeting the date of which Lennox will know. I have a fine lyrical opening to the play.[1] I hope to do the rest of the lyrical

---

[2] The Yeats Library includes Hermes Trismegistus, *Hermetica*, ed. with translation and notes by Walter Scott, 3 vols. (Oxford, 1924), vol. i of which includes numerous marginalia.

[1] On 30 and 31 Mar. 1924 the DDL had performed *At the Hawk's Well* during an 'At Home' for special guests at 82 Merrion Square; LR was the producer and, according to an unpublished lecture by Dermott MacManus in 1963, Madame Bannard Cogley, 'Toto' (b. 1883), founder of the Studio Arts Club and later one of the founders of the Gate Theatre, performed the dance. *The Resurrection* was not produced until July 1934.

[2] Percy J. Gillespie (1891–?1948) had been an accountant to the Irish Agricultural Organization (1914–18) and manager of the *Irish Homestead* (1917–23), then business manager (1923–8) of the revived *Irish Statesman*, edited by AE, before moving to London as manager of *City Press* in 1929; LR was a member of the advisory committee of the *Irish Statesman*.

[1] An early draft of 'Two Songs from a Play', first published in *October Blast* (1927), is recorded in *Journals*, ii. 12.

part before we meet. The worst is that the lyric has without any intention of mine become much less Christian than the play.

Yrs

WB Yeats

[ALS]   82, MERRION SQUARE, S. | DUBLIN.

Nov 3 [1925]

My dear Dobbs: I have got back my usual good spirits. I did not write on Sunday for the world was still rather black. Of course this new fact is there & like other such facts to be borne in mind. Long neglect of his work, at any rate its very inadequate recognition, & an incapacity to make new friends has I think probably undermined Jacks sense of reality.[1]

I have had a really grateful letter from Lolly grateful to excess.[2]

I have had a friendly letter from Jameson. He is in London but returns to day. I lunch with him on Sunday. His house is still half burned out.[3]

I enclose a bill from Heal that may be a shock to you. I think now that my large ballance at the bank may have been left there to meet it, but as things stand I cannot do so. Can you meet it, & charge to me either the whole ultimately or the part that was to pay for the things in my room. Or would you prefer that I sold out something? I am most anxious that you sell out nothing more—you must keep a rampart round the children. At any rate please write to Heal & say that this bill will have immediate attention, or what ever the proper thing is. I did not write as I do not know what to

---

[1] WBY's younger brother the artist, novelist, and playwright Jack Butler Yeats (1871–1957) had been a staunch supporter of his sisters' work at Cuala since the beginning. However, in a letter to WBY on 31 Oct. 1925 he refused to continue his practice of contributing drawings for prints to the press, adding, 'If I had the ready money I would try and buy up the copyrights of all the prints of mine which Cuala publishes.... You say that my painting is now "great". Great is a word that may mean so many different things. But I know I am the first living painter in the world. And the second is so far away that I am only able to make him out faintly' (Bruce Arnold, *Jack Yeats* (New Haven, 1998), 234). Jack's last designs for Cuala were produced in February 1926, but he did contribute illustrations for his brother's new series of *Broadsides* in 1935 and 1937.

[2] On 29 Oct. 1925 WBY wrote a formal letter to his sisters stating that he had paid off their overdraft of £2,010.11.1 and guaranteed a future overdraft of no less than £100 to each of their departments.

[3] Former southern Unionist Andrew Jameson, PC (1855–1941), of Sutton House, Howth, governor of the Bank of Ireland (1896–8), Senator (1922–36), and chairman of the whiskey distillers John Jameson & Son (1905–41), whose house was burned during the Irish Civil War, had been a friend and patron of JBY and became a mentor to WBY on political and financial matters.

say, or exactly how soon we can meet this bill. You might have to make a part payment now & the rest a little later.

There are various other letters for you—a great many drama league letters which as they are in official envelopes probably mean subscriptions. I will ask the maid what arrangement you have made about letters. Meanwhile I enclose nothing but this Heal thunderbolt.[4]

Gogorty came in last night & though bursting with news would not say a word because Ryan[5]—the street child philanthropist—was here. 'I wont say a word it would get round'—great dissapointment as a hungry flock had come.

Yours affly
W.B.Yeats

[ALS]   82, MERRION SQUARE, S. | DUBLIN.
                                      Nov 3 [1925]

My dear Dobs:

I saw Craig of Hamilton & Craig[1] this morning. That matter is now finished. They will keep the Sligo certificates in their safe for us, but the money will be paid direct to Lilly & Lolly. As it will not pass through our hands there will be no question of income tax.

I also saw Keller.[2] The lost document is not a bearer bond but a cer[ti]ficate of Registration which cannot be transferred without my signature. The danger is that it should be transferred by forged signature & perhaps negociated abroad some one taking it over in good faith. The risk is not great & many people lose them. If I ask any body to go surety a simple note undertaking liability should be sufficient. I asked if you would do as surety. He said he thought the bank would accept you & that if so that would be the best solution. If therefore you a gree I will write to the bank. I could give you a note exactly as if you were a stranger which would keep

---

[4] Enclosure is missing. GY, who had gone to London to look after a Cuala embroidery sale at the Drapers Hall, was away from 31 October to 11 November.

[5] The American businessman and philanthropist Thomas Fortune Ryan (1851–1928) was reputed at his death to be the tenth wealthiest man in the United States.

[1] Thomas H. R. Craig and his partner Everard Hamilton of 30 South Frederick Street were long-established Dublin solicitors.

[2] Thomas Goodwin Keohler, later Keller (1874–1942), solicitor, poet, and theosophist, had been a member and auditor of the Irish National Theatre accounts before seceding; he published 'The Irish Theatre Movement' in the Dublin *Sunday Independent* in January 1929.

me from extravangence. If not I will ask Arthur Jackson[3] when he comes up for the Senate—we meet next week.

> Yours affecly
> WBYeats

[ALS]   82, MERRION SQUARE, S. | DUBLIN.
                                                    Nov 5 [1925]

My dear Dobbs: All going well. Stuarts came last night & I got Francis Stuart to tell me about his work. His second novel has been rejected & he is now writing a book on 'The Immortality of the Soul'.[1] On Thursday I dressed in what I thought was my new dress suit went to the O Neills & on finding they had not dressed pleaded the newness of my suit. And in truth after a bad moment, during which I thought it pinched me under the arms, I felt in great elegence & looked with satisfaction in several mirrors. Next morning when I took it from the chair to pack it away I found that it was the old suit & was covered with hairs not having been brushed of late. I wonder what Mrs O Neill thought of my veracity.

I have finished except for the typing my work on the Autobiographies. I have repaired Macgregor but I am afraid his wife will think I have made the account worse.[2]

> Yours affecly
> WB Yeats

I have given your wire to Nurse but send this to Knightsbridge as I suppose you will be there still.[3]

---

[3] Arthur Jackson (1853–1938), WBY's uncle by marriage and a successful entrepreneur in charge of the Pollexfen family firm in Sligo, was considered the financial genius of the family; chairman of the Harbour Commission for Sligo, he was like WBY a presidential nominee to the Senate, serving 1922–8.

[1] Stuart's fourteen-page pamphlet *Mystics and Mysticism* was published by the Catholic Truth Society of Ireland on 5 Aug. 1929; his first published novel, *Women and God* (1931), unsuccessfully attempted to incorporate his current obsession with religion.

[2] Doubtless spurred by her charge that WBY had misinterpreted his character, in July 1926 in a new preface to a new edition of MacGregor Mathers's *The Kabbalah Unveiled* Mrs Mathers reaffirmed her belief in her husband's teachings.

[3] For the Cuala sale GY was staying at the Knightsbridge Hotel, south-west London.

[ALS]   SAVILE CLUB, | 107, PICCADILLY.W.1.
                                           Nov 28 [1925]

My dear George: Thanks for your wire. I have seen nobody yet except the
faithful MacGreevy who turned up last night & apologised for not having
met the train. He is established in the 'Conniseur' for some months as the
editor has gone to America for that time & the subeditor has become editor & he has filled the vacancy so made.[1] I had a cold & windy passage but
am none the worse. I am to have tea with Olivia but have made no other
plans as yet.

I have just got out an old letter of Lady Gregorys to answer & the first
sentence is 'Can you help me in this. Richard has been given a rifle' etc.
I think you said you would write to Mrs General Murphy[2] about it. I dare
not write to Lady Gregory without saying something of the kind. I shall say
that I think you are doing so. If I am wrong I must see about the matter in
some other way.

                                                     Yours affectly
                                                     WBYeats

[ALS]   KNIGHTSBRIDGE HOTEL, | LONDON, S.W.
                                            Nov 29 [1925]

My dear Dobbs
    I have come here from the Savile driven out by the cold. Turner[1] a new
member & so an enthusiast said he did not mind it as he always went every
now & then to a deserted greenhouse & skipped for a few minuites. So far
I have only seen the Dulacs, Whaley & Olivia but am just off to Mrs Woodmass.[2] O yes, I say MacGreevy who came in on Friday night & apologised

---

[1] MacGreevy, who had moved to London about May 1925, wrote freelance criticism for
various literary journals; from November 1925 to February 1927 he was assistant editor of *The
Connoisseur*, a journal of the arts, continuing as Paris correspondent when he moved in January
1927 to teach at the École Normale Supérieure (Paris) as *lecteur d'anglais*, a position he held
until July 1930.
[2] A slip for General Mulcahy, former chief of defence, whose wife Mary Josephine 'Min'
Mulcahy was politically influential in her own right; AG's grandson had been given a rifle and
she was anxious to receive a permit for its use.
[1] Walter James Redfern Turner (1884–1946), outspoken and unconventional Australian
poet, playwright, and novelist. At this time he was music critic for the *New Statesman* (1915–40)
and drama critic for the *London Mercury* (1919–23), and would later work closely with WBY in
his BBC poetry programmes; his novel *The Aesthetes* (1927) deeply offended Ottoline Morrell
and would indirectly cause a rift between her and WBY when he praised it in his introduction
to the *Oxford Book of Modern Verse* (pp. xxviii–ix).
[2] GY's grandmother.

for not having met the train. I am only just beggining to get warm so this letter a little congealed. Olivia had no news except that the Pounds seemed well & happy—Ezra generally better. I meet Bessie[3] there on Friday afternoon.

Yrs affecly
WB Yeats

[ALS]   82, MERRION SQUARE, S. | DUBLIN.
Friday [Saturday] Dec 4 [1925]

My dear Willy

I send you a couple of papers & the Irish statesman. That brute AE has divided up your speech. I am so cross with him. He might just as well have put it all in—Its so short.[1]

I hear from Tom that all went very well at the dinner.[2]

Great excitement in the Theatre over the marriage of McCormick & Miss Crowe![3] They did it secretely on Wednesday morning.

In haste to catch evening post

Love. G.

[3] Maud Elizabeth Furse Barnes ('Bessie'), née Radcliffe (1886–1954), who in 1922 married Ronald Gorell Barnes, 3rd Baron Gorell (1884–1963), had been involved with WBY and Eva Fowler in experiments with automatic writing during the years 1913–15 and apparently continued her mediumistic activities throughout her lifetime; see GHL's first letter.

[1] WBY's speech of 30 November to the Irish Literary Society on 'The Child and the State' was published by AE in the *Irish Statesman* in two parts, on 5 and 12 Dec. 1925.

[2] WBY was guest of honour as one of the founding members at the dinner given by the Irish Literary Society at the Florence Restaurant, 56 Rupert Street, W 1.

[3] Peter Judge (1890–1947), whose stage name was F. J. McCormick, was considered the greatest actor of his generation; he had been acting at the Abbey since 1918 and performed in more than 500 plays during his career. Eileen Crowe had been at the Abbey since 1921 (see 30 Jan. 1923).

1926

MUCKROSS HOUSE, | MUCKROSS, | CO. KERRY,
IRELAND.
August 22 [1926]

My dear George: Michaels birthday but by this time the candles will have
been blown out & the cake cut. Here[1] the heat is over powering & all but
me are away at a boat race. I remained behind to work at my poem.[2]

Shane Leslie & his wife[3] are here & an American or English high Church
clergyman, & a young girl who came down in the same carriage with me.
'She is got up' Vincent said 'as shere Mont-Martre—she does it to shock the
county.' She is about 17 has a pale face—'London season'—scarlet lips & an
electric eye but is quite innocent.[4] Then there is the Vincent girl of about
the same age, & some younger children who come & go in the distance.[5]
Shane Leslie wears a kilt & talks well. Yesterday the Chinese letter was read
out with great laughter but its authenticity doubted—'It is too perfect.'[6]

---

[1] While GY was arranging a party for MBY whose birthday was on 22 August, WBY
escaped the family gathering by visiting Muckross House, home of Maud Chase, née Bowers
Bourn (1883–1929), and Arthur Rose Vincent (1876–1956), a barrister, JP, and later Senator
(1928–34).

[2] While at Muckross House WBY began work on what would become 'Sailing to Byzantium' and wrote 'Parting' and 'Her Vision in the Wood'.

[3] Sir John Randolph 'Shane' Leslie, 3rd Baronet (1885–1971), poet, biographer, critic, and
first cousin of Winston Churchill, and his American wife Lady Marjorie, née Ide (1881–1951),
were strong Irish nationalists while maintaining a high social profile in London; a prolific
writer, supporter of the Gaelic League, and world traveller, like the Yeatses he had a keen
interest in the paranormal; in 1933 he was elected an associate member of the Irish Academy
of Letters.

[4] Perhaps the 'Miss Eley' who left a sketch of WBY during this visit (Foster ii. 724 n. 101).

[5] The Vincents had two children, Elizabeth Rose (1915–83) and Arthur William Bourn
'Billy' (b. 1919).

[6] 'To Honourable Editor Irish Statesman. Honoured Sir,—Identical post brought me Irish
newspaper with speeches about Lane Pictures and letter from my nephew in Liao-Yang. My
nephew though comparatively young man is convinced supporter of old Chinese Political System he writing that great-grand-daughter of last Great Chinese Empress being educated near
him and she showing already strong blood of her race, in truth her present Advisor is fifth all
others went away despairing. Yeats speech and nephew's letter connect in my mind though
knowing nothing of pictures of which he speak. As man of pure Chinese race another art
pleases me, but I was excited by words in which he was sorrowful that Gracious Majesty King
of Commonwealth did not in quarrel between two nations have consultation with Ministers of
both. I said I am of pure Chinese race but am British citizen and hope my children will rule
over restaurant made by my father eighteen years ago in obscure corner of Empire having
fled from Chinese Democracy. His Gracious Majesty has opportunity which no Emperor of
East or West had for three hundred years for only He can tie together independent nations

There are salmon & trout in the lake—Kerry lakes have no pike—& I shall go fishing if there is a likely day. Meanwhile the view from my window, a Californian pine in the foreground, is pure Santa Barbara.[7]

I wish for you constantly for I want to talk about everybody & everything. I cant go up to a stranger & say 'your manners & looks have stirred me to this profound meditation'—

Yours affecly
W. B. Y.

[ALS]   MUCKROSS HOUSE, | MUCKROSS, | CO. KERRY,
IRELAND.
Thursday [26 Aug. 1926]

My dear Dobbs:

I go to Coole to-morrow & expect to return Monday. I wish you could have come—you would have seen the most beautiful gardens I have seen—rock garden's especially—in a place more beautiful than Moloya.[1] The Vincents are very pleasant people & Mrs Vincent is a clever woman.[2]

---

of Commonwealth. This He can only do if plain to all He does not listen to one more than to others. Our great statesman Tung Ch'i-ch'ang said to make great emperors three things needed: A long time to look ahead, solitude, clever women in marriage. Because it is hard to find those clever women my nephew's letter and Irish paper connected in my head. Kung Pan-ch'ien. Sun-Never-Sets Restaurant, Kyrenia, Cyprus' (*Irish Statesman*, 21 Aug. 1926, 658).

[7] He is probably recalling the Maryland Hotel in Pasadena, where during his 1920 lecture tour they stayed for some time in a separate bungalow in a garden setting and continued the automatic writing; they then moved on to Santa Barbara.

[1] The Vincents spent considerable energy and money on developing the grounds: in 1915 the Sunken Garden, designed by Wallace and Co. of Colchester, was laid out; the Rock Garden was developed on a natural outcrop of Carboniferous limestone; and the Stream Garden was also landscaped. Moyola Park is the country estate of 450 acres at Shanemullagh, Castledawson, Magherafelt, close by the north-western shore of Lough Neagh in Northern Ireland; it was inherited by Marion Carolina Dehra Chichester (1904–76), wife of Captain James Jackson Lenox-Conyngham Chichester-Clark (1884–1933), MP for Northern Ireland (1929–33) and president of the Royal Ulster Agricultural Society. Moyola House was built in 1713 by Joshua Dawson, Chief Secretary under Queen Anne, who also built the Mansion House on Dawson Street, now the official residence of the Lord Mayor of Dublin. GY wrote to LR from Ballymoney, Co. Antrim, in June 1926, so she (and perhaps WBY) may have visited Moyola Park on that journey; Ballymoney was the home of the popular Abbey dramatist George Shiels whose play *Professor Tim* had been a great success in September 1925, but there is no record of a visit by the Yeatses to the wheelchair-bound playwright.

[2] Maud Chase Vincent (1883–1929), whose father William Bowers Bourne II, a wealthy Californian mining magnate, purchased the Muckross estate from Lord Ardilaun in 1910 and presented it as a wedding gift to his daughter and son-in-law. Three years after the death of his wife Vincent presented Muckross House and its surrounding 11,000 acres to the state as the first Irish National Park.

This morning deer's liver for breakfast but tastes much like any other liver.

I hear the neighborhood is going to vote for Browne, who fishes here & for the Marquess who has canvassed it.³

Yours affectionately
W. B. Yeats

[ALS]   MUCKROSS HOUSE, | MUCKROSS, | CO. KERRY,

IRELAND.
Friday [27 Aug. 1926]

My dear Dobbs: I thank you very much for arranging with Lady Gregory. Here it is incomparably beautiful & my poem is not quite finished. On Monday the Leslies go back too so I shall have fellow travelers (Shane Leslie you will be glad to hear has decided that the Chinaman's letter in The Statesman is quite genuine). Will you ask Lennox, Russell, & Lady Gregory to come in Monday evening. I am asking the Leslies. They will dine at the Hibernian¹ & come in afterwards I suppose about nine. I shall get out my velveteen coat & Leslie will probably dress. I have got to like Leslie very much—he is quite simple & friendly & is regarded by his wife very much as Gogorty is by his wife.

My committee meets on Tuesday morning²—I cannot remember when— so I had better arrange for Lady Gregory to lunch some where if she will.³

Yrs—
WB Yeats

³ Samuel Lombard Brown, who was co-opted to fill the vacancy in the Senate caused by the death of Lord Dunraven in 1926, was a keen angler, and a regular visitor to Caragh Lake, Co. Kerry. The canvasser may have been Henry William Edmund Petty-Fitzmaurice, 6th Marquess of Lansdowne (1872–1936), or Geoffrey Thomas Taylour (1878–1943), the 4th Marquess of Headfort, also a Senator.

¹ The Hibernian Restaurant, 49 Dawson Street, was run by the Hibernian Hotel.

² On 19 May 1926, WBY was invited to chair a coinage committee to advise 'firstly, as to the steps which should be taken with a view to getting designs submitted, and, secondly, as to which of the designs that may be submitted are the most suitable for adoption'; other members of the committee were Dermod O'Brien, president of the Royal Hibernian Academy, architect Lucius O'Callaghan (1877–1954) who was director of the National Gallery 1923–7, art historian Thomas Patrick Bodkin (1887–1961), one of the governors of the National Gallery, subsequently its director 1927–35, and Barry M. Egan (d. 1954), a jeweller and TD for the City of Cork.

³ AG went to Dublin to consult WBY about a new pamphlet she had drafted concerning the Lane pictures; while there she unexpectedly underwent further surgery for breast cancer on 31 August.

[ALS]   ORCHARD HOTEL | PORTMAN STREET,
                                            MARBLE ARCH, W. 1
                                                Oct 12 [1926]

My dear Dobbs

Manning Robertson[1] comes to London Monday & I shall try to see him & get such a modification of dates as will make it possible for our man to meet ministers. We can then decide about public dinner. I would think the most desirable thing would be public dinner (speaches & good reports in papers) & a small lunch party or dinner as well at which he could meet Blythe O Higgins & Gillingham,[2] let us say. It will be desirable to have photographs of his work in the papers.

I have at last got Milles[3] to compete—I shall get his formal [submission] to night. Palmstierna[4] thinks that the trouble was that Milles hates Meistreirch (how is that spelt).[5]

I thought I get back Monday night but stay to meet Churchill at dinner on Tuesday night. I meet members of Labour party at high commissioners on Monday.

                                                        Yrs ev
                                                     WB Yeats

Lady Londonderry is forming committee. I see Tom this afternoon & talk his post over.[6] I am too busy to write more at the moment.

---

[1] Manning Durdin Robertson (1888–1945), prominent architect and town planner whose offices were at 3/4 College Street; his wife Nora Kathleen Robertson wrote a number of books on salmon fishing along the River Slaney near their home at Clonegal (now Huntington) Castle, Co. Carlow, and together they published *Approach to Architecture* (1948). See 15 Nov. 1926 for plans to entertain the Swedish architect Ragnar Östberg.

[2] Kevin O'Higgins was Vice-President of the Executive Council and Patrick MacGilligan was Minister for Industry and Commerce; Ernest Blythe was at this time Minister of Finance.

[3] Carl Milles (1875–1955) one of Sweden's most famous sculptors, born Carl Emil Wilhelm Andersson near Uppsala, Sweden, lived in Paris from 1897 to 1904 where he was at one time Rodin's assistant, travelled to the Netherlands, Belgium, and Germany, and in 1905 married painter Olga Granner with whom he returned to Stockholm; from 1931 to 1951 he was Director of Sculpture for Cranbrook Academy of Art in Michigan but returned to Sweden in 1951. WBY admired his work and invited him to submit a design for the new Irish coinage.

[4] Baron Palmstierna, the Swedish Minister in London; see 1 Sept. 1924.

[5] Ivan Mestrovic (1883–1962), Croatian expressionist sculptor living in America, was one of the artists invited to submit designs, but his reply came too late.

[6] MacGreevy's position as *lecteur* at the École Normale Supérieure was extended from July 1927 until Samuel Beckett took over in November 1929, but the temporary nature of the appointment made him anxious to seek another more permanent post. WBY, who admired his knowledge of paintings, regularly supported MacGreevy's search for appropriate work; see 27 May 1927 concerning his application as director of the National Gallery of Ireland.

What will Gosse say about the new Nobel award.[7]

Should be no public dinner unless sure of good & representative attendance

[ALS]   82, MERRION SQUARE, S. | DUBLIN.
[?1 Nov. 1926]

This is what you want
W.B.Y[1]

—<Neither the tyrants that spat>
   Neither the slaves that were spat on
   Nor the tyrants that spat—
   John Synge & those people of Grattan
   That give though free to refuse,
   Pride like that of the morn
   Casting its strange light loose,
   Or that of the Fabulous Horn,
   Or that of the sudden shower
   When all streams are dry,
   Or that of the hour
   When the swan must fix his eye
   Upon a fading gleam,
   Float out upon a long
   Last reach of glittering stream
   And there sing his last song.

[ALS]   82 Merrion Square | Dublin
November 12. 1926

My dear Willy

I half hoped to get a letter from you this morning, but not having got one means I suppose that you are in the thick of it.

That wretched Nursery Garden has sent all the rose trees I ordered for Ballylee so I will have to go there on Monday—I cant ask Lady G. to have me at such short notice so I have wired to [?] to have fires lit & I shall sleep

---

[7] Gosse's review of *The Bounty of Sweden* in *The Sunday Times*, 26 July 1925, had dismissed WBY's Nobel award as 'all just a little incongruous' and derided the 'dreamer who ought not to meddle in public affairs'. The 1926 Nobel laureate, Sardinian novelist and poet Grazia Deledda (1871–1936), was only the second woman to be awarded the prize.

[1] Draft of 'The Tower' (first published June 1927), dated by GY '1 Nov 1926'.

in Anne's room which is always the driest. In fact it never gets damp at all & has the only fireplace that never smokes! I shall return on <u>Thursday</u> here.

I shall take the pug for company!¹ I know he will love the fires on the floor! How are you getting on?

There were great rumpusses here last night for Armistice, but little has got into the papers.

I go tonight with Lennox to the Valkyrie (Wagner opera) otherwise I am doing little but going to bed early & getting up v. late—

Love. G.

[ALS]   SAVILE CLUB | 107, PICCADILLY. W
                                         Nov 15 [1926]

My dear Dobbs: I have seen Manning Robertson. He has secured Blythe & O'Sullivan for the Monday & is to bring Ostberg to see Cosgrave.¹ He also hopes to get MacGilligan. On Tuesday the architects give Ostberg a public lunch. So I think we must confine our efforts to a private dinner on Tuesday night as the Architects seem to be doing the publicity.²

I hope to return on Thursday (travelling by day) but stay as long as your work requires at Ballylee. I am doing fairly well but it is slow work. O'Higgins said to day that Balfour³ told him that he was entirely in favour of the return of the pictures & would say so when the time came. I lunch

---

¹ The current household dog, brought back to Dublin by GY from England, as described by WBY: 'She once tried to smuggle a pug puppy through in her pocket; she had known nothing of the regulation until she reached Holyhead. She was found out, but as it was so small that it had to be spoon-fed the customs at Dun Laoghaire decided that it was "no dog"' (WBY to T. J. Kiernan, 19 Oct. 1932).

¹ Ragnar Östberg (1866–1945), Swedish architect of the National Romantic school, was being honoured by the Royal Institute of British Architects, presented with the Gold Medal by the then Prince of Wales at their annual dinner at the Guildhall in London on Tuesday 23 Nov. 1926. Best known for his design of the Stockholm Town Hall, 'a poem in brick' long in the making but recently completed in 1923 when Yeats praised it in his address to the Swedish Royal Academy, comparing the method and achievement to the Italian Renaissance. During his career, Östberg also worked as a stage designer, painter, etcher, and professor at the Swedish College of Arts; he was later awarded the Gold Medals by the American Institute of Architects in 1933. Ernest Blythe was Minister of Finance. Seumas O'Sullivan was the pen name of the poet and essayist James Sullivan Starkey (1879–1958), founding editor of the influential *Dublin Magazine* and later president of the Irish PEN and a founding member of the Irish Academy of Letters; he was married to the painter Estella F. Solomon (1882–1968).

² On 30 November Östberg was guest of honour at a dinner at Merrion Square catered by a chef; among those also invited were LR, the Gogartys, the O'Higginses, the Jamesons, and the Cosgraves.

³ Arthur James Balfour, 1st Earl of Balfour of Whittingehame (1848–1930), urbane statesman and philosopher and former president of the Society for Psychical Research (1892–94); as

with Bracken to-morrow[4] (to meet I think Lutchens who is ready to build the gallery for nothing) & in the evening with Beaverbrook to meet Churchill. I am now going to buy a detective story called 'The Invisable Adversary' if I can get it going to bed for an hour or so.

I long for you & peace & regular work. By the by I spent the morning over Wundts work & the London Library is sending a number of his books to you in Dublin.[5]

Yrs affly
WB Yeats

[ALS]   SAVILE CLUB | 107, PICCADILLY. W
                                              Nov 16 [1926]

My dear Dobbs: I have wired to tell you I shall not return till Thursday. I could not pay postrage because you cannot do that from England. I did not want you to feel that you must hurry back. I shall really finish to day but it is just as well to give myself the extra day. I lunch with Bracken in a few minuites I think to meet Lutchens, who is ready to design the Dublin gallery for nothing Lutchens says. Yesterday I heard O Higgins inform people that the new coinage would be out before Xmas. It will take a year, so far as I can see, or if we hurry everbody to the utmost nine months.[1] I am too busy to have any thoughts except that I want greatly to be back home with you drinking a bottle of Muskatel & telling you all the news.

Yrs ev
WB Yeats

I shall travel by day on Thursday

Chief Secretary for Ireland (1887–91) he was referred to as 'Bloody Balfour' for the coercive New Crimes Act of 1887, but was also responsible for the creation of the Congested Districts Board in 1890. He became leader of the Conservative Party (1891–1911), Prime Minister (1902–5), First Lord of the Admiralty in the coalition government in 1915, Foreign Secretary in David Lloyd George's cabinet (1916–19; during which time the Balfour Declaration promised Zionists a national home in Palestine), and Lord President of the Council (1919–22 and 1925–9). During these weeks while WBY was in London Balfour was chairing the committee on Inter-Imperial Relations at the Imperial Conference of British Empire leaders, whose report established autonomy for the dominions in all matters of internal and external affairs.

⁴ Brendan Bracken, 1st Viscount Bracken of Christchurch (1901–58), energetic Irish-born businessman and publisher, founding editor of *The Banker* (1926), later chair of the *Financial Times* (1945–58); elected an MP in 1929, since 1923 he had been a strong supporter of Winston Churchill who would later appoint him Minister of Information (1941–5).

⁵ German philosopher and psychologist Wilhelm Maximilian Wundt (1832–1920), whose *Principles of Physiological Psychology* (1874) GY had read before her marriage. Strongly influenced by the experimental psychologist Gustav Fechner (1801–87), who is mentioned in GY's automatic script, Wundt's ten-volume *Social Psychology*, which outlined four stages of cultural development, was published in 1920.

¹ The coins were not approved until 1928.

1927

[ALS]   SAVILE CLUB, | 107, PICCADILLY. W.1
                                   Tuesday [17 May 1927]

My dear Dobbs: Lennox has just gone, enthusiastic about the films and
also wants tecnical committee—is full of projects.[1] He goes to Dublin on
Wednesday & will I hope see Mrs Macneill.[2] Lady Londonderry is not in
London, but I shall see Harmsworth[3] at 4 this afternoon—perhaps he can
arrange.

Never will I travel by night again except by Liverpool. Ticket Office
man in Dublin never wired to reserve me a sleeper & all sleepers were full.
I return ticket as you might like to demand restitution. I sat bolt-upright
until 5.45 when we reached Holihead. Could not get room at Euston but
got one here by turning Hugh Law out at 11. Slept for a couple of hours &
feel quite fresh.

Present Film project is—W.B.Y. Chairman of advisory body & so
with ex-official post on tecnical committee. Tecnical committee Lennox,

[1] WBY was appointed chairman of the Provisional Committee to advise British Authors
Productions Limited on Irish films; nothing seems to have come of these plans and the company was dissolved on 3 Feb. 1933.

[2] Josephine McNeill, née Aherne (1895–1969), wife of James McNeill (1869–1938) who
was Irish High Commissioner in London until in 1928 he was appointed the second
Governor-General of the Irish Free State; an active Republican, in 1950 she was named
Envoy Extraordinary and Minister Plenipotentiary of Ireland to the Netherlands, the
first appointment by the Irish government of a woman to a post of head of mission, later
Minister to Sweden in 1955, and from 1956 held a joint appointment to Switzerland and
Austria.

[3] TCD graduate Cecil Bisshop Harmsworth (1869–1948), created 1st Baron of Egham in
1939, was at this time retired after a distinguished career as a Liberal MP, Under-Secretary
of State for Foreign Affairs under Lloyd George's coalition government, and British Member of the Council of the League of Nations. He and his brothers the late Lord Northcliffe
and Harold Sidney Harmsworth, 1st Viscount Rothermere (1868–1940), both newspaper
magnates, were supportive of the attempt to retrieve the Lane pictures for Ireland; his
nephew Esmond Cecil Harmsworth (1898–1978) was instrumental in supporting the Irish
Academy of Letters.

Arthur Shields[4] (to be in London Film Studio for six weeks), Mont-gomery.[5]

Dolly[6] (not engaged to Lennox I think) cut cards for Lennox last week & the Films were in it.

Yrs affly
WB Yeats

[ALS]   SAVILE CLUB | 107, PICCADILLY. W
                                        Saturday [21 May 1927]

My dear Dobbs: I did not write because I have not yet been to Cam-bridge. I go there to-day for the Matinee show.[1] I have seen Dorothy & Olivia. Dorothy left Omer in Paris as he had measels (or is it meazels or Meazles) but he is to be fetched—probably by Olivia I think—in June.[2] He is recovering from the measels. Last night I dined with Dulac, & that so far is all I have to report except a visit to Macmillan. I saw Sir

---

[4] Arthur 'Boss' Shields (1896–1970) took classes at the Abbey Theatre in 1913 and joined the company in 1914 where, except for a brief imprisonment as a participant in the 1916 Easter Rising, for over twenty-two years he played close to 200 parts, directed twenty plays, was stage manager and tour manager for the three Abbey tours in the USA 1931–5; he also performed with the DDL. Having occasionally performed in silent movies since 1910, he moved permanently to Hollywood in 1936, where he was in John Ford's production of O'Casey's *The Plough and the Stars* and many other well-known films; he frequently acted alongside his older brother Barry Fitzgerald on stage and in film and television. See also below 16 Mar. 1937.

[5] F. James M. ('Jimmy') Montgomery (1870–1943) was the first film Censor (1923–1941), and, claiming to take the Ten Commandments as his code, banned almost 50% of submit-ted films in the early years. A strong nationalist, he proclaimed that 'One of the greatest dangers of our time is not the Anglicisation, but the Los Angelesation of Ireland'. Despite little formal schooling and a career as a clerk in the Dublin Gas Company 1886–1923, he was a close friend of Arthur Griffith, Seamus O'Sullivan, and James Stephens. Known for his wit, Montgomery wrote the facetious 'George's Key', soon accepted as a traditional street ballad.

[6] Dorothy ('Dolly') Travers Smith who would marry LR in 1931, was, like her mother Hester Dowden (Mrs Richard Travers Smith), a medium.

[1] WBY's *The Player Queen* was produced by Terence Gray at the Festival Theatre at Cam-bridge 16–21 May 1927 in a programme with *The Red Knights of Tcheka*, a Grand Guignol 'thriller' by André de Lorde and Henri Bauche, translated by Gray, and dance selections by Ninette de Valois's students.

[2] Dorothy's son Omar Shakespear Pound was born on 10 Sept. 1926 in the American Hos-pital in Neuilly outside Paris and spent all of his young life in England under the supervision of his grandmother, with lengthy summer visits from his mother; he attended Norland Nurseries in London before going to Charterhouse. EP did not see Omar after his birth until after OS had died. Omar died in 2010.

Fredrick.[3] I do not think he will print in Ireland. He will print my poems in a form quite seperate from that of Collected Edition with Sturge Moore cover & frontispiece of Tower, & he wants 'Oedipus the King' at once. He says he prefers to print the two translations seperately. I promised to send MSS on my return.

I will write to-morrow about 'Player Queen'

Yrs ev

WBYeats

[ALS]   SAVILE CLUB | 107, PICCADILLY. W

Monday [23 May 1927[1]]

My dear Dobbs

I went to Cambridge Saturday & liked the afternoon performance so much that I stayed for the evening one. Terrence Gray[2] put me up & I returned here on Sunday. The acting was as a whole good amateur acting—very good sometimes—but one man—the man who played the old man who wants straw—gave a beautiful performance—grotesque phantastic & distinguished.[3] However what impressed me was the staging, that was just

---

[3] 'Gentleman-publisher' Sir Frederick Orridge Macmillan (1851–1936), eldest son of co-founder Daniel Macmillan, became a partner of the bookselling and publishing firm Macmillan and Company in 1876 and first chairman in 1893; his partners were his younger brothers Maurice Crawford Macmillan (1853–1936), whose sons succeeded Sir Frederick, and George Augustin Macmillan (1855–1936). Knighted in 1909 for his charitable work, as president of the Publishers Association (1900–2 and 1911–13) Sir Frederick was involved in framing the Copyright Act of 1911, but perhaps his most lasting contribution was his role in the establishment of the Net Book Agreement (1900), which guaranteed price stability to both authors and the publishing trade.

[1] Dated 20 May 1927 by GY.

[2] Terence Gray (1895–1986), a wealthy racehorse owner and vineyard proprietor, previously trained as an Egyptologist, was influenced by German expressionist theatre practice and Gordon Craig's theories, and in partnership with metallurgist C. Harold Ridge established an experimental Festival Theatre in 1926 by transforming a Georgian theatre into an open stage space with the most advanced lighting and staging facilities in the United Kingdom at the time, abolishing both the proscenium arch and footlights and introducing a revolving stage and cyclorama. The theatre opened in November 1926 with *The Oresteia of Aeschylus*, with the chorus produced by his cousin Ninette de Valois (see note below). In the same year Gray published his theories in *Dance Drama: Experiments in the Art of the Theatre*; among many avant-garde productions, he included some of his own plays. By 1931 he had become 'Quetzalcoatl,' and in 1933 after his final seasons directing at the Festival Theatre, he travelled extensively in India; in 1958, as 'Wei Wu Wei', he published the first of a series of seven books on Buddhist philosophy culminating in a final eighth book in 1974 under the pen name 'O.O.O.'

[3] Walter Alexander Meyjes (1905–1987) performed in a number of the Festival plays during the 1927–8 season while a student at Trinity College, Cambridge. Ordained in 1930, he was later co-author of the annual Westminster Passion Play, filmed in 1951 as *The Westminster Passion Play: Behold the Man!*

what I had dreamed of The beasts—they streamed in through the audience—were a delight. After my play came dancing, the work of a woman who has, I think, inventive genius.[4] She is Irish & a friend of the Maudes[5]-her people have a place at B[l]essington—& has spent some years with the Russian ballet. I travelled up with her brother & got his address—as we might want her in Dublin if we continue to prosper. I think you must go to this theatre & study it. It is apparently the one centre of scenic & lighting experiment now in England. Terrence Gray who pays for it is a rich man, an Egyptologist by trade with a big country house near Cambridge. He is obviously rich & will I understand be much richer. The Festival Theatre seets about 460. Audiences are thin during first half of week but house is a always packed on Friday & Saturday.

Grey & various members of his company spoke to me of 'Bailes Strand' which seems to have had a great success.[6] The Fool & Blind Man—the same man played him & man who wants stray [straw]—in their masks were the great excitement.

Yrs affly

WB Yeats

Savile is moving to 69 Brook St—central heating in 15 bedrooms instead of 4.

---

[4] Ninette de Valois (1898–2001), later dame and CH, was the stage name of Edris Stannus, whose family home was Baltiboys, near Blessington, Co. Wicklow; after working with Leonide Massine's Company in Covent Garden in 1921 and as soloist in Serge Diaghilev's Ballets Russes 1923–5 where she worked closely with the choreographer Bronislava Nijinska, in 1926 she founded the Academy of Choreographic Art in London, which performed once a term in her cousin's Cambridge Experimental Theatre and was at the same time associated with Lilian Baylis at the Old Vic in London. From 1931 she directed the Vic-Wells Ballet, later to become the Sadler's Wells Royal Ballet Company, and eventually Covent Garden's Royal Ballet. She published two autobiographies, *Invitation to the Ballet* (1937) and *Come Dance with Me* (1957).

[5] Nancy Campbell, née Maude (1886–1974), a school friend of DP, married the poet Joseph Campbell in 1910 against her family's wishes; she was a descendant of Mary Tudor, and had strong Anglo-Irish connections.

[6] As his second production in the Festival Theatre, the week of 31 Jan. 1927, Gray had chosen a four-part programme opening with Dunsany's *The Glittering Gate*, followed by Strindberg's *The Stronger*. WBY's play was described in 'Variety at the Festival', *Cambridge Daily News*, 1 Feb. 1927: 'The lighting and stagecraft resources of the theatre made "On Baile's Strand", an example of poetic drama by Mr. W. B. Yeats, a thing of remarkable beauty and barbaric splendour, and the producer, Mr. Norman Marshall, is to be commended on his admirable work. Grotesque masks are worn in this piece, these having been designed by Mr. Hedley Briggs, who himself plays the Fool with undoubted ability, while special music has been written by Florence Farr. Mr T. G. Saville's musical voice enhanced the poetic beauty of the lines, while Mr. Walter Meyjes did some effective work as the blind man.' The evening concluded with six dance cameos presented by Ninette de Valois and her company, with music arranged for two pianos by Arthur Bliss.

[ALS]   SAVILE CLUB | 107, PICCADILLY. W
                                                    May 27 [1927]

My dear Dobbs: I shall return Tuesday leaving here that morning. I have
dined with Cecil Harmsworth & Dulac been at a couple of lunch parties & so
on and been reasonably contented. Last night I dined as Cecil Harmsworths
guest at the Annual 'T C dinner' (Trinity College dinner). Was asked to
speak & refused & then a memorial, signed by about 30 names, was sent
up & I did speak & I think well. What was more important—keep this
private—I made suggestions to Cecil Harmsworth as to possible journalists
support for the Irish government. He said he would like to discuss the matter at greater length & has asked me to see him next Monday afternoon.
I think he means to see his brother on the matter.¹ My point was that
O'Higgins, MacGilligan & Hogan are the government,² & that they have
no reliable support from either the 'Irish Times' or the 'Independent.' That
the future of Ireland may depend on there getting that support. I told him
that an English owned newspaper must not touch certain political questions
but that there were a mass of questions which it could touch. He is aware
of the difficulties for he had dissuaded his brother from buying a French
Newspaper. My suggestion will probably come to nothing—the majority of
suggestions do—but he spoke quite definately of going into the matter with
his board.

   Dorothy goes to Paris again in July to fetch Omer—Omers very vivid
photo is on Olivia mantle piece stuck into one corner of a photo of Ezra so
I suppose likeness is being traced.³ MacGreevy has sent me (Mrs Duncan
sends a supporting letter) a most unwise document. Instead of simply sending
in his name & credentials and asking for the post; he attacks the proposal to
select a 'half-time' director which is not his business at all, but the business
of the board.⁴ Furthermore it is, of course, an attack on Bodkin which also
is most certainly not his business. The form of his application will do him
great injury & if I could I would get him to withdraw the whole thing but
he would never understand & in any case I imagine it is now too late.

   ¹ Harold, Lord Rothermere (1868–1940), right-wing Conservative owner of the *Daily Mail*,
Daily Mirror, and *Evening News* and friend of Lord Beaverbrook, who controlled the *Daily Express*
and the *Evening Express*; he was reputed to be the third richest man in Britain at this time.
   ² See notes to 10 Feb. 1923 and 18 June 1924.
   ³ EP was not Omar's biological father, whose identity has never been revealed.
   ⁴ WBY was on the Board of the National Gallery of Ireland which was once again seeking a
new director, a post anxiously sought by MacGreevy and eventually secured in 1950, succeed-
ing Thomas Bodkin (1927–35), who went on to be founding director of the Barbour Institute of
Fine Arts, University of Birmingham, and George Furlong (1935–50), who followed Bodkin.

His document, taken as a whole, has a queer impudent air & will make the board believe that he has no judgement. I am afraid Dermuid O Brien[5], who is a goose & has been in Paris lately, is reponsible. I had said to him <u>that the board might,</u> if he & other governours thought well, consider whether it wanted a half time or a whole time man. He could not have done MacGreevy a greater injury. The Lord protect us & our children from geese.

Yours affly
WB Yeats

Two days ago I felt so lonely that I all but started for home, & would have but I had written to Ottoline. Now I find the Morrels are in London & Garsington let furnished.

[ALS[1]] Savile Club | 107 Piccadilly
[27 May 1927]

My dear Dobbs: I wronged MacGreevy reading him late last night after the public dinner. The remarks about 'half-time' were in a covering letter to me. I find also that he asks me to send on his application. Please read it & send it on to O'Calligan[2] or to the Register.

Yours e
WB Yeats

[ALS] Coole Park
June 15 [?1927]

My dear George

I have just had enclosed from Lolly (Telegraph office prefers the more familiar Lally). I send it[1] as it may mean that the lost type-script has turned up & so save you work to-morrow. I shall take this letter to Gort & post it there (or re-telegraph) as I was too stupid to give it to the messanger boy

[5] Dermod O'Brien, president of the Royal Hibernian Academy and member of the Board of the National Gallery.

[1] On the stationery of Olivia's club, 'Albermarle Club | 37 Dover Street. W 1' with address struck out.

[2] Lucius O'Callaghan, a member of the committee advising on coinage.

[1] Enclosure missing

who brought the wire. Lady Gregory has driven over to Castle Taylor where Mrs John Shawe Taylor has arrived.[2]

Much better

Yours very affecly
WBYeats

[ALS]   KILDARE STREET CLUB. | DUBLIN.

June 28 [1927]

My dear Dobbs. I went to Hogan at 3.[1] He said tooth should come out, so out it came—local anesthetic—then bleeding—I forgot to warn him.[2] He said if this did not stop I was to return at nine. It did not stop so I returned, leaving an excellent Monday evening—Cruise O Brien, Shemus O Sullivaun, Lennox, an American—got home again a little after 10 to find all except Lennox going—O Sullivan drunk through a single very strong drink poured out by Lennox. All went. This morning I went to Hogan again. Last night he had stopped the bleeding but as it may return I am not to go back to Galway till Thursday. I have a swollen check but feel quite comfortable. Going back home to 2 & 4 as at 4:30 Lennox comes to help set up those Japenese dolls.[3]

Yrs
WBY.

---

[2] Amy Eleonora (née Norman; c.1880–1938), mother of Michael and widow of Captain John Shawe-Taylor (1866–1911), one of the prime movers of the Wyndham Land Act; see p. 202.

[1] James Edward Hogan (1885–1960) of 16 Upper Fitzwilliam Street was house surgeon and member of the Management Committee of the Dublin Dental Hospital in Lincoln Place and first president of the original Dental Board, established in 1928. GY and WBY were spending a quiet time together at Ballylee.

[2] WBY had a tendency to haemophilia.

[3] The Japanese poet, translator, and essayist Dr Yano Kazumi, 'Hōjin Yano' (1893–1988), presented WBY with a print and two *dairi-bina,* Japanese festival dolls; he was invited to Ballylee on 30 July 1927 (Shotaro Oshima, *W. B. Yeats and Japan* (Tokyo, 1965), 102). Yano sought help from WBY for the commentary for his edition, *Select Poems of William Butler Yeats* (Tokyo, 1928) and from AG for a projected translation of some of her plays.

Part Five

Changes
1928–1933

In December 1926 George had complained to her friend Tom MacGreevy, 'Nothing has been happening here except work and work and work and the children alternately in bed!'[1] WBY was also overworked, and after a serious bout of pneumonia in October 1927 he was advised to spend the winter in a warmer climate. After a disastrous beginning in Spain when he became seriously ill with congestion of the lungs, George took him to Rapallo where Dorothy and Ezra Pound were already settled; he then contracted Malta fever, and George found an apartment that would become their winter home for the next few years. Michael's health was also a worry, and he was sent to school in Switzerland, where Anne soon joined him. Torn between concern over her ailing husband and her children's needs, George turned more and more to their old friend Lennox Robinson for help. Once back in Dublin in 1928, they sold 82 Merrion Square and moved to a flat at 42 Fitzwilliam Square. But more changes were to come—Lady Gregory was becoming much frailer, her body racked by cancer; while George 'kept all Willy's irons hot' in Dublin, WBY spent most of his time at Coole assisting his old friend and colleague. From there he was introduced to the challenges of broadcasting, and although no longer in the Senate was actively involved in the controversy over the oath of allegiance. His concern over the censorship introduced by de Valera's new government led to his next new project, the establishment of an Irish Academy of Letters, and at the same time he was introduced to the writings of Shri Purohit Swami. Both these enthusiasms would engulf him and George for the next seven years. Shortly after Lady Gregory's death they moved again, to a charming house in Rathfarnham, just outside of Dublin. To raise funds for this new expense, and for his Academy of Letters, WBY made one last lecture tour to America, this time leaving George to deal with responsibilities at home.

[1] *BG*, 378.

1928

[ALS]   Albergo Rapallo | Rapallo | Italy[1]
                                             Saturday [25 Feb. 1928]

My dear George: All well. To night Ezra & Dorothy bring me to dine with
a Mrs Stein & her daughter & her son in law who is an Italian Prince of the
Holy Roman Empire, & descended from from Charlemagne.[2] They have
a villa out on a headland. Mrs Stein is of course an American the widow,
I gather, of several millionaires. Ezra has spent several hours explaining the
structure of his Cantos, & all I know is that there is a structure & that it is
founded on that of a Fugue[3]—that word looks wrong.

   Olivia has written to Dorothy that Anne is charming & has the most
excellent manners. Annes Masterpiece was however on her arrival in Dublin. She went to see Lily & Lolly & asked them to lunch & when one of the
work-girls asked 'What did you like best abroad'? replied 'The boat I came
back on.'[4]

   Lennox writes enclosing a letter from Antheil which I send you.[5] It sounds
like a welcome to continental art. With Antheils music perhaps the Dutch
may like to use their masks again.[6]

   [1] WBY was staying in the hotel next to the Pounds while GY took MBY, discovered to
have a tubercular gland, to l'Alpe Fleurie in Villars sur Bex, Switzerland, a school which was
part nursing home.
   [2] Unidentified.
   [3] EP was annoyed by WBY's description of his Cantos in *A Packet for Ezra Pound*, claiming
that the 'blighter never knew WHAT a fugue was anyhow'; WBY probably did not understand
the principle of the fugue, many-voiced writing in which a theme or subject is announced,
followed by an 'answer' in another voice, then imitated by one or more other voices, in the
manner of a flight (hence its name) and pursuit—the primary melody often playing hide-and-seek
among various voices.
   [4] ABY returned to Ireland accompanied by the children's nurse, Florence 'Nana' Reade
(b. *c.*1901), who trained as a midwife at the Rotunda after the children went to school in
Switzerland in 1929.
   [5] The letter is missing. While in Paris LR had approached George Antheil (1900–59), avant-
garde American pianist and composer, asking him if he would be interested in writing the
music for WBY's *Fighting the Waves*, his ballet-drama based on the earlier play *The Only Jealousy
of Emer* and written especially with Ninette de Valois in mind. Antheil, whose *ballet mécanique*
with its heavy percussion and multiple pianos had caused an uproar on its first performance
in Paris in 1926, was greatly admired by EP as representative of the 'new music', 'a musical
world…of steel bars, not of old stone and ivy'; he had orchestrated EP's opera *The Testament
of François Villon* (1923).
   [6] WBY was sent photographs of the production of a Dutch translation of *The Only Jealousy
of Emer* (*Vrouwe Emer's Groote Strijd*) produced by the actor-manager Albert van Dalsum in 1922
and revived in 1923, 1924, and 1926. Excited by the masks of Cuchulain and Bricriu designed
by Hildo Krop, WBY later borrowed them for the 1929 production of *Fighting the Waves* which

Ezra has written for Cocteau's 'Antigone'. Cocteau has made it into a powerful play for the modern stage & a translation of it for Dublin would complete our Sophoclean Trilogy.[7] The chorus does not appear. Some large masks hang upon the back wall, & a voice speaks through them.

This place is as much a delight as ever & I am so much better that I long for your return that we may explore it together.

It [is] now 11 & I am dressed & must shortly join Dorothy who will take me to the Library to find more base fiction.

Yours affecly
WB Yeats

I have written to Mrs Asquith[8] & done most of my duties

[ALS] Ambergo Rapallo | Rapallo
Feb 27 [1928]

My dear Dobbs

I wrote Friday last. All well here—Ezra explains his cantos, & reads me Cavalcanti & we argue about it quite amicably.[1] We have twice dined to get variety at another hotel—almost under our trees—where he purloins sraps that he may feed a black & two grey cats who wait for him about fifty yards from the hotel. He has been feeding them for quite a considerable time & brags of there fatness. I think my self entirely recovered & I walk for nearly an hour at a time without fateague.

when published was dedicated to 'Hildo von Krop who made the masks'. See Liam Miller, *The Noble Drama of W. B. Yeats* (Dublin, 1977), plates XVIII–XXII for illustrations of Krop's five masks.

[7] EP admired the work of French avant-garde poet and artist Jean Cocteau (1889–1963), whom he had first met in Paris in 1921; he had reviewed Cocteau's adaptation of Sophocles' *Antigone* ('to the rhythm of our times'), which was first produced (and heckled by the Dadaists) in 1922 at the experimental Théâtre de l'Atelier in Montmarte, with Antonin Artaud performing Tiresias, set design and masks by Picasso, costumes by Coco Chanel, and incidental music by Arthur Honegger (1892–1955), who then composed a full-scale opera version of *Antigone* with libretto by Cocteau (first performed in December 1927 in Brussels). An Irish production of *Antigone* did not take place.

[8] On 25 Feb. 1928 he wrote a letter of condolence to Margot, Lady Asquith, on the death of her husband on 15 February.

[1] Guido Cavalcanti (*c.*1255–1300), Italian poet who was a close friend of Dante, both of whose translations were featured in *The Early Italian Poets* (1861) by Dante Gabriel Rossetti; EP published his own translations in 1912, in 1936 edited his works in *Rime*, and composed a three-act opera, *Cavalcanti*, which though commissioned by the BBC was never produced. GY deplored EP's preference for Cavalcanti over Dante.

All the news I have will be better for waiting your arrival when you can get it in detail. The mother in law of the descendant of Charlemagne was ill so we did not dine there, & Tom has written praising above all other public dancers James Joyces daughter.[2] We may use her someday.

Yours affecly

WB Yeats

This is so short because yesterday I lost my fountain-pen, & only found it this morning, & I am afraid of missing you if I delay

[ALS]   SAVILE CLUB | 69, BROOK STREET. W.1.

June 26 [1928]

My dear George: All has gone pleasanty. I have seen only friends & that without fateague—friends & the Sitwells whose acquaintence I made last Saturday. Miss Sitwell pleasant & sincere & as ugly as the devil—I shall hear all recite tomorrow night.[1] I am just off to the Dulacs. Tomorrow I see Shaw to ask him to join an Irish Academy[2] & this afternoon I ordered a large box for prints in a queer shop in a back street where they make such things for the British Museum (ordered it but the enthusiast in the shop refused to make it until I send him the size of my largest print). I find the Sevile a friendly place full of conversation.

---

[2] Lucia Joyce (1907–82) studied dance from 1926 to 1929 with various innovative teachers including Jacques Dalcroze (1865–1950), Raymond Duncan (1874–1966), brother of Isadora, and Lubov Egorova (1880–1972), Diaghilev's colleague. By 1931 her brief professional career ended when she began showing signs of schizophrenia. By this time Tom MacGreevy was a member of the Joyce circle in Paris.

[1] WBY was in London while GY went to Switzerland to fetch MBY home for the summer. Edith Louisa Sitwell, later dame (1887–1964), political poet and biographer, was famous for her striking recitations; her best-known works are *Façade* (1922) and *Gold Coast Customs* (1929), of which WBY wrote to Wyndham Lewis, 'something absent from all literature for a generation was back again, and in a form rare in the literature of all generations, passion enobled by intensity, by endurance, by wisdom' (Wade, 776). Dame Edith's brothers Sir Osbert Sitwell (1892–1969) and Sacheverell Sitwell, later 6th Baronet (1897–1988), were also prolific poets and critics. *The Times* notes that Edith Sitwell's recital at the Arts Theatre Club was broadcast on the BBC on 27 June 1928.

[2] Enraged by the proposed 'Censorship of Publications Bill, 1928', WBY published several broadsides criticizing the Free State government and Roman Catholicism in general; his failure to defeat the bill led to his determination to establish an Irish Academy of Letters in order to combat censorship, and he, AE, and Starkie approached Ernest Blythe, Minister of Finance, to gain his support. However, because of his ill health, it was not until 1932 that the Academy was finally founded with Bernard Shaw's assistance (see letters of 6 and 7 April 1932).

I have done some writing at the system & corrected those proofs.[3]
Stephens[4] thinks 'Winding Stair' better than 'The Tower'[5]
To day I was interviewed by the Daily Express about Lane Pictures which
suggests that it is time to get home[6]

Yrs affectionly
WBY

[ALS]   COOLE PARK, | GORT, CO. GALWAY.
[16 Aug. 1928]

My dear George: Many thanks for the Balzac, it comes in the nick of time
for I have begun my essay on Ezra. To day I find however that the envelope
with 'Cavalcanti' written on it contains only the Italian. There is another,
which I read lately, with the translation & notes. I am so sorry to trouble
you but I do rather want it. It may be at Howth.[1]
Yesterday that stupid young German,[2] who was at the Abbey, turned
up with an introduction from AE. Lady Gregory suffered from 11 to 1.30,

---

[3] As soon as *A Vision* was published in 1925, he set about revising it; the proofs were for the
limited edition commissioned by Crosby Gaige (see below).

[4] James Stephens (1880/2–1950), poet, playwright, and novelist, perhaps best known for his
book *The Crock of Gold* (1912), for which he was awarded the Polignac Prize from the Royal
Society of Literature, *Deirdre* (1923), which received the Tailteann prize for literature, and in
later life his broadcasts for the BBC. Of his poetry Yeats wrote, 'I like you always best where
you are trying to create beauty', but he was also a captivating teller of tales and much sought
after for literary gatherings. After a few years in Paris he returned to Dublin in 1917 to take
up the position of registrar of the National Gallery, but after two successful lecture tours in
America in 1925 settled permanently in London.

[5] *The Tower* was published in February 1928 and immediately became, in the words of *The
Observer*, 'a best seller'; WBY must have shown Stephens the poems written for *The Winding
Stair*, a limited edition commissioned by the American theatrical producer and publisher
Crosby Gaige (1882–1949) and finally published in 1929 by Fountain Press (see Colin Smythe,
'Crosby Gaige and WB Yeats's *The Winding Stair*', in Warwick Gould (ed.), *Yeats Annual No. 13*
(London, 1998), 317–28).

[6] The 'Daily Express' art critic published an interview with WBY on 27 June 1928 entitled
'Irish Claim to Tate Pictures. Lane Collection in Dispute. Legacy Problem'.

[1] WBY had stayed at Brook Lawn, Howth, while GY was arranging the move of their
belongings from 82 Merrion Square, which had recently been sold for £1,500 to the architect
Rudolph Maximilian Butler (1872–1943), head of architecture in University College Dublin
(1924–42). Some of the furnishings went to 42 Fitzwilliam Square, a house owned by Bethel
Solomons, and some to their newly leased flat in Rapallo. He went to stay at Coole 14–31
Aug. 1928.

[2] Erich Gottgetreu (1903–81), a Jewish socialist and journalist who had recently visited a
kibbutz in Palestine and emigrated to Jerusalem in 1933, was the author of many works on
Zionism including *Das Lande der Soehne* (1934), *Maximilian Harden: Ways and Errors of a Publicist*
(1962), and, posthumously, *The 37th Siege of Jerusalem* (1985); during the Second World War he
served in the British army psychological warfare branch in Cairo.

then I stormed at him through lunch—Upton Sinclair is his ideal novelist, 'Masses & Men' his ideal play[3]—then Lady Gregory, having remarked 'as for propeganda our servants will do that for us'[4]—he thought all literature should serve some good cause—took him & dispatched him home. He had plainly intended to stay the afternoon.

All is green & flowering here & I am well & busy but not too busy

Yrs ev
WB Yeats

Mike Dooley[5] daughter is in jail awaiting trial for the murder of her second illegitimate infant. She was the result of preyer at a Holy Well.

Dont put yourself to too much pains to find the Cavalcanti I can finish the first part of the essay & on Monday or Tuesday I will have the photographs of the coins to work on.[6]

[ALS]   COOLE PARK, | GORT, CO. GALWAY.
Friday [17 Aug. 1928]

My dear George: I am so sorry but I have found those notes you have been searching for in one of those Italian MSS books. They were not in the leather bound book I put you looking for. I am ashamed on my self. Next time you are in Dublin send me the fourth Plotinus volume for it is to that they refer. I have finished all my 'Player Queen' revision & now no dancer has to speak

---

[3] Upton Beall Sinclair, Jr. (1878–1968), American novelist and political activist, was also interested in psychic phenomena. Among his many books publicizing the fate of immigrant workers, *The Jungle* (1906) and *Oil!* (1927) are most popular. Ernst Toller (1893–1939), German expressionist whose play *Masses and Men*, in seven scenes of unrhymed verse, was first produced in 1920 and translated into English in 1923, was popular with the Workers' Theatre Movement and other political groups; one of its dream scenes included a dance of death. WBY tactfully did not mention a third hero, Charlie Chaplin, whose films GY enjoyed (*Journals*, ii. 306).

[4] A parody of the line in *Axel* (1890) by Auguste Villiers de l'Isle-Adam (1838–89), 'as for living our servants will do that for us'. WBY had been deeply impressed when he first saw a production in Paris and in 1924 he wrote an introduction to H. P. R. Finberg's translation of the play.

[5] Lizzie Dooley (b. 1903), daughter of Michael 'Mike John' Dooley of Coolebeg (1859–1943), AG's gamekeeper since 1895, worked in the Great Southern Hotel, Galway; *The Connacht Tribune*, 21 July 1928, reported that she was awaiting trial for having concealed the birth of a stillborn baby in June. She later emigrated to England (information courtesy Sister de Lourdes Fahy).

[6] Designs for the new Irish currency, to feature eight different animals, had been presented anonymously to the committee, who unanimously selected the work of Percy Metcalfe (1895–1970), an English artist.

I send this to Howth thinking it may save you a journey to Dublin as well as a search there.

Yrs ev
WB Yeats

PS.
I am writing in a hurry for post

[ALS]   COOLE PARK, | GORT, CO. GALWAY.
Monday [?20 Aug. 1928]

My dear Dobbs: I [am] working at my Ezra essay. Some days ago the Warrens & Poppy Gough (she is really Lady Something or other for she is married)[1] came to tea, & I began to explain the nature of Nirvana, inspired by Poppy Goughs pleased & animated eye—when she first made her first [will] she shocked her intimates by leaving money to the Abbey—& still more by the spite of Mrs Warren. The result was I suddenly saw that Cavalcanti poem in a new light that enables me to connect it with Ezra.[2]

I am reading Ludwics 'Bismarck'. I have taken, not to Ludwick who has a commonplace mind but to Bismarck. Bismarck was so much the country-man that he had the peasants land hunger, & when ever he fell out with the King he seems to have remembered that the Hollonzollens, some hundreds of years before, had robbed his family of certain lands. Once he reproached the king with it. He wrote & talked in the most vivid way & thought constantly of trees & dogs & horses.[3]

The country quiet or rather would if you were here

Yours affecly
WBY.

---

[1] '17 August. The Warrens to tea yesterday, and Poppy Guthrie and a friend (Lady Mary Carnegie). And Yeats talked Buddhism at tea. Mrs. Warren listening uneasily as he apparently belittled the Christian active virtues and preached contemplation the emptying of the mind, and passivity of the body' (*Journals*, ii. 307). Guy Gough's youngest sister Kathleen Mona ('Poppy') Gough (d. 1963), who was married to Col. Ivan Douglas Guthrie, belonged to the Yeatses' social circle in Dublin; Revd H. G. Warren was the local clergyman in Gort; he met his wife Mona ('a nice pleasant mannered woman') in Japan where she had been a missionary (*Journals*, ii. 141).

[2] The essay he planned to write on EP and Cavalcanti was never completed; see 26 Aug. 1928.

[3] Doubtless instigated by AG, who read Emil Ludwig's biography *Kaiser Wilhelm II* (1922–4, trans. 1926), and in January 1928 Ludwig's play *Bismarck, the Trilogy of a Fighter* (1926, trans. 1927). Count Otto Eduard Leopold Bismarck (1815–98) was known as 'The Iron Chancellor' for his role in achieving the unification of Germany. The Yeatses would later meet the popular biographer Emil Ludwig, né Cohn (1881–1948), in Rapallo.

[ALS]   COOLE PARK, | GORT, CO. GALWAY.
                                              August 26 [1928]

My dear Dobbs

I have finished the first draft of my coinage essay—nothing now to be done but copy it out & improve the style.[1] I have had communications from Minister of Finance & nothing is yet settled as to date of that meeting. It may be Sept 4 or any of the three following days. You told Mrs Philomore[2] I think that I would have to go to Dublin for rehersals. However I have written to her.

I have written to Ezra & told him that though I have practically finished my essay on him I cannot use his Cavalcanti.[3] I have told him I shall use my essay with other things of my own, or, if he will let me, with a little selection from his poetry. When I got the essay from you I found that to make it clear, or even readable I should have to risk an interpetation, so little in the mood of that time as I understand it so much in accord with Ezras words that both Ezras accuracy as a translator & my scholourship would stand accused. Ezra could have made a fine translation if he thought, however mistakenly, he understood his original, but as he was quite sure he did not the translation is enfuriating. <Yet I understand all that was thought & that I can touch on but if my guess sounds plausible at where Ezra…illegible…trouble this would look, for it makes him artfully obscure> If I could get a literal prose version I could do something with it.

Lady Gregory speaks of her dissapointment at not having the children here this year, and as I hope I told you she will be delighted to put you up when ever you come to have a look at Ballylee. She reads Trollope's 'Rachel Ray' to me at night, & is working on her little essays on the wood, the library & the garden which I am to have for Cuala.[4]

---

[1] 'What we did or tried to do' was published in *Coinage of Saorstát Éireann* (Dublin, 1928), 1–7.

[2] GY had arranged for WBY to visit Lucy ('Lion') Phillimore, Mrs Robert Charles, née Fitzpatrick (1869–1957), of Kilmacurragh, Kilbride, Co. Wicklow, while she and the children remained at Howth; in March 1929 the Yeatses stayed with her in Monte Carlo, but there was always tension and argument between WBY and Mrs Phillimore.

[3] On 23 September he wrote to EP again: 'I am worried about that translation of yours Donna mi Prega. I worked hard until I found myself plunging into solutions that seemed impossible for the period, & realised that as I could not read the Italian & even if I could lacked historical knowledge, nobody would accept me as interpreter. On the other hand your verse translation is far from explaining itself, & people would want to know why what they regarded as a work of art—verse translations are always so regarded—was not sufficient to itself' (*CL InteLex*, acc. 5161). EP's translation of 'Donna mi Prega' was published in *The Dial* in 1928; he reworked it again for Canto 36.

[4] These final essays by AG were published in *Coole* by the Cuala Press in July 1931 with WBY's poem 'Coole Park' (Sept. 1929) as introduction.

I have read all that matters to me of Ludwig's Bismarck (plays & biography) & his William II. I am now reading Shawn Leslie on Swift.⁵ The damp in my throat deprives me of cigarettes—I have those two boxes intact or almost so—& I have made friends with an old grey dog. When I came here he was sick, thought to be dying, but the coach man declared that nothing ailed him but dissapation & that he would soon be all right. After four or five days he began to rat again, & now he swims out into the lake after sticks.

Give my love to Ann & Micheal. I shall [come] up on the day you said

Yrs affectionly
W.B. Yeats

[ALS]   COOLE PARK, | GORT, CO. GALWAY.
Tuesday [28 Aug. 1928] 10.45

My dear George: Lady G has just come to tell that the post is going—it goes much later as a rule.

I am so sorry about Anne,¹ & sorry too for the trouble & anxiety you have under gone. Write again & tell me how she is.

You will have had my letter by this. I come up Friday as arranged. Lady G is writing.

Yrs affecly
WB Yeats

[ALS]   Coole Park | Gort | Co Galway
August 28 [1928]

My dear Dobbs: I wrote in great haste this morning & in bed. I hope poor Anne is better & that you are exempt—that is my chief anxiety.

Yesterday I had tea at Guy Gough's—he has a most quiet & beautifully furnished little house made out of old stables & hay lofts & outside a pond of gold fish & beyond that the lake & a little to one side the deserted castle. When the Castle was inhabited all looked the creation of yesterday but now with the castle as background & some old furniture all seems centuries old. Margeret¹ arranged everything I understand. I found Guy Gough looking in

⁵ *The Skull of Swift: An Extempore Exhumation* by Shane Leslie, which dealt in detail with the relationship between Swift, Vanessa, and Stella, was published in 1928 and may well have influenced WBY's *The Words upon the Window-Pane*, begun in August 1930.

¹ ABY was ill with dysentery and pneumonia, but well enough by 15 September to join MBY at his school in Switzerland.

¹ Margaret Gregory, Robert Gregory's widow, soon to be Mrs Guy Gough; Jack Yeats frequently showed his paintings in Ireland as well as in England.

humble but puzzled misunderstanding at a picture of Jacks somebody had presented to him.

Lady Gregory sees more people than she ever did—all more or less pilgrims. Kearnan a government official & his wife have just arrived.[2] He is not a pilgrim—he helps Lady Gregory with her Income Tax, & Lady Gregory in gratitude has invited [them] to stay. I hear his voice & hers. They are returning from the garden.

I have finished my coinage essay. My love to Anne.

Yrs ev
WB Yeats

[ALS]   SAVILE CLUB, | 69, BROOK STREET, W.i.
Thursday [18 Oct. 1928]

My dear Dobbs

You will see by above I gave you a wrong address—96 instead of 69.

I have been given Lady Harcourts bed-room.[1] It is a large room with a bath all to itself; and I had a comfortable journey & am not tired. Last time I was a couple of days recovering.

As yet I have seen nobody. I am just about to look up that jacket maker— I wonder if he is under J or Y.[2]

---

[2] Dr Thomas Joseph Kiernan (1897–1967), who was the first Irish ambassador to Australia and whose last post before retirement in 1964 was Irish ambassador to the United States, became one of AG's literary executors. He began his distinguished career as a tax collector in Galway and in 1924 was appointed secretary to the Irish High Commissioner in London, where he also worked towards a doctorate in economics from University College London. From 1935 to 1941 he was Director of Broadcasting at Radio Éireann, on secondment from the Department of External Affairs, and in 1941 he became Irish ambassador to the Vatican. In 1924 he married the Irish folk singer Delia Murphy (1902–71).

[1] In 1927 the Savile Club purchased 69 Brook Street from American-born Mary Ethel, Viscountess Harcourt, née Burns (c.1874–1961), niece of millionaire J. Pierpont Morgan and widow of Lewis Vernon 'Loulou' Harcourt, 1st Viscount Harcourt (1863–1922), a Liberal Cabinet minister who had committed suicide to avoid sexual scandal.

[2] In the 1920s Jaeger's, which advertised a 'healthy' line of clothing made exclusively of fine yarns and natural fibres, could be found in Selfridge's Department Store in Oxford Street; later it had an independent store in Regent's Street.

James Douglas in the 'Daily Express' is advocating a form of censorship but not 'the reactionary Irish form'³ Let me have papers with the Dublin debate. I shall put off 'The Sunday Times' till I get them.⁴ Here they no longer take 'The Irish Times'—at least I have not found it.

Yours affectionly

WBY

³ James Douglas (1867–1940), journalist and critic, editor of the *Sunday Express* since 1920. On 18 Oct. 1928, two months after his editorial denouncing *The Well of Loneliness* by Radclyffe Hall as 'a book that must be suppressed', his article in the *Daily Express* entitled 'There is Too Much Licence in Fiction' advocates a voluntary unofficial board of literary censors which 'would cleanse fiction of a great mass of dismal and disgusting stuff' and yet avoid the 'intolerable' reactionary state censorship of the Irish Free State. In 1923 the Censorship of Films Act had been passed in Ireland, followed by public and private campaigns including book burnings, culminating in the 1926 recommendation of 'the Committee of Enquiry on Evil Literature' and, finally, the Censorship of Publications Bill, 1928. Although WBY had retired from the Senate on 28 Sept. 1928, he vigorously protested the bill in letters and articles to the *Irish Independent, Irish Statesman,* and *The Spectator.*

⁴ The *Irish Times* faithfully reported the extensive debates in the Dáil on the Irish Censorship Bill from 19 Oct. 1928 until the final reading was passed on 22 Mar. 1929.

1929

May 5 [1929]

My dear George: I have seen Fielding[1] & the Ghosts Club, Olivia, Wyndham
Lewis,[2] Dulac, Sturge Moore & Ricketts. This exausts my revelry so far.
I have only found Olivia, Dulac, Sturge Moore & the Ghosts good company
& so shall probably hasten my return to Dublin, the Savile 'wash' permit-
ting. However one never knows. Ricketts has given his new book, wonderfully bound & illustrated—'he only published for sale'—Sturge Moore tells
me—'enough copies to pay for those he has given to his friends'[3] A characteristic magnificence that secures the ultimate value of each copy he has
given. 'The Ghosts' recieved my accout of the philosophy & its origin with
enthusiasm—Ionides especially—he was the friend of Crooks & has translated a Proclus fragment.[4]

　　I am well but not inclined to do much.[5] Tomorrow night the Dulacs &
Miss De Valois dine with me at the Ivy. Dulac is now most prosperous—he

[1] The Hon. Francis Henry Everard Joseph Feilding (or Fielding) (1867–1936), a prominent
member of the Society for Psychical Research who in 1919 married the Polish medium Sta-
nislawa Janina Tomczyk (d. 1975), was one of the investigators with WBY and MG of the
bleeding pictures of Mirebeau in 1914 (see 19 Mar. 1922); his *Sittings with Eusapio Palladino and
Other Studies* (1911) revealed considerable trickery. The Ghosts Club, founded in 1862, claims to
be the oldest organisation in the world associated with psychical research
[2] Percy Wyndham Lewis (1882–1957), the Canadian-born writer and painter who founded
the Vorticist movement, edited the short-lived *Blast* (1914–15) with EP; his ideas in *Time and
Western Man* (1927) and the novel *Childermass* (1928) excited WBY, who then read the autobiographical *Tarr* (1928) before leaving Rapallo. In August 1917 GHL had bought one of his
paintings for £12, the sale arranged by EP.
[3] Ricketts published *Beyond the Threshold* under the pseudonym Jean Paul Raymond; written,
illustrated, and designed by him and bound in goatskin and tooled in gold, it was published
privately at the Curwen Press in 1929.
[4] Alexander Constantine Ionides (1862–1931), author and translator of Proclus, engineer
and stockbroker, co-founder in 1913 of the Anglo-Hellenic league, and a good friend of OS.
He inherited the family home at No. 1 Holland Park, decorated by his father's friends Philip
Webb, William Morris, and Walter Crane. Sir William Crookes (1832–1919), physicist noted
for his work on radiation, was a serious student of spiritualism as were his scientific friends
Marie and Pierre Curie.
[5] After a stay of almost six months the Yeatses left Rapallo on 27 April, and after a night
in Paris went on to London, where WBY remained until 16 May while GY returned immediately to Dublin.

has done magnificent designs to the Apocolypse & is decorating & furnishing etc the saloon of a Pacific liner.[6] You fortold Miss Beauclerks success with the cards.[7]

Yrs affecly
WB Yeats

[ALS]   SAVILE CLUB, | 69, BROOK STREET, W.1.
                Thursday [9 May 1929]

My dear George

I shall come home Monday or Tuesday—I have my room till Tuesday—I shall wire.

I have spent an hour or so to day at the Round Pond. I went there to get the name of a maker of model yacts—I had Micael in mind. I got the name of the most admired maker from an old man who had a beautiful boat. A great change from my day is that there are now a number of little steam boats. One man had an Atlantic liner which went as fast as one could walk. He never started it without blowing its whistle. As I came back in a taxi through Hyde Park the taxi suddenly stopped. I heard the taxi man say over & over again 'now come on, come on.' When I looked out to see who was taking so long to cross the road I saw two ducks from the Serpentine.

I have seen Sturge twice, Dulac twice, Lady Ottoline twice & been to a couple of mediums. At the last medium somebody, who seemed to be my father, came & said 'You have a son who is slow to learn but he is slow & sure. When older he will be brilliant.'

Yours affly
WB Yeats

Lora Riding is alive. Did she entice Phibbs to her 'funeral' & if so has she kept him.[1]

[6] After a lapse of three years, Dulac was again designing covers for the *American Weekly*, an arrangement which continued sporadically until 1951; in addition he did designs for Helen Beauclerk's new novel, *The Love of the Foolish Angel*, designed a play, *The Shadow of the East*, and an advertisement—not a ship—for the Canadian Pacific Line. The following year he supervised the decoration of the Chelsea Arts Ball and the Cathay Lounge, a smoking-room for the Canadian Pacific Liner *The Empress of Britain*; two illustrations to *The Book of Revelation* were completed in 1930.

[7] GY was adept at reading the Tarot cards; Helen Beauclerk's second novel, *The Love of the Foolish Angel*, was published by Collins in 1929.

[1] When the Yeatses arrived in London news was circulating of the complicated lives and attempted suicides a few days earlier of the poets and lovers Laura Riding (1901–91) and Robert Graves (1895–1985), son of WBY's old collaborator and sometime critic Alfred Perceval Graves (1846–1931), who were embroiled in a triangular relationship with Graves's wife the painter and fashion designer Nancy Nicholson (1899–1977) which was in turn exacerbated

[ALS[1]]   Coole Park, Gort, Co Galway
                                              Wednesday [17 July 1929]

My dear George: Yesterday we drove to Castle Taylor, where Michael
Shawe Taylor is setting all to rights & settling down for all the year round.[2]
We called at Tullyra, getting in through an old disused avenue, which opens
into the yard—but the Hemphills were away—expected back in a day or
two.[3] The only visible life was an incredible old slattern. Her protestant
equivalent at Castle Taylor was a neat, clean & rather quatrocento looking
old woman. To day there are callers from Lough Cutra[4]—Anne Gregory
& who else I do not know as so far I but hear there distant voices. In the
evening Lady Gregory reads out Anthony Trollopes 'American Senator.'
    My work goes well & I am well—except that I cannot spell.

                                              Yours affecly
                                              WB Yeats

by the recent arrival of Geoffrey Phibbs from Ireland. American poet and short story writer
Laura Riding, née Reichenthal, had divorced her first husband Louis Gottschalk in 1925 and
moved to Europe, where she collaborated with Robert Graves on *A Survey of Modernist Poetry*
(1927) and *A Pamphlet against Anthologies* (1928). The two then settled in Majorca where they
established the Seizin press and edited the literary journal *Epilogue*. In 1936 she and Graves
moved to the United States where their volatile relationship soon foundered; Graves returned
to England while Riding remained in America, marrying poet and critic Schuyler B. Jackson
in 1939. Meanwhile Irish poet Geoffrey Phibbs (1900–56) and Nicholson (who would eventually divorce Graves in 1949) were living in Wiltshire and collaborating on the Poulk Press.
Phibbs, who published under the pseudonym 'R. Fitzurse' and from 1930 legally changed his
name to 'Geoffrey Basil Taylor', had worked with LR and MacGreevy as an organizer for
the Carnegie Libraries and had in 1924 married the Irish artist Norah McGuinness (1901–80)
whom he divorced in 1929. After five years he and Nicholson separated; in 1935 he married Mary Dillwyn (1909–56), and returned to Ireland in 1940. Graves meanwhile eventually
returned to Majorca with a new wife, Beryl Hodge, their four children, and a flourishing
career as poet, critic, translator, and novelist, perhaps best known for *I, Claudius* (1934) and
The White Goddess (1948).

    [1] Printed address '42, Fitzwilliam Square, Dublin' struck out.
    [2] Walter Michael Shawe-Taylor (1906–*c*.1950), son of Captain John (1866–1911) and nephew
of Francis 'Frank' (1869–1920) who had been ambushed and killed in March 1920 for refusing
to give up his grazing land, was the grandson of Walter Shawe-Taylor (1832–1912) and AG's
sister Elizabeth Persse (d. 1896). According to Mick Martyn, a gardener at Castle Taylor,
after his mother's death 'Master Michael' spent from March to October in Ireland, but did
not work the land, concentrating only on the gardens; his sister Eleonora Elizabeth Aileen
(1910–86), who also came to Castle Taylor regularly, worked with the film industry in France.
I am indebted to Sister de Lourdes Fahy for this information.
    [3] The late Edward Martyn's property, Tillyra, had been inherited by Mary, daughter of
Andrew Martyn, and her husband Baron Fitzroy Hemphill (1860–1930), barrister and JP for
Co. Galway; they also had residences in London and Dublin.
    [4] Lady Gregory's daughter-in-law Margaret married Captain Guy Gough of Lough Cutra
on 8 Sept. 1928; see 28 Aug. 1928.

[ALS]   Coole Park | Gort
                                          Tuesday¹ [23 July 1929]

My dear George

No events except Lennox & Emperor Jones on Sunday.² They went off after dinner to break their journey at Ballinasloe Jones said that the price of an assasination in Clare is still something between £5 & £10—apparently it has stood at that price for years. There is a sort of Mafia there & has been for years. He is writing us a play & told me the plot & so far as I could make out the one valuabl idea had been put in by Lennox. His dialogue & character drawing will however probably be excellent³—I have done all the troubl some part of the system now—after a little tidying up tomorrow I shall begin to copy out what I have done.⁴ The other night I tried to get some instruction on the religeous side of it all in my dreams. Result—a magnificent Cathedral & a man in it who started to prey for my conversion. I got perfectly furious & told him that such a preyer was an insult. I hope he was not Dionurtes.⁵

When do you want me back? When do you start for Switzerland? When do you bring the children here? How long do they stay?⁶ Etc etc etc. I have forgotten all dates.

The flies in the garden are unendurabl but all else is very pleasant.

At Athenry station, when I was coming down, a girl jumped out of the train & ran to where I was sitting, & said 'O have you done a book with 'Good & Evil' in the name? Its in a cross word puzzle' I said 'yes. Ideas of

---

¹ On 42, Fitzwilliam Square stationery struck out; Monday struck out.

² AG had entertained LR and Rutherford Mayne for dinner and tea at Coole on Sunday 23 July. Mayne was one of the pseudonyms (another was 'Neil Gallina') of playwright and actor Samuel John Waddell (1878–1967) who in January 1927 had performed the title role at the Abbey Theatre in Eugene O'Neill's *The Emperor Jones*. One of the founders of the Ulster Literary Theatre in 1902 and a member of the breakaway group The Theatre of Ireland 1906–12, he was the author of over a dozen plays most of which were premiered by the Ulster Literary Theatre, who performed his *The Drone* in 1908, and *Red Turf* in 1911 at the Abbey Theatre. Married to Joseph Campbell's sister Josephine and brother of the scholar Helen Waddell, he was a qualified engineer who worked for the Irish Land Commission and was involved in discussions over the sale of Coole Park.

³ After many years Mayne returned to playwriting, and the Abbey produced *Peter* in 1930 and in 1934 *Bridge Head*, which won the Casement Prize for the best Irish play of 1934/5; both plays were directed by LR.

⁴ The second version of *A Vision*.

⁵ Dionertes was GY's principal Instructor during her automatic writing and dream speaking.

⁶ GY left at the end of July to bring back MBY and ABY from their school, l'Alpe Fleurie in Villars sur Bex, Switzerland, returning to Dublin on Monday 5 August.

Good & Evil' & she ran off to her carriage afraid to be left behind. Theres
decission of character—all on the spur of the moment.

Yours affectionly
WB Yeats

P.T.O

Anne Gregory has just come from Lough Cutra with enfuriating news.
Seventeen shots were fired into Castle Taylor last night—troubl a dissmissed
steward aparently. They waited it seems till Micael Shaw Taylor's grand
mother arrived—she arrived yesterday.[7] Her room was one of those fired into.
Michael brought her, & her hysterical maid, to Lough Cutra & asked them to
take her in. He himself is at Castle Taylor & will remain there—all the family
obstinancy active in him.

[ALS]   Coole Park | Gort | Co Galway[1]
                                              July 26 [1929]

My dear Dobbs

The account of the Castle Taylor schooting in to days 'Independent' is
correct except that the number of the shots is exagerated.[2] There were 17 or
20. Nobody knows anything for certain except that Michael Shaw Taylor
has a bad manner & is disliked & that he put a drunken refugee from Ulster
out of the Stewards Lodge & put in a sober protestant.[3] This was a stupidity
considering that the house was once a center of prosletising. The refugee
was violenly elequent about the penal laws. Meanwhile Coole & Coutra live
in terror at the thought of the old grandmother coming to stay. By taking
out the kitchen range Lough Coutra has evaded her & she is back at Castle
Taylor. She is a masterful bore of 83 or 84 & was very disatisfied at at not
being in the newspapers. 'The Independent' has perhaps been informed in
her interest. Her maid thought it was an air-raid.

---

[7] Amy Shawe-Taylor's mother, Eleanora (Mrs Gerard) Norman (1851–1936).

[1] On 42 Fitzwilliam Square stationery, struck out.

[2] The *Irish Independent*, 26 July 1929, reported that at 1 a.m. a fifteen-minute volley of shots
were fired into Walter Shawe-Taylor's bedroom at Castle Taylor, and that when the Civic
Guards were summoned they discovered '80 sporting gun cartridge cases and spent rifle and
revolver bullets' in the vicinity of the house, in which several windows were shattered, and
twenty bombs hidden in a drainpipe in a disused mill at Gort.

[3] 'Poor Michael, he had done so much to house and garden and had been so proud to show
it to his grandmother and hoped she might stay on there. The people had seemed glad at his
return and his intention to keep up his home. It was probably that Northern, Cogan, who
had been dismissed and his house given to Sullivan the late caretaker at Garryland' (*Journals*,
ii, 24 July 1929, 453).

I am copying out the philosophy now—it runs smoothly. The grand children come about something or other practically every day & that Dutch woman who was looking up questions in the British Museum is on her way.[4] Other wise I see nothing & hear nothing. I have had one letter from a neglectful wife who is in the midst of the world

Yours affly
WB Yeats

Yes I shall come up on August 4.
Micael Shaw Taylor is a goose. He gave the blind piper a cup of tea & not a penny peice & asked him to come again. He sold a man a tree for 30/- & when the man had cut it, wanted some of it back because the price was too small. However 17 shots at dead of night seems excessive even for a goose.[5]

Yours affecly
WB Yeats

[ALS] 42, FITZWILLIAM SQUARE, | DUBLIN.

Wednesday [?28 Aug. 1929]

My dear Dobbs: Your ring was found in the hall. I have written also c/o Walsh hoping to reach you before you go to Galway. It was found this morning. I wish I could have gone to Galway with you and would if you had been alone.[1] I am planing out a long poem to you—my dear—about the length of the Byzantium poem I think,—an apology for much seeming inatention caused by absorbtion in my thought[2]

Yrs affly
WB Yeats

---

[4] 'the Dutchwoman who is writing on Yeats came for two nights—quite nice—but urgent for facts for her book' (*Journals*, ii, 7 Aug. 1929, 455). This was Rebecca P. C. Brugsma (1889–1968), whose Ph.D. dissertation for the University of Amsterdam was defended on 1 July 1933 and whose impressive collection of first editions of WBY's works was bequeathed to the University Library of Gronigen. Her small book *The Beginnings of the Irish Revival Part I*, published in 1933, thanks AG for her hospitality (Roselinde Supheert, *Yeats in Holland: The Reception of the Work of W. B. Yeats in the Netherlands before World War Two*, Costerus New Series 104 (Amsterdam, 1995), 90–5).

[5] Walter Michael Shawe-Taylor was, however, popular on the racing circuit and had made a generous donation to the Memorial Hall in Labane; despite the firings, he remained at Castle Taylor until 1951.

[1] GY went down to Coole with the children for a week before they joined WBY at Rosses Point; meanwhile he went to Markree Castle, near Collooney (see next letter).

[2] Probably 'Coole Park 1929'.

[ALS]   MARKREE CASTLE, | COLLOONEY.[1]
                              Wed [28 Aug. 1929]

My dear Dobbs
'Ewings Hotel' Rosses Point but leave that to me. Mrs Cooper is phoning this after noon from Cooloney to engage 3 rooms from Wednesday next. The Point is crowded this time of year.
'The Grand Hotel' Sligo but that is not likely to be crowded however if it is fall back on 'The Railway Hotel'. I leave that to you out of force of habit.[2]
Mrs Erickson[3] is here & a silent Welsh man.

                                        Yrs ev
                                        WB Yeats

[ALS]   MARKREE CASTLE, | COLLOONEY.
                              Thursday [29 Aug. 1929]

My dear George
We have three rooms at Ewings Hotel Rosses Point from Thursday which will give us a couple of days sight seeing at Sligo.[1]
I have done another stanza of the poems for Lady Gregory book & so I am idling to day. Mrs Cooper is driving me into Sligo & round the lake.
This is a pleasant house.

                                        Yrs affecly
                                        WB Yeats

[1] WBY was staying at Markree Castle, Collooney, just south of Sligo, the country home of Senator Bryan Ricco Cooper (1884–1930). Cooper's book *The Tenth (Irish) Division in Gallipoli* (1918) described his experiences as a Connaught Ranger in the First World War, after which he was appointed Press Censor for Britain in Ireland; he served as Unionist MP for South Dublin in 1910 and in 1923, supported by WBY, was elected as an Independent, then joining Cumann na nGaedheal for his third term as TD. In 1931, after his death, Mrs Lillian Stella Cooper, née Hewson (d. 1966), presented a half-size reproduction of the ancient Lough Lene bell to Dáil Éireann and it has since been the bell of the Ceann Comhairle (chairman) of Dáil Éireann.
[2] They were planning a tour with the children of WBY's old haunts.
[3] Margit Eriksson, wife of the Swedish consul Herr Harry Eriksson, lived in 17 Fitzwilliam Square but had been anxious to move to a flat in 82 Merrion Square the previous year when GY briefly considered renting rather than selling. Harry Eriksson (1892–1957) was with the Swedish Consulate in Dublin from 1926 to 1937 and was a member of the DDL committee.
[1] Ewing's Golf Links Hotel, Rosses Point.

[ALS]   COOLE PARK, | GORT, CO. GALWAY.
                                            Monday [16 Sept. 1929]

My dear Dobbs

I thought of you yesterday with some anxiety as the wind was gusty & the
sky full of clouds. As the Newspaper has not recorded a disaster you have
no doubt reached home.[1]

I shall go up Wednesday—that will give you a clear day to disport your
freedom in.

I have written verse—Swifts epitaph as verse & some more of the poem for
Lady Gregorys book & gone on with the correction of the account of system.

The news I pick up about the Lough Cutra affair is none of it good—
Gough's stupidity & Margeret's malice have probably boiled that pot.[2]

                                                                    Yrs ev
                                                                  WB Yeats

[ALS]   SAVILE CLUB | 69, BROOK STREET. W.1
                                            Thursday [24 Oct. 1929]

My dear George

I have had a very pleasant afternoon at the Mac Kenzies—I like both
of them greatly.[1] The philosopher Broad is also in the order—a 5–6.[2] They

[1] WB was staying at Coole while GY took the children back to Switzerland.

[2] Early in September there had been a strike at Lough Cutra because Guy Gough had
dismissed a worker who had struck the foreman; the foreman, whose strong language was the
origin of the trouble, was then also dismissed, but despite AG's pleas that the men be taken
back, the Goughs had left for Dublin.

[1] Mr and Mrs McKenzie, both spiritualists, lived at 59 Holland Park, London W 11. James
Hewat McKenzie (1870–1929), author of *Spirit Intercourse: Its Theory and Practice* (1916), and a pamphlet *If a Soldier Die* (1916), founded in 1920 and largely funded the British College of Psychic
Science at 15 Queen's Gate, London, a rigidly disciplined resident college for mediums similar in
aims to the Institut Métapsychique of Paris. Among the mediums he worked with were Gladys
Osborne Leonard (1882–1968), with whom GHL and WBY independently had numerous sittings before their marriage, Eileen Garrett (1893–1970), whose sittings they attended in the 1920s,
and Blanche Cooper. After James Hewat died his wife and collaborator the medium Barbara
McKenzie, née Hendry (1870–1963), who had investigated WBY's favoured physical medium
Evan Powell, continued their study of the paranormal and became especially interested in 'direct
drawing'. In 1938 the college amalgamated with the International Institute for Psychical Investigation (Jenny Hazelgrove, *Spiritualism and British Society between the Wars* (Manchester, 2000)). Mrs
McKenzie was also president of the Women's Adult School Movement in Britain.

[2] Charlie Dunbar Broad (1887–1971), Professor of Moral Philosophy at Cambridge, was
keenly interested in psychical research, joining the SPR in 1920 and serving as president of the
Society in 1935 and 1958; although his name does not appear on any surviving list of Golden
Dawn members, as late as 1949 he was publishing on 'The Relevance of Psychical Research
to Philosophy'.

seem to have got something about the sources of order through Steiner. I go
to Bristol (not Cardif) to-morrow & return on Sunday.[3]

Have you the roller?[4] If it is sendible—send it—if not bring it. I am doing
my old exercises. We both forgot it.

Yrs ev

WB Yeats

[ALS]   SAVILE CLUB | 69, BROOK STREET. W.1

Oct 25 [1929]

My dear George

This morning when the Valet was setting out my shirt etc we discovered
that I had only one vest which is in need of a wash. Can you send me one—
if not wire & I will buy one.

Geogorty has sent me my preface back that I may defend 'Ringsend' etc
against his enemies.[1] I shall do nothing until I get to Italy. I think I shall
leave him without an answer for a few days.

I am discovering the most curious things about the Order. I have seen
Dr Dixon (or Dickson) & am to see him again on Sunday, to go through
papers of Wescotts[2] He has Westcotts diary. Freulein Sprengel was authentic

---

[3] In search of more information about Golden Dawn affairs, especially its origins, WBY
planned a visit to the Hermes Temple in Bristol (R. A. Gilbert (comp.), *The Golden Dawn Companion* (Wellingborough, 1986), 42). The confusion over whether WBY should go to Cardiff or
Bristol probably concerned Mrs Hettie Millicent Mackenzie (1862–1942), 'Magna Est Veritas',
one of the first three chiefs of the Hermes Temple in Bristol, which was established by Felkin
in 1916 and remained active (closing each year from November to February) until the 1960s.
Author of *Hegel's Educational Theory and Practice* (1909), in 1904 she was the first woman to be
appointed a professor in the UK, at Cardiff University, and in 1918 again made history when
she unsuccessfully stood for Parliament as a Labour MP. A follower of Rudolf Steiner, the
founder of the Anthroposophical Movement, in 1922 she hosted a conference on education at
Oxford to which Steiner was invited.

[4] Used by WBY for his 'Swedish exercises', a combination of movement and massage
introduced by the Swedish teacher of fencing and gymnastics Pehr Henrik Ling (1760–1839),
which gained such widespread popularity that they were introduced into the British schools
in the 1870s.

[1] WBY wrote a preface to Gogarty's *Wild Apples*, published by Cuala in 1928; it includes the
poem 'Ringsend' (after reading Tolstoy), which begins 'I will live in Ringsend | With a red-
headed whore, | And the fan-light gone in | Where it lights the hall-door, | And listen each
night | For her querulous shout, | As at last she streels in | And the pubs empty out.'

[2] For Dr Dickson see note to 8 May 1921. Dr William Wynn Westcott (1848–1925), 'Sapere
Aude', coroner for the north-east of London (*c.*1880–1910), a high-grade Freemason, Ros-
icrucian, member of Mme Blavatsky's Theosophical Society, and, with Dr William Robert
Woodman (1828–91), 'Vincit Omnium Veritas', and Samuel Liddell MacGregor Mathers,
one of the first chiefs of the London-based Isis-Urania Temple of the Hermetic Order of the
Golden Dawn. The Golden Dawn Cipher Manuscripts were said to have been discovered in

I also have the name of another Third order person. I was greatly struck by what I learned in Bristol—a most able group—that clergyman who is on the lonely Island where the survivors of the mutiny of the 'Bounty' are was one.[3] He volunteered. Dr Broad the philosopher belongs also. This all very private of course. Better destroy this.

Yrs ev
WB Yeats

[ALS] SAVILE CLUB | 69, BROOK STREET. W.1
Saturday [26 Oct. 1929]

My dear Dobbs

I am a bad lier—& worst of all on the telephone. Mrs Cecil Harmsworth phoned this morning 'are you & your wife free on Tuesday evening?' I was vague—'I think we are not free as we are leaving next morning' That was hopeless, & she said 'well if you are free let me send to the Hotel for you you need not dress' Then I promised to find out. 'Are you free on Tuesday evening if so wire or phone to club that day. They will take a message.

There is a chance that Mrs Harmsworth may get her husband to come home a day sooner & in that case it will be Monday.[1]

Yrs
WB Yeats

a cupboard and handed over to Westcott who recognized the similarities of five summarized grade initiations to Masonic rituals; he in turn commissioned Mathers, knowledgeable in occult lore, to rewrite the summaries into the new Order's grade structure of three ascending orders. Westcott's multiple responsibilities in the early years of the Golden Dawn led to a great many instruction documents which enhanced his already extensive occult and metaphysical library. One of many rifts in the Society led to the establishment of a breakaway group loyal to Mathers, and Westcott remained loyal despite Mathers's attempt to undermine his authority by claiming that his correspondence with the mysterious Fräulein Sprengel had been a forgery (see *CL II*, 541–4).

[3] Some survivors of the mutiny settled first on Pitcairn Island, then later moved to Norfolk Island; *Crockfords Clerical Directory* (1929) identifies Chaplain F. Berry as the Church of England missionary on Norfolk Island, but all residents remaining on Pitcairn were Seventh Day Adventists.

[1] The dinner engagement with Emilie Alberta Harmsworth, née Maffett (1874–1942), does not appear to have taken place.

[ALS]   SAVILE CLUB | 69, BROOK STREET. W.1
                                                Oct 30 [1929]

My dear Dobbs

I have done my various duties. I have got three stalls for 'Tassie'[1] & have ordered the big trunck. I dined with Dulac last night—keep <u>Sunday week</u> free for the Filum Society—the famous Russian filum Potemkin—Dulac is getting us tickets.[2] To night I dine with Beaverbrook—he discovered I was in London & sends his motor to fetch me.

Did I tell you that I am finding out a good deal about the origin of the Order. I have met Dr Dickson & dine with him on Sunday. I am delighted that you are going to the Halls.[3] I am tired & am going to bed until it is time for Beaverbrooke.

                                                        Yrs affec
                                                        WB Yeats

I have written into my big MSS book several schemes for poems.
The Maid at the Sevile unasked mended my sleeping jacket. She found a bit of stuff to match it. I have only one vest that I came in—so bring me another

[ALS]   SAVILE CLUB | 69, BROOK STREET. W.1
                                                Oct 31 [1929]

My dear Dobbs

I have accepted. I have however an engagement on Tuesday evening to dine with Dulac.

I dined last night with Beaverbrook. Four of us including the host. A silver Table in a vast room. Two rooms off an orcestra. The orcestra practices

---

[1] Sean O'Casey's *The Silver Tassie*, having been rejected by the Abbey Theatre, opened at the Apollo Theatre in London on 11 October produced by C. B. Cochran, designed by Augustus John, and directed by Raymond Massey, with Charles Laughton playing the lead. AG saw it and was pleased, though she thought the Abbey would have done it better; in the end, WBY was too ill to attend before the run ended on 7 December.

[2] Dulac was on the council of the Film Society, founded in October 1925 to screen avant-garde works and other 'quality films', and succeeded the film director Ivor Montague as chair. *Battleship Potemkin*, the revolutionary propaganda silent film by Sergei Michailovich Eisenstein (1898–1948), a homage to the aborted 1905 Russian naval mutiny, which premiered in Berlin in 1926 and was officially banned in the UK until 1954, was shown at the New Gallery Kinema in Regent Street on 10 Nov. 1929, along with John Grierson's *Drifters*.

[3] The Yeatses had met John Hall (1870–1930), a prominent wealthy British industrialist and amateur photographer, and his Canadian wife Jean Isobel Hall, née Nesbitt (1888–1970), on the boat to Algeciras in November 1927, and the two couples remained friendly, the Yeatses visiting their home in Stafford as well as the London flat in St James's Place; Jean Hall, like GY considerably younger than her husband, had been a concert pianist until her marriage.

every morning & plays from 9 to 12 every evening. No body ever listens. It is a faint back ground for conversation. After dinner for a half hour stocks & shares were discussed—the true appetite—the howling of the beasts at the Zooe. All very pleasant & amusing

Yrs ev
WB Yeats

[ALS[1]]

Savile Club
[3 Nov. 1929]

My dear George: I have had a slight set back in my health as result of a low cold. A good deal of blood. I got Dickson (Dickson of the order) to examine me. I was dining with him in any case & it came on about an hour before I was due at his house. On his advice I am seeing a specialist to-morrow.[2] I have no reason to think it serious, but I shall have to give up theatre, Etc for the present. You will find me at Mrs Halls flat or I will find you there. I will bring the tickets but there will be a ticket for somebody as I shall not go.

Yrs ev
WB Yeats

I am writing this at Dicksons.

[ALS]

VIA AMERICHE 12–8 | RAPALLO | ITALY

Last Will & Testament[1]

Dec 21, 1929

I bequeath whatever I may die possessed of to my wife Bertha, Georgie Yeats, knowing that she will employ it, according to my known wishes, for the benefit of my children.

William Butler Yeats

Dorothy Pound
34. Abingdon Court W. 8. London

Basil Bunting
5 Osnaburgh Terrace London NW 1

[1] On stationery of 7 Upper Harley Street, London NW 1, address struck out.

[2] Robert Arthur Young, later Sir (1871–1959), physician at the Brompton Hospital and a distinguished specialist in chest diseases, had been called in to consult on SMY's condition in 1923.

[1] WBY was seriously ill with what was finally diagnosed as brucellosis or Malta fever, usually transmitted to humans by unpasteurized milk or contaminated cheese. They remained in Italy until early July 1930.

[ALS]   VIA AMERICHE 12–8 | RAPALLO | ITALY
                                                        Dec 21, 1929

I bequeath whatever I may die possessed of to my wife Bertha, Georgie, Yeats to be employed by her, according to my known wishes, for the benefit of my children.

                                        William Butler Yeats
                                        William Butler Yeats[1]

              Witnesses   Basil Bunting
                                        5 Osnaburgh Terrace NW1
                                        Ezra Pound
                                        Marsala 12/5 | Rapallo

  [1] On 28 Nov. 1934 WBY signed a further will, drawn up by his Dublin solicitor, providing specific details of his bequests to his children and once again naming GY the sole executrix; the 1934 will was probated after his death in 1939.

1930

[ALS]   SAVILE CLUB, | 69, BROOK STREET. W.1
                                                    July 9 [1930]

My dear Dobbs: I enclose a letter from Eva Ducat.[1] It is I think invitation
for to-morrow—Thursday—July 10—7.30. I am accepting for myself. Olivia
is ill—bronchitis—& cannot see me. She has arranged this invitation from
Eva Ducat I think. I have tried to get you on phone in vain.
    I am comfortabl here.

                                                          Yrs ev
                                                        WB Yeats

[ALS]   SAVILE CLUB, | 69, BROOK STREET. W.1
                                              Friday [11 July 1930]

My dear George
    I am sorry not to see you. All is well I am not tired & am enjoying life. I have
just come from Lady Ottolines & met James Stephens[1] there. He dines with
me here on Sunday night. This evening I shall, I hope, see Ricketts. I saw Miss
Grigsby[2] yesterday & an Monday afternoon she will take me in her motor to the
Academy. I see the poet Turner here & gather much news. I have dined twice
with Dulac. The first time I met Mrs Rummell, charming, & charmingly dressed
& just cast off by Rummell who has found another lady & is convinced that his
wife was bad for his soul.[3] She wants to go on the stage to earn some money.
    Give my love to Michael[4]

                                                          Yrs ev
                                                        WB Yeats

[1] Enclosure missing. At this time Eva Ducat, an old friend of GY, her mother, and OS, was
living at 1 Cheniston Gardens Studio, London W 8 (see note to 18 Aug. 1918). The Yeatses
had returned from Rapallo by sea, arriving in London about 9 July.

[1] Between frequent lecture tours to America, Stephens had been living in London since 1925.

[2] Emilie Grigsby (1880–1964) of 3 Curzon Place, who was the model for Berenice Fleming in
Theodore Dreiser's novel *The Stoic* (1947), inherited her great wealth from the American millionaire
Charles T. Yerkes Jr., whose mistress she was until his death in 1905. After a trip to India she lived
for many years in England, where in addition to her salon in Park Lane she entertained government and military leaders at her country home 'Old Meadows' near West Drayton, Middlesex.

[3] See 9 May 1921 for Rummel's previous relationships. In December 1925, he married an
Englishwoman, Sarah Suzanne ('Patricia') Hetherington (1902–77), but by 1927 had met and was
living in Paris with the Russian poet Amanda Françoise ('Francesca') Erik (1896–1977), reputed
to have been the mistress of King Leopold III, who became his third wife after his divorce in
November 1930. Under his influence, both wives joined the Anthroposophical Society.

[4] GY had gone on to Dublin, leaving WBY in London until 17 July.

[TLS]   42 Fitzwilliam Square | Dublin
                                      Wednesday [23 July 1930]

My dear Willy, I hope you arrived safely at Pakenham, enjoyed an evening
of frivolous conversation and did not allow the more serious side of your
head to get into political weighty conversation with 'The Earl', as Lady
Fingal used to allude to her husband....¹

No newses here but for the thrill of our dustbin being stolen yesterday
evening from the pavement between the hours of eightthirty and ten. McCoy²
was most puzzled this morning when he went out to fetch it in and found
nothing to fetch, and filled with vehement righteous indignation when I told
him that I had observed on returning home last night at 10.15 that it was not
there. He insisted on my telephoning to the police at Lad Lane....I rather felt
that anyone who could pinch a large galvanised iron dustbin filled to the brim
with rubbish during the combined light of twilight and street lamp deserved to
get that dustbin! I hope the lady or gentleman who snaffled that bin will not
be discovered; I should dislike extremely to make my first appearance in the
Dublin Police Courts on a matter about which I feel so frivolously, in fact
I am not sure that if this horrid eventuality occurred I would not turn Republican and refuse to recognise the Courts. Of course it was only from, out of,
or because of, the worst kind of moral cowardice that I telephoned to the
police; but there was McCoy, so eloquent,—if this sort of thing was allowed
to pass unnoticed ALL the Dustbins on the Square might be stolen, fortunately
there was nothing in 'the doctor's' dustbin so he had not put it out yesterday
(I refrained from the obvious retort that 'the doctor's' was an antique no one
could covet). 'There's a lot of police regulations that are never enforced' says
the police at the other end of the telephone 'but there's a regulation that bins
shouldnt be put out as early as that'. 'Do you think the police took it' says I.
'O no' says he 'They wouldnt take it. They'd notify.' Then, 'When they take

---

¹ WBY was staying overnight at Pakenham Hall (now Tullynally Castle) in Westmeath
as guest of Edward Arthur Henry Pakenham (1902–61), 6th Earl of Longford, and Lady
Longford, née Christine Patti Trew (1900–80). From 1931 to 1936 the Longfords worked with
Hilton Robert Hugh Edwards (1903–82) and Micheál MacLiammóir, né Alfred Lee Willmore
(1899–1978), at the Gate Theatre, then founded Longford Productions, which during the next
25 years produced over 150 plays at The Gate and on tours around Ireland. Lord Longford
wrote a number of plays and served as a Senator 1946–8. In 1931 Christine Longford pub-
lished an autobiographical novel, *Making Conversation*, and later other novels, but is best known
as the author of more than two dozen plays (see letter of 19 Mar. 1932). Elizabeth Mary
Margaret, Countess of Fingall, née Daisy Burke (1866–1944), was married to Francis James
Plunkett, 11th Earl of Fingall, 4th Baron Fingall (1859–1929), of Killeen Castle, Co. Meath;
Seventy Years Young, her memories as told to Pamela Hinkson (the daughter of WBY's old friend
Katharine Tynan), was published in 1937.
² The caretaker at 42 Fitzwilliam Square, to which they had moved after selling 82 Merrion
Square. The house belonged to Bethel Solomons, master of the Rotunda, where he main-
tained a surgery on the ground floor and the Yeatses rented the two upper floors.

them they generally empty them out on the pavement, did they empty out yours?' 'They did not' says I. 'They must have had a handcart with them' says he. 'Do you mean the Garda would have emptied it out' says I. 'No, the people who take the dustbins' says he; so it is evidently one of the unregistered occupations like the stealing of doormats, washbaskets and umbrellas.

The flat resounds with hammers and files on copper tubing, and your new gas fire in the study looks grand, and your new bedroom almost has its gas fire and electric fire; you'll find a salamander heat in your two rooms when you return.

I go to the Viceregal Garden Party tomorrow with your sisters—hate going to these things alone, dont know why I am going anyhow unless its in the hope of gathering a little frivolous conversation though the Lord knows experience might have taught me that one never finds it in crowds. Perhaps I really want an excuse for wearing a brand new large hat even though it must top an old, old, dress. I showed you the new stuff for your new bedroom curtains and quite forgot to show you the lovely—or so I think—length of brocade in many colours that I got in London for my new evening dress. It is getting made up now and pray heaven someone will ask us to dinner that I may wear it! One of the nuisances of the world is that one must have an 'evening dress' (for me one in three years would be enough!) and before you have a chance of wearing it sufficiently providence has changed the fashions and the dress has gone gaga. However this new one of mine will be so long in the skirts that whatever providence arranges summat can be done with it!

Please dont go and get colds or nuisances of that sort and do control your dislike of giving trouble by remembering that milk and biscuits for the night and hot water bottles for the day give very little trouble, and that there really isnt anyone who wouldnt be glad to take that little trouble for you!

I have written to Lady Gregory to ask her to write you the name and address of the man she gets her car from (I've forgotten it) so will you please wire to him as soon as you know when you're going to Coole that he may fetch you from the Station at GALWAY. If you havent enough money to pay for the car from Galway to Coole you can tip the man, and ask him how much the car costs, and send the money in by Lady G's messenger later.

Yours forever
George.

[ALS]   RENVYLE HOUSE HOTEL | RENVYLE, CONNEMARA | CO. GALWAY
Wednesday April [July] 23 [1930]

My dear Dobbs: Arrived about an hour ago. This is a most charming house—nothing could be in better taste & there is real ingenuity & enterprise everywhere.[1] John[2] has not yet come in, is 'out with some friends'. Lord Longford his wife, & two girl friends of Lady Longford's, one Prof Griersons[3] daughter are here & very good company. In spite of some opportunities I have not caught a cold & my room is comfortabl & the fire set.

If you see my slippers lying about you might send them to me.

Yrs affly
WB Yeats

[ALS]
RENVYLE HOUSE HOTEL | RENVYLE,
CONNEMARA | CO. GALWAY
July [*c*.25, 1930]

My dear Dobbs

The portrait promises to be a masterpiece—amusing—a self I do not know but am delighted to know, a self that I could never have found out for my self, a gay, whimsical person which I could never find in the solemnity of the looking-glass. Is it my self?—it is certainly what I would like to be.

This hotel is exceedingly comfortabl. I cannot tell why but even my legs are not cold. The fire is set in my room but I have not yet lit it though the weather is vile. I shall probably lit it this afternoon however.

Yours ev
WB Yeats

[1] Renvyle House, which had been a hotel since 1883 until Gogarty purchased it in 1917, had been burned down in February 1923 by Republican forces during the Civil War; the Gogartys restored it and reopened it as a hotel in March 1930. In 1919 while visiting the house, known to be haunted, the Yeatses had spoken sternly to the apparition, who was unhappy at strangers in his house (*BG*, 226).

[2] Gogarty had invited the flamboyant Welsh artist Augustus Edwin John (1878–1961) to be his guest while he painted WBY's portrait; John's first portrait of WBY was done in 1907 and had recently been turned down by the Cork Municipal Art Gallery when Gogarty tried to sell it, on the grounds that WBY 'insulted Daniel O'Connell' during his speech on divorce. Other guests at the hotel during John's visit included the Philadelphia socialite Hope (Mrs Edgar) Scott (1904–95) of Philadelphia, Lady Dorothea Louise Ashley-Cooper (b. 1907) and her sister Mrs Sturt, Lady Mary Sibell, Baroness Alington of Crichel (1902–36); see Augustus John, *Chiaroscuro: Fragments of Autobiography* (1952), 89.

[3] Probably authors and translators Flora Lucy Margaret Grierson (1899–1966) and Joan Mary Shelmerdine (1899–1994), founders of the private Samson Press and fellow students at Somerville College with Christine Longford, who had met her husband while living in Oxford.

[ALS]   RENVYLE HOUSE HOTEL | RENVYLE,
                         CONNEMARA | CO. GALWAY
                         Sunday [27 July 1930]

My dear Dobbs
    Here is my letter to Lewis for him to publish.¹ Please type it & return it
that I may send it on. Correct spelling & punctuation I cannot get letters
even moderately right after noon & it is now tea time.
    John somewhat spoiled that portrait & has laid it aside—I tell him he will
endow it later with vice or virtue according to mood having got me out of sight
after the manner of Lewis. He started another much larger portrait to do [?day]
which is more 'monumental'—his word—has less comedy. It is a fine thing.
                                                         Yrs ev
                                                         WB Yeats

[ALS]   RENVYLE HOUSE HOTEL | RENVYLE,
                         CONNEMARA | CO. GALWAY
                         July 30 [1930]

My dear Dobbs
    No letter & I am famished for news. John is at Galway races & I have
done a great days work & packed up what I have brought down of 'Vision'
& declared the book finished. Now poems.
    John has done a big oil portrait of me—I am in a chair in the open air
my leggs in the fur bag & my hat on my knees & my hair flying. It is a fine
thing.¹ I think he will want two or three more sittings but I may get off on
Monday or Tuesday. I have written this to Lady Gregory
    I wonder what you thought of my Wyndham Lewis paragraph.
                                                         Yrs affly
                                                         WB Yeats

¹ On 24 Mar. 1927 WBY, who had been reading Lewis's *The Enemy*, commented to OS,
'Lewis has some profound judgments—where he analyzes public opinions or some definite
work or art—& often a vivid phrase.' In September 1928 Lewis had asked permission to
quote a passage from WBY's letter praising *Childermass* (*LWBY 2*, 484); now he wrote asking
that he might include WBY's comments on *The Apes of God* in his pamphlet *Satire and Fiction:
Enemy Pamphlets No. 1* (1930), which attacked the English book reviewing establishment. WBY's
paragraph concluded, 'I felt…on first reading The Apes of God, that something absent from
all literature for a generation was back again, and in a form rare in the literature of all generations, passion enobled by intensity, by endurance, by wisdom.' In a revealing letter to LR
on 29 June 1930, GY described the impact Lewis's work had: 'I maintain that the book is a
realistic novel: William maintains that it is a satirical pamphlet; we quarrelled about it, about
that terminology, until 11.30 last night'.

¹ Gogarty sold the painting to the Glasgow Art Gallery.

[ALS]   RENVYLE HOUSE HOTEL | RENVYLE,
                                CONNEMARA | CO. GALWAY
                                Sunday [3] August [1930]

My dear Dobbs: Let me know how you are but write to Coole.¹ I hope to
be there Tuesday or Wednesday. I should have been there to-morrow but
John took three days off for Galway races & attendant activities. 'How did
the races go yesterday' said John to a man in the street. 'Grand—we had the
ambulences out' 'Who for?' 'O lots of people' 'What was wrong with them'
'Collapsed from too great enjoyment.'

Mrs Pillomore [Phillimore] has come & gone & we got on admirably—
once established that we are enemies we were in great amity. 'Why do
you hate me?' she said. 'Because you crush my chickens before they are
hatched'

The Lewis paragraph was a short open letter to Lewis, meant for publication, which I enclosed in a letter to you & asked you to type for me. There
appear to have been two notes of mine which you have not recieved. I got
your letter about the dust-bin. I began dinner that night by saying solemnly
'I have just had news that my dust-bin has been stollen with all its contents.'
Lord Longford gave a great shout of laughter and said, 'All—all what all
its contents.'

I shall get Lady G. to type the Lewis letter as that will be rather quicker
I think.

                                                              Yrs aff
                                                              WB Yeats

[ALS]   42, FITZWILLIAM SQUARE, | DUBLIN.
                                Wednesday [6 Aug. 1930]

My dear George: I have just wired 'arriving Dublin to-morrow second train'
writing. I am doing this because Lady Gregory has just come in to say, that
wants to go to Dublin to see Slattery <not I think the old complaint by the
soun> not the 'rheumatism' but some disturbance in the old place.¹ She is
waiting for this letter.

                                                              Yrs affly
                                                              WB Yeats

¹ GY was once again in the hands of the dentist.

¹ Dr Richard Vincent Slattery (1881–1940) of 75 Merrion Square, and consulting surgeon
to Richmond Hospital, had performed a mastectomy on AG in 1926 with Gogarty in attendance.

[ALS]   COOLE PARK, GORT, CO. GALWAY
                                          Thursday. [7 Aug. 1930]

My dear Dobbs: Lady Gregory must go to Dublin Monday. She has a
growth again in the old scar & there must be an operation. She found it on
Sunday & would have gone up on Monday but to my distress waited for
me. Naturally I have urged her to go up to-morrow but she wont go until
Monday.[1]

If Lennox is back[2] she wants to have a directors meeting on Monday.
Please wire if Lennox is back & I will wire him hour & place of meeting. It
will probably mean getting Tulloch[3] too. If Lennox is not back she wants
a meeting when she is out of Hospital. The problem is Dennis Johnston.
Yesterday she accepted him without difficulty but to day she has gone back
on it.[4] She will I think take Tulloch's opinion as final & he spoke to her of
a possible new director. In her heart she hopes he meant only 'a business
director'. She knows that some thing must be done but her suggestion is
to get Sally Allgood back which I do not want, unless she came for a very
short time.[5]

Lady Gregory looks old & thin & both Margeret & Catherine (or was it
Anne) who were at lunch at Renvyle on Saturday thought her ill. Though
she herself did not find the lump till next day. I shall of course come up with
Lady Gregory, but if you do not feel capable of coping with things please
let me go to the club.

                                                              Yrs ev
                                                           WB Yeats
Lady Gregory hopes to see Slattery on Monday at 3. She would probably
have meeting at 4 or 5.

                                                                 Yrs

---

[1] AG was once again operated on for breast cancer.
[2] From April to July 1930 LR was a visiting producer at Amherst College, the Carnegie
Institute of Technology, and the University of Michigan, concluding his tour at the University
of Montana as visiting professor and producer where he also taught a summer school class on
the history of the Abbey Theatre and a seminar on playwriting; he sailed from New York on
30 July and stopped over in London.
[3] George Hill Tulloch (1873–1957), a member of the United Arts Club and senior partner of
the chartered accounting firm of Craig, Gardner and Associates, 41 Dame Street Dublin, had
been in charge of the Abbey Theatre's financial records since 1923 and was also accountant
for the Cuala Press; a director of the Bank of Ireland (1935–57), in 1944 he was nominated to
the Industrial and Commercial Panel of the Senate.
[4] LR and WBY were recommending that the playwright Denis Johnston (author of *The
Old Lady Says No!* which they rejected for the Abbey) be made a co-director, a position vacant
since the death of Synge.
[5] Although performing regularly on stage in London and in films, Sara Allgood was still
interested in returning to the Abbey Theatre, as a 'guest artist' if not more permanently.

[ALCS] STEPHEN'S GREEN CLUB, | DUBLIN.
Friday [29 Aug. 1930]

My dear George
 I will call about 11:30 that you may have some sleep after your journey[1]
but if you want me before that telephone here.

Yrs ev
WBY.

Hour Glass successful at Abbey. Masks wonderful[2]

[ALS] Coole Park[1]
Sept 13 [1930]

My dear Dobbs
 I do not yet know how long I am to stay I have been waiting until Lady
Gregory heard from Jack or Masefield.[2] She heard to day—neither can
come. I will seize a good oppertunity & raise the question—probably to
night. The trouble is that Lady Gregory wants me to stay as long as possible
so I shall have to set the limit.
 Have been writing notes in diary & correcting Robartes.[3] Robarts is
finished—they get me a registered envelope in Gort to day. I will send it
on Monday.
 Thank you very much for sending the books & the throat gargale. You
never forget anything
 I have written in my diary an imaginary letter to Michaels school master
which will amuse you.[4] Lady Gregory wants me to put it into verse.

---

[1] GY had gone to England.

[2] There was a revival at the Abbey Theatre on 25 Aug. 1930 of WBY's *The Hour-Glass* with
masks by the Dutch artist Hildo Krop and the screens designed for the Abbey Theatre by
Gordon Craig.

[1] On Fitzwilliam Square stationery address struck out; WBY was at Coole from 10 Sept. to
17 Oct. 1930 while AG was still in considerable pain.

[2] Jack and Cottie Yeats made annual visits to Coole; John Masefield came less often.

[3] In 1929 WBY started thinking about a new version of the Michael Robartes stories; *Stories of Michael Robartes and his Friends: An Extract from a Record made by his Pupils*, signed by John
Duddon, was published by Cuala Press along with his play *The Resurrection* in March 1932. On
26 July 1936 he wrote to DW, 'I have for years been creat[ing] a group of strange disorderly
people on whom Michael Robartes confers the wisdom of the east'; *Stories of Michael Robartes
and his Friends* was then included with an additional passage in *A Vision* (1937).

[4] 'A Letter to Michael's Schoolmaster' was published in *Pages from a Diary Written in Nineteen
Hundred and Thirty* by Cuala Press in 1944 with a note by GY; in it he orders that MBY be
taught Greek at once 'by the Berlitz method' but 'not one word of Latin', and learn mathematics but no geography or science; MBY and ABY were still at school in Switzerland.

I am about to start on the Swift play.⁵

Yrs affectionly
WB Yeats

[ALS]   COOLE PARK, | GORT, CO. GALWAY.
[?14 Sept. 1930]

My dear Dobbs
    Bring Swifts verse when you come. You remember the one volume edition
I got a year ago.¹ I want it for the Swift play on which I am now working.
    I am in favour. I wrote a poem, half mocking & wholly complimentary
about Anne Gregorys 'yellow hair'—three verses of which this is the last

> I heard an old religeous man
> Yesternight declare
> That he had found a test to prove
> That only god, my dear,
> Could love you for your self alone
> And not your yellow hair.²

Lady Gregory made me read it to her six times in the course of one evening,
& would have insisted upon a seventh had not bed time come.
    It is quite impossible to discuss with Lady Gregory when I am to leave—
she said when I spoke of it 'You cannot possibly say—you do not know what
the weather or your health will be like or how your work will go on. Leave
that until George comes. I imagine she expects quite a long visit from you'
I told her it would be short but she has forgotten. If I told her again she
would again forget.

Yrs affecly
WB Yeats

[ALS¹]   at Coole | Gort
Monday [15 Sept. 1930]

My dear Dobbs,
    I send script of Robartes. I couldnt get a re[g]istered envelope—when
asked for their largest the Gort Porst Office sent one for letters. Had no

---

⁵ *The Words upon a Window-Pane,* WBY's play about a séance that conjures up the spirit of
Jonathan Swift, was first produced at the Abbey on 17 Nov. 1930.
    ¹ This one-volume edition of Swift is no longer in the Yeats Library.
    ² This version of the last stanza of 'For Anne Gregory' is very close to that published in *The
Winding Stair and Other Poems* (1933).
    ¹ On Fitzwilliam Square stationery, address struck out.

other I suppose. I am writing a poem, another of those 'poems for music' & shall probably write that on Michaels eductation.[2] I am well—no colds. I have said nothing yet about the length of my visit. I rather shrink from the moment when I must do so. Lady G is a good deal shaken by her recent operation, & has a good deal of pain from time to time from those spots but of course, as always, is cheerful. I have done little at the play A first draft is always a hateful job & one puts off.

Yrs ev
WB Yeats

I shall send this for the pleasure of using a beutiful seal I have found in Lady Gregory bundle of seals—
'Let me know if you get Robartes'

[TLS]   42 Fitzwilliam Square | Dublin
                                              Saturday [20 Sept. 1930]

My dear Willy

I suppose I shall see you almost as soon as you see this letter.[1] The Robartes has arrived safely. I hope to finish my clean, nice, tidied out copies in time to bring one with me to Coole on Tuesday.

Tremendous houses at the Abbey. Personally I do not like the play,[2] hate the play, am bored by it, despise its detection (but then—when one has read all the first class detection of the world…!) Anyhow, everyone else seems to be loving it, and the box office receipts must be Terrrrrifficccc. I only hope that they will be so large that when added to the past weeks of profit there may be during the next six months—as a result of these accumulated hundreds—some play I DO want to see!

The pettest old things have errupted into the Abbey—the Lord knows from what suburb or province of Dublin. Ancient white haired, fearfully eighteenth century old things, with diamond stars in their hair, or white lace caps (diamond stars and brooches in them also) and lorgnettes, and faces marvellously made up in the fashion of fifteen years ago, the fashion that

    [2] The text remained 'a letter', not a poem; see 'A Letter to Michael's Schoolmaster', *Pages from a Diary written in 1930* (Dublin, 1944) reprinted in *Explorations*, 320–1.

    [1] GY returned from Switzerland on 19 September and went to Coole on 23 September for two nights.

    [2] *Let the Credit Go*, an Irish detective play by Bryan Cooper, who had died the previous July, was premiered on 15 September; in 1920 he published *The Collar of Gold and Other Fantasies*, a collection of plays, and translated Paul Claudel's *L'Otage* as *The Hostage* for production by the DDL 17 and 18 Feb. 1924; in 1931 LR published *Bryan Cooper*, a biography.

wanted to deceive—all the old Minnie Fitzgeralds[3] and things of that sort and they all had a grand evening. Nothing dangerous, suggestive, (they giggled so much at the mild digs at Rathmines and Rathgar that I think they did not emerge from that part of Suburban Dublin) no politics, no thought, nothing to agitate them, and in spite of three shockingly wet nights they could all go home and go to bed with hot water bottles, certain of a night of tranquil sleep. When I said 'no politics' I forgot the very milk and water, no, watered milk, Republican. But then, he, too, was so unassuming and reassuring in his Republicanism that he could not have fluttered the most sensitive heart. I saw the damned thing on Monday, but having had two shockingly late nights on Saturday and Sunday I was so tired that I could not be sure whether my annoyance was mere fatigue. So I went again last night.

I am bringing you down a little extra clothing, as I think you may need it. I shall stay two or three nights. Lady Gregory suggested I did that and then came down later on again. You will probably like to stay on a week or two <u>after</u> I leave.

George.

[ALS]   COOLE PARK, | GORT, CO. GALWAY.
Sept 27 [1930]

My dear Dobbs

Lady Gregory tells me that somebody else has used the name 'The Winding Stair'.[1] Shall I change it & call my book of poems 'Byzantium'. In that case I can send Sturge Moore the new Byzantium poem (I have it here) which will give him a mass of symbols. 'Byzantium' would follow up my old 'Sailing to Byzantium' which people liked.

After you left I shortened by a whole page the Swift exposition & read what I have written to Lady Gregory. She was enthusiastic, & has several times returned to the subject. She says there is not a word too much, that it is 'powerful' & full of a sense of something coming.

---

[3] A reference to the class represented by Miss Minnie Fitzgerald (d. 1937), popular philanthropist known for her work with the wounded during the First World War, the St. John Ambulance Brigade, and as a Life Governor of the Royal Hospital for Incurables; she was also an active follower of the Ward Union hounds, the Meath Hunt, and the Devon and Somerset Staghounds. I am indebted to Christopher Murray and Lisa Coen for assistance in tracking down Miss Fitzgerald.

[1] The novel *The Winding Stair* by the popular author Alfred Edward Woodley Mason (1865–1948) was published by Hodder & Stoughton in 1923 and produced as a film the following year.

If you can lay your hand on 'Chambers Biographical Dictionary' which should be in the study you might let me know when Joe Biggar & when O'Gorman Mahon² died.

Yours
WB Yeats

I wrote to Sturge Moore yesterday but have written today asking him to do nothing until I write again.³

[ALS]   COOLE PARK, | GORT, CO. GALWAY.

[?4 Oct. 1930]

My dear Dobbs: I have finished the play as completely as it can be finished without your criticism. Could you bring down your type-writer, & let me dictate a clean copy. It could then go to Starkie & Lennox & if they approve be put on at the Abbey at once. I have sent 'Byzantium' to Sturge-Moore he can find all the symbols he wants there. If that type-writer would be nuisance, dont bother about it. I shall have to find somebody in Dublin who can take dictation & the sooner I enquire about it the better. I have the philosophy to dictate.

Swift or as I call it 'Words Upon the Window Pane' being finished I am enjoying a pleasant day of idleness. It was very good of you to send me that poem¹ I am afraid you had to copy it twice—once in the National Library & then upon the type-writer.

Yours affectionly
WB Yeats

---

² Joseph Gillis Biggar (1828–90) was an Irish nationalist politician from Belfast noted for his obstructionist techniques in the House of Commons. Charles James Patrick 'the O'Gorman Mahon' (1900–91) was an Irish nationalist journalist, adventurer, and barrister whose quarrel with Daniel O'Connell stifled his first attempt at a parliamentary career, but whose support of Parnell in later years made him the oldest MP in Parliament. In a draft dictated to GY to be included in *Dramatis Personae* but never published, WBY refers to 'the O'Gorman Mahon…with his two and twenty duels', but does not seem to have incorporated Biggar (*CL II*, 709).

³ WBY reverted to his original title.

¹ Probably the poem 'Stella to Dr. Swift on his birth-day November 30, 1721' by Esther Johnson (1687–1728); in *The Words upon the Window-Pane* the young scholar John Corbet quotes the lines 'You taught how I might youth prolong | By knowing what is right or wrong; | How from my heart to bring supplies | Of lustre to my fading eyes'; AG also found the poem in her library, quoted by Samuel Johnson (*Journals*, ii. 554).

[TLS]   42, FITZWILLIAM SQUARE, | DUBLIN.
                                                            [1 Nov. 1930]

My dear Willy, you left your shaving brush here—I didnt know what to do, whether to wire to you, whether to send it on.[1] Then I thought, if I wire he will dash out to buy one after he finds the telegram at the Club when he arrives on Friday evening; by that time most of the shops will be shut and he will get very tired hunting for one that is open. If I post it on he will not get it until Monday and in any case it is high time, as I told him before (!) that he bought a new one! He will shave on Saturday morning by fluffing up his shaving soap with a sponge, and later in the morning he will prance out and buy this much needed new brush. Anyway, my lad, don't you tell me anymore in a fierce voice that 'I will see to the packing of my own dressing case'. Horrible thought.... did you secretly buy a new shaving brush? It never occurred to me until this moment that you might deliberately have left the old brush behind!

I am just off to lunch with Lolly; then I go to 'Tosca' (with Lennox)[2] and tomorrow I go to tea at Dundrum, having asked myself there thinking that Lolly was to be away in Belfast for the week end. She only goes to Belfast on Monday...[3]

I hope you posted that letter to May Morris. If you go over there do remember to talk to her about those two lovely poems in the Quinn letters especially that one with the refrain 'O how lone, how lone it is.'[4] I can see her point of view that her letters to Quinn were private letters, that they both agreed to 'burn them', but Quinn did not 'burn' hers, perhaps because he felt that one cannot burn and destroy works of art. She wrote beautiful letters; damnable perhaps that he did not burn them, although had I been able to write letters like that my personal vanity would have been pleased that they survived seeing that they contained so much that was impersonal, so little that was personal, so much praise of a man who gave her birth and of his house and of his friends—even his and her criticism of his friends, in

---

[1] WBY went to London on 31 Oct. 1930 and stayed until 12 November; GY collected their children from Switzerland at the end of November.

[2] *Tosca* by Giacomo Puccini was given a matinée performance by the Carl Rosa Opera Company at the Gaiety Theatre on 1 Nov. 1930.

[3] Cuala was represented each year at the annual Arts and Crafts Society exhibition and sale in the YMCA Minor Hall, Belfast, patronized by Lady Londonderry. I am grateful to Dr Joseph McBrinn of the School of Art and Design, University of Ulster, for assistance.

[4] The refrain to the poem 'A sweet garden by the sea' by William Morris (1834–96). LR had been asked to edit the letters of the New York lawyer John Quinn, whose epistolary affairs included those with Lady Gregory and William Morris's daughter May (1862–1938) who was in the process of editing her father's correspondence; LR's project eventually fell through (see *On Poetry, Painting and Politics: The Letters of May Morris and John Quinn*, ed. Janis Londraville, Cranbury, NJ, 1997).

those letters, had such nobility and justice that it was impersonal. Her own criticism of your gestures, lecturing, was justified, although she cut it, because she did not know you well enough to know that you do it unconsciously in private life. Anyway, if she isnt going to give that poem, those two poems, to the Quinn book, put the fear of God into her and make her publish them.. we've read the prose part of that whole edition, and maybe you nor I have found all the poems in the verse part; perhaps she has already put them in. The damn thing is all save two volumes are at Rapallo.

Lunching with Lolly today. Teaing at Dundrum tomorrow.

A hell of a lot of letters up from the Abbey today and yesterday. One I enclose; you must deal with it.[5]

Love to all, I like to think that you are staying with Masefield,[6] you must have met him for the first time just about the time you first stayed with Lady G. (I send on a letter from her which came today) If you get the opportunity look up Force Stead at Worcester College, and if you go there, look up Sheagan Dorman,[7] Lennox's nephew and take him to Fullers to feed on ices and cream buns! You wont get any value out of him, but you like ices, and he adores cream buns!

                                                              George

[ALS]   SAVILE CLUB, | 69, BROOK STREET.W.1
                                                    Nov 3 [1930]

My dear Dobbs: I am setting out for Oxford in a few minuites now. I have seen Lady Ottoline & Dulac & am to see May Morris on Wednesday. I posted my letter to Kelmscott at 6.30 the night I arrived & had an answer at 10 next morning. All well & no news

                                                              Yrs ev
                                                         WB Yeats

    [5] Enclosure is missing.
    [6] WBY was visiting John Masefield in Oxford to commemorate the thirtieth anniversary of their first meeting (see 8 Nov. 1930).
    [7] William Force Stead (1884–1967), who was a regular visitor at WBY's Monday evening 'At Homes' in Oxford from 1920, was an American diplomat who became an Anglican clergyman and after some time in Italy returned to earn an MA at Oxford, where he was chaplain of Worcester College 1926–33, during which time he baptized his friend T. S. Eliot. He published a number of volumes of poetry, edited *The Poetry of the Bible* (London, 1938), was an authority on the 18th-century poet Christopher Smart, one of whose unpublished poems he discovered, and contributed articles to leading English and American periodicals; WBY included two of his poems in the *Oxford Book of English Verse*; at this time his emotional life was in turmoil (see note to 28 May 1931 and *LWBY 2*, 507). Sean Dorman (1911–99) after graduating from Oxford became a freelance journalist, novelist, teacher, and publisher, whose memoirs of his uncle LR and theatre life in Dublin, *Limelight over the Liffey* (1983) and *My Uncle Lennox* (1986), were published by Raffeen Press, named after the Robinson family home in Kinsale.

[ALS]　　　　　　　　　　SAVILE CLUB, | 69, BROOK STREET.W.1

Nov 8 [1930]

My dear Dobbs: I have taken my room here until Wednesday morning but may return sooner. I am delighted to hear about the Hones house.[1] Did you get a letter from me on the back of the envelope of which I asked for the address of the man, who would make a box for the Chaucer.[2] You might wire address.

I had a rather moving experience at Masefields. At his little theatre he made a long eulogy on my work & my self—very embarrassing—& then five girls with beatiful voices recited my lyrics for three quarters of an hour. I do not think the whole audience could hear but to me it was strangely over whelming. The next day we went to Kelmscott—quite a small but very lovely. Those poems are in the Collected Edition.

Yesterday I met De-la-Mare & Virginia Wolf at Lady Ottolines and here is the upshot of my talk at a metephore of Lady Ottoline's

> We that had such thought,
> That such deeds have done,
> Must ramble on—thinned out
> Like milk on a flat stone.[3]

Yours affectly
WB Yeats

[ALS]　　　　　　　　　　SAVILE CLUB, | 69, BROOK STREET.W.1

Thursday [13 Nov. 1930]

My dear Dobbs: Are you a letter-writer? No youre not.

I think I will return Monday. I am impatient to get to work again; & have seen most of my friends & spent most of my money.

[1] Joseph Maunsell Hone (1882–1959), biographer, critic, translator, and historian, edited the quarterly *Shanachie* (1906–7), wrote *Irishmen of To-day* (1915), *WB Yeats: The Poet in Contemporary Ireland* (1916), *The Life of George Moore* (1936), and would be asked by GY to write the official biography of WBY, published in 1948; see letters of August 1931 for his collaboration with Mario Manlio Rossi on Bishop Berkeley and WBY's involvement. GY had arranged to rent Joseph Hone's house in Killiney for the spring of 1931 since Ballylee was considered too damp and too expensive to open.

[2] For WBY's 40th birthday on 13 June 1905, AG and twenty-five other friends had presented him with the Kelmscott edition of the works of Chaucer, printed by William Morris (1834–96).

[3] Revised and published as 'Spilt Milk'.

Last night I was at Mrs Traver Smith.¹ Dolly there wonderfully trans-formed—slim, very slim, red lips, a manifest charmer. Result I suppose of the self confidence of work.² Quite a crowd of people all interested in psychics, one old millionaire, very dull & very earnest, & a face like Don Quixotte. He prefers mediums to race-horses.³

That Rapallo relation of Olivia a Johnston has been expelled from Italy—his morals were it seems eccentric.⁴

Yrs affly
WB Yeats

¹ Hester Meredith Travers Smith (1868–1949), daughter of JBY's old friend Professor Edward Dowden of TCD, reverted to her maiden name Hester Dowden after separating from her husband Dr Robert Montgomery Travers-Smith (1872–1945). A concert pianist and well-known Dublin medium, she had moved to London in 1921, and continued to practise automatism with her control 'Shamar' while supplementing her income by taking lodgers, including MacGreevy; she published *Voices from the Void* (1919) and *Oscar Wilde from Purgatory: Psychic Messages* (1924). Neither GY nor SMY (who nicknamed her 'the cobra') liked Hester, but like LR, WBY had been a regular visitor at séances since her Dublin days, and served with her on the committee arranging Sunday lectures at the Abbey Theatre.

² An artist and stage designer, Dorothy 'Dolly' Travers Smith (1901–77), Hester Dowden's daughter, was a close friend of MacGreevy and LR, whom she was to marry in 1931.

³ A reference to the character 'Cornelius Patterson' in *The Words upon the Window-Pane*, who sought assurance that 'they race horses and whippets in the other world'.

⁴ Unidentified.

1931

[TLS]   42, FITZWILLIAM SQUARE, | DUBLIN.

Saturday [24 Jan. 1931]

My dear Willy

Anne and Michael are both up today for a little—Michael says his legs feel funny when he walks, but he liked being up very much! In the meantime Vera Hone has gone to her bed with bronchitis!! So the delay in our getting to Killiney will be once more their fault! Joe rang up this morning, and said he thought it would be a week before she could move....

I enclose a letter, an interminable letter the gist of which is that the writer asks you to send a 'word of greeting' to Professor Baker, as a public dinner is being given to him on February 15th to commemorate the work he has done for drama in America....[1]

A second letter explains itself.[2]

Hope you are well, and not working too much yet,

Yours ever

George.

[ALS]   at | COOLE PARK, GORT, CO. GALWAY.

Jan 26 [1931] Private

Private

My dear George: My work goes on well & I am not doing too much. Lady Gregory had a shooting party here before she went up to Dublin. Her nephew (Roxborough Persse) came & his wife. She found the nephew selfish & greedy in all sorts of ways & no longer regrets Roxborough's destruction but was delighted with the wife. And now Margeret says the wife had a most scandelous <career> existence before marriage & the wife herself writes that

---

[1] George Pierce Baker (1866–1935), theatre scholar and educator, whose '47 Workshop' at Harvard (1905–25) began as a playwriting course to which was added an experimental workshop in production, encouraged many young American playwrights, directors, and designers, including Eugene O'Neill, George Abbott, Philip Barry, S. N. Behrman, and Donald Oenslager. In 1925 he became director of the University Theatre at Yale and chairman of the postgraduate department of drama, which evolved into the Yale School of Drama; he retired in 1933, having suffered from ill health for several years.

[2] Enclosures missing.

Lady Gregory is the only member of 'that terrible family' who likes her. Lady Gregory's feelings are very mixed.[1]

I find it hard to make out what MacGreevy wants me to do but what ever it is I wont do it. I shall wate to hear however.[2]

It is good news that the children are better—write me when you can.[3]

Yours affectly
WBYeats

[ALS]

COOLE PARK, GORT, CO. GALWAY.
Feb 2 [1931]

My dear Dobbs: You must overflow with news & you do not write a word. How is Michael? How are the Hones? When do you want me? I can go or stay as it seems best to you. Lord Monteagle[1] comes here on Thursday & goes I think on Saturday, I must stay for him. I am writing daily, reading Goldsmith & Trevelyan's 'Blenheim'[2] & taking exercise—& that is all my news but then somebody said 'the happy man has no history' or something of the sort. At the moment Ann Gregory is expected every moment from a distant hunt & it so late that I can see Lady Gregory is anxious. I write with my ear cocked for the sound of wheels.

Yours always
WB Yeats

Feb 3

Anne turned up very late. A certain Lady Nelson[3] had been thrown & had broken three ribs. Anne brought her to hospital in Galway & all the way she was raving 'giving out tips for the Grand National.'

---

[1] 'My head is tired with entertaining my house guests—their manners of the invading type...A little overpowered by my guests' (*Journals*, ii. 585). Her guests were her great-nephew Major Dudley William Arthur Persse (1901–76), his American wife Olivia ('Olive') Barclay, née Boysen, their friend Capt. John Valpy Filleul (1898–1979), and two dogs; the Persses divorced in 1937.

[2] In his role as secretary to the editor of the fine arts journal *Formes*, MacGreevy had asked WBY to write an article on the portraits of Edgar Degas, a subject MacGreevy himself refers to in his monograph *T. S. Eliot: A Study* which was published by Chatto & Windus in January 1931.

[3] Both ABY and MBY had the measles.

[1] Thomas Aubrey Spring-Rice, Baron Monteagle (1883–1934) of Mount Trenchard, Foynes, Co. Limerick, was first secretary in the diplomatic service and a strong supporter of the Abbey Theatre.

[2] 'I had been reading Macaulays essay on Goldsmith—& he [WBY] took it to his room to read' (*Journals*, ii. 592). *Blenheim* (1930) was the first volume of *England under Queen Anne* by George Macaulay Trevelyan (1876–1962), great-nephew of Thomas Babington Macaulay and like him a staunch believer in the Whig tradition.

[3] Lady Anne Cathleen Elizabeth Nelson (1899–1989), née Loftus Bryan, wife of Sir James Hope Nelson (1883–1960) of Craughwell Castle, hunted with the Galway Blazers and piloted her own plane.

[ALS]   COOLE PARK, GORT, CO. GALWAY.
                                              Feb 4 [1931]

My dear Dobbs: I have wired 'Monday'—I would sooner have returned on
Saturday while you are all in the first excitement of your new house but Lady
Gregory has made rather a point of my waiting until Monday—speaking of it
several times. I think she wants me here after Monteagle has gone. We shall
look at Ballylee on Saturday. You say nothing about the key and I suppose
we can see all that is necessary without it, but if you want the thatch of the
garden side searched for rat holes I shall want the garden key. I thought that
it was I who had the greivance about letters. You in the midst of the great
world every moment bursting with news & I with nothing to tell.

    Lady Nelson had only one rib broken & a strained back last time—some
months ago—she broke two & in a fortnight was out hunting again, 'all
bound up in splints'—now that is the sort of thing that happens here or is
said to happen & you expect me to write letters.

    To the best of my beleif 'Vision' is finished & I am reading Oliver Gold-
smith in great peace of mind.

                                                      Yrs ev
                                                   WB Yeats

I give Ezra leave for those but wont you have to ask Macmillan or must I
or Watt.[1]

[TLS]   42, FITZWILLIAM SQUARE, | DUBLIN.
                                          Thursday [5 Feb. 1931]

Dear Willy
    When you return I will tell you all about that fantastic 'Great World' in
which you imagine I am living. Alan[1] writes that he will be over on Monday.

---

    [1] EP had written on 24 Jan. 1931 requesting permission to quote 'The Bald Heads' ['The
Scholars'] and 'one or two later poems if possible' for an anthology he was compiling; *Profile:
An Anthology Collected in MCMXXXI* (1932), 'a collection of poems which have stuck in my memory and which may possibly define their epoch, or at least rectify current ideas of it in respect
of at least one contour', was a limited edition of 250 published in Milan by John Scheiwiller;
'The Scholars' was the only poem by Yeats which was included, the same poem with which
EP had opened his *Catholic Anthology* in 1915 'as it were under Yeats' *patronato*, at least it started
with a poem in his then newer manner, which might be regarded as a turning point from the
twilit to his more strong and later phase' (p. 47).
    [1] Captain Alan George Duncan (1895–1943), son of Ellen Duncan who founded the Dublin
Arts Club and a friend of MacGreevy, had been living in Paris with his wife the painter Isabel
('Belinda') Atkinson; he was to spend a few weeks in Killiney as WB's secretary. The Yeatses
were in South Hill, Killiney, for three months from mid-February.

I shall expect you <u>here</u> by—I suppose—the second train. We can arrange about when he starts work etc on Monday evening. Michael seems to be perfectly well now, he says that his legs are not at all 'wobbly' today. He will want looking after for another couple of weeks.

You need not bother about the back of the thatch. You can observe all that is necessary from the front. The Kelly's have the keys of the garden. I forgot that you would probably not know that!

Yours
George.

[ALS]   SAVILE CLUB, | 69, BROOK STREET, W.1.
Saturday. 7. PM [23 May 1931]

My dear Dobbs

I have just wired 'Who do I lunch with on Tuesday'? I think the letter is in the holder with the John portrait. I meant to bring the holder & its contents & forgot. If you cannot find it I shall have to try & find out in Oxford on Monday. I go there to-morrow afternoon.[1]

I am sorry to have been so stupid. I am just off to Dulacs for supper. I lunched with Olivia, went to Academy. Then came in & went to bed so I shall not be too tired.

Yrs ev
WB Yeats

I have got the letter about the Wadham dinner.

[ALS]   SAVILE CLUB, | 69, BROOK STREET, W.1.
Thursday [28 May 1931]

My dear George: I had a pleasant busy time at Oxford. On Tuesday lunch, and the festival, & dinner at Wadham (a large gathering of men & women to whom I read out from 'The Winding Stair & then The Tower & was asked what had of recent years so deepened my poetry).[1] On Wednesday Force

---

[1] WBY was to receive a D.Litt. from Oxford on 26 May.

[1] Guests at the dinner, hosted by Cecil Maurice Bowra (1898–1971), classical scholar and warden of Wadham College in Oxford, included art historian and curator Kenneth Clark (1903–83), Coleridge and Chaucer scholar John Livingston Lowes (1867–1945), poet and historian Theodore Wade-Gery (1888–1972), Irish novelist and short story writer Elizabeth Bowen (1899–1973), critic and book collector John Sparrow (1906–92), and socialite novelist and biographer Nancy Mitford (1904–73) (see C. M. Bowra, *Memories 1898–1939* (London, 1966), 235–6).

Stead to lunch. You were right he wanted help & it is just possibl I may go down there again before I return, though I suppose unlikely.² I have been wonderfully well & vigerous & today for the first time am pleasantly tired. I shall see Watt in the afternoon. I have not yet been to Macmillan.

I wore my brown suit at the degree giving, having told the vice-chancellor that prolonged inactivity & gluttony—how does one spell that rare medieval word—had made my dark cloths impossible.

A Miss Lee asked to be remembered to you, & a pretty Miss Starkey spoke of her desire to get her brother established at Oxford.³

There has been a burglery at our Rapallo flat.⁴ All Mrs Pounds jewelry was taken out of the unlocked drawer where she kept it. Nothing else was touched.

Yrs affly
WB Yeats

[ALS]   SAVILE CLUB, | 69, BROOK STREET, W.1.
                               5. P.M. Thursday [28 May 1931]

My dear Dobbs I have just seen Watt & dealt with all letters except enclosed. Watt is inclined to be stern about it but I thought I should ask you about the translator. There was a German you thought rather good. I don't much like refusing leave to print a translation of the limited & private kind proposed. Return enclosed & let me know if know anything about the late Herr von Heiseler.¹ Watt hates him because of his interminable letters.

---

² Stead, who was separated from his wife, had fallen hopelessly in love with a young woman (his 'Nymph') half his age and a cousin of the Goughs; at this time he was also contemplating becoming a Roman Catholic, and in August 1933 resigned his fellowship at Worcester College to do so. The following year he enlisted WBY and other well-known literary friends to support his application to teach at the University of Cairo; instead, he visited the Yeatses in Dublin in the autumn of 1935 and by 1939 was on his way to the United States where he taught at Trinity College, Washington, DC, until 1958 (see George Mills Harper, 'William Force Stead's Friendship with Yeats and Eliot', *Massachusetts Review*, 21/1 (Spring 1980), 9–38).

³ I have been unable to identify Miss Lee. Enid Mary Starkie (1897–1970), critic and biographer of Baudelaire, Gide, and Rimbaud, was a fellow of Somerville College and reader in French literature at Oxford; her brother was Walter Starkie.

⁴ GY had sublet their flat to EP's parents.

¹ Henry von Heiseler (1875–1928), Russian-born German writer who between 1914 and 1922 translated into German ten of WBY's plays, but despite frequent appeals was not given the publication rights which went to the Austrian poet and translator Herberth Egon Herlitschka (1893–1970); after von Heiseler's death his son Bernt published a limited edition of 250 copies of *Irische Schaubühne* in 1933 (see AE to WBY, 14 May 1924, *LWBY* 2, 454–5). The enclosure is missing.

I am to see Macmillan on Monday. Don't bother about the Abbey copy of Oedipus² the corrections are all in the 1/- copy which I conclude is in the MSS. If it is not I will write next post.

Yrs ev
WB Yeats

[ALS]   SAVILE CLUB, | 69, BROOK STREET. W.1.
6. PM.. Thursday [28 May 1931]

My dear Dobbs

The little shilling Oedipus is not in the copy for Macmillan. I did not give it to Lennox. I gave Lennox a typed page with a very few corrections for the first page & that was all. The shilling Oedipus with my corrections was always in a left hand drawer of the writing Table at Southill.¹ Try & find it for me for it is full of corrections, some in the verse choruses. Let me have it before Monday if you can. If you cannot find it let me know by wire or letter before Monday. I will get another copy [and] revise it as fully as I can.

I am having two inches added to the waist of my dress trowsers & waist-coat—alas. They come in there amended form to-morrow.

Yrs ev
WB Yeats

[ALS]   SAVILE CLUB, | 69, BROOK STREET. W.1.
June 1 [1931]

My dear George

I have just seen Macmillan. The printing will take months & he does not expect to publish until the Autumn of 1932, but is prepared to advance the money expected from book at any time. There is no hurry about Vol VII.¹ I made no suggestion about portraits. He talks of the John among others. He knows 'a scholour on W B Yeats' & expects to have a lot of questions to send me.

The corrected 'Oedipus' arrived this morning. You spoke last week of sending my pen. Did you do so? It has not come. I have had all my clothes let out. I dont think I have grown much in the last six months or since I got my light brown suit. It seems to have been the time from the start of my

² Macmillan had published a separate edition of WBY's *King Oedipus* in 1928.

¹ South Hill, the Hones' house in Killiney.

¹ Sir Frederick Macmillan was planning to issue an Edition de Luxe of WBY's works, origi-nally promised for the autumn of 1931, but finally never completed.

illness to six months ago, that made me compete with Michael in growing out of my clothes. Strange that age & infancy should be so much a like.

I feel rather light in the head now that I have deposited that great heap of manuscript on Macmillans office floor. I am intoxicated with leisure.

Yrs affly

WB Yeats

[TLS]   42, FITZWILLIAM SQUARE, | DUBLIN.

Derby Day [3 June 1931]

My dear Willy

I'm not very sure of the date but I know to my sorrow that it is Derby day—not that I have lost, in fact on the day's transactions I am sixpence 'up'. But that is only because I backed beasts in the first and last races who won, but my Derby day is wrecked by the collapse of my fancy for the big race!¹

There's so much news that I do not know where to start. The news that amuses me most is perhaps that A.E. went down to the Abbey this morning and asked for Lennox, and Lennox thought it must be something very interesting and special. But no, 'tell me all the gossip' says AE. So after half an hour of this Lennox decided that he really could not interrupt rehearsals, and made AE come to rehearsals of the new show. I gather (and I think this is *private*) that AE made just under £3000² (expenses and American income tax paid) but I repeat this under seal of privacy. Lennox told the saga to me on the telephone this evening saying 'AE will of course tell Willy,...but...)

Then I met Dossy Wright who told me that Window Pane had got a very good reception in Belfast and that there was a good house last night at the Abbey (the Abbey was broadcasting Monday night)³ Then, there was a rather nightmarish lunch yesterday with that Miss Daking.⁴ I thought of everything that might excuse me from it, but nothing but flight to England

¹ The Epsom Derby, named after the 12th Earl of Derby, who first organized the event for his friends in 1780, is the biggest race in the United Kingdom, a flat horse race run each year in early June; in 1931 'Cameronian' won at 2.36.60.

² From September 1930 to May 1931 AE was lecturing in the United States to raise money for the medical fees incurred by his wife's lengthy illness; Violet Russell died on 3 Feb. 1932.

³ Udolphus ('Dossie') Wright (1887–1952) was theatre electrician, producer, and occasional actor from 1903 until his death (see *Ireland's Abbey Theatre: A History, 1899–1951*, compiled by Lennox Robinson (London, 1951), 76–7). *The Words upon the Window-Pane* was performed by the Abbey Theatre Company on 18 May 1931 in the Grand Opera House, Belfast. *Autumn Fire* by T. C. Murray was broadcast by the Abbey players from the Belfast studio of the BBC on 1 June 1931.

⁴ Daisy Caroline Daking (1884–1942), author of *Feed my Sheep*, 'a primer on human nature' (1932), and *Jungian Psychology and Modern Spiritual Thought* (1933), comparative studies in psychology published by the Anglo-Eastern Publishing Company, the first of which quotes a passage

could have postponed the evil. She came at one o'clock. At 5.30 I said—quite truthfully—that I must go as I had to meet Michael at Westland Row at 5.45. So she departed. She interests me tremendously as a human being but lord god in heaven William no one who talks so much can think, and that woman talked incessantly from one to five thirty, that's four and a half hours; honestly I don't think I said more than 50 words, perhaps less, during the sitting. I got down to my most English sub-soil and said 'quite' that I might alternate the 'yes, yes.' or 'no, no' which were necessary as punctuations. Had I not been compelled to meet Michael the interview would have been even longer and I am sure I would have begun punctuating with 'how true'. She spills out overflowing and wasted stuff that is adorably interesting—the entire history of her life, her sister's life, the life of the nephew for who she is responsible—and wrecks all her material with a philosophical psychology or psychological philosophy which is as full of holes as the Hone's sheets. I hate her hands. I suppose you did not look at them? Queer curtailed fingers, short in the third joint with the very short nails that mean obsession, or the half-developed. No, perhaps that is too personal a judgment; I've known three people with those short, abnormally short, nails who were obsessed.

She is convinced that her visit to Dundrum—I forget if I told you that she has been staying there, Friday to Thursday...—has been most fruitful. Lolly and Lily are both regenerated beings, the rhythm of conception and birth applies also to the spiritual life, in nine months time fate will see that she (Miss Daking) returns to Ireland on a 'job' and she will then be able to take up the work again. BUT, it may be a year. (If circumstances prove unpropitious the gestation is delayed.) Meanwhile, Lolly rings me up daily and does not seem to me either regenerated or in a process of spiritual gestation. Sad. The situation, says Lolly on the telephone today, is so difficult and tiresome that 'I get sea-sick in my bath'. Miss Daking, I am sure, would develope a most interesting interpretation from this phenomena, I cant do that; it just seems to me a very tragic business.[5]

More newses. I've decided that it would be better for Michael to go to a day school until he can be taken at Baymount than to have a governess. I've arranged for him to go to Miss Sweeny's (very protestant, she's the daughter,

on dreams and visions from WBY's *Ideas of Good and Evil*. Before the First World War she was well known in Oxford as a teacher of Old English and morris dancing, and then participated in the Lena Ashwell Concert Parties for the troops in France; described as no more than three feet tall, she served as model for 'the Pixie' character in the Abbey Girls series by Elsie Jeanette Oxenham. She seems never to have had a permanent home and worked at whatever job she could get, either in the London or Oxford area; GY's assessment is sadly accurate, for she committed suicide in 1942.

[5] Despite SMY's efforts to move elsewhere, the two sisters, locked in enmity, were forced because of their limited incomes to spend their lives together.

sister, aunt, of vast hordes of protestant clergy!) where there are four little
boys who go to Baymount at the same time as Michael.[6] He starts on June
8th. He seems pleased and excited, and I think he needs companionship
of people of his own age. He is much better without Anne, but she is 2½
years older and very 'bossy', in spite of all that he is very lonely without her.
Anyway, its worth trying, I think?

Yours as always George.

This is an interminable letter. The next part is really the only part that matters. The Cuala book 'Michael Robartes and his friends' only makes three
eights. That means that it is a very small book. Even with the prints and the
poems it will come to only about 28–30 pages. Will you write to Lolly about
it? I've racked my brains to think of any enlargements but the book seems
to me so complete in itself that I cannot imagine how any more pages can
be grafted in.[7]

[ALCS]   COOLE PARK, GORT, CO. GALWAY.

Tuesday [28 July 1931]

My dear Dobbs: Have written two poems—queer & I think good.[1] Race day
in Galway, writing in a hurry that maids may post on the way there. I have
four vests & no drawers except those on me. If I did not change in Dublin,
& I don't think I did, please send me a pair.

   Lady G greatly pleased over Lennox marriage—she said quite unexpectedly when we were talking of some thing else 'I am delighted—delighted
about Lennox'[2]

Yrs ev
WB Yeats

---

[6] After the children returned from their school in Switzerland, MBY went each day by
tram to Mount Temple Preparatory School for Girls and Boys, run by Miss Ellen T. Sweeny
of 3 Palmerston Park, Rathmines, until he entered Baymount in May 1932. On 1 May 1931
ABY became a boarder at Hillcourt Glenageary School (now Rathdown) in Dun Laoghaire,
returning home one day a week.

   [7] *Stories of Michael Robartes and his Friends: An Extract from a Record Made by his Pupils and a Play
in Prose* [*The Resurrection*] was finished at Cuala on All Hallows' Eve, 1931; pp. 47–56 were left
blank.

   [1] Probably 'Tom the Lunatic' and 'Tom at Cruachan'.
   [2] See next letter.

[TLS] 42, FITZWILLIAM SQUARE, | DUBLIN.
Wednesday [29 July 1931]

Dear Willy

You're a great letter writer. So glad to hear all the news from you.[1]

Anne returned on Monday for holidays, very pleased because she is to be 'moved up' next term to form 3b.[2] and had done quite well in exams...First in French, with 98 out of 100 which is good because spelling and writing counted. She is also pleased because in the examination for drawing (Royal drawing society, London) she got two 'Honours' certificates.

She brought back some of her examinations questions and answers (they were for a whole year, Anne had only one term) the answers were mostly the sort of thing you do say in exams, but for the question 'what do you most admire in the character of Desdemona' she wrote 'I admire Desdemona because of her singular love for a black man; most people have a peculiar dislike and distrust of black men', and this answer still, after a whole day, makes me laugh.

Several letters from Dolly: she and Hester had it all out on Saturday,[3] Dolly writes 'the situation is that we have decided unfortunately to remain friends, tho' any sign of going back on that and I depart', and the next day 'the storm over and the outlook greatly improved....but any more nonsense and I ups and go...the stomach milder too'. All this is PRIVATE. I wrote Dolly a very cold bath of a letter on Sunday advising her to eat soda-mint tablets after meals and take phospherine three times a day; today I got a letter, a rather indignant letter saying 'I don't often do it and having done it I now see it is very bad value and have decided to stop' So I hope all is well. I wrote a frigid letter because I dont think she has a chance in a competition of throwing fits with Hester—Hester has far more experience.

For Heaven's sake don't forget that you have GOT to be here on Thursday of next week for dinner at the McNeills.[4]

Yours
George.

[1] Some of WBY's letters seem to be missing, as he had returned to Coole by 27 July.

[2] That is, the second stream of third year in the post primary or secondary school system; in the 1940s she would return to Hillcourt, now incorporated in Rathdown and Park House schools, to teach art.

[3] On 20 July LR had secretly told GY of his engagement to Dolly Travers Smith, which Dolly's mother Hester Dowden, an old friend herself of LR, felt was inappropriate (LR is 44, Dolly 29); the engagement was announced in the *Irish Times* on 1 August and the marriage took place in London on 8 September, the day of WBY's broadcast in Belfast.

[4] The Governor-General James McNeill and his wife entertained a large party to dinner before going on to a reception at the French Legation on Thursday 6 August; The *Irish Times* noted that among the ladies present 'Mrs W B Yeats was in an effective black net gown' (7 Aug. 1931).

[TLS & MS]   42, FITZWILLIAM SQUARE, | DUBLIN.
                                            Friday [31 July 1931]

My dear William, DID you get a letter I forwarded to you last Tuesday from the BBC, Belfast? I sent it straight on to you without opening it (I concluded it was BBC as it had a Belfast postmark). Mr Bullock[1] rang up from Belfast today terribly anxious for an answer. I thought it better to arrange at once as he has to fix up his programmes seven weeks ahead. The arrangements are that you are to broadcast a 'talk' about your version of Oedipus the King, referring to the fact that it is to be broadcast from Belfast a week later (Sept. 15) and that the players are going to America, making a sort of 'farewell' windup to the 'talk'[2]. (This for publicity for the Abbey)[3] At 8.40 you are to do fifteen minutes readings from your own poetry. I asked Bullock if you could do the readings with commentary, and he said you could do anything you liked! He also said that he proposed to add five guineas to the fee originally arranged as you were to broadcast the 'talk' as well as the readings! So you will get thirtyfive guineas....

I think you must write him at once 'to confirm' these arrangements—you might perhaps say you will be glad of the opportunity of meeting him again! (He told me on the phone that he had met you in the Abbey years ago when the Ulster players were there...[4]

By law it is necessary for you to send a copy of your 'talk' to be vetted. I have written to Mr Bullock to ask him to write to you at Coole IF HE WANTS THE COPY BEFORE FRIDAY NEXT.[5] I think it will be time enough when you get to Dublin. You could dictate it. You'll have to keep closely to the fifteen minutes in both cases—you can try the 'talk' out on me.

[1] Samuel Arthur Malcolm Bulloch (1879–1950), one of the founding members in 1923 of the Northern Drama League which emulated the aims of the DDL, was drama assistant for the BBC regional division in Belfast 1931–7; during that period he produced many plays by Irish playwrights, beginning with LR's *The Whiteheaded Boy* by the Abbey players (17 Feb. 1930), followed by WBY and AG's *Kathleen ni Houlihan* (17 Mar. 1930); a linen merchant, he was also involved in the purchase and sale of paintings.

[2] The BBC had established a broadcasting station in Belfast in 1924. WBY's first radio broadcast was to take place from the Belfast offices of the BBC on 8 Sept. 1931; a full report of his speech was published in the *Irish Times*, 8 Sept. 1931, under the title 'Greek Play over Radio. Abbey Players in Belfast. Mr. Yeats Explains the Broadcast'. The Abbey Theatre company was planning a tour of the United States and Canada from October 1931 to April 1932, their first return to North America since April 1914.

[3] The sentence is in MS in the margin; the broadcast and news of the company's tour received considerable newspaper attention.

[4] The Ulster Literary Theatre, founded in 1902 by Bulmer Hobson and David Parkhill ('Lewis Purcell'), from 1915 to 1934 known as the Ulster Theatre or Ulster Players, annually performed in Dublin at the Gaiety or Abbey Theatre. On 24 Apr. 1908, the Ulster Literary Theatre produced two plays at the Abbey, one of which was Rutherford Mayne's *The Drone*, in which 'Sam Bullock' was one of the actors.

[5] 'IF' underlined four times.

I asked him if it would be possible to have a try-out on the microphone before you actually do the thing, and he said it could easily be arranged & very much approved of the idea.[6] As your two doings are to be radiated from the London centres and you havent broadcasted before I think a try-out might be an advantage—you wont be able to tiger up and down the room as you usually do when you speak!

Heaven knows what Bullock's initials are...I couldnt get hold of Lennox or Perrin[7] to ask and had to write at once to confirm the telephone conversation. I made a squiggle which looked faintly like S T but not enough so as to be traceable. B.B.C. Belfast.

Please let me know when you come up and by what train, for Horse show starts on Tuesday and my hands will be very full![8]

George.

[MS] Met Jack today. He says he has <u>never</u> seen you in such good health![9]

[ALS]   COOLE PARK, GORT, CO. GALWAY.
                                          [1 Aug. 1931]

My dear Dobbs

I never got the B.B.C letter. I have written confirming your talk on the phone. If I am to send that talk for Friday I shall go to Dublin on Tuesday dictate it to you if I may on Wednesday. I could not do it here. I dont want to write it. I want to dictate it, that I may feel I am talking.

I have paid Rafferty bill £7.15.6

                                                    Yrs affly
                                                    WB Yeats

Lady G. sometimes asks the same question several times then remembers that she has done so & laughs. Her judgement is vigerous but her memory comes & goes.

---

[6] This last clause in MS.

[7] John Henry Perrin (1900–55) was secretary of the Abbey Theatre from 1925 and from 1926 also business manager, until replaced in 1932 by Frederick Eric Gorman (1882–1971), an actor in the company since 1908, who served as secretary for 32 years.

[8] During Horse Show week in early August Cuala always had a stall in the Royal Dublin Society exhibition hall.

[9] Jack and his devoted wife the artist Mary Cottenham 'Cottie' Yeats, née White (1863–1947), had paid one of their annual visits to Coole on 18 July 1931 and did not leave until after WBY arrived.

[ALS]   COOLE PARK, GORT, CO. GALWAY.
                                   ?Staturday or Sunday [1 or 2 Aug. 1931]

My dear Dobbs: For the last three days I have been tired with the effort of
my two poems & had a slight touch of 'poison day' & so disinclined to write
letters or do anything but make vague beginnings of my next poem. To day
I am full of life & hope to finish the poem.

   Last night Guy Gough & Margeret were alone with me in the breakfast
room & Guy said something to Margeret & I heard Margeret answer 'No
we could not ask that'. Presenly Margeret went out & I asked Guy what it
was & he said 'We think somebody should be with Lady Gregory as much
as possible' I suggested that as she wants to arrange old letters & continue
her memoirs she might be glad of a typist, & this typist if the right person
might to some extent watch over her. He went away very taken with the
idea. He seems anxious because Lady G. gets attacks of bleeding from the
nose. I think I convinced both Guy and Margeret that they have no sufficient reason to think Lady Gregorys pains are more than rheumatism. They
may be more—but she has had even more violent pains from rheumatism.
Last night I spoke to her of the typist, but she said she will wait till she is
better.[1] I am afraid therefore I shall have to be here a good deal not continuously but from time to time until we know more. Lady G wants you &
the children but not until the grapes are fit to eat. She says there is nothing
now worth eating in the garden.

   I was delighted with your letter & Annes admiration for Desdemona.
I hope however that she herself has not idealised Othello's complexion It
might be an embarassment in five years time.

   I have not forgotten about the Vice regal dinner. Will it be time enough
if I come up on Wednesday?

                                                       Yrs affecly
                                                       WB Yeats

[ALS]   COOLE PARK, GORT, CO. GALWAY.
                                              Saturday [15 Aug. 1931]

My dear Dobbs: I have just noticed that my post card for Anne was not
posted.[1] This was not my fault—except that I should have remembered that

---

   [1] Eventually AG acquiesced sufficiently to invite Charles Simpson Millington (?1884–1965),
to Coole for the week-end of 10–12 Oct. 1931 to work on some of her correspondence and discuss her diaries. Appointed business manager and secretary of the Abbey Theatre in 1918, he
left in 1926 to become a journalist and eventually editor of the *Farmer's Gazette*. He remained a
trusted friend and adviser to AG, and after her death was invited to edit her letters.

   [1] On 10 Aug. ABY was in Elpis nursing home having a septic ingrown toenail removed.

Lady G. forgets. I have just had confirmation from Slattery (private) of my view that Lady G has rheumatism & nothing else, & given this information to Guy Gough & Margeret. His message (in a letter from Gogarty) was marked confidential but it is right that you should know

I came back from Renvylle yesterday I saw both my plays & both went well.² The Hotel was quite full. Today we lunched at Lough Cutra & am longing for quiet & routine. You write charming letters—that bit about Anne & the underground is a delight.³

I enclose the Cobden-Sanderson letter. I also enclose a letter from somebody in Belfast.⁴ I thought of answering it—but you may have already as he speaks of another letter.

I brought away with me the typed copy of my 'patter'.⁵

> Yours affly
> WBYeats

[ALS]   COOLE PARK, GORT, CO. GALWAY.
                                          [17] August [1931]

My dear Dobbs: I have returned proofs to Cobden Sanderson¹, & said that I hope their words about paying so much a page do not mean that they are paying for verse & prose at the same rate. I wonder what their origonal letter said.

---

² After opening Renvyle as a hotel in 1930, Gogarty wanted to create 'an Irish Bayreuth', 'to get rid of jazz, and to give visitors to the beautiful scenery of the West an opportunity to see, too, the outcome of such scenery in the world of Irish art' (*Irish Times*, 12 Aug. 1931, 13). From 11 to 18 Aug. 1931 the Abbey Theatre Ballet and the Abbey players performed two of WBY's Noh plays, *The Only Jealousy of Emer* and *The Cat and the Moon*, at the hotel before their production at the Abbey on 21 Sept. 1931. Although advertised as the first production, *The Cat and the Moon* had been produced on the Abbey stage with *The Only Jealousy of Emer* on 9 May 1926 for a DDL annual general meeting.

³ This letter from GY is missing.

⁴ Both enclosures missing.

⁵ What he was planning to say in his broadcast in Belfast on 8 Sept. 1931, but not a finished prepared speech; later he would use the same word to describe a method of reading verse half-way between singing and speaking.

¹ Richard Cobden-Sanderson (1884–1964), son of the artist and book-binder Thomas James Cobden-Sanderson (1840–1922), who under the influence of William Morris founded the Doves Press with Emery Walker, established his own publishing house in London, publishing Eliot's *The Waste Land* among other modernist works. Yeats contributed 'Lullaby' to his anthology *The New Keepsake* (Nov. 1931), which was illustrated by Rex Whistler.

Rossi[2] goes to morrow. He is a charming person very pleasing to Lady Gregory. MacLaughlin[3] turned up yesterday quite as stony & egotistical as I expected, Lady G. faded out of the room very early in his visit but I doubt if he even noticed. I felt that he was going round a kind of golf course & that Coole was one of the holes. He had a young Oxford student with him, timid & shy. He was standing near Lord Longford when Lord Longford hit the man in the face for singing 'God save the King'. Then the man he hit said 'I will apologise to any English man present but to no Irish man'. His 'God save the King' came when the band played at the beginning; I did not gather what he had to apologise for. There seemed to have been general confusion, and much petting & pacifying.

Rossi was very troubled at lunch—the 17th is his unluccky day & he upset the salt & yesterday upset a teacup, got wet in the rain & had to wear dress-clothes all day. 'Three times I have been shamed' he said. Round about the 17th every month such things are liable to happen.

Yrs ev
WB Yeats

[ALS]   Coole Park | Gort | Co Galway
                                          Wednesday [19 Aug. 1931]

My dear Dobbs

Let me know if you want me up for any particular day. As Lady G. despairs of the fruit ripening, she asks to bring the children here when ever you like. (could we not take Vincent & Killarney in the trip).[1] Great peace has descended upon us, yesterday & the day before there were American & I was Cooks guide.[2] Yesterday morning Rossi left. I have never known Lady G. take to any stranger as she took to Rossi. He is certainly a cheerful lucid

---

[2] Mario Manlio Rossi (1895–1971), an Italian philosopher and scholar whose annotated editions of the philosopher George Berkeley's *The Commonplace Book* (1924) and *The Principles of Human Knowledge* (1925) led Joseph Hone to invite him to collaborate on *Bishop Berkeley: His Life, Writings and Philosophy* (1931) to which WBY wrote an introduction. Having been invited to join WBY at Coole for a few days, his reminiscences of the visit and the deep impression both his hosts made on him were published in *Viaggio in Irlanda* (Milan, 1932), translated by Joseph Hone for the Cuala Press (1933). Later works included *Swift, or the Egotist* (1934) and *Storia d'Inghilterra* (1944, 4 vols.). I am indebted to Professor Fiorenzo Fantaccini for details of Rossi's life and work.

[3] Unidentified but described by AG: 'Sunday was spoiled however by a visitor of Yeats…He was English, very loud voiced & common. I slipped away as soon as I had poured out tea' (*Journals*, ii. 622–3).

[1] WBY had been a guest of the Vincents of Muckross House in 1926, before Mrs Vincent's death (see 26 Aug. 1926).

[2] AG's *Journal* mentions an unidentified Miss McHaye.

person & his English is no longer a strain. Yesterday one visitor was Mrs Brandenburg³ (she interviewed me in Dublin & came that I might correct the result) a harmless, likabl creature, dull by nature but not like MacLaughlen dull by human contrivance. I have just finished breakfast, I am in bed & idle. Yesterday I finished the poem I have worked on since I arrived & to begin a new one want a quotation from MacKenna's translation of Plotinus⁴ & to get that I should have to go into the Drawing Room in my pjamas. The morning is blessed. Owing to Gogorty furious driving⁵—our Ford passed every thing on the road, including a Rolls Royce—my head hit the top of the car twice. I had a headache until last night, now it is gone.

Yours affly
WB Yeats

[ALS]   Coole Park | Gort | Co Galway
August 30¹ [1931]

My dear Dobbs: The children have now quite ousted Rossi in Lady Gregorys mind. She speaks often of 'those dear children'.² Last night she said 'I like them, not merely because they are your children but for their own sake, they are dear good children.' Mrs Leach (Rita Daly) was here yesterday & she was in Gort that day. Do you remember Anne saying they had not seen her & your saying, she must have been some where about. She saw Anne & Michael quarrelling as to who should drive the poney & the driver take the rains himself that he might turn round the trap; after that she lost sight of them. I have begun a new poem to day, the reduction in the amount of meat having restored my vigour.³

The Play Lennox was asking about is a masterpiece. The best play we have been sent in years. The Scene is a public house in a little country town, & the speach & life of both is represented with obvious accurecy & fullness of knowledge, & yet the writer seems to me educated, to think like a continental dramatist. Why on earth did not Lennox say so insted of leaving me with the impression that it was some new Cork discovery. All he said

---

³ Possibly Rebecca Brugsma, see letter of 26 July 1929 and note.
⁴ The poem was probably 'The Delphic Oracle on Plotinus'. Stephen MacKenna (1872–1935), journalist, Gaelic nationalist, and close friend of Synge, is best known for his translation of Plotinus, to which he devoted much of his life; in 1924, after he had left Ireland for good, he refused the medal awarded him by the Royal Irish Academy and would later reject nomination to the Irish Academy of Letters.
⁵ Apparently Gogarty, a daredevil pilot whether in his car or an aeroplane, drove WBY to Coole from Renvyle the previous week.

¹ On Fitzwilliam Square stationery, crossed out; dated both 29 and 30 August.
² GY, ABY, and MBY were at Coole 23–8 August.
³ 'Remorse for Intemperate Speech'.

was that 'he rather likes it'. It should have gone into the bill weekes ago & it might have changed everything⁴

If you are sending pants (which you need not as I shall be in Dublin on Friday) send pjama trowsers also. I have three pjama jackets & one pair of pjama trowsers. Of course I only use the trowsers as a dressing gown but the maids may not know that & be shocked. I merely record this matter that we may not forget.

Yrs affly
WB Yeats

I have an immense wad of your penny stamps

[ALS]   COOLE PARK, | GORT, CO. GALWAY.

Sept 2 [1931]

My dear Dobbs
    I forgot that womans type written book—Mrs Dacher, or Dackle or Dachel.¹ The woman Lilly did the panel picture for. You might send it me registered & her address. No news here. I had a pleasant journey.

Yrs ev
WB Yeats

[ALS]   42, FITZWILLIAM SQUARE, | DUBLIN.¹

Sept 12 [1931]

My dear Dobbs: I have been re-writing 'The Mother of God' poem, & am in the middle of a new poem. I have heard from Miss Grigsby & your mother praising my broadcast & Lady Gregory has had a letter from Francis Hackett²

---

⁴ *Things that are Caesar's* by Paul Vincent Carroll (1899–1968) shared the Abbey Theatre prize for new plays in 1931 with *Temporal Powers* by Teresa Deevy (1894–1963), and was first produced at the Abbey on 15 Aug. 1932; his play *The Watched Pot* had been produced by the Experimental Theatre in the Peacock Theatre on 17 Nov. 1930, directed by LR. Four more plays by Carroll would be produced by the Abbey over the next twelve years including *Shadow and Substance* (1936) which won awards both in New York and Dublin; the rejection of *The White Steed* in 1938 (which won the New York Drama Critics' Circle award) led to a temporary break with the Abbey. In 1942 Carroll helped found the Glasgow Citizens' Theatre.

¹ GY has annotated this 'Daking'; see GY's letter 3 June 1931.

¹ Although on this stationery, written from Coole.

² See 11 July 1930 for Miss Grigsby; Francis Dominick Hackett (1883–1962), novelist, historian, and former literary critic for the *New Republic*, lived 1928–37 in Co. Wicklow with his wife novelist Signe Toksvig (1891–1983); reminiscences of their time in Ireland are published in *Signe Toksvig's Irish Diaries 1926–1937*, ed. Lis Pihl (Dublin, 1999).

also praising it. Robin Flower[3], the gaelic scholour is here, quite a pleasant person; Lady Gregory does not know how long he is staying. Lady Gregory is not so well, more crippled, & this morning had bleeding from the nose, & her memory a little worse. Yesterday I heard her tell somebody that she had been crippled with rheumatism 'for the last fortneight'. I shall not come up until the 18th—as I shall lie down at once—I shall be quite fresh for the ball[4]—that I may take the burden of visitors a little longer. When I come up I have told Lady Gregory I will see Gogorty about her bleeding from the nose. So far as I can make out she never spoke of it to Gogorty or Slattery.

You might show Lilly that tinted paper in the 'Vision'—Lolly is away—that steps may be taken to get similar paper without delay.[5]

Tell me how Anne liked 'the Underground' when she saw it near.[6]

Yours affly
WB Yeats

Lady G's comment on the photograph of Lennox & his bride in 'The Irish Press' was 'like an "f" and an i—if'. She added 'I would have thought a permanent engagement might have been better'.[7]

[ALS]   COOLE PARK, GORT, CO. GALWAY.
Thursday [17 Sept. 1931]

My dear George—I return to-morrow <u>by the first train</u>. So I shall be with you about two. I cannot write more as Lady Gregory is waiting for this. I plan to get back here second train on Saturday

Yrs ev
WB Yeats

Lady G decided for first train—she takes it herself[1]

---

[3] Robin Ernest William Flower, 'Bláithín' (1881–1946), deputy keeper of MSS in the British Museum, was a poet and translator who spent much of his time on the Dingle peninsula and is now perhaps best known for his translation of *The Islandman* by Tomás Ó Criomthain [O'Crohan], published in 1934, and the much-anthologized 'Pangur Bán'.

[4] A farewell supper dance was being held in the Metropole Ballroom for the Abbey players on 18 September before they sailed on 7 October from Southampton on the *Aquitania* for their North American tour, the first since 1914; approximately 500 attended, and the dancing did not end until 3 a.m.

[5] Perhaps for his *Stories of Michael Robartes and his Friends* being set by Cuala; the drawings by Dulac for *A Vision* (1925) were printed on brown tinted paper to give the impression of age.

[6] As part of their school holidays GY took MBY and ABY to London for five days after WBY's broadcast in Belfast on 8 September.

[7] LR was always suspected of being homosexual; although the Robinsons remained together, the marriage was not entirely happy.

[1] AG was suffering from so much pain that when WBY went up for the Abbey ball, she

[ALS¹]   Coole Park | Gort | Co Galway
                                              Tuesday [6 Oct. 1931]

My dear Dobbs: please send me some paper for loose-leaf book (I enclose
page). I think you will find a package in the drawer in my desk. I know
there a lot some where. Please also phone Hodges & Figgis² & ask why they
have not yet sent me Ciceros Letters (Loeb Series). I have written to Michael
apologising for not having said good by.³

    We had an easy journey, & I have done a good days work.

                                                              Yrs ev
                                                           WB Yeats

Just heard a story of Dr Coyne.⁴ In a state of intoxacation he drove his
motor car into a wall so that his wife fell through the glass wind-screne.
He forgot her existence drove home & went to bed. She was picked up
on the road side, brought into a cottage, & sent to hospital. She came
out after some weeks her face all scarred & batterd. They are devoted to
one another & when ever he gets a good look at her he swears off drink
for ever. He is hesitating whether he will support the new government
(Republican I suppose) or the old; as he has it seems good offers from
both.

    Please send me some note paper.

went to Dublin to see Dr Slattery, who admitted he could do nothing for her except prescribe
drugs, which she was reluctant to accept.

    ¹ On Fitzwilliam Square stationery with address struck out. He accompanied AG back to
Coole on 5 October and from now until mid-March WBY remained at Coole, with only a
few brief trips back to Dublin.

    ² Hodges & Figgis of Dawson Street was Dublin's oldest and largest bookshop, established
in the 18th century.

    ³ See next letter.

    ⁴ Gerard Morgan Coyne (?1899–1970), dispensary doctor for Ballinasloe and Aughrim for
forty years, was well known for his violent temper and determined stands on principle. A few
months later he was chastised by the local hospital board for refusing to continue attendance
on a child whose parents rejected hospitalization. In 1946 he was charged with careless driving
and breach of the peace, when he was represented by Sean MacBride, SC, and he continued
to make headlines throughout his career.

[ALCS¹]   at | Coole Park | Gort
                                                     Tuesday [6 Oct. 1931]

Dear Michael: I am so sorry I did not say good by to you. I was in a hurry
at the last, the taxi came too soon so I forgot.

Lady Gregory was very sorry you could not go to see her on Sunday² &
both she & I hope your cold is better. Forgive my only sending you a card
but I have run short of note paper.³

                                                     Yours affectionly
                                                     WB Yeats

[ALS]   COOLE PARK, | GORT, CO. GALWAY.
                                                     Oct. 13 [1931]

My dear Dobbs:

I have said each day, I wont write until to morrow because I am sure to
get a letter next post However I remember that I am the superior sex &
must set you a good example.

I have now finished—all but the bit from Cicero—the section of the
Great Year.¹ All that remains is some revision of 'A Packet for Ezra Pound'
and a few final paragraphs to wind up the book. All my coming together, all
my besetting problems solved [h]as given me a sense of power & joy I have
not had for a long time. I shall be soon back at verse—I did a new lyric the
other day, quite good but not much attempted.

> Things out of perfection sail
> And all their swelling canvas wear;
> Nor can the self-begotten fail,
> Though man's bitter heart suppose
> Building yard, storm beaten shore,
> Winding sheet & swadling clothes.

It is a 'Tom the Lunatic' poem & a reply to the Dancers song about the
'One that is perfect' 'among birds beasts & men'²

---

¹ Written on Fitzwilliam Square stationery, address struck out.

² AG had gone to Dublin with WBY to consult Dr Slattery.

³ AG has written at the sides of the card 'He has plenty of notepaper here when I saw this
I took him a supply. AG.'

¹ 'Book IV: The Great Year of the Ancients', Section III, begins with a quotation from
Cicero, 'By common consent men measure the year…by the return of the sun' (245–6 of *A
Vision 1937*) and in Section VII refers to Cicero's belief that the Great Year began 'with an
eclipse at the time of Romulus' (p. 251).

² An early draft of 'Old Tom Again' in the series 'Words for Music Perhaps', which when
published follows 'The Dancer at Cruachan and Cro-Patrick'.

Here is the latest chronicle of Coole. Some time ago the cook reported that Ellen the house maid had 'two suspicious characters' whom she named to visit her after dark. Lady Gregory admonished Ellen who denied all. A few days later the two men called to say they had never been near the house after dark. Then the cook wrote to Margeret that the two men had met the kitchen-maid on the avenue one afternoon pitched into her for tale-bearing & sent her home in tears. Last night Margeret came to say Guy Gough was going to see the C.I.D. about it to day. This morning, after a sleepless night, Lady Gregory decided that she would not have the milatery called out to keep order in her kitchen & sent a letter to Guy to say. Now she has had Ellen up. Ellen admits 'the suspicious characters' but says she is engaged to one of them, that they are to be married after Xmass & that the Cook & the kitchen maid are her enemies. For the moment we are happy but Margeret is expected.

Yours affly
WB Yeats

Thanks greatly about the Cicero[3], but I want manuscript paper for the loose leaf book. There is a packet in the study.

[TLS & MS]   42, FITZWILLIAM SQUARE, | DUBLIN.
October 15 [1931]

My dear William, do you know that you pocketed without even opening a letter from dear Mr O'Donovan (the income tax inspector)[1] addressed to ME, pocketted it in the inner pocket of your dark brown coat? I found it today because I was feeling that Peggy[2] had nothing to do and so might mend the lining which I had remembered was torn. Now that letter came when you were up for the Abbey farewell dance! I have taken all the blame on myself—except to Tulloch who is dealing with our claim now for reasons too long and complicated to go into—reasons forced on by that pocketted letter, incidentally.

I suppose you wont have contrite heart because you didnt mean to pocket the letter, didnt know you pocketted the letter, and so on, like Michael who used to refuse to apologise for accidentally kicking people on the grounds 'I didnt do it on purpose'.

[3] GY may have sent him annotations from George Pollexfen's volume of *Collectanea Hermetica*, ed. W. Wynn Westcott, a volume annotated by WBY, containing *Somnium Scipionis, The Golden Verses of Pythagoras*, and *The Symbols of Pythagoras* (the Yeats Library).

[1] D. O'Donovan, Income Tax surveyor for Dublin's 1st district.
[2] One of the two household maids.

Incidentally, Michael got a star for another 'composition', and has been told that he is a very good 'goal' (hockey).

Hope the lamps arrived, also writing paper, loose leaf, etc.

I like that poem—but I'm not sure if Ive misread the fourth line. You might re-write it to me.

[MS] 'Though man's bitter heart suppose?'[3]

G.

[TLS]   42, FITZWILLIAM SQUARE, | DUBLIN.
                                               October 16 [1931]

My dear Willy

I post you under separate cover the Berkeley[1] which arrived this morning—Its a nice handsome looking book, and it is most self-sacrificing of me to post it on to you at once instead of keeping it to look at over the week-end. However I'm amusing myself with the Drennan Letters[2] which came four days ago, and which are decidedly not of handsome appearance. Paper like the paper of Dail reports, a hideous navy-blue cover made of that slightly bumpy material which makes a mousey noise when scratched with the fingernail. The letters themselves are both 'amusing and instructive' as I was told on being given Mrs Gatty's 'Parables from Nature' as a school prize.[3] No, that's hardly fair on the Letters—they're amusing and interesting, at least to me who knows very little of that part of history. I've asked the Stationery Office Belfast to post a copy to Lady G. You can read 'em from her copy.

Great excitement in Dublin over the Coercion bill. I met Mrs O'Higgins twice—she told me a very interesting thing which I cannot tell you in a letter.[4]

³ WBY revised this line in 'Old Tom Again' to 'Though fantastic men suppose'.

¹ WBY had written an introduction for *Bishop Berkeley: His Life, Writings and Philosophy* (1931) by Joseph Hone and Mario Rossi, which was published by Faber and Faber in October 1931.

² *The Letters of William Drennan Being a Selection of the Correspondence ... between William Drennan, M.D., and his brother-in-law and sister, Samuel and Martha McTier during the years 1776–1819*, ed. D. A. Chart, were published by Her Majesty's Stationery Office in Belfast in 1931; William Drennan (1754–1820), a member of the Irish Volunteers, was a nationalist and poet who is said to have been the first to refer in print to Ireland as 'the emerald isle'.

³ Margaret Gatty, née Scott (1809–73), 19th-century author of books for children whose five-volume series *Parables from Nature* (1855–71) was internationally renowned, was also editor of a children's journal, *Aunt Judy's Magazine*.

⁴ Brigid Mary O'Higgins, née Cole (1898–1961), before her marriage a Professor of English at Knockbeg College in Carlow, was the widow of Kevin O'Higgins who, one of the ablest ministers in the Cosgrave administration, had been assassinated in July 1927. The government, under the leadership of William T. Cosgrave's beleaguered Cumann na nGaedheal Party, had recently pushed through the Constitutional Amendment Bill to set up the Military Tribunal to try political offences; debates referred to it as another 'coercion bill'.

I was not able to find O'Connell's[5] address. It is probably in your address book. IF IT IS NOT 24 Trafalgar Terrace Monkstown will you please write to her and tell her the correct address. I told her the number in T. Terrace from my imperfect memory. Her address is Knockbeg, Cowper Gardens, Rathmines. In the meantime she is writing a non-commital letter asking him to come and see her, a letter which can be returned through the dead letter office.

Jack and Cottie are keeping themselves to themselves at the moment. …although on Saturday when Anne and Michael and I were returning home we saw him in the distance and the children said with one voice 'he is crossing the road to speak to us!'

Have you been reading the Scala sweepstake case?[6] The morning papers did not give as full an account as the evening ones. One very pet thing was Mrs Apicella's evidence about the seance that Scala held to enquire of the spirits whether he held a winning ticket. 'He kept on calling on Rasputin, and I thought he said rice pudding and he got so angry he wanted to turn me out of the room.'

When I have [not] been prancing[7] in the evenings I've been going to bed at 8.30 or 9 every evening (surrounded with base fiction) and I feel very much the better for it.

Yours affly
George.

[ALS[1]]   at Coole Park | Gort | Co Galway
Saturday [17 Oct. 1931]

My dear Dobbs: Jepson O'Connell's address is 21 Trafalgar Terrace, Monkstown. Berkeley has not come yet. The electric lamp came some days ago (you say lamps. Were there two?) & is most useful, though such things have too brief a life for a reading lamp.

I am very contrite endeed about that letter. I have no memory of it. I must have found it on the hall-table. I hope it has not up set things. You should have put the blame on me.

Russell is here, arrived yesterday but I doubt if there is any grain in the mill at present.[2]

[5] Lt.-General Jephson 'Ginger' O'Connell (1887–1944), deputy chief of the Free State Army and assistant to Mulcahy during the Civil War, was at this time director of the Intelligence Branch, later director of the Military Archives; he was introduced to WBY by Dermott MacManus, his fellow officer in the Free State army.

[6] For three months Dublin and London newspapers carried details of a case being heard in Dublin's High Court concerning the suit of two London hairdressers, Antonio Apicella and Matteo Constantino, against café proprietor Emilio Scala, also of London, claiming a share of the first prize in the Irish Hospitals Sweepstake on the Grand National.

[7] A favourite word of GY's for a pleasant activity.

[1] On Fitzwilliam Square stationery, address crossed out.

[2] WBY was hoping to persuade AE to collaborate on the foundation of an Irish Academy of Letters.

To day I found that all I had to do to 'The Packet for Ezra Pound' was to shorten & that I did so when I hear about Cicero I shall be through. Imagine the shock when I got Cicero in six volumes, 10/- each. As I could not find the letter I mention I wrote to Pursur[3] & if I hear in time I think I shall send back half of them on some excuse—30/- is quite enough to pay for verefying a reference.

Lady Gregory has the door's locked every night at about 8.30, so Ellen will probably upset a window-box one of these evenings. She said it was quite right to lock the door these dark nights & suggested that she herself should keep the key. This was not allowed. The trouble about her seems to be that she is in no need of the advice Wilfred Blunt[4] used to give his women friends 'get engaged but never get married'.

You write most amusing letters

Yours affecly
WB Yeats

Yes I meant

'Though mans bitter heart suppose'. Is it wrong? I felt a doubt. 'Does suppose', <would perhaps be all right> with 'does' left out <Perhaps I should> write

No here is a better version
First two lines unchanged then
'Nor may the self-begotten fail
Though fantastic men suppose
Building-yard & stormy shore,
Winding-sheet & swadling-clothes.'

Monday
Russell has gone to Dublin. A wire came to say Brian had got a job and was leaving for England to day & Russell could not leave the invalided Mrs Russell alone.[5]

---

[3] Louis Claude Purser (1854–1932), fellow and vice-provost (1924–7) of TCD, Professor of Latin with special expertise in Cicero, was, like his sister the artist Sarah Henrietta Purser (1848–1943), an old family friend; at one time considered 'interested' in ECY, he occasionally served as proof-reader for Cuala publications and patiently answered WBY's queries concerning classical references.

[4] Wilfrid Scawen Blunt (1840–1922), poet and activist who had been imprisoned in Galway jail in 1888; the Yeatses were apparently unaware that AG herself had had an affair with him.

[5] There remains some confusion over AE's eldest son, as there might have been two Brians, one of whom, Brian William Angus Russell, born 30 Jan. 1899, may have died in infancy; the second, Bryan Hartley Russell (*CL II* and *IV*), who died in 1977, had for a number of years worked in India and Australia but finally settled and married in England. AE's other surviving son Diarmuid ('Dermot') Conor Russell (1902–73) was assistant to his father on the *Irish Statesman* for three years before joining his brother in India in 1926, then in 1929 settling in the United States, where he married and became a successful literary agent. AE's wife Violet Rose, née Hunt (1869–1932), died of cancer on 3 Feb. 1932 after an illness of almost ten years.

[ALS¹]   Coole Park | Gort
                                                  Tuesday [20 Oct. 1931]

My dear Dobbs: I enclose a letter of Pursers.² Could you look in Cudworths
'Intellectual Systems of the World'. You will find it under 'sibyl' or 'sibyl-
lene Oracle' in the Index. Cicero speaks of Ceasar in connection with the
great year & uses the words that 'neither gods nor men would tolerate a
king in Rome'. Ceasar had thought of having himself repres[ent]ed as the
king fortold by the Oracle. We have two copies of Cudworth but the one
with an index is in three volumes, an eighteenth century or early nineteenth
century edition.³ If the referrence is precise do not trouble Purser but if it
is, as I expect, merely to a letter to 'Atticus' you might ask his help. There
are 3 vols of letters to 'Atticus'. I don't want the passage I want merely the
referrence. I am writing to Purser.

No Berkeley yet. The Drennan letters came yesterday. Lady G. will write
& thank you.

Russell went to Dublin yesterday. He has changed very much. Powers
himself in superlatives, but came in from the lake with descriptions of the
spirits as in old days. As in old days too he resented any suggestion that they
were not just what they seemed to be.

You saw I have no doubt that Charles Ricketts died a weak or so ago of
sudden heart failure. I wrote a letter of condolence to Sturge Moore but as
he has not replied & as his wifes name & not his was among the names of
people at the Memoreal Service I am afraid he is ill.

Gerald Heard⁴ has written to ask me if I would like to broadcast in London on my next visit. I am writing to say I would. I hope therefore to earn
my expenses.

                                                    Yours affectionly
                                                    WB Yeats

¹ On Fitzwilliam Square stationery, address struck out.
² Louis Purser replied on 19 October asking for the reference in Cudworth that led WBY
to Cicero.
³ The 1678 edition of Ralph Cudworth, *The True Intellectual System of the Universe* (London,
1678), presented to WBY by Emery Walker in 1917, and the three-volume edition (London,
1845) are both in the Yeats Library.
⁴ Henry FitzGerald 'Gerald' Heard (1889–1971), prolific author of historical and theological
studies, a psychical researcher, mystic, and philosopher, was secretary to Horace Plunkett in
Dublin and London from 1919 until 1929 when his own career as lecturer took over; 1930–4
he was the BBC's first science commentator; in 1937 he accompanied his friend Aldous Huxley
to America, where he lectured briefly at Duke University on historical anthropology before,
inspired by Vedanta teaching, he founded Trabuco College in California, devoted to the
study of comparative religions. WBY was especially interested in Heard's *The Ascent of Humanity* (1929), a study of the evolution of human consciousness which was awarded the British
Academy's Hertz prize.

[ALS]   42, FITZWILLIAM SQUARE, | DUBLIN.[1]
                                            Oct 22 [1931]

My dear Dobbs: Purser has sent me all I want & I have now finished 'The Vision'. Still no sign of the Berkeley but a pleasant letter from Rossi to day praising my Swift.[2] I have also had a long letter from Sturge-Moore. He has been asked to write the official biography Have you an 'Observer' with his article on Ricketts?[3] He sent it to me, at 42 I suppose for it has not come here.

There [is] no news of any kind.

                                            Yours affly
                                            WB Yeats

[TLS]   42, FITZWILLIAM SQUARE, | DUBLIN.
                                          October 26 [1931]

My dear William

Here are two very important questions which you <u>must</u> answer, and answer at once.

I. Will you be able to produce 'The Dreaming of the Bones'. (for Sunday Nov 29)

II. Are you coming up to see Miss de Valois when she comes over the first week of November?

These two things are inseparable.[1] <u>IF YOU DO NOT FEEL THAT YOU CAN COME TO DUBLIN YOU MUST LET ME KNOW AT ONCE</u>. I think you are probably feeling that you cannot leave Coole, but I must know quite definitely. If you do not think that you can come up to produce 'Dreaming of the Bones' I must see Miss de Valois, and must also try to work up some people to go to the Ballet.—the Lodge, the Alphands[2] etc.

[1] GY has noted 'from Coole'.

[2] On 8 Oct. 1931 WBY had sent Rossi a copy of the *Dublin Magazine* (October–December 1931), which included the first half of his 'Commentary' to *The Words upon the Window-Pane*.

[3] T. Sturge Moore, 'Charles Ricketts, his Life and his Friends: "A Marvellous Human Relationship"', *The Observer*, Sunday 11 Oct. 1931, describes the 'incomparable' Ricketts, his generosity, and his long-time partnership with Charles Shannon.

[1] The Abbey School of Ballet had been established in 1927 and the first dance performance was in January 1928, by students from the School performing with de Valois's students from London. While the Abbey players were on their American tour, the directors instituted an occasional series of performances, entitled 'Mainly ballet: The Abbey Directors' Sunday Entertainments'. WBY's dance play *The Dreaming of the Bones*, written in 1917 and published in 1919, received its first production at the Abbey on 6 Dec. 1931.

[2] 'the Lodge' refers to the residence of the Governor-General, James McNeill. Charles H. Alphand (1879–1942) was the first French Minister Plenipotentiary appointed to the Irish Free State, serving 1930–2, and was later ambassador to Russia and Switzerland.

If you are not coming up for the first week of November I want to know in order that I may arrange to come to Coole. I want to be in Dublin for <u>November 18th</u> for a meeting of the French Society. You make things a little difficult by not writing any sort of plans. If you cannot make 'plans', I think you must say so in order that I may know what to do about a number of problems that I find difficult.

I want a definite answer about my problems <u>I</u> and <u>II</u>.

Please do not think that I am 'feeling neglected'—your own phrase!

Dobbs.

[ALS]   COOLE PARK, | GORT, CO. GALWAY.
Oct 27 [1931]

My dear Dobbs

Yes I will come up to see Miss de Valois? Margeret is in Dublin to day but returns I think to-morrow. She should be here daily when I am away. I told her I should be in Dublin first week in November. Wire date of Miss de Valois arrival

I can start 'Dreaming of the Bones' & then come up in time to take last rehersals; or at worst to see a dress rehersal etc.

I have been waiting to hear from you about Miss De Valois & other things. I wrote you several letters which may or may not have reached you.

Margeret is excited about the recent exhibition of embroidery in London—there is still another exhibition there now—its coming into fashion again.[1] I asked her for a list of possible things for Lilly to make. She told me some but said she would wait until you came down & talk it over with you.

Yrs affectly
WB Yeats

---

[1] *The Times* of 3 Oct. 1931 described a retrospective exhibition at the Batsford Gallery of the architectural drawings, furniture, fabrics, and other decorations by C. F. Annesley Voysey (1857–1941), a pioneer of the Arts and Crafts movement. On 24 Oct. 1931 *The Times* gave an extensive account of the Exhibition of Contemporary Needlecraft at 16 Bruton Street, under the patronage of the Queen, who lent some pieces from her collection; on 26 October the Lord Mayor opened an exhibition and sale of British handicrafts at the Drapers' Hall, organized by the Home Arts and Industries Association.

[TLS]   42, FITZWILLIAM SQUARE, | DUBLIN.
                                          Thursday [29 Oct. 1931]

My dear William

I have just wired to you 'Valois arrives November seven performance postponed until December six'. She is bringing over the new ballet mistress and
I dont think the ballet could be got into trim—granted the change of teacher
etc—in time for the 29th Nov. I rang up Perrin and he entirely agreed. I did
not know until yesterday that Miss de Valois was not arriving until the 7th.

If you will come up on the 9th (she arrives on 7th and probably will be
busy all Sunday going through things with Miss Patrick[1]) I will fix up a meeting for Tuesday 10th with you and Walter[2] and her.

Unless I hear to the contrary I shall expect you by the first train on <u>Mon-
day November 9th</u> and shall meet you at Broadstone.

I didnt send the Berkeley because after I had written to you I glanced at
the end of it and found that the last thirty odd pages had been bound with
a different book altogether! I returned the copy to Faber and asked them to
post you another. It was an 'advance copy' so they may have had to wait
for the general edition. Do you remember how we once bought a crime
fiction because of its name and when opening it at home found a ghastly
sentimental novel within the cover 'The Eternal Love' or something similar,
whereas the cover said 'Murder at Keyes'.

I hear that all 'the girls' in the Abbey Company were most terribly sea-
sick on their journey over and that poor Delaney[3] lost nearly two stone—
this is not of course strictly true, but let us hope there is some truth in the
statement! Their first month has had to be completely altered as regards
performances as some of the places they were going to have 'diseases' and

[1] de Valois sent over her most promising students, with Vivienne Bennett (1905–78) who
opened the School, and Sara Patrick, née Payne, Mrs Dermot Kelly (1907–93), daughter
of Ben Iden Payne, as the first ballet teacher; Bennett later turned to classical acting and
created The Market Theatre, and Patrick moved on to become choreographer at the
Cambridge Festival Theatre and later taught at the Royal Ballet School, continuing to
work closely with de Valois. Patrick was replaced at the Abbey by Nesta Chilcote Brooking
(1906–2006), who was trained in the Cecchetti method, danced at the Old Vic, co-founded
the Dance Theatre which was active during the Second World War, and then established
the highly successful Brooking School of Ballet and General Education in London. De
Valois occasionally performed herself, while arranging the choreography for most of WBYs
dance plays during this period.

[2] Walter Starkie.

[3] Maureen Delany (1888–1961) had first performed with the 'second company' when the
theatre last visited America in 1914 and remained one of the Abbey's most popular comic
actors until her death in 1961.

are therefore 'in quarantine'. However the Alber people[4] got out new advertisements etc and made new bookings.

> Yours affly
> Dobbs.

[TLS]   42, FITZWILLIAM SQUARE, | DUBLIN.
                                               [?31 Oct. 1931]

My dear William

If you want a rehearsal or more than one rehearsal while you are in Dublin from November 9th, please wire by return stating your ideas about the cast. These people are all very busy and must have notice. To say nothing of the fact that you may not agree to my suggestions!

Young Man	O'Gorman (Lame Beggar, in Cat and Moon)
Young woman	Hilda Lynch
Stranger	Stephenson
First Musician	O'Neill (1st. Mus. in Cat)[1]

Hilda Lynch may not do, but was v. good in school of acting. Might be given a try-out anyway.

I suggest O'Gorman for the Young Man rather than Stephenson because O'Gorman speaks well but with a terrific natural accent! And as he was 'in the Post Office' in the play...etc...

---

[4] The extensive Abbey Theatre tour (seventy-nine centres from October 1931 to April 1932, but avoiding New York and Chicago) had been arranged by Alber & Wickes of Boston and New York, 'Managers of World Celebrities', responsible for managing all four of the Abbey Theatre tours 1931–8. Elbert A Wickes (1884–1975) and his co-manager Louis John Alber (1879–1962) were theatrical impresarios, producers, and concert and lecture managers.

[1] Performers remaining in Dublin were those not on permanent contract or who had recently graduated from the Abbey School of Acting. William 'Billy' O'Gorman (1903–66), who was a member of the company for twenty years, would later co-produce Lyric Theatre productions with Austin Clarke (1896–1974) and as president of the Catholic Stage Guild become a well-known adjudicator, did perform the role of the Young Man. The Stranger was John Stephenson (1889–1963) who had for some years performed in DDL productions and at the Abbey, as early as 1925 earning Joseph Holloway's admiration for his clear speaking and singing voice and later selected by WBY to sing his ballads, eventually leaving the Abbey to work as a freelance producer before joining the Radio Eireann Drama Department, where he was a producer and actor from 1947 to his death. The Singer (First Musician) was Joseph O'Neill, a newcomer who had performed in WBY's play *The Cat and the Moon* and would also dance with the ballet company. Hilda Lynch (b. 1908) does not seem to have joined the company and the part of the Young Woman was performed by Nesta Brooking, newly appointed teacher to the School of Ballet. WBY's *The Cat and the Moon* had its first performance at the Abbey on 21 Sept. 1931, alongside *Fanny's First Play* by Bernard Shaw.

Do do something about it all! No letter this morning

G.

Parts are all typed.

[ALS[1]] 42, FITZWILLIAM SQUARE, | DUBLIN.
Nov 1 [1931]

My dear Dobbs: I will come up on the day you say. I have just finished a beautiful & exciting second part to my commentary on the Swift play. I will bring it up & you can type it perhaps & O'Sullivan[2] can have it if he likes. It is an interpretation of the sceance in the light of Plotinus—Ennead V. 7—& is a thought that has been exciting me for weeks.[3] Those 'Wheels' will be very fine if I trundle them a little longer. I have a poem running vaguely in my head but it depends on a correspondence I am carrying on with Purser about a certain incident in Roman history

Lamp has come—What oil do I put in it.

That Mrs Pearson[4] who plaged us at Killiney a year ago has written to Lady Gregory from Scotland the same sort of vague letter. Lady Gregory wired 'regret impossible to see you' Then came another long vague letter proposing herself for the end of this week & yesterday Lady Gregory wired 'cannot recieve your visit.'

Lady Gregorys rheumetism has gone to the other side & up into her back & her left wrist has swollen up so it is I conclude just rheumatism. She gets about with difficulty but has just been round the place in her donkey cart. She reads Trollope to me every evening. I am working harder than I have worked for a long time being very well; but I hate not seeing you. Still I would not have you come down here till it is necessary—for I think you see much more of life when you are not burdened by my distaste for late hours & many voices. There is really no hurry about this vol VII of my

---

[1] Written from Coole.

[2] Both parts of the commentary to *The Words upon the Window-Pane* were destined for his volume *Wheels and Butterflies*, where the 'wheels' were the four introductions planned as 'a scheme of intellectual nationalism'; the first part was published in Seumas O'Sullivan's *The Dublin Magazine* (October–December 1931) and the second part in the January–March 1932 issue.

[3] WBY considered Stephen MacKenna 'the consummate translator of Plotinus'; here he is working from volume iv: *The Divine Mind, Being the Treatises of the Fifth Ennead* (London, 1926), with specific reference to the Seventh Tractate, 'Is There an Ideal Archetype of Particular Beings?'; in his Notes to *The Words upon the Window-Pane* he quotes from the last line of the first section: 'There is no need to baulk at this limitlessness in the Intellectual; it is an infinitude having nothing to do with number or part; what we may think of it as its outgoing is no other than its characteristic Act.'

[4] Unidentified.

collected edition, unless Macmillan says there is. But write some times Your
letters are the best I have ever recieved they are so gay & vivid
        Love to Anne & Micael

                                        Yrs affly
                                     WB Yeats

[ALS]   42, FITZWILLIAM SQUARE, | DUBLIN.
                                    Sunday [1 Nov. 1931]

My dear Willy

    I have posted to you by the same post a large envelope marked <u>immediate</u>.

    You will see that the claim is (Gt. Britain) for 467 pounds odd. This (minus
agents' fee) will help very much in the 1931–32 year—what with Cuala and
London Macmillan whose account for this year is £104....(Watt's commission not deducted). So I want it sent off immediately! And, do get it registered! When I say 'immediately', I only mean that I want it sent off by the
first convenient post; I dont mean that I want you to walk to Gort in order
to send it off after the usual messenger has left.

    Posts are so inconsequent that I dont know whether you will get this letter
first or the large envelope first.

    As you know, I dont want to get an 'advance' from Macmillan this year,
because I want to have the cash from the Collected Edition kept beautifully
isolated.

    Various newses—which I will keep until you arrive—from U.S.A. In
Dublin, Dossie Wright has a new daughter; Mr and Mrs Dermod O'Brien
went to the Arts Ball as '<u>Fig Leaves</u>'!; Denis Johnston went down to the
Abbey to ask permission to stay there for Hallowe'en night to lay the ghost.[1]
Now for God's sake keep this last piece of news to yourself and dont impart
it to Lady G. I havent heard yet what happened, if anything happened etc.
If you repeat this I shall never again write you a letter to Coole containing
anything frivolous or serious. Perrin rang me up yesterday (Saturday) to say
Denis was in the office asking if he could stay all night in the Abbey and
Starkie[2] was away, and he (Perrin) did not feel that he could give permission

---

  [1] Perhaps because of its earlier manifestation as a morgue, the Abbey Theatre had always
been considered haunted. William Denis Johnston (1901–84), a member of the DDL, had
achieved notoriety with the 1929 Gate Theatre production of his play *The Old Lady Says 'No!'*;
the Abbey directors invited him to direct *King Lear*, and in April 1931 produced his play *The
Moon in the Yellow River*; he was later a BBC writer and producer with distinguished service as
a war correspondent in the Second World War.
  [2] Walter Starkie.

on his own So I said I was sure that if you were in Dublin that you would give permission subject to Denis seeing that the premises were securely locked up on his departure from the Theatre. His father is, in any case, a Free State Judge, and one does not suspect Denis of republican or communist tendencies!

I may get a letter from you tomorrow (Monday) saying that you come up on the 9th—

Yours affly
G.

[ALS¹]   Coole Park | Gort | Co Galway
Tuesday [3 Nov. 1931]

My dear Dobbs: I enclose a letter which I opened by mistake. I think the caste for 'Dreaming of the Bones' excellent but I should like one rehersal while I am in Dublin. I must also have a talk with the stage manager about constumes etc. The young woman need have no lines to speak. I arranged so that her lines could be transferred to the Stranger. Only her dancing power has to be considered

I got your letter about income tax yesterday evening & this morning the document went off registered

Of course I shall be up on Monday 9th first train, & I very pleased with the thought that you meet the train

I think I must have written but I overworked last week, & got rather slack as a result.

Mrs Gregory says that needle-work is all the fashion in London now—two exhibitions—& that when you come here she can give a lot of suggestions²
Russell is painting 'a Woman of the Sidhe' as an idea for embroidery & American tourists.³

Yours affecly
WB Yeats

¹ On Fitzwilliam Square stationery, address struck out.

² Although she had married Guy Gough in September 1928, WBY continued to refer to Margaret as 'Mrs Gregory'. Exhibitions in London included Contemporary Needlecraft, which opened on 24 Oct. 1931 at 16 Bruton Street under the patronage of the Queen; and an exhibition and sale of British handicrafts, which was opened by the Lord Mayor on 26 October at the Drapers' Hall.

³ In an effort to help her financially, WBY had asked AE to provide a subject for SMY to embroider.

[TLS]   42, FITZWILLIAM SQUARE, | DUBLIN.
                                              Tuesday, Nov. 3 [1931]

My dear William

Delighted to hear about the second part to the Swift. I am very excited to hear it. For Heaven's sake dont forget to bring it up with you. You can read it to me, and dictate it.

The lamp of course consumes lamp oil, paraffin. What in Heaven's name else <u>could</u> it consume?! Its very form shouts paraffin oil; you could surely not have imagined that it demanded Sanctuary oil, or olive oil?

I think I wrote to you that Denis had asked permission to make vigil at the Abbey Halloween night? He and Perrin stayed together, Perrin frankly admits that he slept—like Peter in the Garden of Gethsemane—Denis watched, found nothing to watch, and at the witching hour of three aroused the sleeping Perrin in order that they might adjourn to the gas ring and cook eggs and bacon....

I have asked the Starkies and Colum[1] to dine on Friday (13th). Starkie will be away until then—I shall fix up a meeting of you and Miss de Valois on <u>Tuesday</u> Other arrangements depend on my hearing from you....I hate bothering you about the Dreaming of the Bones, but if it is to be done it must be got going—anyway, have you thought out who is going to shake dem bones when you is gone back to Coole? ('bones' is a name negroes give to dice—shaking the 'bones'...very low)

                                                        Yours affly
                                                            George.

[ALS[1]]   42, FITZWILLIAM SQUARE, | DUBLIN.
                                              Thursday [5 Nov. 1931]

My dear George

I wonder if you got my letter approving your casting of the play. I think Stephenson should be made stage-manager. Nothing can be done about costume till I know what the dancer is to wear. Then we can dress the Stranger. I may perhaps put the other character into a bawneen[2] as he is

---

[1] Walter Starkie's wife was Italia Augusta, née Porchietti, of Buenos Aires and Genoa. Padraic Colum (1881–1972) was a prolific author who had been one of the founding members of the Irish dramatic movement; he and his wife the critic Mary Catherine Colum, née Maguire (1887–1957), were at this time spending most of their time in France where they were close friends of James Joyce, but frequently returned to Dublin.

[1] Address struck out, and GY has annotated 'From Coole.'

[2] From the Irish *báinín*, an unlined jacket made of undyed white sheep's wool.

in hiding, but it depends on the colors wanted somewhat. Has any body looked at the music?

I have been working very hard

Yrs affly
WB Yeats

Your letter has just come. <I think Stephenson will be best. Consult him about getting. I do not neglect your letters> I do not neglect your letters I replied to each letter about play the day it came.

Dossy Wright will do as stage manager, if you have already spoken to him.³ I cannot say anything about the zither. Can the musician do Rummells music without it?⁴ If they can leave it out.

[ALS¹]   Coole Park | Gort | Co Galway
Nov 17 [1931]

My dear Dobbs: All here as usual. The evening I arrived Lady Gregory had an attack of bleeding from the nose, which lasted two hours, it was the second that day & she had had one the day before.² On Sunday however she seemed none the worse. On Sunday evening she read out Trollopes 'Can You forgive her' & said when she closed the book for the evening 'I see we shall be in better society in the next chapter, I dislike those English middle-classes. I think very little of them.' (The conscientious heroine had been pre-occupied with her future for severel chapters). Lady Gregory always thinks people unworthy of attention unless they have an inherited code which makes fussy thinking unnecessary. That I imagine is why she always refuses to read any modern intellectual novels; she has by her side in the breakfast-room at present Arabia Deserta³ & The New-testament in Irish. She has just added a forgotten novel published in the seventies of last century & called 'Charley Houstans Aunt' I asked what it was about & she said 'The hero is a young doctor. He goes into the disecting room to disect a

---

³ In the end, Dossie Wright was stage manager for the production.

⁴ Music for *The Dreaming of the Bones* was originally written in 1917 by Walter Rummel, for four musicians playing a plucked instrument (harp or zither), flute, a bowed instrument, and a drum (*The Collected Works of W. B. Yeats*, ii: *The Plays*, ed. David R. Clark and Rosalind E. Clark (New York, 2001), appendix B, pp. 784–97). The programme for 6 Dec. 1931 states that the music was by J. F. Larchet (but see 12 Apr. 1932).

¹ On Fitzwilliam Square stationery, address struck out.

² WBY returned to Coole on Saturday 14 November.

³ The two-volume *Travels in Arabia Deserta* by the English poet and traveller Charles Montagu Doughty (1843–1926) was considered one of the finest books on Arabia ever written; first published in 1888, it was reissued by Jonathan Cape and the Medici Society in 1921 with an introduction by T. E. Lawrence; a 1923 edition is in the Yeats Library.

body and finds that it is his own aunt.' She seems to have known the author, a once well known doctor.[4]

I forgot to dictate to you the piece about 'The Dreaming of the Bones' for the programe. I have it in the white-book & will send it in good while.

Olivia says that Ezras opera was bad on the wireless, certain instruments failed to get through.[5] The Cavalcanti[6] may be out any day. It was delayed by the bankruptcy of the publisher. Dorothy has left London I suppose for Rapallo. She & Olivia went to the B.B.C. place to hear the Opera.

Yours affly
WB Yeats

[TLS & MS]   42 Fitzwilliam Square | Dublin
                                             November 18 1931

My dear Willy

I send you the copy of introd: to Fighting the Waves which I want you to correct and return to me.... (envelope and stamps enclosed). One of the 'see back's has been completely crossed out but the subsequent pages—i.e. p. 4 'I would have Caesar compel' etc is unexplained without a former line or two? I have also queried in blue pencil, p.4. 'knows that it | would | be Latin' should not that 'would' be 'should'?[1]

---

[4] *Charlie Kingston's Aunt* (1885), one of two novels using the pseudonym 'Pen Oliver', was written by Sir Henry Thompson (1820–1904), distinguished surgeon, astronomer, artist, early advocate of cremation, and well-known host to London society with his 'octaves', eight-course dinners for eight people at eight o'clock; in *Seventy Years* (268) AG recommends him as publisher's reader of her edition of *The Autobiography of Sir William Gregory*.

[5] EP's opera *Le Testament*, first written 1920–1 and revised several times with the assistance of George Antheil and others, was based on excerpts from the poetry of François Villon (1431–?1463); it was produced by the BBC on 26 Oct. 1931.

[6] Aquila Press of London went bankrupt with only a part of EP's translation of Cavalcanti printed; *Guido Cavalcanti Rime*, an edition of Cavalcanti with essays in English, was published by Edizione Marsano in Genoa in 1932.

[1] *Fighting the Waves*, Yeats's ballet-drama based on his earlier play *The Only Jealousy of Emer*, was first produced at the Abbey Theatre on 13 Aug. 1929 with music by George Antheil, masks designed by Hildo van Krop, curtain and costumes by Dorothy Travers Smith, and choreography by Ninette de Valois, who danced the part of Fand. WBY's newly written introduction was published in the *Dublin Magazine*, April–June 1932. In the published version the lines preceding 'Only a Caesar could do what I want ...' (Section II) lament that there is no literary school which would substitute 'positive desires for the negative passion of a national movement beaten down into party politics'. Section III includes the discussion of Latin, the grammar as corrected by GY.

Let me have it back soon that I may send it to Starkey². The streets resound with newsboys shouting the first stop press of the Sweepstake draw.³ I was a fool not to buy a ticket and so share in the excitement!

[MS] In haste for post

Love G—

[ALS¹]

Coole Park | Gort Co Galway
Nov 19 [1931]

My dear George: Margeret has just told me that Lady G. finds that her flesh from the waist down to the middle thigh on both sides is painful to the touch. Her comment is 'inflamation of the nerves. Could Mrs Yeats find out anything that would ease it.' I promised to ask you. Could you consult Gogerty.

Yrs ev
WB Yeats

How are the rehersals?

[TLS]

42, FITZWILLIAM SQUARE, | DUBLIN.
Nov. 24 [1931]

My dear William

For some reason or other I thought I'd sort out all your letters to me this morning—all undated—and among them I found one written from the Savile Club about your waking to the sound of two volleys—'Childers is dead'—Then the post came with a letter from Dulce Philpotts (who was Dulce Childers) then I saw—an hour later—the Irish Press notice. Dulce wrote to me about nothing at all, but it just happens that she wrote on the very day, Nov. 22, that we last met, when she was in Dublin before Childers was shot.¹ That was all only the sort of coincidence that so frequently

---

² James Starkey ('Seamus O'Sullivan'), founding editor of the *Dublin Magazine*.

³ 'The world's greatest sweepstake draw', the Irish Hospitals' Sweepstake on the Manchester November Handicap, began annually on 18 November and continued for two days; GY usually bought a ticket.

¹ On Fitzwilliam Square stationery, address struck out.

¹ Dulcibella Mary 'Dulce' Childers (1878–1945), who was married to Dr Henry Austin Philpot (1878–1982), and lived at 7 South Eaton Place in London, gave her name to the boat in her brother's novel *The Riddle of the Sands*. The 24 November issue of *The Irish Press* carried a lengthy memorial article on her brother Robert Erskine Childers, who had been executed 24 Nov. 1922 by a Free State firing squad. See letters of 23 and 24 Nov. 1922.

happens—one sees a new word in some book, meets it again three or four times within twentyfour hours; the 'dramatisation' perhaps of which you write in that Part II of the 'Windowpane.'

Maud has been terrifically busy! She got in a meeting that had been banned twentyfour hours earlier than the banned one[2]....

Anne has been in profound disgrace at school for not working; she wrote to me 'Miss Palmer blew me up and made me go to late prep: every day last week. I think the results were good for I got 8 out of 10 for arithmetic, 14 out of 15 for Geometry, 10 out of 10 for French, 12 out of 15 for Algebra, but dont think that I shall be much higher in the class because I didnt work at the other subjects'.[3]

I sent off the 'Windowpane' and 'Fighting the Waves' commentaries to Starkey. I think that the reason I did not very much like Part II Windowpane is that your argument—the dramatisation [of] the secondary and tertiary personalities of the medium, seem so close to the old psychical research theory of the 'subconscious' or at least that I cannot personally understand what you mean except in those terms. If I had to interpret that 'commentary' I could not say that any 'spirit' were present at any seance, that spirits were present at a seance only as impersonations created by a medium out of material in a world record just as wireless photography or television are created; that all communicating spirits are mere dramatisations of that record; that all spirits in fact are not, so far as psychic communications are concerned, spirits at all, are only memory. I say 'memory' deliberately, because 'memory' is so large a part of all psychic phenomena. I dont remember any case in which a spirit (communicating through a medium) had during the latter part of his life or during any part of his life been cut off from that every day faculty of memory. Those people who were wounded in the head during war—they dont come—the insane dont come???—the spirits who tell us about their houses, their horse racing, their whiskeys and sodas, their children, their aunts and God knows whatnots, their suicides, were all mainly preoccupied during their lives with those things. Have we any record of a spirit communicating who had been at any period of his life been so physically or mentally incapacitated that memory, even 'subconscious memory', had been obliterated?

---

[2] Maud Gonne, from whom WBY had been estranged over political differences, had spoken on 21 November at a meeting of The People's Rights Association protesting treatment of prisoners arrested under the Constitution Act; a meeting for the same purpose arranged for the following day had been proclaimed by the Minister for Justice.

[3] ABY, now 12 years old, remained for five terms at Hillcourt Glenageary School, run by the Misses Phyllis and Gladys Palmer; a third sister, Eileen, ran a boarding house for the students.

Apologies for this diatribe—it all comes out of an idea I had lately that small nations have long memories, big nations have short memories, small nations make Empires.

Yours affly
G.

[ALS] COOLE PARK, | GORT, CO. GALWAY.
Wednesday [25 Nov. 1931]

My dear Dobbs: I am greatly stirred by your letter. Most by what you quote from Anne. She could not have written like that if she was afraid of you, or if she did not want to please. There was nobody I could have written to like that. I would have been afraid to tell of my short comings, & I would not have thought of them as Anne does with out moral fuss. I cannot tell you how much it has pleased me.

I like your comment on my note. My difficulty has been that <our whole system etc. seems> we have been told that the dead recover memory from us, that they have seperated themselves from the 'acquired faculties'. They can see in the <u>Passionate Body</u> but all names, all logic, & all that we call memory is from us. I enclose a page of comment. I half think of giving your letter (without your name) as a footnote with the comment I send or something like it.

I go up Friday morning. I hope you will be able to meet me & take me to the Gresham. I hope there will be a dress-rehearsal for me on Friday or Saturday or Sunday.

Lady G expects you to return here with me. She suffers a great deal of pain now.

Yrs ev
WB Yeats

[Encl¹]
Note on G Y's letter
I do not consider the fully seperated spirit a passive mirror of timeless images but as a timeless act. This act appears to us through the antimony of past & future, & loss of memory in the living man would be present in the act also. It may make communication difficult. If I think of John Smith who lost his memory from a blow on his head, I not only transfer that loss to the dramatization, in so far as that dramatization is from my suggestion, but think of him in just that part of his life which is absent from his present state. If my 'subconscious' could think of him as he was when most alive,

---

¹ Later copied by GY on Fitzwilliam Square stationery, with minor alterations.

most completely himself, and do so with as great intensity as it now thinks of his tragedy he would enter & direct the dramatization. It is because whatever is in time, is also in the timeless moment, that one is compelled in the pursuit of moral coherence to beleve in re-birth. I admit the difficulty of timeless moments, that in some sense them selves but parts of time; but what can one do with antimonies but symbolise their solution by some kind of Platonic Myth.

G Y's letter

a different comment

Remember how many of what seem the laws of spirit life are but the pre-possessions of the living. A number of communicators have warned us against cremation on the ground that it is a shock to the departed spirit yet to think so would be to think that Eastern Races who have studied these things for centuries are more ignorant than we who have hardly studied at all. If I think of a <spirit> man as having lost his memory from a blow on the head, my 'un-conscious' rejects him as possible testimony. < no more thinks of him, that it would of a dumb man as a possible communicater.> I am more moved by my correspondents statement that I have turned a sce-ance into a kind of wire-less apparatus & denied that the spirits are there at all. If I drop that word 'unconscious', adopted out of mere politeness I may be better understood: The Daimon of a living man is a dramatist—what am I but my daimons most persistant drama—it dramatizes its fancies—characters out of fiction have written through the planchette—it dramatises its knowledge, & when that is knowledge of other daimons it is as though it had lent them its dramatic power. The Spirit is then present in a repre-sentation which is <may dramatise the will of the dead. The spirit is then present> The resultant representation will be the child of the living and of the dead. The seperated daimon is not a passive timeless mirror but a time-less act which with your <our> help enters time once more. [MS concluding GY's TS[2]] <Nothing can separate a spirit from its own actions.> If I want to remember somebody I knew years ago I think 'how tall was he' 'what kind of hair & nose' & so on. <I make a series of judgements, & by them> The act of remembering is a series of judgments, which make me aware of my own timeless act & knowledge. No bodily injury could seperate my spirit from either, though it could from the language, from the logical construction that makes judgement possible. I suggest that it is <the logic of their lan-guage and merely there language, where we offer thought dramatization to the dead making them present in our dramatizations which create separate daimons for the dead to re-enter time> because they are a main part of our dramatic power, that seperated daimons can re-enter time.

---

[2] WBY later revised and added to GY's typescript; his revisions and additions are marked with < >.

[TLS & MS]   FITZWILLIAM SQUARE, | DUBLIN.
                                          Friday [27 Nov. 1931]

My dear Willy

Your two letters came this morning; I havent had time to digest the two commentaries as Michael's school is having a sale tomorrow and he has the sweet stall...so I have had to make fudge and make it all up into pretty little parcels! Tonight I dine with the Gogartys—on Tuesday I go to tea with Mrs Erskine Childers!-![1]

The rehearsals seem to be going well. On Tuesday morning I have an assignation with Miss Devoy[2] to look out dresses. I'll tell Dossie that you come up on Friday so that he can arrange for dress rehearsal.

I've asked the Alphands and one or two others to come and return with us after the performance for supper. Hope you wont find this too tiring. Michael has developed a passion for Suzanne Alphand—he heard her 'conference' at the French Society and never took his eyes off her for a moment. Afterwards he said 'She's very like Anne Gregory but I think she's even prettier. She is pretty'. And later on 'I dont wonder she's engaged, she wouldnt be difficult to engage.'![3]

About Coole; do you think Lady Gregory is well enough to stand the strain of a visitor? In any case I hope you have not forgotten that you told me she is using Margarets room and that I should feel very upset if I found I had been put into that room.

[MS] I am afraid that she may find my coming adds to her burdens.

                                                        Yours
                                                          G.

---

[1] Robert Erskine Childers's widow Mary 'Molly' Alden Childers, née Osgood (1877–1964), shared her late husband's Republican fervour, and was still active in the Fianna Fáil party, having worked closely with Michael Collins and served as honorary treasurer of the Republican Daily Press Fund which assisted in founding the *Irish Press* in 1931. In July 1914 she and her husband and Mary Spring-Rice had smuggled to Howth German arms (which would later arm the Irish Volunteers in Easter 1916) in the yacht *Asgard*, which had been given to the Erskines as a wedding gift by her wealthy American father. Her statement to the press after her husband's death was: 'His sacrifice is as much a gift to me as it is to his comrades who serve Ireland's cause.' Her son Erskine Hamilton Childers (1905–74) was elected fourth President of the Republic of Ireland in 1973.

[2] Costumes for *The Dreaming of the Bones*, which was to be produced on 6 Dec. 1931; Dorothy Devoy was the Abbey Theatre costumes mistress.

[3] Suzanne Alphand, daughter of the French Minister Charles Alphand (1879–1942), spoke to the French Society in the Russell Hotel on 25 Nov. 1931 on 'L'Irlande vue par les Français'. In April 1932 at the All White Ball in honour of her marriage to Michael E. Fitzgerald (1904–63), 'well known in Irish legal and hunting circles', a diplomatic incident occurred when the arrival of the Governor-General resulted in the abrupt departure of all the representatives of the Fianna Fáil party (*Irish Times*, 26 Apr. 1932*)*. The Fitzgeralds were both later employees of Aer Lingus in Paris, and in 1974 Suzanne received a Remy Martin Franco-Irish trophy as 'outstanding ambassador for Irish tourism in France'.

[ALS]   COOLE PARK, | GORT, CO. GALWAY.
                                              Sunday [29 Nov. 1931]

My dear Dobbs

Here are the press-cuttings. I suggest a slip put in to programmes, printed on both sides & headed 'Abbey Players in America'.[1]

Lady G is deep in Brian Cooper[2], which she is liking greatly.

Gerald Heard writes that I shall hear from the BBC & that he is sure they will agree to my proposal to submit a typed copy of my broad cast. I hope to earn my London expenses.

                                                          Yours ev
                                                          WB Yeats

[TLS]   42 Fitzwilliam Square | Dublin
                                         Dec. 15 or so [14 Dec. 1931]

My dear Willy

I enclose an income tax form which I want you to sign in the two places marked in blue pencil and return, in stamped envelope.

I send also a letter from Dr Crone.[1] Its a pity he says February or March—

Lennox writes 'I am convinced that W.B. and Tulloch think I am blueing all the proceeds—I wish there was half a chance of doing so' (He is feeling poor) 'the money question is still stringent but will straighten out soon.' He has evidently had a pretty bad time with his back.[2]

I wired to the impertinent person whose letter I enclose—'Harry Watts'[3] to say 'regret cannot give permission Yeats'

We had a good drive up, lunched at Athlone, and arrived in Dublin at four. (We didnt leave Lough Cutra until well after 10.30—)[4]

---

[1] News of the Abbey's success from their opening performances of 21 October in Philadelphia was regularly reported in the Dublin newspapers.

[2] LR's biography of Bryan Cooper was published in the autumn of 1931.

[1] John Smyth Crone (1858–1945), medical doctor, editor of *Irish Book Lover* (1909–24) and *Concise Dictionary of Irish Biography* (1928), was president of the Irish Literary Society, London 1918–25; WBY was asked to speak at the Society's annual dinner, which finally took place on 3 Apr. 1932.

[2] LR, who was in charge of the Abbey tour, had hurt his back while opening a window.

[3] Enclosure missing. The London telephone directory for 1931 lists a Harry Watts in Streatham Common, but I have been unable to discover anything further.

[4] GY, who accompanied WBY back after the production of *Dreaming of the Bones* (6 Dec. 1931), had been at Coole for the previous week; she motored to Dublin with Guy Gough of Lough Cutra.

This letter is all new paragraphs because it is all information—the unfinished play will reach you by registered parcel post as it is in one of the old loose leaf books. It was really very pet and nice of you to be up when I was going yesterday, thankyou. I found Michael very well, bursting to tell all his doings during the week—the plot of the play at the French Society—the lion cubs at the zoo and the charms of Rupert...(your cousin⁵) the conversation he had with someone at the French Society 'I didnt know him, he was French, and I dont think he knew me, I like talking to people I dont know'....A thrilling cinema (gunmen) and a star for composition! Two mice caught in his cupboard, his crocusses all much bigger, thank goodness painting classes were over for the term, how many hours until Anne returned from school on Friday, what was a moon's nebula (that stumped me), kippers for breakfast twice, no chicken since I went away, and so on ad infinitum. Very pleased with his book—he writes to thank for it himself, but probably not until Wednesday or Thursday as he has two late days at school—Tuesday and possible Wed: also.

Yours affly
G.

[ALS¹]
at | Coole Park | Gort | Co Galway
Dec 15 [1931]

My dear Dobbs: I send you my glasses—yesterday an hour after you left I broke one of the leggs or limbs or what ever they are. If you can get them to stick it in a gain the slight shortening wont matter. I have my reading glasses.

Nothing has happened except that I miss you greatly

Yrs ev
WB Yeats

[TL & ALS]
42, FITZWILLIAM SQUARE, | DUBLIN.
Tuesday [22 Dec. 1931]

My dear Willy

I've just written an awful scrawl to Lady Gregory but I cant compose a proper 'roofer'¹ being too tired to think. That unfortunate Anne came home

---

⁵ Dr Rupert 'Tim' Gordon was the son of JBY's sister Frances Armstrong ('Fannie') Yeats and Dr Samuel Thomas Gordon, vice-president of the Royal College of Physicians of Ireland, and surgeon in the Royal Irish Constabulary; GY was especially fond of Rupert's sister Violet.

¹ On Fitzwilliam Square stationery, address struck out.

¹ GY's slang for a letter of thanks for hospitality.

ill (better today) with a terrific temp: and throat, and it was only certain yesterday that she was NOT developing diptheria! We had to have three different lots of swabs tried out at the laboratory.... anyway, its just a very bad sceptic throat. The doc thought the temp. was too high for diptheria, but had to make sure. She'll be in bed for Xmas poor child but I hope she['ll] be well enough by then to enjoy presents. Her temp. was down today to just under 101. She really is unlucky.

Write and tell me the news, such as it is.

Yours affly
G.

[MS] Please write to her about her 'linotype' & dont forget to read the inscription on the back of the calendar! She wrote it before getting ill, but in bed so writing is atrocious! A lino-type is <u>cut</u> in linoleum—she cut it herself but did not print it herself[2]

[ALS[1]]   at Coole Park | Gort | Co Galway
                                                   Dec 22 [1931]

My dear Dobbs

I forgot to give you the money for the childrens presents. Please tell me how much & I will send you a checque. How about Lilly & Lolly. Shall I give them a checque of a pound each?— it goes against the grain?[2] I enclose checques— no I have only three checques left in my checque-book & I have some bills to pay. If you give them a present—I forget what we did last year—tell me what it costs when you write to me about the childrens presents. There should be an unused checque book of mine on the desk or table. If you can find it post it to me by return; if you cannot send me a card & I will write Bank. I dont want to accumulate checque books because I long for one of those very little books which are evidently to be got only by personal application & insistens.

I have written the first three stanzas—eight lines each—of my new poem 'Wisdom'. I have now to do two short lyrical sections. What I have written is in the meatre of Byzantium. I want to exorcise that slut 'Crazy Jane', whose language has grown unendurable.[3] I am pleased with what I have

[2] ABY was already exhibiting exceptional artistic talent, regularly gaining honours standard and first place in various competitions.

[1] On Fitzwilliam Square stationery, address struck out.

[2] They had just bailed out Cuala once again, at the cost of £1,800.

[3] GY has written 'Vacillation' at the top of the page; by time it was published in *The Winding Stair and Other Poems* (1933) the poem had eight sections; the shorter 'Wisdom' was published in *The Tower* (1928). The Crazy Jane poems were first published by Cuala in *Words for Music Perhaps and Other Poems* (1932).

written. For days I could get nothing & thought I was finished & now I have found a new life. I am reading Balzac with all my old delight, picking up old acquaintances, & reading Shelley 'Prometheus Unbound' with thoughts of an essay, not Irish notes but something you can send to 'The Criterian'⁴

Where did Anne learn stencil making. I have her calendar by the mantle piece. I hear she is ill—please give me news.

Yrs ev
WB Yeats

Get Punch for Dec 16 & see W Birds caricature of Dolly.⁵

[ALS]   at | Coole Park | Gort | Co Galway
23 December [1931]

My dear Michael.

I thank you for the salted almonds. I have already eaten so many that Lady Gregory tells me that I shall make myself ill. They are excellent salted almonds, no cook in the world could have made better

Your affectionate father
WB Yeats

[ALS]   42, FITZWILLIAM SQUARE, | DUBLIN.¹
Dec 24 [1931]

My dear Dobbs: I promised to write later in day but did not because I got absorbed in my poem. I sometimes wonder how I have retained any sense of punctual[it]y & order after so many years of verse. I return Michael's 'report', a product doubtless of the teachers desire to flatter the parent without injuring the child. However I doubt that any teachers desire to flatter ever gave me so good a report. He will probably lack always observing power—I suppose that 'nature study' like drawing needs that.² He will

⁴ WBY's 'Prometheus Unbound' was first published in *The Spectator*, 17 Mar. 1933, and included in *Essays 1931 to 1936* (Cuala, 1937). See pg. 288 for his admiration of Balzac.

⁵ 'W Bird' was Jack Yeats's pseudonym for his drawings in *Punch* (1910–48); the only W. Bird drawing of the issue for 16 Dec. 1931 is on p. 645, a cartoon entitled 'Modern Wine Merchant (dictating catalogue for the Christmas trade)' where the secretary may have some resemblance to Dolly Robinson.

¹ GY has annotated this 'Written from Coole.'

² The report for the term ending Christmas 1931 from the Mount Temple School describes Michael's work as 'Very good' in English and History, 'Good' in Geography and Arithmetic, 'a very good beginning in Latin', but only 'Fair' in Nature Study, and as for Drawing and Painting 'original ideas, but work often spoilt through lack of observation'.

learn by doing things, which is perhaps the right way for man began so. Yes I wrote to both children. Annes lynotype seems to me very good indeed. I would have praised it more, but I dont feel I know how it was made. Did she copy a picture made by somebody else? If it is her own design, & if the treatment of wall & ground is her invention it is very remarkable. I hope she will send me—as her rhyme promises—a picture of Ballylee.

No you never told me how Lennox got his strained back.

I am anxious about the American tour. I see from a letter in yesterdays Irish press that there is the old Irish American opposition helped this time by Republican dislike of 'The Free State Theatre'.[3] I do not think there will [be] any serious disturbance, but there may be no money.

Yrs affly
WB Yeats

[ALS[1]]   Coole Park | Gort | Co Galway
                                             Wednesday [30 Dec. 1931]

My dear George: Nothing from you. You had promised me a wire & of course I am anxious about Anne. I should have written before but I have knocked up—bad cold, consequent exaustion. Am better to day—up to this I have done little but sleep. Perhaps a letter will come from you next post.

I enclose Michaels school report which I thought I had returned.

I hope to be back at verse writing to-morrow

Yours
WB Yeats

[ALS]   COOLE PARK, GORT, CO. GALWAY.
                                             Thursday [31 Dec. 1931]

My dear Dobbs: Your letters have come. Let me know about Anne. Post-cards will do.

I wonder if you could tell me one or two things I want to know. I am thinking of that 'Spectator' article. They pay rather well & I might be able to do an article that I could reprint. When was 'Ulysses' published? You will find a book about Joyce in one of the book racks on my table. If it came out as I think in 1921 or the next year, & so came into the ten years I might start

---

[3] The Abbey was now receiving an annual government subsidy, after many years of independence.

[1] On Fitzwilliam Square stationery, address struck out.

my theme with it. Then if you happen to know when did James Stephens publish his 'Land of Youth'. I am not sure that I have an article in me, or one that I could write here, away from my books, but I may have & it would come as a rest after a little more verse.[1]

The bed jacket came, & is very satisfactory, more comfortable because less braided than the other. I thank you also for the detective story. I have begun on Balzac again & have finished the two volumes I brought down. I wonder if you could post me another Balzac. Any Balzac that you please. I shall probably go through the lot again.

Yrs ev

WB Yeats

[1] James Joyce's *Ulysses* was published in Paris in 1922; James Stephens's *In the Land of Youth* in New York and London in 1924. WBY's article 'Ireland 1921–1931' was published in *The Spectator* on 30 Jan. 1932.

1932

[ALS¹]   Coole Park | Gort | Co Galway
                                                      Jan 1 [1932]

My dear Dobbs: Your letter was a great releif. I was growing more & more
anxious. All you tell me is interesting. The more I look at Anne['s] Lino-
type—it is up before me on the mantle piece—the better it seems. You ask
about my verse. I was working well until my cold began & since then was
unfit for anything until to day which I have tried to spend writing letters.
I think however I found a new lyrical theme, which I am elaborating in little
poems. Some thing with notes to a Chinease book started me off. I will soon
send you a short series of poems, grouped under a common name, which you
should find markateble.² Did Frank O Connor acknowledge those poems?³ I
have heard nothing & Lolly will one of these days call out for copy. Did you
find that checque book of mind? I have only one cheque left & dont want to
get a new book until I have used the one in Dublin (I covet a very little book
which I cannot get out of them by letter it seems). Could you also send me
an engagement book? I want to begin to put down my London engagements
B B.C, Irish Literary dinner etc. This is an ungracious letter all questions &
request but I have been writing business letters all morning & one letter to
a young poet⁴ which [I] re-wrote completely five times that I might neither
unduly discourage or encourage (no I wrote that yesterday, my head is in a
mist). I send a lot of autographs you wanted.⁵ The new dectective story came
this morning, & is most welcome. I finished the last of the old set last night
at two in the morning (hence perhaps the mist).

                                                      Yours affectionly
                                                      WB Yeats

I have kept back some autograph forms to think of quotations. I enclose an
old addressed envelope of yours—which it is possible though unlikely that
you may want.

---

    ¹ On Fitzwilliam Square stationery, address struck out.
    ² 'Vacillation' which when completed had eight sections.
    ³ In 1932 the Cuala Press published *The Wild Bird's Nest*, Poems from the Irish by Frank
O'Connor, pen name of Michael Francis O'Connor O'Donovan (1903–66) novelist, short
story writer, and translator, who later became a director of the Abbey Theatre and, for a
number years from 1941, co-editor with GY of the Cuala Press.
    ⁴ Unidentified.
    ⁵ WBY was in the custom of autographing, frequently with a line from his poetry, a label
designed by Sturge Moore which could be pasted into one of his books.

42, FITZWILLIAM SQUARE, | DUBLIN.

January 2 1932

My dear Willy, very distressed to hear you had such a bad cold. I hope you are quite well again???? Anne managed to get a cold in her head in spite of extreme precautions and so had to return to bed again after being up for one hour, two hours and three hours on three consecutive days! She is better tonight and her temp. is lower than this morning. Michael extremely well. He and I went to see Colum's 'Mogu of the desert' last night.¹ (I left Peggy in charge of Anne) Colum was there. He and his wife had to come to Dublin on some other business for a week, or so he said, and they arrived last night. It was a bad performance, the music was quite intolerable, it turned the play into something approaching light opera although there was not a great deal of it. The music should have been flute only, the songs almost spoken. No difference was made between the dressing of the Romans and that of the Persians, nor was their acting different so one lost a most necessary sense of balance in the first act and in the 3rd. Hilton Edwards played Mogu as he played the jew in Jew Suss,² the women were atrocious, the scenery and lighting excellent, the dresses and colours ditto; Colum said to me as we were going out 'I dont recognise my play'. (They had cut an essential part of the second act, he told me)

Poor Anne is missing everything—children's parties, pantomimimes etc—its rotten luck for her.

A very queer thing happened on the day after Christmas (Boxing Day) the telephone rang about 5 to nine. I answered it but instead of a reply I heard Italian opera being sung; I seized a chair and sat and listened. Presently, when I. Op. had ceased, a voice said 'this is 2 RN' then an announcement of a pantomime that was to be broadcast. Then a sort of preliminary song and the telephone suddenly cut off! I have been trying to find out what could have happened to make my telephone wire cut in on a broadcast, but so far without success.

I havent seen anyone except Colum and relations so havent any gossip. Nor have I been to see anything but Colum's play. Nor have I read anything but detective stories and some of Burns' verses (to Anne who had learnt some at school and liked 'em) or the encyclopaedia to answer Michael's intolerable questions, and 'Marius'³ in bed for tranquility of mind,

¹ The Gate Theatre, founded by Hilton Edwards and Micheál MacLiammóir in 1928, produced Padraic Colum's play *Mogu of the Desert* on 29 Dec. 1931, with setting and costumes designed by MacLiammóir.

² Ashley Duke's *Jew Suss* had been produced in October 1931; Orson Welles performed in the plays by Colum and Duke.

³ The 1902 two-volume edition of Walter Pater's *Marius the Epicurean* is in the Yeats Library.

and that one excellent detective story which I got Peggy to post to you when I heard you had a cold!

Various people have telephoned. The Gogarty's, who at one time asked me round time and time again have not uttered. Either something queer happened about that night at the Abbey on Dec. 6 or they are in Galway?

I posted on to you a letter from the Spectator—it had an English stamp but had not been through the post—which was left here this afternoon. Had you received from them the letter they mention having addressed to the Kildare St Club?

When you write tell me facts, how you are, how Lady Gregory is, did you get a new bed-coat sent to you from Horton's (Grafton St)[4] is there anything you need?

Dobbs.

[ALS]   COOLE PARK, | GORT, CO. GALWAY.
Jan 4 [1932]

My dear Dobbs: I enclose a letter which has just come in a envelope marked 'urgent'.[1] You will know what to do.

Do not bother about the checque-book I have written to the bank.

Yrs ev
WB Yeats

[TLS]   42 Fitzwilliam Square | Dublin
Jan. 4 1932

My dear Willy, alas, Anne's illness put O'Connor out of my head, and your letter today reminded me of my deficiencies. I have posted his poems to him today with an explanatory letter.

Anne is still in bed—she had two days of a normal temp. and was lively and active and up for two or three hours each day—got a slight cold and returned to temperatures and headaches and post-nasal nuisances. Tom Graham[1] came in this evening and punctured her right anterrim (he shoved in cocaine first). When it was all over he said in a most casual way 'I think that's worth a shilling isnt it?' Anne obviously didnt know what to answer. He shoved his hand into his pocket 'I hope I've got one!' Brought it out with a shilling. All of course

---

[4] Horton's outfitters, 105–6 Grafton Street, Dublin.

[1] Enclosure missing.

[1] Thomas Ottwell ('Togo') Graham (1881–1966) was a senior eye, ear, and throat surgeon in Dublin.

carefully pre-arranged, I'm sure he does it with all his young patients, but Anne who had got over three pounds for Xmas presents is treasuring that shilling as no other shilling was ever treasured! I hope that the cleaning out of the anterrim will have stopped what ever was the origin of the sceptic poisoning.

Cuala is wound up—the embroidery I mean. I have paid all the bills except the overdraft at the Bank which could not be cleared up until, after Jan 2 (Xmas and Bank holidays etc) Sara Hyland and May Courtney have decided to try and carry on as a 'Mendery and dressmaking establishment'[2] They pay their rent to Lolly, and bear their proportion of telephone. As they said to me—'the only other expense is our wages and our firing' and as May has 10/- a week from the Carnegie Libraries—she is librarian of the Carnegie library at Dundrum—and Sara gets some similar sum or perhaps more from organising Irish classes—they are prepared to do work at a very much lower rate than in the days when they were under the control of 'Cuala'. They undertake 'mending'—rates sixpence upwards—etc. They are going to issue a printed circular shortly. They will act as agents for Lily's embroidered pictures, banners, Stations of the Cross, etc. I think it is a courageous idea and I am doing everything I can to circulate the idea. It is easy to do propaganda when propaganda is altruistic! Lily sold her first 'Customs House' last Friday.[3] She will now have the job of doing another for exhibition.

Walter rang up today about that translation of his,[4] I said you were at Coole, he said shall I send the first act to Mr Yeats at Coole, and I said yes! Later the Irish Press rang up to enquire for Lady Gregory. I said that I had seen her recently and that she was well.

Yours affly
Dobbs.

[ALS[1]]   Coole Park, Gort, Co Galway
                                                    Jan 5 [1932]

My dear Dobbs
    I am writing much poetry. There are now three of the four sections of 'Wisdom', & yester day I wrote a little scrap of verse which is not a part of

[2] The embroidery division of Cuala Industries had been under GY's management since Lily Yeats's illness in 1923; in addition to SMY, Sara Hyland (1893–1972) and May Courtney (b. 1895), who had won various medals for their needlework, worked in embroidery from designs contributed by a great many Irish artists including Cottie (Mrs Jack B.) Yeats, AE, and occasionally GY herself; May left in 1933 and from 1934 worked in the Carnegie Library, Dundrum. I am grateful to Maureen Murphy for information.

[3] At WBY's suggestion, SMY was embroidering a series of pictures of famous buildings, chiefly for the American market.

[4] In 1964 Starkie published *Eight Spanish Plays of the Golden Age*, but none of these translations appears to have been performed at the Abbey Theatre.

[1] On Fitzmaurice Square stationery, address struck out.

the series. I send it.[2] There is no change here—Lady G is no worse. Endeed the night before last she had her first night without pain. She says that any thing very hot or cold to drink starts the pain & that it is in 'sciatic nerve'.

If you have not found the checque book do not trouble further but let me know. I have used up my last checque-form.

I am facinated by the Gandi drama. How completely he has the 'ugliness' the system attributes to the saints. The head of the 'red-shirts' upon the other hand is no saint but to judge by a 'Times' photograph is a magnificent person.[3]

<'The Spectator' has asked for an article on some phase of Ireland during the ten years just closed>

Tell me about Anne. I have had no news for a week.

When do you go to Glen gariffe[4]

Yrs affectly
WB Yeats

Mrs Gregory was generally admiring about Annes picture & urged me to get it framed

[ALS[1]]   at | Coole Park | Gort | Co Galway
Jan 10 [1932]

My dear Dobbs: I have just paid Pollock & Co[2] account in full after some cross purposes. As far as I can make out my personal share in bill was

---

[2] Enclosure missing, but probably Section VII, a version of which he sent to OS on 3 Jan. 1932. The sequence of poems written during this period is discussed in *Words for Music Perhaps and Other Poems: Manuscript Materials by W. B. Yeats*, ed. David R. Clark (Ithaca, NY, 1999), pp. xlii–xliii, 611–12.

[3] *The Times* of 29 Dec. 1931 published a photograph of Abdul Ghaffar 'Badshah' Khan (1890–1988), a Pashtun Muslim inspired by Gandhi's ideas on civil disobedience and non-violence and founder of the Khudai Khidmatgar movement (a 100,000-strong non-violent army on what is now the Afghan/Pakistan border comprised of men, women, and youngsters from the multi-ethnic traditions of Afghanistan and India, whose uniform included red shirts). An editorial in *The Times*, 5 Jan. 1932, reported the arrest of Mahatma (Mohandas Karamchand) Gandhi (1869–1948), founder of the Civil Disobedience Movement, on his return to Bombay from London where he had alone represented the Indian National Congress at the second Round Table Conference held to negotiate about self-government. A few months later, Khan was also arrested by the British government under the command of Lord Willingdon, newly appointed Viceroy of India, and his Red Shirts declared an illegal organization; he was twice nominated for the Nobel Peace Prize. In the philosophic system of WBY's *A Vision* the Saint, who is all purity and simplicity, was assigned to Phase 27, where Unity with God was at last possible; Socrates and Pascal are given as examples.

[4] GY was planning a holiday in Killarney so that ABY might recuperate.

[1] Fitzwilliam Square stationery, address struck out.

[2] Pollock & Co., oculists, opticians, and spectacle makers of 50 Grafton Street, Dublin.

£5.12.0. (new glasses, mending old glasses, new case) so you should credit me with £5.2.0 (£10.17.0–£5.12 0) which you can deduct from the bill you send me for Lilly.[3]

Richard[4] was here yesterday with two Cambridge friends. Richard thinks that it is quite possible that your telephone wire got the wireless wave (one of the others said before he came in that they make use of the telephone wires in relaying) or that you may have been rung in mistake for another number by some body at the Dublin Wireless Centre & heard the lound-speaker. One of the other men suggested that a joking friend rang you up & then held his reciever up against his wireless set.

Lady Gregory has had a good deal of pain the last few days, then last night a very good night. She is I think in the same state as when you were here. I judge by the fact that she reads out for about the same lenght of time & without greater difficulty. She had a bad period about a fortnight ago which coincided with the worst part of my cold. I found it rather painful to watch her difficulty in arranging my food, she could not remember what she had ordered—at one moment I saw her struggling against tears; but now she is better than she then was, at any rate. I have a letter to day from Lady Londonderry asking for news of her—Gogorty accounts I suppose have spread.

I have finished the four sections of my poem 'Wisdom' & have not yet decided either to write another poem I have in my head [or] to re-start the play

Perhaps next post may bring me a letter with news of Anne.

Yrs affly
WB Yeats

I enclose Pollocks account,[5] & will send you his reciept when it comes.

[ALS]   42, FITZWILLIAM SQUARE, / DUBLIN
[c.18 Jan. 1932]

My dear Dobbs
        Here is a better version of those lines

---

[3] On closing down the embroidery section of Cuala, WBY and GY agreed to contribute an allowance of £7 a month to SMY.

[4] Richard Gregory, Lady Gregory's grandson, who received a BA in engineering at Cambridge, was commissioned into the Royal Engineers at the Woolwich Academy in 1929.

[5] Enclosure missing.

'Healing from her lettered slab. Those self same hands perchance
Eternalise the body of a modern saint that once
Made Pharoh's sacred mummy, but though heart might find relief'

then on as you have it.[1]

I send you a bill from Hatchards[2] which I opened by mistake, & a letter
from Sally. Perhaps you had better wire Sally.[3]

Nothing has happened here

Yrs ev
WB Yeats

[TLS]   42, FITZWILLIAM SQUARE, / DUBLIN.[1]
                                      Thursday [21 Jan. 1932]

My dear Willy

Hope you arrived safely back to Coole and had not too bad a time with
Hogan?[2]

We had an excellent journey—arrived in gales, storms and floods! No
front rooms overlooking the lake could be used because the wind so terrific. The next morning dead calm, some sun, floods vanishing. Today
a summer's day, and the lake dead smooth and transparent and the
children have gone off with an old boatman for a 'grand tour' which is
to take 3–4 hours! We had a long drive yesterday (outside car) all round
the Muckross estate up to Torca Mountain etc.[3] Anne has done a quite
excellent sketch from the covered in verandah, and proposes to start
another tomorrow so as to get two done! She is getting back her colour
and energy.

No news—we shall be back in Dublin on Monday evening and A. returns
to school on Tuesday.

Love,
George.

---

[1] These lines from Section VII of 'Vacillation' when published were further altered to read
'Healing from its lettered slab. Those self-same hands perchance | Eternalised the body of a
modern saint that once | Had scooped out Pharaoh's mummy. I—though heart might find
relief'

[2] GY regularly ordered books from Hatchard's of Piccadilly, 'booksellers since 1797'.

[3] Possibly a request from Sara Allgood for news of AG, who was fond of Sally.

[1] From a hotel in Killarney, where GY had taken ABY, still too weak to return to school,
from about 18 to 25 January; GY must have taken her typewriter with her.

[2] WBY was in Dublin from about 16 to 19 January, during which time he visited his dentist,
James Edward Hogan.

[3] WBY had been a guest at Muckross House when Mrs Bourne Vincent was still alive (see
22–7 Aug. 1926).

[ALS] at | COOLE PARK, GORT, CO. GALWAY.
Sunday [24 Jan. 1932]

My dear Dobbs: I hope the weather at Killarney has been as good as it has been here. I have finished my group of poems which I now call 'Vacilation'—there are seven poems; & I have written all my recent verse into the big MSS in such a way that you will have a good MSS—21 poems in all—one however is only four lines.[1] My article is I think to be in this weeks 'Spectator'.[2] I sent proof back yesterday.

I got just after you left a bill from Piggotts shop for £2.7.0 & threatening a summons.[3] I paid it so you owe me that amount.

No news except that a friend of Anne Gregory's (a Mrs Nelson) has run over a Civic-Guard & killed him.[4]

Yrs affecly
WB Yeats.

[TLS] 42, FITZWILLIAM SQUARE, | DUBLIN.
Jan. 25 1932 (Monday)

My dear Willy

I see, on going through my letters tonight, that you have paid £2.7.0 to Pigott's; a sum I paid in 1930 and for which I have the receipt. I will reclaim your £2.7.0 and refund it to you.

Anne has returned from Killarney looking pink and well and fatter. We had amazing summer weather; arrived in tremendous storm and flood, drove on Wednesday all round the middle and lower lakes going, on part of the road, through floods so deep that the foot rest of the outside car almost touched the water.

Swans swam over what the hotel had once hoped to make a tennis lawn! We had the hotel entirely to ourselves. As it was not 'the season' the Manager and his daughter were able to entertain in the house all their dogs—ages 3 months to five years, species varied—and a regally colossal black cat. During the season the proprietors of the hotel ban animals, and the animals are banished to the stables. Such is German discipline—the manager is a German—that the animals, or so I was told, understand that

---

[1] Probably 'Three Movements' or 'Gratitude to the Unknown Instructors'. 'The big MSS' is what is now known as 'the White Vellum Notebook', in private hands.

[2] 'Ireland—1921–1931' appeared in *The Spectator*, 30 Jan. 1932, 137–8.

[3] Pigott and Co. Ltd., music and musical instrument dealers, 112 Grafton Street.

[4] Notorious for her daring, in May 1932 Lady Nelson was acquitted of manslaughter when the car she was driving on 20 Jan. 1932 struck and killed John Murnaghan, a local Civic Guard; see above 2 and 4 Feb. 1931 for other exploits.

from Whitsun until September 15 they must cease to be house dogs and cats I doubt very much that the cat would permit this code to be imposed upon him, he did not seem at all obedient. He was a very determined cat. Cobden Sanderson has just published a forgotten and unprinted fragment of Maria Edgeworth's. It is called 'The Most Unfortunate Day of My Life' Printed in fine type on handsome paper it seems an incomparable piece of style—of its own kind—the grandfather and grandmother of all the Virginia Woolf's and Stella Bensons and of all those modern novelists who seem to write with the astonished eyes of an imaginary child.[1]

I had hoped, when I arrived home this evening, to find a letter from you.

Yours affly
George.

[ALS] | COOLE PARK, GORT, CO. GALWAY.
Jan 25 [1932]

My dear Dobbs
I send you a checque & statement from Watt. I have endorsed checque.

Yrs ev
WB Yeats

[ALS] | COOLE PARK, GORT, CO. GALWAY.
Jan 28 [1932]

My dear Dobbs: I thank you for your delightful letter—you are much the best letter writer I know, or have known—your letters have so much unstrained animation, so much natural joyousness.

---

[1] Maria Edgeworth (1768–1849), feminist, novelist, playwright, and short story writer, whose *Castle Rackrent* (1800) catapulted her into fame and who, after a series of successful novels, towards the end of her career wrote books for and about children; *The Most Unfortunate Day of my Life* was published in 1931 by Richard Cobden-Sanderson of London with illustrations by Irish artist Norah McGuinness, who had in 1927 illustrated WBYs *Stories of Red Hanrahan and the Secret Rose*. Stella Benson (1892–1933), feminist, travel writer, journalist, novelist, and short story writer, wrote seven novels, including *Tobit Transplanted* (*The Far-Away Bride*), which won the Femina-Vie Heureuse Prize and the silver medal of the Royal Society of Literature in 1932; a copy of *Kwan-Yin* (San Francisco, 1922), her short poetic drama set in the temple of the Buddhist Goddess of Mercy, is in the Yeats Library. Virginia Woolf, née Stephen (1882–1941), feminist, publisher, novelist, biographer, and essayist, had by now published the novels *The Voyage Out* (1915), *Night and Day* (1919), *Jacob's Room* (1922), *Mrs Dalloway* (1925), *To the Lighthouse* (1927), which won the Femina-Vie Heureuse Prize, and *Orlando* (1928), as well as several collections of essays and stories.

1. W. B. Yeats's ring designed with a butterfly and hawk by Edmund Dulac in 1918, commissioned by George Yeats, with their astrological symbols engraved inside: 'And wisdom is a butterfly | And not a gloomy bird of prey' (WBY, 'Tom O'Roughley'), photograph by Nicola Gordon Bowe

2. Georgie Hyde Lees in 1910, courtesy of the late Dr Grace Jaffe, George's cousin

3. W. B. Yeats c.1914, courtesy of Philip Marcus

4. Portrait by Edmund
Dulac of Mrs W B Yeats,
1919, reproduced by
permission of Hodder
Children's, of Hachette
Children's Books,   London

5. George Yeats photographed by E. C. ('Lolly') Yeats in the garden of Gurteen Dhas,
Dundrum, in March 1918

6. S. M. ('Lily') Yeats and E. C. ('Lolly') Yeats in the Cuala Industries office, Dundrum

7. Lady Gregory *c*.1915, Alice
Boughton, New York, courtesy of
Colin Smythe

8. (*above*) On the upper deck of the *SS Carmania* in a heavy snowstorm as the Yeatses
arrived in New York on 24 January 1920
9. (*below left*) Studio portrait of George Yeats, Underwood & Underwood, New York, 1920
10. (*below right*) Studio portrait of W. B. Yeats, Underwood & Underwood, New York, 1920

11. (*left*) Studio portrait of George
and W. B. Yeats, probably
Underwood & Underwood, New
York 1920
12.(*right*) George and W. B. Yeats in
San Antonio, Texas, in front of the
Mission Concepción, 14 April 1920,
courtesy of Mrs J. H. Savage

13. John Butler Yeats in his room at
the Petitpas' boarding house, New
York

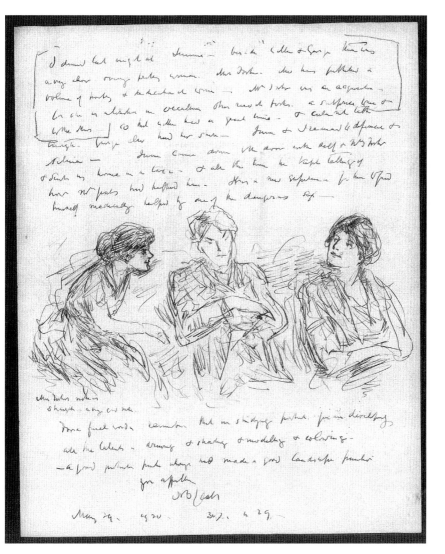

14. Letter of John Butler Yeats to Mrs Jack B. ('Cottie') Yeats, 29 May 1920: 'I dined last night at Quinns—besides Willie & George there was a very clever & very pretty woman Mrs Foster who has published a volume of poetry & dedicated it to me—Mrs Foster was an acquisition—for she is interested in occultism & has read the books. A Surprise to me & to the others', courtesy of the National Gallery of Ireland

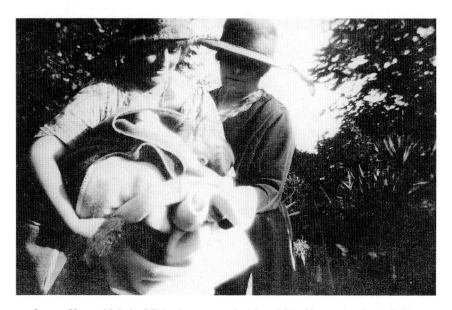

15. George Yeats with baby Michael, one month old, and Lily Yeats, taken by Lolly Yeats at Dundrum, September 1921

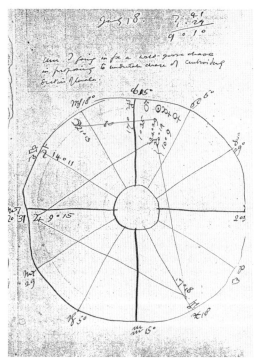

16. George Yeats's horary for 18 July 1923 before deciding to take charge of the embroidery section of Cuala during Lily Yeats's illness

17. The Yeatses in Algeciras, early November 1927, with Mrs Jean Hall (centre), a still from a film by John Hall, courtesy of Ann Saddlemyer

18. Anne and Michael on the beach in Cannes, December 1927

19. 'L'Alpe Fleurie' in Villars sur Bex, Switzerland, where Anne and Michael went to school for three years from 1928

20. Michael at Villars sur Bex, photograph by George Yeats

21. (*left*) Anne and Michael at
Villars sur Bex, photograph by
George Yeats
22. (*right*) Anne and Michael on the
beach in Rapallo

23. Anne in Dundrum, photograph
by Lolly Yeats

24. W. B. Yeats and Joseph
Hone at 'Sorrento', home of
Lennox Robinson in Dalkey,
during a Dublin Drama
League performance of
Euripides' *Ulysses*, summer of
1926

25. George with Michael and
his godfather Lennox Robinson
26. Anne at Gurteen Dhas
with Aunt Lily in the doorway,
Easter Saturday 1928,
photograph by Lolly Yeats

Coole Park,

Gort, Co. Galway.

August 26

1928

28. Michael at Gurteen Dhas, photograph
by Lolly Yeats
29. Three street photographs of George
and W. B. Yeats
30. Studio portrait of Anne and Michael
1929, photograph by Graphic Studio,
Dublin
31. W. B. Yeats and Jack B. Yeats leaving
Gurteen Dhas after a tea party, photograph
by Lolly Yeats

32. W. B. Yeats delivering his first BBC Belfast broadcast, September 1931, photograph by A. R. Hogg, 81 High Street, Belfast

33. W. B. Yeats and Shri Purohit Swami in Majorca, 1936

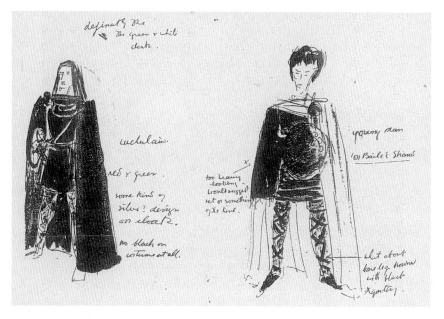

34. Anne Yeats's designs for the Abbey Theatre production of her father's play *On Baile's Strand*, 1938

35. George and Willy's last resting place in Drumcliffe churchyard, photograph © Keith Parsons

Would you tell me something about 'Antiphone'.¹ Lady Gregory has been very much better—though does not admit it—for some time. I know because she reads out to me for nearly an hour without her voice failing; & she could not do this a few weeks ago. But she has had a very bad day & night & to day when I said something about 'Antiphone' she said 'yes that might be some good'. Probably she will have no such thought when better, but you had better tell me about it. Is it morphia? Does it stupefy? Etc.

I have read an advance copy of Stuarts book 'Pidgeon Irish' & think good, much better than the others.² The publisher wants an opinion from me. The post goes very early to day

Yrs ev
WB Yeats

Have you heard from Lennox

[ALS] | COOLE PARK, GORT, CO. GALWAY.

Jan 29 [1932]

My dear Dobbs: April 3 has now been settled as the date of my London dinner.¹ I shall probably go there on April 1 to get a days rest first.

Stuart's publisher asked me to write an opinion of Stuarts book 'Pigeon Irish' which could be used as an advertment. I have just done this. The book is remarkable much better than the others. When I doubt his future as a novelist, which I sometimes do, it is because he is sensuous but never passionate. He is sensuous & spiritual. His characters always keep themselves with difficulty from throwing themselves, on the spur of the moment, into one anothers arms, or into the arms of God. It was Shelleys temprement, it was perhaps that of the saints when they set out. His work has lovely moments & a profound idea. Is his temprement that of spiritual objectivity.²

Lady Gregory had a good night & is normal again. She has just sent Micael a pheasant.

Yrs affecly
WB Yeats

---

¹ I have been unable to find any information about this drug.

² *Pigeon Irish* by Francis ('Harry') Stuart, IG's husband, was published by Victor Gollancz in 1932. Set in an imaginary future with one character based on St Catherine of Siena, it describes an Ireland which represents 'the last stronghold of Western Culture against the expansion of over-civilisation'.

¹ The Irish Literary Society dinner (see 14 Dec. 1931).

² 'From Phase 26 to Phase 28 is Spiritual Objectivity' (*A Vision*, Part II).

[TLS]   42, FITZWILLIAM SQUARE, | DUBLIN.
                                                    Feb 1 [1932]

My dear Willy

Glad to get yours this morning—and glad that you like Harry Stuart's new novel.

Anne was here yesterday and looks very much better in spite of a septic toe (on her other <u>foot</u>, the one which did not have its big toenail removed!) She is evidently having a happy time and, so far, is finding herself very popular! In fact everything is beautiful in the garden, even maths. for which she got five out of ten. This may not seem much to <u>you</u> but her last term was frequently nought out of ten! She is still being crowed and cooed over by the Miss Palmers and matron and cossetted by the 'dormitory' although to my eyes she now looks quite well!

I dined with Joe Hone last Thursday—he rang up to say he was in Dublin and he had had Rossi's introductory chapter to his book on Ireland and would I come and dine at the K[ildare] St. Club so that he could hear the latest news of you and Lady G. So I dined, and not only had Joe no other diner but no one else was dining or sitting, so we had those two vast rooms to ourselves. Joe discoursed at length on religion, death and so on. I am afraid the poor man thinks he hasnt very long to live. If you feel inclined you might write to him St Ann's Hydro, Blarney, and ask him about his book on Swift.[1]

I saw Walter on Thursday also—he came in very late to a committee of the French Drama League and stayed on afterwards to gossip. He had heard nothing about the Abbey since the meeting you and he had. I handed him the letter from Tulloch (which he had not seen) that I found lying around in your bedroom. Poor Walter does so feel that he is a cardboard and cottonwool director and does so like to be consulted![2]

'Family Failing'—I never saw it before last Friday, a lifeless production about lifeless people. 'Queer Ones' a lifeless prod: also. Not Dossie's strong point, production? A sprinkling of people on Friday night, most of them looked like friends' friends. I didnt even agree with the casting. Frolie Mulhern would have been far better than Gertie Quinn (I think that's her name) and O'Gorman (who played your cat and moon and dreaming of the bones) had been done nothing with. He needs stimulus and obviously hadnt

---

[1] Joseph Hone was collaborating on *Swift; or, The Egoist* with Mario Rossi, who was now back in Italy.

[2] Walter Starkie, the government appointee to the Abbey Board of Directors, had made headlines in 1928 when he disagreed with the decision to reject O'Casey's play *The Silver Tassie*.

got it. Peter Nolan and Tom Moran, old Abbey people, were half asleep too.[3] NO, NO!

I am posting you on a novel sent you by Lady Lavery.[4] She enclosed a letter, it came today. I smelt the novel between the unwrapping and the re-wrapping, and I dont think you need bring it home <u>when</u> you come. I posted to you also a letter from the B.B.C.

Now the B.B.C. is important, and you must come up in good time to dictate your piece. I think in any case that you should come up before your dash to London. I think you should come up in two or three weeks time for a week. I want to take you out to Baymount when I go to see Mr Scott about Michael (he goes there in May)[5]

Yours G.

[ALFrag]   at | COOLE PARK, GORT, CO. GALWAY.
Feb 3 [1932]

My dear Dobbs: I am writing to you instead of starting on my days work. I am tired owing to the fact that I have at last found a rich theme for verse. I am turning the introductory verses to Lady Gregorys 'Coole' (Cuala) into a poem of some lenght—various sections with more or less symbolic subject

---

[3] A scratch company, many drawn from the DDL, under the direction of Dossie Wright continued to keep the Abbey open while the permanent company was on the American tour: *Family Failing* by William Boyle (1853–1923) had first been produced in March 1912, his first play for the Abbey since withdrawing his popular works because of his objection to *The Playboy of the Western World*; *Queer Ones*, a curtain-raiser by journalist and novelist Con O'Leary (1887–1958), in October 1919. Frances 'Frolie' Mulhern first began performing with the Abbey in 1929, joining the American tours, and was active until a month before her death in November 1939. Gertrude Quinn, who was a frequent performer in radio drama and had been a student in the Abbey School of Acting, was never a permanent member of the company, but performed sporadically from 1928. Peter Nolan (d. 1937) of Dollard's Printworks was performing at the Abbey by 1916 and also later with the DDL. Tom Moran, an auctioneer at the City Fruit Market who had performed at the Abbey since 1924, also acted frequently with the DDL, appearing in both *The Only Jealousy of Emer* and *The Cat and the Moon* at the DDL annual general meeting on 9 May 1926; however, he first appeared in film, starring in *Cruiskeen Lawn* (1922), Irish Photo-Plays Ltd. William 'Billy' O'Gorman had a small part in LR's adaptation of Sheridan's *The Critic*, which opened on 6 Jan. 1931; a recent student in the Abbey School of Acting, he had been praised for his performances as the Lame Man in WBY's *The Cat and the Moon*, 21 Sept. 1931, and the Young Man in WBY's *The Dreaming of the Bones*, 6 Dec. 1931.

[4] The novel sent by well-known hostess, artist, and Republican sympathizer Hazel Lavery (1886–1935) was probably by one of her protégés; the portrait of her as a romantic Kathleen ni Houlihan by her husband, Sir John Lavery, decorated Irish banknotes from 1928 to 1996.

[5] MBY attended Baymount Castle Preparatory School, 414 Clontarf Road, Dollymount (founded by Lord Ardilaun in 1898), as a boarder under headmaster William Lucas Scott (1871–1950) from 1932 until he enrolled in St Columba's College in September 1935.

matter. Yesterday I wrote an account of the sudden ascent of a swan—a symbol of inspiration I think.[1]

I must come to Dublin to vote, as soon as I know the date of the general election[2] I will arrange to spend a week in Dublin. I have written to the Broad Casting People to tell them of change of plan (The Irish Lit Society dinner is on April 3 so I must broad-cast after that)

I have nothing to read. Can you send me Balzacs 'Harlots Progress vol 11' I have just finished Vol 1. I want to go right through Balzac again he has fascinated me as he did thirty years ago. In some ways I see more in him than I did, he is the voice of the last subjective phases, of individuation in its exaltation.[3] When I read of Lucians return to his native town & his brief triumph there I see Wilde, in his manner of speach & remember that Wilde was a Balzac scholour, perhaps a Balzac diciple—so perhaps were we all. Yet his world was closer to reality than a Goya characture.[4]

When the new rules of the Kildare St Club are passed you will be entitled, as a members wife, to become a member by the payment of two guineas a year. You can then invite your own guests & make war on that electric light.[5]

[ALS]   at | COOLE PARK, GORT, CO. GALWAY.
                                                   Feb 3 [1932]

My dear Anne

I hear you are almost well again. I have no news except that the head forrester here a little while ago counted sixty two wild swans on the Lake,

---

[1] The poem became 'Coole Park and Ballylee'; see his letter to ABY below.

[2] The general election took place on 16 Feb. 1932.

[3] In *A Vision* Balzac is cited along with Shakespeare and Napoleon, as an example of Phase Twenty, 'the Concrete Man'.

[4] WBY purchased the forty-volume edition of 'The Human Comedy' by Honoré de Balzac (1799–1850) in 1905; *A Harlot's Progress* is the longest in the set. The Spanish court painter and printmaker Francisco José de Goya y Lucientes (1746–1828) in his long career reflected the transition from classicism to romanticism, becoming increasingly dark in subject and context.

[5] The conclusion to this letter is missing, but both of them preferred candlelight or gaslight to the harsher electric light. Members of the conservative Kildare Street Club, founded by Irish landlords in 1782, finally voted to allow women to be entertained as guests in 1929 and in 1932 as associate (Lady Voucher) members (R. B. McDowell, *Land & Learning: Two Irish Clubs* (Dublin, 1983), 102). In 1861 the club had moved from 6 Kildare Street to new premises at the corner of Leinster and Kildare Streets designed by the architects Benjamin Deane and Sir Thomas Deane in Italian Gothic style with carved animals (including a pair of billiard-playing monkeys) on the external limestone columns and one of the finest interiors in 19th-century Dublin, with a magnificent staircase, since demolished. In April 1921 the anti-Treaty faction of the IRA occupied the building. The Club eventually merged with the University Club, and the building was taken over by the National Library of Ireland and the Heraldic Museum.

that is seven or eight more than I ever saw. A little before that he saw a flight of twenty five herons rising from the bank & I never saw more than two or three. He says that wild swans & herons are increasing all through the west of Ireland & explains it by the greater gentleness towards beasts & birds of the people especially the children. I have been writing a poem which contains a description of a wild swan suddenly flying up from the side of the Lake[1]

Your affectionate Father
WB Yeats

[ALS] at | COOLE PARK, GORT, CO. GALWAY.

Feb 5 [1932]

My dear Dobbs: I enclose the Spectator checque also bill from Hatchards which I opened by mistake.

De Blacam has had an article on An[g]lo Ireland in the Irish Press which starts from Hones work, Lennoxs & mine.[1] He has sent it me (I had already seen it) with a letter saying that he wrote it because of what I had recently written (essays in Dublin Magazine probably) seems to be alarmed lest we should bring about two Irelands corresponding to French Belgium & Flemish Belgium. I have replied & sent his letter & articl to Hone. I think it will do something to make Hone feel that his work is important & therefore put him into better spirits

I have sent my Spectator articl to de Blacam[2]

I have written to Anne

Yrs affecly
WB Yeats

---

[1] 'Coole and Ballylee, 1932'.

[1] Aodh de Blácam (born Hugh Saunders Blackham; 1891–1951), journalist, playwright, and critic, later director of publicity for the Department of Health, wrote for the *Irish Press* under the pseudonym 'Roddy the Rover'. As a convert to the Gaelic League and Roman Catholicism, and always critical of WBY's Anglo-Irish Protestant stance, in his signed article 'The Rise and Fall of Anglo-Ireland...: A Race That Passed Away—Why?', *Irish Press*, 3 Feb. 1932, he chastises the Anglo-Irish Protestants for their rejection of national allegiance; reference is made directly to LR's biography of Bryan Cooper, Joseph Hone's writings on Swift and Berkeley, and WBY's recent commentary on *The Words upon the Window-Pane* in the *Dublin Magazine*.

[2] In 'Ireland, 1921–1931', published in *The Spectator*, 30 Jan. 1932, WBY writes of his conversion to the importance of the 18th century, especially the writings of Swift and the anti-Unionist stance of Henry Grattan (1746–1820).

[ALS¹]   42, FITZWILLIAM SQUARE, | DUBLIN.
                                                            Feb 8 [1932]

My dear Dobbs: Forgive this dirty outside sheet of paper. I hear general
election is on 16th but would like to know for certain. You are a vile
corrspondent not to have answered my last letter on the subject. Do you
know if we are on the register? Unless I get some information to the contrary expect me up about Feb 14.²

I have just had the first 3rd of the Indian Monks Autobiography³—a masterpiece. A book the like of which does not exist, written with the greatest
possible simplic[it]y—mahatmas, cows, children, miracles, a sort of cinema
film to the Glory of God. I have agreed to write the preface but have urged
that Sturge Moore is the proper person.

Lady Gregory is certainly better—I know by her voice when she reads out
& she sleaps better. On the other hand she suffers very great pain, generally after any phisical exertain, climbing stairs of the like, & shows signs of
increasing age. She will ask the same question several times over within five
minutes. She is acute & amusing on any theme that takes hold of her but little does. Old age, as I see it in her, suggests somebody passing into trance.

My poem on Coole may grow into the finest I have written for some
years.

Did you get any further information about the pain killing drug.

                                                                    Yrs
                                                            WB Yeats

I never thanked you for sending me those ciggarettes & matches I am very
glad to have them

[ALS¹]   at Coole Park, | Gort, | Co Galway
                                                            Feb 8 [28 Feb. 1932]

My dear Dobbs: I enclose a note for Anne, please read it & if the birth-day
is over please cross out the word 'almost'.²

    ¹ Written at Coole.
    ² WBY went to Dublin on 15 February, returning to Coole on 24 February.
    ³ *An Indian Monk*, a translation of the autobiography of Shri Bhagwân Hamsa, his master,
by Shri Purohit Swami (1882–1941), had been sent to WBY at the suggestion of T. Sturge
Moore. This led to a literary collaboration between WBY and Purohit Swami, culminating in
the visit to Majorca where they translated *The Ten Principal Upanishads*; see below, especially
December 1935.

    ¹ On Fitzwilliam Square stationery, address struck out.
    ² ABY was born on 26 Feb. 1919.

Emery Walkers address is

16 Cliffords Inn

Fleet St

London E.C

I am writing him to say you are sending the block.

I am making a good essay about Russells book—an essay I can re-publish but such things are wasteful journalism they take too long to write[3]

I am lost in curiosity as what Walter Starkey had to say about the Academy.[4]

Do you know if my protest came out in the Manchester Guardian?[5]

Do not forget about the pain-killer. I think Lady G would like it—The pain has been very bad lately. Yesterday she was talking again of the possability of going into the hospital

Yrs affecly

WB Yeats

[ALS]   at | Coole Park, Gort, Co Galway

March 8 [28 Feb. 1932]

My dear Anne: I have just looked up the date on your calender, the one with the cottages. It is hanging over the mantlepiece. I have been so busy that I had <almost> forgotten your birthday. Many happy returns of the day.

I find that flock of herons was even larger than I thought. There were thirty two, & nobody before that ever saw more than one.

Yours ever

WB Yeats

[3] WBY was writing a review article on AE's *Song and its Fountains* (London, 1932), in which AE provided autobiographical settings and discussions for a number of his poems. Acknowledging the turbulent relationship with his old friend, WBY 'began by hating the book for its language' yet 'came to love the book for its thought'. 'My Friend's Book' appeared in *The Spectator* on 9 Apr. 1932 and was republished with minor corrections in *Spectator's Gallery: Essays, Sketches, Short Stories & Poems from The Spectator 1932*, ed. Peter Fleming and Derek Verschoyle (London, June 1933), 335–41, then collected in *Essays 1931 to 1936* (Cuala, 1937), and republished in *Essays and Introductions* (London, 1961).

[4] WBY was intent on establishing the Irish Academy of Letters and hoped that Walter Starkie would be of assistance in establishing relationships with other national academies (see 1 May 1932).

[5] The *Manchester Guardian*, 26 Feb. 1932, printed a lengthy interview headed ' "The Puritan" Mr. O'Flaherty's Novel Mr. W. B. Yeats's Protest "Grotesque" Charge', in which WBY is apparently quoted verbatim with a detailed criticism of the charge of censorship and the novel itself, concluding 'He is a great novelist, and no opposition can prevent him from doing much to mould the next two generations.'

[TLS & MS]   42, FITZWILLIAM SQUARE, | DUBLIN.
                                                     Feb 29 1932

(No 2 letter)   P R I V A T E[1]
My dear Willy

   Starkie has just gone. He entirely agrees that the Irish Academy should be independent of Government, in fact he thinks it is the only way in which the Academy could be made a success. I know he tends to agree with everything anyone says but he spoke with real passion about it. He made various suggestions about the Abbey which were I think very sound, but they must be talked about, not written.

   He is evidently anxious about his position, as Abbey Director. The Gate Theatre have been spreading rumours that now Fianna Fáil is in Starkie will be booted out and Murray or F.Hugh O'Donnell put in, or Norman Reddin. I do not imagine that the directors of the Abbey would stand an 'imposed' government director?[2] Starkie asked me if I thought he ought to resign before the problem arose. I told him that I would write to you. I do very much wish that I could see you to talk over a few of these things now that the political situation is clearer. If you think that you cannot come to Dublin again before you go to London, I wonder if you could come to Galway for a night—I would make an excuse to go there.. a friend.. because I dont think Lady G. ought to have the burden of a visitor. I really do believe that this is the moment to start things off, and the few people I have seen since you went away all say the same thing—we are tired of politics, we want an intellectual movement politics are the death of passion and passion is the food of the intellect.

   *Please do agree that either you come up, or we have an assignation in Galway! I have marked this letter PRIVATE.

   [1] GY's previous letter is missing; 'PRIVATE' is written in very large letters.
   [2] The general election defeated Cosgrave's government and brought in Fianna Fáil under the leadership of Éamon de Valera, thereby causing some doubts as to the future of the Abbey Theatre's subsidy and WBY's plans to establish an Irish Academy of Letters. The possible replacements for Walter Starkie as government-appointed director were LR's fellow Corkman the playwright Thomas Cornelius Murray (1873–1959), soon to retire as headmaster of the Model School, Inchicore, Co. Dublin; Murray's friend the businessman, playwright, and critic Frank J. Hugh O'Donnell (1894–1976), who was keenly interested in amateur theatre and was appointed to the Senate in 1943; and Gerard Norman Reddin (1896–1942), a solicitor who had been associated with The Irish Theatre (1914–20) and who, with his two brothers and mother, was a strong supporter of the Dublin literary scene; both O'Donnell and Reddin had in recent years debated the role of the theatre with WBY at Dublin Literary Society meetings, while Murray was known to be very conservative in his views. In the event, the government nominee was Richard Francis Hayes (1882–1958), medical practitioner and military historian who had been jailed for his part in the 1916 Rising, was a TD in the first Dáil, and although he became the second Film Censor in 1940 remained on the Abbey Board of Directors until his death in 1958; meanwhile WBY appointed Starkie an ordinary shareholding member of the Board.

Incidentally, the fact that Denis Johnston is now a director of the Gate marks him off the list as a possible director of the Abbey! The Gate, is either playing for the Abbey Audience or playing for a subsidy from the new government (this is not Starkie's gossip) They announced at the party to Sally[3] that they were going, in future to specialise in Irish plays.

Anne was home yesterday—she celebrated her birthday—was enchanted with her mahogany chest of drawers, a present from you and me. It is a nice thing, with charming handles and nice wood. I got it on the Quays.[4]

It is most horribly cold, north-east wind, the kitchen is the only really warm room. I envy Lennox and Dolly in Florida! Dolly writes that New Orleans is worth it all, by which I imagine that she means worth all the train journeys and horrible cities. Lennox writes very cheerfully and sends me a story of Edith Wharton's which he says I wont like but he does! They are both evidently feeling warm and pussy in sunlight.

Yours ever George.

[MS](Among the directors of the Gate Theatre are—Longford, Denis Johnston, F.H.O'Donnell Norman Reddin—)

[ALS] COOLE PARK, GORT, CO. GALWAY.
March 1 [1932]

My Dear Dobbs: Have wired 'will come up Saturday agree about everything writing' I could not make out from your letter whether I had to give some decession or not about Miss Draper getting the Abbey.[1] You have however Lady Gregory decission & mine to leave that matter to you & Starkey.[2]

You could have stayed here without upsetting Lady G in any way but I conclude there are matters I can better do in Dublin. The new Executive Council will I gather be appointed on March 9 or soon after. We shall have to find out under what Minister the Abbey comes & who he may be.[3] Keep Starkey quiet—nothing can be done for the present. All that talk set loose by the Gate means nothing. Dublin loves to talk in a crisis.

---

[3] Actress Sara Allgood was performing in a touring production of *The Chocolate Soldier* at the Gaiety Theatre in Dublin.

[4] There were numerous secondhand book and furniture shops along the Liffey quays.

[1] It had been suggested that American monologuist Ruth Draper, who was performing at the Gaiety Theatre, should appear at the Abbey in the Directors' special Sunday evening series.

[2] Walter Starkie.

[3] The new Minister of Finance was Séan MacEntee (1889–1984), who replaced Ernest Blythe.

I shall bring up my Russell essay to dictate.

Yrs ev
WB Yeats

[TLS]   42, FITZWILLIAM SQUARE, | DUBLIN.
March 2 [1932]

My dear Willy

I have just seen Perrin about the arrangements for Sunday night. Miss Draper's manager was at the Abbey this morning to make arrangements.... Perrin tooted him around and showed him the Peacock and so on![1] Prices of back stall & front gallery seats are being raised, postcards are being printed to circularise. Free list entirely suspended. I told Perrin that the Abbey Directors (and wives) would pay for their seats so that there should be no question about free lists...my joy that Holloway[2] will have to pay!

I wrote to Slattery again this morning—I wrote the day after you left but got no answer.[3] I think he will answer the letter I wrote him this morning, it was extremely tactful...he would perhaps send a prescription himself...

Starkie has buzzed off to England, will be back on Thursday, returns to England on Saturday....

Miss Draper lunches at 1.30 on Sunday and asked me if I would mind asking Francis Hackett to lunch as she had meant to go to Wicklow to see him on Sunday until she got our invitation. So I wrote to him.

I sent on your letter to Anne, crossing out the 'almost' and commenting in a letter of my own on the fact that you had dated your letter March 8....I told her that you had asked me to read it to 'see if it was legible', and that I hoped she would be as amused as I was to see that you lived always a week or two behind time or in advance of time. (She wont mind the date because she will remember that you came to Dublin a week too early once!)

Here is what Michael's present headmistress says about him: 'I never knew so nice a little boy, he is so solemn and yet merry, so innocent, but he's clever'. Its like an epitaph on an eighteenth century tomb.[4]

---

[1] The Peacock Theatre, designed by architect and occasional Abbey actor Michael Scott, was built in 1927 and housed the Abbey School of Acting and School of Ballet; it was frequently let to other groups and had been the home of the Gate Theatre from 1928 to 1930 until they secured their own premises.

[2] Joseph Holloway (1861–1944), avid theatregoer and persistent collector who had been the original architect for the Abbey Theatre and whose 221 volumes of 'Impressions of a Dublin Playgoer' (NLI MSS 1794–1890) have been a rich resource for researchers, appears to have forgone the Sunday night performance, attending a Gaiety performance instead. He had a reputation for requesting free 'press' tickets.

[3] WBY had been in Dublin 15–24 February.

[4] Michael was soon to leave Miss Sweeny's Mount Temple School for Baymount.

I want you to stay here until Tuesday,⁵ because I want you to see Starkie. I have excellent reasons for wanting you to see Starkie, which I will tell you when I see you on Saturday. I shall of course meet you at the station.

Yours ever affly
Dobbs.

[ALS¹]   at Coole Park | Gort; Co Galway
March 5 [1932]

My dear Dobbs: I think I wrote to you yesterday & gave you a correction for a poem but I am not sure. 'The Lord of Chou' is correct—'Chow' is wrong as you said.²

I have been trying to get new copies of my 'Book plate'. The block cannot be found and Emery Walker asks if we have it. Do you remember anything about it?

I am inclined to ask Emery Walker if block does not turn up to make me a book plate out of the 'end paper' design of a unicorn, cave, hawk etc Ricketts designed—the one in all my books. He would merely have to make a quite cheap 'zyncotipe block' & put my name under it. What do you think of the idea.

Yrs ev
WB Yeats

[ALS]   at | COOLE PARK, GORT, CO. GALWAY.
Wednesday [9 Mar. 1932]

My dear Dobbs
Here is the quotation.

'I know
No nurse had ever crooned a lullaby
So softly as Thou the music that guides the loud
Tempest on it[s] going forth"¹

Post is here

Yrs ev
WB Yeats

⁵ WBY returned to Dublin on 7 March.

¹ On Fitzwilliam Square stationery.

² Line 3 of Section VI (originally numbered V) of 'Vacillation' reads 'the great lord of Chou'.

¹ Lines 27–30 of 'Will O' the Wisp' from *Vale and Other Poems* (1931) by AE, quoted by WBY in 'My Friend's Book', review of *Song and its Fountains*, published in *The Spectator*, 9 Apr. 1932.

[ALS]   at | COOLE PARK, GORT, CO. GALWAY.
March 10 [1932]

My dear Dobbs

<I wrote yesterday & gave you the right quotation but forgot to say that the title of the book is 'Song and its Fountains'. I know you are at Glendalough but write when the mood takes me as because I fear to forget.>

The Second instalment of the Indian ascetics mss has come & I am overwhelmed by it. It seems to me one of the great books of the world, a book that must affect every thought men have about the east. It rises to a kind of lyrical intensity as spiritual vision comes. There is a wonderful description of life in the forest & his relation to birds & snakes.

The new medecine & so far has worked wonders. Last night Lady G was able to read out again. To day however she has had some pain but had a good night & the pain may lessen or dissapere as the tablets take effect.

Yours affly
WB Yeats

March 10 [11]
Lady Gregory has a great deal of pain this morning but the medicene will probably remove it as the day goes on. She read out to me again last night & had no pain in the latter part of day.

[ALS]   COOLE PARK, GORT, CO. GALWAY.
March 11 [1932]

My dear Dobbs: I write because I have found a note of yours asking for Emery Walker's address. I enclose his letter.[1]

I wrote to you an hour ago & sent letter with typed script of essay & nothing has happened since—I [am] writing & tearing up letters partly because instauled in the downstairs room where I have less space.

Yrs ev
WB Yeats

[on back of envelope] Have you written about Ezra Cavalcanti it is described as 'beautifully got up & printed & very learned' or have you deceded not to. It may be a limited edition.[2] W.B.Y.

---

[1] Walker's letter of 22 Feb. 1932 explained that they do not have the wood block of his bookplate, and that Sturge Moore cannot find it either.

[2] Cavalcanti's *Rime*, edited by EP, was presented by him to GY in 1934.

[ALS]   at | COOLE PARK, GORT, CO. GALWAY.
                                                      March 13 [1932]

My dear Dobbs: Can you get the chemist to make up another box of the
Tablets numbered 2392 (the other box is different). Lady G. has very few
left & there is the chance that the other box may not be as good. The
prescription says 3 a day so, though Lady G. never takes them unless
the pain threatens to be very bad a box does not last long. They have
taken away the worst bouts of pain—she is reading out to me again every
evening.

   Did I tell you that I have another big mss of the Indians Auto biography—one of the great books of the world I think. It rises to great hights of
intensity. I think it will make as great a sensation as Tagores first books. It
is more fundemental, more unique.

                                                           Yrs affly
                                                         WB Yeats

Great quantities of primroses in the wood.

[ALS]   at | COOLE PARK, GORT, CO. GALWAY.
                                                      March 14 [1932]

My dear Dobbs: I have asked the Kildare St Club sec to send you your
'vouchers' (they must be ready now) you will have to ask somebody the
extent of your privileges. I enclose rule as first proposed.[1] <I believe you can
take Anne & woman friend.> Some extension was made. I am not quite
clear what beyond that, when Michael is a little old you can take him <but
whether you can take any other male I do not know. Probably not, another
male member>. I am doing nothing but working through arrears of letters,
plays etc & that keeps me very busy. Yrs ev WB Yeats

[ALS]   COOLE PARK, GORT, CO. GALWAY.
                                                      [16 Mar. 1932]

My dear Dobbs: I just got the MSS ready in time for post. I had not time to
write a letter, but first about those Club Vouchers. You will see by enclosed
note from secretary that there will be some weeks delay.[1]

---

[1] Enclosure missing; see letter of 3 Feb. 1932.
[1] Enclosure missing, but see letter of 3 Feb. 1932.

You will find if you turn over the MSS that I have added several poems. If they are legablle leave Lolly's Girls to puzzle them out. I think this collection & 'The Winding Stair', when combined, will make the best of my books of verse. Until I went through this typed script I had not realized how much I had enriched it lately. Lolly might call her book simply 'New Poems' & should not publish too large an edition unless I hear that Macmillan will post pone his for some time.[2] When Macmillans edition de Luxe is out I shall want to issue my book in the ordinary way. I shall write Lolly a preface of some sort.

Yrs affly WB Yeats
March 16.

[ALS]   at | COOLE PARK, GORT, CO. GALWAY.

[17 Mar. 1932]

My dear Dobbs: I want you to put the poem 'For Anne Gregory' after the Second Coole poem. Its present place has no meaning. It is some where towards the end of the poems before 'Words for Music perhaps'. I wonder will Lolly think the book small. It cannot be enlarged except that I shall send her a preface or front note of a couple of pages. No news of any kind here & none of my own except that I got a wire yesterday from B B C London asking if I could give my 'talk' on April 3 the one impossible date. This was in answer to a letter from me. They had written to me six weeks ago & the letter was lost in the post, they have sent me a copy. The carelessness of the post office may have lost me my London 'talks'.

Yrs affly
WB Yeats
March 17

One of the servants has left a large bunch of shamrocks on my plate so I am properly arrayed, despite my 'Spectator' protest.[1]

---

[2] Cuala published an edition of 450 of *Words for Music Perhaps and Other Poems* in November 1932; Macmillan published *The Winding Stair and Other Poems* in September 1933.

[1] The first section of 'Ireland, 1921–1931', *The Spectator* (30 Jan. 1932), refers to his disgust at the shamrock 'with its association of drink and jocularity' which was engraved on a medal of WBY by the American artist Theodore Spicer-Simson (1871–1956). However, an envelope of dried shamrocks exists among the Yeats papers, labelled '4 leaved shamrocks etc'.

[TLS]   42, FITZWILLIAM SQUARE, | DUBLIN.
                                                    March 19 [1932]

My dear Willy

Many thanks for the registered envelope with poems...I will type the MSS part—Lolly isnt ready yet, she had a big order for prints from Boston which have kept the press busy.[1]

I hope you got the two boxes of tablets?

What a nuisance about the BBC. I do hope they can fit you in later. By the way, you have got it firmly in your head that April 3 is a SUNDAY?

I went last night to The Gate to see Christine Longford's play. I had to stay to the end because the Longfords were sitting rather close and the theatre was not full enough to cover departure! The Currans sked-daddled after the end of the second act, but they were sitting further back....[2]

Tomorrow Anne is bringing four children from her school (Mrs Cooper's[3] niece among them) for a picnic and home for tea. A long day—we start at 11 and they leave at 5.30! Anne would I think have liked to have the full day which is 10.30 to 7.30, but I told her firmly that it was too long....I hope to heaven it will be fine.

I asked you in a letter if I was to send the Russell article direct to the Spectator, and as you didnt reply I have done so, asking them to send the proof direct to you at Coole.[4]

Yours ever
George.

[ALS]   at | COOLE PARK, GORT, CO. GALWAY.
                                                    [21 Mar. 1932]

My dear Dobbs: I shall go to Dublin on Saturday next—March 26—as Monday is a bank holiday. If this inconvenieces you—it occurs to me

---

[1] The Cuala Press did not finish printing *Words for Music Perhaps and Other Poems* until September 1932.

[2] Christine Longford's comedy *Queens and Emperors* received its first performance at the Gate Theatre on 15 March. Constantine Peter 'Con' Curran (1883–1972), lawyer, journalist, architectural critic, and lifelong friend of James Joyce, was registrar of the Supreme Court; his wife Helen S. Laird (1887–1957), a teacher at Alexandra College, was one of the original founders of the Irish National Theatre, as 'Honor Lavelle' performing Maurya in the first production of *Riders to the Sea*, and then joined the Theatre of Ireland.

[3] Probably the niece of Lillian Stella Cooper (d. 1966), the widow of Major Bryan Cooper.

[4] See letter and note of 9 March 1932.

that you & Dolly may have some week end arrangement¹—I shall go
to the Club. Shaw² is returning from South Africa & it is just possible
I might have to go to London a day earlier to see him before my Irish
Literary Speach. Mr & Mrs Gough came over yesterday & <arranged
to> said they had decided to stay at Lough Cutra while I was away & to
come here constantly. I said I should not return until the end of April as
I must spend some time in Dublin both going & coming. If Lady G gets
suddenly worse they are to wire me and I am to return at once. I think
it probable that Lady G in another four or five weeks will be bedridden,
& in charge of nurse. She may be very near the end. I will however
arrange when I see you a scheme of life which will enable me to be a
certain time in Dublin a certain time here. <There seems a break with
Mrs Gough.³> I am Lady G sole link with her old interests but it may
be the link will break as she grows weaker. She gets up for a shorter &
shorter time but I see her as far as possible at the old times. After breakfast, after lunch when the papers come—she never opens them until
I join her—after tea & again after dinner that she may read out to me.
She reads out 'Shirley'⁴

Lilly writes that she is lunching with you to morrow & that you 'give her
courage' She says that Michael school mistress says he is 'the most delightful
little boy, so intelligent, obedient and merry'

Yours ev
WB Yeats
March 21

[ALS] | COOLE PARK, GORT, CO. GALWAY.
[22 Mar. 1932]

My dear Dobbs: I have just given Lady G a little bottle of tablets. The bottles are number 2392. The other prescription is numberd 2391. You might

¹ Dolly Robinson, now a close friend of GY, had returned from America ahead of LR.
² WBY was anxious to receive Bernard Shaw's support for the establishment of the Irish Academy of Letters.
³ Lough Cutra Castle, designed by John Nash in the early 19th century, was owned by the Gough family, but the main buildings were closed and a residence converted from the stables. AG's relationship with her daughter-in-law, now living with her husband Guy Gough at Celbridge Abbey in Co. Kildare, remained uneasy: 'I do not desire the extension of life. I have had my day—and had not rested when there was work to be done that I could do. I do not like to think of a deserted Coole & will stay here while strength permits, or till the pressure of Celbridge is too strong for my weakness' (*Journals*, ii, 14 Feb. 1932, 629).
⁴ The second novel written by Charlotte Brontë (1816–55), published in 1849, was set in a Yorkshire community in the early 19th century during the time of the Napoleonic wars and Luddite riots.

some tablets of that number sent. The two bottles will not last Lady G very long. They are now a necessity of life. She thought though it was probably fancy that 2391 was the best.

I dont think the Swami will come to Dublin. He was probably in a hurry to get his now finished book passed that he might start for America. I have told him that I returned the 'chapters' to Sturge-Moore three days ago, and that would be in London next week.

My 'broad casting' is fixed for April 10. I will have to dictate the 'patter' to you in Dublin.

Yours affly
WB Yeats

[ALS] SAVILE CLUB, | 69, BROOK STREET. W. 1.
Thursday [31 Mar. 1932]

My dear Dobbs: These are the events of the Sturge-Moore Swamy quarrel. I have seen both also Mrs Foden.[1] Swamy some where in middle winter recieved £20 from India & sent £10 as a present to Sturge Moore for his work. Sturge Moore who had never asked for anything or expected anything was furious. Returned the £10 & said that if the saint wanted to pay him the proper way was a share of his royalties. Meanwhile Mrs Foden & perhaps other admirers had gathered round the hitherto 'starving' (Mrs Fodens word) saint. They choose a literary agent for the Saint Sturge-Moore hears that they have chosen a lawyer and is still more furious, especially as somebody rings him up on the phone & accuses him of asking 'half' Swamy royalties. Sturge Moore then writes a letter refusing to take anything for his work and demanding an apology. Meanwhile Sturge Moore has put himself in the wrong by asking to have his name on the title page. I think there will be peace. He has agreed to accept some acknowledgement in the preface or my introduction instead of mention on title page & a letter of thanks from Swamy instead of apology. He must also see the final manuscript. The whole trouble has come I think from Swamy ignorance of our ways, his deciples ignorance of what was owing to a man of Sturge-Moores position & from Sturge Moore own temper. I have now the final section. I shall read it to-morrow & go through it

[1] Gwyneth Foden (Mrs Gertrude Hilda Riddell, née Woolcott; c.1885–1965) was for a time Shri Purohit's companion and self-styled protector, but would soon stir up a 'witches' cauldron' involving false accusations and possibly attempts at blackmail (see John Harwood, 'Appendix: Yeats, Shri Purohit Swami and Mrs Foden', in Warwick Gould (ed.), *Yeats Annual No. 6* (London, 1988), 102–7 and John Harwood, *Olivia Shakespear and W. B. Yeats* (London, 1989), 174–7 and below 1934–7).

with Sturge-Moore on Saturday night. I lunch with Mrs Foden & Swamy next Thursday.

Yrs always
WB Yeats

[ALS]   SAVILE CLUB, | 69, BROOK STREET. W. 1.
Wednesday [6 Apr. 1932]

My dear Dobbs: I have just seen Shaw. All settled about Academy Shaw agrees to nominate etc. I see him next weak with draft circuler. Years seem to have passed since my arrival here,—so much has been packed into the days. Endless telephone interviews about the Oath.[1] Making peace between Swamy & Sturge Moore, to day just before I set out to go to Shaw the High Commissioner[2] called. There are things he wants me to say if I meet anybody to say them to. His call however was pure friendliness. Endless messages from Lady Lavery. She is to arrange when I come next for my readings to raise money for an Academy (Shaw offers to pay preliminary expenses). I have lots of interesting thing to say but I am too tired. Tell Anne I will write to her (I did wire)[3] when I am not too tired. I have talked from 11 to 4 to day.

Yrs ev
WB Yeats

[ALS]   SAVILE CLUB, | 69, BROOK STREET. W. 1.
April 7 [1932]

P r i v a t e

My dear Dobbs: Here is a note for Anne which please read and give her if suitable. To day I am quite rested but the last few days have been a rush. Yesterday at 11 came a young man, one of Beaverbrooks leader writers who spent an hour with me. At 12 came the High Commissioner & he stayed till 1.40. He has been completely ostracised by the English Government since the first note about the Oath. There were one or two things

---

[1] The Irish government was quarrelling with England over the oath of allegiance, which de Valera had promised he would abolish if returned to power during the March 1932 election.

[2] John Whelan Dulanty (1883–1955), a consummate networker who in 1928 was appointed Irish Commissioner for Trade in Britain, then High Commissioner for Ireland in 1930 and, just before retirement in 1950, the first ambassador of the Irish Republic to the United Kingdom.

[3] Anne was once again in the nursing home having the septic toenail on her other foot removed.

I should say if I met any person of importance. At 1.40 I got to Shaw (10 minuites late for lunch) He has agreed to nominate with me the Academy & offers to pay preliminary expenses. Then at 4.30 when I was back here Lady Lavery got me on the phone. I was to make no binding engagement for the moment. I might have to go to Downing St 'for Irelands sake'. Half a hour later she rang me up again my visit to Downing St posponed till after Sunday. I dont think it will take place for I gather Downing St is in a state of fury. 'Is Ireland going to break up the Empire'? etc. I am amused & flattered—amused that I of all people should be selected to temper the wind to the shorn Republican lamb—or to some lamb for it is not quite clear who is shorn. I was at 'The Ghost Club' last night. One curious tale which will wait. I lunch to day with Mrs Foden & the Swamy then go to Lady Ottolines. I have a letter from Tom[1] & other things which must wait

Yrs affly
WB Yeats

I have just had a phone to say I am to 'meet incognito' at a house in Queens Gate at 3 to morrow somebody whom I believe to be the Prime Ministers son.[2]

[ALS Encl] SAVILE CLUB, | 69, BROOK STREET. W. 1.
April 7 [1932]

My dear Anne: I am so glad to hear you are better but I do not know if you are still in hospital so I will send this to Fitzwilliam Square. I hope you are at home again for it is very dull to be in hospital. When I was there a horrible old nurse seemed to take an especial pleasure in opening the window in cold weather. I said to one of the other nurses that I would not have minded the draft if any body else had opened the window. I have no news to send you for here there are no herons & the only swans are those tame creatures in the parks. However there are lots of nice things in the shop window that I would like to buy if I were rich enough.

When you are a little older you will come to London with me & be my secretary perhaps & speak to people on the telephone & I will get very lazy.

Yrs affecly
WB Yeats

---

[1] Thomas MacGreevy.
[2] Malcolm John MacDonald; see 10 Apr. 1932.

[ALS] SAVILE CLUB, | 69, BROOK STREET. W. 1.
[10 Apr. 1932]

Private

My dear Dobbs: I saw Malcolm Macdonald & Sir Richard Harding[1] on Friday after noon & put my case against the Oath & discribed what was I believed the Irish situation. I think I convinced them, but one or the other said that they had to consider their own wild men. I got the impression that the wild men are for the moment in control & that there will be very acute conflict between Ireland & England.[2] I find I have changed that I am much more self-possessed & potent than I used to be. I spoke well. The next day the High Commissioner called to hear the result. He offers to raise money for the Academy so I have earned his gratitude. I am resting to day to be ready for the broad cast.

I am worried lest Lady G. may run short of tablets. If she takes 3 a day they go quickly, though I do not think she takes them every day. I think you might send her some more, writing with them.

Yrs ev
WB Yeats

[TLS] 42, FITZWILLIAM SQUARE, / DUBLIN.
April 12 [1932]

My dear Willy

Your news is very interesting! Dolly and I listened to your broadcast[1]—the machine was working badly and your voice was unrecognisable, so I couldnt judge of it at all. I thought it was too slow, so very much slower than you lecture or read. We went on to the Abbey for the ballet etc. Just missed Dreaming of the Bones, but I was told that it went very much better than the last time.[2]

---

[1] Malcolm John MacDonald (1901–81), National Labour MP and at this time Under-Secretary of State for Dominion Affairs in the coalition government under his father, Prime Minister Ramsay MacDonald, and later Secretary of State for the Colonies under Stanley Baldwin; in 1937 he negotiated a new set of agreements with the Republic of Ireland to resolve disputes over trade, compensation, and the Treaty Ports, later holding many diplomatic posts including High Commissioner to Canada and India. 'Sir Richard Harding' (the title of a children's novel by Edith Nesbit) is a slip for Sir Edward John Harding (1880–1954), Permanent Under-Secretary of State for the Dominions (1930–9).

[2] On 3 May 1933 the Removal of Oath Act was passed under Fianna Fáil.

[1] WBY's programme, 'Poems about Women', was broadcast on the BBC on the evening of 10 April.

[2] See letter of 26 Oct. 1931.

Larchet[3] had altered the music for songs a little. There was a good house, not packed, but good. Ballet <u>very</u> much better than last time.

No news. I went to the opening of the Hibernian Academy yesterday— the usual crowd, and four lovely Jack pictures, two especially so.

Anne is beginning to walk about but not much yet. The toe, however, doesnt hurt her, so she can manage to amuse herself quite a lot.

This is a terribly dull letter, cant help it!

Yours ever
George.

[ALS]   SAVILE CLUB, | 69, BROOK STREET. W. 1.

April 14 [1932]

My dear Dobbs

Through flurry & confusion of mind I accept on the telephone this morning a dinner invitation for April 21, so will not be able to return till April 22. (I had marked April 20 for my limit), probably it is for the best as my life has been so crowded with work (the Indian Monk, my own business, & politics) that I have scarcely seen my friends. Yesterday I was at Macmillans. The have begun to print my <u>Edition de luxe</u> but will not issue it until autumn or next spring according to prospects in the publishing trade. I shall have proofs at once. I saw some handsom pages. As I have asked for proofs of the Indians book (not [?now] at last finished) I shall spend the spring & summer with proofs & getting 'the Vision' into final shape. I send a copy of the Indians horoscope.[1] Yesterday he said I do everything in excess & then said speking of his life before he began the Monkish life 'Once I ate 240 bannanas (or is it bananas) in a day, once I drank 14 pots of cream, once I ate 180 oranges. When I married (he had to beget a son as a religeous duty) I lay beside my wife for six months without touching her but teaching her religeon & then for six months I was sexually so excessive that I never slept until dawn had come'. His book ends with these words 'I declare with

---

[3] Dr John Francis Larchet (1884–1967), popular composer, violinist, pianist, expert in Irish music, was director of music at the Abbey Theatre from 1907 to 1934, during which time he contributed music to a number of WBY's plays, including also *The Land of Heart's Desire, Deirdre,* and *The Cat and the Moon.* He was Professor of Harmony, Counterpoint, and Composition at the Royal Irish Academy of Music (1920–55), Professor of Music at University College Dublin (1921–58), and among other public responsibilities first president of the Dublin Grand Opera Society. The original music for *The Dreaming of the Bones* was written by Walter Morse Rummel in 1917, but Dr Larchet contributed new music for the 1931 productions.

[1] Based on a copy of another astrologer's horoscope, the birth date not given.

all the fervour of which I am capable that great as is my faith in God it is
not so great as is my faith in my Master'.

Yours affly

WB Yeats

[ALS]   SAVILE CLUB, | 69, BROOK STREET. W. 1.

Friday April 15 [1932]

My dear Dobbs: to day lunched with Shaw. He has written a letter which he
& I are to sign, a letter to persons selected for Irish Academy of Letters; and
insisted on giving a checque of £50 for preliminary expenses. The Academy
to have 20 members.

Yesterday left Indian Saints MSS with Macmillan. On Monday will probably introduce Dulac & the Saint as I have suggested Macmillan getting him
to do Saints portrait. Would go back to Dublin then if I [had] not accepted
that damn dinner engagement. May get a wire calling me back to Dublin
and bolt.

Think my broad cast was successful. Broad cast people liked it & said they
would always fit me in if they could if I suggested myself.

Yrs ev

WB Yeats

[ALS]   SAVILE CLUB, | 69, BROOK STREET. W. 1

[17 Apr. 1932]

My dear Dobbs: I am getting tired which means I am going to Dublin
on Wednesday (or perhaps Tuesday). I have created urgent business there
to get out of that Thursday dinner party (Mrs Clifton).[1] All my work here
seems finished or will be if I can get to the London Library & it is now too
late to start on a social jaunt. I shall have some busy days in Dublin launching the Academy.

Yours affly

WB Yeats

---

[1] Probably Violet Mary Clifton, née Beauclerk (1883–1961), the widow of John Talbot
Clifton (1868–1928) and reputed to be a descendant of Charles II and Nell Gwynn; her name
('Peristeria Elata') appears in the list of Waite's breakaway Outer Order in June 1910 (R. A.
Gilbert, *The Golden Dawn Companion* (Wellingborough, 1986), 171). Her eccentric son Henry
'Harry' Talbot de Vere Clifton (1907–79), who dissipated the vast family fortune, would
present WBY with a Chinese carving in lapis lazuli on his 70th birthday, giving rise to the
poem 'Lapis Lazuli'.

[ALS]   SAVILE CLUB, | 69, BROOK STREET. W. 1.
                                              April 18 [1932]

My dear Dobbs: I do not yet know whether I shall to Dublin on Wednesday
or Thursday night. Sturge Moore comes to lunch that I may make what
will I hope be a final attempt to clear up the mess he has made of the
arrangements about the Saints book. He engaged an incompetant assistant
& promised him that his made [?name] would go on the title page (I take
it he had no right to do) & the incompetant assistant may turn out to be a
very competant rogue. It is a long story & must wait. At 4 I bring the Saint
to Dulacs for the plan is get Dulac to do the Saints portrait for the book
& turn a couple of photographs into line drawings, one a photograph of
Saints Master. Mrs Foden, a rich woman who is to endow a kind of Indian
monastry for the Saint has given me for you two Indian shawls, one of great
beauty.[1]

I have just had a wire from Wright saying that somebody wanted the
Abbey to produce Eugene O Neills 'Love under the Elms' & that he &
Starkey thought we should refuse. As I had not read the play I could only
wire that Starkey must decide.[2]

When I get to Dublin I shall want a meeting of certain persons who must
make a provisional Committee for Academy. We have decided to make
both Frank O Connor and Francis Stuart Academicians (keep this to yourself). I do not want any discussion as to names until the 20 chosen men have
recieved their letters of invitation.

                                                        Yrs ev
                                                        WB Yeats

[ALS[1]]   at Coole Park, Gort, Co Galway
                                              April 28 [1932]

My dear Dobbs: I enclose a letter from AE[2] <which you might send to
Frank O Connor. I know>. O Connor had told me that AE was in what
O Connor thought a difficult position—'he had so committed himself'—
He seems upset about him. But AE has knowledge that we want. If AE

[1] See note to 31 Mar. 1932; Mrs Foden's promises tended to evaporate.
[2] That is, Walter Starkie. O'Neill's *Desire under the Elms* does not appear to have been produced at the Abbey; the DDL, under LR's and GY's control, had presented *The Emperor Jones*
16–17 Jan. 1927 with a striking design by Dorothy Travers Smith (later Mrs LR), the production picked up by the Abbey a week later, and in April 1934 the Abbey produced O'Neill's
Days without End.
[1] On Fitzwilliam Square stationery, address struck out.
[2] Enclosure missing, see 30 Apr. 1932.

would act on the sub-committee O'Connor will have to work things out
with Starkie & my self, unless you can think of somebody else on our list
of Academicians who could help. I will be little use for I am not in Dublin. If O Connor cannot get AE to reconsider his refusal, he might still be
able to get his informal help. I have asked him to see AE & said I might
ask you to talk things over with him. Would O Sullivaun³ be any use with
the rules.

   Lady Gregory seems rather better. She is very wasted but does not seem
to have so much pain. She seems to stay up a little longer—probably warmer weather helps or the hope it brings.

Yrs ev
WB Yeats.

PS 1
I enclose Michaels clothes list. You put it in my charge for safe keeping, &
forgot
PS.2
I cannot find AE letter. I said nothing can be done in a country 'governed
by louts' & that it is no use fighting for any thing where the press is domi-
nated by fear of the priests⁴

[ALS¹]   at | Coole Park | Gort | Co Galway
April 30 [1932]

My dear Dobbs: Here is AE letter from which you can judge his state of
depression.² I want his help with the preliminary work badly as he knows all
about friendly Societs & their rules. I have asked Michael O Donovan³ to
do what he could You may hear from him.

   ³ Seumas O'Sullivan (James Starkey), editor of the *Dublin Magazine*.
   ⁴ See next letter.

   ¹ On Fitzwilliam Square stationery, address struck out.
   ² AE had written, 'I do not at the moment feel interested in controversies or in societies
started for that purpose. I am trying to write a book and I do not wish to have my mind
deflected to other matters. Since I stopped the Irish Statesman I have taken little interest in
Irish affairs and am very glad that I have not the task of writing about them. There is nothing
to interest me in a nation run by louts and your Academy of Letters will not have the slightest effect in a country where all the papers are united in fears of clerical denunciation. I may
think differently later on, but just now I feel alien to everything except the earth itself and if it
was not for that love I would leave Ireland' (*LWBY* 2, 532). He soon regained his pleasure in
controversy sufficiently to write a series of letters to the *Irish Times* in November and December
1932 in defence of the Academy, but by August 1933 he had resigned as honorary secretary
and moved to England.
   ³ Frank O'Connor.

I thank you for hair brush. It has made me realize, that all my life I have wanted to scratch my head & never have been able to do so hitherto. No news by post or other wise

Yrs ev
WB Yeats

I have done nothing but write letters

[ALS] at Coole Park¹ | Gort | Co Galway
April 30 [1932]

My dear Dobbs: Here are two letters which I want you attend to. <I have told the Eastborn man that you would send him a poem if you could find anything suitable, if you do.> If you think well of it send the Eastbourn man something, & send the Surrey lady a signed label.² I have still masses of unanswered letters.

Yrs ev
WB Yeats

[ALS¹] at | Coole Park | Gort | Co Galway
[*c*.1 May 1932]

My dear Dobbs

I enclose a note I have just got from O'Donovan.² If necessary I shall have to drop Starkie on the ground that we have decided not to put in the <u>first nominations</u> any body who had not done Irish work <(if it should exclude any body who has)> & this excludes both Starkie & Stephen MacKenna.³ Certain men are certain to refuse & the Academy could then elect who it liked. It would certainly elect MacKenna for one. Has Russell heard of Starkie as a possible member? I dont think I mentioned Starkeys name to AE—I am practicaly certain I did not. I am struck by O Connors strong objection. My origonal idea was that Starkie would be useful

¹ On Fitzwilliam Square stationery, address struck out; WBY.
² Unidentified petitioners.

¹ On Fitzwilliam Square stationery, address struck out.
² Enclosure from Frank O'Connor is missing; see 30 Apr. 1932.
³ Stephen MacKenna refused to accept nomination; Walter Starkie was made an Associate member.

with foreign Academies—Edwin Ellis' father[4] did the correspondence with foreign learned bodies for the Royal Society of which he was a member. I also thought Starkie could have acted as Hon Secretary & <lately I have begun to doubt him in that capacity> I thought of it as unpaid work will take on a paid typist. I can only however drop Starkie if <u>necessary</u>— Russells refusal would create a necessity. I told Shaw that Starkie could only be justified by his utility as secretary. Do you think him impossible in that capacity. I want your ideas on the subject—I am afraid of my own impulsiveness. I do not want to seem to be faithless. If there was a wish on the part (say) of Russell, O Donovan etc that we should confine nominations to those who had written about Ireland, or that such should be given first claim Shaw would of course accept the principle

Yrs affly
WB Yeats

The essential thing is a working body in Dublin. O Sullivan (remembering his magazine) might be very useful

[ALS¹]   at Coole Park, Gort, Co Galway.
                                                                       May 4 [1932]

My dear Dobbs: Dossy Wright writes that players are expected back on April [May] 10 or 11 but not Lennox. Do you [know] when he comes. I should probably should go up for the players but dont want to be in Dublin a considerable time waiting for Lennox. I have suggested that the Abbey re-open with 'Juno' or 'Far Away Hills' or 'White Headed Boy'² that wont have to reherse much in their first day or two. If I go up it will be to decide what new work to put them at.

I am coming to the conclusion about the Academy that we shall have make it a first consideration to get an efficent Dublin executive, & that we

---

⁴ Edwin John Ellis (1848–1916), poet and illustrator and with JBY and John Trivett Nettleship students together at Heatherley's Art School and members of 'The Brotherhood', who were admirers of the Pre-Raphaelites. In 1889 WBY and Ellis began work on the three-volume *Works of William Blake: Symbolic and Critical* (1893) and in 1892 the 2nd edition of WBY's *The Wanderings of Oisin* included as a new frontispiece a lithograph by Ellis; WBY's *The King's Threshold* borrows from Ellis's *Sancan the Bard* (1895). His father Alexander John Ellis (né Sharpe), FRS, FSA (1814–90), philologist, mathematician, and music theorist with a special interest in phonetics, was one of the models for Henry Higgins in Bernard Shaw's *Pygmalion* and influenced the work of Alexander Graham Bell; he was twice president of the Philological Society.

¹ Fitzwilliam Square stationery, address struck out.

² *Juno and the Paycock* by Sean O'Casey was first produced on 3 Mar. 1924; *The Whiteheaded Boy* and *The Far-Off Hills*, both by LR, on 13 Dec. 1916 and 22 Oct. 1928 respectively.

can do this without excluding obviously better people else where & send out more than 20 letters. Probably not more than 20 will except but if they do—there will have to be 25 or 30 Academicians. I would then have among the Dublin Academicians both Starkey & O Sullivan without having to exclude Miss Somerville³ or any body else of value.

Please write about Lennox Etc.

Yrs ev
WB Yeats

[ALS¹]   at Coole Park, Gort, Co Galway
April [May] 7 [1932]

My dear Dobbs: Dossy Wright says Lennox returns on May 11. I shall probably be up that day or the next as we shall have to decide what is to be the first Abbey new production. T C Murray has sent in a fine play—probably his best.² Lolly writes 'We could begin to set up your book any time now.' I have told her I would let you know. So far I have added only one short paragraph to 'A Vision'. You have told me nothing of your house-hunting³ & or endeed of anything else except for one short note about Michael & his bicycle. Yours affecly

WB Yeats

[ALS¹]   at Coole Park, Gort, Co Galway
May 9 [1932]

My dear Dobbs: I shall come up Wednesday unless I hear something next post that makes decide for Tuesday. In either case I shall wire. Abbey business of all sorts.

---

³ Edith Anna Œnone Somerville (1858–1949), Irish novelist and artist who with her cousin Violet Martin, 'Martin Ross' (1862–1915), collaborated in fourteen books, including the popular series of stories initiated by *Some Experiences of an Irish R.M.* (1899), travel sketches, and the outstanding novel *The Real Charlotte* (1894); after Martin Ross's death Somerville, a spiritualist, wrote a further fifteen books under their joint name. A founding member of the Irish Academy of Letters, she was awarded the Academy's Gregory Medal in 1941. An ardent feminist and equestrian, in 1903 she became the first woman Master of Foxhounds.

¹ On Fitzmaurice Square stationery with address struck out.
² *Michaelmas Eve* by T. C. Murray received its first performance at the Abbey Theatre on 27 June 1932.
³ On WBY's return from London the search for a house with garden began; eventually they discovered Riversdale (see 11 July 1932).

¹ On Fitzmaurice Square stationery with address struck out.

Edith Sitwell writes that London for the last three days has talked of nothing but the great scandal, which has come 'Echoing from America' & she is herself very pleased because she foresaw it all years about [ago] when she described the lady in question as Lady Bamburger in 'Gold Coast Customs'.[2] What has happened is that Nancy Cunard is has been living in a negro hotel in Harlem telling all to a multitude of reporters who are too shocked—or their editors are—to print the details. She is now however in 'a rooming house in Harlem' owing to the fact that the emmense publicity made the inhabitants of negro hotel shy. She was entreated to leave.[3] There is the post

Yrs ev
WB Yeats

[ALS[1]]   at Coole Park, Gort, Co Galway
May 10 [1932]

My dear George: I have wired 'Must delay till Thursday writing letter important.' I did this fearing that otherwise you might be at Dalkey perhaps when this letter arrived.

Last night Lady Gregory told me that the lump in her breast had grown very much bigger 'especially in the last few days' She wanted to go to Dublin to see Slattery. I persuaded her to wait until she had heard from him (He had told me 'there would be no question of an operation') This morning I wrote to Slattery & asked him to wire. I want you to telephone him to-morrow & find out if Lady Gregory is to come up. If she must do so please meet the train, & have some kind of wheeled chair to bring Lady G from the carriage to the taxi. I am afraid in any case she will have a

---

[2] See 26 June 1928 for WBY's first meeting with Edith Sitwell, whose experimental poem 'Gold Coast Customs' (1929) rhythmically excoriates society's barbarism and decadence in the 'rotting parties and death-slack ease' of 'Lady Bamburgher'; WBY would select six poems (18 pages) from Sitwell's work, including extracts from 'Gold Coast Customs', for publication in his *Oxford Book of Modern Verse 1892–1936* (1936).

[3] Nancy Clare Cunard (1896–1965), daughter of WBY's influential friend Lady Cunard and friend of George Moore, was a poet, social activist, journalist, and founder of the Hours Press in Paris which published EP's *A Draft of XXX Cantos* and Samuel Beckett's first separately published work, his poem *Whoroscope*. In the 1930s she began a relationship with the black jazz musician Henry Crowder, and became an activist for racial equality and civil rights, leading to her fight against fascism; her polemical pamphlet *Black Man and White Ladyship* (1931) explicitly attacked her mother and the social circles of London; in 1934 she edited *Negro: An Anthology*. When she stayed in a hotel in New York's Harlem district during her visit in April 1932, newspapers such as the *Daily Mirror* and the *Daily News* and the newsreel *Movietone News* headlined and scurrilously attacked her every move.

[1] On Fitzmaurice Square stationery with address struck out.

very painful journey. She can go to Athenry by motor but the getting from motor to train will be painful. She is stronger than she was, sits up longer, but much more crippled. Yesterday after noon she had a desire to get down to the library & tried to, leaning on my arm, but had to give it up. She had however on Sunday morning for the first time for months got down stairs & out in front of the house where she sat for a few minuites. I now think she was testing herself with the thought of this journey. The effort brought on some pain. It is characteristic of her that all these months she has never spoken of the lump in the breast (I knew from Margeret that it was still there) & that last night after speaking of it for two or three minuites & the journey to Dublin she said 'We will now dismiss the subject' & began to read out Charlotte Bronte.

Slattery may bring her to Dublin to keep her under his eye. In that case she will in a very short time find a return here impossible.[2]

Yrs affly
WB Yeats

[ALS]   COOLE PARK, | GORT, CO. GALWAY.
                                        Monday 2.30 [23 May 1932]

My dear George: Lady Gregory died last night about 12.30. She became ill on Friday, Yesterday seemed a little better & got up at her usual hour & went into the children play room, which has been her sitting room of late, & sat there most of the day. Margeret was with her. Margeret thought she suffered much pain. They got her to go to bed, & when there she seemed better for a time. Laterly she was almost unconcious but asked Katherine[1] to say the Lords Preyer.

Mrs Gregory had phoned for me yesterday morning & thought Keller said he had 'got through'.[2] She thought I could have motered down. She thinks that at the end Lady Gregory thought 'Everybody was there'.

I am giving this to Guy who is going to Galway with Margeret to choose a grave. Margeret has asked me to stay here as she 'does not want to be

---

[2] AG did not go back to Dublin, but on 12 May WBY returned on Abbey business, meeting the players on their return from America, discussing AG's condition with her doctor, and arranging the purchase of 'Riversdale'.

[1] Catherine Gregory, her granddaughter.

[2] Keller (T. G. Keohler) was AG's solicitor. On 19 June 1932 WBY drafted a detailed, highly personal description of her last days, edited and published by Colin Smythe (see 'The Death of Lady Gregory' and 'Afterword' in *Journals*, ii. 632–60).

alone' (Guy & the grand children are at Lough Cutra) She is afraid among
other things of press-men coming. Richard could not be reached in time.

Yrs affly

WB Yeats

[ALS]   42, FITZWILLIAM SQUARE, | DUBLIN.

July 6 [1932]

My dear Anne

I have heard how well you are doing at School, & I have been very glad
endeed. Your mother is tired out putting things into bundles & boxes to take
them to Rathfarnham. As I am greatly in the way she is sending me to Glen
da lough to-morrow where I shall stay for more than a weak getting more
& more impatient for my new study. The study walls are to be all yellow
like a butter cup

Yours ever

WB Yeats

[ALS[1]]   Royal Hotel, Glendalough

July 11 [1932]

My dear Dobbs

I am at work on my 'Modern Ireland' lecture & am making discoveries as
I write.[2] I think it will be an essay for the new collected edition. I am a little bored—Iseult has gone to Roebuck House to see Madam Gonne before
Mrs Despard gets back[3] & I find Frances Stuart alone rather flat—but in
excellent health those pains that alarmed me have almost gone. I am able to
step in & out of the house as I did at Coole & so get much exercise without
noticing it. Iseult comes back to morrow & I dine there.[4] Frances Stuart
always agrees with me or pretends to & that is very dull & he has a young

---

[1] On Fitzwilliam Square stationery, address struck out.

[2] Some of this lecture for his American tour was incorporated in 'Commentary on "A
Parnellite at Parnell's Funeral"', *The King of the Great Clock Tower* (1934); the entire lecture was
edited by Curtis Bradford and first published in the *Massachusetts Review*, Winter 1964.

[3] MG and Madame Despard had together purchased 'Roebuck House', Clonskeagh, Co.
Dublin, in August 1922, where they established several small businesses to give employ-
ment to ex-prisoners. In 1933 Mrs Despard moved into Dublin and the following year to
Belfast, but MG remained at Roebuck House with her son and his family; see note to 28
Nov. 1922.

[4] The Stuarts were living in 'Laragh Castle', a former barracks in Glendalough, where
Francis had established, then in 1932 sold, a poultry farm.

art student with him called 'Lulu' who never opens her mouth.[5] The hotel is pleasant & quiet & I have a writing table in my room.

Yours affectionly
WB Yeats

Frances Stuart gradually let out first that he new who wrote 'Tara Hall' & then that he himself at the request of Mary Manning had written in to it some sentences of horsy dialogue.[6] He had evidently not told Iseult about it. I gather that the communist cook is a reality. She was selected by Mrs Despard.

What on earth is the correspondence which the Governor General asked the Irish Times to publish, & the Executive Council declares 'a State secret'?[7]

[TLS]   42, FITZWILLIAM SQUARE, | DUBLIN.
Monday [11 July 1932]

My dear Willy

I dont know if you have favoured me with a letter because I had to come in to the flat on Sunday night to collect the 'gas fires'—the gas fitters declared that their work would be 'delayed' if they did not get them today....and as all work has been so much delayed....[1]

Mrs Gogarty[2] rang up to know if you could lunch today. I told her that as far as I knew you were at Glendalough...I was a little vague purposely,

[5] Unidentified.
[6] Stuart was intensely interested in horse-racing, and had owned a horse himself. I have been unable to trace 'Tara Hall'. Mary Elizabeth Manning (1905–99), novelist, playwright, actor, and critic, was a student of the Abbey Acting School and had performed in two plays by the DDL before becoming publicity manager for the Gate Theatre which produced her plays *Youth's the Season...?* (1931, assisted by her childhood friend Samuel Beckett) and *Happy Family* (1934); she emigrated to Boston in 1935, married Harvard law professor Mark de Wolfe Howe, and helped found the Poet's Theater in Cambridge where *The Voice of Shem*, her play based on Joyce's *Finnegan's Wake*, was produced in 1955. After her husband's death in 1967 she returned to Dublin to become theatre critic for the *Irish Times;* her adaptation of Frank O'Connor's *The Saint and Mary Kate* was produced at the Abbey Theatre in 1968; in 1980 she married American lawyer Faneuil Adams of Cambridge, Mass.
[7] A brief message appeared in the *Irish Times*, 11 July 1932, explaining that at 1.15 a.m. that morning the editors had received a message from the Minister for Justice (James Geoghagan) prohibiting the publication of a correspondence between Governor-General James McNeill and Éamon de Valera, recently appointed President of the Executive Council, although the Governor-General himself had earlier sent copies requesting publication, which were published in full the following day. The dispute between the representative of the British crown and the Republican Fianna Fáil government was during this time highly public.

[1] By late July the move to Riversdale, Willbrook, Rathfarnham was completed.
[2] Martha Mary 'Neenie' Gogarty, née Duane (1876–1958), wife of Dr Gogarty.

said you might be at the Club, because I did not want to offen[d] Gogarty with the statement that you were at Glendalough until...when?

I feel that I am getting too old for this kind of thing: my pace is got slow, I dont get through things with the rapidity that I managed even five years ago! Of course when we moved five years ago it was Dublin to Dublin which made a difference.

The garden looks perfect. I made John[3] arrange so that we could leave open the gates into the lawn when we have a party without fear of the hens escaping. <There is a small> This has been done most skilfully!

Yours

G.

[ALS[1]]   Royal Hotel | Glendalough

July 11 [1932]

My dear Dobbs: I forgot to say that I gave directions, & was advised, to sell out the 500 war loan & pay off overdraft; Today I noticed in the paper that if I converted it it would bring me 3½ per cent & I would get one per cent bonus. And further I seem to remember that I was told that all I pay the bank for that part of my overdraft is 3 per cent. If this is so, I lose one half per cent per annum on 500 pounds (£2.10.0 per annum) & one per cent on whole £5. If you think this sum worth bothering about this letter gives you full power to countermand my order to sell if it be not too late. I am a goose in these things because my head is full of other things. I am sorry if I have made a mess

Yrs affly

WB Yeats

No pains to night—am I think quite well again

[ALS]   42, FITZWILLIAM SQUARE, | DUBLIN.[1]

[13] July [1932]

My dear Dobbs: If tomorrow is rainy I shall go back to Dublin and to the club. This hotel is full of children who keep running up & down stairs & past my door. There are, I think, three families. The worst consists of six so much the same in size & voice that I am certain all six were born at a single birth. They are very good children but intolerable. Yesterday was bad

---

[3] John Henry Free (b. 1910), a young local man who was the gardener at Rathfarnham.

[1] On Fitzwilliam Square stationery, address struck out.

[1] Annotated by GY 'From Royal Hotel, Glendalough.'

enough but to day, when they cannot get out, exceeds imagination. Probaby I would bolt at once, but I have asked the Stuarts to dine. I have done a good days work on 'Modern Ireland'. Yesterday Gogorty phoned me to come to lunch but I refused, two hours of the buss either way.

Ah if only the children were not here how beatiful this place would be, the Stuarts want me to stay but I should bore them & talk my self stupid. We have not enough in common to give back a splash when I drop a stone. Every second day I can with great pleasure sit on the well-side <& drop in my stones,> & applaud my own stone.

Yrs affecly
WB Yeats

[ALS] Royal Hotel | Glendalough | Co Wicklow
July 14 [1932]

My dear Dobbs

Francis Stuart & Iseult dined with me last night. Lulu had been out fishing & got wet & did not come. The conversation was profound & gave me great help in my 'Modern Ireland' Lulus absence & Iseults presence made the diffrence. I dine with them to night. They want me to stay with them if I find the children too much, but I shall either stay here, or go back to Dublin. My pains are all gone & my essay is going well.

Yrs ev
WB Yeats

[ALS] Glendalough
July 15 [1932]

My dear Dobbs

Noise too great so I am moving after lunch to the Stuarts. On Monday I shall go to town probably first buss & will be at Club. I shall come here to-morrow for letters & [if] there is none from you then, I shall expect one at club.

Yrs ev
WB Yeats

[ALS] SAVILE CLUB, | 69, BROOK STREET. W. 1.
Tuesday [11 Oct. 1932]

My dear Dobbs: Your letters have just come. I will not write more than a word as I developing a cold.

I want you to bring to London a copy of the letters giving the terms of my lecture tour.¹ I shall want it in U.S.A.

Yrs ev
WB Yeats

Would you mind locking up the sword in some safe place.²

[ALS]   SAVILE CLUB, | 69, BROOK STREET. W. 1.

Oct 13 [1932]

My dear Dobbs: I too have had a cold—yesterday & part of the day before in bed. To day no great things but lunched with Sturge Moore. I will call at 'The Orchard Hotel' to-morrow about 2.30 unless you phone to contrary or invite me to lunch

Yrs affly
WB Yeats

[TLS & MS]   RIVERSDALE, | WILLBROOK, |

RATHFARNHAM, | DUBLIN.¹
October 24 1932

My dear Willy

I enclose a couple of extracts from Irish Times and one from Irish Press. Not that they are particularly interesting but they act as ballast for your pills which came here three hours after we had left on Friday....opened by the customs.

You will have got a wireless from me containing no news except a demand for your New York address and affectionate greetings. I hope you havent had too bad a journey and that you picked up something elegant and pleasing to talk to! !

---

¹ WBY was leaving on 21 Oct. 1932 to lecture in the United States and Canada, his last extended tour, to raise funds for the Irish Academy of Letters and for expenses of the move to Riversdale.

² While in Portland, Oregon, in March 1920 during his previous tour of the United States, WBY was given the 600-year-old short sword 'Motoshigé' by Junzo Sato (1897–?1988), a young Japanese member of the Ministry of Agriculture and Commerce who later as a diplomat in Europe took a special interest in the arts; see 'A Sketch of my Life by Junzo Sato', in Shotaro Oshima, *W. B. Yeats and Japan* (1965), 131–3. I am grateful to Professor Yoko Chiba for sharing her research on Sato.

¹ Written from London.

Sidmouth was pleasant—19[2] was being sane and sensible bar the fact that she insisted on motoring me to Exeter that I might catch a train which left twenty minutes later than the one I had intended to take from Sidmouth on the grounds that it would bring me to London at nine PM instead of at 10 PM. Actually the train stopped at every station and arrived in London at ten minutes to 11. I examined my conscience severely and finally decided not to tell her; if she does it to anyone else its their own fault for not looking up the train themselves!! She and Harry came to the station (Exeter) and it seemed heartless to write and say 'your train dont arrive at 9 PM'—Harry is taking his uncle-hood to Omar seriously. He solemnly asked me, when we were alone 'At what age did Michael read?' And I said 'about five' upon which Harry sighed heavily, and looked worried and finally said 'Omar cant read anything, he was six in October'. I said 'He has probably decided he prefers being read to' upon which Harry cheered up a little and then got depressed again and said 'he ought to be coerced. He is spoilt'. From what I hear Omar is the most spoilt of all only children, but I am inclined to think also from what I hear that in about a year, or maybe two, Dorothy, who apparently Omar obeys where he obeys no one else, will import him to 'school abroad'.[3]

I hope you are looking after yourself; yesterday I tracked down Eric Gill's 'Four Gospels' (it is 'out of print' and the Cockrel Press had no copy) at Dulau's.[4] I had been to 8 bookshops. I looked at it and when I had quite decided that we must have it I said 'It is twelve guineas I think' whereon Dulau said 'O no, it was published at eight guineas and we have not put up the price because we bought it at sale price'. You will find it at Riversdale when you return. It is a lovely book. Dulau said to me 'I think it is one of the best pieces of typography since the Chelmscott Press Chaucer'. Apart

[2] EET, GY's mother, was always referred to according to the Phase in *A Vision* to which WBY and GY thought she corresponded: 'the beginning of the artificial, the abstract, the fragmentary, and the dramatic. Unity of Being is no longer possible…governed by conviction, instead of by a ruling mood…so to use an intellect which turns easily to declamation, emotional emphasis' (*Vision A*, 148).

[3] Omar Pound (1926–2010) went as an infant to the Norland Institute in London under the care of his grandmother, OS; in 1933 he attended a Montessori School in Sussex, and 1940–3 was a student at Charterhouse School in Sussex. Later he was to serve in the US Army of Occupation in Germany before taking up an academic career as a specialist in Islamic studies, producing a number of books and poems and translations from the Persian and Arabic, and editions of the correspondence of EP and his mother.

[4] Dulau's, 32 Old Bond Street, an antiquarian bookshop founded in 1792, was by now a limited company with no member of the original family involved. The sculptor and wood engraver Arthur Eric Rowton Gill (1882–1940) designed his first original typeface for the Golden Cockerel Press limited edition of *The Four Gospels* (1931), considered the finest example of Gill's design and illustrations.

from the fact that it may increase in value it is a most lovely book (the binding by the way is Sangorski and Sutcliffe's⁵)

Yours most affectionately

George Yeats.

I go to Dublin tonight.

[ALS]　　　　　　　　　　　　　　　　　D. 'EUROPA' NORD LLOYD

Tuesday [25 Oct. 1932]

My dear Dobbs: This is the first day of little wind, people look cheerful &
I have just met a strange thing on wheels like a vacuum cleaner used to
pump air into the seasick. But the weather has never seemed to me bad,
though that ladies unhappy secretary, who came to tea yesterday, after a
pale anxious hour set out to return to her own part of the ship escorted
by Alan¹ & did not get there safely I have been comfortable except for an
encounter with the clam the very first day at dinner. Alan said of the fish
sauce 'this may be the enemy'. Forgetful of past experience I tasted it to see
with the usual results.

I have met a couple of acquaintances on board, one a man returning
from Constantinople where he has been employed as an archeologist upon
the mozaics of St Sophia. He says 'at last we have a series of mozaics from
the time of Justinian down to the last dynasty which are all the work of
great masters.'

Yrs affly

WB Yeats

I have sent the children a couple of post-cards each.

[TLS Dict]　　　　　　　　　　　WALDORF-ASTORIA | NEW YORK

Oct. 28th. 1932.

My dear George,

We arrived in a dense fog, or rather we lay anchored in it for hours, and
finished our journey when it cleared off. We reached this hotel at 12 o'clock

---

⁵ The hand book bindery established in 1901 by George Herbert Sutcliffe (1878–1943) and
Francis Longius Sangorski (1875–1912). On WBY's 40th birthday friends, spearheaded by AG,
presented WBY with a copy of *The Works of Geoffrey Chaucer* (1896), edited by F. S. Ellis and
designed by William Morris at his Kelmscott Press.

¹ Alan Duncan accompanied WBY as secretary; among WBY's papers is a typed accounting of money advanced to Duncan and spent in preparation for the journey; see note to 5
Feb. 1931.

at night. Next day there were various interviewers, at night a dinner at the Authors Club.¹ Today I was interviewed and my portrait drawn and a charming young man son of the old reprobate Brett² came from the Macmillan Coy to arrange about the Guaranty Trust Fund, and to talk about my books. Tonight I go to see 'Words on the Window pane'.³ The telephone goes all day long (Alan interpolates 'Indeed it does') I have seized a spare quarter of an hour while waiting some young people who are getting up a play of mine, to dictate this letter. My lecture tour is all filled up, 25 or 26 lectures. I find that I have forgotten the envelope containing the addresses of my Toronto relatives.⁴ Would you mind sending me those addresses at once; it seems unlikely that I shall lecture there after all, but I shall be at Montreal on the 27 and 28 of November—Since writing this I have decided to cable you for the addresses.

This letter was interrupted this afternoon by people who came to question me about one of my plays; I have just come in from the theatre where 'The Words upon the Window Pane' was played before a vast audience, every seat sold and people standing. It was followed by the 'Playboy', but I was tired and came back here with Alan who must hurry back to the theatre in a few minutes to see Mrs Martin who entertained us at Lakeview in Chicago;⁵ she sent round a note giving the number of her seat; she wants me to dine with her. I made a speech at the end of my play. Tomorrow morning at ten thirty Russell's friend Judge Campbell⁶ calls, and at a quarter to twelve a motor comes to take me into the country that I may stay with a society leader Bracken

¹ On 27 Oct. 1932 WBY was guest of honour at the Authors Club, 48 West 76th St, on the occasion of his election as an honorary member, the 36th in the last fifty years, preceded by Hauptmann, Tagore, Masefield, and Galsworthy; he was introduced at the dinner by Louis J. Alber of the Alber & Wickes Lecture Bureau (see 29 Oct. 1931). In his interviews WBY concentrated on his plans for the Irish Academy of Letters.

² George Platt Brett (1859–1936), president of The Macmillan Company in New York, had first published WBY's works in 1903; in 1931 his son, George Platt Brett, Jr. (1893–1984), became president and, on the death of his father, chief executive officer.

³ The Abbey Theatre players, who were on an American tour October 1931–April 1932, performed Yeats's *The Words upon the Window-Pane* and Synge's *The Playboy of the Western World* in a double bill at the Martin Beck Theatre, 45th Street W. and 8th Avenue; the critic Brooks Atkinson of the *New York Times* remarked of WBY's appearance on the stage, 'It is remarkably stimulating, in the midst of hackneyed theatricals, to have both a strange play and a passion.' Other plays advertised for New York were LR's *The Far-Off Hills*, AG and WBY's *Kathleen ni Houlihan*, and O'Casey's *The Shadow of a Gunman*.

⁴ See 25 Nov. 1932.

⁵ During WBY's previous lecture tour he and GY were in Chicago in early March 1920, but I have been unable to trace Mrs Martin.

⁶ Richard Campbell (1872–1935), a close friend of AE, was born in Larne, Co. Antrim, and emigrated as a child, working as a newspaper reporter in New York before studying law; he served as a Judge of the First Instance in the Philippines until retiring in 1917 to pursue a private law practice in New York, and was a member of the executive committee of the American Commission for Relief in Ireland which was established in 1921.

introduced me to⁷: I hope to get both her and Judge Campbell's help for my
Academy lectures. On Monday I start on my lecture tour in good earnest.

Yours ev

WB Yeats

[MS] I meant to add something to this but Allan is waiting with a pile of
letters
PS.
[TS] Somebody said in a speech last night at the Authors Club that in his
experience the New York press had never been so enthusiastic about any
theatrical event as they have been about the Abbey plays and players.

W.B.Y.

[TLS]   RIVERSDALE, | WILLBROOK, |
                                      RATHFARNHAM, | DUBLIN.
                                              November 2 1932

My dear Willy

I had a faint hope that I might get a postcard from you on todays American Mail. I expect you have been rather snowed under this first week. I am
writing to Alan to tell him that part of his secretarial duties is to report to
me once a week, either by letter or night cable, how you are.

When I got back here our gate lodge tenant came up to say that he had
got a job at Crumlin WITH GATE LODGE!!!!!! They moved out yesterday.
Really God is very good at times. Chrissie and I went down this morning to
brush and clean out—you never saw anything like the filth of the place. We
tore off all the damp wallpaper from the bedroom walls, (three layers) opened
windows that had not been opened for time immemorial, sprayed jeyes fluid
over all, and had a huge bonfire. I got Roberts¹ to send out a man to report
on the roof etc (for damp) and to estimate for a door to what he called 'the
privvy'. The present 'privvy' hath no door and hath been used for a rubbish heap of bycycles (all broken) disused clocks, jam jars, empty bottles, and
portions of bedsteads and mattresses. Question how did the Rileys (our last
tenants) manage?! The roof does not need much, chiefly a little pointing, but
the gutter system has to be inaugurated for at present the rain has no trap
and so gently and persuasively runs into the walls—hence damp—
Your cat is adorable, he is very affectionate, perfectly square, and since I
beat him for trying to pounce on a wren he turns his face away from all
sitting birds, this may not last but future smacks await him.

---

⁷ Mrs Harrison Williams; see note to 4 Nov. 1932.

¹ Albert Roberts & Co. of 133 Baggot Street, Dublin, builders and decorators.

Anne was here on Sunday, she looked very well and very tall. She had 'gone up' five and a half pounds last holidays when weighed at school but as she had also grown just over ½ inch in three months I dont think that matters! She looked thinnish in the face which becomes her. She comes home on Saturday for the half term week-end. On Sunday your sisters are having a party to which I go—with Anne—

The Spectator has your Prometheus Essay,[2] and poems—Macmillan has The Vision and diagrams,—all sorts of nuisances have been replied to.... BUT <u>DID I TELL YOU THAT THE BODKIN HUGH LANE BOOK ARRIVED?????</u>[3] I dont think I did, and it is most important that you write to thank for it. You can dictate the letter to Alan. I enclose on separate sheet a copy of the letter which arrived with the book.[4] I am not sure if you should write to the President's Private Secretary or to himself. You will be the best judge of this. I have acknowledged with thanks to the Secretary, explaining that you are in USA.

Yours ever
George Dobbs.

[ALS]   ELMWOOD HOTEL | WATERVILLE MAINE
Nov 4 [1932]

My dear George: I have a moment of leisure at this little university town.[1] This is a big sunny room in the hotel over looking leasurly streets & detached wooden houses. It is the end of a hard week, the hardest I shall have probably, two lectures a day on two of the days, one lecture a day on the other days. To morrow I return to New York, a long journey, spend the day there & start off again on Monday. But next week there are only two lectures & the long journey to Chicago. If I do not find myself tired when I get to New York to morrow night I shall accept a proposal of 'Alber Wicks'[2] to stay on after Xmas & give more lectures. I picture to myself the little house in the yard put in perfect order, a play room there.[3] If I stay on I shall keep

---

[2] 'Prometheus Unbound' was published by *The Spectator*, 17 Mar. 1933, and reprinted in *Essays 1931 to 1936* (Cuala, 1937); the revised version of *A Vision* was published by Macmillan in 1937.

[3] *Hugh Lane and his Pictures* by Thomas Bodkin, director of the National Gallery, was published by the Government of Saorstat Eireann in the autumn of 1932, with the 400 copies presented by President de Valera to various libraries, art institutions, and individuals.

[4] Enclosure missing.

[1] Colby College, a private liberal arts college, was founded in Waterville in 1813.

[2] The Alber & Wickes Bureau; see 29 Oct. 1931.

[3] Riversdale, the Yeatses' last home together, was a 'rather squat and square' creeper-covered 17th-century farmhouse, only two storeys high, and the rooms small in comparison with those of Merrion Square, but WBY's study, the former conservatory, looked out upon fine walled gardens and lawns inviting croquet and other games, while the old stables became the children's playrooms (see *BG*, 451–4 ff.).

Allan. I shall send the children some post cards as soon as I find any but there are none, or none that would mean anything, in these little university towns. I had a charming week end at Mrs Harrison Williams but I think I told you. A great house by the sea with fine pictures, great gardens & a large covered tennis court & swimming pool—yes I remember I told you. Did I describe the room by the swimming pool, a great high room, made out of pointed arches covered with silver leaf, fine frescos over the mantle pieces by some Spaniard, Goya like things made to tone in with the general silver & brown.[4]

Allan is a great help, life here would be impossible without him. Give the children my love.

I have finished D. H. Lawrence 'Women in Love' a beautiful enigmatic book. I feel in sympathy with him as I do not with Virginia Woolf.[5] He is full enquiery & very courageous. His language is too romantic his metephors often seem to me worn out while his thought is new & vivid

Yrs affly
WB Yeats

[TLS]
RIVERSDALE, | WILLBROOK, | RATHFARNHAM, | DUBLIN.
November 8 1932

My dear Willy

Your letter arrived just as I had sealed up mine to you. I was starting off for Dublin, so I didnt open it to add any remarks—not that there were any beyond surprise that you investigated the clam sauce!!!!!!!!

I see you were dining at the Authors Club. A press cutting came to the Abbey with a horrid flashlight photograph of you which made you look very

---

[4] Mona Schlesinger Bush Williams, née Mona Travis Strader (1897–1983), whose third husband was the multi-millionaire utilities executive Harrison Charles Williams (1873–1953), was famous not only as a society hostess and 'the best-dressed woman in the world', but as an astute patron of the arts; their 94-acre estate and 80-room mansion 'Oak Point', Bayville, Long Island (one of three houses owned by Williams at that time), was noted for the antiques and Chinese porcelain Mrs Williams had selected on their frequent voyages around the world, and also the frescoes in the sports pavilion which had been commissioned from the Spanish artist Jose Maria Sert Y Badia (1874–1945). After Harrison Williams's death she married Count Edward Albert Bismarck, the grandson of Germany's Iron Chancellor Otto von Bismarck, and after his death Count Umberto de Martini, whom she also survived.

[5] David Herbert Lawrence (1885–1930), novelist, short story writer, critic, artist, and playwright, had with Woolf been a frequent guest at Garsington, along with others who often became characters in his works; his major novels—*Sons and Lovers* (1912), *The Rainbow* (1915), *Women in Love* (1920), *Lady Chatterley's Lover* (1928)—were banned as obscene because of his courageous insistence upon sexual freedom and its expression.

stern and very thin in the face. I hope that does not mean that you are having too much entertainment and are getting done up.

The Sweepticket play[1] seems to have been a success; there was great
enthusiasm on Monday night and roars of laughter. Personally I also
roared.... the post has just come with a letter from you. You are very good
to write when you are in such a rush. I hope Bracken's lady will give you a
quiet weekend—or is it only a night.[2]

Lily is coming to stay on Saturday for a few days. She isnt very well and
a change may do her good. She needs stirring up or perhaps cheering up.
I shall put her in your room as she can have her gas fire for breakfast in
bed.

With love
Dobbs

[APS[1]] DEARBORN ENGINEERING LABORATORY AND AIRPORT
Dearborn, Mich.
[11 Nov. 1932]

Today I have been through the Ford works at Detroit. When ever I go to
any big town there is a car called a Lincoln with its chauffer to take me
where I wish. It is leant me by the Ford Company Detroit
WB Yeats

[ALS] BOOK-CADILLAC HOTEL | DETROIT
Nov 12 [1932]

My dear Dobbs: I am hourly expecting the telegram that is to tell me
whether I am to go to Chicago or not. Wicks has fallen out with a turbul-
lent Scotsman called Fergusson—Lennox would tell you all about him—&
unles the unforseen happens my four Chicago lectures are abolished. Fergusson wrote me a preposterous half man [mad] letter. He wanted me to
break my contract with Wicks & give the four lectures under him. If the
Chicago lectures are abolished I shall be stranded somewhere for the next
eight days. I shall have more than twenty lecturs in any case. I shall stay in

[1] *The Big Sweep* by Matthew Michael Brennan, whose short comedy *The Young Man from Rathmines* (1922) was an Abbey favourite, opened on 7 Nov. 1932.
[2] Mrs Harrison Williams (see note to 4 Nov. 1932).

[1] A postcard showing the Ford Engineering laboratory and Ford Airport, addressed to Michael Yeats Riversdale, Willbrook Rathfarnham Dublin Ireland, address struck out and 'Baymount school Dollymount' added.

New York for last half of December & lecture in drawing rooms for the Irish Academy—Judge Cambell[1] has arranged 3 lectures & promises others—then I may return to Europe or stay on for part of January. I said I would stay if eight more lectures were got for me. I want to bring you after all expenses have been paid five or six hundred pounds & a couple of hundred for the Academy (I may get more).

I look forward to being home with great excitement. Perhaps I shall ask you to meet me somewhere, where we can be together for a little without distracting business. I shall deserve that reward if I bring you five or six hundred. I have had no letter but I am comforted because Allan also has heard nothing from his wife

I have sent Michael & Anne photograph post cards of the Ford works. The Ford Company has put at my disposal a Lincoln car in all the chief towns. I have the drivers who drove Churchill.[2] I thought it but needful politeness to accept an invitation to go through works. They are the most efficient of factories but also what Ford builds in the corner of the room with his box of bricks. There is the first house that was lit with electricity; Edisons birth place, his first laboratory, all taken up with the earth they stood on & transplanted from some other state—Endless shows of the same kind.

Yours affectionately
WB Yeats

[ALS]   NETHERLAND PLAZA | CINCINNATI | OHIO
[18 Nov. 1932]

My dear Dobbs: This is a beautiful hotel. Furniture well designed & of beautiful wood.[1] We have three rooms, one room a sitting room & these rooms are 'complementary' (Alber Wicks want to make up I suppose for that collapse of my four Chicago lectures). I am getting through this torrid American winter with the help of iced water & shower baths. I am not tired but bored. I will never come again without you—I long for you perpetually.

If I do not get ill—and I am very well—I shall have earned, Allan says, £500 over all expenses by Dec 15. Then I give half a dozen drawing room lectures for Academy. I shall take expenses for Allan & my self. Then will come 8 or 10 more public lectures adding say £200 more to our £500. Then

---

[1] Judge Richard Campbell; see 28 Oct. 1932.

[2] Winston Churchill made an extensive lecture tour of the USA and Canada in 1929, and returned in December 1931, when his tour was cut short when he was struck by a taxi in New York; on both visits he was entertained lavishly by prominent businessmen.

[1] Now the Hilton Cincinnati Netherland Plaza, the hotel, known for its French Art Deco design and furnishings, opened in 1931.

in middle January we shall return. If Alber Wicks fail to get lectures for January I shall return at end of December.

I go to day for a couple of days to a Mr Howes[2]—James Stephens is staying with him. This is Friday & we stay in this neighbourhood until Tuesday (Nov 22).

I am reading D H Lawrence with great excitement. He has brought back the material of literature, after the error of the last 30 years. He is often clumsy in style, almost ungramatical now & again, but there is passion as Shakespeare understood it. I have read 'The Rainbow' 'Women in Love' & am in the middle of 'Sons & Lovers' My only dread is that I may find him monotonous but I have not so far.

Yrs affecly
WB Yeats

[TLS]   Riversdale | Rathfarnham | Dublin.
                                            PHONE Terenure 758
                                                Nov. 23 [1932]

My dear Willy

Many thanks for your letter from Detroit. But surely you will have had some letters now?? I posted one from London which contained some Irish press cuttings, addressed to Macmillan's. The other letters were <u>all</u> posted in Dublin, two of them at the GPO. When you arrive back to Southampton I shall meet you and we can do a little jaunt somewhere—I suggest not London—then you might return here for a few weeks and do your London Academy lectures in April or May. I do think London is much nicer then, also you would be less cold and foggy.

The gate lodge has been done up and looks extremely nice. <u>John</u> is going into it!!! He asked Chrissie if she thought he had a chance, and she asked me and I of course leapt at the idea. The rent is to be deducted from his wages! His own arrangement. I gave him carte blanche to do what he liked with the ground round it, the result was that he spent his last Saturday half holiday with his two immense brothers clearing out all the half cut down holly trees, and the general mess in front. Today he is going to clear some more. Then he plans to 'continue the lawn' down from the cypress tree so that 'the lodge will set off the house'. I think we shall have a model lodge!

---

[2] William Thomas Hildrup Howe (1874–1939) of Cincinnati, a former Yale professor and mineralogical chemist, assembled over forty years a collection of 16,000 books and MSS which at his death was purchased by fellow collector Dr Albert A. Berg; he became president of the American Book Company (founded 1890), at that time the world's leading publisher of educational materials. James Stephens visited him regularly in Cincinnati and at his country home in Freelands, Kentucky.

He is making most of his own furniture—has made a very good kitchen table and a washstand in our tool shed working there after he finishes with us at six pm. When I first asked him if he had any furniture for the lodge he said 'well, I've got a lot of pictures'. Michael was out here last Sunday. He looked well. He has had more sceptic outbreaks and the doc: thinks that if they continue he should be inoculated against them. Lily was staying for a long week-end and enjoyed seeing him. Lolly came out for two days and one night earlier in the week and managed to keep off all controversial subjects the entire time, which was remarkable.

The cat continues to be angelic! Last night he could not be found and as it was fearfully wet and a wind that cut one in half was blowing I left him out and left open my half door in the pantry and locked the inner door. This morning again he was nowhere, we all hunted and called, no reply until at last John went into the shed where the chicken food is kept in large bins with very heavy tops. John called, 'miaow, miaow' from a bin! He had somehow managed to get inside the corn bin, although how he had pushed up the heavy cover with his head I cant imagine and the lid had fallen and he was trapped in the corn:: A good thing, as John remarked, that he hadnt tried the bran bin for it was very full and he would have suffocated very quickly without air. In future that door will have to be kept shut!!

You wont know the house when you come back!

Yours ever affly
Dobbs.

[TS Dict]   CANADIAN PACIFIC HOTELS
ROYAL YORK HOTEL | TORONTO
November 25th. 1932.

My dear George,

I dictate this to Alan in the large sitting room in our suite of three rooms. The room, as far as the invention of electric light will permit, takes all its details out of Dutch pictures. The day before yesterday I gave the best lecture I have given since I came to America in the most beautiful auditorium I have seen, the work of a French architect of the most modern school.[1] Yesterday I gave up to seeing my relatives (your letter with their

---

[1] WBY lectured on 'The Irish National Theatre' to a meeting of the recently established Canadian Authors' Foundation in the seventh floor Art Deco Auditorium of Eaton's department store, on College Street in the centre of Toronto; the auditorium/concert hall seating 1,275 and with excellent acoustics, was designed by Jacques Carlu (1890–1976) and opened in 1931.

names has not arrived, but one of them wrote a couple of weeks ago). One of them, Mrs. St. Lawrence, an old woman that I played with when she was a child, paints; her relations say very well, and hides everything she does in a cellar. She is simple and natural, and still a woman of the countryside.² Two of them are married to professors—a professor of Theology and a professor of German literature.³ This afternoon I go to see Eugene O'Neill's play Mourning becomes Electra: it lasts five hours with an interval for dinner in the middle.⁴ So far I have had no fatigue, but in a few days from now I shall be lecturing nearly every day. It seems pretty certain now that I will stay into January, but I will not do so unless I have a guarantee of at least eight lectures. At the first possible moment I will write a real letter with my own hand and when I do so I will say complimentary things about Duncan which I cannot say behind his back while he stoops over the typewriter.

Yrs ev
WB Yeats

[ALS]   THE COLGATE INN | HAMILTON | NEW YORK
Dec 1 [1932]

My dear Dobbs: I am on my way from Montreal to Boston by car. I have the same car & driver Churchill had leant by the Ford Company. I have stopped at Hamilton to give a lecture & start again in the

---

² Their common ancestor was Revd John Yeats (1774–1846), whose son Revd William Butler Yeats (1806–62) was JBY's father, and whose son Thomas Yeats (1808–79) was father of Mathew Yeats (1819–88) who married Annie Grace Marie Drew ('Gracie', whose portrait was painted by JBY); Mathew and Grace's daughter Laura, 'Lolly', who trained as a nurse, married James St Lawrence in 1905 and had been living in Toronto since 1926; she had two sons, Tom and George St Lawrence, both of whom lived in Toronto.

³ Two of Laura St Lawrence's brothers were J. Edwin Yeats, a banker whose children were Frank and Grace B. Yeats of Toronto, both of whom remained unmarried, and Dr John Francis ('Frank') Yeats (1860–1923), who practised medicine in Dunham, Quebec, and had five daughters and one son. JBY corresponded with Dr Frank Yeats, and WBY was probably thinking of these relatives when in 1931 he wrote in his introduction to *The Words upon the Window-Pane* of 'the family tree before it was burnt by Canadian Indians' (*Explorations*, selected by Mrs W. B. Yeats (London, 1962), 347 n. 1). I have been unable to trace the two professors who married into the family.

⁴ Eugene O'Neill's trilogy *Mourning Becomes Electra*, a modernization of *Oresteia* by Aeschylus which had premiered at the Guild Theater in New York in 1931 where it ran for 150 performances, was produced at the Royal Alexandra Theatre in Toronto by a company of well-known American actors, including Robert Strange, Elizabeth Risdon, Leona Hogarth, and Lee Baker.

morning. We have passed through fine wild scenery, once the seat of Indian wars & of the last of the Mohocans.[1]

I enclose some photographs of myself taken when I landed in New York in 1903. The Oceanic is the background (I think so). They must have been taken by some reporter. They are copies the origonal belong to a Mr Howe, in whose house I met James Stephens. Take care of them.

I expect every moment a letter from 'Alber Wicks Burreau' saying if they will guarrantee a minimum of 8 new lectures if I stay until Jan 15.

No letter from you for some time—probably one awaits me at Boston If I get this garrantee I shall bring home about £700

Yours affly
WB Yeats

Allan is invaluable, friendly intelligent & never a bore.

In the photo with hat I look such a good young cleric

[ALS[1]]   Willbrook | Rathfarnham | Dublin
                                        December 6. 1932

My dear Willy

Many thanks for your letter from Toronto. I sent you Mrs St Lawrence's address the day after I got your cable. That was the only one Lily gave me. However you evidently met her. I do wish I knew what letters you have had from me!

We are expecting a railway & bus strike at any moment! Actually, Sunday next is the date fixed for it to start unless negociations in between now & then settle things temporarily.

The new Governor-General ('Seneschal', I beg his pardon) is going to conduct all his private & formal duties through the medium of the Irish language!!![2] I wonder will there be an Official Interpreter for the occasions when Foreign Ministers visit this country to sign Treaties?

I have just been to the Cuala annual sale—the usual depressing affair, the only point of interest being that Mrs Reddin spent 5/9. This is, I think,

---

[1] *The Last of the Mohicans* is a romantic historical novel by James Fenimore Cooper (1789–1851); published in 1826, the fictional story takes place in 1757 during the Seven Years War between France and Great Britain for control of the American colonies.

[1] On Fitzwilliam Square stationery, address struck out.

[2] The third and last Governor-General or Seanascal of the Irish Free State was Domhnall Ua Buachalla (in English, Donal Buckley) (1866–1963), an Irish language activist who had been imprisoned after Easter 1916 and opposed the Treaty; he served in the first Dáil and was re-elected to the second, then was chosen by de Valera to replace James McNeill after the latter's resignation in November 1932.

the first time on record that she has bought anything—As a rule she 'takes tea'—[3]

The youngest Childers—'Bobby'[4] has engaged himself to Mary Manning's sister——

Anne & Michael well—

Love

George

What a lot of money!

[TLS[1]]   RIVERSDALE. WILLBROOK. RATHFARNHAM. DUBLIN

December 9 1932

My dear Willy

Just got your cable. When the Macmillan cheque comes I will keep it until the exchange is at its best, or rather ask the Bank to cash in on the best. I will tell Lennox about the cheque for railway, or rather steamship, expenses when I see him. He went to the Macmanus's[2] for ten days or so

---

[3] Mrs Teresa Reddin (1873–?1949), first treasurer of Cumann na mBan, the 'League of Women' founded in 1914 as auxiliary corps to the Irish Volunteers, and one of the founders of St Ultan's Infant Hospital, was an original subscriber to the Abbey Theatre and one of the founders of the Gate Theatre; she was a supporter of Arthur Griffith and Sinn Féin, and held a salon in Artane every Sunday. The house, which was frequently raided by British forces and where she and her sons were arrested in April 1916, finally burned down during the Civil War in 1922. Later in her double drawing room at 45 Fitzwilliam Square she held a monthly Sunday salon at which her sons produced plays on a fully equipped and lighted stage. Three of her sons were active in the theatre: Kerry (1893–1954), a doctor who frequently performed with Edward Martyn's Irish Theatre and the DDL, District Justice John Kenneth Sheils (1894–1967), who wrote for the Abbey as 'Kenneth Sarr', and Gerard Norman (1896–1942), a lawyer (see note to 29 Feb. 1932).

[4] Robert Alden 'Bobby' Childers (1910–96), who later left his career as a businessman in London to live in the Barton family home of Glendalough House, Annamoe, Co. Wicklow, married Christabel Susan (1910–88), daughter of Dr James Fitzmaurice Manning, on 16 June 1933; Christabel Childers was secretary of the Friends of the Irish Academy of Letters.

[1] On Fitzwilliam Square stationery, address struck out.

[2] Diarmuid 'Dermott' Arthur MacManus (1892–1975), folklorist and formerly an officer in the English army in India where he became interested in Tantrism and Hindu philosophy. Now fervidly Republican after participation in the IRA and the Free State army, he was romantically described by WBY as 'a gunman' and for a brief time encouraged WBY's fascist interests; he dedicated *The Middle Kingdom: The Faerie World of Ireland* (1959) to WBY. The MacManus family took in paying guests at Woodville Grange, Granard, Co. Longford, and the Yeatses spent eight days there in September 1933 with GY teaching the children to row on the lake. Replying to his letter of condolence on WBY's death, GY wrote, 'You were one of the few men for whom WBY had a real affection.'

and was to have returned today. He has written a new three act comedy[3]— did it in six days at the Macmanus's. . . . Dolly stayed here a night while he was away but would not stay more. I think she was hoping that he might suddenly turn up at Sorrento[4] having got bored with Longford depths of country.

I went last night to 'The Dark Saint' by Curel at the Peacock. A lovely play and lovely performance.[5] Miss Young as the returned Nun was quite unlike the Elizabeth Young I have been accustomed to see; I can imagine the part better played but I cant think of anyone who could do it better.[6] Ann Clements, one of the Abbey School of Acting people who has been playing in the 2nd company took the part of Christine and was charming and <u>was</u> sixteen, which she is supposed to be![7] Shelah Richards, who had a quite small part looked delightful but as usual didnt know her words perfectly. She is a tiresome dog that young woman[8]. . . . very bad audiences. The papers mostly grumbled that the play was 'murky', what murky means I am not very clear.

Today I lunched with the Childers, Mrs Osgood made lunch intolerable by breaking in on all conversation started either by her daughter or her grandson Bobby.[9] Bobby is rather nice. Mrs O. announces continually that

---

[3] *Drama at Inish* by LR was produced at the Abbey Theatre on 6 Feb. 1933, then in London with the title *Is Life Worth Living?*

[4] 'Sorrento Cottage' was the name of LR's home in Dalkey.

[5] When the Abbey company was not playing, both theatres were let to other producers; a translation of *The Dark Saint* by the French novelist and dramatist François de Curel (1854–1928) was produced by Elizabeth Young at the Peacock Theatre during the week of 5 Dec. 1932.

[6] Elizabeth Young, 'Violet Mervyn', the sister of MG's good friend the poet and folklorist Ella Young (1867–1956), remembered for playing the title role in AE's *Deirdre* in 1902 before performing for some years professionally in England; she returned to Dublin in 1910 and, although never a permanent member of the Abbey company, performed with the DDL and in many radio and stage productions.

[7] GY has mixed up the names of two young actors who began their career with the Second Company in 1932, Ann Clery and Dorothy Clement; the latter performed in *The Dark Saint* and unlike Clery did not continue as a permanent member of the Abbey company.

[8] Shelah Richards (1903–85), actor, director, and producer in theatre, film, and television, was a member of the DDL before joining the Abbey company in 1924, playing the role of Nora Clitheroe in the first production of *The Plough and the Stars* (1926) and chosen by WBY to perform the title role in the Abbey's revival of *The Player Queen*. She became one of the Gate Theatre's leading actors, performing also in Irish films; she married playwright Denis Johnston in 1928 and for a time ran the Abbey School of Acting. After performing in New York she returned to establish with Nigel Heseltine (Michael Walsh) an independent company for new plays at the Olympia Theatre, serving as director and producer, including the world première of O'Casey's *Red Roses for Me* and a production of Synge's *The Playboy of the Western World* starring Siobhán McKenna; she was one of the first drama producers for Telefís Éireann when it was established in 1962.

[9] Molly Childers's widowed mother Mrs Hamilton Osgood of Boston lived with her daughter in Dublin from 1921 until her death in 1934.

at her age one renounces the world, there is no 'I' left; I, mine, possessions, desires, all must fade into—I suppose—a preparation for the next world. Gosh, what she needs as a preparation for Eternity is a Trappist Nunnery.

Two days ago I dined with Nora Dorman.[10] Sean was there, opened the door to me, I said 'Hullo Sean' and Sean in a most disappointed voice said 'O, did you recognise me!' He has grown face fur, only a mustache. I suggested that for complete disguise a beard was essential. Mustaches must be in fashion again. Denis Johnston has one, and I notice slight growths on the faces of many young men. <u>DONT YOU DARE TRY IT</u>.

Bobby Childers told me a nice tale of some friends of his who took a maid from a drunkard's Home (the Childers <u>would</u> know people who have these kind but sentimental aspirations) and she cleaned and she cleaned and she sang and she prayed as she cleaned, and then one day she decided that the only way to polish under a particularly low bed was to lie flat on her stomach and wriggle under it. Then she couldnt wriggle out again, and she lay there a full threequarters of an hour praying to Our Lord and to the Blessed Virgin and at last she got out 'And sure to God I don't know which of Them it was pulled me out'. Her last effort was to fling the statue of St Anthony out of the window 'I gave you your sixpence, NOW perhaps you'll find me my brooch'. (You know, you give St Anthony sixpence when you want to find something you have lost.

Six days more and you'll be through—unless you give those extra eight lectures. PLEASE dont forget that you must cable the name of the boat that you are sailing on. I would so like to come and meet you.

Love
Dobbs

[TLS Dict] THE COPLEY-PLAZA | BOSTON MASSACHUSETTS
December 11th. 1932.

My dear George,

I have just wired to you as follows:—

> 'Mcmaster wires for Oedipus rights. Make enquiries and decide. Tell Lennox to send copy last year's Abbey American contract to Waldorf New York.'

I had already wired to Mcmaster 'Cannot decide now' and then Alan remembered that Mcmaster had brought Mrs. Campbell to Dublin which

---

[10] LR's sister, Mrs William Stewart Hobart Dorman (d. 1961), was the author of a number of radio plays, a children's book with a setting in India where she had lived with her husband for some years, and, with her two brothers, the family reminiscences *Three Homes* (1938). See note to 1 Nov. 1930 for her son Sean.

made me take him more seriously.[1] Hence I have left the matter to you. A week ago I sent you by post a cheque for the Macmillan money. In my wire I have asked you to get Lennox to post me a copy of that contract because I intend to get a legal opinion upon it in New York. I am on the best of terms with Alber-Wickes; they have kept all their promises so far as I am concerned, and they are making a success of the Abbey tour, but I think it necessary to have all relevant information before the final settlement. Lennox is a goose. I wired him to find out if the money advanced for my tickets etc. had been repaid, and was careful to put my address, Waldorf Astoria. He did precisely what I did not want him to do, sent the answer through Alber-Wickes.

I am in the midst of the busiest part of my tour, but have managed to fit in a seance with Mrs. Crandon tonight.[2] I will write to you the results tomorrow (not dictating). There are four professional dancers in Washington who have cherished for years a conviction that they are related to us. They have adopted as their professional name their mother's name, Yates (their grandfather adopted the 'American spelling'). The eldest, aged 24 (married with a son aged six), sends me a newspaper picture of her three sisters, aged 17, 18 and 19; they are dressed alike, all in the same pose, and all exactly alike, and all smiling. Their mother, too, was a professional dancer. The eldest of the sisters claims that all have always kept themselves posted in my movements, to have known when I was in Dublin, when I was in the South of France, etc. Their question is, Are we really related? I shall make enquiries.[3] One of my grandfather's brothers altered the spelling of the name 'because he could not fight the whole world'.

Yours affecly
WB Yeats

[1] Andrew 'Anew' McMaster, 'Martin Doran' (1891–1962), one of the last actor-managers, toured his company throughout Ireland from 1925 until 1959, performing most of the major Shakespearian roles, and when it was available, renting the Abbey Theatre. The proposed performance of WBY's *Oedipus* does not appear to have taken place: 1932–3 he was performing in London and Stratford-on-Avon, and then took his company on a tour of the Near East, returning to perform at the Dublin Gate Theatre in April 1935. Hilton Edwards and Micheál MacLiammóir, whose sister Marjorie Willmore was married to McMaster, met while touring with McMaster. Harold Pinter published a memoir of his two years with the company in *Mac* (1968). Mrs Patrick Campbell performed Mrs Alving in *Ghosts* and Lady Macbeth in the McMaster productions at the Abbey Theatre in December 1929.

[2] Mina 'Margery' Crandon, née Stinson (1888–1941), the third wife of Boston surgeon LeRoi Goddard Crandon (1873–1939), was a popular direct voice and telekinetic medium whose control was her late brother Walter; despite accusations of fraud from observers including a team of Harvard professors and the magician Harry Houdini, she continued to hold regular séances, exhibiting a wide range of phenomena, until her early death.

[3] The four Yates Sisters danced professionally in Washington, DC, from 1930 to 1940, in 1934 performing in the White House for President Roosevelt; I have found no record of their relationship to WBY.

[ALS]   THE COPLEY-PLAZA / BOSTON MASSACHUSETTS
                                    [12] Dec [1932]

My dear Dobbs: I have had my first cold. Dr Crandon cured me with tabloids & whiskey & now I have nothing but exaustion. I shall be able to lecture to night after an afternoon in bed. Cold the result of the first snowfall of the winter. Scence very remarkable. They have been experementing with two seperate wooden rings made of different woods which the spirits are to lock into each other ⊙. At an early scence the rings vanished & at the different sceance they return (I saw & handled them last night; they were interlocked) then they vanish again. The aim of the controll is to get the rings so seperated from Medium (a process compared to that of birth) that they may not vanish but remain interlocked. Zollners theories of four dimensional 'spirit action' are involved[1] Then Alan & I selected by chance leaves from a calander & put them in envelopes without looking at dates chosen. My envelope was gummed up. After the scence during which control seemed to handle envelopes Mrs Crandon & another, writing automatticaly, gave the days of the month we had chosen—14 & 16—correctly. Mrs Crandon held in her mouth the mouth peice of a curious instrument which would have showed by the movement of a luminous stopper if her tongue had not remained in contact with a certain hole. While medium was gagged in this way the direct voice[2] continued as loud as ever. The instrument was made by the man who discovered how to prevent enteric fever in armies. Owing to his work there was no enteric in the great war. He was present & directed the sceance. Mrs Crandon & her husband are very charming people, the whole circle was intelligent & pleasant.

I am now delivering the last four lectures of my first tour. On Thursday I give the first of my Academy lectures. Except for this cold I have had good health—in fact I am better than I have been for years. By the by after sceance last night Mrs Crandon said to me, just as Dionertes used to, 'drink water' & then she added 'drink water every sixty minuites' I said to Dr Crandon 'should I really do what she says' & he said 'yes'

                                              Yours affectionly
                                              WB Yeats

[1] Johann Karl Friedrich Zöllner (1834–82), German astrophysicist who discovered the perceptual illusion named after him, where cross-hatching disturbs the perception of parallel lines, making them appear diagonal; his book *Transcendental Physics: An Account of Experimental Investigations from the Scientific Treatises*, translated into English in 1880 and admired by Blavatsky, discussed supernatural phenomena occurring in a fourth dimension of space, including slate-writing and interlocking wooden rings. He was a professor at Leipzig at the same time as his colleague the experimental psychologist Fechner (see note to 15 Nov. 1926).

[2] In 'direct voice' the speech appears to come through the medium directly from the control.

That I long for you I think you know. I constanly picture to my self our meeting.

[TLS Dict]   THE WALDORF-ASTORIA | NEW YORK
December 18. 1932.

My dear George,

I have had five letters from you in all, sent upon Oct 24, Nov 2, Nov 8, Nov 23 and Dec 6 respectively. I had no letter giving me Mrs. St. Lawrence's address. It seems to me that letters between Nov 8 and Nov 23 must have gone astray. I shall make enquiries at the Macmillan Company tomorrow, but some hotel may have forgotten to forward them or forwarded them wrong. Alan on one occasion was for over three weeks without hearing from his wife. I hope you have had all my letters, including the cheque for the Macmillan money. It is still undecided whether I remain on after the first of January. Meanwhile I am occupied with the Acadamy. I give my third drawing room lecture on the subject tonight. Last night I spoke to typical Irish-American men and women, and answered questions about the 'Playboy' and so on. There seems a prospect that quite a considerable sum will be raised for the Acadamy, but that largely depends upon one rich woman: I have as it is enough to have justified my activities. Dr. McCartan[1] and Judge Campbell are my great support here.

Yrs affly
WB Yeats

[TLS]
RIVERSDALE, | WILLBROOK, | RATHFARNHAM, | DUBLIN.
December 21 [1932]

My dear Willy

Two letters from you today—one dictated to Alan, one in your own hand telling me that you have had a bad cold. Your account of the Mrs Crandon

---

[1] Dr Patrick McCartan (1878–1963), Irish-born Republican who for many years worked closely with the Irish Republican Brotherhood; elected to the first Dáil, he was appointed Sinn Féin's representative in the United States, and thereafter travelled between the two countries. Adept at raising funds from his wealthy American friends for Irish causes, he was a staunch supporter of WBY's plans for the Academy and later was a prime mover in the founding of the 'Testimonial Committee for W. B. Yeats' which sought to guarantee WBY enough money to provide security and comfort for the rest of his life (see letters of 19 June 1937 ff. and *Yeats and Patrick McCartan: A Fenian Friendship*, ed. John Unterecker, No. X of the Dolmen Press Yeats Centenary Papers (1967)). McCartan unsuccessfully contested the presidency of Ireland in 1945 and 1948–51 was an appointee to the Seanad.

seance is very interesting; especially interesting in the mechanical control of the tongue by the instrument during the 'direct voice'. I wish you had escaped this cold until you had finished your lectures—

I saw Macmaster's agent about the Oedipus business. Macmaster thought your cable meant that there was nothing to be done about it. The agent wired at once to him, but I am afraid that in the interval Macmaster had told the syndicate that was backing him for the 'west end' production that it was impossible. Anyway, I havent heard anything further. There is just a possibility of a February production at, I think, the Ambassadors Theatre.[1]

Lennox goes to London directly after Xmas to produce 'Things that are Caesars' (Sally Allgood, and an amalgamated group of old Abbey players).[2] He says he will be away 'about ten days'. Dolly had telephoned to me about two hours before he told me to say 'Lennox is going away for several weeks after Xmas'. So whether Lennox is going to prance elsewhere afterwards I don't know.... They, the Lennoxes, are blowing a party on Friday at 8.30 pm.... I was asked by Dolly to stay the night so am doing so. I gather that we all stay in bed until at least 11 am on the following day as Sean Dorman will be sleeping in the bathroom and no power can awake him before eleven.[3] I think the guest room, unlike the other bedrooms, has a basin and jug in it and if I find it hasnt I shall brush my teeth and wash my face into the kitchen sink! OR yank Sean out of bed. OR bribe Sean to exchange beds. I really dont like to leap into an astonished world as late as all that...on Xmas eve...when one remembers all the things one has forgotten to buy.

Anne came home as usual with a sore throat, cold, cough, looking pale and rather thin. She has got rid of the throat, and her cough is better. Michael comes home tomorrow. I havent seen him for a month but I gather that he is very fit. Mrs McClelland, the mother of another boy at the school, rang me up to ask if she might motor him home as she had a car and it would save us a taxi! Michael taught young McClelland to play chess during the summer term and was of course able to beat him every time, but during the summer holidays McClelland 'swotted' so hard on chess that he can now beat Michael. Michael told me this himself; remarking 'his mother

[1] No record of a production of Yeats's *Oedipus* plays by McMaster has been found.

[2] *Things That are Caesar's* by Paul Vincent Carroll was produced by LR at the Arts Theatre on 11 Jan. 1933, with a cast of many of the early Abbey players, including Sara Allgood, Maire O'Neill (Molly Allgood, 1885–1952), Cathleen (Kathleen) Drago (Mrs E. J. Kennedy, *c*.1894–1938), Fred O'Donovan, J. A. O'Rourke (1882–1937), Henry E. Hutchinson (1892–1980), Tony Quinn (1899–1967), Felix M. P. Irwin (1893–1950), and Joyce Chancellor (Mrs Fred O'Donovan, b. 1906); see WBY's letter of 30 Aug. 1931.

[3] LR's nephew.

played with him perpeturally', and whether this was a hint to me or not I dont know.[4]

One day last week I lunched at the Kildare St Club, the Goughs were there and asked me to lunch with them...Guy said a thing that amazed me and that still amazes and puzzles me. We were talking about the new Governor General—Seaneschal as he prefers to call himself—and I said 'I have never seen any man so changed as McNeill is since he ceased to be GG.' and I enlarged on the theme because the change IS remarkable, his voice so improved, his face pink and lively, his carriage so improved and so on. Guy said 'He always looked as if he were crouching from a bullet, yet I dont think the man is a coward' and he repeated again later 'I dont think the man is a coward', each time with a questioning doubt in his voice. For fear that they might think I had spoken of the change in McNeills appearance because I thought it due to a now fearless life I spread myself out on the theme of his interest in his dairy and cow occupations, and so on, but O no, 'I suppose he always went in fear of his life'. I think I now understand why they would like to suppress Lady Gregory's later Diaries.[5]

I havent sent you all the rather stupid Irish Times correspondence about the Irish Academy of Letters because Lennox told me that he had done so. I have kept the cuttings as you may lose or throw them away in USA. I dont think AE's letters were particularly intelligent.[6] Did you?

Harry Stuart has sent in a play to the Abbey. A great deal of it—as retailed by L.R.—sounds uninteresting, a very second-hand London cocock-tail (this is a combination of cocotte and cocktail) life which has never been, I imagine, observed by Harry, and which, in any case, only existed in an entirely unintelligent world and was not a world into which Our Hero the Irish Gunman shaper of an Irish Ireland would or could have penetrated. But, according to the synopsis LR gave me, there are queer interesting things in the part of the play which does not deal with cocktail life.

---

[4] Richard Leeper McClelland (1922–2004) went on to school in England, returning to Trinity College to train as a doctor before making a successful career in film and television as Richard Leech; his parents Isabella Frances, née Leeper, and Herbert Saunderson McClelland, a solicitor, lived at 18 Palmerston Park.

[5] AG's journals repeatedly comment on her appreciation of McNeill's support and kindness.

[6] On 15 Nov. 1932 AE joyfully entered into a prolonged argument with two Jesuit priests and others, disputing their objections to the establishment of the Irish Academy of Letters. The correspondence in the *Irish Times* continued, until after 13 December AE lost interest in rebutting; on 17 Dec. 1932 he wrote to WBY, 'You wanted a fighting Academy and I have done my best to supply pugnacity in your absence,' and on 31 Dec. 1932, 'I find my old talent as a controversialist had not deserted me, and when you are back and I am refreshed by Donegal we may start a fresh excitement' (*LWBY* 2, 547–8).

Lennox made no comment whatever on the play. He sent it on to Starkie and I gather that he is for doing it. Starkie hasnt yet returned it.[7]

> With love
> George.

[TLS Dict]   THE WALDORF-ASTORIA | NEW YORK
                                        December 24th. 1932.

My dear George,

I saw the representative of the Macmillan Company a couple of days ago, and he was anxious about the American copyright of the poems just published, or just to be published, in the Cuala Press. He wanted to know if Watt had taken out interim copyright in America, and seemed to doubt if he had. Please look into this matter with Watt. I have just sent £300 to the Bank of Ireland for the Acadamy of Letters; I have a good deal more promised. Alan Duncan tells me to let you know that all the money due for my tour has been paid up to date. This is dictated on a very crowded day; I will write with my own hand as soon as I can.

> Yours affly
> WB Yeats

[ALS]   THE WALDORF-ASTORIA | NEW YORK
                                         Xmas Day [1932]

My dear Dobbs: Not yet certain when I return as the new contract has not come but all indications suggest Jan 15 or 16. I am longing for you & constantly picture our meeting. How generous of you to promise to come to Southampton. Inddeed that meeting there is part of the impulse to prolong my tour, for if I return on Jan 1 instead you will not, perhaps, be able to get away from the children in time. I am better than I can remember having been. Most days I go to the swimming bath that being the only form of exercise convenient in this crowded traffic. Nearly all the money I have sent to the Irish Academy is Irish Catholic money & the jesuit attack in Dublin helps.[1] I am promised contribution in the future

---

[7] *Men Crowd me Round* by Francis Stuart ('Harry') was produced at the Abbey on 13 Mar. 1933 to a sparse and tepid audience; Joseph Holloway objected to the 'air of artificiality' and 'vulgar language' (*Joseph Holloway's Irish Theatre*, ii: *1932–1937* (Dixon, Calif., 1969), 24). A second play by Stuart, *Strange Guest*, was produced by the Abbey on 9 Dec. 1940.

[1] See note to 21 Dec. 1932.

from time to time.[2] I heard one subscriber tell another that he was certain the letters in the Dublin press, signed by such names as 'Byrne' & 'Walsh', were all written by Jesuits. I have a long series of lunch parties—I eat my Xmas dinner—at 1 o clock—with Bush of the Bush Terminal, the man who bought the mountain to grow coffee that is 'never sold' but is given to his friends.[3] Alan Duncan is the perfect secretary, firm, good humoured & self-possessed.

My love to the children. I hope they have had the post cards. I have sent several

Yrs affecly
WB Yeats

PS.
I send a fine photograph of myself from January 'Mayfair'. Keep it safely. It is by the best photographer in the States. He works for 'Mayfair' alone & if one wants a seperate print of one of the photographs it costs fifteen dollars.

I thank you & Ann & Micael for the telegram. Alan asks me to give you his thanks.

Yrs ev
WBY.

[TLS]   RIVERSDALE, | WILLBROOK, |
                                  RATHFARNHAM, | DUBLIN.
                                          Dec. 29 1932

My dear Willy
Lordy but you should have had far more letters than five—I suppose they have been sent on to hotels and not forwarded. Just got your cable giving date of return. Please no, stupid of me, you wont of course have time to reply! Christmas went off well, children seemed pleased with everything. I gave them ten shillings each from you and a box of chocolates.

---

[2] A typed memo in the Yeats papers by Alan Duncan reports that £700 was raised for the Academy, £425 of which were brought in by WBY's own lectures.

[3] Irving T. Bush (1869–1948), wealthy entrepreneur, businessman, and art collector who built the Bush Terminal in Brooklyn, an intermodal hub for railways and cargo ships, Bush Tower, a skyscraper in Manhattan, and Bush House in London; at this time he was living in the seventeen-storey tower at 280 Park Avenue with his third wife, philanthropist, artist, and former dentist Marian Spore Bush (1878–1946), who believed that her unusual and striking paintings were inspired by artists long dead. WBY's coffee story is inaccurate: in August 1931 the Federal Farm Board arranged a trade of surplus wheat for Brazilian coffee, which was stored in the Bush Terminal with the understanding that it would not be sold by the Farm Board for at least a year.

Vincent has written a long letter to all the papers asking Cosgrave and McDermott to ally and form a National progressive party.[1] I gather that no one has any intention of doing anything of the sort. Alfie Byrne blew off three days later with a meeting at the Mansion House with a new 'party' of his own![2] I don't see any enthusiasm about that either!

I shall be counting the days now until we meet—I wonder if I am to meet you at Southampton or if you are coming straight home? I shall cable to you about it.

Michael is making friends at school. Tomorrow he goes to a party with Alan Browne,[3] next week McClelland and some others lunch here. Its queer that he makes friends and Anne didnt, though that may be because the boys at Michael's school are on the whole a more intelligent lot than Anne's girls were.

With much love
George

[1] Arthur Rose Vincent, member of the Seanad 1928–34, whose home WBY visited in 1926; W. T. Cosgrave, President of the Executive Council until 1932, was leader of the pro-Treaty party Cumann na nGaedheal and its successor Fine Gael until he retired in 1944; Francis Charles 'Frank' MacDermot (1886–1975) was an Independent in the Dáil 1932–3, and helped found the short-lived National Centre Party, which merged with Fine Gael in 1933.

[2] Alfred Byrne (1882–1956), an Independent in the Dáil since 1922, was elected Mayor of Dublin for nine successive years (1930–9) and again 1954–5; in 1928 he was elected to the Seanad, returning to the Dáil in 1932.

[3] Alan Browne (1923–2010) attended Mount Temple and Baymount Schools with MBY; his later career included the mastership of the Rotunda Maternity Hospital (1960–6) and authorship of a history of the Rotunda (1979). As Professor of Obstetrics and Gynaecology in the Royal College of Surgeons in Ireland he was active in the promotion of sex education.

1933

RIVERSDALE, | WILLBROOK, |
RATHFARNHAM, | DUBLIN.
Sunday Jan 8 [1933]

My dear Willy

Your wire came yesterday—the Terenure exchange rang up at 8.30 in the morning to say that there was a cable and was Riversdale the correct address—so Chrissie said 'yes'... but for all that we didnt get it until a quarter past ten. We have all been devastated by flu!! Anne started it two days after Christmas and two days later I fell. I had to have a nurse because neither Anne nor I could get out of bed without fainting dead off.... then last Wednesday Michael got it! He has had a slight attack. I was the first 'up', yesterday; Anne was up today, in her room; I got up because I couldnt stand the nurse any longer. She stays until tomorrow and then the children's old nana[1] is coming for a week. I got old Dr Croly to look after Anne and he then took us all on in turn as we collapsed. He is a great old pet, in 'his ninetieth year'.[2] His hobbies are gardening and clocks, and he tells me that the Ballast Office is no longer the clock it once was, time should be regulated from the North Wall clock, but Father something or other in Rathfarnham gets Dunsink time[3] for the midday Angelus and that bell is quite dependable. Apart from the north Wall and Father ..XX..'s Angelus the next best (and 'most reliable') is the Beaumont Laundray hooter. Now we hastily set our clocks when the 8.30 am laundry hooter goes and he invariably looks at them (Anne's and mine) and compares them with his watch. I told him that you were our timekeeper and that when you were away we all went astray. This seemed to surprise and please him! He says that Anne 'is a very sweet child'.

So you see I have no news, not having seen a soul.. Dolly writes that the recent storms and high seas threw up a dead donkey on to the Sorrento rocks... this news interested the children more than me... and today I hear that the Corporation sent five men to remove it and that it was towed out to sea at the end of a rope by the said five men in a row boat! Michael wants to know if Dolly can inform us 'how long it had been dead'.

---

[1] Florence Reade, who trained at the Rotunda Hospital after the children went to Switzerland; see note to 25 Feb. 1928.

[2] Their neighbour Dr Albert J. Croly (1850–1934), fellow of the Royal College of Physicians, who lived at Silver Acre, Rathfarnham.

[3] The 18th-century Dunsink Observatory, in Castleknock in north-west Dublin; until 1916, the official Dublin Mean Time was twenty-five minutes behind Greenwich Mean Time.

I think De Valera will get his majority without any doubt—Cork threw stones at Cosgrave last night, not serious stones, but still stones. Dr O'Higgins was booed in—I think—Limerick and the Army Comrades approached the booers. O'Higgins held up his hand to the A.C. and proceeded to say that if the Cumann na Ghadael were not allowed free speech at their meetings he would see to it that no other party got free speech.[4] Upon which there was silence.

[continued in MS] Erskine Childers is standing for South County Dublin— Fianna Fail tried to get Bob Barton as a candidate but he refused. As a Treaty Signatory his position would have been a little difficult & I am glad he has kept out of things.[5]

Hope you are well—

Love G.

[AL]   THE WALDORF-ASTORIA | NEW YORK
                                    [*c.*10] Jan [1933]

My dear Dobbs: Just back from a lecture near Chicago ('Notre Dame' Catholic University where the Fathers turned the conversation to psychical research & questioned me eagerly) I have got your letter in which you say you will wire whether I am 'to go straight home' or whether you are to meet me at Southampton, I hope you will meet me there (your mind will be made up before you get this) I want to be alone away from everybody (no AE dropping in to know how much money I have for the Academy.[1] I thought of a few days in some country place. I too count the days, then London for a few days, you must want to buy clothes[2]

Yrs affecly

---

[4] Dr Thomas F. O'Higgins (1890–1953) had been a TD since 1929, first as a member of Cumann na nGaedhael, then as Fine Gael for Laois-Offaly; a brother of the assassinated Kevin O'Higgins, he was founder of the Army Comrades Association, the quasi-fascist organization which for a short time intrigued WBY. In later governments he served as Minister for Defence (1948–51) and briefly as Minister for Industry and Commerce (1951). In this election Fianna Fáil won almost 50% of the seats.

[5] Robert Childers Barton (1881–1975) was a member of the committee sent to London to negotiate the Treaty, which he signed 'as the lesser of two outrages forced upon me', and while he remained loyal to de Valera, did not take his seat though elected to the third Dáil; his cousin Erskine Hamilton Childers (1905–74) was not elected until 1938 and rapidly rose through various ministries of Fianna Fáil until elected the President of Ireland in 1973.

[1] AE as honorary secretary was now actively campaigning for the welfare of the Irish Academy of Letters.

[2] WBY sailed on 21 January but, because of the family's illnesses, GY did not meet him en route; he was back in Dublin by the 28th and almost immediately also succumbed to the flu.

At Mrs Crandons this time—I stayed four days—I got perfect levitation of a basket. I & president of 'American Psycical Research Society'[3] alone with medium. We stood holding hands. Basket (painted with luminous spots) rose up from table & hit the ceiling several times & floated above of heads.

No time for more than this scrawl. I am off to lunch with French,[4] who wants to print the Swift play. Then to see a rich woman who may endow Academy.[5]

Strange melodramatic things happened at Mrs Crandons—she was walking about in a somnambulistic state for hours. Three people who were dying some where at a distance had asked the help of her control. The trance began by her going to the telephone & asking the post office why a telegram that was there for her had not been sent. 3/4 of an hour later the telegram came. The friends of a dying man telegraphed for the help of her control. She was in trance with a break of a few minutes from about 4 till 12 that night. Her forces were being used to help the dying.

[ALS]   SAVILE CLUB, | 69, BROOK STREET. W. 1.
                                         Friday [21 Apr. 1933]

My dear Dobbs
    I enclose a checque & account from Watts.
    The moment I arrived the hall-porter handed me a parcel & a telegram. The telegram was the one you sent me about meeting me at Kingstown when I arrived from U.S.A. & the parcel contained my dress-coat which had been sent last October.
    I have seen Dulac & Olivia & various people here at Club. Appart from that I have done nothing but read Lady Gregorys MSS.[1]

                                         Yrs ev
                                         WB Yeats

    [3] A report by W. H. Button, president of the American Society for Psychical Research, Inc. NY confirms this description (*LWBY* 2, 549,551).

    [4] Samuel French, play publishers and authors' representatives since 1830.

    [5] Mary Harriman Rumsey (1881–1934), wealthy widow of the sculptor Charles Cary Rumsey, an activist in the Settlement Movement, was appointed by Theodore Roosevelt in 1933 to chair the Consumer Advisory Board of the National Recovery Administration. Influenced by AE's book *The National Being*, she was one of the founders of Farm Foundation. Although her donation to the Academy fund was such that the American fundraisers originally wished to have the Academy medal named after her or her husband, it was finally agreed it should be called 'the Gregory medal'.

    [1] AG's will had stipulated that WBY have 'the final decision as to arrangement and publication' of any unpublished autobiographical material, though Margaret Gregory and T. J. Kiernan were trustees and executors of the estate.

[TLS]   RIVERSDALE, | WILLBROOK, |
                                         RATHFARNHAM, | DUBLIN.
                                                        April 24 1933

My dear Willy

I wired to you on Saturday asking you to ring up Kiernan. I enclose his letter.

Nothing much has happened here—Michael has still a cough, quite slight, and is having Malt extract. I went into the Abbey on Friday night and to my disgust found only one seat disengaged—a bad seat—and a wildly enthusiastic house! I heard two young men talking in the second interval, one said 'There's nothing in the play' and the other said 'Its years since I laughed so much' and the first said 'I've seen it three times and I laughed as much this evening as I did before, but there isn't anything in it' and the other said 'Its so true to Irish country hotels' and the first said 'that's just it, there's nothing in it'. I moved away. There isnt anything 'in' it, but it is a great success...goes on three days this week 'by special request'.[1]

Tomorrow, I regret to tell you, I go to Punchestown with Dolly and Lennox....that is because on Thursday last Lennox got a cheque for £400 from Alber Wickes....I have insisted that I pay my own expenses; hope to recover them by mug punting of the 'blind prick' sort! Added of course to slight following of form and instinct guided by seeing the annimules prancing round the paddock before each race.[2] I am taking a limited amount of cash with fivepence earmarked for my bus fare from Dublin to Willbrook.

We have at last had some good rain—I spent three hours on Saturday evening watering the most drooping parts of the garden (the tulips were dying, and the peonies all drooping) and on Saturday night we had terrific rain, rain most of Sunday, all Sunday night, today half rain. The garden looks terrific now, and the late tulips have shot up and thickened their buds so that they will be fine when you come back. I am taking in twelve dozen today—without leaving much bare space! Next year I shall have about two thousand under the fruit trees which will people that bare space and die down before the trees grow thick in green. We have only six chickens out of the dozen eggs; the hen trampled on one rotten egg thereby killing five infants who were ready to get out of egg....(they were tapping and chirruping inside the eggs, Anne and I listened to them!) The fumes from that one egg went to her head—if hens have our sense of smell?—and she trampled down the poor remaining un-rotten.

---

[1] *Drama at Inish : an exaggeration in three acts* by LR.

[2] Vol. i of Radhakrishnan's *Indian Philosophy p.* 452 in the Yeats Library is underlined at 'The shifting nature of the world conceals the stable reality' 'Marked by my wife who had opened the book at random to find what horse would win at Punchestown. W.B.Y.'

Later. John has just come in saying that we have a 'clucking' hen (i.e. a broody hen) and he wants to put down eggs of our own to sit on. I told him frankly that I did not think our eggs would be fertile as our cock is very young and has been with us only three weeks; I said 'I'd bet you one thousand to one in pennies that the eggs wouldnt hatch out'. So I stand to win one penny or lose £4.3.4.

Sybil Childers is coming over tomorrow. She is staying with Molly[3]; as neither of them like each other much I may ask Sybil to come here for a night or two; that rather depends on my getting back from Millar and Beatty[4] your mattress which had to go to be re-covered. When you come home we will seriously go into the question of the lofts : and when we go into that question we shall also have to see about the heating of the 'Vinery'.[5] It might be possible to do it quite cheaply.

I dont like, as you know, the idea of Una Pope-Hennessey doing the 'Life', etc.[6] Mrs Childers, to whom I have not spoken of the thing at all in its private aspects, said to me that you were the only person who could do it, and that if you could not undertake it the only other person 'who would not do it as hurdy gurdy barrell organ' was L. A. G. Strong. Strong is perhaps worth considering?[7] He would submit all he did to your judgment.

Yours as ever
George

[ALCS]   SAVILE CLUB, | 69, BROOK STREET. W.1.
Tuesday [25 Apr. 1933]

My dear Dobbs: No news except that Cambridge has phoned to say they have written me two letters (one to Kildare St Club & one to Abbey) offering me

---

[3] Sybil Rose Culling Childers (1871–1954), Robert Erskine Childers's sister, whose name in the Order of the Golden Dawn was 'Rosa in cruce Restat iter coelo', had been one of the officers to whom GHL applied when seeking membership in the Stella Matutina branch in 1914. She paid a visit to Ceylon in 1916, and returned from a lengthy stay in India in 1925, but now resided once again in London.

[4] Millar and Beatty Ltd., house furnishers at 13 and 14 Grafton Street.

[5] The outbuildings in what had been the stable yard.

[6] Dame Una Constance Pope-Hennessy, née Una Constance Birch (1876–1949), was a historian and prolific biographer and a friend of AG, whom she used to visit at Coole as a child.
In the end, instead of a biography WBY's memoirs of AG were included in *Dramatis Personae* (Cuala, 1935; London, 1936); LR, whom WBY had at one time recommended as AG's biographer, edited a selection from the Journals 1916–30 (1946), and James Pethica edited the Diaries for the years 1892–1902 (1995); Daniel J. Murphy edited the Journals in their entirety in two volumes (1978, 1987). AG's autobiography, published as *Seventy Years*, was edited by Colin Smythe (1974).

[7] L. A. G. Strong first met the Yeatses in Oxford when he was a student; although the author of a number of biographies, including of Thomas Moore, J. M. Synge, and John Masefield, he was not selected; see note to 27 Nov. 1922.

an honarary degree on June 8. & that Margeret Gregory has been to Putnams and made a blazing row because Huntingdon[1] would not accept Una Pope-Hennessey as Lady Gregory editor. Said she would withdraw all MSS which she has no power to do. I spend most of my time reading diaries. Always interesting & often touching. One records Lady G's depression when I am ill in Italy. She notes one day that she must write to Cooks[2] & found out what a ticket to Rapallo would cost. She wanted to help you in taking care of me (thought she might read me Trollope). But all the time the old wounds in her breast are giving her pain, the trouble there starting again. Then she gives up the thought of the journey fearing that she might be taken ill in the train

Yrs ev
WB Yeats

[ALS] SAVILE CLUB, | 69, BROOK STREET. W.1.

April 28 [1933]

My dear Dobbs

I shall have to over-stay my two weeks. I breakfast in bed at 8.30 & then from 9 till 11.30 I read the Gregory Diaries & then every day, except about twice when very busy, I read them an other hour or two in the afternoon. I begin to think I shall have to do this book. I cannot decide anything until I see Huntingdon. I am asking to see him next Wednesday. I should have got through the material by that time. There are many ullusions in the diaries to Anne & Michael. In one passage she mentions their presence at Coole, as one of the justifications for the house. She speaks of your kindness. One gets through out the impression of her nobility. She <often> repeats several times this sentence from Aristotle: 'To think like a wise man but to express oneself like the common people'.

I have seen nothing of 'society' but to day I lunch with Lady Lavery. I have Dulac a number of times & am on the track of a brass-knocker.[1]

Here is a conversation between my self & Mrs Philamore, recorded by Lady Gregory Mrs Philamore 'why cant you read Bertram Russell?' WBY. 'I could no more read Bertram Russell than I could make love to a bald-headed woman' Mrs Philamore 'Why could you not make love to a bald-headed woman' I appear to have let the subject drop at that point

Yrs affly
WB Yeats

---

[1] Constant Davis Huntington (1876–1962), American-born managing director of G. P. Putnam's Sons Ltd., AG's London publishers.

[2] Thomas Cook Travel Inc., 'the oldest travel agency in the world'.

[1] When GY left Rathfarnham she took with her the brass knocker, engraved with the single name 'Yeats'.

I enclose checque from Watt

[ALS]   SAVILE CLUB, | 69, BROOK STREET. W.I.
                                                        April 29 [1933]

My dear Dobbs
   I have got that fit of homesickness I always get after ten days of London but I cannot get away yet. I have just written to Huntington saying
that I shall have read enough of the MSS by Monday to talk things over.
I have still to sign those pages for Macmillan & arrange an interview with
him. I think too I shall have to see Cecil Harmsworth to thank him for his
families benefaction to the Academy.[1] My last engagement at the moment
is for Wednesday evening. It looks as if I may get away about Friday if that
will suit you. (How about Sybil Childers? Do not hesitate to say if you are
using my room. I can always linger on here if I have a good conscience.)
I may be delayed.

                                                            Yrs ev
                                                            WB Yeats

[ALS]   SAVILE CLUB, | 69, BROOK STREET. W.I.
                                                           May 2 [1933]

My dear Dobbs: That is a horrible story about your finger. What a piece of
ill-luck. Of course you can have the new ring when you please.[1]
   I may return Saturday morning. I think I shall have got through all business by then. I have offered to do the Lady Gregory book my self but asked
if I may use in my own autobiography any chapter of mine I like. A good
deal will suit both books. I saw Watt to day & asked him to arrange terms.[2]
I see Macmillan to-morrow.
   If Sibyl Childers is with you & you want my room please wire post pone
my return. I have an essay I can write here

                                                            Yrs ev
                                                            WB Yeats

---

   [1] The Academy Harmsworth Award of £100 annually 'for the best work of imaginative prose' was established by the Harmsworth family, and organized by Esmond Cecil
Harmsworth, son of the 1st Viscount Rothermere, nephew of WBY's friend Cecil Bisshop
Harmsworth.
   [1] Incident unknown.
   [2] WBY did not write the biography of AG after all; instead, his reminiscences are included
in *Dramatis Personae* (Cuala, 1935; London, 1936).

[TLS & MS]   RIVERSDALE. | WILLBROOK, |
                              RATHFARNHAM, | DUBLIN.
                              Saturday June 3 1933

My dear Willy

I send you some letters—one from the Anglo-Swedish Society from which you will gather that the 'reception' is on Friday June 23rd at 10 o'clock.[1] Please note that the secretary is a 'Mrs'! White ties and decorations I conclude. Then there is a much delayed letter from the Lyceum club—when writing enclose their envelope! A letter from USA.

No newses here. Roberts deposited a vast quantity of sand and sand and lime mixed, slates, and general whatnots in the courtyard as preparation for work on Tuesday. John promptly put a padlock on the fruit garden gate....chicken[s] have hatched out and ducklings due tomorrow. Robert Wilson[2] came to tea on Friday and brought Jack White's daughter[3]....a small little person of seventeen or eighteen who hadnt much to say. I didnt know who she was until she remarked on the number of books in the study (and so many big books) and how she was often given books but they always got lost because she never stayed anywhere for more than a month, Daddy was always on the move. Upon which I said 'are you Jack White's daughter'? 'I am' said she 'What pestiferousness is he u[p] to now'? said I, at which she giggled cheerfully and I gathered that a flat in Edinburgh was the next move—why, I dont know—and a few minutes later a telegram was telephoned through to her here (evidently events had been sufficiently hot for her to leave evidence of movement with her host and hostess) saying that she must 'wire position before taking flat'. Both she and Robert seemed vague as to 'position'. Robert is trying for Sean O'Faolain's position in the Jesuit College at Strawberry Hill—shades of Walpole.[4] S. O'F has apparently decided

---

[1] *The Times* of 24 June 1933 reported that Sir Harold Wernher, chairman of the Anglo-Swedish Society, and Lady Zia Wernher held a reception at Someries House, Regent's Park, in honour of the Nobel Prize winners of Great Britain and Ireland; among those present along with WBY were Rudyard Kipling and Bernard Shaw.

[2] Robert Noble Denison (1899–1953), 'Robin Wilson', sent copies of *The Holy Wells of Orris and Other Poems* (London, 1927) and *Equinox* to WBY in 1937. His brother Lawrence Wilson published a further selection, *Raghley, O Raghley and Other Poems*, after Denison's death.

[3] Captain James Robert 'Jack' White (1879–1946), a Boer War veteran, then trade unionist, was one of the co-founders with James Connolly of the Irish Citizen Army in 1913 and in the 1930s in London was a member of Sylvia Pankhurst's anti-parliament Workers Socialist Federation. Ave White was his daughter by his first wife, Mercedes Dollie Mosley, whom he married while serving in Gibraltar (1901–5).

[4] Seán Proinsias Ó'Faoláin, né John Francis Whelan (1900–91), short story writer who on his return from Harvard in 1929 taught at St Mary's University College in Twickenham, which in 1925 had moved to Strawberry Hill, the house originally built by Robert Walpole's son the Gothic novelist Horace Walpole (1717–97). In 1940 he founded and edited *The Bell*, a literary magazine, and in 1964 his autobiography *Vive Moi* describes his early experiences as a Republican in the Gaelic League and a member of the Irish Volunteers and the IRA during the Civil War. From 1957 to 1959 he served as director of the Arts Council of Ireland.

that he cant stay out of Ireland any longer. Robert is taking Derek Verschoyle's place for the biography of Madam Marchiewicz....[5] he is doing the part up to 1910. I wonder have you any memories that would be any use to him? He has been seeing people and says that he can get nothing but anecdotes. He spent a long afternoon with AE. AE was painting a picture. The picture's painting was a rapid process, the panorama on the canvas was complete within an hour but the elucidation of AE's memories of Con Marchiewicz amounted to little else than pictures of Casimir.[6] That slow-minded Robert was appalled at the rapidity of AE's painting 'it must be so expensive, all those canvasses'.

Please send postcards to both children. Michael's address is Baymount School, Dollymount, Co Dublin. picture postcards of London, Oxford and Cambridge with appropriate remarks!

Yours affly
Dobbs

O—I forgot an adorable incident, see next page![7]

[ALS]   SAVILE CLUB, | 69, BROOK STREET. W.1.
Wednesday [7 June 1933]

My dear Dobbs

I am back from Oxford & start in an hour or so to Cambridge.[1] I dined last night with the Christ Church Dons—Cooke[2] my host—& saw a new flower in the College garden. I sent it you in a large envelope. It is a blue poppy which has just arrived from China

Yesterday some young man said 'Do you like Guy Gough?' I said 'Yes he is very simple & friendly', then he said 'Do you like Mrs Gough' I said 'No' Then he said 'She is a bully. She bullies Guy & gives her two children a most unhappy life'. I do not in the least know who the young man was. He was upset about Anne Gregory teath which spoilt her & 'nothing could be done for them now.'

---

[5] Derek Hugo Verschoyle (1911–73), poet and diplomat who later founded his own publishing house, was editor of *The Spectator* (1932–9); neither Verschoyle nor Wilson appears to have written about this passionate artist-activist, but in 1934 Ó'Faoláin published *Constance Markievicz, or The Average Revolutionary* (Jonathan Cape), the first of many biographies.

[6] 'Count' Casimir Dunin-Markievicz (1874–1932), a Polish artist intimately involved with the artistic and social circles of Dublin, left Ireland in 1913 and became a journalist, returning only to be by his dying wife's bedside.

[7] Unfortunately this page is missing.

[1] WBY gave a reading to the Oxford University English Club on 5 June 1933; one of his hosts was the poet and critic Edmund Charles Blunden (1896–1974), now a fellow of Merton College after returning from Japan where he was Professor of Poetry at Tokyo University (1924–7). On 8 June WBY received an honorary degree from Cambridge University.

[2] Revd Dr George Albert Cooke (1865–1934), Regius Professor of Hebrew and Canon of Christ Church, Oxford.

It was pleasant at Oxford

Yrs ev
WB Yeats

[ALS]   RIVERSDALE, | WILLBROOK, |
RATHFARNHAM, | DUBLIN.
[*c.*13 June 1933]

My dear Willy

Many happy returns of your birthday—Did you arrange your little dinner party? I'm sure you didnt—you needed a firm hand behind your pen
to make the ink flow.

Now. Do please write to Robert Childers to say how sorry you are that
you cannot come to his reception (after wedding to Christine Manning) on
June 16th.

Robert Childers
12 Bushy Park Road
Dublin.

We shall have to pack up some sort of a wedding gift—later—

Michael was here yesterday—very well & cheerful. Says the Scholarship
Exam for St. Columba's is the easiest in Europe. A boy from Castle Park
School got a 'scholar'¹ & only got 2 out of 10 for geometry!

Anne very brown & bathing a lot.

Love G.

[ALS]   SAVILE CLUB, | 69, BROOK STREET. W.1.
June 14 [1933]

My dear Dobbs: I gave the party. Palmstierna, Dulac, Squire, James
Stephens, Turner, Keirnan. Ellis Roberts could not come.¹ Stephens was

---

¹ St Columba's College traditionally awarded entrance scholarships, for which the appli-
cants sat a competitive examination set by the College; gaining a scholarship was considered
highly prestigious.

¹ Sir John Collings Squire, pseud. 'Solomon Eagle' (1884–1958), anthologist and one of the
poets published in Edward Marsh's *Georgian Poetry* collections, began his career as an essayist in 1909 as a parodist for the *New Age*, was the literary editor for the *New Statesman* (1913)
before founding the *London Mercury* which he edited 1919–34; 1922–8 he was chairman of the
Architecture Club, and later a reviewer for the *Illustrated London News* (1937); in 1927 he was
an early radio commentator on Wimbledon, was knighted in 1933, and became a reader for
Macmillans in 1934. Richard Ellis Roberts (1879–1953), critic, poet, and translator of Ibsen,
was literary editor of the *New Statesman* 1930–2.

magnificent. We all conspired to keep his fountain flowing This morning I am tired. (I had a long pleasant lunch party at Emily Grigsbys as well as the dinner) trying to do nothing for the present as I shall spend the evening with the Swami. Kearnan is now reading through Lady Gregorys memoirs for which I am thankful. Margeret is now asking for their publication instead of a 'life', Kearnan has intercepted a violent letter from Keller, in Margerets name, to Huntington. If some publication of the memoirs could be arranged, the Goughs perhaps guarranteeing Putnams against loss, I should be well content. The book is formless but full of valuable history. I have not yet seen Huntington

Yrs ev
WB Yeats

Cannot spell—too tired

[ALS]   SAVILE CLUB, | 69, BROOK STREET. W.1.
16 June [1933]

My dear Dobbs

I saw Huntington yesterday. Margeret who said to him a couple of months ago 'I know the material you have is not suitable for publication except as material for a life' and proposed Mrs Pope Hennesey to write it, now insists, through Keller, that she will not permit anything but the publication of what Lady Gregory has herself written. This to prevent me writing the life. I have told Huntington to reply as follows 'Mr Yeats feels that he must in loyalty to Lady Gregory's memory write her life. As he is old though now in vigerous health he cannot delay. He will start writing at once. This life, or if too long a condensation of it, will be published as an introduction to the diaries. Mr Yeats will ultimately publish the whole life among his own works. He hopes that he will be permitted to use her letters & the other material mentioned in the codecil, but at the same time does not consider this material essential'. The sport in all this is that Margeret's main object (according to Huntington) is to suppres the black & tan parts of the diaries & that she can do nothing.[1] I propose to write the whole book in my own language except where I quote some convesation, & to use the material as a guide to memory. This will leave Huntington to publish or not to publish as he pleases Lady Gregory's Autobiography. I will also I think make it impossible for Margeret to make an unseemly quarrell.

---

[1] In fact, AG had published extracts from her diaries anonymously in *The Nation* from 16 Oct. 1920 to 1 Jan. 1921, recording some of the atrocities she herself had observed carried out by the Black and Tans.

My dinner cost £9.5.0 more than half being the wine (hock and sherry) [and] the whiskey. It was an excellent dinner & I took the advice of the club steward through out. You may expect me back on June 24 (day after Nobel prise affair) I told the Club it can have my room then.

Yrs ev
WB Yeats

[APS¹]   London
[19 June 1933]

Here the most famous and sacred mountain of Japan.² I went yesterday to the British Museum to see the Chinease and Japanese pictures & bought this at the door. Thank you for that nice letter

WB Yeats

[APS¹]   London
21 June 1933]

Got this at the Picture Gallery to day. It is by Augustus John.² I have sat to him several times

WB Yeats

Did you look like this picture when you played the violin³

[ALS]   SAVILE CLUB, | 69, BROOK STREET. W.1.
[22] June [1933]

My dear Dobbs
     Another twist in the Lady Gregory affair. I have just written to Huntington (& told Keirnan) that I shall write the life without making any use of the documents & Kearnan says 'it is the right' solution (he was thinking of resigning his post as executor through dissagreement with Mrs Gough. These are my reasons

---

¹ Addressed to 'Miss Anne Yeats | Riversdale | Willbrook | Rathfarnham | Co Dublin'.
² Photograph of 'Hokusai Fuji above the Lightning', British Museum B.104.

¹ Addressed to 'Miss Anne Yeats | Riversdale | Willbrook | Rathfarnham | Co Dublin'.
² Photograph of 'Madame Suggia' (Guilhermina Suggia, 1888–1950) at her cello by Augustus John, in the National Gallery.
³ AY studied the violin while at Hillcourt School.

(1) The documents would be mere helps to memory

(2) I should have to give half the royalty to the family (half of 15 percent) instead of getting 20 per cent from Macmillan.

(3) The Gregory family would feel that my book was substitution for Lady Gregorys own words.

(4) I dont want a personal quarrell (public quarrels may be the salt of life)

I have been brought to this conclusion partly because Huntington repented of the proposal that I should use a condensed version of 'the Life' to introduce an abridged version of the 'diaries', thus leaving later partial publication of the 'Autobiography' for later consideration. My book was to be substituted for all other publication

Expect me Saturday

Yrs ev
WB Yeats

[TLS]
RIVERSDALE, | WILLBROOK, | RATHFARNHAM, | DUBLIN.
December 9 1933

My dear Willy

What are you up to? Having a gay time I hope.[1] Anne came in this evening at 7.15 in great joy after a long day with Charles[2] and Mrs Wilson (Canon Wilson's wife who christened A, the Canon[3] I mean of course!) at a drag hunt near Naas.... the chief achievement of the day seems to have been that two people offered Anne cigarettes! I neednt say that Anne was following on foot, not on horse. I had expected her to come home starved and had arranged for a hot meal to be ready immediately she arrived. She looked at it and sighed: 'I havent stopped eating since I left this morning'. I gather that bars of chocolate and ham sandwiches alternated throughout the day and that her only regret was that the only available liquid came out of flasks or puddles. Her strong hygenic sense had disdained the puddles, and she drank glasses and glasses of water throughout the evening like a dog that has stolen a ham.

---

[1] WBY was in London from 4 to 21 December to attend a PEN Club dinner, but spent part of the time in bed with a bad cold, so saw very few people.

[2] Charlotte Ruth Lane Poole (later Mrs Gerald Burston), known always as Charles (1913–2007), eldest daughter of WBY's cousin Ruth Lane Poole, was staying with SMY while attending TCD, then studying landscaping at Glasnevin Gardens.

[3] Revd Canon D. F. R. Wilson, Rector of St Mary's Donnybrook, who when later Dean of St Patrick's Cathedral unsuccessfully urged GY to allow WBY to be buried there.

Thank God I can now sit down again, I never appreciated a chair so much.[4] John has been painting the walls of the bathroom and Aunt Jane;[5] the first coat was finished yesterday; today John asked me as a personal favour not to have any hot baths run in the bathroom. Apparently no one can have a hot bath until two days after the second coat has been put on. This will bring us to next Wednesday; John prefers Thursday. Anne feels that God is being really delightfully good. He cleaned out the tank which supplies us with all our water: this was done on Tuesday, and as I was in bed until Thursday he kept for my inspection all the treasure he found therein. I am sorry that he did so. The tank is now covered with good ply wood but it will be some time before I shall think that water has any qualities as a drink. There was a most handsome wasps nest in the rafters just above the tank which accounts for the dead wasps that poured into the bath through the cold water tap.

I hear, though it may be untrue, that Keating (the painter) has bought the McFadden's house next door to us. I cant quite believe it because it is a very large house with some seventeen acres and many newly built outhouses and I cant believe that our Keating has enough cash. It may be that it is Keatinge the house painter who has bought it. I once met Keatinge at the Cahill's and on being introduced I said 'the painter?' and he said 'the house-painter'. The House-painter-Keatinge is quite a nice person. Anyway, either Keating or Keatinge will be an amiable neighbour.[6]

Lennox lectured yesterday (Friday) at the RDS. I couldnt go because I couldnt face sitting in busses and those hard seats in the lecture hall! From the Irish Times report I gather that his lecture was mainly reminiscence of early years—Kinsale and so on—so perhaps he has got into the mood of writing his early autobiography.[7] You will find the report in the copy of the Irish Times I send you under separate cover. I mention this because if you want a book for the Cuala Press he might be gingered up.

I havent seen anyone since you left, having been delightfully comfortably luxuriatingly in cot—until this afternoon, when, being Saturday,

[4] By now GY was suffering with rheumatism and arthritis; see letter of 30 June 1934.
[5] Slang for WC.
[6] J. F. Keatinge and Sons Ltd. were contractors for building, painting and plumbing, and electrical engineering works in Dublin. Their neighbour was indeed John (later Sean) Keating RHA (1889–1977), whose address in Thom's 1935 Directory is 'Ait-an-Cuain',Willbrook, Rathfarnham. James McFadden lived nearby at 'Fairbrook', Willbrook.
[7] LR spoke at the Royal Dublin Society, Ballsbridge, in connection with a sale of work; in 1938 he and his two siblings published their early family reminiscences, *Three Homes*, but no other autobiographical work.

three people called, and Mrs Dix[8] being the first the rest got let in. There was a certain amount of pleasant aimless gossip of an entirely political kind.

Yours—
George

[ALS]   SAVILE CLUB, | 69, BROOK STREET. W.1.

Friday [15 Dec. 1933]

My dear Dobbs

I am slowly casting off the cold. Had a really good night last night & hope to be able finish my work on Monday or Tuesday.

Two days ago a man introduced himself. He said that four or five years [?days] ago he had a wire from U.S A 'Yeats seriously ill get obituary'. He told St John Ervine who wrote 1¾ collumns which he had set up for 'Observer' & gave my informant a proof. My informant had the proof in his pocket that he might telegraph it later when he came into the Savile & there I was.

Forgive me [not] writing more but though the cold is practically gone it has left me very lazy. I am tired out talking to a man I want to review Higgins book. I had, by the by, wired for 2 copies of it as <u>Cuala</u> sent me one copy & one copy of Rossi's book[1] which I dont want. I had hoped to give the second copy to Squire.

Yrs ev
WB Yeats

My dear you are a worst correspondent than I am. I am hoping to have the energy on Monday to get that star-map for Anne.

---

[8] Probably Elizabeth Rachel Dix, whose husband Ernest Reginald McClintock Dix (1857–1936) was a solicitor and noted bibliophile, whose residence was Coolevin, Butterfield Road, Rathfarnham; Saturday was traditionally GY's 'At Home' day.

[1] *Arable Holdings* by F. R. Higgins was published by Cuala Press in November 1933; *Pilgrimage in the West* by Mario M. Rossi, trans. J. M. Hone, was published in July 1933.

Part Six
Adjustments
1934-1936

Convinced that he could now tolerate winters in Dublin, WBY and George made one last trip to Rapallo to close their apartment; it was the last time the Yeatses and the Pounds would be together. But recurring bouts of congestion of the lungs continued to plague WBY. In February 1935 he reported to Olivia Shakespear, 'Certain societies are preparing for my next birthday. The alarmed sec of one called on George. "O Mrs Yeats" he said, "dont let him slip away before June"'.[1] The loss of Coole and Ballylee after Lady Gregory's death also weighed heavily, as did the fear that he had lost his creativity. When he learned therefore that the Steinach 'rejuvenation' operation (actually a vasoligature and vasectomy) promised revived sexual potency, he was, encouraged by George, convinced that poetry would follow.[2] It did, in renewed bursts of energy and a corresponding enthusiasm for sexual relationships. His first dalliance was with the young actress and poet Margot Ruddock, rapidly followed by a less sentimental alliance with the novelist Ethel Mannin. Despite some guileless attempts to hide his London adventures from George, she was fully aware of the source of his excitement. During one of WBY's more serious relapses she sought Gogarty's help, confiding, 'I do not want Willy to be made an invalid or a fool. I think too that if any of these things are serious, I would rather he died in happiness than in invalidism. He may not have told you of all his past 18th months activities. One of them is that he has been very much in love with a woman in London. I tell you this that you may understand why I am most anxious that he should not be tied to an unnecessary invalidism.'[3]

Complicating these clandestine arrangements were other more legitimate reasons for his absence from Dublin. Work on an Oxford anthology of modern poetry led to a friendship with the poet Dorothy Wellesley, whose Sussex home he hoped would replace the loss of Coole. Plans to establish a poet's theatre in London came to nothing, despite his renewed interest in verse plays. Excitement over his discovery of the mystical philosophy of Shri Purohit Swami led to a journey to Majorca to collaborate on a translation of the *Upanishads*. Work on *The Oxford Book of Modern Verse* brought the Yeatses even closer together. But as always George, bound to Dublin by family, household, and WBY's publishing responsibilities, was sympathetic to his need for fresh stimulus, despite the frequency with which she was required to rush to her ailing husband's bedside and extricate him from a

[1] WBY to OS, 5 Feb. 1935 (Wade, 831).
[2] See *BG*, 475–7.
[3] GY to Gogarty, 29 Jan. 1935, courtesy of Professor Philip Marcus.

few embarrassing situations. From Majorca she confided to her sister-in-law that 'she feels like a child of five left in charge of a Tiger in a wire cage, and she is tired of being sent for when the Tiger escapes'.[4] Though during one illness WBY 'burned all personal letters not knowing what the end would be',[5] the surviving letters continue to chart activities in Dublin and elsewhere, his writing and theatre projects, and George's close eye on the Abbey, the children, and the Yeats industry.

[4] *BG*, 502.
[5] WBY to Dorothy Wellesley, 26 Apr. 1936, in fear that Gwyneth Foden would read and publicize his correspondence (*CL InteLex*, acc. 6542).

1934

[TLS]   Riversdale | Rathfarnham | Dublin
                                              Saturday [14 Apr. 1934]

My dear Willy

I wired to you today 'all news good' adding that the Abbey made a profit of £83 on 'Grogan and the Ferret'.¹ I hear that McCormack is playing John Loving and Boss Shields the mask—so that is well.²

If you are able to see Macmillan on Tuesday or Wednesday I imagine you will travel Thursday night staying at Queens Hotel Chester the night. Dont forget to wire for room WHY DONT YOU GET A SLEEPER FROM LONDON TO CHESTER? Dont think of the fifteen shillings! It would be well worth it for the sake of being able to lie down.³

You ought to arrange at once for your reservations. Send me a wire saying if you start Wednesday, Thursday or when.

Hope you are feeling better on your legs today. I had a fearful crossing—had to hold on to prevent falling out of my bunk, but was not seasick at all. This wind will have blown itself out by the time you start.

I enclose a letter from Lambert.⁴ You had better send him a wire in reply to his question about exhibiting the medal at his show at the Lefevre galleries.

                                                        Love
                                                        George

¹ *Grogan and the Ferret*, a comedy in three acts by George Shiels, was first produced 13 Nov. 1933 with Eileen Crowe, F. J. McCormick, Michael J. Dolan, and Barry Fitzgerald as performers.

² Major characters in *Days Without End* by Eugene O'Neill, produced at the Abbey Theatre 16 Apr. 1934, directed by LR.

³ WBY was in Beaumont House Hospital, London, recovering from the Steinach operation of 5 April; GY, who accompanied him, returned to Dublin a week later (see Foster ii. 498–9; *BG*, 475–6).

⁴ Maurice Prosper Lambert (1901–64), British sculptor and brother of the musician Constant Lambert, was by now well known along with Henry Moore and Barbara Hepworth for his experimentation with materials and the contemporary movements of Surrealism and Art Deco; he had been invited by WBY to submit a design for the Gregory medal for the Irish Academy of Letters, called by him 'Aengus and the birds' but by WBY 'Inspiration' or 'Genius' 'as I dont want to be involved in controversies as to the number, species, or existence of the birds'. Lambert wished to show the cast at his exhibition of sculpture at The Lefevre Galleries, London, which opened 8 May 1934; seventeen copies were cast in bronze in 1934, and the mould then destroyed; AE, Shaw, and WBY were the first recipients, awarded by the Academy in 1934 although the ceremony making the actual presentation did not occur until 26 May 1937.

[ALS] SAVILE CLUB, | 69, BROOK STREET. W.1.

Saturday [30 June 1934]

My dear Dobbs

I saw Dr Smith. Blood-pressure 204. Dr Smith is going to Dublin to see friends will be there at end of next week & show you how to give me that injection.[1]

Turner the musical critic not of Ezras opinion about my verses, says that they are excellent songs, that I understand the simplicity of the song as distinct from lyric & so on.[2] I am in great vigour, seeing everbody no longer taking taxis & so on.

Dined with Olivia & Dorothy last night. They discussed Mrs Foden. Dorothy thought her 'suburban' or some thing of that kind & Olivia said 'Yes Willy called her a Cleopatra of the suburbs but we had a shock the other night at the Swamis Indian Institute. Some body read out the list of members & came to "Lady Gwyneth Foden" upon which the Chairman said You must not call her that she asks us to call her "Mrs Foden". She does not use her title.'[3] One wonders what is the mystery. I saw her & the Swami yesterday & found him very luminous.

I have seen Lady Ottoline & Dulac, Stephens dines with me to night. Miss Grigsby asked me to spend Sunday at her Cottage but I could not give the time so I see her Monday after noon.[4]

How is your back.?

Yrs affecly
WB Yeats

You promised to write & tell me about your back
Remember me to your Mother & Harry Tucker[5]

[1] Possibly Richard Travers Smith (1872–1945), a Trinity College graduate and a specialist in heart disease; Professor of Surgical Pharmacy 1915–17, he left Dublin and his wife Hester Dowden, who divorced him in 1922, and established a practice at 45 Wimpole Street, London.

[2] While they were together in Rapallo for the last time, EP had pronounced WBY's verses 'putrid', written in 'nobody language'.

[3] As with so many of her stories, Mrs Foden's title seems to have been an invention.

[4] See letter of 11 July 1930.

[5] From 6 to 25 June 1934 they were in Rapallo closing their apartment and choosing which furniture should go to Riversdale; on their return WBY spent a week in London while GY visited the Tuckers in Sidmouth.

[ALS]   SAVILE CLUB, | 69, BROOK STREET. W.1.
                                                    Oct 23 [1934]

My dear George

I am doing great work here—seeing all kinds of people, dancers, musicians, actors & think there will be no difficulty in launching here just such a theatre for 'No plays' as I have described & always wanted.[1] I have not yet seen Lady Londonderry. She has wired 'Alas am away until end of month, going Mount Stewart Saturday can you call there on way to Dublin'. She evidently thinks that everybody goes to Ireland via Larne.[2] I have wired to ask on which day she comes to London, and add that if I cannot stay for it I will go to Mount Stewart

I have been asked to edit 'The Oxford Book of Modern Verse'—poetry since 1900. I shall put Watt on to it. It might bring a great deal of money. It would not take me much trouble. The publisher will send me a mass of material.

Please send me papers etc about 'Macbeth'[3]—I shall get back some time next week—what day depends on Lady Londonderry—in time for last performances. Perhaps I did not say that I want to give the first 'No plays' for benefit of 'Irish Academy' in her house.

I go to day to tea with Olivia. She is the first friend I shall have seen. All the rest of my time I have been seeing people about the new project.[4]

I wonder what sort of passage you had.[5] I had the worst channel crossing I have known—I was sick.

                                                    Yrs affectly
                                                    WB Yeats

[1] On 4 Oct. 1934 WBY contacted the actress and poet Margot Collis, née Ruddock, Mrs Raymond Lovell (1907–51), who had written to him about her poetry and the possibility of establishing a poet's theatre; they arranged a meeting on his return from Rome, where he and GY had been invited to the 4th Congress of the Alessandro Volta Foundation and he had spoken on Ireland's national theatre.

[2] The Marchioness of Londonderry was spending more and more time at Mount Stewart, the family estate, near Newtonwards, Co. Down, in Northern Ireland, where she continued to develop the gardens.

[3] On 25 October the Abbey produced *Macbeth*, directed by the new appointee Bladon Peake (see 18 Dec. 1934).

[4] A somewhat disingenuous statement; by now he and Margot were probably lovers. At her suggestion he had taken furnished rooms for a week from 17 October at 44 Seymour Street, run by Miss Elizabeth O'Dea.

[5] GY stayed on in Italy until 20 October to see the mosaics at Ravenna and then went directly back to Dublin.

[ALS]   RIVERSDALE. | WILLBROOK, |
                               RATHFARNHAM, | DUBLIN.
                                         Friday [26 Oct. 1934]

My dear Willy
    I enclose the newspaper cuttings of Macbeth. The papers have been kind.[1]
I was sitting in the 4th row & could neither <u>See</u> nor <u>hear</u>![2] Pet Wilson[3] in the
front row of Gallery said she could not hear a word, nor see. It was played
in almost complete obscurity, far darker than Johnston's 'King Lear'—the
costumes might have been interesting if one could have seen them!
    Am going tonight with Olive Craig.[4] Hope a little more light as Lennox
felt the obscurity trying.

                                                        In haste
                                                        G.

[ALS]   SAVILE CLUB, | 69, BROOK STREET. W.1.
                                         Friday [26 Oct. 1934]

My dear George
    The reproaches crossed each other—we both had expected letters & had
not had them.
    I [?swim] from little theatre to little theatre & have no[w] decided to work
with what is called 'the group theatre'.[1] They are about to get up displays of
work by Elliot & Auden[2] & are I believe highly skilled. They will in future play
not in a theatre but in a large room which suits my 'No plays'. I go to see that

---

[1] Enclosures missing. The *Irish Times* described the production as 'very disappointing', but
that 'the gloom was quite effective at times' (26 Oct. 1934, 8).

[2] Both words underlined twice.

[3] Hermione Lytton ('Pet') Wilson (d. 1965) of 'Kayos', Greenfield Park, Stillorgan Road, Donnybrook, was WBY's Dublin typist from the early 1930s and with GY a member of the executive
committee of the DDL. A close friend of Shelah Richards, she was one of the editors of the silent
film *Guests of the Nation* (1933–5) which was directed by Richards's husband Denis Johnston.

[4] Olive (Mrs Francis Brownrigg) Craig of 45 Leeson Park, a close friend who could be
counted on to look after ABY when GY was away, and whom GY later used to visit in her
cottage in Malahide, was acting honorary secretary of the DDL in 1928.

[1] 'The Group Theatre' (1932–9), not to be confused with the New York theatre collective
of the same name, was founded as 'an actors' cooperative' by the dancer Rupert Doone, né
Ernest Reginald Wollfield (1903–66), who had worked with the Experimental Theatre in Cambridge, and his partner the artist Charles Owen Robert Medley (1905–94).

[2] Wystan Hugh Auden (1907–73), poet, dramatist, and journalist, at this time a schoolmaster
at the Downs School in the Malvern Hills, a preparatory school for boys with a heavy concentration on the arts; his first book was the privately printed *Poems* (1930), followed by *The Orators:
An English Study* (1932), which included both prose and verse. The Group Theatre produced his
play *The Dance of Death* (1933), a verse drama written in the style of a musical revue reflecting
his left-wing politics and described as 'a satire on modern life'.

room to day. I want to combine a performance in such a room with one for benefit of Irish Academy in Lady Londonderry drawing room. I may however not wait here long enough to see her at the moment. She returns here Nov 1. My plans are the new version sketched in Rome of the dance with severed head music by Dulac, Miss De Valois as dancer. Dulac agrees. 'Fighting the Waves' for flute, drum & gong, music probaly by Constant Lambert.[3] 'The Resurection' I am to write an article for the journal of 'The Group' theatre explaining what I propose to do. This means that they allow me to direct their policy to some extent. I hope to get more origonal music & better masks than I can get in Dublin except by some fluke, and to use these in Dublin later There is great tecnical skill in the little theatres & this is the moment to use it

I have had to spend a good deal of money asking people to lunch or dinner. 'The Gate Theatre' here,[4] where there is fine acting would have taken my work & that organization is richer than 'The Group' but seemed the wrong audience. I think I am almost at the end of my work here—but I want to see Audin if possible & perhaps have a final meeting with Ninette de Valois who is enthusiastic

I am full of energy & health

Yrs ev
WB Yeats

'The Group' talks of taking one of my plays to Germany.

[ALS]   SAVILE CLUB, | 69, BROOK STREET. W.1.
Saturday [27 Oct. 1934]

My dear George

'Macbeth' is evidently a disaster. I told Peak[1] not to make a dark stage & said from the designs that 'Macbeth' looked dark. He said it was not.

---

[3] Leonard Constant Lambert (1905–51), composer, conductor, and critic, whose career began with a commission to write the ballet *Romeo and Juliet* for Serge Diaghilev's Ballets Russes (1925), followed by the success of *The Rio Grande*, a choral work based on a poem by Sacheverell Sitwell, conducted Antheil's music for de Valois's revival of *Fighting the Waves* at the Lyric Theatre, Hammersmith, on 28 Mar. 1930. His book *Music Ho! A Study of Music in Decline* (1934) was a witty study of contemporary music in the context of modern European culture. The artist Maurice Prosper Lambert was his brother.

[4] The Gate Theatre Studio was founded in 1925 by actor, clown, and director Peter Godfrey (1899–1970) and his wife actress Molly Veness (1898–1985) to produce contemporary experimental plays. Originally called the Gate Theatre Salon, it reopened in 1927 at 16A Villiers Street, 'underneath the arches' near Charing Cross Station; by operating as a theatre club it was able to avoid censorship by the Lord Chamberlain's Office, producing Wilde's *Salome* in 1931 and plays by Schnitzler, Kaiser, Toller, and Bruckner.

[1] Bladon Peake, whose first production at the Abbey was *Macbeth* in October 1934, had been trained at the Maddermarket Theatre in Norwich, which had been founded in 1921 by Nugent

Darkness & inaudality are the worst form of 'darkest Kensington before the tambourine'.[2] I feel I should return at once but may not be able to do so for a couple of days. A little gathering of friends at Dulacs last night decided that 'The Group Theatre' should act and produce my plays but that a public theatre must be found for the performances. He and I are to see Lady Cunard to find out if I can raise a hundred pounds or so by a lecture at her house. They also object to my working with Audin & Elliot as they say comparisons between rival schools prevents a proper understanding. I must have the assent of Elliot, Ashton Ninette de Valois and one or two others.

Yrs ev
WB Yeats

[ALS]   SAVILE CLUB, | 69, BROOK STREET. W.1.
                              Tuesday [30 Oct. 1934]

My dear George

I cannot get away until to-morrow night. I had meant to cross to night. I am tired but triumphant. An attempt is to be made to found a poetical theatre. Ashley Dukes of the Mercury theatre (a little theatre in Notting Hill) has undertaken all expense.[1] It will open with 'Fighting the Waves' 'Player Queen' (costumes by Dulac) & my new version of The Clock Tower (music by Dulac). 'Fighting the Waves' will have new music (drum, gong, flute & zither, & new masks, all suitable for a small theatre. The music will

Monck (1877–1958), who doubtless was responsible for recommending him to the Abbey directors. After leaving the Abbey Theatre in January 1935 Peake was residing in Birmingham before becoming producer of the Northampton Repertory Players (1935–7), then moving to a career in film, producing a number of documentary films during the 1940s and eventually in the 1950s continuing his career in South Africa.

[2] On 17 Sept. 1934 WBY sent OS a quatrain he had written about the talented painter, illustrator, and theatre designer Norah McGuinness, who after her divorce from Geoffrey Phibbs in 1929 was associated with the avant-garde London Group of artists. Claiming that she 'has changed her artistic aim with each lover', he made the following quatrain:

> Where has she gone that gave up all for art?
> Nature has gifted her, without, within;
> What new salvationist has won her heart?
> In darkest Kensington what Tambourine?

[1] Ashley Dukes (1885–1959), playwright and theatre manager who purchased an old church in Notting Hill Gate, converted it into studios and auditorium, and founded the Mercury Theatre partly as a venue for the ballet company run by his wife, Marie Rambert (1888–1982).

I hope be by Lambert. I have insisted on the inclusion in repertory of the poetical left—3 evenings of me, then 3 evenings of Auden & T. S. Elliot. Tomorrow I meet Aston[2] & Ninette de Valois to arrange details. 'The Group Theatre' (its representative has just left me) will do Auden & Elliot. My aim is to get Masks & music & costume I can use in Dublin, & describe or picture in my books.

Yours affecly
WB Yeats

Organizing is like a bumble-bee in a bottle. One tries all directions until one finds the neck.

[ALS]   SAVILE CLUB, / 69, BROOK STREET. W.1.

Second letter   Tuesday [30 Oct. 1934]

My dear George
   I shall return to-morrow night by Liverpool, probably stay in bed as long as they let me & then take a taxi to Rathfarnham. The fare will seem a trifle compared to what I have spent here on inviting people to lunch etc. Now that the bea has got out of the bottle I am feeling rather slack.

Yrs ev
WB Yeats

[TLS]   RIVERSDALE, | WILLBROOK, |
                    RATHFARNHAM, | DUBLIN.
                    Tuesday Dec.11 1934[1]

My dear Willy
   Last night at the end of Canavans the pit stamped with their feet (unanimously) as well as clapping. That ought to mean a good week. A very good performance from Linnane as Anthony and Stephenson as the Miller. Anne

---

   [2] Frederick William Mallandaine Ashton, later Sir (1904–1988), dancer and choreographer who began his career with Ballet Rambert, then moved on to work with de Valois's Vic-Wells Ballet, now The Royal Ballet; during his distinguished career he was responsible for the choreography of almost 100 works.

   [1] WBY had returned to London on 7 Dec. 1934, again staying in a flat at 44 Seymour Street, and remained until 11 Jan. 1935.

Clery very good, Chris Hayden dull.[2] The scene in the castle was admirable, the house rocked with laughter. I didnt much like the setting for the Mill room. It was all painted like brand-new pitch pine though not so yellow, which somehow looked wrong when they speak of the 'thatch' overhead. Headley had a very fine costume, Anthony's good, miller too elaborate, and a magnificent get-up for Queen Elizabeth in the Castle prison![3] I dont think I ever saw Dolly laugh as she did in that scene.

I enclose the press cuttings—the Irish Times are unfair to the production. John is bringing the Independent from Rathfarnham so I have not seen it yet. (John just back, no Independent to be got. I will post this letter in Dublin and slip in the cutting there.)

Neither Hayes nor Starkie were at the Theatre![4] I am going tonight for Canavans only and will let you know what the house is like. Poor last night. Back pit well filled, not much in front pit, back stalls fair.

Yours
George.

[ALS]   SAVILE CLUB, | 69, BROOK STREET. W.1.
                                       Thursday [13 Dec. 1934]

My dear Dobbs
Could you wire me the full title of O Connells book.[1] He has asked me to get him a review in 'The Times' & 'The Observer'. I can get him a review in 'The Times' at any rate, but I must know the name of the book. His letter

---

[2] This revival of *The Canavans* by AG was performed with John Stephenson, Joseph 'old Joe' Linnane (d. 1981), who became well known as a popular radio producer, and Fred Johnson (1899–1971), who after performing with Anew MacMaster and the Gate company, began his twenty-year career with the Abbey in 1929, eventually in the mid-1940s moving to England where he performed on stage, films, and television. Anne Clery (d. 1985), who was also known for her acting in films and radio, had begun her lengthy career with the Second Company in 1932; Christine Hayden, Mrs Eric Gorman (1890–1977), performed with the Abbey Theatre in 1917 until her retirement in 1951.

[3] Enclosure missing. The *Irish Times* pronounced the play bad but charming, and the settings 'novel and effective'; these were by Francis James Bould (1908–80), who had been brought over to Dublin by Peake as designer and received an exaggeratedly positive review in the *New York Times* (22 Nov. 1934) for the 'fantastic extravagance and unreality' of his designs for Peake's production of Molière's *The School for Wives* and Arthur Schnitzler's *The Gallant Cassian* (week of 12 November), in contrast to the 'drab, dowdy settings' of the previous production of *Macbeth* (week of 25 October). From the late 1940s until the early 1970s Peake was a production designer and set designer for numerous television shows, including the Sherlock Holmes series, BBC Sunday Night Theatre, and *Are You Being Served?*

[4] See note to 29 Feb. 1932.

[1] Jephson Byrne O'Connell, *The Financial Administration of Saorstat Eireann with an Epitome of the Reports from the Committee of Public Accounts 1922–1932* (Dublin, 1934).

does not give the name but says he has sent a copy. You will probably find the book at 'Riversdale'.

Little here to report except a pleasant life. I am re-writing 'The Clock Tower' in verse, substituting a new and more philosophic lyric for that containing 'What says the Clock' which becomes a seperate poem. I dine with Ashley Dukes tonight to talk over details Tomorrow I lunch with T. S. Elliot.

Yours affly
WB Yeats

Thanks for letter about Abbey. I want to know if the audience increases.

[ALS]   SAVILE CLUB, | 69, BROOK STREET. W.1.
16. XII. 34

My dear Dobbs: Nothing to report except that I am writing poetry & recovering from it by conversation and idleness. In about two months I should have a new book of verse, without including any of the prose parts of 'The Clock Tower'—that play I am writing in verse. Dulac has made a model theatre for his designs for 'The Player Queen'. He has set up the first scene on it. He does not like my new severed head play,[1] thinks it too realistic & bloody, prefers the old 'Clock Tower', but this may only mean that he shrinks from writing music for a play that is too 'wet' for his 'dry' temprement.

There has been some trouble at the Abbey about the engagement of a English acter.[2] Lennox wrote. It has probably been alredy smoothed over but I have written Lennox a vehement letter on the subject, which he can <show if nece> talk about if necessary. I have suggested desolving the company, which is the last thing I expect to happen.

I am longing to know what houses 'Canavans' drew

Yrs ev
WB Yeats

Remind Anne to write about Canavans

[TLS]   [Riversdale, Willbrook, Rathfarnham, Dublin]
Dec 18 1934

My dear Willy
Many thanks for your letter. Yes, I had heard from Lennox that there had been trouble at the Abbey but nothing more than that. [insert from below]

---

[1] *A Full Moon in March.*
[2] J. Geoffrey Davids; see 28 Dec. 1934 for GY's opinion.

I think the less I say about anything the better, so I shall avoid talking about it. You say in your letter 'I have written Lennox a vehement letter which he can talk about if necessary'.[1] Not, I think, to George! I cant help feeling that until Peake departs there will be neither peace nor houses. I suppose Macbeth prejudiced this very prejudicial country. I think I told you that I had ascertained from Italia[2] (in the course of a general conversation) that Starkie had seen neither the Pirandello nor the Canavans.[3] I dont know if Hayes had been down to either.

I think L.R. is really being very sober. I stayed a night there and for the first time for some months it was very pleasant—the two of them were not being on each other's nerves. I didnt naturally mention the theatre to Dolly seeing that L.R. had so recently made the gesture of resigning.! I saw her a few days later and she began on it herself and I gathered that they were now discussing together all these things, an excellent sign dont you think? They are having a party (of a large kind) next Saturday. It is to start at 5 pm and I am bidden to stay the night which I am doing.

You will have had my letter giving you four houses of Canavans, and Anne wrote last week, I forget which day.[4] She asked me to look at the letter but I told her I thought you wouldnt know whether her spelling was correct or not and refused to look at it!

Michael has done very well in his exams: first in History, 2nd in Geometry, and 1st in some other lesson which I forget, and 1st in Latin. The other results are not in yet.

I have a cheque for you from The Mercury £5.5.0 and one from the Spectator £4.14.6. I am not sending them on unless you ask me to do so.

Last Saturday I went to Howth for the night to Mrs Gasking[5]—when you are away people think I am lonely and entertain me. I told you Sorrento Cottage[6] always asked me when you were away. When we were in Dublin the Dermod O'Brien's used to do it and a couple of times the Marquis McSwineys—and, did you see his mother died—'The Countess McSwiney'

---

[1] 'I do not think we can surrender the right to employ what artist we please. We may have to take stern measures. I will come over if necessary. It may even be necessary to dismiss Stephenson or to dissolve the second company & let the theatre' (WBY to LR, 16 Dec. 1934, *CL InteLex*, acc. 6148).

[2] Italia Augusta, Mrs Walter Starkie.

[3] The Abbey Theatre had performed a translation of *Six Characters in Search of an Author* by Italian playwright and Nobel laureate Luigi Pirandello, directed by Bladon Peake, the week of 3 Dec. 1934, with Shelah Richards and Fred Johnson in the cast; AG's play *The Canavans* was revived the following week, see GY's letter of 11 December.

[4] Apparently WBY never received GY's letter.

[5] Jean Stewart Gasking (Mrs Robert J. M.) (d. 1945) lived at 'Innisfree', Carrickbrack Road, Baily, Co. Dublin.

[6] Home of LR and his wife in Dalkey.

at Pau, leaving him some £19,000 odd.⁷ That will give them a lift up. I believe they've been very hard up for some years. And talking about money, everyone is asking 'WHO is the woman who lost £400 gambling with Mrs Erriksson and who offered to settle up for £50?'⁸

Lily, Lolly and, I hope, Charles,⁹ come over on St Stephens Day for lunch and so on. Charles may have a 'hunt' but for my own sake I hope not for if she comes I can more easily separate off the controversialists. In the evening Charles, Anne, Michael and I all go to 'Lady Precious Stream'¹⁰ that Chinese play of Hsiung which I liked very much in the reading—I forget if you read it—

[MS] Yours affly

G.

(The turf fire side of the study has been re-yellow washed by John. It was very dirty.)

[ALS]   SAVILE CLUB, | 69, BROOK STREET. W.1.
                                                Dec 19 [1934]

Dear Dobbs

I enclose checque etc.

I am getting thi[ng]s arranged here. Our plays will in all liklihood be given April 29 to May 19. There will be controlling board consisting of T. S. Elliot, Dulac, Ashton & myself. I shall probably give a programe consisting of Ressurection, Player Queen, Full Moon in March. To alternate (a weak each) with T. S. Elliots Sweeny Agonistes & a new Ballet play by Auden.¹ My next work to get the committe to meet. I intend to write verse for two months & then do 'The Oxford Book of Modern Verse'

Yrs affly

WB Yeats

---

⁷ *The Times*, 17 Dec. 1934 includes notice of the will of Emma Isabella Konarska, Countess MacSwiney, of Pau, France, whose estate in England was valued at £19,287.

⁸ Mrs Eriksson's gambling partner has not been identified.

⁹ Charles Lane-Poole, Ruth Pollexfen's daughter and WBY's second cousin from Australia, who was boarding with SMY and ECY.

¹⁰ *Lady Precious Stream*, based on a Chinese story by Shih I. Hsiung (1902–91), actor, scholar, and translator, opened at the Gate Theatre on 26 Dec. 1934 with actor James Mason (1909–84) as 'the Honourable Reader'; when produced in London in 1935 at Nancy Price's 'Little Theatre', the play received glowing reviews and ran for 1,000 nights.

¹ *The Dance of Death* (1933).

[ALS]   SAVILE CLUB, | 69, BROOK STREET. W.1.
                                        Sunday [23 Dec. 1934]

My dear Dobbs

A young man, Rupert Doone, has gone, to whom I have read 'A Full Moon in March.' He is to produce it & has made most strange & imaginative suggestions. Early next week our Committee holds its first meeting. I go daily to Norman Haire for injections¹—now is the time to get my body back to the normal. I am full of themes for poems & have promised to let Watt have the new book of verse in two months after which I shall work at the Anthology I write verse every morning.

Tell Anne that I thank her for her letter about Canavans but I wanted more. Why she liked the play & so on.

All the seasonal greetings to you all.

                                                      W.B.Y.

[ALS]   SAVILE CLUB, | 69, BROOK STREET. W.1.
                                        Boxing Day [26 Dec. 1934]

My dear Dobbs

I thank you & the children for the Xmas wire of greetings. I shall get back to Dublin about Jan 5. I will then have been here exactly a month. I have written three lyrics & put The Clock Tower into verse, have formed my committee & in the next day or two it will meet. Befor I return I shall, I hope, have a properly typed 'Full Moon in March' & the lyrics in Watts hands.

Can you tell me when Lolly will want the rest of the Auto biography.¹ Do you remember the date on which I am to lecture to the London Institution.² Some time early in March I think. I was to see Christy³ (or were you to

---

¹ WBY has drawn a thick line down the margin of this sentence, and one line is heavily deleted. Norman Haire, né Zions (1892–1952), Australian sexologist, gynaecologist, and sexual reformer who performed the vasoligature and vasectomy believed to stimulate male sex hormones, a surgical procedure developed by the Austrian physiologist Eugen Steinach (1861–1944); after operating on WBY on 5 Apr. 1934, Haire continued to be an influential figure in encouraging his 'rejuvenation' (see Foster ii. 498–9; BG, 475–6).

¹ *Dramatis Personae* was finished at Cuala in October 1935 and published in December 1935.

² A planned lecture on 1 Mar. 1935 to the Royal Institution of Great Britain, 'the oldest independent research body in the world', and a planned lecture tour, had to be cancelled due to WBY's illness.

³ Probably Christy and Moore Ltd., literary agents, 225–7 Strand WC, who arranged WBY's lecture tours in Britain.

arrange by post) & arrange about some lectures before that date, in which were are to share.

Have you had the Aviery made?[4] That is one [of] the events I look forward to

Yrs ev
WB Yeats

[ALS]   SAVILE CLUB, | 69, BROOK STREET. W.1.
Dec 27 [1934]

My dear Dobbs

Would you phone <u>Cuala</u> & find out how many copies of <u>Clock</u> <u>Tower</u> are left. I think it might be well to publish a book of poems with Macmillan just before the plays at <u>The Mercury Theatre</u>, that is to say in April. When I have written one more lyric I shall have a book with a certain unity

I want you also to phone Abbey and find out how <u>Mrs Beam</u> has done. Because of the bad houses for <u>Canavans</u> & because we seemd to have no plays that would draw I suggested closing Peakes engagement at once.[1] I want Peake if possabl however to do <u>O'Donnell's</u> play and <u>Zozimus</u>.[2] This was an afterthought & Peakes arrangements may rule it out

Yrs ev
WB Yeats

[TLS]   [Riversdale, Willbrook, Rathfarnham, Dublin]
Dec. 28th [1934]

My dear Willy

---

[4] They were both keen breeders of canaries.

[1] After the *Macbeth* disaster, WBY had been impressed by Peake's production and Bould's designs for *The School for Wives* (12 Nov. 1934), but the audiences remained thin. *At Mrs Beam's* by C. K. Munro (d. 1973), pseudonym of Charles Walden Kirkpatrick MacMullan, was produced at the Abbey Theatre on 26 Dec. 1934, the last play produced for the Abbey by Peake.

[2] Peadar O'Donnell (1893–1986), native Irish speaker, socialist, and Republican who was one of the anti-Treaty IRA men who took over the Four Courts building in 1922 and was imprisoned; formerly an organizer in the Irish Transport and General Workers Union, he was elected as a Sinn Féin candidate in 1923 while still in prison; disillusioned by the IRA programme under de Valera, he founded the Republican Congress in 1934, then joined the Spanish Republican militia in 1936 and on his return devoted himself to writing novels and plays and as editor of literary journal *The Bell* (1946–54). His first novel *Storm* was published in 1925; the Abbey Theatre produced his play *Wrack* in November 1932, directed by LR; *Zozimus*, the proposed second play by O'Donnell, has never surfaced.

I enclose a letter from Sturm which arrived on Christmas day (about 11 pm...the first post...) Have you taken the MSS to Macmillan?

I send also a Christmas card of Peake's which does seem to me bloody bumptiousness!!

The houses for At Mrs Beam's were, Wednesday (St Stephen's Day) £57.5.6. Thursday, £29.11.0. I gather that Bould leaves Dublin any moment; Peake at the end of the week. As LENNOX GOES TO USA on Thursday next this is probably a blessing as the company would undoubtedly burst unless he were here to comfort and cajole them. Lennox only just heard about USA.

I enclose two press cuttings.[1] I thought At Mrs Beam's firstly an intolerable play, secondly abominably cast. The 'Vamp' who is not married to the hero-villain was played by Irene Murphy whose only quality is a good pair of leggs which she showed by means of slit dresses! Sheelah should of course have been in the part. The hero-villain was played by an Englishman, I dont know where he was picked up but he had every defect that English male actors can have. The chief part, that of Miss Chew (or Shoe) was played by Madeleine Ross, one of the old Drama League actresses who play also in Mrs Carey's plays.[2] She was not at all bad but her voice drives me mad, it has a nasal quality which, in a very long part, becomes a nightmare. The boarding house scenes, created for the play, were not any better than any of the Abbey existing scenes for boarding houses....In fact, as you can see, I was disgusted to the roots of my soul both by the play, by the acting (Chris Hayden the only relief) and the scene.

Cuala has 138 copies of 'Clock Tower' left.

I HAVE FOUND THE MISSING VOLUME OF MORRIS.[3]

Yours
George.

[1] Enclosure missing; the reviewer for the *Irish Times*, 28 Dec. 1934, thought the production moved 'a little too slowly to be quite effective' and that Madeleine Ross lacked liveliness.

[2] While the first company was on tour in America, it was necessary to draft performers from the large pool of actors in Dublin. J. Geoffrey Davids, the English actor whose appointment had raised objections in the company, seems to have performed in only two Abbey productions. Irene Murphy, whom GY thought less suited to the role than Shelah Richards, who performed with the Gate Theatre and at the Abbey 1921–4, returning for the 1934 season. Madeleine Ross (d. 1971), secretary of the Irishwomen's Writers' Society, not only acted in numerous Dublin companies but was producer of the New Players. May, Mrs W. D. Carey (1880–1966), a founder member of the Gate Theatre, who had trained with William Poel's Shakespearian company before moving to Ireland, also had her own company, which frequently rented the Abbey Theatre, was a director of the Dublin Theatre Guild, and one of the founders of the Irish Film Society.

[3] As a Christmas gift to each other in 1919, WBY and GY bought the 24-volume set of *The Complete Works of William Morris* (1910–15).

1935

[TLS]   [Riversdale, Willbrook, Rathfarnham, Dublin.]
                                                        Jan 1. 1935

My dear Willy
    Edwards[1] came out here yesterday, Dec. 31st at 4 pm and stayed until
about 10.35pm. This morning he came just in time for our eleven o'clock
cup of tea and left at 10.40 pm. And lordy I do know so much more than
I ever knew about your life! In the last 48 hours I have done more research
for 'data' than I ever did since I took on with you. I think I did it with
great discretion. I nearly fell into temptation and opened the packet of
your private memoirs that I might find out the date when you first went to
Woburn Buildings, but refrained. I looked for this date in the three packets of your letters to Lady G. for 1897–8; otherwise I did not open those
packets. I allowed him to make copies of three letters of James Joyce's
but he understands he must ask your permission to use any extract from
these. As a matter of fact I need not have said anything about it to him
because I dont think he has in any sense the journalist's mind. I showed
him Masefield's Ship, the book 'The Wanderer',[2] the Berkeley that Lennox
gave you,[3] I corrected your statement to him that Sato had given you the
sword in San Francisco (it was in Portland, Oregon) I told him about Pollock's book and how you had made him eliminate all references to M.G.[4]
He went through all the Scott designs for Ballylee, discoursed on which
of three Gort Forges had made the iron-work; the timber we used for our
furniture in the Tower;[5].... This a very small part of the notes and searches
the poor lamb made.

[1] Oliver H. Edwards (b. 1900), who had taught at Hull University 1928–34, had recently
signed a contract with Wishart & Co. to write WBY's biography after Austin Clarke withdrew from the project; the book was never completed, but Edwards and GY became firm
friends.
    [2] In December 1930 Masefield presented WBY with a model brig named *The George and
William*, which he had made himself as a tribute; he also inscribed no. 11 of a limited edition
of *The Wanderer of Liverpool* (London, 1930), embellished with original drawings and additional
poems, 'For W. B. Yeats, from John Masefield. November 5th, 1930, Being the 30th anniversary of their meeting'. GY left the book in her will to ABY.
    [3] The Yeats Library has two copies of *Berkeley's Commonplace Book*, ed. G. A. Johnston
(London, 1930), and *The Works of George Berkeley*, 2 vols. (Dublin, 1784).
    [4] *W. B. Yeats* by poet, playwright, and short story writer John Hackett Pollock (1867–1964)
('An Philibin') was to be published in 1935 by Talbot Press in Dublin.
    [5] See letters of 1918–19 and *BG*, 169–70 for details of the restoration of Ballylee.

He left me a magazine with a poem of his own which is psychically extraordinarily interesting.[6] I made some notes after he left this evening which, with poem, I keep till you return.

Can you remember the date you got the book test with Mrs Cooper, the Euripides? I have not been able to find them. (You had told him about it.) The Dante-Blake 48–84[7] he was able to verify here.

This is all long-winded and dull to you, but it hasnt been dull to me because all these investigations have quickened my memory of the strange, chaotic, varied and completely unified personality that you are.

Yours
George.

[TLS Dict[1]]   Savile Club, | London.
3rd Jan., 1935.

My dear Dobbs
I thank you for your toil over my biography, you would not have found anything of value in those secret reminiscences. I abandoned them because I found it impossible to write for posterity. One has to have some living man in one's eye. They are a mere first draft plus a few indiscretions of my pub-lished book. You might get both Edmonds (if that is his name) and Keller to write to me to the Savile; I go there every day at one o'clock for letters and lunch.[2] I am sorry to be delayed in London for I am getting homesick, but even if you had not made an appointment with me for the biographer, I should almost certainly have had to stay.

Last Wednesday we had the first meeting of our dramatic committee. Edmund Dulac, Rupert Doone (ballet master and producer), T. S. Elliot, myself, Margot Collis's secretary. Ashton was absent dancing somewhere. Next morning I 'phoned to Dulac: 'I won't have Rupert Doone spread-ing mustard and molasses over my brown bread, I shall produce all my own plays'. Result, a visit from Dulac to Ashley Dukes, who owns the theatre we are to play in and who supplies the finances, and to Ashton. General agreement that I don't know enough about London actors to cast my plays—somebody else has to be found. We are now in pursuit of that

---

[6] I have been unable to trace this poem.

[7] During the 1920s the medium Mrs Blanche Cooper had provided WBY with a number of book tests (see 13 Feb. 1923); the Blake book test occurred during a session in London in October 1926.

[1] Dictated to a typist with salutation, signature, and a few minor emendations in WBY's hand.

[2] Once again he had taken furnished rooms at 44 Seymour Street, Marble Arch.

somebody else, and there is to be a committee meeting on Tuesday. It has been decided that the actual performance of the plays will be from April 29th to May 19th, or longer if we have a success, and the rehearsals will take about a month.

The Abbey wants me back to meet Starkey and Hayes over a proposal of Peak's to run a touring company of Abbey work.[3] I would be very glad if you would get the Abbey secretary on the 'phone and explain that I will get back either at the end of next week, or as early as possible in the week following.

I am very well, but tired of being rather idle. Five or six days ago I finished the last poem I had in my head. All will be well if another comes, meanwhile I am trying to dictate for an hour a day the continuance of the Memoirs and have had proper copies made of 'A Full Moon in March'.

Yrs ev
WB Yeats

[TLS]   [Riversdale, Willbrook, Rathfarnham, Dublin.]

January 5 1934 [1935]

My dear Willy

Many thanks for your long letter; I am glad to see you have found yourself a typist!

Edwards (not Edmonds as you write) lunches with you at the Savile Club on Friday at 1.30. I told him I would let you know as he is moving about for the next few days. So expect him to turn up!

I dont think I have given him anything you would not want published. This is a list of actual material I supplied (apart from conversational dates and so on of which he took notes.

3 letters of James Joyce.

2 letters from you to your father. a. in which you describe at some length your reading The Player Queen to Mrs Campbell and your meeting with Lord Cromer and Asquith at Gosse's dinner party. b. a dullish letter which has a reference to Mrs Asquith and her house.[1] I told him I wasnt sure if you would want that reference mentioned!

---

[3] This plan did not materialize.

[1] WBY to JBY, 17 July 1911, 'I have just come from lunching with Mrs. Asquith. Her house in Downing Street is an interesting old house, full of uninteresting copies of famous pictures. I was next Mrs. Asquith who asked me a lot of questions about Lady Gregory....I didn't think Mrs. Asquith herself had much capacity, but she was interested in everything.'

a copy of your quatrain you call a recent incident: Rousseau that threw babies in etc. He had your rubber goods one which you repeated at the dinner Myles Dillon gave to you, Gogarty and Edwards.[2]

I also gave him the MSS of Byzantium with all its corrections to get photographed. This being as an example of your method of work. He returned the MSS.

Anne has roped Michael into theatre work.[3] He suggested she should stage a scene from the Merchant of Venice and has in consequence found himself set down to learn five parts and use a different voice for each! He also re-set all her electric lights with proper bulb holders so that the bulbs can be changed for coloured light if necessary.[4] The present programme is Merchant of Venice and Dark Lady of the Sonnets....We have arranged the old tent poles so that it is possible in two minutes to put them together and have the whole end of the nursery curtained off with an opening for the theatre itself. I dyed old sheets black for curtains. Olive Craig introduced Anne to Betty Fitzgibbon, Judge Fitzgibbon's daughter[5] who is also a theatre devotee. She is to come out on Tuesday, and I suppose Anne will have her learning parts...

I enclose an envelope with Press Cuttings which McCartan sends. No letter was enclosed.

Love G.

[ALS]   SAVILE CLUB, | 69, BROOK STREET. W.1.
Sunday [6 Jan. 1935]

My dear Dobbs

I shall return on Thursday or Friday (10 or 11th). My last letter was written in a misunderstanding. I thought I was to see biographer here on Friday.

---

[2] WBY sent the quatrain to AG on 24 Apr. 1931, the 'recent incident' 'a protestant mother, whos[e] yelling children were taken from her in open court to be taken to catholic institutions': 'When Rousseau dropped his babies in | The foundling-basket it was sin; | But who dare call it that, if Rome | Prefer the basket to the home.' Myles Patrick Dillon (1900–72), son of the MP John Dillon, the last leader of the Irish Parliamentary Party, was a philologist and Gaelic scholar, at this time a reader in Sanskrit at TCD, later director of the Celtic School in the Dublin Institute of Advanced Studies.

[3] ABY's interest in theatre design began very early, judging from the following programme dated 21 Dec. 1934: 'The Pegasus Play House Will Present "Hamlet" & "The Needle" 6 o'clock The performance will take place at Riversdale, Willbrook, Rathfarnham, in the "Theatre Room"'. This performance was followed by 'Act I Scene III from "The Merchant of Venice"' with the following cast: 'Shylock, a rich Jew M. B. Yeats, Bassanio, friend to Antonio, B. FitzGibbon, Antonio, a merchant of Venice A. B. Yeats.'

[4] Since the house was lit by gas, ABY's lighting system must have been run by battery.

[5] Gerald Fitzgibbon (1866–1942), judge of the Supreme Court (1924–38); by May 1935 Betty Fitzgibbon had gone to school in Switzerland.

I find now you said Wednesday. I am homesick, idle & tired, longing for garden, canaries, country roads, Higgins's stories[1] etc. etc. Norman Haire has done me much good, I expect increased working powers etc. I am happy

I am delighted the lost Morris has been [found] I feel it is a good omen. Its loss worried me.

Yrs ev
WB Yeats

[TLS Dict] Savile Club, | 69, Brook Street, | London, W.
7th January, 1935.

My dear Dobbs

I interrupt the dictation of my Memoirs to dictate this. Yesterday I found your letter of January 2nd, and found that it was indeed Friday the 11th upon which I am to see my biographer. I submit, though I haven't heard a word from him. Expect me back on Saturday.

To-morrow evening we have a committee meeting at Dulac's which should, I think, complete the preliminary arrangements for the plays. On Wednesday I give a dinner party at the 'Ivy', necessary return to people who have given me dinner.[1] (Alas! I had expected to get back to Dublin on the Thursday, or if worst, on the Friday.)

I have exhausted London for the moment and am homesick for hearth and home.

Yrs ev
WB Yeats

[ALS[1]] 45 Seymour St | Marble Arch
[c.30 Mar. 1935]

My dear Dobbs

I came here on Tuesday. I am just oppossite my old lodging—Miss O Dea who was full up sent me here. My room here has no gass fire—result I woke up on Wednesday with sore throat & exaustion. Got taxies saw Dulac &

---

[1] Frederick Robert Higgins (1896–1941), poet and companion to WBY, who relished the Rabelaisian stories Higgins obligingly provided; the editor of a number of trade and union journals, in April 1935 he was appointed to the Abbey Board of Directors.

[1] His guests included a new friend, Ethel Edith Mannin (1900–84), left-wing journalist and prolific novelist, to whom he introduced the Dulacs; by now, encouraged by Norman Haire as part of his 'cure', they were lovers.

[1] On Savile Club stationery, address crossed out.

Ashley Dukes & did much essentale busines. Thursday could only crawl about & had a struggle to keep Dulac from packing me off to a Nursing Home. But admitted a doctor. Doctor says I shall be all right in a few days Have now no temerature. I will return to Dublin before April 8 & then come back here for May, when rehersals begin. Peak seems likely to be our producer

My visit here was necessary—there were things I only could decide.

Forgive me for not writing. This is the first day on which it would not have been a misery to write

Yrs affectionly
WB Yeats

[ALS]   SAVILE CLUB, | 69, BROOK STREET. W.1.
Sunday [31 Mar. 1935]

My dear Dobbs

I am just recovering from one of my worst colds. I spent Friday in bed & Saturday on my bed. Hence I have not written. I am still dazed & week

Do you remember my conversation with Beroda[1] (I hope I spell it right). I spoke against conducting all higher Indian education through English. The old Prince, turned to the Swami & said 'Do you agree' The Sami said 'yes'. Well the old Prince went back to India & ordered all the education in his kingdom to be conducted in the vernacular & made a decree that Hindi was the language of his Court. He had probably been thinking of the thing for years so you must not say that either I or the Swami did it. He is like an old country gentleman, very modest & simple just the type of man who does nothing on impulse.

I will write later when my head clears

Yrs ev
WB Yeats

[ALS[1]]   45 Seymour St | Marble Arch
Sunday Evening [31 Mar. 1935]

My dear Dobbs

In writing this morning I forgot to ask to send two things on that I forgot

---

[1] Sayajirao Gaekwad III (Shrimant Gopalrao Gaekwad) (1863–1939), the Maharaja of Baroda (1875–1939), was the first Indian ruler to introduce compulsory free education; a zealous reformer, patron of the arts, he used to visit England every year to seek out promising young people who could further his modernization of the state, and made a lengthy stay in England from the autumn of 1934 through 1935.

[1] On Savile Club stationery, address struck out.

(1) The razor strop from my bed room door.
(2) My black dress-waistcoat

Am feeling better than for days

Yrs ev
WB Yeats

[ALS¹]   45 Seymour St | Marble Arch | London
Thursday [4 Apr. 1935]

My dear Dobbs

I am well now but the doctor hates my going out; however I have got his leave to dine with Dulac to night. These last two days of vigour have been packed with work, people coming & going about the theatre project & sometimes the Swami, rather irrelevant as wisdom must be. The doctor says I will not be fit to travel back until early next week. I will go then if I can. Peak who will probably produce for us has just gone, taking T. S. Elliots play, no play but magnificent speach.² There are difficulties but I hope all will be right before I return to Dublin

Yrs ev
WB Yeats

Parcels came today

[ALS¹]   45 Seymour Street | Marble Arch
Monday [8 Apr. 1935]

My dear Dobbs: I think you are right. Certainly to day I feel very unfit for the journey. The worst of my cold has gone but left a cough & some sleaplessness. Why dont you come over & have a week or fortnight of London & put me into better spirits. Mrs Foden is going to Russia (where her brother is being sent by the Foreign Office) & she has lent me her flat from April 20 to May 12. I could not put you up but we could ask friends there—there is a great handsome room. There is something I want which you must bring or send regestered & insured. I forgot that black leather Italian note-book you gave me. It contains the poems for my new book. Then it is somewhere

---

¹ On Savile Club stationery, address struck out.
² *Murder in the Cathedral*; see note to 10 Apr. 1935.

¹ On Savile Club stationery, address struck out.

in my room that unbound copy <u>The Clock Tower</u> I got from Watt but did not use. I want that. Thirdly there is an evelope in my cup-board with typed script of the Swami's.

I am very tired. I wired Audin to come up from Birmingham to settle a point about his play. There has been a long lunch at the Ivy and after that old Oliver Onions[2] has been to call. Then I had a bad night.

I am working at the essay for the <u>Criterion</u> & am about one third through.[3] I am also reading steadily for the Cambridge Book of Modern Verse[4]

Yrs ev
WB Yeats

I pay £2 a week here which includes breakfast. I could get you a room.

[ALCS[1]]   [10 Apr. 1935]

First card
I think you had better send me the proofs of diagrams with the proof of the letter press. You are certainly all right about C.M. Maske etc but it would be easy to be mistaken about the correct place in text.[2] I brought frontispiece (John Etching) to Macmillan.[3]

The theatre project has I think broken down. Ashley Duke has insisted on the Elliot play & we do not feal that we could make a success with[out] cuts & that in any case for Elliots sake Canterbury should come first[4]. Ashley Duke has rejected all counter proposals; but talks of himself

(WBY)

---

[2] Identity uncertain. Although younger than WBY, possibly the novelist and short story writer George Oliver Onions, later George Oliver (1873–1961), whose ghost story 'The Beckoning Fair One' in his collection *Widdershins* (1911) is considered by many the best horror fiction ever written.

[3] 'Mandookya Upanishad with an Introduction by William Butler Yeats' appeared in *The Criterion*, July 1935.

[4] That is, the *Oxford Book of Modern Verse*.

[1] Both cards originally addressed to 'Mrs Yeats Fitzwilliam Square', then readdressed to Riversdale, are apparently cards pre-addressed by GY for future use; both are date stamped Paddington W2 10 Apr. 1935.

[2] The diagrams for the new edition of *A Vision* included one—'the historical cones'—from the first edition.

[3] WBY had suggested using the etching by Augustus John done of him in 1907 as a frontispiece to the second edition of *A Vision*.

[4] The first performance of *Murder in the Cathedral* was in the Chapter House of Canterbury Cathedral on 15 June 1935, a production encouraged by George Bell, the Bishop of Chichester, who had been responsible for the collaboration between Eliot and E. Martin Browne on the historical pageant *The Rock* in 1934. It was agreed that the production would then move to London.

Second card

establishing a poets theatre. I shall stay on for a bit partly because I do not want to break off until I have finished the <u>Criterion</u> essay which grows important & because I would like to start (here where I am near to book sellers) the Anthology. Last night Sir John Squire who has made several most successful anthologies from my period[5] offered to read my proofs.

I hope I shall hear that you are coming over

W B Y

[ALS]   SAVILE CLUB, | 69, BROOK STREET. W. 1.
                                            Monday [15 Apr. 1935]

My dear Dobbs

Early last week theatre project went Smash—T. S. Elliots new play cannot be done before Canterbury performance, & Ashley Dukes wanted it first. General despair! On Thursday I got Dukes to dine at Savile and started project again. He was struck by a letter from Peake about Elliot's play & has asked him to come to London at his expense. If their talk is satisfactory, simultanious London & Canterbury performances of Elliot. Peake general producer & Ashley Dukes in general charge. I much prefer this arrangement. Ashley Dukes at Peakes suggestion is to give two weeks of my plays to celebrate my 70th birthday—then comes Elliot. Then after an interval will come other poets plays mainly new school Auden etc. It may mean much of my work in London. Elliots play is about the murder of Becket, half play half religeous service as spoken poetry exceedingly impressive. I had proposed cutting it but Peake says no & is perhaps right. I only understand the play on a Greek or Ibsen model, a single action. It will require magnificent speaking, its oretory is swift & powerful.

This is a good day I have climbed the stairs without getting out of breath. All last week I was crawling about & panting—dilated heart from broncial guitar [catarrh] (how does one spell it? I have no dictionary at Seymour St) the doctor says. I have however managed to finish my essay for 'The Criterion' & am just off to dictate it to Miss Jacobs.

I find I have 2 pants and 2 vests. Is that right, or have two vests been stollen (I want those 2 vests for night wear). The house-maid has warned me to lock my door when I go out.

---

[5] See note to 14 June 1933; among Squire's anthologies, some edited with the pseudonym 'Solomon Eagle', are *Selections from Modern Poets* (1921, 1924), *The Comic Muse: An Anthology of Humorous Verse* (1925), *Apes and Parrots: An Anthology of Parodies* (1928), *The Augustan Book of Modern Poetry* (1925), and *Younger Poets of To-day* (1932).

On Friday I shall move to Mrs Foodens flat—a big handsome room where I can see my friends.

> Yours affecly
> WB Yeats

I am reasonably happy & as yet without my wild desire to return to Dublin at all costs—probably the prosect of that big room next the Park. I am well enough to look up my friends

[AL¹]   19 Lancaster Gate Terrace | W. 2
                                         Monday [22 Apr. 1935]

Dear Dobbs

I am in this very pleasant flat, a great room with Chineas tapestries, a golden Bandolit,² a bad painting of the Scots School—mountain & mist. Very large but not unpleasant. My bed & breakfast are paid for & I can get other meals for about eighteen pense. I have been really very ill. I did not tell you until it was over but even last week there were days worse than any I have had in Dublin except the very very worst there. The doctor who still comes to give me injections & charges 10/6 a visit says I suffered from nervous exaustion after broncial trouble. My evenings still tend to get a little bad but with the doctors approval I make an evening meal of bread, olives & burgundy & if there is somebody to talk to (& there always is at the Savile) I forget my troubles. I am so much better to day that I am hoping to break the habit of bad evenings (I am dining with Dulac). <u>King of Great Clock Tower</u> etc has come, Vests will no dout come to morrow (I have 3 pants & 2 vests)

I seem to have pulled the Mercury Theatre project out of the mire but will not feel it is safe for a day or two (I dread Ashley Dukes changability). It is post poned to June 11. I may return to Dublin next week or wait a little longer.³ I need some days of my restored health to finish off my business (Huntingdon etc) & with the exception of Dulac I have not seen any friends. Even if I could have left the Mercury project to chaos & was not

---

¹ Unsigned on Savile Club notepaper, address struck out.

² Possibly an ornamental bandolier, a pocketed belt such as the one used for holding ammunition, usually worn slung over the chest.

³ WBY's health worsened, and Dulac wired to GY who went to London immediately, staying until WBY was well enough to travel on 8 June 1935. On 27 June the Dublin branch of PEN marked his 70th birthday with a banquet at the Hibernian Hotel.

well enough to return until this week. To day life seems good & I am full of energy & this great room pleasant

[ALS]   PENNS IN THE ROCKS, | WITHYHAM, | SUSSEX.
                                Monday August 19 [1935]

My dear Dobbs: Anne & I stay here until Friday.[1] Anne is very happy— there are two girls of her own age. Last night however she played crocket with Lady Dorothy myself & two grown up guests. In the first game she was worst. Then Lady Dorothy took her as partner (she had seen that Anne was nervous) & began to encourage her & praise her. Anne soon had that joyous animated look she gets & beat everybody including Lady Dorothy. Lady Dorothy has corrected my selection from Kipling, showing me certain delightful things.[2] In return I have made a selection from her poems which I want her to offer to Faber & Faber. I finished it yesterday. I cut long passages out of certain poems & got her to re-write others. Such a volume, about 80 pages, should establish her fame.[3] I am work- ing at Sacheverel Sitwell as well as I can in this delightful place, where there is fine talk & beautiful gardens I am better than I have been for a long time

Yours affecly
WB Yeats

What are your plans. When does Michael reach Stratford? I shall I suppose send Anne there on Friday.[4]

---

[1] Delighted by her poetry, which he was reading for inclusion in *The Oxford Book of Modern Verse*, WBY was introduced to Dorothy, Lady Gerald Wellesley, née Ashton (1889–1956), poet, biographer, and essayist, who had purchased Penns in the Rocks after separating from her husband; GY, who declined the invitation, arranged that Ottoline Morrell accompany WBY and ABY on this first trip to Penns.

[2] Thirty years before WBY had dismissed poet and novelist Rudyard Kipling (1865–1936), whom he had never met, as 'a kind of imperialist journalist in prose and verse' (*CL III*, 467); the two poems by Kipling, chosen by DW, were the only ones in the anthology not personally selected by WBY.

[3] *Selections from the Poems of Dorothy Wellesley* with an introduction by W. B. Yeats and a draw- ing by Sir William Rothenstein was published by Macmillan in 1936. The Hogarth Press, for which DW was a reader, published three works in their Hogarth Living Poets Series (1928, 1930, and 1932), but the volume that had first captured WBY's attention was *Poems of Ten Years, 1924–1934* published by Macmillan in 1934; they would later collaborate on creating poems and on editing the *Broadsides* (see below) and in 1940 DW published *Letters on Poetry from W. B. Yeats to Dorothy Wellesley* (Oxford University Press).

[4] While ABY went with her father to visit DW, GY took MBY away to celebrate his birth- day, then sent him to Stratford to meet up with ABY.

[APS¹] [London W. 1 29 Aug. 1935]

Returning to-morrow Friday night by Liverpool. Have engaged cabin etc. Have read 45 books in British Museum. Got about a dozen or so extra poets. Will wire to-morrow when I am starting (I might be delayed). Have seen Haire, examined heart gives good report.

WBY.

[ALS] SAVILE CLUB, | 69, BROOK STREET. W. 1.
Saturday [26 Oct. 1935]

My dear Dobbs: I am waiting for an interviewer from the Era. I had four interviewers yesday beside an unknown woman who brought a tabl cloth for me to sign.¹ I have seen nobody but have telephoned to all the world. After the play to-morrow night I motor to Penns in the Rocks with Lady Dorothy & Helen Matheson.² I come up Wednesday & probably return there that night for a couple more days.

I am well & not tired. Sorry to bother you about those <u>Broadsides</u>³

Yrs ev
WB Yeats

¹ Picture postcard of William Blake's *The First Book of Urizen* (1794), pl. 2, addressed to 'Mrs Yeats | Riversdale, | Rathfarnham | Dublin'.

¹ 'Three Plays by Yeats', an unsigned squib in *The Sunday Times*, 27 Oct. 1935, reported that 'W. B. Yeats will be at the Little Theatre to-night. He came over from Dublin on Friday for the special performance of three of his short plays, "A Pot of Broth," "The Hour Glass," and "The Player Queen," which the ever-enterprising Nancy Price is presenting. The last has not been seen before in London. Soon after he arrived Mr. Yeats talked to me for half an hour about the Abbey Theatre and the prospect of a revival of interest in the poetic drama. He was amusing about Dublin audiences. "I never expect them to understand me as a poet, but they admire me as a fighter." There will be matinees of the three plays on Monday, Tuesday and Thursday, in addition to to-night's performance' (see letter of 31 Oct. 1935).

² Wellesley's lover Hilda Matheson (1888–1940) had worked as an intelligence officer for MI5 during the First World War (returning in 1939), and then as political secretary to Nancy Astor, the first woman Member of Parliament, before being approached by the newly established BBC to head the Talks Department (1927–31). Responsible for establishing the first News Section, she commissioned many high-profile speakers and also trained readers to write and speak in an informal, conversational style. In 1928 she initiated the programme featuring women in politics, 'The Week in Parliament'; she resigned in 1931 because of her refusal to restrict productions to less controversial subjects, and concentrated on print journalism and publishing until the outbreak of the Second World War when she was appointed director of the Joint Broadcasting Committee. Her influential book *Broadcasting* was published in 1933, and she was primarily responsible for the *African Survey* (1938), a study on British colonial policy for which she was awarded the OBE (Fred Hunter, 'Hilda Matheson and the BBC, 1926–1940', in Sybil Oldfield (ed.), *This Working Day World: Women's Lives and Cultures in Britain* (London, 1994), 169–74).

³ In December 1935 Cuala issued 100 bound volumes of *Broadsides: A Collection of Old and New Songs 1935*, with an introduction signed by the two editors; the series of twelve *Broadsides*, edited by Higgins and WBY, had been issued monthly during 1935.

[TLS]   [Riversdale, | Willbrook, | Rathfarnham, | Dublin.]
                                              Monday Oct 28 [1935]

My dear Willy

I got your wire about the Broadsides after I had posted you a complete set. The Broadsides you took with you together with the proof of the Introduction were in a large manila envelope, and as they were not left in your bedroom I conclude they are in your luggage!! Have you looked in the black leather letter case??

I forward a letter from Edith Sitwell.[1] Housman writes 'If you condescend to edit the collection, I suppose I must not be above contributing to it, and I assent to your taking from LAST POEMS the five pieces you specify. I exact no tribute from anthologists, so there are no "usual terms".' *Do please* write to thank him A. E. Housman Trinity College Cambridge.[2]

Ervine has sent a play 'Boyd's Shop';[3] am I to send it to the Abbey, or keep it until your return? I have acknowledged its arrival.

                                                      Yours
                                                      George

[ALS]   PENNS IN THE ROCKS, | WITHYHAM, | SUSSEX.
                                                      Oct 31 [1935]

My dear Dobbs

The play was successful, when I went back to my seat after the first interval I was applauded & again after the second.[1] Neither I nor nor my friends were pleased, however, The Player Queen (Nancy Price's daughter) was beutiful, never less than a picture postcard of the most popular sort but not a trace of talent.[2] Margot was accomplished, distinguished flawless, & will

---

[1] Enclosure is missing.

[2] Alfred Edward Housman (1859–1936), poet and classical scholar who was Professor of Latin at Cambridge; WBY included the five poems in the Oxford anthology, but none from Housman's previous volume, the popular *A Shropshire Lad* (1896).

[3] *Boyd's Shop* by St John Ervine was produced at the Abbey Theatre 24 Feb. 1936.

[1] *The Player Queen* was produced at the Little Theatre, London, followed by *The Hour Glass: A Morality Play* with Abbey actor Fred O'Donovan as the Wise Man; see next note.

[2] Lillian Nancy Bache Price (1880–1970), an established stage and film actress, playwright, producer, and essayist, in 1932 founded the People's National Theatre at the Little Theatre, John Adam Street, and produced over 50 plays before the theatre was badly damaged in 1940; when the Mercury project dissolved, Price decided to present a 'Yeats Festival' to celebrate his 70th birthday, offering matinées on 28, 29, and 31 October while the evenings were devoted to a lengthy run of *Lady Precious Stream*. Joan Maude (1908–98), elder daughter of Price and her husband, actor Charles Maude (1882–1943), was already experienced on stage and film, most famously as Salome in her mother's production at the Savoy Theatre of Wilde's play on its first public performance in Britain in 1931.

be no more praised by the weekly reviews than by the daily.³ Lady Ottoline writes 'she has it' but what is the use it was 'the coming out' party of Nancy Price's daughter & all the press has, or will have played up.⁴ Yet all was pleasant enough, Septimus⁵ good and the audience enthusiastic.

Now an anoyance. Carnegie Dickson insisted on making a fresh blood test, first injecting arsenic, if the result is still negative he wants to give me a stronger injection on Wednesday next & after that I must not travel for two days. If there is a positive result he says I should have injection & other treatment for 3 months. I should hate to keep the Swami, or Mrs Foden in London—I shall have to find out if there is any warm cheap place where I could get injections⁶

I have not found the broadsides—they were certainly not in my luggage. Please tell Lolly that Turner will write about them in the 'New Statesman'. He took away the typed poems & will, I think, do what we want.⁷ I think he will compose one or two tunes himself

Watt writes urgently about seeing me & offers call at the club (promotion for me)

Yrs ev
WB Yeats

[ALS]   SAVILE CLUB, | 69, BROOK STREET. W. 1.
Tuesday [5 Nov. 1935]

My dear Dobbs

In a few minuits I set out for <u>Mercury Theatre</u> to see <u>Murder in the Cathedral</u> I have a very active day, if I told you all I have done you would

<hr>

³ WBY had wanted Margot Ruddock to play Decima, the Player Queen, but she was given the part for the final performance only, playing the real queen on the two previous days (see *Ah, Sweet Dancer: W. B. Yeats, Margot Ruddock: A Correspondence*, ed. Roger McHugh (London, 1970), 56–7). WBY had advised Price on 2 Oct. 1935, 'If Margot Collis proves unsuitable I suggest Gwen Davies. What I dont want is the objective minded comedian. Their tragedy never rises above pathos, and is sometimes disagreeably sentimental. Through all the play Decima in the midst of her farce is keeping down with all the force of her will the hysteria of her tragedy' (Princeton). Gwen Ffrangcon-Davies (1891–1992) was at this time best known as a Shakespearian actor.

⁴ 'H.G.' in a lengthy article in *The Observer* (27 Oct. 1935), and an unsigned article in *The Times* (28 Oct. 1935), both emphasized WBY's 70th birthday as the occasion for the special performances, the latter review extravagantly praising Price's daughter Joan Maude in the title role.

⁵ Septimus, the drunken poet, was performed by the talented actor-manager Robert Newton (1905–56) who later became well known for his character roles in film.

⁶ To avoid the winter in Ireland, plans had been made for WBY to travel somewhere with the Swami to work on an English version of the *Upanishads*; Mrs Foden was to accompany them and then go on with Shree Purohit to India.

⁷ W. J. Turner published his article 'Broadside Songs' in the *New Statesman*, 7 Dec. 1935, 848–50; for the second series of *Broadsides*, edited by WBY and DW, he sent three of his own poems which he set to music.

dissaprove, but then I get a strong injection of arsenic to-morrow & must rest for two days. After that I return to Dublin. I was at Lady Dorothys from Wednesday to Sunday evening, last night I saw a strange exciting play by Turner called <u>The Man Who Ate the Popomax</u>¹ the same matter as in his poems but much wit & comic invention. I have just come from Lady Ottoline, she talks of 'that vulgar woman who played the Player Queen' that is an overstatement but she was common place & all the press has praised her. I have just finished a horrid Dorothy Sayers book which I will not bring home with me. With the ingenuity of a monkey she brings her own hero to the gallows.² So between that & the press praise of <u>The Player Queen</u> Production I have a sense of the pervesity of things

Yrs ev

WB Yeats

I send a letter I wrote you in August.³

[ALS]   SAVILE CLUB, | 69, BROOK STREET. W. 1.
Wednesday [6 Nov. 1935]

My dear Dobbs

Carnegie Dickson did not make his new blood test after all, he gave me the injection Shaw would have given had I been in Dublin.¹ Meanwhile thinking I was to have the strong injection & was bound to rest 2 days I have made one or two appointments for Thursday. I shall return Friday night (or if I wire Friday morning)

Saw <u>Murder in the Cathedral</u> last night. It is to my great surprise a powerful religeous play. It is expected to run until next February. It would succeed at the Abbey. It needs however a chorus of women of five or six they have eight at <u>the Mercury</u>. They [do] not sing but frequently speak in unison. Miss Fogerty admired Florence Farr & no doubt lerned this from her.² The whole cast was about 15.

Yrs ev

WB Yeats

¹ An expressionist drama, *The Man Who Ate the Popomack* by W. J. Turner, opened at the Grafton Theatre, 133 Tottenham Court Road, on 4 Nov. 1935.
² Possibly *The Nine Tailors* (1934) by Dorothy Leigh Sayers (1893–1957), translator, poet, playwright, essayist, and novelist best known for her popular series of detective fiction.
³ Enclosure missing, but perhaps the letter written on 19 Aug. 1935 from Penns in the Rocks.

¹ Probably Dr Richard William 'Dick' Shaw (d. 1971), an anaesthetist to the Rotunda Hospital and for the Children's Hospital, who lived nearby at 51 Rathfarnham Road; see 6 Nov. 1938.
² The chorus for this first production of *Murder in the Cathedral* was trained by Elsie Fogerty (1865–1945), a distinguished voice teacher and founder in 1906 of the Central School of

[ALCS]   SAVILE CLUB, | 69, BROOK STREET. W. 1.
                                                      Nov 6 [1935]

My dear Dobbs: I forgot to say in the letter that I posted half an hour ago
that I am perfectly well, & have been all the time I have been here.

H Watt called on Monday & talked over anthology business—quite
satisfactory.

Turner has the Broadsides & writes on them I think next week. I think he
will do what we want in the next series.¹ He is 'making enquiries'—I think
that was the phrase.

                                                              Yrs
                                                        WB Yeats

[TLS]   RIVERSDALE, | WILLBROOK, |
                                        RATHFARNHAM, | DUBLIN.
                                                      Dec 4 [1935]

My poor William! I am afraid you had a fearful three or four days—the
papers were full of accounts of storms off the Cornish coast. It was bad
enough on Saturday in the Irish channel—one of the worst crossing I have
ever known, accompanied by sheet lightning all the way.¹

I enclose the press cuttings. MacCormack made a very fine performance,
also Dolan. But I DO not like the play.² Production good, scenes good; but
unadulterated religion and self-righteousness all through for nearly three
hours, with no joy in religion and the only sinner not enjoying his sin, is

---

Speech Training and Dramatic Art, who had established a poetry choir for which she adapted
and produced a number of Greek plays; the DDL hoped to stage the play but were forestalled
by the English Players, under the direction of Fogerty, who presented it at the Gate Theatre
25 May–2 June 1936. Florence Farr Emery (1860–1917), actor, playwright, producer, and outspoken feminist, was WBY's one-time lover, his colleague in the Golden Dawn where for a
while she was the Praemonstratrix of the Isis-Urania Temple, and for a number of years collaborator in his theatrical ventures and experiments to set his words to music for the psaltery.
In 1912 she sold all her possessions and moved to Ceylon to teach in a girls' college, and died
there in 1917 of cancer.

¹ WBY and DW were hoping to make Turner the English music advisor for the second
set of *Broadsides*.

¹ GY had accompanied WBY to Liverpool on 28 Nov. 1935, where he was to embark with
the Swami and Mrs Foden for Majorca.

² *A Saint in a Hurry* by the Spanish journalist and poet José Maria Penám (1897–1981), translated by Aodh de Blaćam, opened at the Abbey Theatre on 2 Dec. 1935, produced by LR with
scenery and dresses by Tanya Moiseiwitsch; the large cast included McCormick as Francis
Xavier and Michael J. Dolan (1884–1953), one of the teachers in the Abbey School of Acting
who had been with the company as actor and producer since 1912, as Ignatius de Loyola.

unbearable. There were about 100 priests ('rookies' as Higgins calls them) at the dress rehearsal....

I have the photograph of the Sickert portrait of George Moore and the permission of the Tate Gallery for reproduction subject to Sickert's permission. I have written to him today. Nothing from the Paget's yet.[3]

I forgot to pack you a medecine glass. You and Mrs Foden can get one in Palma—Dont forget to let me have an address, when you have one.

Yours ever
George.

[ALS]   HENDERSON LINE | S. S. [Pegu]
Wednesday [4 Dec. 1935]

My dear Dobbs

On Friday we reach Giberalter a day late. Instead of starting on Friday night we left Saturday morning at 11. At 10.30 Mrs Fooden had begun to work. She protested to the Purser against her cabin. She had not been able to sleap for the cold. He replied 'You would have been all right if [you] had left the Indian where we put him & not changed cabins'? The man was lost; for she knew there were empty cabins. She said 'I have been asked to look after Dr Yeats, who has heart-attacks & Shri Porhuit Swami is Dr Yeats' friend. Dr Yeats has decided that we are all to leave the ship at Giberalter as a protest against your treatment of his friend. So public a protest will not help the Henderson Line' (I had not said a word on the subject) Collapse of Purser. Swami & Mrs Fooden were given good cabins as nearly mid ship as possible & we were asked to dine at the captains table. Mrs Fooden refused this on some polite excuse but really because she wanted to prolong the war. Then, the doctor, young, enthusiastic, on his first voyage came to find all about my heart attacks & I found it hard to keep to the truth without giving Mrs Fooden away. Next morning Mrs Fooden complained to the Purser that the lounge & the cabins were cold no steam in the radiator pipes. Immediate inspection by men in uniform, then almost warm cabins Then, no doubt to the Purser relief, the weather got rough & Mrs Fooden took to her bed. We all did (including the doctor).

---

[3] For the edition of WBY's *Dramatis Personae* to be published by Macmillan in May 1936, they were trying to trace portraits of some of his subjects. Florence Farr Emery's sister Henrietta ('Dum Spiro Spero'), a practising medium, and her husband the artist, illustrator, and amateur actor Henry Marriott Paget (1856–1936) ('In Deo Sumus'), both also early members of the Golden Dawn, had been friends and neighbours of the Yeatses in Bedford Park, and WBY was seeking Paget's portrait of Farr; Florence Farr Emery is not included among the illustrations (see note to 18 Sept. 1937).

I doubt if any passanger remained up except an old retired ship's captain on a pleasure cruise. Sunday, Monday, Tuesday were the worst I have ever known on ship board. I have never seen a ship roll so—comparetive quiet, then a great lurch, then a banging & clanging caused by all the chamberpots on board breaking loose again. Once there came a great crash, then the sound of the stewards swearing in hindustani. On Monday they discovered Swami. He had signed the ships register S P Swami, thinking to keep his incognito as Swami is a surname in Madrass. Now however he is discovered and relays of hindoo stewards call upon him which must anoy him as he is very sick. Mrs Fooden was not completely subdued by the weather as was proved by our getting clean napkins at breakfast. She must be restrained, she has had enough victory My terrible personality has been exploited enough.

I wonder if you will be able to read this. The ship is still rolling though not so badly, & it spoils my usually clear handwriting. I have not been ill but stayed in bed until to day for it was the only place where I was certain not to break a limb. I have corrected a good deal of the essay[1]

> Yrs affecly
> WB Yeats

I will post this at Giberalter

Thursday
Mrs Fooden appeared in the dining room for the first time last night. In the middle of dinner she was suddenly all still alertness. She had seen her roses, the roses you gave her

> (P.T.O.)

adorning the captain's table. She said to the steward 'My roses are on that table bring them to me' Then I interfeared to protect the embarrassed steward I said 'It will do if you get them back before tomorrow'. However it was discovered this morning that they had fallen in pieces. This morning the Swami made his first appeance anywhere since the storm, very magnificent in his pink cloths & turban. Mrs Fooden, sent him below again to shave. Then she put Swami & myself in two chairs side by side in the sun, photographed us, found a baby on which to bestow her energies.

The sea is quiet though not in the words of the steward 'like the pond of the mill'

---

[1] WBY had taken a draft of his introduction to the Oxford Anthology to revise.

[APS[1]]   [en route to Gibraltar
                                                      *c.*4 Dec. 1935]

This is the steamer[2] I am on leaving Gibralter, where I arrive on Friday. This Wednesday & the ship is rolling & has been for days.

                                                      Your affection
                                                          father

[TLS & MS]   [Riversdale, Willbrook, Rathfarnham, Dublin.]
                                          Monday December 9th [1935]

My dear Willy

No word from you yet;* [MS Tuesday morning 10th—Your letter from Gibraltar just arrived—Thanks. Will write later. In haste for post] I had vague hopes you might be so extravagant as to wire when you arrived. I posted you a copy of the weekly Irish Times to Cooks, Palma, but its no use ordering the weekly London Times till I know your address.

I am dying to hear how you got on with the journey. I picture it all as being as wet, blowy and unpleasant as the day I saw you off at Liverpool. I'm sure Mrs Foden thought it most odd of me not to wait to see the boat steam out of the docks. I felt too like the dog who sees his masters going for a walk and leaving him at home.

I made the index of first lines yesterday; it took me 13¼ hours; I got obstinate and determined to finish it, and did! Pet is coming out on Thursday to check it with me.[1] Really the whole thing could go off any day now if that kitty-bitch Margaret Gough would reply...Keller is dealing with her, but I don't think she bothers much about his effusions. Chesterton is also proving obdurate...even his publisher is finding he does not reply to letters. Waley[2] gives delighted permission for The Temple and indicates that he asks no fee.

---

  [1] Addressed to 'Miss Anne Yeats | Riversdale | Willbrook | Rathfarnham | Co Dublin | Irish Free State'.

  [2] Photograph of 'Henderson Line to Egypt and Burma'.

  [1] GY had been left in charge of the business end of the Anthology; see 26 Oct. 1934 for Hermione Lytton 'Pet' Wilson, WBY's Dublin typist. Rumours spread that WBY had not made the selections himself; as late as 1968 GY was forced to protest, 'I had nothing whatsoever to do with the choice of poets or poems included in the "Oxford Book of Modern Verse"—My only connection was that I typed letters dictated to me by WBY, and collected dates of authors' birth' (GY to Michael Yeats, 15 Feb. 1968).

  [2] 'The Temple', a lengthy translation from the Chinese by Arthur Waley included footnotes but not his birth date; Chesterton, who died in 1936 before the anthology was published, is represented by two poems.

Higgins is fearful that ill-gotten wealth may bring back the exiled Austin Clarke to Ireland! He foresees plot after plot being hatched in the volcano O'Sullivan–Clarke.[3] He told me he had quantities of letters from Clarke written during the brief period when Clarke and Starkey were at war. Clarkes always referred to Starkey as 'Shame-us O'Solomon'.

The new Emmet play[4] was on at the Abbey tonight, but as Anne and I both have vile colds I did not go. Will send you the press cuttings.

Charles Madge[5] very pleased that you have added to his poems. He is only 23...he sent a few typed ones, two of which Eliot is printing in the next issue of the Criterion. I told him (Madge) that you were abroad but that I would send them on. If you like any of them they or it might perhaps be added. He is the youngest of our anthology.

I wrote to Waley to ask if he would prefer to be with the dated or the undated. I mentioned that the only un-dated were Michael Field and Edith Sitwell![6] I am curious to know what he will reply. His friends may find some amusement if he stays with the ladies

Love
George.

---

[3] Augustine Joseph 'Austin' Clarke (1896–1974) poet, verse dramatist, and novelist, was a charter member of the Irish Academy of Letters, but when his first novel *The Bright Temptation* (1932) was banned, he moved to London, where he had already been doing considerable work as a reviewer, during which time he contemplated writing a biography of WBY; in the *Dublin Magazine* James Starkey ('Seamus O'Sullivan') published Clarke's poetry and short verse dramas, but GY is doubtless referring to Clarke's critical essay 'Irish Poetry Today', the issue of January–March 1935, in which Clarke blamed WBY for leading Irish poets back to English forms. Clarke did eventually return to live permanently in Ireland, but not until 4 Feb. 1937, after which with Robert Farren he established the Dublin Verse-Speaking Society (1939) and in 1944 formed the Lyric Theatre Company, for which ABY designed. The 'ill-gotten wealth' was presumably the legal settlement in his libel action against Cassell & Co., publisher of *The Journals of Arnold Bennett 1896–1928*, ed. Newman Flower (1932–3), which quotes Clarke vilifying Irish women.

[4] *Summer's Day*, one of two melodramas by Mrs Maura Molloy produced at the Abbey.

[5] WBY included two poems by Charles Madge (1912–96), poet, sociologist, and co-founder of the social experiment 'Mass-Observation'; in 1938 he married the poet Kathleen Raine, but the union did not last.

[6] For Waley see note to 22 Aug. 1924. 'Michael Field' was the pseudonym adopted jointly by Katherine Harris ('Michael') Bradley (1846–1914) and her niece, Edith ('Henry') Cooper (1862–1913); together they wrote close to forty books and a journal, *Works and Days*, which after their deaths was heavily edited and published by T. Sturge Moore. WBY included nine poems in the anthology and GY included their and Sitwell's dates.

[ALS]   c/o Thomas Cook | Majorca
                                  Probably Thursday [*c*.11 Dec. 1935]

My dear Dobbs: Your letter has come, let me know what houses are drawn
by the Saint in a hurry. Yes we had an abominable passage until a day
before Giberalter. We arrived here two days late. A day after we left Giberalter there was a curious exciting event. There was the usual concert &
Mrs Foden had offered to dance Indian dances. She had brought with her
thinking to wear it at a Festa the dress of a sacred Temple dancer (she had
danced in a temple) when she had put on the dress she felt some uncertainty about the proper position of the sari & rang for her hindoo steward.
He spread the news & when she came out of her cabin (I have her account
& Swami's) 'dozens & dozens' of hindoo stewards lined the passage'. All
raised their hands to their foreheads saluting the sacred dress, & the head
steward prostrated himself, touching the deck with his forhead. I think
they had learned of the fight with the Pursur & were giving thanks for her
defence of their coulour. We left the ship in great favour. The Purser said
'Come home on this ship & I

                                                        P.T.O.

will give you a suite of rooms on the upper deck with your own sitting
room.'

When the steamer was rolling there was anxiety among the ships' officers
lest the locomotive engines, there were two aft & one in the bows should
break loose. They were inspected from time to time & their props strength-
ened. We were late because the Captain altered our course from time to
time to lessen the rolling. Though the Swami was very sick he said 'I was
very happy'. He had decided to escape sea sickness by going into contemplation. He called up the form of his Master the ancient sage Deltatreya,
said certain words, then thought 'no I must not trouble my Master about a
natural event like sea-sickness. He always takes care of me'. He thought 'I
have left on the electric light' but when he opened his eyes the cabin was
dark. For four hours that light remained, it was there when ever he closed
his eyes; & when he was not sea-sick he had 'great happiness'

We have not yet got a permanet address, are in a Palermo hotel[1] but
hope to leave it on Saturday. To morrow we go off in a motor to find some
tavern or little hotel where we can have fires, & set up oil stoves. A musician a young woman who has sent me a setting of 'Down by the Salley
Gardens'[2] goes with us in the motor; we shall get further advice from the

---

[1] GY remarked to Lily Yeats, 'He calls "Palma" "Palermo" throughout his letters...very
muddling to future biographers' (18 Dec. 1935).

[2] Unidentified; there have been many settings written for this popular poem.

British Consul who has asked us to tea today. On his cards he has printed in equally large black letters, British Navy. Savile Club.³

I have great confidence in myself. Yesterday morning the last crumple in my play⁴ smoothed it self out & now all is complete in my head, at last my work is all in all in all to me.

I have done that last chapter for the introduction & am now about to make a clean copy for to days post I hope.

Yrs always
WB Yeats

PS
The ships concert was got up by

(P.T.O.)

Collingswood Gee, & a soldier friend of his. Collingswood Gee was a friend of Horne, Bottichelli authority, an old friend of mine.⁵ He & the soldier had left Florence because of the war. I read three poems, introduced with usual patter, & Swami sang a passage from the <u>Upanishads</u> announcing that India had sung it exactly as he did for 5000 years, Mrs Foden danced badly but with contagious good humour. I thought the audience particuley intellegent. We all spoke well.

I doubt if I can finish the introduction to day

[ALS]   C/o Thomas Cook | Palma | Majorca
                                    Thursday [12 Dec. 1935]

My dear Dobbs
    Here is the corrected introduction. I would have asked Mrs Foden to type the little bit in MSS at the end but Swami says her spelling is even worse than her type-writing & proposed to copy it out in his own hand-writing.

---

³ Captain Alan Hugh Hillgarth (1899–1978), having recently retired from the Royal Navy as lieutenant commander, was British vice-consul (1932–7) and later consul at Palma (1937–9). In 1939 during the Spanish Civil War he was able to arrange the peaceful surrender of Minorca and later, having been chiefly responsible for Spanish neutrality, served as chief of British Naval Intelligence, Eastern Theatre (1944–6); for such services he received the OBE in 1937 and in 1943 was appointed CMG. He married the translator Mary Sidney Katherine Almina Hope-Morley (1896–1982) as her third husband in 1929; they were divorced in 1946. He was later consulted during the Foden fracas. See notes to 16 Jan. 1936 and 20 June 1936.

⁴ *The Herne's Egg*; on 25 Nov. 1935 WBY had written to Turner, 'In Majorca,—I leave Liverpool on Friday—I plan to write a three act tragi-comedy in short lines, rhyming now and again, more or less "sprung verse"' (H. W. Hausermann, 'W. B. Yeats and W. J. Turner 1935–1937 (with Unpublished Letters)', *English Studies* (August 1960), 243).

⁵ Collingwood Walter Gee (1879–1946), an artist, returned to Florence where he spent his later years; his painting of D. H. Lawrence reading *Lady Chatterley's Lover* to Reginald Turner, Norman Douglas, and Pino Orioli (1927) is frequently reproduced.

We go to a new address on Saturday but Cook will forward letters. I will write from the new address at once; I have plenty of news and am full of imaginative ideas. I may start my play on Saturday.

Yrs ev
WB Yeats

Mrs Foden says that our new hotel is 'a paradise'

[APS[1]]   [Mallorca Palma
12 Dec. 1935]

We are in this town[2] but in a couple of days go to some country in. To morrow we go by motor to look for it.

Yours ev
WB Yeats

[ALS]   HOTEL TERRAMAR | SAN AGUSTIN
(C'AS CATALÁ) PALMA DE MALLORCA ESPAÑA
Sunday [15 Dec. 1935]

My dear Dobbs

Above is our permanent address. We have been here two days & pay (including ten percent tax) about 2.13.0 a weak.[1] The hotel is new, white & pleasant, the scene from the windows beautiful & my play is getting written. My heart was a little upset by the rolling of the steamer I had to hold on to things so hard & so often but that will soon mend

I hope 'introduction' reachd you. Please put in the correct name of Bridges daughter I left a blank in last paragraph, & do not forget to add Stephens poems in the Anthology that poem from the Gaelic about a ghost in Lennoxs Anthology[2]

We have made friends with the British Consul & he has lent us a mountain cottage where we go on Feb 1, so we shall not spend much money. He has a medieval villa near Palma a vast Ballylea furnished with exquisite taste

---

[1] Addressed to 'Miss Anne Yeats | Riversdale | Rathfarnham | Dublin | Ireland | British Possession'.

[2] Photograph of a view of Palma and the bay.

[1] WBY and Foden had arranged to share the Swami's expenses.

[2] None of the poetry of Mrs Ali Akbar Daryush, née Elizabeth Bridges (1887–1977), appears in WBY's anthology; four poems from the Irish by James Stephens were included, but not 'The Ghost' which WBY remembered from *The Golden Treasury of Irish Verse* (1925) compiled by LR.

& at great expense. I want you to send me a copy of the <u>Cuala</u> <u>Dramatis</u> <u>Personae</u> I want to give it to his wife

My only news is that I have have had only 1 letter from anywhere since I left & I wrote you two long letters

Yrs affly
WB Yeats

[TLS]   RIVERSDALE, | WILLBROOK, |
RATHFARNHAM, | DUBLIN.
Dec 18 1935

My dear Willy

In haste...just going out with Michael to buy some trousers—he returned with no seats in any of them !!!! He was first in exam results. Pet[1] is typing your introduction. She has been doing a little work for me here, checking my index of first lines—I had only missed out one so I felt quite proud of myself. I have some thrillers to send you when I get your address. It might complicate things to post books to Cooks—they would have to pay extra postage probably and might refuse to do so unless you sent them cash.

London Macmillan are going to print your new book of autobiographical papers at once and send proofs to America. This will save a lot of misprints.

In haste

love
G.[2]

[TLS]   RIVERSDALE, | WILLBROOK, |
RATHFARNHAM, | DUBLIN.
Dec. 20 [1935]

My dear Willy

Thanks for your letter dated Sunday—You should have had my second and third letters at any rate. This is number 5. Did you get my letter telling

[1] Hermione Lytton Wilson, WBY's Dublin typist.
[2] On the back of this letter WBY has written

'arrived on the 8th
arranged on
left Hotel T—14th
Arrived Palma 8th
arranged to go H.T.—12
Consul H.T—on 14th'

of de Valera's visit to the Abbey!! (Saint in a hurry....)[1] The houses were so bad that he must have realised Dublin does not like piety outside the Church! Partly of course the bad period before Christmas. All the theatres and even the cinemas have been very empty.

Did you get my letter saying that Michael had been first in the exams? From his letter I thought he had been first in each exam; actually he was first on the total of marks for all the exams. He got an average of 77 out of a hundred. His voice has broken; I havent got accustomed to it yet and keep on thinking there is a strange man in the house.

Nothing is happening here but preparations for Christmas—as usual I shall be glad when it is over.

Turner's article[2] brought in a great many letters and orders. I havent the numbers as Cuala has been so busy with orders of all sorts that I dont want to delay the girls for information. Higgins has gone to London on some business for Thom's.[3] He was to see Turner in London.

Yours ever
George.

[ALS]   HOTEL TERRAMAR | SAN AGUSTIN
                    (C'AS CATALÁ) PALMA DE MALLORCA ESPAÑA
                                        Dec 7 [21 Dec. 1935]

My Dear Dobbs: Yesterday I finished the scenario & to day began writing the play in verse—short lines, rhymed here & there. I think I shall write it quickly, have it all blocked in in a month—3 acts, act 2 with 3 scenes. All I think amusing & strange. There is a donkey, like a childs toy, on wheels but life size, an important character. My days are not long enough for all I have to do. I breakfast at 7.30 & work in bed until 11.30 at 12.30 I go on to the terrace, lunch at 1 & have from 2 to 3 for letters etc, from 3 to 4 I work with the Swami at his translation. He brings me 'They have put a veil upon the face of truth' I send him back to the origonal & we get 'They have put a golden stopper into the neck of truth' He is in great delight when I tell him he may write that, endeed happy when ever something like the origonal & its music emerges. At 4 we have tea & from 5 to 7 I lie down to sleap or read. At 7 I change into my blue clothes for dinner. I am never tired & I am take great care of. When I go upstairs, or down stairs, the Swami, very broad & unpassibl in his pink robes walks in front very slowly that I may

---

[1] This letter is missing; de Valera attended the Abbey during the previous week.

[2] 'Broadside Songs' by W. J. R. Turner in the *New Statesman*, 7 Dec. 1935.

[3] Thom's *Irish Almanac and Official Directory* was first published in 1844. In 1852 it added the Dublin street directory which is still published annually.

not go too fast. There is one other guest in the hotel, an elderly Englishman who puts himself to the trouble of going to a distant bathroom & lavetory to avoid those used by the Swami. On the other hand the Manager is a German 'very fond of philosophy' who had wanted to learn Sanskrit when young 'but had to go into busines instead' He seeks the Swamis society when he can, & is very polite. Mrs Fodens firm eye is on the Englishman, so he to will behave. The hotel is very white an new & clean.

I think I did wrong in letting you write to Mrs Gregory or Keller. Only the two executors can give leave.[1] You might on the other hand write to Putnam, who is the present publisher of <u>The Kiltartan History Books</u>

Please tell me what houses <u>The Saint in a Hurry</u> drew & if there was a loss

I must stop because Mrs Foden has just called to say the Swami is coming round with our first weekly bill. We are spending, I think, when all extras are counted, less than £3.5.0 a week.

I enclose photographs of self & Swami on steamer. Please give the children—endeed I know you will—usual presents in my name.

Yrs affecly
WB Yeats

[APS[1]]   [Mallorca
21 Dec. 1935]

Some where in Majorca. Not unlike where I am. Same still sea[2]
good wishes for Xmas.

WB Yeats

[ALS]   HOTEL TERRAMAR | SAN AGUSTIN
(C'AS CATALÁ) PALMA DE MALLORCA ESPAÑA
Dec 26 [1935]

Letter 5 (I will number letters that you may know if a letter goes astray)
My dear Dobbs

This was to have been our first expedition by motor but it is raining. A few days ago Swami & I had a shock. Mrs Foden went out & did not return

---

[1] Four of AG's translations from the Irish, three by Douglas Hyde and one from Padraic Pearse were included in WBY's Oxford Anthology; Margaret Gregory and T. J. Kiernan were co-executors of AG's estate.

[1] Addressed to 'Miss Anne Yeats | Riversdale | Rathfarnham | Dublin | Irish Free State | B.P.'

[2] Photograph of unidentified hotel on a bay.

until the middle of lunch. She had gone to Church, not her own Church (she is a Catholic) but the protestant church. She had met the English colony, & acquaintances made on the the steamer & was full of gossip. There was no doubt about it, she was bored. Before she went she had paid Swami & me visits but had said nothing about her expedition. That meant she was ashamed. How could Swami and I get on without Mrs Foden? We held an alarmed consultation. If we could remain invalids that would satisfy her energies but that was impossible. I suggested, & Swami accepted the idea, that we were over worked. Once a week she must take us to the cinema, or on an outing by motor, she choose direction & films. Swami told her our idea. Of course he did not suggest that she was bored. We had both suggested, when we first came here, that she might be & had only made her miserable 'You think I have no thoughts' she had said 'that I have no intellect'. The contraversy about the Christian name, by the by, awakens at intervals—I have no settled practice

I am to sign the translation of The Upanishads with Swami, & we are to devide royalties. Our translation will certainly superceed all others & should have a steady sale. It will be finished before we return.

Yrs affecly
WB Yeats

[ALS]   HOTEL TERRAMAR | SAN AGUSTIN
(C'AS CATALÁ) PALMA DE MALLORCA ESPAÑA
6th Letter
[?28] Dec—about 3 days after Xmas [1935]

My dear Dobbs

I have had four letters from you dated Dec 4, 9, 18, 20. I have not had the letter about De Veleras visit to theatre.

This is a mere note to give above facts.

All goes well—beautiful warm weather. Yesterday I rested & to day I am not writing verse. My heart has never quit recovered from the strain of those four days of storm otherwise I am very well & am doing beautiful work.

On Monday—the day after to morrow—the British Consul his wife & daughter lunch with us & the Manager of the hotel is in great excitement. By the by he types the Upanishad & will take no payment.

I always want news of the Abbey. Would it do if Anne took giving me that news as her department. I want to know the gain or loss in each new play.

Yrs affecly
WB Yeats.

I do not think my head was ever so full of imaginative inspiration. I think of a saying in the Upanishad 'I am full of longing. They have put a golden stopper in neck of truth; pull it Lord, let out reality'

[TLS]   [Riversdale, Willbrook, Rathfarnham, Dublin.]
                                                   December 29 [1935]

My dear Willy

Your abode sounds delightful—your energy magnificent. The Englishman disgusting. The Abbey has had good houses for 'The Critic' I enclose two notices.[1] The songs were a great success; they were sung without music, an opening phrase from piano or piano and fiddle only. The children have a lot of parties this year—Michael more than Anne which is unusual. He goes to the Luce's[2] tomorrow. Lily and Lolly spent St Stephens night here 7–11, rather heavy going with Lolly who hasnt the least idea how dull her clothes and etc are to the very young. However, all went off well—and at the moment I have just washed the back of Anne's neck with tremendous results for a party tonight before the Larchet celebration at the Abbey. He is to be given his portrait by Sean O'Sullivan if the funds from tonight's show are large enough. As the house was booked out yesterday, and all services from actors and staff are free I hope he'll get it. Anyway he is sure of a great ovation.[3]

I had a letter from Mrs Foden last night (Saturday) and will write to her tomorrow. I wish she wouldnt call you my 'belovedest' or 'your beloved', but one must endure these things! And I wish you hadnt told her I was writing a novel. You are so indiscreet that I fear you may even mention I dont like you referred to as my 'belovedst', so you had better put this letter in the fire at once, or, failing a fire, down the half-way.[4] How the devil am I to 'write a novel' if people ask how it progresses and I get involved therefore with biographical matter? I am doing it to amuse myself, and if I attempt to publish it shall do so under a pseudonym. Probably it will be burnt, but it is meant as an interest to myself, is not Irish or English, has no autobiographical or biographical associations. So leave me to stew in my solitary juice.[5]

I saw the film of THE INFORMER yesterday; it is the best film I have ever seen, the females were bad because they tried to have an Irish accent and so were unreal. The Informer himself rather magnificently acted by

[1] LR's adaptation of Richard Brinsley Sheridan's *The Critic* was first produced 6 Jan. 1931; the revision on 26 Dec. 1935 was preceded by songs sung by baritone and noted singing teacher Michael O'Higgins (d. 1980); enclosures are missing but the *Irish Times* (27 Dec. 1935) praised the excellence of the acting and the entire production.

[2] Revd Arthur Aston Luce (1882–1977), Professor of Philosophy and fellow of TCD, and an expert on Berkeley, lived in Rathgar; he had two sons, John Victor (b. 1920) and Arthur, both of whom MBY would have known from St Columba's.

[3] After twenty-seven years, Larchet had retired from his position as Director of Music at the Abbey Theatre because of ill health; the special performance raised sufficient funds for the portrait by Sean O'Sullivan (1906–64), which was presented on 25 Oct. 1936.

[4] Another slang expression for the WC. WBY later suspected Foden of reading his mail.

[5] GY's MS has never been discovered.

Victor MacClagen, no sentimentality, no improvised accent, brutal, drunk, coarse, yet one came away with the feeling that he was a 'sympathetic' and rather tremendous person. Very clever sensitive acting and production.[6] The first time brutality on the films hasnt left me with a bad taste in my mouth. The brothel was discreetly called a 'shebeen', this puzzled me a bit; but I did, what I have never done before, an evil act, and sat through the show for a second round! It then dawned on me that the shebeen was of course a brothel. (Incidentally the word brothel was used in 'The Critic' and Michael said in a loud whisper 'What was that?')

Yours affly
Dobbs

[ALS]   HOTEL TERRAMAR | SAN AGUSTIN
(C'AS CATALÁ) PALMA DE MALLORCA ESPAÑA
[30 Dec. 1935]

Letter 7 (or is it 8)

My dear Dobbs

Here is the list of errors & missprints in <u>Dramatis Personnae</u> better correct them in copy for Macmillan. In addition to these there is the correction of first line, and of passage about Dowson—you have these

I have recieved from you 'a wild west' which I am now reading and 'New Statesman' for Nov 7 & Nov 14, no other papers <u>Dramatis Personnae</u> came a few days ago.

Did you get the corrected introduction which I sent a few days after reaching Palma?

Lunch party for British Consul to day, a muskitto bite has made Mrs Fodens left eye close completely. Manager arrayed in his best

Yrs ev
WB Yeats

Have you heard what sales resulted from Turners article
I have finished & am copying out my first act.

---

[6] *The Informer*, based on O'Flaherty's novel and directed by John Ford, was playing at the Capitol Cinema at 2.30, 4.50, 7.10, and 9.30 p.m. The *Irish Times* review of 24 December also praises the film and Victor McLaglen (1886–1959), who won an Oscar for his performance as Gypo Nolan, but mentions that Una O'Connor (née Agnes Teresa McGlade; 1880–1959), a member of the Abbey company who remained in America after the 1912 tour and was now well known as a character actress in cockney and English parts in films, was miscast; other Abbey players in the film were J. M. Kerrigan, who remained in Hollywood, and Denis O'Dea (1903–78), who thereafter combined leading roles at the Abbey with film work.

1936

[TL]   RIVERSDALE | RATHFARNHAM |
                                          CO. DUBLIN | IRELAND
                                          January 6 1935 [1936]

My dear Willy

My activities have been nil for the last few days owing to a fearful cold. I am still rather knocked up. I enclose an income tax paper for you to sign. You have to sign twice; once on front page, once on back. Please send it back by return. The reclaim pays the Irish Free State income tax which will soon be due. (It wont be as much as the amount of the re-claim!!) Please dont remove typed slip on enclosure.

You will remember that in 1934 you got an advance from Macmillan and Co for the journey to Rapallo and return of furniture. That delayed their income tax return claim (why I dont know) so it is included in this year's re-claim. The amount stated is for gross amount, agents fee and income tax not deducted. Our income tax forms are made out on the amount actually received. Thank goodness Mr Radcliffe[1] has to do these things! You need not fill in any details, he does that, and I have supplied him with the dates you were in England etc.

Frightful storms and floods here; I shall have to get the two big chestnuts at the bridge lopped, alas. The Sergeant met me on the road a week or more ago and mentioned them hinting that I might be held responsible if they fell and damaged anyone on the road. So Murphy[2] will have to get on to them directly the wind drops. They cant be done before that.

Michael has gone to stay in Bangor with a school friend.[3] The boy wired on Thursday 'Come on Friday for week-end will meet you Belfast if you wire train'—'Royal Command,' said Michael 'I cannot refuse'.

Coriolanus next week (Professor Tim this week)[4]

---

[1] The officer at the Bank of Ireland in Dublin; Thom's street directory lists a W. L. Radcliffe resident in Rathgar.

[2] A local contractor and handyman.

[3] Arthur Brian Deane Faulkner (1921–77), MBY's closest friend while at St Columba's although their political affiliations were completely opposed; a strong Unionist and member of the Orange Order, he was elected to Parliament in 1949 and was Prime Minister of Northern Ireland 1971–6. The following year he was created a life peer. See MBY, *Cast a Cold Eye* (Dublin, 1999), 21–7 for a record of their friendship.

[4] GY's letter breaks off here, half-way down the page. *Coriolanus*, directed by the new arrival Hugh Hunt and designed by Tanya Moiseiwitsch, opened 13 Jan. 1936; see GY's letter of 21 Jan. 1936. *Professor Tim* by George Shiels (1925) was a perennial favourite.

[ALS]   HOTEL TERRAMAR | SAN AGUSTIN
            (C'AS CATALÁ) PALMA DE MALLORCA ESPAÑA
                                              [?6 Jan. 1936]

Letter 8 (This is a guess but I am making a note of the number so from this on at any rate I shall number my letters correctly)

My dear Dobbs: I am writing in bed after breakfast, the window is wide open & the sun streams in.

You said in your last letter that you were enclosing press cuttings about The Critic but you forgot to do so, this leaves me unable to understand what songs you refer to when you say 'the songs were delightful'. Were they part of the Critic or were they songs from the broadsides sung before or after the play? If part of The Critic are they new songs.

Turner writes that he cannot be English editor—is busy—& asks is he to find somebody. Lady Dorothy Wellesley would I think be English editor. I want you & Higgins to decide & let Higgins write direct to Turner or let me know, that I may write to Lady Dorothy.

No change in life here. I have moved down to a room on the ground floor to avoid all stairs & have finished the first act or scene of my play. It amuses me, a strange faery tale. I shall write a lyric or two before I go on to the second Act

The Swami manages Mrs Foden with great skill, says she must never be checked on the first day of one of her projects, but only on the second & this checking he does firmly but with many bantering complements. However some of her projects are admuribl such as brining me to the ground level & all are benevolent. To day she has invited to lunch a very old, very infirm, but very well informed labour member of the London County Council.

She & the Swami go to India in June next.

I enclose an envelope that contains a Xmas card from Michael. Who is J I Howell who restamped the letter. If a known neighbour should he be thanked. But no I see he put on English stamps. The puzzle is who is how it got into a letter from S. H. Roche[1]

                                                    Yrs affectly
                                                    WB Yeats

I have written rather a fine lyric WBY[2]

---

[1] Both names unknown, though it was possibly a neighbourly gesture by Revd J. S. Roche, Prior of the Augustinian Novitiate College in nearby Rockbrook, Rathfarnham.

[2] Written on back of the envelope.

[TLS]   Riversdale | Willbrook | Rathfarnham | Dublin
                                                    January 9th [1936]

My dear Willy

I enclose some press cuttings of your last book. Also fresh cuttings of THE CRITIC which you say you didnt get.[1] I enclosed them in an envelope separately as I forgot to put them in my letter telling you about them. Anne will write about Coriolanus which begins on Monday and I will send you cuttings.

We are still having storms and torrents of rain....Impossible to go out.

(I forgot to say the songs sung on Abbey stage were all from Broadsides with the exception of one by Frank O'Connor and one by Stephens.)

How on earth did Michael's envelope get into another envelope and get to England—did you notice the Irish stamps were not postmarked?? This sort of things explains letters occasionally going astray!

I had a letter from Dorothy Wellesley saying she would like to correct her own proofs of the anthology poems....that is some time ahead. Pet hasnt finished the three copies of your preface yet; I will send you one for final corrections when I get them; that page in your own writing is difficult—some word or words missing and punctuation definitely needed. As soon as you get one act of your play done you really ought to make a clean copy or you will forget your own writing!

I am posting you tomorrow two more Wild Wests...What do you do all the evenings....have you had any cold? Probably not with all that sun streaming on you.

A piece of gossip...Geoffrey Phibbs is still working with Mrs Robert Graves on linoleum designs and so on but he has married her assistant;[2] they all go on living together....

                                                              Love
                                                              George

---

[1] Enclosures missing.

[2] GY received much of this gossip from Tom MacGreevy; Phibbs, now legally Geoffrey Taylor and divorced from Norah McGuinness, married Mary Dillwyn in 1935 (see note to 17 July 1929).

[ALS]   HOTEL TERRAMAR | SAN AGUSTIN
                    (C'AS CATALÁ) PALMA DE MALLORCA ESPAÑA
                                Jan 16 [1936]

Letter 9

My dear Dobbs: I have not written since Jan 8¹ because I have been ill for the last few days. Breathing became difficult then I got pains, which I beleived to be muscular rheumatism & took to my bed. Swami remarked 'Give grass to a cow & it turns it into milk; give milk to a serpent & it turns it into poison; an old man turns his food into poison' It never occurred to me to connect this remark with my own state. Next day Mrs Foden sent for the doctor, a very able Spaniard recommended by the Consul. He became interested in my 'corporation' said it was in part the result of poisoninng (?poison day) told me how to apply to my self a very drastic treatment which I must keep up always. My heart enlargement is very slight but my heart misses a beat which should be cured in a few weeks. He gave me a medicine to increas the flow of blood but the main trouble is that my food poisons me. At once my pains began to dissapear & now I feel better than I have been since I came to Majorca I am getting up to day & shall know how much I have improved by the distance I can walk.

Mrs Foden is devotion itself now that I am ill, but for all that I am in disgrace—all the fault of a cock tail. We were lunching with the British Consul (author of a very fine novel about Bolivia).² I took a cock tail & it went to my head. I gave his wife ('under the influence') Mrs Fodens little book about Russia with these words 'no writer, but Cook, Observer, Traveller'.³ Had I known that she put the Swami into Coventery for a fort night for calling it 'a homely little book' I would have had more sense. When we got home Mrs Foden went to bed, refused tea, refused dinner, spent the rest of the evening in a darkened room, did not get up next day until lunch, at lunch was monasolabic—both Swami & I were in disgrace (she had obviously remembered the word 'homely'). We saw nothing of her for the rest of the day. 'She is not ill in body' said the Swami 'but in mind' Next day came a diverson. The Englishman, who goes to a distant bathroom rather share one with Swami got the Manager to aske her to ask the Swami to use the distant bath room. She naturaly refused in a blaze of rage. Yesterday she

---

¹ Probably an error for Letter 8.

² Hillgarth's adventure novel *The Black Mountain* (New York, 1933) was about an Indian hero who becomes immersed in Bolivian politics. Other novels include *The Princess and the Perjurer* (1924), *The Passionate Trail* (1925), *The War Maker* (1926), *Change for Heaven* (1929), *What Price Paradise?* (1929), and *Davy Jones* (1936).

³ In 1926 Gwyneth Foden published *A Wife's Secret* (London), a title already used in a well-known 19th-century play, and in 1935 *My Little Russian Journey* (London).

spent looking for a flat but decided in the evening that she would not give the English man the satisfaction of driving us out. I have asked the Manager to come & see me. I dont want Mrs Foden to handle the situation as when angry she is given to threats I shall offer to leave the hotel with my friends if our presence is bad for it but point out that if we stay the Swami must not be insulted. Of course we have not told the Swami what has happened.

The Swami's comment on Mrs Foden is 'I am taking her to India, she will find her work there. I once saw her getting ready to be photographed. There was a peice of expensive silk. She tore off a strip to wrap round her head. She has the genius of destruction. She was born for polotics. It is the destruction in her that makes her unhappy'

I was delighted to get 'the Wild West' & the press-cuttings. I am particularly happy about the success of the songs

I have made a clean copy of my first act.

Yrs affly
WB Yeats

[TLS]   [Riversdale, Willbrook, Rathfarnham, Dublin.]
January 18 1935 [1936]

My dear Willy

I am sending you in two packages of newspapers giving accounts of the last three Senate meetings. Gogarty evidently blew off in characteristic style!!! Bobby Childers was trying to draw out Sean T. O'Kelly at the party the other night on the subject of the Senate, but S.T. said firmly 'I was in my office'.[1]

I heard yesterday (from Mrs Bulmer Hobson) that Frank O'Connor is very ill again and had to be X rayed; the old trouble. Gastric ulcer was suspected. He is one of the very few people who ought to be subsidised to prevent his having to do office work.[2] Neither he nor Higgins were at the

---

[1] On 27 Nov. 1935 de Valera submitted a motion which if passed by the Dáil would have effectively abolished the Seanad because of its 'persistent obstruction' of 'the will of the people'; the motion was debated in the Dáil on 12 December and passed. Gogarty in debate on 1 Jan. 1936 referred to 'the sinking ship of State' and de Valera's 'madcap schemes'; on 16 Jan. 1936 he referred to the President 'as the greatest national fiasco', and as 'suffering from magalomania'. Thomas O'Kelly (1882–1996), who became the second President of Ireland (1945–59), was at this time Vice-President of the Executive Council and Minister of Local Government and Public Health in the Fianna Fáil government, then appointed Tánaiste (deputy prime minister) on the adoption of the 1937 Constitution; in 1902 he joined the Irish Republican Brotherhood, followed by membership in Sinn Féin, participated in the 1916 Rising and the Civil War, and followed de Valera into Fianna Fáil as Vice-President.

[2] In November 1943 GY offered financial assistance to O'Connor and his wife when he was in straitened circumstances, adding, 'Frank O'Connor is a writer who must go on writing.' Bulmer Hobson (1883–1969) was one of the founders of the Ulster Literary Theatre.

first night of Coriolanus—possibly Higgins is also ill, which would account for his prolonged silence about Broadsides.

Michael went back to school yesterday; the taxi got stuck on the hill and would neither go up nor down...slid backwards into a bank and refused to move. The hill was pure ice. The luggage had to be carried up, and finally all hands shoved and we got dislodged, slid gently down into a gate. We blocked the road for about ten minutes with all the other parents' cars hooting and flashing headlights. This about 8.30 pm—Johnson's[3] tyres are of course too smooth from old age to get a grip.

The children's party here was a success—if one is to judge by noise— Michael as a widow with a baby in her arms was admirable but the play (in which everyone had to improvise their parts from a scenario) ended in a free fight on the floor; no casualties.

The Drama League produces Cocteau's 'Orphee' tomorrow and Monday. (Torch Theatre) future productions at the Gate.[4] The Gate is going to Egypt for six weeks—the Egyptian Government wishes to have Shakespeare plays....let us hope some of their small audiences will now come to the Abbey. Their audiences have been very bad lately. Dolly bought a notice at Woolworths to put on the gate at Sorrento Cottage, painted in black on white 'SHUT THE GATE' Lennox came home and saw it 'O if only we could write Hilton Edwards name on the back and send it through the post.'[5]

I see in today's paper that Kipling died yesterday after a sudden operation for gastric ulcer; the King is also very ill, and judging by the bulletin issued by his doctors I should say he is not expected to live; bronchial trouble with cardiac complications. The royal family will all move up one like taxis on a cab rank.[6]

I am inaugurating a third war against our neighbours, the Weldons.[7] This one is going to be strictly silent. Their maid has for the past three weeks

[3] A local taxi driver, possibly associated with C. J. Johnston, Dublin motor haulage contractor.

[4] The DDL, which had disbanded in 1928, was revived in 1936 by LR, GY, the Earl of Longford, and Olive Craig to fill the gap caused by the absence of MacLiammóir and Edwards's company at the Gate Theatre. Its first production, 19–20 Jan. 1936, in the recently established Torch Theatre on Capel Street, was *His Widow's Husband* by Jacinto Benevente, produced by Ria Mooney, followed by *Orpheus* by Jean Cocteau, produced by LR and Shelah Richards. After this 1936 season the DDL once again lapsed, to be briefly revived for the last time in December 1941, with LR president once again, GY general secretary, and Ernest Blythe treasurer.

[5] By now there were two production companies operating out of the Gate Theatre, the Edwards–MacLiammóir group, who were going to Egypt, and the Longford group.

[6] George V died on 20 Jan. 1936 and Edward ascended the throne.

[7] James Patrick Weldon (1874–1950), who in the 1890s founded a jewellery shop in Upper O'Connell Street, lived next door to the Yeatses at Edenbrook, Willbrook, Rathfarnham; although labelled a 'Blueshirt' supporter by GY and WBY, he was a strong supporter of

been climbing into our premises and taking wood from our river walk and upper field (some cut up by us) she does this quite regularly on Wednesday, Saturday and Sunday. I am having John barb-wire the gaps in the fence between us and them. John is afraid to speak to her about it because he says 'she'd say I hit her'. The Weldons have far more timber than we have, and in any case I dont see why <u>we</u> should keep them in fuel for their fires!! I think I told you we had a cattle feud; their hungry cattle breaking in to us for 'oats', incidentally through the same hole that the maid has now re-opened for her raids! Mary, in a vigorous denouncement of the maid's behaviour ended up 'no wonder their cattle break in' (i.e. bad example given by human being)[8]

Yours affly

G.

[ALS]   HOTEL TERRAMAR | SAN AGUSTIN
(C'AS CATALÁ) PALMA DE MALLORCA ESPAÑA
['Jan 20. 1936.'[1]]

Letter 10

My dear Dobbs

   I enclose a letter & checque from Bender which please send to the right quarter. I would have sent them to Con Curran who is probably the right person if I had his address. I have thanked Bender[2]

Collins and Griffith and a lifelong friend of the Cosgraves. The first 'war' had been over the disappearance of one of GY's hens, which she believed had been killed by the Weldons' collie dog; when GY complained, a note of apology was sent saying four dogs had been destroyed; but the following week much to her embarrassment GY's hen returned and the story, retold several times by WBY as 'the fascist dog and the democratic hen', was incorporated in 'Three Songs to the Same Tune': '"Drown all the dogs" said the fierce young woman' (WBY to OS, 27 Feb. 1934). The Weldons' jewellery shop is still in the family.

   [8] Mary Martin of Monasterevin came as housekeeper from Fitzwilliam Square and remained with GY until after she moved to Palmerston Road.

   [1] Dated in GY's hand.

   [2] Albert Maurice Bender (1866–1941), Dublin-born San Francisco millionaire and insurance broker and generous patron of the arts with a particular interest in fine printing; WBY's hand-written letter of thanks for Bender's 'generous contribution to the A E memorial'—an award presented to writers under 35 for their work in the previous five years—describes his work with Shree Purohit Swami on their translation of the *Upanishads*. Previous gifts from Bender to WBY included *Life of Dante*, trans. Philip Henry Wicksteed (1922) and a volume of translations of Villon, a facsimile of 'The Lake Isle of Innisfree' in WBY's hand (1924), printed by John Henry Nash in San Francisco, and a cheque on the occasion of WBY's 70th birthday. He continued to order books from the Cuala Press until it closed down (Albert M. Bender Papers, Special Collections, F. W. Olin Library, Mills College).

The supposed attempt to make Swami change his bathroom etc turned out a mare-nest of Mrs Fodens. She wept at intervals & was in a black temper without intervals for a week after my slip of the tongue. At last I told Swami that if she did not return to normal in a few days I would ask her to go back to London. Then Swami had a series of long interviews with her & then announced that I would now find her normal. She is & when she is good she is very very good—if it would only last.

My attack of illness is over I think

One 'Willd West' has come & is a treasure but you said two

Yrs ev
WB Yeats

[TLS]   [Riversdale, Willbrook, Rathfarnham, Dublin.]
Monday Jan 20 [1936]

My dear Willy

I have been a little worried about you. Six nights ago I suddenly woke up and heard you saying 'O,O,O,O,' continuously like a groan, forgetting that you were away I ran into your bedroom to find Michael fast asleep. I hope you havent had a return of your congestion of the lung? I havent had a letter except the envelope containing the income tax paper for twelve days. I very nearly wired, but decided not to. Anyway if you were ill Mrs Foden would let me know and get you a doctor and so on. The British Consul would know all about doctors and nurses. I didnt write all this before because I hate to seem fussy.

Very good performance of Cocteau's 'Orpheus' last night. Very well produced and acted—I didnt like the woman Lennox had got to play the part of Euridice—Esme Biddle—a competent actress with no imagination or invention; and STOUT!! Why will he put fat woman into the part of heroine! An inexperienced actress like Sheelah May would have looked lovely in the part and would have made it credible that Orpheus would follow her into Hades and Heaven.[1] (the final scene is in Heaven)

---

[1] Esme Biddle (d. 1951), one of the 'Famous Beauties' featured in collectable cigarette cards, performed with F. R. Benson at Stratford and the Ben Greet Players in 1923 before joining Anew McMaster's Shakespearian company who gave several lengthy winter seasons at the Abbey in the late 1920s, performing with the Gate Theatre and other companies until about 1950. Her first husband was H. V. Neilson, producer and former manager of the F. R. Benson company; with her second husband Ian Priestley Mitchell, actor, producer, and radio performer, she toured Ireland with their own company. Sheila May, daughter of Dublin music store owners, played in the 1934 film *Some Say Chance*, and began her stage career with the Gate Theatre in 1936; she also designed settings for DDL productions; her final career, before her death in the early 1970s, was as a political journalist.

I may get a letter from you on the post when it comes—or tomorrow—we have four inches of snow. I am just putting on galoshes to go to post; John is too busy clearing snow. No paper yet and no busses running on our road. No post of course either.

I have been working hard on the AE letters. So many of them are 'a yard wide and all <u>wool</u>' but I think I have selected a bunch which are interesting as a whole book.[2] I am putting in very little of the cloudy supernatural, they are so very badly written. They start in 1896, hardly any are dated and I have had to refer to your letters to Lady G to date them. That is all done now. He seems to have started dating letters fully about 1923!

Love

G.

[TLS]   RIVERSDALE | RATHFARNHAM | DUBLIN
Tuesday Jan. 21 [1936]

My dear Willy

A letter from you this morning saying that you had been laid up with food poisoning but were better. Hope you are now up and about again. I wrote yesterday and sent the letter by air mail (posted 11.45 am at Rathfarnham January 20th) to see how long it takes compared with the ordinary post. The postoffice <u>says</u> it takes two and a half days instead of five. It cost twopence halfpenny extra. If you didnt happen to notice the envelope please notice this one which will be posted tomorrow Jan 22 at Rathfarnham at 11.45 am. I am very curious to know how long it takes.

I havent any news to write about, in fact writing at all is part of an act of defiance and challenge to a poltergeist[1] who has three times since four o'clock today thrown a brass ash-tray from my typewriting table to the floor with a loud clang. The last occasion occurred about 11.15 pm when I had carefully placed said ashtray in the middle of the table so that I might be sure that the vibrations caused by the machine were not the agent or propeller of its action! I have now lit one of Swamiji's incense sticks, put on a kettle for a hot water bottle, a mug of bovril, with which I shall retire to bed, plus a further incense stick—its a little like the story of Father Benson who went to investigate a haunted room armed with a piece of the True Cross and a

---

[2] The Cuala Press published *Passages from the Letters of AE to W. B. Yeats* in June 1936; page proofs with autograph corrections and notes by GY survive, but her name is not included as editor.

[1] A spirit, usually mischievous, that moves objects or makes noises and bad smells to make itself manifest.

revolver[2]—as soon as I feel I have not succumbed to fright. Needless to say the darned thing only jumped off the table when my mind was completely absorbed in my work. I have been working since ten this morning on the AE letters—I began to wonder if the passages I was typing when it jumped had anything to do with the matter. It didnt do it while Anne was in the room (7.30 to after 10)

Gogarty telephoned this evening a propos of nothing at all except a desire, I think, to say that the flag on Government buildings was lowered for the King's death and that he was surprised that 'those vulgarians' had done it, adding that they had followed the lead of the consulates.... this I believe to be pure fiction!! I told him I had sent you papers with his farewell speech to the Senate which pleased him, he said 'The Irish Press had a leader on it' and I said 'I sent him that too' and he seemed still more pleased. An English publisher has taken his poems, has advanced him £225 on account of royalties and he is to get 20% after the first 5000 'But I shall be driven out of the country or quenched before that'. I think he's waving his red flag at a bull which has been de-horned; he ought to try the Papal bull for a change; the Irish pulpit has a much larger range of invective than the poor parliamentarian.

I notice that no one has thought of closing any Dublin Cinema or Theatre for the King's death! In London all the cinemas theatre and so on closed down when they got the news last night that the King was dying. John had his wireless on and at 10.10 pm it was announced that it was closing down as 'the king had taken a bad turn' to use John's phrase!

Well, I think I shall go to my bed!

Wednesday morning

Just heard that Stephenson slipped up in the snow on his way to the Abbey last night and broke his arm. Hunt played his part last night, but they are taking off Coriolanus and finishing the week with Paul Twyning.[3]

No further poltergeistery!

Yours
G.

[2] GY may be referring to the fiction of Monsignor Robert Hugh Benson (1871–1914), a convert to Roman Catholicism; or this may be a slip for Father Brown, the detective priest created by G. K. Chesterton.

[3] Hugh Sydney Hunt (1911–93) came to the Abbey Theatre in August 1935 as artistic director from the Maddermarket Theatre in Norwich and Croydon Repertory Theatre on the recommendation of Masefield, remaining until the Second World War; subsequently he was the first director of the Bristol Old Vic (1945–8), the London Old Vic (1949–53), the Elizabethan Theatre Trust in Australia (1955–60), and while the first Professor of Drama at Manchester University (1961–73) returned as artistic director to the Abbey (1969–71). For the Abbey Theatre he collaborated with Frank O'Connor on *The Invincibles* and *In the Train* (1937), and *Moses' Rock* (1938); his books include *The Director in the Theatre* (1954), *The Making of Australian Theatre* (1960), and *The Abbey: Ireland's National Theatre 1904–1979* (1979).

[TLS]   [Riversdale, Willbrook, Rathfarnham, Dublin.]
                                                              [?*c.*23 Jan. 1936]

Dear Willy

As I have not heard from you about the Elizabeth Bridges (Daryush) poems I am afraid the material I sent you may have gone astray. I now send you duplicate copies of her two books, and a fresh copy of her letter to Milford.¹ I have asked her to send to you suggestions of her own as she proposes in letter. I want to get this settled as soon as possible as the material can then all go to OUP.

Macmillan are rather tiresome. They want you to cut down to say one fourth the two poems of Roy Campbell's which I enclose. They say that Campbell's book is so small that they are obliged to ask this. I see their point. If you don't think you can cut they might let you include the whole of one poem.²

Do let me have back this stuff as soon as you can. We shant be safe until the material is at the OUP!! I also badly need that excuse for the people who are constantly sending manuscript poems for your 'consideration' for the Anthology!!

Hope to hear you are quite well again.

                                                                        George.

I am enclosing also the copy of her poems you chose; as she wont give permission for them you can scrap them!³

[ALS]   HOTEL TERRAMAR | SAN AGUSTIN
                                  (C'AS CATALÁ) PALMA DE MALLORCA ESPAÑA
                                            ? Jan 24 [postmark 27 Jan. 1936]

Letter 11

My dear Dobbs

I have had your letter with its curious, &, at the time, accurate vision & the letter about 'Orpeus' & the fat lady. When you had your vision I was not actually groaning (that was dream dramatization) but I was ill & in pain.

---

¹ Humphrey Sumner Milford (1877–1952), publisher to Oxford University and the managing director of the Press.

² Roy Campbell (1901–57), South African poet and satirist, is represented by four poems in WBY's anthology.

³ There are no selections in the anthology from the poetry of Elizabeth Daryush, Mrs Ali Akbar Daryush the daughter of Robert Bridges, because she refused publication of the one poem WBY wanted.

Every breath was painful the doctor here discovered that what I thought muscular rheumatism was food poisoning. He cured me in a couple of days but not of the difficulty of breathing. I am quite well except that a slight phisical exertion makes me pant. He has stopped my creative work & says it must not be resumed until my breathing has improved. He permits my work on the Upanishads

What has happened about my various new books? What about the Scribner-Macmillan collected edition? What about 'Autobiographical papers' or what ever we called it?[1] How many broadsides have now been published?

Yesterday I sat in the warm sunlight for 3 hours—the sea very blue. There is a little villa with terrace & charming garden belonging to the owner of this hotel. I am allowed to sit on its terrace & do so daily Some few feet below spreads a very blue sea, with green & purple patches. One or two days have been wet or misty, no day has been cold

Yrs affly
WB Yeats

I enclose a violet plucked in the villa garden on Jan 8 but there are other flowers

[ALS Dict[1]]   HOTEL TERRAMAR | SAN AGUSTIN
(C'AS CATALÁ) PALMA DE MALLORCA ESPAÑA
[29 Jan. 1936]

Dictated to the Swami

My dear George,
    I am dictating this to the Swami; for the moment I rather shrink from writing. In any case I want simply to state facts.
    A couple of days ago, my breathing got very difficult, and remained so for a part of each day. The doctor has just been, and I asked him to talk my case over to the Swami. The doctor says that my heart is very much better & the beat is now regular and that my very distressing panting is caused by weak circulation and in order to get complete rest I am now confined to my

---

[1] 'Dramatis Personae' was serialized in the *London Mercury*, 2 Nov. and 7 Dec. 1935, 4 Jan. 1936, and in the New Republic 26 Feb., 11 and 25 Mar., and 8 and 22 Apr. 1936; it was then reprinted by Cuala Press December 1935 and by Macmillan in May 1936 with *Estrangement, The Death of Synge*, and *The Bounty of Sweden*. In November 1935 Charles Scribner first approached Macmillan of New York suggesting a subscription set of WBY's works which would offer a large sum in royalties; although in 1936 WBY wrote new essays for this edition, the project never materialized.

[1] GY has written on the envelope, which is postmarked 29 Jan. 1936, 'arrived after I had left for Majorca'.

bed. The doctor says my complete cure is only a matter of time, but that to go to England or Ireland at present would kill me. I must wait for the warm weather. Now here is the substance of the letter. I must have some one to look after me, who will nurse me & report to the doctor. I can get a professional nurse here for 20 Piestas (12 shillings) a day. Now the question is would you care to come out?[2] You could live here for a good deal less that I shall pay the professional nurse. Probably so much less that it would save the amount of your ticket. You could take me back when the weather was warm. I do not want to press you in any way, for I know how difficult it is to find a fitting abode for Anne in Dublin.[3] And there are of course Michael's holidays to be considered.

[In WBY's hand] I hate writing so upsetting a letter but there is no help for it—do not hesitate to say that I should get the nurse. I cannot go into a nursing home for all are Spanish & speak Spanish.

I have told you everything in this letter—I am keeping nothing back.

Yrs affly
WB Yeats

[TLS]   [Riversdale, Willbrook, Rathfarnham, Dublin.]
                                         Wednesday [10 June 1936]

Dear Willy

Hope you are less tired—Anne and I and three hundredweight of luggage (had to pay overweight!) arrived safely.[1] Garden looking good—animals all well and so on and thank heaven no more rabbits—a disappointment for Michael but no one else!

I had a registered letter from Mrs F. this morning. It contained copies of Swami's daughter's letters (to Mrs F presumably) They all began 'Dear' or 'Dearest' with no name, which made me suspect at first that they might be compositions of Mrs F's, but on closer examination the style was too good! I dont send them to you. They are mostly attacks on Hamsa.[2] The lady is

---

[2] After receiving a wire on 28 January from the Swami on the doctor's orders, she flew to Majorca, arriving on Sunday morning 2 Feb. 1936.

[3] ABY went to stay in Leeson Park with Frank and Olive Craig, who had a son and daughter, until she travelled to Majorca on her own, sailing on the *Pegu* from Birkenhead 20 Mar. 1936. MBY, who was a boarder at St Columba's, followed by train, also on his own, on 26 March after his confirmation at the College, held by the Archbishop of Dublin, on the 21st.

[1] The three Yeatses finally left Majorca on 26 May, arriving in London 2 June. WBY went on to DW's while ABY and GY returned to Dublin. Michael, who had returned earlier, was back at St Columba's but in quarantine for scarlet fever.

[2] Purohit Swami's estranged daughter was the writer and activist for women's education Mrinalini Chitale, who later translated *An Indian Monk* into Marathi. Swami's master was

evidently a hysterical suburban prude. Mrs F's letter to me merely said 'If Mrs Foden is indebted to Mrs W.B. Yeats for returning the silver cup and saucer she lent Mr Shankar Purohit she thanks her...' This unusual terseness suggests that she is not going to waste any more stamps and stationery upon me, for which the lord be praised.

I spent most of yesterday answering the telephone. All your relations—except your aunt Jenny![3]—rang up and discoursed at great length. Lolly is going away for a week or so on Monday, so I may be able to avoid a seance with her. She and Violet Gordon[4] were full of curiosity about the Barcelona episode (Evening Herald) and I was of course full of ignorance on the subject[5]— The Gate Theatre has had a grand bust up—Dublin seems to be divided into the Longford party and the 'Boys' party, the 'boys' being MacLiamoir and Hilton Edwards. So far I have only heard the gossip of the 'Boys' party![6]

Lennox has let his house to Sean MacEntee[7] for July and August, and seems to have vague plans of going to Finland...

The cat has been ratting again and looks more disreputable than ever. This is all very choppy bits of news. I have been making out the list of acknowledgements. They have to go to O.U.P. at once!! I saw Watt in London and he says they are howling daily on the telephone to him about it.

Yours
G.

Bhagwân Shree Hamsa (1878–1937); WBY was greatly excited by Hamsa's autobiography *The Holy Mountain Being the Story of a Pilgrimage to Lake Manas and of Initiation on Mount Kailas in Tibet*, trans. Shree Purohit Swami and published by Faber and Faber in 1934 with an introduction by WBY.

[3] JBY's unmarried sister Jane Grace Yeats (1847–1938).

[4] Violet Montgomery Gordon (d. 1945), WBY's cousin, daughter of Frances 'Fannie' Gordon.

[5] Although WBY was increasingly cautious of his relationship with Margot Ruddock, he continued to encourage her writing and performing; however, she became more erratic and emotionally unstable, finally turning up unexpectedly at the Yeatses' villa in mid-May, explaining that 'Yeats will tell me if I am a good poet, Shree Purohit Swami if I have a right to live'. The following day she moved on to Barcelona, and after a series of adventures broke her leg, and ended up in hospital; the British consul appealed to WBY and GY who at their expense sent her back to England in charge of a nurse. Numerous reports appeared in the London papers (see WBY's introduction to Ruddock's *The Lemon Tree*, 1937).

[6] Since 1931 Lord Longford had kept the Gate Theatre financially afloat, but costs for the large-scale productions kept rising and finally Edwards and MacLiammóir insisted on accepting a tour in Egypt, taking half of the company with them. On 23 Feb. 1936 Longford Productions, supported by Shelah Richards and Denis Johnston, offered its first play, and when Edwards and MacLiammóir returned, a formal agreement allowed for each company to lease the Gate for six months a year, both depending upon touring to augment the Dublin performances.

[7] Seán Francis MacEntee (1889–1984), an IRA commander during the Civil War and a member of every Fianna Fáil cabinet from 1932 to 1965, was at this time Minister of Finance (1932–9), the first of various ministerial positions held during his long tenure as TD; his daughter is the Irish poet and scholar Máire Mhac an tSaoi.

[ALS]   PENNS IN THE ROCKS, | WITHYHAM, | SUSSEX.
                                              June 14 [1936]

My dear Dobbs
    I shall be here another weak & then spend two or three days in London.
I am well, my attacks of fateague are lessening. Here it is delightfully quii-
et—a few guests all chosen to fit into my interests.¹ I think we are making
progress with <u>Broadsides</u>. Turner who came down for a night promises two
poems of his, with their settings, in a few days, Lady Dorothy has written two
fine songs & for these & for three or four poems of mine he will send settings
by some body else. We are about to ask Belloc for a song of his I have heard
him sing but which has never been published.² There was a little gathering
of folk-musicians here a couple of days ago & all were excited over the published <u>Broadsides</u> & some of the songs sung. Miss Matheson of the BBC who
lives in a cottage on this estate is a great help her mind like Lady Dorothys is
full of folk tunes.³ She will write to Auden for us. Please let me know if Lolly
has many sets unsold. Suggests have been made as to their sale
                                              Yours affecly
                                              WB Yeats

I have posted the signed autograph labels
Lady Dorothy is very thoughtful. She phoned Carnegie Dickson to get a
sleeping draft for me & has I find had a letter from Young⁴ (that however
you I suppose arranged)

[ALS]   PENNS IN THE ROCKS, | WITHYHAM, | SUSSEX.
                                              June 14 [1936]

My dear Anne
    I thank you for your letter though 71 is a lamentable age.¹
    Here both lady Dorothy & her daughter ask many questions about you.

---

    ¹ While GY and ABY returned to Dublin, WBY went to visit DW in Sussex; other guests
at Penns in the Rocks included Turner, William Rothenstein, and—for one day only—Margot
Ruddock.
    ² Hilaire Belloc (1870–1953), poet, novelist, essayist, and historian, also the popular author
of *Cautionary Tales for Children*, contributed 'Mrs Rhys', along with his own music, to the February 1937 issue of the new series of *Broadsides*.
    ³ WBY would eventually discover that Hilda Matheson was DW's lesbian lover. Her house
on DW's estate was aptly named 'Rock Cottage'.
    ⁴ Sir Robert Arthur Young (1871–1959), distinguished as a specialist in the diseases of the
chest, and an exceptionally gifted teacher, was a physician to the Middlesex Hospital; he had
been consulted concerning SMY in 1923.
    ¹ WBY's birthday was 13 June.

See the crocquet ground is in order. I shall I think be home about ten days

Yours ever
WB Yeats

[TLS]   [Riversdale, Willbrook, Rathfarnham, Dublin.]

Monday June 15 [1936]

My dear Willy

I thought I might get a letter from you this morning explaining your wire, but didnt. <u>Are</u> you returning on Saturday, because if so, <u>please wire at once</u>. I am rather puzzled, firstly because your wire was sent off from London, and secondly because it is signed 'WILLIE' and never have I had a wire signed anything but 'YEATS' before!! and secondly because it was sent from London.

I will meet you at Holyhead and arrange from here for a cabin on boat—

I am busy correcting proofs of the O.U.P. anthology. Except for the printer's suggestions, which are all inaccurate, they are very good proofs. The printer cannot bear Hopkins' accents and queries them…I have checked them all with the OUP edition of the Poems and they are correct. I send you the proofs of your own introduction. Please return them through Watt, not direct to Press.

I was at Mrs Nolan's yesterday afternoon—they have lived in the house for twentyfive years and it still looks as though it had just been delivered from the shop—no traces anywhere of the residents—and and and the ornaments!![1] Anne went with me but I gathered it was not a house she had any desire to return to…the young Gogartys were there and the usual gangs of tea-party people. The ostensible reason for going was to arrange the Drama League 'Fete'.[2] Everybody was largely photographed. I refused. I dont think newspaper photographs as 'advance publicity' are the least use (except for the theatre) and I loathe them. Anne was photographed by herself examining a bird-bath or sun-dial kind of object.

I enclose the missing letter from Joyce, also one from Mrs F. which I opened (having recognised the writing on the envelope as being the one she uses—possibly a friend does it for her—to ensure her letters being opened.) It is harmless.[3]

Yours
G.

[1] Hilda J. Nolan (b. 1891), whose husband William Robert Nolan was chairman and managing director of the publishing and printing company Browne & Nolan, was a member of the DDL; her home was 'Corbawn' in Shankill.

[2] At this time GY was a member of the DDL committee; 'At Homes' were hosted in various houses in order to attract new members, but the League activities lapsed after a production in April 1936 and were not taken up again until 1941 when GY became general secretary.

[3] Foden continued to write threatening letters accusing Swami, and by association WBY, of unfounded charges; GY, who dismissed her as 'a very hysterical and unpleasant person', refused to reply but preserved all the correspondence.

[TLS]   [Riversdale, Willbrook, Rathfarnham, Dublin.]
                                                                June 17 1936

Dear Willy

Please thank Lady Dorothy for her wire. I was a little anxious about you because you were so very tired when I saw you off at Charing Cross, and I heard nothing of you until yesterday—Tuesday—morning post, except for the wire.

I gather that you are NOT returning for another week at least and that you are well. No, I didnt suggest the telephone message to Carnegie Dickson about the sleeping draught; it was a brilliant thought of D.W's own.

I had immoral ideas of sending the list of acknowledgements to the OUP without letting you see them, but decided that you might want to alter the opening phrase (!) and perhaps add a word of two at the end about help from friends... If you make any alterations please do not make them <u>between</u> my pencil marks. Where names of authors and publishers are concerned I have adhered strictly to the forms of acknowledgement required by <u>a</u>. general usage in previous O.U.P. anthologies; <u>b</u>. forms specially requested by authors or publishers for this anthology (see Masefield, for example!!)

IF YOU ARE MAKING ANY ALTERATIONS OR ADDITIONS PLEASE SEND ME THIS COPY WITH YOUR NOTES BY RETURN.

I am sorry to bother you with these things, but they have to be done.

D.W's proofs will of course be sent to her (as she asked) when they come from the Press. So far I have only had the people up to 1870.

Anne very pleased to get a letter from you.

I will let you know about the number of 'sets' still unsold (Broadsides) tomorrow. Have asked Cuala to look it up.

                                                                Yours
                                                                George.

[TLS]   [Riversdale, Willbrook, Rathfarnham, Dublin.]
                                                                June 17 [1936]

Dear Willy

There are only 24 bound sets left, and 13 sets of the unbound!! So Cuala has nothing to complain of. If we can get the new numbers out more punctually it ought to ensure a good year for Cuala.

The AE book is nearly ready; am going in tomorrow to see about the block for title page. Lolly is away for a week—she took all her clothes except one dress and wrote to Lily the next day to have it posted!!

Higgins is attacking O'Connor's book of verse[1]—he and O'Connor have quarrelled at the moment partly over the book and partly over the rejection of Lennox's play by the Abbey!![2] Blythe and O'Connor voted against it and O'Connor made the rejection the occasion for an attack on Lennox's work in general, whereupon Higgins bit O'Connor hard and as he says 'It is very funny but Lennox and I are now thrown together again!'

Yours
G.

[TLS & MS]   [Riversdale, Willbrook, Rathfarnham, Dublin.]
Friday [?19 June 1936]

Dear Willy

The fees for each poem of Kipling's is fifteen guineas, (five for England, five for Canada and five for USA) IF YOU ARE ADDING ONE OR TWO YOU MUST WIRE OXFORD UNIVERSITY PRESS AT ONCE THROUGH WATT ASKING THEM TO HOLD UP PROOFS AND LIST OF ACKNOWLEDGEMENTS UNTIL EXTRA KIPLING POEMS ARE SENT. Please also WIRE TO ME, [MS] stating which poems you are adding[1]

In haste to get the post.

G.

[ALS]   PENNS IN THE ROCKS, | WITHYHAM, | SUSSEX.
Saturday [20 June 1936]

My dear Dobbs

---

[1] O'Connor's *Three Old Brothers and Other Poems* was published by Thomas Nelson in 1936.

[2] Although there had been many revivals of earlier plays by LR, his *Killycreggs in Twilight*, produced on 19 Apr. 1937, was the first new play produced by the Abbey since *Church Street*, 21 May 1934. The rejected play was probably LR's *When Lovely Woman: A Comedy in Three Acts*, which was produced by Hilton Edwards at the Gate Theatre 18 Aug. 1936, and described disapprovingly as 'one of Robinson's astounding failures and as unwholesome as a play could be' (*Joseph Holloway's Irish Theatre*, ii: *1932–1937*, ed. Robert Hogan and Michael J. O'Neill (1969), 59).

[1] Kipling is represented in the anthology by two poems, 'A St. Helena Lullaby' and 'The Looking-Glass (A Country Dance)'; see 26 Mar. 1937.

To morrow Sunday I return to London. I shall stay in London about a week, number of days depending upon Dulacs report about the C I.D.[1] I must also see Turner, Sturge Moore etc The proof of Anthology came last night. <I shall send> I notise a misprint in second York Powell poem 'day' instead of 'clay'. You have probably corrected it. One of Wilfred Blunts poems is I think too long & should be condensed.[2] I shall go into the question of Kipling again with Lady Dorothy as soon as I hear the price he charges

I have finished all my play except last scene & a few lines in the scene just before it & I have a subject for a ballad.

If Higgins could suggest a poem or two from his own work (Has he begun his gypsey dance play?)[3] one or two from Gogorty & Stephens & one from Fran O Connor <also some other young poet>, we will have all the literary material for our first six Broadsides & <I think all the music except for the> all most all the music

Yrs ev
WB Yeats

[ALS] SAVILE CLUB, | 69, BROOK STREET. W. 1.

Tuesday [23 June 1936]

My dear Dobbs

I came up Sunday & expect to get back on Monday. As I can do little in the day I cannot get away sooner. I am working at my play—I read it on Thursday to Dulac[1]

Dulac has been to C. I D. They have nothing a gainst the Swami & never sent anybody to Mrs Foden

I have had a naive letter from the Swami—full of happiness at seeing his Master again. He took the labels off his luggage that nobody might know he was back 'Soon I will tell them' he says 'and retire'[2]

---

[1] Among her many mischievous denunciations, Mrs Foden had claimed to Dulac and Commander Hillgarth, who was now in England, that the Criminal Investigation Department was investigating the Swami's activities. In addition, Margot Ruddock's husband Raymond Lovell had written to the police in Bombay making enquiries about the ashram run by Shri Bhagwân Hamsa (*Ah, Sweet Dancer*, 113).

[2] WBY printed selections from 'The Wisdom of Merlyn' (1914) by Wilfrid Scawen Blunt.

[3] The only recorded play by Higgins is *A Deuce of Jacks*, a comedy with ballads and dance, produced at the Abbey on 16 Sept. 1935.

[1] A draft of *The Herne's Egg*, which is not published until 1938.

[2] Shree Purohit Swami left Majorca on 16 May; WBY, GY and ABY returned to London by steamer on 26 May and WBY went to stay with DW in Sussex until 23 June. GY met him at Holyhead on 29 June to accompany him back to Dublin, managing to keep out of the photographs taken of the group meeting him on the pier when he disembarked.

The heat is immense. I am in my silk dressing gown

> Yrs ev
> WB Yeats

I have put 'St Helens Lulleby' & 'Looking Glass' instead of 'Danny Deaver'³

[TLS]
RIVERSDALE, | WILLBROOK, |
RATHFARNHAM, | DUBLIN
August 14 1936

My dear Anne

Thank you for returning my black sand-shoes; most gratefully received!!!!!! I hope you got two books I sent you. As I said in note enclosed in the 'Silent Woman' I have a reason for asking you to do what I suggested and if you arent doing it you can kick yourself.¹ It does not matter in the least that you have not got books to help you with the 'period'. Go ahead with designs and damn history. 'Deirdre' was bloody (I am assuming that neither you nor Olive will give voice to my true opinion on that play—).² The production was bloody, the 'famous actress' was, as your father wrote in his own pen-work to MacLiammoir, 'a Camberwell canary, a Blackpool sparrow' and I forget the other epithets. The costumes were HELL:: Deirdre wore large golden hair plaited for about two feet below her ears and ending, as far as I can remember in about six inches of wound gold coils and about nine inches of curls below; her dress was of the purest white (in my young days you would call the material nun's veiling) embroidered with tre-foils (disguised shamrocks) in scarlet and gold. You may remember that she and Naisi arrived on horseback. We had the horses hoofs most realistically portrayed off-stage by Barney.³ For some reason unknown to me her incredible nun's-veiling-scarlet-and gold costume had a bright green tongue-leaved

---

³ Added at the top of the page; his first choice for Kipling's verse in the anthology was the popular Barrack-Room Ballad 'Danny Deever' (1890).

¹ ABY was staying with GY's friend Olive Craig in her cottage at Malahide. *Epicœne, or The Silent Woman* was a comedy by Ben Jonson (1572–1637), first performed in 1609. See GY to ABY, 21 Aug. 1936 for her reasons for suggesting ABY complete a design.

² WBY's *Deirdre*, directed by Hugh Hunt, designed by Tanya Moiseiwitsch, with music composed by the new music director Frederick May (1911–85) was produced at the Abbey on 10 Aug. 1936, with MacLiammóir playing Naisi and the English actress Jean Forbes-Robertson Deirdre. WBY ordered the play to be withdrawn, and after the week's run the Yeatses had a lunch at Riversdale on 16 August with the unfortunate actress as guest of honour.

³ Bernard 'Barney' Murphy (d. 1938), prompter and stagehand with the company for more than thirty years, was one of seven members of the Abbey who took part in the 1916 Rising and remained active in the IRA until 1921; he was associated with O'Casey in the Saint Lawrence O'Toole Pipe Band.

edge.. This may have been because the costume maker had created the costume two inches too short.... Anyway Deirdre had ridden a-horseback for many miles—side-saddle of course as the dress was very narrow—and her gold crown and so on and so forth were speckless.

Naisi was killed (off scene) with a scimitar (probably a scimitar used in 'HASSAN')[1] and the very curious thing was that in the final death scene Naisi's throat had not been cut. Now this was curious because we had a marvellous exhibition of blood on scimitar (see diagram enclosed A) which suggested head being cut off. The death exhibit was most beautiful. Naisi lay dead complete with Deirdre in a lighted square (see diagram B) flood-light from right. Torches came from right also. Poor lambs, poor torches! Madame Tussauds chamber of horrors, (black curtains framed their background)

The public has adored it.

Yours affly
George Yeats

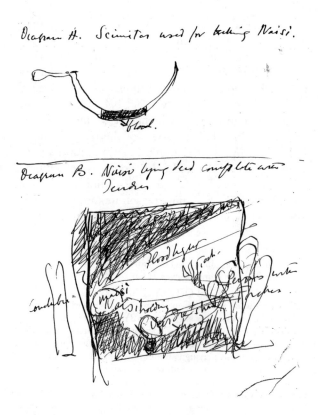

[1] *Hassan* by James Elroy Flecker had been produced by the Abbey on 1 June 1936.

[ALS]   Riversdale | Rathfarnham | Dublin
                                                        August 21. 1936

My dear Anne

Unless you refuse & I don't think you will!!, you go from Monday September 7th every day from 11–1.30 to work on scene painting, designing, etc. at Abbey Theatre. Miss Moisewitch[1] is to teach you all she knows, with a view to your being employed at Abbey in her place when she leaves. This will not be for a year probably. For the first 3 months you will not be paid. After 3 months <u>unless you are thrown out</u>, you will be paid a pound a week; <u>if</u> you are taken on when she leaves, you will probably get £4 a week.[2]

When you get £1 a week it will be your dress allowance. <u>When</u> you get £4 you will contribute part to me for living expenses unless you decide to have a flat of your own.

You will go to art school every afternoon for the present.

I didnt tell you anything about it before because I hadnt made final arrangements with Hunt. About 2 weeks ago the question of an art student to work under Moisewitsch arose (2 previous ones sent by Atkinson Metropolitan S. of Art[3] left Abbey because they really wanted to be portrait painters) & so I ransacked all your drawers etc to find any theatre work to submit!!

I hope you will like this idea as much as I think you will!!

You will sometimes have to work in the evenings at Abbey & in any case will <u>always</u> have to be at Abbey for dress rehearsals. *You will have an opportunity of really learning <u>all</u> the theatre work etc. & if you will work & use your head, it will be the beginning of a career.*

I felt I must put a parental exordium into this letter* ! ! ! !

Please let me know what you think of this scheme.

                                                        Yours
                                                        George Yeats

Typewriter lost a spring—alas!—

[1] Tanya Moiseiwitsch (1914–2003) had recently been appointed the first head of design at the Abbey Theatre; working closely with Hugh Hunt, artistic director, she designed over 50 productions before returning in January 1939 to England where she established a reputation as one of the most significant stage and costume designers of the century. ABY's first responsibility was to assist Tanya in designing a production of Dunsany's *The Glittering Gate* in August 1936.

[2] For the first three months as assistant, she received no salary, then was paid 10s. a week, 30s. a few months before Moiseiwitsch left, and as Abbey Stage Designer £3.

[3] George Atkinson (1880–1941), engraver and designer and director of the Dublin Metropolitan School of Art, later renamed the National College of Art; both WBY and AE were students at the School in the mid-1880s.

[TLS]   RIVERSDALE, | WILLBROOK, |
                                                 RATHFARNHAM, | DUBLIN.
                                                 Wednesday September 30 [1936]

Dear Willy

I have sent broadcast direct to BBC.[1] As I am not sure from your wire about the four anthology pages—you say 'choose four'—if you meant me to choose and send them direct, I send you my four pages with the O.U. Press form filled up. If you do not like the four pages I have chosen please wire suggestions and I will send you by wire the numbers of the pages of your suggestions. AND KEEP THE OXFORD UNIVERSITY PRESS FORM SO THAT YOU CAN CHANGE THE NUMBERS AND SAVE YOURSELF TROUBLE.* See end of letter.

I enclose the BBC letter (the latest, giving their change of the hour.)[2]

I am so sorry that I sent you off with so incomplete papers etc. I let myself get distracted with that Broadcast and all its alterations, and then, too, with Anne in bed, I hadnt an assistant.

I hope you are looking after yourself, and that you will remember that if you get a cold I would rather come over at once and not wait until you are very ill! ! I have a suitcase ready packed and English money, so you will probably NOT get a cold. On previous occasions I was unprepared, and to be unprepared is tempting misfortune. You were so well I dont expect a 'wire', but you must not be cross with me if I telephone to Dulac (cheap rates at night after nine) to ask how you are. You can always explain it by saying 'my wife is very fussy'.

I am going to the Robinsons for Sunday night—Lennox is celebrating a 'fiftieth' birthday.. am to stay the night. Apart from that I am getting teeth stopped, a new dress and coat, and so on. Michael has still got 'bugs' in his throat; I am afraid we may have him with us another month. When Dr Collis[3] gives me a definite sort of date I shall have to think about a tutor.

Anne went in the Abbey yesterday at 10.30. Tanya Moiseiwitsch turned up at 1 pm—hadnt been expecting Anne! She earns (Tanya) her salary easily! If

---

[1] WBY had been asked by the BBC to give the eighteenth National Lecture on Modern Poetry, to be delivered on 11 Oct. 1936; *Modern Poetry* (London, 1936) first appeared in *The Listener*, 14 Oct. 1936.

[2] Enclosure missing.

[3] Michael contracted scarlet fever while at school in June and was quarantined for six weeks, but his problems were compounded by trouble with his glands. Dr William Robert Fitzgerald Collis (1900–75), paediatrician at the Meath Hospital, was a specialist in rheumatic fever; author of two plays produced by the Gate Theatre, his first play, *Marrow Bone Lane*, was such a success that he was able to establish a fund for tubercular children; on his return from working for the Red Cross in Bergen-Belsen concentration camp he established Cerebral Palsy Ireland (now Enable Ireland), where his first patient was Christy Brown, author of *My Left Foot*.

Anne is ever taken on in her place I think you will have to go into that five pounds a week. OR superintend, through me, Anne's activities when there is nothing for her to do at Abbey. Otherwise Anne will dilute her energy with green room gossip. As it seems impossible for Anne to go with any regularity to the '2 to 4' life classes at the Hibernian Academy, I have told her that she must go three evenings a week to the night schools at the School of Art. On the days that she has to work in the afternoons at the Abbey she will have, if she is going to School of Art class in the evening, to have a dinner in Dublin. I am <u>absolutely determined</u> that she must continue her drawing at one art school or another, and I know you will back me up in this. The difficulty about irregular attendance at the Hibernian Academy etc is that she will take up the place of a regular student, and as she may be irregular it does not seem to me to be fair. I have told Dermod O'Brien about this difficulty.⁴

Yours
George Yeats.

[MS]*I chose these pages to illustrate preface (dealing with Kipling & William Watson): Hopkins: York Powell: Eliot:

[ALS]   SAVILE CLUB, | 69, BROOK STREET. W.1
                        Thursday [1 Oct. 1936]

My dear Dobbs

All goes well. This afternoon at 5.30 I read the play to Spate (if this is his name—Becket I mean) Maurice Brown, Turner, Collis, the Dulacs in Dulacs studio.¹

I could not get a good green for a shirt—we shall have to get that in Dublin under your eye but I have ordered two red shirts. I have bought the needful socks etc.

Turner goes to Penns in the Rocks after my broadcast & Lady Dorothy has appealed to him to help her to make me carry out your directions for my wellfare.² He thinks she is much desturbed.

---

⁴ Dermod O'Brien as president of the Academy was in charge of the Royal Hibernian Academy Schools.

¹ Robert Speaight (1904–76), by now a notable Shakespearian actor, had performed Thomas à Becket in Eliot's *Murder in the Cathedral*, which had been directed by E. Martin Browne (1900–80), specialist in religious and verse drama.

² WBY had been ill again in mid-August and on 19 September GY wrote to DW, enclosing a typed slip with diet: 'About "rests"—very difficult to say. At present he lives in a routine: comes down at 3 pm, goes for a drive or walk in his "pram" or wanders about garden. Sees people & always rests after a couple of hours of talk. That is to say he is firmly left alone.—But when he is away I don't believe he'll stay in bed until 3. So he probably ought to lie down or sit by himself for at least 2 hours between tea & dinner & one hour at least between lunch

Your ham sandwich enabled me to make the acquaintance of 'Gypsey Nina'[3] She sat opposite me in the train. When the ticket collector came she had no ticket. Perhaps she had ment to go third & found carrages full, or did not know you could book through. She seemed horrified at the price. Half an hour later she said 'I told the waiter I was having lunch. Now I dont want any lunch. Will I have to pay?' I said 'no' & offered her a ham-sandwich. I guessed that having paid for her ticket she could not offord lunch. She ate the sandwich & was plainly very hungry. When she saw me drink milk she got a glass for her self. Then came all her life history I had time to draw out—you remember my habit in that matter which used to shock Lady Gregory—I soon had to stop talking fearing to get tired. She was returning from the Theatre Royal where she had sung & played the accordian. She was from the middle west had crossed the atlantic half a dozen times & that night was going to write a long letter to her mother & found 'life very expensive'. Then regretfully just when the talk looked like getting interesting I thought it wise to pretend that I must sleep.

Yours always
WB Yeats

[ALS]   SAVILE CLUB, | 69, BROOK STREET. W.1

Sunday [4 Oct. 1936]

My dear Dobbs

All goes well. I have nothing of illness about me except that I soon tire. I have just had lunch—rice pudding, & a salad—too night I shall probably have an apple or two. Yesterday I had chicken.

I read my play to 'Beckett' & to Maurice Brown at Dulacks. Both young men enthusiastic I am to send play to Ashley Dukes. 'Just the kind of play he likes'[1]

I agree with your page from Preface (XII) also the page with Powell (30). I do not much care for the Hopkins or the Ellot. Could you send me the pages of the Michael Field's & of Turners 'Mannequins' (your own suggestion)

Now about Anne. I most passionately object to Anne staying at Abbey with nothing to do but to gossip in the Green Room. She should 'by her fathers

---

& tea! However, as Edmund Dulac said to me, "He is the most obstinate man I have ever known". I find the only way to make him rest is to plant him in a room by himself with a detective story and leave him sternly alone. I am glad he can go to England now, because I doubt very much if he will be able to go over again, at any rate unaccompanied.* In any case he will have to 'stay put' from abt October 20 to mid-April...*This is of course private.'

³ 'Gypsy Nina', née Helen M. Swan (*c.*1901–1939), was a professional accordionist, born in Illinois, who spent most of her professional life performing in Europe.

¹ Although Dukes continued to make vague promises of interest as late as 28 Dec. 1936 when he acknowledged receipt of *The Herne's Egg*, none of WBY's plays was produced by the Mercury Theatre (*LWBY* 2, 587).

orders' wait at one half hour & then come home. I will bring the matter before the board on my return & have fixed hours insisted upon. Both must have an hour of arrival fixed. It may not be so easy to say when their work must end

I go to Penns in the Rocks to-morrow. I am reading Aldous Huxley new book—not so far very good—I am at about page 60.[2]

Ever affecly
WB Yeats

[TLS]

RIVERSDALE, | WILLBROOK, |
RATHFARNHAM, | DUBLIN.
October 5 [1936]

Dear Willy

The page with Turner's Mannequins, and the Michael Fields were cut up for your broadcast. I am sending you the remains of all paged proofs, to choose from. I am sorry, but I asked you at the time about using the proofs for the broadcast and you agreed.

I have told Anne that you object to her sitting about in the Green Room, and that if she does not make definite arrangements with Tanya about her work you will have to get the Board to arrange regular hours. She was very much alarmed and says it will not happen again!! At present she is on a job of painting all alone so is fully occupied all day. I gather the reason Tanya did not turn up was that she had not realised Anne was coming in as Anne had been away with a cold....

Edmund[1] may have told you that he told me on the telephone last Saturday that you were 'exceedingly well, very much better than you were in London last June' Tell Lady Dorothy this.

Yours
G.

[ALS]

PENNS IN THE ROCKS, | WITHYHAM, | SUSSEX.
Friday [9 Oct. 1936]

My dear Dobbs

I am very well in every way. I did not go to London for rehersal as two B.B.C were coming here. Last night Miss Matheson reahersed me. I shall be

---

[2] Aldous Leonard Huxley (1894–1963), prolific essayist, novelist, humanist, and pacifist, had published his dystopian vision in *Brave New World* (1932) and followed this in 1936 with *Eyeless in Gaza* which reflects his increased interest in mysticism; a close friend of D. H. Lawrence, he had, like the Yeatses, been a regular visitor to Garsington Manor.

[1] Despite the Dulacs' assistance in furthering WBY's amours, GY appreciated their friendship.

motored up to morrow afternoon, and fetched next morning. I have spent the last two days adding three pages—asked for by BBC to Broadcast & this afternoon Miss Matheson does the typing

I find that the trouble about the corrected ballad is that some reviewer said that <u>Fire</u> showed traces of my style & so too might the corrected ballad. It is certainly nonsense about Fire.[1]

Last night we had collecten of Rothensteins—son, sons wife, sons wife sister all collected because Dorothy misread a letter of W. Rothensteins & thought they could find tunes for ballads—Rothenstein ment a different member of his family all to geather.[2] Dorothy very bored is sending them back to town by an early train. Rothensteins son has married a neice of Desmond Fitzgerald's. She is an artist as is her sister —they speak with great respect of their uncle, the great man of the family, but have never seen him. They are well read & generally advanced but I suspect the Catholic cow is still there behind their pretty very painted masks. They are twins & astonishing alike.[3] Last night Dorothy who is <incredibly emotional when one reads poetry, & gives> the most emotional audience possible kept me reading out bits of the antholgy Blunts 'Wisdom of Merlyn', all the Gogorty poems, most of her own, most of mine; I suspect that the rest of the audience was merely polite She is sending you some rare plant or bush. It must root and grow.

I am glad that Anne has taken my directions about Abbey attendance seriously. Find out if the same thing happens again

Yrs affly
WB Yeats
P.T.O.

My chief addition the broadcast is a paregraph about Irish literature & account—with quotations <of>—Gogorty

Yrs ev

---

[1] WBY was in the habit of revising other's poetry as well as his own; the ballad referred to is probably 'The Ballad of Reading Gaol' by Oscar Wilde, which he rather heavily edited for publication in the anthology. 'Fire' was the long poem by DW which led his selections from her work.

[2] The portrait artist William Rothenstein (1872–1943), knighted in 1931, was principal of the Royal College of Art in London 1920–35; his three-volume autobiography records friendships with most of the distinguished names in literary and artistic circles of the 1890s throughout the first half of the 20th century. Rothenstein had suggested that his daughter Rachel (1903–89) could sing some ballads for WBY and DW. WBY first sat for him in 1898, and frequently thereafter; see *Since Fifty Men and Memories, 1922–1938: Recollections of William Rothenstein* (London, 1939).

[3] William Rothenstein's son, the printmaker and painter Michael (also known as 'Billy') (1908–93), married the artist Elizabeth 'Betty' 'Duffy' Fitzgerald (b. 1919) in 1936; they were later divorced and Elizabeth, who had an identical twin sister, married the graphic artist and typographer Eric Ayers (1921–2001), continuing to paint as 'Duffy Ayers'.

[ALCS[1]]   SAVILE CLUB, | 69, BROOK STREET. W.1
                                                    Oct 12 [1936]

My dear Dobbs: All went well. With the new passages I was exactly my
time. I am getting you a wireless through the B.B.C, I get a discount which
should pay the tax, & [as] they are getting it should be the best
                                                    Yrs ev
                                                    WB Yeats

I return in an hour by motor to Penns in the Rocks, Turner comes with
me.

                                                    P.T.O.

I was motored up yesterday & motored to the B.B.C & then back here I had
no fateague

[TLS]   RIVERSDALE, | WILLBROOK, |
                             RATHFARNHAM, | DUBLIN.
                                     Tuesday [13 Oct. 1936]

My dear Willy
    Your broadcast came through extremely well—very clear. Your letter
came this morning; I am very excited about the wireless. Thank you so very
much. I hope you told the BBC that we have not got electric light so cannot
have an instrument which 'plugs into' a main. It would save a lot of delay
at the customs when I meet you if it was sent direct from London; otherwise
we would probably be kept waiting for half an hour or more.
    I am sending some press cuttings from a New York paper called 'Time'
which may amuse you... they give photographs of the king with Mrs Simpson
on his recent holiday!![1] Also the reviews of the new George Shiels play at
the Abbey.[2] Sheelah was rather a bore; overdid it, and was rather too well
dressed for the part which made her over-acting seem worse. The house is
sure to be full all the week.

---

[1] On Savile Club letter card, but from Penns in the Rocks.

[1] Unlike the English press, American newspapers and journals felt no compunction about
publishing accounts and photographs of Edward VIII on holiday that summer with the
divorcée Wallis Simpson on board the steamboat *Nahlin* in the eastern Mediterranean.

[2] Enclosures missing. *The Jailbird* by George Shiels opened 12 Oct. 1936 with Shelah Richards playing one of the major roles; *The Times* spoke of her 'brave attempt' at the role, but
Holloway was even more scathing.

Denis Johnston says that Frank O'Connor has written to Nelson's to say that his (D.J's) collection of recent Irish plays will not do at all and that they must not publish the book as it stands....I could not find out what Denis proposes to do about it as Frank O'Connor came up at that moment. Is Frank O'Connor one of Nelson's readers,[3] or is it just high-hattedness?

Yours
George.

[TLS]

RIVERSDALE, | WILLBROOK, |
RATHFARNHAM, | DUBLIN.
October 19 [1936]

Dear Willy

I enclose two letters from the O.U.P. The one I have marked 'A' has ommitted <u>The Irish Press</u> and as it includes the Independent and Irish Times you might add the Irish Press? Also among the list of societies to be circularised the Irish Academy of Letters is omitted whereas The Dublin Literary Society is included. When writing to Gerard Hopkins[1] remember to address it to the London address.

I enclose a letter from Sir Arnold Wilson—(the <u>Nineteenth Century</u> man.[2]) which needs an answer.

I send this to Penns—how much longer do you stay there? Let me know so that I can send letters to Club where I suppose you will stay for a few days or a week.

Dr MacCartan[3] gave a large dinner party at the Shelbourne last week (private room) and I hear made a long speech which was all about you, chiefly attacking Ireland and the Irish for their treatment of you—their lack of appreciation, their fifty years of attack, etc. He had ministers past and present, protestants and catholics, in fact a good mixture! Wish I had heard it.

Yours affly
George.

---

[3] Nelson and Company had published O'Connor's recent book of poems.

[1] Presumably to the executors, the Society of Jesus, c/o the London address of Oxford University Press, publishers of Gerard Manley Hopkins.

[2] Sir Arnold Talbot Wilson (b. 1884), editor of the journal *The Nineteenth Century and After*, was managing director of d'Arcy Health Research Board, chairman of the International Exhibition of Persian Art (1929–30), and in 1939 became chairman of the Board of Trade Cinema Films Advisory Committee; see letter of 26 Mar. 1937.

[3] Patrick MacCartan, see letter of 18 Dec. 1932.

[ALS]   SAVILE CLUB, | 69, BROOK STREET. W.1
                                                    Oct 22 [1936]

My dear Dobbs: Last Saturday I was motored up to London—Dorothy having to visit relations. I got a violent cold & for some days was confined to
my room at the Savile, yesterday (Wednesday) I emerged, quite well again
& began my London round—lunched with Elizabeth Pelham¹ stayed till tea
discussing Foden, dined with Dulac. Today I give lunch to Hilda Matheson
& head of 'talks department' BBC, to consider a scheme of which more
later.² To night I dine with Turner to continue said scheme, to morrow
Dulac etc. On Saturday I return to Dorothy for week end. Then after seeing Olivia I shall return to Dublin unless stopped by the unforseen. My cold
complicated all my plans.
   'The Mercury Theatre' has read my play &, subject to the Censor, wants
to do it
   The Broad-cast has drawn blood. On Tuesday Turner saw Seigfried Sassoon in the Park. Sassoon crossed road to avoid Turner, Turner followed, Sassoon turned his back, Turner prodded him in the back with umbrella. Sassoon
turned & said 'Poetry is dead & Yeats has given it the last kick' 'Why'? 'Praising
Edith Sitwell & Ricketts like that' (real reason Turner quoted & not Sassoon)³
                                                          Yrs affly
                                                          WB Yeats

[ALS]   SAVILE CLUB, | 69, BROOK STREET. W.1
                                                    Oct 24 [1936]

My dear Dobbs
   Unless I write to the contrary I shall return on Friday next.
   Your wireless set is being sent direct.

   ¹ Lady Elizabeth ('Betty') Jocelyn Pelham (1899–1975), eldest daughter of Sir Jocelyn
Brudenell Pelham, 6th Earl of Chichester and a devoted follower of the Swami's master
Bhagwân Shree Hamsa, with whom she studied in India in 1935; she co-founded the
Institute of Mysticism which was established as a London base for Shree Purohit Swami's
work. WBY became infatuated with her but in 1937 she gently rejected his suggestion that
they travel to India together, and in 1948 she married Captain Charles Murray Beazley.
   ² Matheson had already resigned from the BBC but still had considerable influence; the
other guest was George Reginald Barnes (1904–60), BBC Radio Talks producer from 1935 and
in 1950 director of BBC Television, who later wrote an account of his collaboration with WBY
(see 'George Barnes's "W. B. Yeats and Broadcasting" 1940', *YA5*, 189–94).
   ³ WBY included four poems by Siegfried Loraine Sassoon (1886–1967), friend of Robert
Graves and Rupert Brooke, neither of whom was represented in the anthology; Sassoon's
autobiographical novels vividly recount his experiences in the First World War; he became
friends of pacifists Bertrand Russell and the Morrells, and briefly visited the Yeatses in Rapallo.
Twelve poems by W. J. R. Turner were included and WBY praised him in the introduction.

The present idea is to send my new play to America with 'Player Queen' & 'Murder in the Cathedral' by Ashley to a very changable man.

Miss Matheson, Turner, Margot Colles & Watkins, verse-speaker valued by BBC & quite good,[1] are working out a series of recitations, combinations of singing & speaking. I am to get my final letter of acceptance or rejection from the B.B.C next week. I think they will accept. I am to introduce & recommend scheme but need [not] be present. I can gramaphone my few words in Dublin. The first rehersal last Thursday was quite beautiful. Richpins song (Trenches translation)[2] by Watkings. Lionel Johnsons 'What are the winds'[3] by two voices, Watkins speaking & Margot singing, my 'Three things' & 'I am of Ireland' mixed singing & speaking by Margot, two songs by Dorothy sung by Margot. There will be several recitations without singing by Watkins to be decided on later. In all cases music will be used between poems & sometimes between verses. If our two experiment performance succeed there will be twelve of Modern Poetry & everbody will get a little money.

I am just off to Penns in the Rocks where I stay until Tuesday & am longing for the rest, at the same time I wonderfully well & much congratulated upon my improved appearance.

Yrs ev
WB Yeats

I have seen Watt & as I have now heard from Swami Watt can go a head with all my business.

[ALS]
RIVERSDALE, | WILLBROOK, |
RATHFARNHAM, | DUBLIN.
Monday [26 Oct. 1936]

Dear Willy

Glad to hear your cold is quite gone. <u>Friday</u> is a very bad to travel as it is the day of the <u>cheap weekend</u> excursion. But unless you wire to contrary

---

[1] Arthur Ronald Dare Watkins (1904–2001) had been a poetry and prose reader at the BBC until 1932, when he began a long illustrious teaching career at Harrow, distinguished by his Shakespeare productions in which scenery and lighting were eschewed in favour of emphasis on the poetry; he continued to work occasionally for the BBC and later gave a series of lecture tours in the United States, Canada, and Italy.

[2] A translation of 'La Chanson de Marie-des-Anges' by the French poet, novelist and dramatist Jean Richepin (1849–1926) was published by Frederic Herbert Trench as 'Jean Richepin's Song' in *New Poems* (1907); there were many musical settings of the poem.

[3] The title as given in WBY's anthology is 'To Morfydd' by Lionel Pigot Johnson (1867–1902), OS's cousin and WBY's old friend, a fellow member of the Rhymers' Club.

I will meet you at Holyhead that day. You may find yourself delayed by the B.B.C. arrangement, but I hope for not too long. Anne is working very hard at Abbey & I think is getting on well.

Yours
G.

[ALS]   SAVILE CLUB, | 69, BROOK STREET. W.1
Thursday [29 Oct. 1936]

My dear Dobbs

I shall cross next Tuesday. I doubt if Saturday is any better than Friday & Macneices <u>Agamemnon</u> is Sunday night[1], for which I may have to dress, which would interfere with packing—hence Tuesday.

I am exceeding well except for a cough which is irritating but not important. When you wired I was already uncertain about wisdom of crossing until it was better

I saw Faber & Faber to day—<u>Upanishads</u> in January; Macmillan want <u>Vision</u> at once, Scribner pressing for their expensive edition, & Dent have taken Margot[2] & with the <u>Broadsides</u> on top of the rest I shall be busy the moment I get back; & am pleased to prolong present idleness. No final letter yet from B.B.C but should come this week

Yrs ev
WB Yeats

Watt says there will be much money in Scribner edition

---

[1] Irish poet and playwright, Frederick Louis MacNeice (1907–63) had published his first volume of verse with Faber and Faber in 1935 and was now lecturing in the Department of Greek at Bedford College for Women, University of London. The *Agamemnon* of Aeschylus, translated by Louis MacNeice, with music by Benjamin Britten and masks and costumes by Robert Medley, was produced by the Group Theatre at the Westminster Theatre on 1 Nov. 1936; the director was Rupert Doone, Robert Speaight played Agamemnon, Veronica Turleigh Clytemnestra, and Vivienne Bennett Cassandra.

[2] *The Lemon Tree*, a collection of twenty poems by Margot Ruddock (Collis), was published by Dent in 1937 with WBY's poem, 'At Barcelona' and introductory essays by both WBY and Margot with varying descriptions of how they met and the incidents in Majorca and Barcelona.

Part Seven
Endings
1937—1939

'I have a suitcase ready packed and English money, so you will probably NOT get a cold.' But despite this warning from George and his extraordinary vitality, WBY suffered from intermittent illnesses and general fatigue. This did not prevent him from continuing work on the Broadsides, exchanging poetry with Wellesley, making ambitious plans for a series of broadcasts for the BBC, enlisting support for the establishment of the Irish Academy of Letters, and attempting to put both the Abbey Theatre and the Cuala Press on a stronger footing. Money continued to be a worry, eased at last by funds raised in the United States by the indefatigable Patrick McCartan.

In June 1937 WBY embarked on what would be his last love affair, with Edith Shackleton Heald, a friend of the Dulacs. For the next two and a half years he spent less and less time in Ireland, alternating between Wellesley's Sussex home, Penns in the Rocks, where artists and writers were invited to establish a new 'modernity', and respites at the Heald sisters' country home, The Chantry House. Resigned to this last alliance, and even grateful for help in caring for the ageing tiger, George encouraged more frequent visits to England while she watched over the children, tended to the Cuala Press and other social and publishing affairs in a Dublin increasingly less attractive to both of them. But with his daughter now embarking on a career in theatre design, WBY's attention returned to the dramatic form, culminating in the magnificent *Purgatory*, which Anne designed for the Abbey Theatre. Verse continued to flow until his final days.

His last two winters, assisted by the generosity of his American admirers, were spent in the south of France, with either Edith or George in attendance. Together in Menton, where Michael joined them for the school holidays, George once again took dictation from the inspired poet. Now Anne was enlisted in the keeping of all Willy's irons hot in Dublin. When the end came it was sudden and, although long feared, a surprise.

1937

[ALS]   THE ATHENÆUM, | PALL MALL, S.W.I.
                                  Monday [7 Mar. 1937]

My dear George
    This Club is a delight to me.¹ I have a telephone at my bed side so when
friend's telephone I have no to go out on to a cold corridor as at the Savile.
Then I can get in the light-lunchen room exactly the food I want & there is
the library where there is almost everything one can reasonably want—there
are two great reading rooms.
    I ordered my new suit—I thought I got the old stuff until Dulac spoke of
the old as oat meal colour & I think there is a hint of red in what I have
got.
    Could you send me that brilliant shirt. I have ordered blue shirts but they
may not be done as soon as the new suit. Then I have 'a pullover' which
is I think exactly right—it is dull read—to harmonise that bright red shirt
with the rest of me.
    Then please send me two of each <u>Broadside</u>. They were forgotten
    I have started writing verse—but it may come to nothing

                                                        Yrs ev
                                                        WB Yeats

[ALS]   THE ATHENÆUM, | PALL MALL, S.W.I.
                                     March 10 [1937]

My dear Dobbs
    I have quarrelled with Ottoline. I enclose her last & a copy of my last, up
to this last letter I have been very polite.

    ¹ For some years WBY had discussed with William Rothenstein the possibility of being
nominated a member of The Athenaeum, known for its excellent library, and founded in 1824
as an 'association of individuals known for their scientific and literary attainments, artists of
eminence in any class of the fine arts and noblemen and gentlemen distinguished as liberal
patrons of science, literature or the arts'. On 16 Feb. 1937 he was elected a member under
Rule 2, restricted to 'a certain number of persons of distinguished eminence in their particular
fields', which meant that no entrance fee was required and that the annual subscription was
reduced by two-thirds.

All well—I am keeping well—obviously improving in health & I dine out nightly without fateague.

Yrs ev
WB Yeats

I have countless letters to write—alas

[ALS Encl]   THE ATHENÆUM, | PALL MALL, S.W.1.
March 11 [1937]

Copy
Dear Ottoline
You would not have minded, it seems, if I had praised Turner & left out that sentence condemning his attack upon you. But even if I had forseen your anger I would have written that sentence.[1] When I praise a man of genius I cannot allow it to be thought that I am indifferent to his offences against manners, morals or taste (if I consider these offences of importance) I had to meet the same obstruction when I wrote of Dowson & Lionel Johnson only there the motive behind the obstruction was more respectable, being family & neighbourly affection[2] but the result was the same, a conspiracy against vital reality. This kind of refusal to face facts has made much English criticism notoriously worthless.

You have been cruelly & stupidly attacked by several men, & your defense is not an futile silence imposed upon your friends (the works of Huxley & Lawrence are in everybodys hands[3]) but that those friends among whom I still count myself hold you in honour and affection

Yrs ev
WBY

<I have not read the whole of <u>The Aesthetes</u> but what I did read was bad enough. It is possible therefore that I should strengthened the sentence>

[1] The offending sentence included the words 'a rich-natured friendly man he has in his satirical platonic dialogue *The Aesthetes* shot upon forbidden ground', that being Turner's satire on the Morrells, especially Ottoline as 'Lady Virginia Caraway' in *The Aesthetes* (1927).

[2] WBY's references to the Rhymers' Club were more politic: 'Some drank, drinking not as happy men drink but in solitude.... Some turned Catholic—that too was a tradition.... Lionel Johnson was the first convert; Dowson adopted a Catholic point of view without, I think, joining that church, an act requiring energy and decision.' Lionel Johnson, an alcoholic and repressed homosexual, was the cousin of OS, and Ernest Christopher Dowson (1867–1900), who died of alcoholism, was his good friend.

[3] Ottoline Morrell was satirized as 'Priscilla Wimbush' in *Crome Yellow* (1921), 'Mrs Aldwinkle' in *Those Barren Leaves* (1925), and 'Mrs Bidlake' in *Point Counter Point* (1928), all by Aldous Huxley, and 'Hermione Roddice' in *Women in Love* (1920) by D. H. Lawrence.

I only glanced through <u>The Aesthetes</u>, I had not known for instance that it attacked your husband. If I read the whole, it is possible I would have written more strongly but that would have increased publicity

[TLS¹]   RIVERSDALE, | WILLBROOK, |
                                              RATHFARNHAM, | DUBLIN.
                                              Thursday [11 Mar. 1937]

My dear Willy

I dont think I can get this note to the post today as we are snowed in...I was very glad to hear that you are comfortable at the Athenaeum.

I had a very pleasant week end with Bunch², rather hectic, seem to have spent most of the time in motors (the film of GREEN PASTURES³ was advertised as appearing in Southport so we rushed over there only to find it was to start three days later!) and since then I have been doing teeth and not very much else, with the exception of some measured diagrams to Anne's picture for the first play to be produced by the Abbey 'Experimental Theatre'⁴ which she hadnt time for. Tanya went to London to see her real father before he departed for his year and a half tour. She may stay here this week end, but her mother (Mrs Drinkwater)⁵ was badly injured in a motor accident last night so Tanya may not return.

Lennox writes that he has finished his new play, a comedy. I do hope it is not one of his plays for a London theatre.⁶ He returns about March 21, Dolly I believe stays somewhere en route. Dolly seems to have enjoyed Cannes in spite of the fact that Lennox had invited his entire family, or rather the entire family of his sister, to stay in the villa in relays!!

No nominations have come in, with the exception of the one for Miss Somerville, for the Academy. I am seeing Higgins tomorrow, Friday. I gather

---

    ¹ WBY has written 'Answered' at the top of this letter.
    ² The Shakespear family's nickname for Harry Tucker, GY's stepfather; as usual GY had accompanied WBY to London, taking the opportunity to visit her mother in Sidmouth.
    ³ The 1936 film based on the play by author and actor Marc Connelly, né Marcus Cook (1890–1980), who won a Pulitzer Prize for the 1930 stage production.
    ⁴ Established by a group of students in Ria Mooney's Abbey Theatre acting class in April 1937 to give young practitioners an opportunity to work and to produce plays that did not fall within the Abbey Theatre's range; their first productions were *The Phoenix* by 'N.O.B.' and *Alarm Among the Clerks*, by novelist and short story writer Mervyn Eugene Welply Wall (1908–97), both on 5 Apr. 1937 with designs by Gerald Hickey; on 5 June 1939 they produced *Harlequin's Positions*, by Jack B. Yeats, designed by ABY (see note to 6 Apr. 1938).
    ⁵ After divorcing the Ukrainian pianist Benno Moiseiwitsch (1890–1963), in 1924 the Australian violinist Daisy Kennedy (1893–1981) married the poet, dramatist, and manager of the Birmingham Repertory Theatre, John Drinkwater (1882–1937).
    ⁶ *Killycreggs in Twilight* by LR was produced at the Abbey Theatre on 19 Apr. 1937.

that he is still taking great care of his teeth which were taken out about ten days ago. I have a vast amount of gossip, Theatre gossip from Anne, and other gossip from indignant writers in 'Ireland Today' who have been attacked by the CHURCH in the usual underground manner,[7] but my mouth is so sore I do not feel lively enough to relate any of it.

Yours affly
George.

[ALS]   THE ATHENÆUM, | PALL MALL, S.W.1.
March 13 [1937]

My dear Dobbs

I enclose checque & account entery received from Watt.

The trouble with Ottoline, I think, is that I have praised Turner & perhaps lifted an enemy out of obscurity. She may feel too that I have neglected her for Dorothy Wellesley. My conscience has been a little disturbed on that point especially as it was she who introduced us.

Yrs ev
WB Yeats

[ALS]   THE ATHENÆUM, | PALL MALL, S.W.1.
March 14 [1937]

My dear Dobbs

Ottoline has made peace—she has written to advise me to see the Indian Ballet at the Savoy.[1] That letter of mine did the feat—she could not bear being classed among the obscurantists or obstructors. At least think it must have been that—that was the object of my simulated indignation.

My BBC broadcasted poems will be excellent—one man & two instruments.

---

[7] *Ireland Today*, a left-wing literary magazine edited by former IRA volunteer James L. O'Donovan (1896–1979) with contributions from Sean Ó'Faoláin, who was its first books editor, Frank O'Connor, Patrick Kavanagh, Bulmer Hobson, and Peadar O'Donnell among others, lasted from June 1936 to March 1938; one of the magazine's financial backers was WBY's friend and supporter Patrick McCartan of New York (Frank Shovlin, *The Irish Literary Periodical, 1923–1958* (London, 2004), 68–92).

[1] Uday Shankar and his company of Indian dancers and musicians performed at the Savoy Theatre the week of 9 Mar. 1937 and WBY attended on Friday 12 March. Formerly a student of painting under Sir William Rothenstein, Shankar (1900–77) was persuaded by the Russian ballerina Anna Pavlova (1881–1931) to pursue a dancing career instead.

Please send the red shirt—I have a dull-red pull-over & I want to test the combination.

I am keeping wonderfully well.

Yrs ev

WB Yeats

[TLS¹]   RIVERSDALE, | WILLBROOK, |
                                          RATHFARNHAM, | DUBLIN.
                                              March 15 [1937]

My dear Willy

Two letters postmarked March 11 arrived this morning, one containing cheque from Watt and one your correspondence with Ottoline. I am sorry about the quarrel. Had you seen her or was it all done by correspondance?

Anne is I am afraid disappointed because someone else's designs for the Experimental Theatre have been accepted instead of hers; the producer had practically said he would take hers. I think the reason may be that the other designer, a man called Hickie, had submitted highly finished work, whereas Anne only showed a rather rough picture. She is apparently to do the painting etc of the sets.² She went last night to a meeting of the cast, producer author etc. Tanya returns today; I hear that Mrs Drinkwater was badly cut in the face but was otherwise uninjured.

The snow has ceased today thank goodness. Our telephone is repaired and postal services seem to be recovering. We got no post on Friday or Saturday, why I do not know. It was very fortunate that you were away, for I dont imagine London was much afflicted by storms and in any case you were better off at the Club.

I am told that 'The Mothers' Unions' of England have sent a letter to the King's Proctor asking that Mrs Simpson's divorce should not be made absolute! Is this true? What frightful hypocrites people are. The author and producer of a film called 'We Three' was prosecuted in USA on the grounds that a child of fourteen ought not to have been allowed to act in such a film. They lost their case, but appealed and won on the grounds that the Judge had neither read the book nor seen the film!³

---

¹ WBY has written 'answered' at top of the letter.

² The chosen designs were by Gerard Hickey (Gearoid O hIceadha), brother of the Belfast producer Mary O'Malley (1918–2006) and later an architect; the producers were Frank Carney and Cecil Ford (1911–80) who later became a TV and film producer.

³ *These Three* (1936), a Hollywood film starring Merle Oberon, Miriam Hopkins, and Joel McCrea, was based on *The Children's Hour* (1934), a controversial play by Lillian Hellman (1905–84)

Good houses last week for Heffernans[4] in spite of the snow, or so I hear from the Abbey. That was for the first three days, but bookings may have been cancelled at the end of the week.

Yours
G.

[ALS]   THE ATHENÆUM, | PALL MALL, S.W.1.
March 16 [1937]

My dear Dobbs

At last I have got my correspondence up to date & without a typist or other help I finished it all yesterday morning.

No I have not seen Ottoline. I wrote to asked if I might come to see her & she replied by saying she did not think she ever wanted to see me again; but now all is peace.[1]

I enclose a naive article by Mrs Foden Swami says 'Mrs Foden has sent it as a circular letter to all the important daileys in India as is her custom'.[2]

Here is what happened at the Abbey which reduced Miss O Connor to such tears. Boss has an impossible wife he has started an affair with Miss O'Connor.[3] Some virtuous member of the company sent an anonimous letter to Miss O Connor's father who turned her out; & to Boss Shield's wife who came to the theatre & slapped Miss O Connor. I have sworn not to tell any body how I know.

What about that red shirt if you only saw my dull red pull-over you would under stand my passionate desire for that shirt.

Yrs affly
WB Yeats

where a child antagonist accuses her two headmistresses of being lesbian lovers; the screenplay, adapted by Hellman herself, replaced the charge of lesbianism with a heterosexual triangle, but retained the schoolgirls, played by young actresses Bonita Granville and Marcia Mae Jones.

[4] *Look at the Heffernans!* (1926) was a perennially popular comedy by novelist, playwright, and one-time Abbey actor Brinsley MacNamara (1890–1963), one of the pen names used by John Weldon, who resigned from the Abbey Board of Directors after quarrelling over the production in August 1935 of Sean O'Casey's play *The Silver Tassie*.

[1] WBY and Ottoline Morrell do not seem to have met again; she died the following year.

[2] On 21 Mar. 1937 WBY wrote to the Swami, 'I read with pleasure Mrs Fodens naive review of the Anthology. I do not think any intelligent reader would fail to note that she writes because of some personal grievance and that she is full of Malice. The more articles of that kind she writes the better. Fifteen thousand copies of the anthology have been sold in three months and the sale goes on' (*CL InteLex*, acc. 6873).

[3] After the death of his first wife Basie 'Mac' Magee in 1943, Arthur ('Boss') Shields married Una 'Aideen' O'Connor (1913–50) with whom he had been acting since 1934, and who is described by Holloway in August 1936 as Hunt's secretary.

[ALS]   THE ATHENÆUM, | PALL MALL, S.W.1.
                                                March 18 [1937]

My dear Dobbs

I enclose note from Macmillan.[1] Please send them <u>A Vision</u>. There is some muddle which I could put right if the Scots printers would send me my last proofs but please send the book.

I got on phone to Faber & Faber & found to my surprise that they had never received the <u>Patangali</u>. They had written to me to Dublin a weak ago but I have not had their letter. I asked them to write to you direct. The typed script of <u>Patanjali</u> may or may not be replacable but the drawings of the positions are not.[2] You have no doubt alredy enquired at the post office.

The red shirts arrived just in time as the clothes have come & I have only one blue shirt. With the new blue shirt (I have ordered two more) I feel very handsome.

                                                        Yrs ev
                                                        WB Yeats

[TLS]   RIVERSDALE, | WILLBROOK, |
                                    RATHFARNHAM, | DUBLIN.
                                                March 19 [1937]

My dear Willy

I forwarded you a letter which I thought was from Faber and Faber (yellow envelope) about a week ago. I didnt open it because I was so sure it was from them. I have not sent Patanjali—I thought it had gone before you left. Am sending it by registered post today.

Your letter of 16th interesting! Aideen O'Connor has gone to Cork for a fortnight's holiday. She has not been permanently turned out of her father's house for Anne was there last Sunday week! This was after the row. Anne['s] description of the house was highly entertaining. She went to the lavatory and the seat came apart in three pieces 'like a jigsaw puzzle', filthy kitchen, general delapidation and breakage everywhere 'and Mr O'Connor is Master of the Port'. There seems to be no female of any sort in charge except one rather grubby servant. As you heard this saga you will probably also have heard that the Abbey was rent apart because when Hunt returned

---

[1] Enclosure is missing.

[2] *Aphorisms of Yoga* by Bhagwân Shree Patanjali, done into English from the original in Sanskrit with a commentary by Shree Purohit Swami and an introduction by WBY, was published by Faber and Faber in June 1938.

to Dublin from Oxford Tanya had not found a lodging and so Hunt said she had better stay on in his cottage, which she did for the weekend and was solemnly taken to Church by Hunt. I gather this was the first time Tanya had ever been to Church. I think her mother must be a Jewess, for Tanya was allowed when a child to learn the Lord's Prayer because her mother thought it had been written by Moses. She was sent to a Christian Science school but did not know it was C.S. until she discovered why you did not have bed and doctors if you were ill...Hunt's landlady went to the Vicar of Malahide to complain about Tanya and Aideen staying at Hunt's cottage (they thought that each would be chaperoning the other....) 'So sorry I am for those poor innocent girls'.

John is just going to post.

G.

[APS¹]   [London
                                                                    21 Mar. 1937]

Where is that photograph. I have to write to the lady & I must not keep her waiting. I have not seen her for thirty years & I doubt if her temper has improved.²

WBY.

[TLS]   RIVERSDALE, | WILLBROOK, |
                                               RATHFARNHAM, | DUBLIN.
                                                            March 24 1937

My dear Willy

I send a package entrusted to me by Lolly. I was at Cuala yesterday and then took her out to tea. She talked without stopping for two and a quarter hours and then when I got up to go, said 'I am sure I have forgotten all the things I wanted to tell you, I'll ring up when I get home if I remember anything...'.

Anne is doing the costumes (1740) for a one act play the Peacock is doing and also painting the sets for both plays.¹ They are making their own flats,

---

¹ Post card with National Gallery photograph of *Ophelia* by J. E. Millais, addressed to 'Miss Anne Yeats | Riversdale | Rathfarnham | Co Dublin'.

² Annie Horniman, who died in August 1937; see WBY's explanation in letter of 26 Mar. 1937.

¹ *The Phoenix* by 'N.O.B.' dealt with Oliver Goldsmith's life as a student in TCD; the critic of *The Irish Times* (6 Apr. 1937) considered the one-act play 'too much rough-and-tumble', though 'some of the dialogue was good'.

and told her yesterday that she could start painting any time. So she went with the designer, who is also making the flats, to see them and found that one flat was made but not canvassed!! The plays are to appear on April 4th, so she will probably be sleeping at the Peacock for some nights next week! She got a postcard from you (which she asked me to read to her) about a photograph. She doesnt remember your asking her to send one. Did you? The Lafayette ones[2] are not ready yet and she doesnt want to send an old snapshot. Who is the lady who will be angry if you do not send it soon??? We are both very curious.

One peach tree is in blossom; very foolish of it as we are still having snow, hail, frost and then torrential rains. The river is in permanent flood; the weather is very foul, one fine day since you left, and nothing can be done in the garden damn it.

Hope you are keeping well.

The Abbey is glad that Lent is nearly over. The Protestant section of it, because apparently Eric Gorman's form of penance in Lent is to be extremely cross with all Protestants who go up to the office![3] Anne has only had to go once and got off lightly, but Hunt, Ann Clery[4] and others shake in their shoes!

Yrs affly
George.

[ALS]   THE ATHENÆUM, | PALL MALL, S.W.1.
March 26 [1937]

My dear Dobbs

I wanted Annes photograph for Miss Horniman.[1] She has not asked for it, but she has spoken about Anne in her letter in a way that shows she woul be interested.<I had far sooner send a snap shot. I dont want the theatre to be important.> A snap-shot would have done quite well—however I cannot delay any longer answering Miss Hornimans letter.

---

[2] The Lafayette Photographic Studio of Dublin was established in 1880 and operated continuously under the same family until 1951 when most of the negatives were destroyed.

[3] According to ABY, Eric Gorman (1882–1971), an actor in the company since 1908, who served as secretary for thirty-two years, was bad-tempered because he gave up smoking for Lent.

[4] Ann Clery (d. 1985), who started with the Second Company in 1932, performed at the Abbey Theatre until 1938.

[1] Annie Elizabeth Fredrika Horniman (1860–1937), with WBY one of the early members of the Golden Dawn, had funded the Abbey Theatre for its first seven years; the relationship, always bordering on acrimony because of her insistence on 'no politics', ended in 1909 when the Theatre did not close upon the news of the king's death. She went on to found the Gaiety Theatre in Manchester, the first regional repertory theatre in Britain.

My broad-cast as I probably told you is April 2 (9.20–9.40) It is called The Poets Pub. The BBC asks me to get as many people as possible to listen in—all music arranged under Turners eye.

I have been telling everybody that my ticket is up on April 8 but I find it is up on April 4 so I shall have to get it extended. I want to go to Dorothys (she is just back) after the Broad-cast for a few days. As Margot has thrown up her part in that provincial company. <she was on the telephone & I have seen her since> (she had, she said, lost all interest in the work & could not learn her part—she seems in excellent health) I shall have to work 'The Poets Garden' (my Second Programme) from London. The First rehersal is on March 30 but they are almost certain to put off the performance until June.[2]

I have seen Robert Nichols[3] & he brings Aldous Huxley to see me on Tuesday. Huxley has taken up Astrology.

H Watt has woken up about Anthologies rather too vigerously. I have had a letter from Calcutta University complaining of a charge of £5-5.0 a poem.

As a result of my Ezra Pound, Kipling remark,[4] Pound has written an abusive letter to the press & Mrs Kipling reduced her prices from this out to £3.3.0.

Further more Watt has announced that the price of Yeats poem when published in a magazine is £7.7.0

How are the lily pond & the animals?

Wilson, the editor of the Nineteenth Century & After who was at TCD lately came to see me & he offers three times the usual rates for a reply to my anthology critics.[5] I may do it while I am doing the prefaces to the Edition deluxe, which I shall do at latest the moment I reach Dublin

Upanishads come out on April 8.

Yrs ev
WB Yeats

---

[2] 'In the Poet's Parlour', broadcast 22 Apr. 1937, began with Margot's speaking/lilting of the poem WBY had written about her, 'Ah, sweet dancer'.

[3] Robert Malise Bowyer Nichols (1893–1944), poet, playwright, and later a broadcaster and inventor, was a friend of Siegfried Sassoon; his collections of war poetry, *Ardours and Endurances* (1917) and *A Faun's Holiday & Poems & Phantasies* (1917), were followed by a successful Broadway play, *Wings over Europe* (1928).

[4] In a letter to *The Spectator*, 4 Dec. 1936, in defence of his few selections from Kipling and EP in the anthology, WBY wrote, 'The book has been immensely expensive because all the contents are copyright. As I had a fixed sum for payment of authors I decided on my own responsibility that I could not afford more of these expensive writers.'

[5] Nothing by WBY seems to have appeared in *The Nineteenth Century and After*, see 19 Oct. 1936.

[ALS]   RIVERSDALE, | WILLBROOK, |
RATHFARNHAM, | DUBLIN.
Monday March 29. 1936 [1937]

Dear Willy

Many thanks for letter. I am glad you are staying longer in England. It
is still very cold here & wettish, & it would be much better to return to
somewhat warmer weather.

Have you got your valet to have the lock on your suit-case mended? If
not, do it soon! Also, did you get the <u>Jaeger sleeping suit trousers</u>?

If you want to have the old green suit posted back you can do so safely
as it was <u>Made in Ireland</u>, & travel in the new one.

Michael was here yesterday: they have measles at St Columba's—but
I hope he will not get them: he has had one variety. Term ends on April 1st.
He looked very well—I enclose a photograph that came out in Irish Times
(taken by the father of one of the boys—) Obviously taken from below so
that he looks very elongated[1], although he is now 5.11¼.

               Yours
               George.

[ALS]   THE ATHENÆUM, | PALL MALL, S.W.1.
April 1 [1937]

My dear Dobbs

Dont forget to listen to-morrow night (April 2) from 9.20 to 9.40. Please
also send me your impressions c/o Dorothy (Lady. G.W. Penns in the
Rocks, Withyham, Sussex) I go there on Saturday. She has asked to stay
until April 8 on which day she thinks I go back to Dublin. I will stay longer
if she will have me as the BBC want to have their second programme at
once. I wont wait for the performance, but I shall have to take another
rehearsal. I am to arrange the date from Penns in the Rocks. They pay me
15.15.0 for each.

By the by my price for a poem is now £7.7.0

In your letter of March 24 you say 'I send a packet entrusted me by
Lolly'—you forgot to send it. At any rate it has not come.

I am wonderfully well—to day I seem as well as I have ever been &
so I have felt for two or three days. It makes everything easy—I keep my
papers tidy without thinking about it & answer letters

---

[1] Photograph with caption 'Michael Yeats, son of Dr. W. B. Yeats, the famous Irish poet
and dramatist, enjoying winter sports on the Dublin Mountains during the recent snowfall,'
'A Sportsman's Review', *Irish Times*, 17 Mar. 1937, 4.

Yesterday I had tea with Miss Horniman—after 30 years—little changed except for infirmity. Much talk of old times—she hears the Dublin news from Holleway

I am hiring a locker in the club (10/ a year) & shall leave some of my clothes in it—my black evening cape & some new softfronted dress shirts & perhaps one pair of trowsers be[long]ing to new suit etc. I would leave the new suit except for a desire to display it to your eyes. I got my new dress shirts because they go in instantly no struggle with studs.

Yrs always
WB Yeats

I enclose a Watt checque etc
Wilson at Pumpus is ready to distribute some thousands of circulars about <u>Broadsides</u> but may want to correct Lollys circular first. I have written Lolly for her circular[1]

[ALS] THE ATHENÆUM, | PALL MALL, S.W.1.

April 1 [1937]

My dear Dobbs

I got the Yagger suit yesterday—or rather was measured for it. It will be sent here on Saturday I think. Shall I leave it in my locker here (or leave the jacket here: my memory is that the trowsers of my old suit are worn out—the old jacket is still survisable.) If I leave the whole suit in the locker I will bring to London next June the old & get it repaired

I go to Penns in the Rocks to-morrow. I must stay for a BBC rehersal on March [April] 12. I will not fix date of return until I see Dorothy. The BBC are delighted with to-nights programme & talk of a third Programme in June.

I have finished one poem—a ballad—& am in the middle of another.

The sheets for my signature for Scribners edition are being sent to Penns in the Rocks.

When I have finished my present poem, which is a sort of introduction, I shall have finished my book of poems.[1] I shall do then the introductions for Scribner

Yrs ev
WB Yeats

---

[1] John Gideon Wilson (1876–1963), chairman and managing director of the fashionable John & Edward Bumpus Booksellers of Oxford street, founded in the 18th century and 'devoted to the dissemination of good literature on a big scale'; a bookseller to royalty, Wilson was also responsible for finding subscribers to the limited edition of *Seven Pillars of Wisdom* by T. E. Lawrence.

[1] His ballad was 'The Wild Old Wicked Man'; 'The Gyres' opened *New Poems* (1938).

I suppose the third Broadside is out now & that I shall find it at Penns in the Rocks[2]

[TLS]   RIVERSDALE | RATHFARNHAM | DUBLIN
                                        Saturday April 3 [1937]

My dear Willy

I wired to you today. The Broadcast was entirely delightful: I dont like most of the pomes, as you know, but the result of the performance seemed to me most exciting. You spoke in your natural un-restrained voice, a voice very unlike the artificial one of the 'Modern Poetry', and whatever listeners thought of any other portion of the twenty minutes a whole lot of people will have been glad to hear the real Yeats evidently enjoying himself. The whole production during its twenty minutes sounded as if you and the speaker and the drums[1] were really enjoying yourselves and that you had locked the door on the solemn portentous BBC and had no intention of unlocking the door until you had your final laugh—which we heard <u>very</u> distinctly! I should not have said that I do not like 'most of the pomes'. The ones I dont like are the Newbolt and the Chesterton, and I did not much like Clinton Baddeley's 'The Sailor and the Shark' because it did not come through very well (whether that was because less well 'rendered' or reception not so good I dont know).[2] From certain intonations I believe you were the 'chorus'?? Michael said 'I prefer poetry done that way' which is the nearest he ever got to any statement about 'poetry'. (He knew all the pomes so I think he must have been secretly reading your anthology.)

In my wire of today I said it would be 'nice' if you would wire to the Abbey Experimentalists[3] for their opening night. I know you hate doing this sort of thing, but after all you are the person responsible for the creation of

---

[2] The third *Broadside* of the new series, with 'The Three Bushes' by WBY and 'Lass, is your heart dead?' by DW, is dated March 1937.

[1] Victor Clinton Clinton-Baddeley (1900–70), playwright, travel writer, critic, and novelist, whom WBY taught to 'patter', that is, to read poetry somewhere between singing and speaking, and who became one of his favoured readers. Drum-rolls marked the intervals, but music was used sparingly, though some was written by Turner especially for the broadcast.

[2] 'Drake's Drum' by Henry Newbolt (1862–1938), 'The Rolling English Road', omitting the last two stanzas, by G. K. Chesterton, and 'The Sailor and the Shark' by Paul Fort (1872–1960), trans. from the French by Frederick York Powell (1850–1904).

[3] See GY's letters of 11, 15, and 24 Mar. 1937. The Abbey provided the use of the Peacock Theatre, cash for scenery, and a young man to act as stage manager; ABY designed costumes and painted the set for *The Phoenix* by 'N.O.B.', which was directed by Frank Carney (1902–77), an actor with the Abbey and later to become famous for his long-running play *The Righteous Are Bold*, and for *Alarm Among the Clerks* by Mervyn Wall, which was directed by Cecil Ford, one of the students in Ria Mooney's acting class.

the Peacock Theatre, and I believe I am right when I say that you created it partly as a theatre which would 'try out' plays rejected by the Abbey. The 'Experimentalists' have been working with the enthusiasm of fanatics and the sense which fanatics do not usually possess; as they have no money they are making all their own costumes, their own 'flats' (carpenter being one of the school of acting) and for the last four days all the male cast are labouring for eight hours a day, apart from their natural occupations, as carpenters; canvassing the 'flats', priming them (to save Anne who is doing the painting) etc. Anne's only fear is that they are 'over-rehearsed'. They have very good bookings for the week, but of course they wont get good bookings in the future if they dont put up an efficient show. Unfortunately Tanya is away until Monday. I say 'unfortunately' because Anne is under the difficulty of having to wait for the flats, and has to do a hell of a lot of work at the last moment. Very good for her in experience but exasperating to her for her first solo flight.

Yes: keep the new JAEGER suit at the Club. But please bring back the new ointment coloured suit, I must see it! Your old YAEGER trous: are being re-seated here by Bell's.[4]

I cannot read your writing in your letter of April 1 about fixing date of return.... when is the second BBC poetry stunt? You say there is a 'rehearsal on March 12' (sic. obviously April 12) Why not stay over for the next production?

Yours
George Y.

[ALS]   PENNS IN THE ROCKS, | WITHYHAM, | SUSSEX.
April 9 [1937]

My dear Dobbs

I go to the Athenaeum to morrow for a Tuesday rehersal—may wait a few days as Dorothy will be shopping then I shall return here. I shall not go back to Dublin until after April 22 which is the date of the new Broad cast. They were going to reduce my fee by five pounds, if I did not, & I want a clear understanding that my lowest fee is £15.15. I am also most anxious to make these broad casts as good as possible as they about pay for my legitimate London expenses—I mean by legitimate not purchase of clothes etc.

I enclose a letter from Watt about Blundens fee. I have promised to let Watt know at once. <—the worst of it is that I cannot remember whether I told him to pay or not. Please reply on the supposition that I told him not to. If I told him to pay you will have to make out in big checque-book

---

[4] Bells Dyers and Cleaners Ltd. of 2 St Stephens Green and 123 Lower Rathmines Road.

a checque for the amount payable to yourself—I will find out which I did when I hear from you.> (Found letter to Watt—hence crossing out)[1]

I am exceedinly well—working easily. Dorothy says she has never seen me so well.

Lady Colefax a detestable person is here an obvious parvenu very jealous of Dorothy. Her face was an amusing sight when after she had talked of her seat for the Corination Dorothy said she had refused a seat.[2] (So had I by the by—the High Commissioner has offered me one.) Fisher, the ex-minister of education & Ashton—I think that is the name—the expert who arranged the Chineas Exhibition, a very charming person, are here also.[3] Turner was down during the week.

Your wire about the Academy was a great relief—no letter from Higgins

Wilson (Bumpus) promises to send out 'thousands' of circulars about the Broadsides & Turner is thinking of an article on the general question of the singing & speaking of verse with a paragraph on the Broadsides[4]

Yours affly

WB Yeats

I grow impatient to get home but I stay on.

I have written two poems & am about to start on the general introduction to the Scribner edition

[ALS]   THE ATHENÆUM, | PALL MALL, S.W.1.

April 18 [1937]

My dear Dobbs

I propose to return on Saturday morning (April 24). I had ment to return on April 23 the day after my BBC programe but as there is an emmense rehersal on Thursday I am afraid of the fateague of returning on Friday (23). I change the programe a few days ago & this has made the emmense

---

[1] WBY had understood that Blunden had refused fees for the use of his six poems in the anthology, but there appears to have been some confusion among the agents.

[2] The coronation of George VI took place on 12 May 1937.

[3] The recently widowed Lady Sybil Colfax, née Halsey (1874–1950), was a fashionable London hostess and interior decorator. Herbert Albert Laurens Fisher (1865–1940), MP 1916–26, and now warden of New College, Oxford, was as president of the Board of Education in Lloyd George's government responsible for the 1918 Education Act making attendance at school compulsory for children up to 14; his publications included *The Republican Tradition in Europe* (1911), *Napoleon* (1913), and a three-volume *History of Europe* (1935). Sir Arthur Leigh Bolland Ashton (1897–1983), a scholar of Chinese art at the Victoria and Albert Museum and later its director (1945–55), was largely responsible for the 1935 International Exhibition of Chinese Art and Crafts by the Royal Academy at Burlington House which significantly altered the west's view of eastern art.

[4] Turner's article 'Music and Words', *New Statesman*, 24 July 1937, speaks of the relation between poetry and song in WBY's poetry.

rehersal necessary. I require these BBC performances to make my expensive English expeditions possible. For three weeks now I have been longing for Dublin. I should have kept to my plan of going back on April 8. The lure was the broad cast & my visit to Sussex. I am here now because Dorothy has been put to bed by her doctor with orders not to see any body (coronation strain & Toil)

I have been wonderfully well except for the last few days. I began to have some breathing difficulty in Sussex made it worse by a heavy rehersal but now I am all right again. Two or three people have congratulated me on my improved appearance—especially on my skin 'which looks as if I lived in the open air' (diet I expect)

I have begun my 'General Introduction' to the Scribner edition, signed the 700 pages, & am correcting paged proofs of 'A Vision'.

You never wrote me about Blunden. I think, if I do not hear to-morrow I should tell Watt to pay the money.

We were all wrong about the 'lily pond'. Dorothy says John should put back all the mud, baskets should be sunk in mud, & left 'to rot away' but that the right time for planting is May. She promised a scientific account & then went to bed with arthritis & general collapse. I will get the account out of Hilda Matheson if I remember. She comes to rehersals

O how I long for house the cat & the dog,[1] you & Anne Higgins & the local gossip.

Yrs ev
WB Yeats

Fisher (head of 'All Souls' & late Minister of Education was at Dorothys. He opened the subject of 'The Upanishads' & said that Swamis book & mine was ideally good translation & in beautiful English.[2]

[ALS]
RIVERSDALE, | WILLBROOK, |
RATHFARNHAM, | DUBLIN.
Wednesday [21 Apr. 1937]

My dear Willy

Unless you wire on <u>Friday</u> will meet you as usual.[1] I had no letter from you about Blunden, in fact I had no letter for nearly two weeks. Was beginning to be afraid you had a cold or something! Gogarty is going round

---

[1] A succession of dogs and cats in the Yeats household were all named Ahi and Pangur.

[2] See letter of 9 Apr. 1937.

[1] WBY returned to Dublin on 24 April, GY having travelled over to meet him.

Dublin saying 'What does the Bard think of my book?[2] I darent go out to Rathfarnham until I know'. I told him you werent back yet & had not yet seen his book (I have it) as you were waiting to read it at home—

Yours
G.

[ALS]   THE ATHENÆUM, | PALL MALL, S.W.1.
Wednesday [9 June 1937]

My dear Dobbs

Had a pleasant easy journey & ten minutes after I arrived Dulac telephoned arranging a meeting between himself myself & Barnes for Saturday.

Would you ask Anne to bring over that London Library Book (life of Bach—is that right spelling no—too simple).[1] This will be easier than sending it by post.

You did not like the two 'himselfs' at end of first verse of How goes the Weather. I suggest these two lines.

> 'He himself wrote out the word
> And he was christened in blood'[2]

If you think that better.

Yrs ev
WB Yeats

[ALS]   THE ATHENÆUM, / PALL MALL, S.W.1.
Thursday [10 June 1937]

My dear Dobbs

I have signed all letters & sent off all except this to Duff.[1] You did not send me his address. I have therefore to send it back to you.

---

[2] WBY did not care for *As I Was Going Down Sackville Street: A Phantasy in Fact*, the first of a number of volumes of reminiscences by Gogarty; in November 1937 Gogarty was sued for libel over references in the book, and lost the case.

[1] ABY, on holiday from the Abbey, was in London from 11 June to early July 1937. At this time the London Library had in its catalogue two biographies of Bach in English: by Johann Nikolaus Forkel, trans. Charles Sanford Terry (1920), and C. H. Bitter, trans. Janet E. Kay-Shuttleworth (1873).

[2] An early draft of his poem 'The O'Rahilly'.

[1] Arthur Knox Duff (1899–1956), composer, arranger, organist, conductor, and playwright, had been musical editor of the first series of *Broadsides* in 1935; he composed incidental music for five of WBY's plays, and was later assistant music director at Radio Éireann.

Yesterday I saw Dulac. On Saturday I dine with him to discuss 'broad cast' with him & George Barnes. He proposes to set 'Cromwell' 'Mad as the Mist & Snow' & 'He & She' which is more than I hoped for. George Barnes he says has a great respect for me as producer & was afraid to make some suggestion about the music between songs as he thought my ideas were quite settled. I who am feeling my way in complete musical ignorance

On Sunday Dulac, Helen Beauclerk & I motor to some where in Sussex to spend what is left of the week end with Dulacs friend Edith Shackleton.[2]

Dulac has carved beautifully in wood a back scratcher for Helen Beauclerk. He said 'she needed it'

Yrs ev
WB Yeats

[TLS & MS]   RIVERSDALE, | WILLBROOK, | RATHFARNHAM, | DUBLIN.
June 11 1937

My dear Willy

Thank you for the Duff letter which I have sent on. I think, on the whole I prefer the two 'himself' in the O'Rahilly poem and have therefore left it. I am posting today by registered post the POEMS to Watt. I concluded that you wanted the second version of the Casement poem (Alfred Noyes name left out).[1]

Anne went this morning. She didnt at all want all meals as she thought she would spend all her time going home to eat! The room in Sussex Gardens was recommended by D. Barrett,[2] he was on the boat when I took you over, who said it was newly opened and a cousin of his had stayed there a week and thought it clean etc. It is expensive—£2.10.0 a week includ-

---

[2] Edith Shackleton Heald (*c.*1885–1976), journalist, drama critic, and leader writer on the *Evening Standard*, noted for being the first female reporter in the House of Lords, had recently moved to an 18th-century Georgian country house in West Sussex where she lived with her sister Nora (d. 1961), also a journalist.

[1] Sir Roger David Casement (1864–1916), Anglo-Irish diplomat who was admired internationally for his humanitarian service in the Congo, Peru, and Brazil, was charged with treason and executed by the British for appealing to German sentiments in the cause of Irish independence. Enraged by the arguments in William J. Maloney's recently published book *The Forged Casement Diaries* (1937) convincing him that the English Home Office had deliberately used diaries found among Casement's possessions which contained references to homosexual practices in order to blacken his name and prevent any reprieve, WBY wrote the Ballad 'Roger Casement', in which the first version accused the poet Alfred Noyes (1880–1958) of responsibility for circulating the diaries. The poem was sung from the Abbey stage and published in the *Irish Press* before Noyes published 'a noble letter' of apology and explanation.

[2] Denis Barrett, see letter of 16 June 1924.

ing breakfast, but that is less than she would pay in a hotel. She has her money in the form of Cooks Travellers' cheques. Interminable speeches at yesterday's Prize Giving at St Columba's...³ Every boy except one had been allowed to choose his own prize, and that wretched child who is 15 and got a prize in biology was given a thirteen volume edition of 'Ancient Religions'. What HAS biology got to do with 'Ancient Religions'??

[MS] I enclose some photopages from Lily.⁴

Yours
G.

[TLS & MS]   RIVERSDALE, | WILLBROOK, |
                                    RATHFARNHAM, | DUBLIN.
                                         June 12 1937

My dear Willy

I hope you will not dislike the re-arrangement I made in 'Plays II' as the result of your wire. I think it makes a better sequence while preserving the chronological order. Each <u>set</u> of plays for dancers comes together under the date of the Macmillan and Co first edition, each play dated separately. Perhaps you will not think it necessary to give each play its own date, but students of your work may be glad of it. Cat and Moon for instance obviously belongs to the earlier sequence of dance plays allthough in a different mood. I have checked all the dates by <u>YOUR OWN SIGNED</u> dates on final versions! Also the two Oedipusses follow each other which pleases me. IF YOU WANT TO MAKE SOME OTHER ARRANGEMENT TELEPHONE TO WATT AT ONCE AS I POST THE COPY ON MONDAY. It is all packed up ready to go.

I had great difficulty in finding the rewritten brown and yellow beer and enclose a copy.¹ If incorrect, please send Watt a correction. The version I enclose is typed into the note to THE HOUR GLASS.

Yours ever
G.

---

³ Each year while attending St Columba's MBY received an award: Warden's Prize for General Knowledge and a prize for mathematics (1936); a form prize (1937); a prize in mathematics (1938); Mr Wright's Prize for French Reading, and the Junior Todd Prize, awarded to the second most distinguished examination candidate in the most senior form in the College (1939).

⁴ Enclosure missing.

¹ WBY's note to the prose version reads, 'One sometimes has need of a few words for the Pupils to sing at their first or second entrance, and I have put into English rhyme three of the many verses of a Gaelic Ballad.' There follow three stanzas beginning 'I was going the road one day | (O the brown and the yellow beer) | And I met with a man that was no right man | (O my dear, O my dear)'. The note is dated 1907–22.

[MS] I also like getting the <u>verse</u> Hour-Glass into vol I, in its proper setting!

[TLS]   RIVERSDALE, | WILLBROOK, |
                         RATHFARNHAM, | DUBLIN.
                                Sunday June 13 1937

My dear Willy,

Your birthday today; I hope you were enjoying it with the Dulacs and Miss Shackleton.

I am posting to you the material for PLAYS II. I was re-reading the 'Introductions' to the Wheels and Butterfly plays, and I grew more and more discontented at the thought of separating the 'Introductions' from the plays, The Cat and Moon, Fighting the Waves and Resurrection especially. I had at one time numbered them as NOTES, and then when going through the material for Essays I saw that you had put them in that list. If you want to keep them for ESSAYS please return them to me, (they are pinned together separately). The copy for PLAYS II to go direct to Watt of course.

The parcel I send registered to the Athenaeum. You will get this letter first.

                                                        Yrs
                                                        G.

[ALS]   PENNS IN THE ROCKS, | WITHYHAM, | SUSSEX.
                              Wednesday June 16 [1937]

My dear Dobbs

On Sunday I went with the Dulacs & went to the Shackletons. They have a charming old house with an emmense garden in the middle of an old country town—house, furniture, pictures, garden all perfectly apropriate. They are two elderly women. Yesterday the younger of them motored me here. To morrow I go to London & collect my things & go the flat—52 Hollond Park, W11.[1] Probably there is a letter or letters from you at the Club—I pick them up there to-morrow.

Dorothy has a wounded foot. Some man wearing a spur trod on it at a Court ball.

                                                        Yrs ev
                                                        WB Yeats

[1] On Turner's recommendation, Dulac had arranged for the rental of this flat so that WBY could have privacy for his hoped-for meetings with Edith Shackleton Heald.

Anne is being introduced to the right people. She is at Dulacs to night &
next week meets Norah Shackleton[2] I hope & will be introduced to young
people alredy distinguished stage designers.

Yrs

[TLS[1]]   RIVERSDALE, | WILLBROOK, |
RATHFARNHAM, | DUBLIN.
June 16 [1937]

My dear Willy

I have marked this 'proofs', urgent. Please return to <u>me</u>, as if you make corrections you may mis-spell some word...I am anxious to get all these proofs
through as soon as possible as we are waiting for the final proofs for the Scribner
edition of ESSAYS. If possible mark when you can 'PRESS AFTER CORREC-
TIONS'. I can go into Cuala to see that the corrections are properly done.

Duff sent in two songs and writes that he is going to the BBC for six weeks.
So I am now trying to get hold of Higgins to see about substitute musician.

I heard a pleasant story about MacCran.[2] A young man at Trinity failed
to pass in English owing to his spelling, and MacCran went over his paper
with him. 'Now' said MacCran, 'when you meet a difficult word like 'peb-
ble' why not write instead 'a small stone'?'

Yours
G.

[ALS]   THE ATHENÆUM, | PALL MALL, S.W.1.
Saturday [Friday 18 June 1937]

My dear Dobbs

Please look through these, or at any rate through to where there are passages you will have to refer to the introduction to the Macmillan book. They

---

[2] The older of the Shackleton sisters, Nora had been editor of *The Queen* and later *The Lady*
and was an authority on art and architecture.

[1] WBY has written 'Answered' at the top of the letter.

[2] Henry Stewart Macran (d. 1937), Professor of Moral Philosophy at TCD (1901–34) and
of the History of Philosophy (1934–7), an authority on Greek music and translator and commentator of two works by the influential German philosopher Georg Wilhelm Friedrich Hegel
(1770–1831), whose philosophical system was of interest to both the Yeatses. He and his wife
lived at 2 Sorrento Terrace, Dalkey, close by LR. According to his colleagues, 'He was a
popular member of a circle of semi-bohemian literary figures including Gogarty, and perhaps
that was one reason why he did not achieve more, for the fatal connexion between Irish literary talent and alcohol had by then been formed, and Macran spent much of his later life in a
battle against alcoholism' (R. B. McDowell and D. A. Webb, *Trinity College, Dublin, 1591–1952:
An Academic History* (Cambridge, 1982), 459). I am indebted to Professor Barbara Wright and
Faith White for this reference.

may be wrong there—in which case send proof back to me. Do you want the duplicates back?

I am at my flat—a very pleasant spot.¹ Yesterday I came up from Penns in the Rocks. I am on my way to the Escargot Cafe where I give lunch to Hilda Matheson, Edith Shackleton & Turner. I hope next week to get hold of Diana Murphy & show her that embroidery design—there is general condemnation of the design as for those in the photographs, but praise of Lillys work.²

I have turned aside from correcting the General introduction to the Edition de Luxe to write an introduction to the volume of essays etc. It is a kind of creed

Yrs ev
WB Yeats

[ALS]   THE ATHENÆUM, | PALL MALL, S.W.1.
June 19 [1937]

My dear Dobbs

I hear Anne goes to theatre evry night. Dulac introduced her to a girl of her own age or younger of like tastes.¹ On Tuesday next she goes to Norah Shackleton, who will introduce her to some girls of 25 or 26 who already make money & reputations by designing for Old Vic etc.² Yes I would let her stay if she wants to.

---

¹ Written from No. 52 in the block of service flats called Holland Park which was situated at 29 Holland Park Avenue; Kellys Post Office directory of 1937 lists the owner of 52 as Miss Maisie Margetts.

² WBY had brought over to England a sample of SMY's embroidery, designers not identified. For at least twenty years WBY had been encouraging SMY to embroider fine stronger work based on artist's designs. Diana Murphy (1906–76), painter and embroiderer, was suggested by William Rothenstein when WBY was seeking a younger designer to provide his sister with fresh subjects for embroidery; on 22 July 1936 he wrote to her suggesting Tir n'an Og, the Country of the Young: 'It was the old Irish pagan paradise and is generally supposed to be an island. The thing I have in mind is an Irish equivalent to those Chinese pictures of the land of the Gods' (*CL InteLex*, acc. 6620). Murphy also provided two 'Innisfree' designs, the first rejected by WBY as not being sufficiently realistic; this was followed by a design for 'the Happy Townland'; a fourth was asked for but apparently not completed when WBY died.

¹ ABY did not remember who this was.

² Probably 'The Motley Theatre Design Group', three young women who designed for John Gielgud's productions during the 1930s and went on to considerable fame both in the United States and Britain: sisters Audrey Sophia 'Sophie' Harris, later Mrs George Devine (1900–66), and Margaret Frances 'Percy' Harris (1904–2000), and Elizabeth Montgomery, later Mrs Patrick Wilmot (1902–93); 1936–9 'the Motleys' also taught theatre design at Michel St Denis's London Theatre Studio.

At the same time I admit that she lunched with me once at the Athenaeum when I first arrived & that I have not seen her since. I was out of London.

> Yrs ev
> WB Yeats

[ALS]   SAVILE CLUB, | 69, BROOK STREET. W.1.
                          Saturday [19 June 1937]

My dear Dobbs: I have recieved a letter—you have probably read it—from the Director of Recruitment about a certain Frances Noel Desmond Scully.[1] Do you know such a man. If so please wire. I never heard of him. If you do not wire that we know him—Noel does not sound like a Ballylee farmer—I shall conclude the letter is meant for the other WB Yeats.[2]

> Yrs ev
> WB Yeats

Cannot write more as I full up with busines & want to post this before I forget it.

The letter from Director of Recruitment was addressed to Ballylee Castle

[ALS]   SAVILE CLUB, | 69, BROOK STREET. W.1.
                          July [June] 19 [1937]

My dear Dobbs

I enclose letter from McCartan[1] I have written to Cork address to say that I shall return to Dublin to meet him on July 5 (my broadcast is July 3) but that I broad cast from here again on August 5

Please get him on phone the moment he returns to Dublin.

I have attended to proofs etc

> Yrs ev
> WB Yeats

---

[1] Thom's Directory of 1937 lists an F. Scully of 8 Killarney Park in Dublin.

[2] Yeates the stationers were situated at 74 Dame Street; another William Yeates resided in Grangemount, Balbriggan.

[1] See note to 18 Dec. 1932; when McCartan arrived in Cobh in mid-June he immediately sent WBY the first instalment of £600 from the 'Testimonial Committee for W. B. Yeats', which had now raised sufficient funds to guarantee enough money for 'security and comfort' for the rest of WBY's life; WBY had not been told of the committee's generous gesture until January 1937. An additional £400 was sent to him in June 1938; in all the committee raised $US6,000.

[on back of envelope] <McCartan may not get my letter if he is moving about so please keep your eye on I had better I have>

[Tel¹]   [London]
                                                                 21 June [1937]

Does McCartan return home at once if so wire go to Dublin by aeroplane and return to rehearse broadcast would see Doctor first.² YEATS

[ALS¹]   52 Holland Park | W.11
                                                            [22 June 1937]

My dear Dobbs: No answer yet to my telegram, however—

Anne had tea with me yesterday & was delighted to hear she had not to go back on Friday. Her extra week brings her to July 2. If I return to Dublin on July 5 & you cared for her to stay on longer yet she could come to my flat for a week or more.

The one play Anne has liked so far is <u>Murder in the Cathedral</u>.

                                                                    Yrs ev
                                                                  WB Yeats

Your telegram has come.² I reherse on Thursday next & again the following Thursday (July 1).

[TLS]   RIVERSDALE, | WILLBROOK, |
                                               RATHFARNHAM, | DUBLIN.
                                                              June 22 1937

Dear William

I dont know why you wrote to McCartan in Cork seeing that he had written his name and address (Shelbourne Hotel, Dublin) largely on the envelope which I forwarded to you! He has now arrived at the Shelbourne

---

¹ Telegram to 'Yeats, Riversdale, Rfm, Db' reprinted in John Unterecker, *Yeats and Patrick McCartan: A Fenian Friendship* (Dublin, 1965), 402.

² When GY forwarded this wire to McCartan she explained that while in Switzerland WBY had suffered from altitude sickness, hence the reference to seeing a doctor before flying.

¹ On Athenaeum stationery with address struck out.

² GY's telegram is missing but it reassured WBY that McCartan planned to stay 'for several weeks'; a second wire explained that although he was to leave Ireland in a few days, he promised to return in August.

and I have written to him enclosing your wire, making, of course, polite remarks of all sorts.

I asked you to let me know if you had decided to keep the introductory Essays from WHEELS AND BUTTERFLIES for Scribner's Volume V 'ESSAYS', but I hear from Watt that you have sent him Vol. IV. PLAYS II,—and you have not replied to my question. I have written today to Watt asking him to look through the material of Vol. IV—PLAYS II and let me know if those introductory essays were included as 'Notes 6–10' or not. Scribners are screaming hotly about 'copy'. I sent each volume separately to Watt enclosing in each a typed copy (of which you have a carbon copy) of contents. But I seem to have called Poems (Volume I) in a letter to Watt 'Volume II'. They, Scribners, in turn are calling Volumes V and VI 'Auto-biographies'. I have now sent Watt my last carbon copy of the contents of the seven volumes so I really do not think any further misunderstandings can occur. In any case you have carbon copies of contents sent. [heavily inked ms in margin: Please do not lose the one I sent you].

I enclose on separate sheet account of the seven volumes.

Have wired Anne that she can have her extra week!!!

G.

[ALS]　　　　　　　　　　　　　　　　52 Hollond Park | W 11
　　　　　　　　　　　　　　　　　　Wednesday [23 June 1937¹]

My dear Dobbs

I accept what you say about the introductions for 'Wheels & Butterflies'; they are far better where you have put them. The material is with Watt. I was most grateful to you for finding those lost verses about 'The brown & the yellow beer'—I thought they were gone for good. I am however getting the volume back; you seem to have left out some verses I wanted kept. The MSS you found probably only contained the new verses & the first verse of the old to show where they went.

I enclose a touching letter from Watt—put it in the file—I like to know I have behaved decently in one case at any rate.²

I saw Macmillan yesterday & did much business & got some information. They have sold 800 copies of 'Collected Poems' in the last year. They will

---

¹ Dated 'June 24. 1937' by GY.

² The literary agent John Hansard Strahan Watt (1877–1960), who had taken over WBY's file in 1916, wrote on 21 June 1937 to inform him of his retirement after 43 years, stating that he has had 'nothing but kindness from you, and you are—not only my most distinguished client—but the one I can think of with real affection'; his older brother and senior partner in the firm, Alexander Strahan Watt, then took over WBY's file; the relationship with A. P. Watt & Son continues to this day.

reprint it next spring—re-arranged so that they can always keep it up to date by adding at the end new poems (these will of course first come out in a seperate volume). They will also bring up to date 'Selected Poems'. They will bring out a large volume of my 'collected essays' & will add to them from time to time in the same way

P.T.O

All this is subject to a letter he is to write me. He is also to send me unbound sheets of a <u>Vision</u> for Scribner.

You have now all my lyrics. The <u>Listener</u> offered £5 for a lyric & would I think give £7 I think you should ask Watt to send them 'The Curse of Cromwell' telling him what month it comes out in <u>Broadside</u>. I think Watt should offer <u>Lapis Lazuli</u>, the poem called 'To D.W.' 'Beutiful Lofty Things', 'Imitated from the Japanese' & 'Gyres' in England & America. They would go well together in a bunch. I think he should offer 'The Pilgrim' to the <u>Irish Times</u> saying when it is coming in <u>Broadsides</u>.[3] Henceforth £7 should be the minimum for a single poem of mine.

I suggest keeping back 'O Rahilly' 'The Wild Old Wicked Man' I can add other folk things later & put them all togeather.

Yrs affectionly
WB Yeats

[TLS & MS]
RIVERSDALE, | WILLBROOK, |
RATHFARNHAM, | DUBLIN.
June 24 [1937]

My dear Willy

I enclose a note from McCartan I received this morning.[1] I rather hope you wont fly over allthough I suppose the aeroplanes are almost as safe as trains, but I always look on them with suspicion as dangerous and inconsequent objects.

Anne seems very pleased about her extra week. She says she is getting fat again as 'there are so many milk bars in London'...

O'Duffy has become 'His Excellency'...he was given an address of welcome read by Liam Walsh beginning 'Your Excellency'. This has caused much ribaldry. His volunteers have split into two groups. One describes the horrors committed by the Reds; and the other describes the mowing down

---

[3] 'The Curse of Cromwell' appeared in *Broadside* No. 8 (August 1937), 'The Pilgrim' in No. 10 (October 1937).

[1] Enclosure is missing, but evidently had to do with McCartan's plans to return.

by Franco of Reds lined up against walls 'with machine guns, starting at their ankles'.[2]

[MS] I may get a wire from you today—

Yours affly

G.

[AL]   52 Hollond Park | W 11
Thursday April 25. 1937[1] [24 June 1937]

My dear Dobbs

Damn all these complications—I had got my self into as good health as I can ever hope to have by solitude & salad & then came this McCartan business. I have written to the BBC to cancel my Dulac debate[2] arranged for August 5. I will come to Dublin when the six weeks for which Dulac took these rooms end—sooner if necessary; and set to work arranging some sort of reception for McCartan. To meet immediate necessities please send me another box of those sleap pills (I had got free not only of them but almost free of senna, damn-damn)

Try to find out through Gogorty if McCartan guarrenteed the money he has sent me? If so I won't have it—I cannot take such a sum from a compartivey poor man. This is a most urgent matter.

Anne tells me that just after I left Dublin a cable came from McCartan saying that he was starting for Dublin. I know it was out of consideration for

---

[2] Eoin O'Duffy (1892–1944), in succession a TD, chief of staff of the IRA, general of the Free State Army, commissioner of An Garda Siochána (the Civic Guard) on the establishment of the Irish Free State, and in 1933 after dismissal by de Valera, leader of the National Guard or 'Blueshirts', which in turn merged with Cumann nGaedheal to form Fine Gael. In July 1933 Dermott MacManus brought O'Duffy to Riversdale, resulting in the composition of 'Three Songs to the Same Tune', but despite WBY's enthusiasm for philosophical revolution he never entirely succumbed to O'Duffy's fascist ambitions, writing to Ethel Mannin on 1 Mar. 1937, 'I am convinced that if the Spanish War goes on, or if ceases & O'Duffy's volunteers return heros my 'pagan' institutions, the theatre, the academy, will be fighting for their lives against combined Catholic & Gaelic bigotry' (Wade, 885; see note to GY's letter 18 Jan. 1936, and Foster ii. 471–83). O'Duffy had organized an Irish Brigade which paid a brief visit to Spain before being sent home by Franco in June 1937, and it is this occasion GY describes in her letter.

[1] This wrong date may have been added by GY later.

[2] On 4 May WBY wrote to Dulac proposing a debate concerning 'modern music and singing' after James Stephens refused the offer: 'I would write a series of vehement propositions about the arts, you would write a reply—I would write another note. Then we would go over it all & elaborate it into a violent row—then one or other would say that he hoped the audience believed we were in earnest & one or other draw attention to the fact that the red signal was still on etc etc' (*CL InteLex*, acc. 6921). As can be seen below (pp. 474–5), their disagreement soon erupted into a heated quarrel.

me that you did not send me that cable but it would have been better <if it had been sent>—I might have got out of my broadcast.

I am going to the Shackletons this evening—my address probably until Monday will be

C/o of
    C/o
        Miss E. S Heald
            The Chantry House
                Steyning
                    Sussex

When I wrote to McCartan at Cork I sent a duplicate letter to the Shelbourne but I will write again

I am rehersing from 5.30 to 6.30 today then I shall be motored down to Steyning. I hope to get Dorothy to take me next week-end now that there is no point in my immediate return to Dublin. Unless Dorothy asks me to stay some days—I am afraid my offer of this flat to Anne is off. There have been great rows between Dulac & BBC[3]—BBC in the wrong final smoothing over to day. Dulac has set four poems of mine.

I arranged for <u>Great Hearne</u> with Macmillan.

Saw Diana Murphy yesterday—is to do an Innisfree design at once

                                            Yrs aff

I ring Anne up from time to time—I am going to do so now—if my landlady has some pennies

[TLS & MS]   RIVERSDALE, | WILLBROOK, |
                                  RATHFARNHAM, | DUBLIN.
                                          June 26 1937

My dear Willy

I send a duplicate of this letter to Holland Park. Please stop worrying about McCartan. Gogarty has seen him and says he does not in the least expect you to come over now. What he wants is to have you here in Horse

---

[3] WBY and Dulac were in disagreement over theories of speaking verse to musical accompaniment, with Dulac insisting that there should be 'a *fixed* new musical basis' and WBY rejecting all instrumental interference with the speaker's voice; the argument escalated over the next eighteen months (see Wayne McKenna, 'W B Yeats, W J Turner and Edmund Dulac: The *Broadsides* and Poetry Broadcasts', in Warwick Gould (ed.), *Yeats Annual No. 8* (London, 1991), 225–34). The row—more with WBY than Barnes of the BBC—appears to have been over a harpist whom Dulac brought in to play chords behind the words of 'Mad as the Mist and Snow' and 'The Curse of Cromwell', to be spoken by Margot Ruddock—thus according to WBY 'making the music too important'.

Show week as some of the Americans will be here then and want to make the presentation of the remainder of the amount. Gogarty tells me that McCartan has either sent or is sending a cheque for £600 and that the remaining £400 is to be presented.

[MS P.T.O. I could not ask Gogarty if McCartan had 'guaranteed the money' he sent—(or is sending?) because G. went to London last night, but Mrs Gogarty assures me this is not the case. The word McCartan used was 'guarantee' in the sense 'I can assure you that this amount will be available'.] I have seen McCartan and he is lunching with me on Sunday at the Kildare St Club (the Macmanuses, Mrs G. Noll and Brenda; Mrs Sowby[1]) and then we all go on to Dalkey.

As McCartan is evidently going to have some sort of party for the presentation to you would it not be better for you NOT to make any advance arrangements for a reception to him such as you suggest in your letter. This could come afterwards. McCartan will probably tell me on Sunday the date he actually expects to be back in Dublin.

Anne will <u>have</u> to return on Saturday July 3rd as she starts work at the Abbey on Monday July 5th. She knows this and is making arrangements for journey etc.

Yours affly
George.

[TLS]
RIVERSDALE, | WILLBROOK, |
RATHFARNHAM, | DUBLIN.
Saturday evening [?27 June 1937]

Dear Willy

Higgins telephoned to me to say he has seen McCartan about the Academy dinner in his honour and says he will write to you; but as he may not do so for some days, this is what he says: McCartan did not seem very enthusiastic and suggested it should be given to James Farrell,[1] so Higgins suggested there should be a joint dinner to both of them and McCartan apparently liked that idea very much. (I think McCartan is a rather diffident person.) There will be a meeting of the Council on Monday and Higgins is

---

[1] Dermott MacManus; 'Mrs G. Noll' and Brenda are Mrs Gogarty and her daughter (1911–86), who became a well-known sculptor and married Desmond J. Williams; Mrs Sowby was the wife of Revd C. W. Sowby, warden of St Columba's College, Rathfarnham, where MBY was a student.

[1] The chairman of the Testimonial Committee was James Augustine Farrell (1863–1943), president of the United States Steel Corporation (1911–32), America's first billion-dollar company, and first chairman of the National Foreign Trade Council.

going to ask that he be given authority to make all the arrangements. I hope this will save you feelings of responsibility; in any case you and Higgins will be able to confer together more easily, than say you and O'Faolain.[2]

The chemist has posted you your sleeping tables direct, you should find them waiting you at Holland Park when you get back on Monday, or whatever day you return there.

Yours affly
G.

[ALS]   <Athenaeum> 52 Hollond Park | W 11
June 28 [1937]

My dear Dobbs

I write from the Shackletons but return to town to day I enclose a photograph of Dulac, myself, Helen Beauclerk & Edith Shackleton in the drawing room here, Norah Shackleton I think took it is so not in the picture. I have had a pleasant time but there have been too many people staying or calling & I have talked too much & am tired. I long for Hollond Park where I shall not speak to a soul until 3.30 when I set out for the club, if I do set out.

Dulac & I have exchanged affectionate letters after one of the greatest rows in my career. Dulac had lost his temper with the BBC people who had left his name out & had denounced them over the phone. He was within his right. When my rehersal began I told him his musical rehersal would follow but he could [not] keep silent. He came up into the little room like a musicians gallery where I was with George Barnes of the BBC & interupted & when I refused to listen said 'You are not in your Abbey Theatre now' & presenty I said 'Take that man away'. He went declaring he would take his music with him. I finished my rehersal in peace, & Helen pacified Dulac. I doubt if the BBC ever saw any body in such a fury as I was, I was full [of] compliments however to the principal reciter who did his work beatifully. I gave up the idea of doing any part my self for fear it might seem a reflection in his skill.[1] <Dulac is to have a full rehersal singing to himself & god knows what will happen next>.

On Saturday evening I got a satisfactory letter from McCartan. He has mistaken one thing—I want the Academy to entertain him for what he has done for the Academy not for what he has done for me. When I get home in the middle of July I shall urge them to this. I my self must entertain

---

[2] Seán Ó'Faoláin was a founder member of the Irish Academy of Letters; the special dinner given by the Irish Academy of Letters, and organized primarily by LR, took place on 17 Aug. 1937.

[1] Clinton-Baddeley, see note to 3 Apr. 1937.

M'Cartan if the Academy does not but that will be private. He returns to Dublin on August 2.

Yrs ev
WB Yeats

\<When Dulac spoke I had>
I never found out what Dulac wanted except that he wanted to interrupt me. \<I rather think> I beleive that I rejected for bad speaking a speaker he wanted rejected for not following his music. When his musical rehersal came he asked for & was granted a professional singer. God help that professional singer next rehersal if she or he attempts to pour humanity out of a bottle.

[ALS]

52 Hollond Park | W. 11
\<June 30> July 1 [1937]

My dear Dobbs

Stormy rehersal to-day. Dulac's professional singer[1] has an extreme distaste for the English language. BBC said they had engaged her. I said I was quite ready to pay her to stay away. Finally I admitted her on the understanding that the producer state that she is produced by Dulac not by me. The Musec[2] is said to be admirable but as I said to Dulac, her words are 'scandalous & rediculous'. George Barnes (BBC) took me aside & said 'Never have anything to do with Musicians' Dulac & he had quarrelled on the phone. I gather that BBC look forward to making much of me—to day they photographed in different poses.

Now that I have finished but for the dictating my three American prefaces my head is full of subject for verse

Yrs ev
WB Yeats

[TLS]

RIVERSDALE, | WILLBROOK, |
RATHFARNHAM, | DUBLIN.
Monday [5 July 1937]

My dear Willy

A hasty note to tell you how very enchanting 'Cromwell' was—the last stanza perhaps not so good, but all the rest quite lovely. A vast improvement

---

[1] Dulac's 'professional singer' was the popular soprano, teacher at the Royal Academy of Music, actor, and composer Olive Groves (Mrs George Baker) (1899-1974), who was a regular BBC performer for many years.

[2] Marie Henriette Goossens (1894-1991), principal harpist with the London Symphony Orchestra and later Professor of the Harp at the Royal College of Music, accompanied Groves, Margot Ruddock, and Victor Clinton-Baddeley to music composed by Dulac.

on her last broadcast.[1] The singer of course impossible, though the music delightful.[2]

Alas; we cant start the study because the builder's strike is still on and no painting can be done until it is over!!

Will write tomorrow.

G

[TLS[1]] RIVERSDALE, | WILLBROOK, |
RATHFARNHAM, | DUBLIN.
July 7 [1937]

Dear Willy

I did not forward enclosed from Ernest Rhys when it arrived because I did not know when you were returning. Your last letter says 'August 22 or 23' but I imagine you meant July. It is mainly a business letter, and you may remember that when Dents made the suggestion—was it two or three years ago?—Watt was rather against the idea. May I suggest that you write a polite note to Rhys and consult Watt again if you want to be in the 'Every-man' series. I rather think Macmillan also did not like the idea.[2]

Anne returned in a state of high combustion and longing to fling paint around, but unfortunately there was nothing to fling paint on—she had today 'off' and so went to have a very necessary new permanent wave. She has re-done most of the designs for the Sara Payne Ballet[3] and I notice there is a great advance in maturity in the new designs. I think she had enjoyed herself tremendously, she had seen & learnt a vast amount; had gone 'to the back' in various theatres to pick up what she could, had gone to Oxford twice and Canterbury once (three visits to MURDER IN THE CATHEDRAL)

You dont say if you and Dulac are friends again. I think you probably are, because you have a genius for remaining the friend of people to whom you say the most abominable things! (I am thinking of your letter in which you tell me you said in the midst of the BBC row 'Take that man away')

---

[1] Margot Ruddock, rehearsed by WBY, spoke 'The Curse of Cromwell'.

[2] 'He and She' was sung by Olive Groves to music composed by Dulac; GY's innocent remark, reported to Dulac, led to further argument between the two friends.

[1] WBY has written 'Answd' at the top of the page.

[2] The enclosure is missing. Ernest Percival Rhys (1859–1946), poet, playwright, essayist, and editor, and a founder member with WBY of the Rhymers' Club in the 1890s, was founding editor in 1910 of the Everyman's Library series of classics published by J. M. Dent; the proposal was politely declined.

[3] Sara Payne had returned to Dublin to establish a school for dance and mime; her Irish ballet *Doomed Cuchulain* opened in the Father Matthew Hall on 13 Nov. 1937, with costumes by ABY. See 20 Nov. 1937 for GY's report to ABY, who was in Paris.

Are you broadcasting with him later? Are you returning to London when you have seen McCartan and Co?? I am going away with Michael for a week during his holidays in August and September, and, on the whole, I would choose a week when you were away. If you are to be here all August and September you could probably instruct Mary to keep off all the Americans who are now beginning to inflict us. There have been eleven in the past six days wanting to shake your hand...The horrid creatures have their cheap trips in the summer months.

Bishop Blunt⁴ was staying at St Columba's lately. He was at the Ousley's (American minister) 'birthday' party.⁵ He asked to be introduced to interesting people (his own phrase) and so met General Brennan.⁶ Polite small talk went on for a few minutes and then Blunt asked Brennan 'have you ever been in my part of the world?' 'Yes, My Lord, I spent a year and a half in Bradford'. 'Where were you staying?' says Blunt. 'In gaol, My Lord' Blunt instantly, without a flicker of an eyelash, 'A few hundred years ago I should now have been in the Tower.'

Yours George Y.

[ALS]   at PENNS IN THE ROCKS, | WITHYHAM, | SUSSEX.
[8 July 1937]

My dear Dobbs

Here life has been a little disturbed through my anxiety about Dorothy. Coronation balls have brought her near complete collapse. Late at night some days ago she rang up Hilda Matheson & this was the conversation: 'I am afraid I shall be too late for the ball' 'what ball?' 'O the ball at Tilbury—Queen Elizabeths ball at Tilbury' 'Go back to bed you are dreaming' Talking to her is sometimes a strain because she forgets what she has said or what I have said. I am urging an immediate nursing home—but probably in vain.

On Monday Edith Shackleton motors over to take me to The Chantry House, Steyning, Sussex. After a week there I go to the Club for two nights & then return to Dublin.

---

⁴ Alfred Walter Frank Blunt (1879–1957), second Bishop of Bradford, whose speech to the Diocesan Conference on 1 Dec. 1936 unintentionally aggravated the abdication crisis of Edward VIII.

⁵ Alvin Mansfield Owsley (1888–1967) who, as the US ambassador to Ireland 1935–7, traditionally held a party on 4 July.

⁶ Michéal Brennan (1896–1986), witty and wily Irish Republican revolutionary, had a long career with the Irish Republican Brotherhood, where he was skilled in guerrilla warfare. Despite his support of the Treaty, he became army chief of staff 1931–40 under de Valera, until prematurely retired after the IRA made away with most of the army's ammunition. In 1980 he published his memoirs, *The War in Clare*.

To morrow morning I finish copying out my introduction to the bound volumes of the <u>Broadsides</u>—a fiery denunciation of the treatment of poetry by modern musicians & Dorothy approves & will sign.

Please if you know tell me what the Academy Council has done—I have not had a word from F R Higgins

The May <u>Broadside</u> expecialy the second picture is delightful.[1] Dorothy says she will buy & give as Xmas presents a lot of the bound volumes—however I cannot imagine all 12 being ready for Xmas.

Yrs ev
WB Yeats

I am much better than I have been for a long time.
I am still quarrelling with Dulac but all will be well

[TLS]   RIVERSDALE, | WILLBROOK, |
                                     RATHFARNHAM, | DUBLIN.
July 14 [1937]

My dear Willy

I hope you received parcel containing book and letter from E. Pelham which I sent on to 52 Holland Park.

The Broadsides could easily be ready for Xmas if Higgins ever does anything about the music. I have Four times written, spoken, or telephoned to him asking about THE JUDAS TREE music which he has now had for over three months... He promised to see Art O'Murnaghan[1] three weeks ago after much polite pressure on my part. I wrote to Higgins again last Saturday saying that the Cork organist who has done similar work for Cuala and others would do it by return IF Higgins would send the music to me. (I knew that he had not seen A. O'Murnaghan) It merely needs copying. No reply. I am sending a wire to him at the Abbey today. The July number is set up, blocks and all, except for this damned Judas music. The illustrations for August and Sept. are promised (and two of them are done) for July 16th.

---

[1] Both colour illustrations for *Broadside* No. 5 (May 1937) were by Irish portrait and landscape painter Maurice Joseph MacGonigal (1900–79), who taught in the Royal Hibernian Art Schools, was a member of the Board of Governors of the National Gallery of Ireland (1936–9), and later president of the Royal Hibernian Academy (1962–77); he designed the sets for the 1935 Abbey Theatre production of *The Silver Tassie*.

[1] Art O'Murnaghan (1872–1954), now noted for his illuminated folios for the manuscript Leaabha na hAiseirghe (Book of Resurrection), wrote plays under the name 'Patrick Kells', was an organist, designer, composer, and actor-manager for the Gate Theatre, and taught drawing at the National College of Art. The music for 'The Judas Tree' (July 1937) was finally provided by Hilda Matheson, but O'Murnaghan arranged the music for the *Broadsides* of October, November, and December 1937.

As he does not reply about above, I cant very well ask him about Academy business. Write him a note to the ABBEY and tell him when you will be back.

The main at Balyboden² broke and so no one in that district and in the whole of Rathfarnham had any water for nearly twentyfour hours. Fortunately we had rainwater in barrels—one does not fancy river water even for washing as our neighbours throw in all their rubbish and dead rats abound!

Did you leave an address at 52 Holland Park for your letters to be forwarded to? I may have sent several there not knowing you were at Penns.

I hope you wont be returning here into a lot of exasperating Academy business, though I suppose you are now off the Council?³

Yours affly
George

[ALS]   THE CHANTRY HOUSE, | STEYNING, | SUSSEX.
Thursday [15 July 1937]

My dear Dobbs

I enclose BBC photographs and a post card of this pleasant village. I am resting here in peace & need it. It was very painful at Dorothys. She was in complete mental collapse. I spoke to her daughter & told her to tell Gerald Wellsely.¹ The result was that the son came & got her to agree to see a docter—whether she will I dont know. She is afraid of what the docter will say. Then there was the Dulac quarell (I have had a pleasant letter this morning) & another matter which was a great shock.² I am very well in body but tired

---

² The Ballyboden Reservoir was one of four water treatment plants supplying the Dublin region.

³ In an effort to concentrate only on his writing, WBY was resigning from as many committees as he could. In March 1937 the Academy was reorganized to, as he explained to McCartan, 'get a more vigerous council', and in May to Heald, 'I have come to the conclusion that my two institutions here—the Theatre & the Academy—both now prosperous will go on better without me. A new generation must feel that it is in complete control. I have set myself free to go where I please' (*CL InteLex*, acc. 6943).

¹ WY seems to have confused father and son; DW's estranged husband was the architect and diplomat Lord Gerald Wellesley (1885–1972), later the 7th Duke of Wellington; their son was Arthur Valerian Wellesley (b. 1915), who became the 8th Duke; their daughter was Lady Elizabeth Wellesley (b. 1918), who later married Major Thomas Clyde.

² In early July WBY discovered that Margot Ruddock had loaned the Swami £100. On 7 July after consulting Elizabeth Pelham he wrote to Purohit asking that this money be repaid as a first charge on royalties from the *Upanishads*; this meant that WBY would not receive the return of £50 he himself had loaned the Swami for his journey back to India.

I shall go to Dublin in the middle of next week.

I must dress or I shall be late for lunch.

My window looks out the village street—behind are large gardens 'cir-cummured with brick'[3]

Yrs
WB Yeats

[ALS]   THE CHANTRY HOUSE, | STEYNING, | SUSSEX.
July 15 [1937]

My dear Dobbs

I thank you for your letter. Yes I shall get to Dublin next Wednesday or Thursday. I go to the Athenaeum on Monday. I will stay long enough to dine with Dulac & seal our renewed friendship.

When I said Dorothy showed 'Mental Collapse' I did not mean her mind was permanently affected, but her state is dangerous. Two days before I left a dream about some friend of her youth had over flowed into life. She thought the friend was present and then accused Hylda Matheson of impersonating that friend & said she would never forgive it. Then suddenly she became all right. The whole thing comes from an attempt to go back, in the interests of her daughter, into a world she had cast off. All now depends on the firmness of her son.

I shall be in Dublin seven or eight weaks at any rate. It largely depends on the BBC

Without letting any body know what I was doing I used our old Order[1] methods of cure with Dorothy & aparently with success for the moment.

I am only just recovering from the strain. Dorothy constantly forgot what she had said or what I said; & then would become quite well. Hylda felt the strain as I did

All this is private

Yrs ever
WB Yeats

Until I spoke to Elizabeth Wellesly she had evidently noticed nothing—the son however had noticed everything though he had done nothing. I have urged an hospital nurse in residence for the present.

---

[3] An ironically apt quotation from Shakespeare's *Measure for Measure* IV. 1, where Isabella describes to the Duke, disguised as a friar, the entrance to Angelo's rooms where the seduction is to take place: 'He hath a garden circummured with brick, | Whose western side is with a vineyard back'd'...'

[1] Rituals from the Hermetic Order of the Golden Dawn.

[ALS]   RIVERSDALE, | WILLBROOK, |
                                        RATHFARNHAM, | DUBLIN.
                                        Friday [16 July 1937]

My dear Willy

Very many thanks for the photographs which are delightful but not flat-
tering! You might let me have a wire to say if you arrive on Wednesday or
Thursday next week—

Hope the music for Broadsides is now going ahead! Higgins tells me he is
going to USA with the Abbey[1]— I have not told Anne this or anyone else
as I dont know how 'private' it is.

I am afraid you have had a worrying three weeks. Sorry.

                                                    Yours affly
                                                        G.

[ALS]   THE CHANTRY HOUSE, | STEYNING, | SUSSEX.
                                        [?18 Sept. 1937]

My dear Dobbs

I came here on Wednesday & go to Penns in the Rocks on Wednesday
next. Hitherto I have done nothing but idle—talk too much & go motor
drives. Life is pleasant and I am well. Norah Shackleton thinks the new
design is better than those I showed her before but still 'unorthy of the con-
sumate workman-ship of the embroidress'[1] Norah Shackleton embroiders a
great deal herself & like Lilly never uses a frame.

Except the Shackletons I have met no body except Sir John Keane[2] &
Starkey who were both at the Club & were scarce worth crossing the water
for.

---

[1] As a new member of the reorganized Board of Directors, Higgins was authorized to go
with the theatre's 'first company' on its extended American tour from September 1937 until
the end of May 1938; see below, 19 Sept. 1937.

[1] In an effort to provide Lily with commissions for her embroidery, WBY had asked
various artists to offer her designs giving her £5 advance for each piece of embroidery
she completed, to be repaid when sold; see below, 27 Sept. 1937 for discussion of Diana
Murphy's design.

[2] Sir John Keane, 5th Baronet (1873–1956), Senator since 1922; Walter Starkie (see next
letter).

I enclose a letter from an old order friend of mine.[3] I have sent £5 for Mrs Heap.[4] The postscript explains it self. I have written to Mrs Rodes & said you would look for the photograph[5] when you got home.

Yrs ev

WB Yeats

Thank you for the postcards. The little railway must have delighted Michael[6]

I have no memory of a photo from Mrs Rodes or of Mrs Rodes herself

[TLS]   RIVERSDALE, | WILLBROOK, | RATHFARNHAM, | DUBLIN.
Sunday Sept. 19 [1937]

My dear Willy

I write to Steyning as I hear you were seen off by Walter 'in a car' from the Athenaeum! (Incidentally Sheelah Richards saw you 'in Pall Mall in a racing car without a hat'.) Michael and I arrived home yesterday; I met Starkie (Walter) at dinner last night, hence information; and today Anne has

---

[3] Mrs Helen Mary Rand, 'Vigilate' (d. 1929), Instructor in Divination in the early years of the Golden Dawn when WBY was Instructor in Mystical Philosophy; a friend of Miss Horniman, she was asked by WBY for information in 1911 during the legal battle with Horniman over the Abbey Theatre. When the Order finally disbanded, she preserved some of the Golden Dawn properties and bequeathed the original Temple Pastos, decorated with paintings by Mrs Mathers, to an Anglican vicar (See George Mills Harper, *Yeats's Golden Dawn* (London, 1974), 155–6).

[4] Probably Mabel Gertrude 'Maiya' Tranchell-Hayes, née Curtis-Webb (d. 1948); as 'Ex Fide Fortis', she was in charge of one of the London Alpha et Omega Lodges of the Stella Matutina in 1919 and later mentor to occultist and author Dion Fortune (1890–1946) and model for Fortune's fictional character Vivian LeFay Morgan. She suffered from a nervous breakdown some time in the 1930s and ceased to be involved in trance sessions, returning after the death of her psychiatrist husband in 1940 to work with Fortune on the Arthurian myth. Some Golden Dawn artefacts which had belonged to her were found on a beach in Sussex in 1966. (See R. A. Gilbert, *The Golden Dawn Twilight of the Magicians* (Wellingborough, 1983), 79, 85.)

[5] Dorothy (Mrs Percy) Rhodes, née Paget (1882–1980), niece of Florence Farr, had performed the Fairy Child in 1894 in the first production of WBY's *The Land of Heart's Desire*, written at Farr's request so that Dorothy might have a role. As her aunt's student of verse-speaking and the psaltery, she had been his first choice five years later for the title role in *The Countess Cathleen*, but was replaced at George Moore's insistence by May Whitty (1865–1948). With her sister she assisted Farr in public exhibitions of chanting to the psaltery in 1902, and she later toured the United States with Johnston Forbes-Robertson's company in Shaw's *Caesar and Cleopatra*, where she met her future husband, American-born actor Percy Rhodes (1870–1956); thereafter she played only minor roles.

[6] After accompanying WBY to Holyhead as usual, GY and Michael went on a walking tour of Wales; there is a railway four miles long, opened in 1896, that travels from Llanberis station to the summit of Mount Snowdon.

gangs coming to tea and dinner, and at 11.30 pm Sheelah and Denis come to listen in to the Abbey Players broadcasting to & from America. I say 'to & from America' because that is the only way the broadcast from Dublin can be heard. RIDERS TO THE SEA.[1] Sheelah rang up this morning to ask if they might come here for it as we have the only 'short wave' they know. Another tribute to your machine.

After we left you at Holyhead we proceeded to Caernarvon, together with some twelve thousand Welsh Nationalists, all going to the Home Rule meeting at Caernarvon to welcome the three men who had been imprisoned etc.[2] Michael insisted on attending the meeting*, but as it was all in Welsh consented to leave after about ½ an hour. We then walked around and got caught up in a huge crowd awaiting the exit of the three heroes. About six police and three ambulance men dealt with the thousands; very unlike Dublin. From 8 pm until after 10.30 we only heard two words in English, from the police at intervals, 'keep back', also very unlike Dublin! The police mainly talked Welsh, flirted with the girls, one chewed gum unceasingly, in fact 'a good time was had by all'. When Lewis emerged from the hall he had to be pushed through the crowd with the assistance of three police and two ambulance men.

Anne went to Amiens St yesterday morning to see the Abbey people off. They all wept, they all arrived with all their infants but I understand the infants did not weep but merely looked solemnly out of well scrubbed faces at their emotional parents (frightful grammar—) May Craig[3] lost one of her five and sent Anne to look for 'Raymond'. Anne chased around asking all male creatures under 20 'Are you May Craig's Raymond' until she found a lanky spectacled youth looking like Lennox who said 'Yeass?' Fred[4] nearly missed the train; everybody kissed everybody, even Barney[5] embraced all and whatnot, Tanya dissolved in tears and was carried off by Hunt and Frank O'Connor for lunch. Aideen O'Connor did not weep because she had wept all night and had no tears left. Eileen Crowe was true to her travelling

---

[1] *Riders to the Sea* by J. M. Synge was performed by the Abbey Theatre players in Dublin and produced by American director Irving Reis (1906–53) as part of his experimental radio anthology programme, Columbia Workshop, a radio series that ran on the Columbia Broadcasting System from 1936 to 1943, returning in 1946–7.

[2] A reception was held in the pavilion for the three Welsh nationalists J. Saunders Lewis (1893–1985), poet and dramatist, Lewis E. Valentine (1893–1986), the first president of Plaid Cymru, and David John Williams (1885–1970), Welsh-language writer, who were released from Wormwood Scrubs the previous month after imprisonment for setting fire to a Royal Air Force Camp in Wales and insisting on speaking Welsh at their trial.

[3] Mary 'May' Craig, Mrs Vincent Power Fardy (1889–1972), who had performed in the original cast of *The Playboy of the Western World* by Synge in 1907, remained with the Abbey Theatre for more than sixty years, participating in all six American tours.

[4] Fred Higgins.

[5] 'Barney' Murphy.

tradition and did not appear at all, she was on the train but unseen. Paddy Carolyn deathly white and almost speechless; Hunt arrived with a huge hat box which he untied and unwrapped to reveal one large bouquet for all the actresses—one was missing, where was she, she must be found—found, bouquet presented. Paddy Carolan[6] left kissing his wife goodbye until the last moment and they kissed through the carriage window, she running along the platform. The Abbey children had collected into a slightly dazed group to be collected later by relations.

I have asked Watt to tell the Macmillan Co USA that you would prefer not to have an advance on future new books. I think this is better as the American Macmillan, when they have paid an advance, do not mention in their accounts the number of books sold. You will no doubt agree to this decision of mine. This new arrangement will cover their publication of THE VISION and HERNE's EGG.

Hope you are well..

G.

*The Caernarvon meeting of Welsh nationalists was held in a colossal building called THE PAVILLION. It is the size and shape of the Mormon Temple at Salt Lake City, but made of galvanised tin, painted black, with small windows painted white. Sound, or rather acoustics, almost as good as the Mormon Temple.[7]

[TLS & MS Dict]   The Chantry House | Steyning.
                                              [21 Sept. 1937]

[MS] My dear Dobbs

[TS] I enclose the preface for the Cuala volume of essays.[1] Lolly can number the opening pages in Roman numcrals. If that should prove impossible you can leave out all my preface down to 'has grown clearer' and put only the essential information which follows. This could go as a short paragraph at the back of a title page. I think, however, the first paragraph

---

[6] P. J. 'Paddy' Carolan (*c.*1900–1938), an actor much admired by AG, had been a member of the company since the early 1920s and performed in many DDL productions as well as the Abbey,

[7] In mid-March 1920, while on WBY's American lecture tour, they had visited Salt Lake City and met with the Elders of the Mormon Church.

[1] *Essays by W. B. Yeats 1931–1936* was finished in the last week of October 1937 and published by Cuala on 14 Dec. 1937. All but the preface and the first essay, 'Parnell', had been previously published in journals, although in the first paragraph—which was not omitted—he insisted that 'Nothing in this book is journalism; nothing was written to please a friend or satisfy an editor, or even to earn money.'

is wanted and will help to sell the book, and will be a help to the reviewers if review copies are sent out.

I can't write a letter now as I have to go unexpectedly to Brighton to get a slight emendation made in my dental plate.

Yrs ev
WB Yeats

[MS] To morrow I go to <u>Penns in the Rocks</u>.

[ALS]   THE CHANTRY HOUSE, | STEYNING | SUSSEX.

Wednesday [22 Sept. 1937]

My dear Dobbs

Just off to <u>Penns in the Rocks</u> will write from there.
Cut enclosed out of New Cronicle this morning[1]

Yrs ev
WB Yeats

[ALS]   PENNS IN THE ROCKS, | WITHYHAM, | SUSSEX.

Sept 24 [1937]

My dear Dobbs,

I return MacCartan & Healy letters.[1] I have written to McCartan to say that you will deal with the matter. So please write to him. You will see by enclosed papers that I have accepted all your suggestions.[2]

I am exceedingly well & life is pleasant here; from early next week I shall be at the Athenaeum for a week.

While I was at Steyning I had to go to Oxford because I had knocked out a tooth with a crust & so a new tooth had to go on to my plate. On the way back we passed—Edith Shackleton was driving me in her motor—a stalwart, yellow haired, young woman on horse back, followed

---

[1] '"Spirit Notes" Reveal Lost Concerto', *News Chronicle*, 22 Sept. 1937, described the discovery of a long-lost Schumann concerto by GY's old friend the violinist Jelly d'Arányi and her sister Adila Fachiri (1889–1962) while employing the 'glass game', a planchette or ouija board; the BBC announced that the concerto would be performed 20 October in the Queen's Hall by d'Arányi with the BBC Symphony Orchestra, Sir Adrian Boult conducting (see *BG*, 473).

[1] James Augustine Healy (1891–1975), a stockbroker and avid collector of Irish literature and paintings, was a member of the Testimonial committee and generous benefactor to both American and Irish libraries and galleries.

[2] Enclosures missing.

by dogs. Some weeks ago a motor grased one of her dogs (the dog was not permanenty injured). The motorist stopped & got out to apologise. She ran at him, trew him down & bit him, put the other dogs at him, jumped into the motor & broke & tore everything she could. The court made her pay £5.

I thank you for your most amusing letter. My univentful life leaves me with nothing to record. Turner & Hilda Matheson come to-morrow. Dorothy has recovered her health & is trying to unite metrical fragments into wholes.

I am very sorry about Lilly.[3]

Yrs ev
WB Yeats

[TLS]
RIVERSDALE, | WILLBROOK, | RATHFARNHAM, | DUBLIN.
Tuesday, Sept 28 1937

Dear William

Your letters do not sound very cheerful, but I hope you will be seeing Turner and Dulac etc....I am doing a mass of dull work, clearing out old typescripts and so on Can I now burn all the old typescripts of 'A VISION'? I will not do so unless you tell me that I may.

I went last night to that play about Mangan at the Abbey. If Clarence Mangan was the cringing, self-pitying, horror, that D'Alton has made of him I dont think he is worth making a play about. If such a play had been presented at any other theatre I would have walked out after the first act. The newspapers today praise it. 'In Siberian wastes,'...'Pain as in a dream' and so on, 'You'll think of me through Daylight's hours, My virgin flower, my flower of flowers, My dark Rosaleen!'[1] Perhaps I hate the play because you have taught me to hate the weak.

Yours affly
George Yeats

---

[3] SMY suffered from a retrosternal goitre, which caused laboured breathing and physical weakness which too frequently prevented her from working at her embroidery.

[1] *The Man in the Cloak*, the first play by Louis Lynch D'Alton (1900–51), who had gained experience as actor and director by touring with his actor-manager father Frank Dalton (1850–1935) and would become one of the Abbey Theatre's most prolific playwrights during the 1940s; for the first five months of 1940 he also served as managing director of the Abbey, but resigned to establish his own touring or 'fit-up' company.

[ALS]   THE ATHENÆUM, | PALL MALL, S.W.1
                                            Sept 29 [1937]

My dear Dobbs

A Vision comes out on Oct 7 so you may destroy all proofs etc. I shall send you three of my six copies as you are part author.[1] Macmillan has sent you an unbound set for the American Edition de Luxe.

I went last night to Richard II. A fine performance except that the great passages had no rythem & the chief character neither charm nor good look. Shakespeare had called him 'sweet lovely rose' & allowed him to speak of his face as 'brittle glory'.[2]

I hear that the Times says Mangan was well played but I have not seen the notice. If so that is very important as almost every body is in America

                                                                    Yrs ev
                                                                    WB Yeats

[ALS]   THE ATHENÆUM, | PALL MALL, S.W.1
                                        Friday Sept 29 [1 Oct. 1937]

My dear Dobbs

I have just seen Dr Yong.[1] Report good. No swelling of ankles, lungs clear, blood-pressure down. He says I am much better than at any of my previous visits. On the other hand there is an increase of albumin. Owing to this last my diet for six days out of seven is to be milk, fruit, salad in fact my own diet. On the seventh day I may eat game, or chicken or fish etc. He thinks the increase of albumen may be temporary (I have been slightly constipated the last couple of days).

Yesterday I saw Diana Murphy. Lilly's work approved but there are some colours to be worked through others to soften harsh contrasts I have full directions.

I met Dulac last night (at dinner with others) & dine with him on Tuesday. All my plans after that are held up because Bowra[2] is away & I want to get that Oxford dinner or lunch off my conscience.

---

[1] Not only was *A Vision* based on GY's automatic script, the philosophy derived from it was discussed between them; the 1937 edition describes her role for the first time.

[2] *Richard II*, the first in a season of 'great plays' at the Queen's Theatre with a permanent company that included Peggy Ashcroft, Alec Guinness, and Michael Redgrave, was produced and directed by John Gielgud (1904–2000), who also performed the title role.

[1] Dr R. A. Young, specialist in chest diseases who had been consulted first with SMY and later WBY; see 3 Nov. 1929.

[2] Bowra had hosted a dinner for WBY at Wadham College when he was given an honorary doctorate from Oxford; see 28 May 1931; however, WBY wished to make amends because he had refused an invitation to lunch which he did not realize had been issued by Bowra (see 1 and 27 Oct. 1937).

I have just had a phone message from Elizabeth Pelham. She has had 'the happiest letter she has ever had from Swami'. It seems that he has at last got a good conscience.

When I was in Steyning a delightful smiling shy man came to tea. He is a country neighbour & has some kind of paralysis that makes him shake perpetually. I drew him out & heard all about his property. He owns three ducks, four geese & an apple tree. One of the geese eats all the fallen apples. He has put barbed-wire all round the apple tree but the goose gets over. He had lived many years in Africa, 'turning the natives into soldiers' where he was the only white man, & he had a pet monkey, & the monkey etc etc. It is years since I have seen any body smile so, timidity, shyness, boundless benovelence. I saw a Chinease actor smile like that.

What did Anne think of the Mangan play

Yrs affly
WB Yeats

[TLS]

RIVERSDALE, | WILLBROOK, |
RATHFARNHAM, | DUBLIN.
October 4 1937

My dear Willy

Thanks for your letter—yes, Mangan was extremely well acted. A woman in the audience was over-heard saying 'The number 2 company are as good as the first company'. The INVINCIBLES comes on on October 18th.[1]

I saw Frank O'Connor on Friday. Baty at last wrote. He has no 'atelier' attached to his theatre, the work is all done in the studio of a friend of his, Bertin. O'Connor's suggestion, which I accepted, was that Anne should go to Paris as soon as possible with introductions to Baty, the Pitoeffs and one or two others; should find out from Baty if she could be taken in to Bertin's workshop and ask his advice generally. Baty was apparently extremely friendly and said that Anne could attend all his rehearsals etc. Anne points out that from the point of view of stage decoration that would not be a great deal of use as most rehearsals would be on an un-set stage.[2] Anne is to

---

[1] *The Invincibles*, 'A Play in Seven Scenes' by Hugh Hunt and Frank O'Connor, produced by Hunt and designed by Moiseiwitsch, received its first production on 18 Oct. 1937.

[2] At Frank O'Connor's suggestion the Abbey Theatre Board had approved a study trip to Paris so that ABY could learn more about scenic design. Gaston Baty (1885–1952) of the Théâtre Montparnasse in Paris, and from 1936 a producer at the Comédie Française, was both a director and playwright, known throughout Europe for his brilliant scenic effects; Émile Bertin (1878–1957), a frequent collaborator with Baty, began his distinguished career as designer of both theatre and opera with André Antoine (1858–1943); Georges Pitoeff (1887–1939), Russian-born actor director, designer, and translator who over the years produced Shaw, Chekhov, and Pirandello as well as contemporary dramatists, and his wife the actress Ludmilla Pitoeff (1895–1951) were at this time running a company at Théâtre des Mathurins in Paris.

try and see O'Connor today or tomorrow and get him to put up a definite proposition to the Board regarding the length of time she is to have, and the allowance they propose to make. I think it better that she should do this herself as an act of independence! His suggestion to me was that she should be allowed £2.10.0 for living expenses and her one pound a week 'pocket money' making £3-10-0 in all. This will of course be supplemented by me. I shall know when I hear from some families I have written to (who take in students) on the advice of M Brière, how much to add.[3]

She is to talk to Tanya today and I am afraid is rather nervous about it. O'Connor has already spoken to Tanya, and with his usual IRA methods told her that Anne was to go at once and not wait to finish the sets for the INVINCIBLES. Anne is going to tell O'Connor that she wishes to stay and finish! It is a very big job and a rather interesting one.

Do you think you could find out from anyone in London about the group and other small theatres in Paris? Dulac might know.

O'Connor told me that Fred May had been suspended for a month…he had the bright idea that the 2nd company should all go up to Carnforth to play to George Shiels.[4] The Directors were not to be asked permission as they would certainly refuse! Anne, when I asked her if she knew, said 'Yes'. She had heard the whole saga from one of the players (I wont say which) and had asked her informant how on earth they would get the costumes, sets etc out of the Abbey and back without being found out!! Her practical mind.…It was to have occurred on a Sunday. Really, the things they think they can get away with are incredible.

I am sorry about the increase of albumen, but it is probably a temporary condition. DID YOU GET YOUR AIR CUSHIONS???

I have got an overwhelming cold and if I had not wanted to let you know at once about Paris would have waited a day or two before writing as my brain is like cotton wool and I have probably written a muddled letter.

Yours

G.

[ALS]   THE ATHENÆUM, | PALL MALL, S.W.1
Oct 2 [4 Oct. 1937]

My dear Dobbs,

I have just come from Watt. He sent you a Yoga Aphorism (Patanjali) Agreement on Sept 16, or rather sent it to me at Riversdale. Please let me

---

³ The French consul; see 11 Oct 1937.

⁴ Composer Frederick May, who had begun his studies with John Larchet, succeeded him as music director at the Abbey Theatre (1936–48). George Shiels was confined to a wheelchair and could not attend performances of his plays at the Abbey Theatre; a revised version of his play *Cartney and Kevney* was to be produced on 8 Nov. 1937.

have it—there has been a muddle & Swami seems to have signed an agreement making me part Author

George Barnes (of BBC) lunched with me to day. He insists that I have not the strength for a whole BBC programme. I have written offering a 20 minuites test.

I go back to Sussex on Thursday & am longing to get away. I find I cannot talk as much as I do here—all necessary or inspiring talk—& work. To morrow Rothenstein lunches here & then takes me to his studio for a new drawing.[1] In the evening I dine with Dulac. On Wednesday I hope to give BBC the test. Then I go to the Shackletons, then I think to Oxford to give that lunch, then again to Penns in the Rocks. Then perhaps a broad cast & home.

Has the Candle-Press set up that speach, poem etc. The act will loose graciousness if too long delayed[2]

Has the Nat Gallery replied yet about the O Leary portrait?[3]

I have been almost a week in London now—damn the place.

Yrs

WB Yeats

Did you get my preface to the Cuala essays?

[ALS]   THE ATHENÆUM, | PALL MALL, S.W.1

Oct 5 [1937]

My dear Dobbs

I am sorry about your cold & sorry I wrote about all that business yesterday.

Two days ago I sent proof of Broadside introduction to Lolly. I think I asked for another proof as I had made a muddle. I will wire if it is correct.

Hilda Matheson spoke of some place in Paris where Anne could stay. I have written to her about it

I see Dulac to night—I dine there & will ask about Paris theatres

---

[1] William Rothenstein did many portraits of WBY, a number of them in later years while visiting their good friend DW at Penns-in-the Rocks (see Robert Speaight, *William Rothenstein: The Portrait of an Artist in his Time* (London, 1962), 383).

[2] *A Speech and Two Poems*, being the text of his speech at the banquet of the Irish Academy of Letters on 17 Aug. 1937 and the poems 'Dedication' and 'The Municipal Gallery Re-Visited', was privately published by WBY in an edition of 70 copies and printed by the Sign of the Three Candles, Ltd., Dublin. Copies were to be sent to the donors of the Testimonial Committee.

[3] JBY's 1904 portrait of the Fenian leader John O'Leary (1830–1907) is considered one of his finest works. After Hugh Lane, who commissioned the portrait, exhibited it in London, it was purchased by John Quinn, and subsequently donated to the National Gallery of Ireland.

My <u>broadcast</u> is fixed for Oct 29. Could you meet me the next day or on Monday Nov 1. We can then go on to the Halls if they can still have us.[1]

> Yrs ev
> WB Yeats

Enclosed is the letter I thought I had sent—mere business dont open it till cold is gone[2]

[ALS]   THE ATHENÆUM, | PALL MALL, S.W.1
                                                        Oct 7 [1937]

My dear Dobbs
    Dulac will give Anne an introduction to the man who arranged all the theatrical exxhibits in the Parris exhibition. If the exhibition is over when Anne gets there this man will be able to introduce her to all Parisian experimental theatres[1]
    3 copies of Vision have just been sent to you.
    I am just off to Chantrey House, Steyning for a few days

> Yrs ev
> WB Yeats

Am in excellent health

[ALS]   THE CHANTRY HOUSE, | STEYNING | SUSSEX.
                                                        Oct 9 [1937]

My dear Dobbs
    I enclose part of a note from Hilda Matheson with information which may be helpful, or may not.[1]
    I have not yet found any press or other errors in <u>A Vision</u> wonderful to say.
    Dulac said of Lilly's embroidery 'She could make a lot of money faking old Chinease embroidery with that stitch of hers'—a great complement from him

> Yrs ev
> WB Yeats

[1] Jean Hall, now a widow, was living with her six children in Charnes Hall, Eccleshall, Staffordshire, while restoring Broughton Hall, a 23-bedroom Elizabethan country house nearby; see 30 Oct. 1929.
[2] Probably his letter of 4 October above.

[1] The Exposition Internationale des Arts et Techniques dans la Vie Moderne was held in Paris from 4 May to 25 Nov. 1937.

[1] Enclosure missing; see next letter.

Did I tell you that Scribner have written to Watt demanding those prefaces.

[TLS]   RIVERSDALE, | WILLBROOK, |
                                         RATHFARNHAM, | DUBLIN.
                                         Monday [11 Oct. 1937]

Dear William

I had to go to cot because I apparently hadnt a cold but had flu. By the end of this week I shall be able to be innocculated against colds flu etc. Helen[1] wrote to me an address of a friend of theirs in Paris. I have written. The French Consul here, M.Briere[2] had already given me the address Miss Matheson tells you of—Institut Britannique—and also several other addresses. I wrote to the Institut Britannique and they sent me all their literature, lists of families who took students, etc, etc. I think the Dulac's friend would be better than any if she will take Anne; in any case I have committed myself to her for the moment—unless she can't have A.

I had already sent to Watt the three prefaces and VOLUME FIVE ESSAYS (your letter of today); there are other outstanding things I have not done <because I thought I had a cold but it was 'flu and last week I had to go to bed>. I am to start being innocculated against such things at the end of this week. Colm O'Lochlainn was to have sent you proofs of the poems and speech to the Irish-Americans.[3] I will go into Dublin tomorrow to see him. Like the Abbey Directors he is unsatisfactory on the telephone.

I return Miss Matheson's letter and have kept the address she gives as a possible home for Anne in case Mme Rexens falls through.[4] In any case it might be useful for Michael; I am not at all inclined to keep him on at St Columba's after the end of this next year (end of summer term 1938 when

[1] Helen Beauclerk.
[2] M. François Brière, secretary to the French Legation in Dublin for five years, left in 1937 to take up the position of independent consul in Boston.
[3] Colm Ó'Lochlainn (1892–1972), founder in 1926 of the publishing company At the Sign of the Three Candles, and later of the Three Candles Press, was a bibliophile and collector of street ballads, many of which he published; 1933–43 he was also Professor of Language and Literature at University College Dublin.
[4] In the end, ABY did stay with Léa Rixens (1885–1985), widow of Dulac's long time friend and fellow art student Émile Rixens, and one of his own favourite models. Active in the Resistance during the war, she was appropriately later the model for Marianne, symbol of the Republic, in the stamp Dulac was commissioned by de Gaulle to design for the 'Free France'; the same image, known as 'Marianne de Londres', was later used on post-war banknotes in France and its colonies.

he will be nearly seventeen) and the Sorbonne might be a better place for him for a year than Germany. I was infuriated to find that he has now been started on 'the Second Book of Virgil' 'which we have to do for School Certificate and Intermediate' with no sense of the construction of The Aeneid. They just have to 'do' the Second book; 'it is five hundred lines'. Damn school. I'm not exalting Virgil but damning a system which gives you '500 lines' and no circumference.

What are you broadcasting? Will arrange if possible with Jean Hall to stay there on our way home.

G.

[TLS]					RIVERSDALE, | WILLBROOK, |
					RATHFARNHAM, | DUBLIN.
					October 13 1937

My dear Willy

I saw Colm O'Lochlainn yesterday. He had been delaying—he said!—because he could not get the paper I had chosen. I selected two others and he has promised proofs 'at once'. He is a conversationalist, one might say a chatterbox.[1] After seeing him I called in to hurry Victor Brown[2] with the December illustration (Terrible Robber men) and found him surrounded by designs for the new stamp. He handed me the 'official' typed material on which designs have to be based, with just one word. 'Religion'. I read it and found it was selections from the opening clause of the new Constitution. He then said 'stamp'. After that he became less monosyllabic and confided that at any rate there need not be much printing on it, but he had only just received the document and the design had to be ready by Monday. I did not like any of his preliminary sketches except perhaps one. But what can you do with a stamp which has to have a large Cross in it?

---

[1] Ŏ' Lochlainn's entry on WBY for 1939 *British Annual of Literature*, ii. 29 reads: 'Like many another of the old Ascendancy he found little to love in the newer order in Ireland. To him the magnificent crimes of the older regime were more noble than the petty virtues of the new. And towards the end his mind was all bemused with strange occult philosophies, theosophy, spiritism; and in play or poem these were given an airing, without even full conviction to defend them.'

[2] Victor Brown (1900–53), political cartoonist for the *Irish Press* as 'Bee', was also one of illustrators to the 1935 *Broadsides*; to the 1937 series he contributed illustrations to Nos. 3 (March), 8 (August), 9 (September), and 11 (November); his illustrations to 'The Terrible Robber Men' by Padraic Colum and 'The Huntsmen' by Walter de la Mare appeared in the November 1937 issue. The postage stamp he was designing was to commemorate the 25th anniversary of the Easter Rising (1941).

I wrote to Jean about our going there on, say Nov. 1st, but have not yet heard from her. She may be away.

Yours
George Y.

[MS] Hope you are well?

[ALS]   THE CHANTRY HOUSE, | STEYNING | SUSSEX.

Oct 13 [1937]

My dear Dobbs

I am certain you are right about Michael. He is being taught Virgil as I was taught it at the High School & I was damnably ill taught.[1] There too the intermediate was the excuse & the real reason was I imagine second rate teachers. I think he should do well at the Sorbonne, as he knows French and would find himself among hard workers. I will ask Dulac about it

To day I am in good spirits. Since I came to England I have been been upset because, though I tried, every day, I could not find a theme for poetry. I thought I was finished. I was inclined to blame the diet which is necessary to my health. Yesterday quite suddenly I found a theme & have written a poem that pleases me[2] & now I have another theme. I am pleased too about something else—I was to have left to day to go to Oxford but Bowra has not written & I have been asked to stay on. Evry day I go for an hour's drive through this green country & shall probably do so until I return to Penns in the Rocks. I get the stimulus I want from occasional visitors

My plans for spring are getting clear. <The Shackletons can> I think of Cap-Martin at Monte Carlo where life just now is cheap, a hotel advertises food & lodging for 8/- a day. The Shackletons can come for one month, any month, can you come before or after? The Scot James[3] may come for a couple of weeks. <Can you come?> It should be pleasant & sunny & Anne will be fairly near. I think of writing a long Noh play on the death of Cuchulain.

I was glad to get your letter. I was just about to telephone to know how your cold was.

---

[1] WBY attended the Erasmus Smith High School, Harcourt Street, Dublin, from the autumn of 1881 until December 1883; the following May he enrolled at the Metropolitan School of Art on Kildare Street, remaining there until April 1886.

[2] 'The Circus Animals' Desertion'.

[3] Rolfe Arnold Scott-James (1878–1959), journalist and literary critic, held editorial positions at the *Daily News* (1902–12), the *Daily Chronicle* (1919–30), *The Spectator* (1933–5, 1939–45), and the *London Mercury* (1934–9), in which he published much of WBY's later writings. His publications included the influential *Modernism and Romance* (1908), *Personality in Literature* (1913), and *The Making of Literature* (1928). His wife was Violet Eleanor, née Brooks (d. 1942).

Please let me have some Abbey news. Has 'The Invincibles' been played yet. Send me the papers about it if you can.

I enclose a letter from Watt[4] with a passage marked

Yrs affecly
WB Yeats

[ALS]   RIVERSDALE, | WILLBROOK, |
RATHFARNHAM, | DUBLIN.
Sunday [17 Oct. 1937]

My dear Willy

Very many thanks for letter & poem which I like—I enclose a typed copy[1]—Of course I would love to join you at Cap Martin—January would be difficult because of Michael's holidays. After that, any time.

I am not sure if I shall be able to go to 'Invincibles' tomorrow night as I have had to go to bed again with fresh chill. Damn. Its such years since I had had colds. I will try & get Anne to write!

Hope the new poem is going well—

Yours
George Y.

[ALS]   THE CHANTRY HOUSE, |
STEYNING | SUSSEX.
Oct 20 [1937]

My dear Dobbs: If a certain date is given correcly in <u>A Vision</u> this must be the Anniversary of our marriage. Last night I had a night mare. I was in a crowded house of horrible people who all said you were dead (I have been anxious about your cold). Then I found you in the form of a large cold cooked chicken. I took you up & then bit by bit you came to life. I woke up very content.

I return to London to day—go from there probably on Friday to 'Penns in the Rocks' & then to London for my 'Broadcast'.

I wonder if you have heard from Mrs Hall. Get Anne to write & tell me. I have a reason for wanting to know

I am writing to Anne for information about your cold

Yrs ev
WB Yeats

[4] Enclosure missing.
[1] Most likely an early draft of 'The Circus Animals' Desertion'.

[TLS]   RIVERSDALE, | WILLBROOK, |
                                   RATHFARNHAM, | DUBLIN.
<See enclosed>   Oct 21 1937
Dear Willy

I enclose some press cuttings about Abbey re-building etc. Anne was told by Frank O'Connor on Tuesday that the papers were going to have remarks, so I ordered them all. Nothing, you see, is out about the possible Gov. grant for the main re-building. They are, I imagine, laying pipe for further announcements. I need hardly say that I have not said anything to anyone (Anne included) about the negociations with the Govt.[1]

I think Tanya has found a possible 'assistant'. At any rate she and Anne have now come to an arrangement of a most amicable kind and I think Anne will proceed to Paris in two weeks time. As I have not yet heard from Jean I am writing again today to ask whether my post or hers is to blame, and I have suggested that Anne and I meet you at either Stafford or Crewe (whichever suits her best) on Monday November 1st and that we all three proceed for a night (or two nights) to Charnes. You can leave London by a reasonably convenient train, <u>not</u> the early Irish Mail, and if your train arrives later than ours Anne and I can disport ourselves in the selected town and meet your train, complete with Jean. I dont want to ask her to do that very long motor journey twice in the day. DO YOU AGREE.

I am feeling revolting, have been in cot for five days, havent seen INVIN-CIBLES, have an ulcerterated throat—at least that will save me telephones for some days—and am generally out of hand.

                                                            Yours
                                                            G.Y.

[ALS]   THE ATHENÆUM, | PALL MALL, S.W.1
                                                      Oct 21 [1937]

Dear Anne

I thank you for your note & the cutting. You say that your mother has sent off 'clippings'. None have come. Your note is the first information I have had. Thank you.

---

[1] Enclosures missing. Since 1924, with the encouragement of Ernest Blythe, the theatre had received an annual subsidy from the government; the *Irish Times* (17 Nov. 1937) included a small squib announcing that Sean McEntee, Minister for Finance, moved 'a supplementary estimate of £2,800 in Dáil Eireann on 27th October for miscellaneous expenses…for a special grant to the National Theatre Ltd., for certain structural alterations to the Abbey Theatre'.

I have wired to you at the theatre & asked you to wire me saying how your mother is.

Will you find out from her if she has heard from Mrs Hall. I want to know at once.

Yours ever
WB Yeats

[ALS]   RIVERSDALE, | WILLBROOK, |
                                               RATHFARNHAM, | DUBLIN.
                                               Friday [22 Oct. 1937]

My dear Willy

No, I have not heard from Jean. I gather your 'reason for asking' is probably that you want to go somewhere else on Nov 1? Let me know at once so that if she <u>does</u> write I could make an alternative date with her.

My cold improving. I was up yesterday & did too much so am tired today & shall probably laze in bed. I write in pencil only because no ink in my pen—

Next week I shall have to start seeing to Anne's clothes, or rather making <u>her</u> see to them—I am certain she will buy none in Paris—all her money will go on books as it did in London. She bought one summer frock because I threatened her with stoppage of allowance if she didnt!

Yours
George

[TLS]   RIVERSDALE | RATHFARNHAM | Co. DUBLIN
                               Monday Oct. 25. 1937

My dear Willy

Jean Hall telephoned yesterday (Sunday) but I was in bed and Mary explained this. I hoped to hear from you this morning about your plans, but no letter came—I do not really feel well enough to 'pay visits' by Nov. 1st—which was your date—and am writing by this post to Jean to explain. I have suggested in my letter that after Nov. 7th we shall have a spare room 'of sorts' and that she might put in a few days with us. I have not done it in quite the stupid way that this typed letter suggests.

When I hear from you about your plans—and addresses—I will be more sure of my ground. I think I have sent many letters to 'Penns' under the impression that you were there. As I look through your letters I see that I did not have any particular address for any particular date!

Pangur died last night which was a slight blow to me—Mary and the gardener think me heartless because I said 'I must get a kitten for myself at once'.[1]

Yours George.

[TLS]   RIVERSDALE, | WILLBROOK, |
                                         RATHFARNHAM, | DUBLIN.
                                                October 25 1937

My dear Willy

Here is a tiresome, but not important, thing. I meant, when I was downstairs last Thursday Oct 21 to send to Richard de la Mare the envelope in
which typescript and proofs of PATANJALI had arrived Wednesday Oct 20th
evening. After doing some necessary letters, I felt ill, and went back to bed. I
came down again this morning and I find that either Mary or Mrs Wilkinson[1]
have destroyed the envelope which I had left on Study table. (I meant to
send it to him to explain that he must send you galley proofs 13–32 IF YOU
HAVE TO SEND A COPY TO SWAMI.) No letter arrived with proofs, and
galleys 13–32 inclusive were missing from packet. I am now sending you by
registered post to The Athenaeum the complete typescript of PATANJALI,
Galley proofs 1–32 which make one complete set; Galley proofs 1–12.

Will you either ring up R. de la Mare[2] or write to asking him to send you
another set of galleys if you have to send one on to Swami. R. de la Mare
may have sent proofs direct to Swami.

ANNE AND MARY ARE BOTH WITNESSES TO CONDITION OF
ENVELOPE WHEN RECEIVED.

GY.

[ALS]   THE CHANTRY HOUSE, | STEYNING | SUSSEX.
                                         Wednesday [27 Oct. 1937]

My dear Dobbs

Your letter written on Friday has only just come. <I have wired
answer.> At the last moment Hilda Matheson wrote that Dorothy was

---

[1] The household never seemed to be without at least one cat.

[1] Mary Martin had been housekeeper at Riversdale since they moved in; Mrs Wilkinson is
presumably a 'daily' or charwoman.

[2] Richard de la Mare (1901–86), son of the poet Walter de la Mare, was joint managing
director and later chairman of Faber & Faber, who had at WBY's suggestion agreed to publish
Purohit Swami's translation of *The Aphorisms of Yoga* by Bhagwân Shree Patanjali.

too ill. The death of her great dane Brutus had caused a relapse. Brutus had become paralysed & she had to order his destruction. So I asked if I might return here. When I wrote to Anne asking your plans I thought if you were not going to Mrs Hall I might give that Oxford lunch on Sunday or Monday I owe to Bowra & his guests. That is not possible now <& anyway I am here> & will do quite well the next time I am in London

I go to London this afternoon & reherse my broadcast to morrow

Yours affectionly
W B Y

PS

I do not write more as I am at work on a poem which is almost finished

I wired to say I would go to Dublin or meet you at Chester on Monday. I am not sure if Chester is the right station

[TLS]
RIVERSDALE, | WILLBROOK, |
RATHFARNHAM, | DUBLIN.
October 27 1937

My dear Willy

I wired to you that I would meet you at Holyhead on Monday. I have written to Jean who wired yesterday 'come whenever you like writing' that owing to complications about Anne's departure to Paris we cant stop this time—I have explained fully to her.

The Abbey Board has to 'authorize' payments to Anne for expenses in Paris. I telephoned to Gorman to know what was being done and he read me a note O'Connor had given him regarding 'expenses' with the remark 'subject to authorisation by Board'. A good deal of unnecessary 'uncomfortableness' having occurred because the Board never officially notified Tanya, etc, etc, I do not feel at all inclined to have Anne start off until the Board has officially passed O'Connor's suggestions. There is no meeting today; the Board is now meeting only once a fortnight. Gorman is to bring the matter up next Wednesday, and if you get here on Monday you might perhaps attend the meeting? I can tell you the various details when I see you. Tanya has found an assistant to take Anne's place, but she cannot start until Monday, so Anne stays at Abbey until the end of this week.

[MS] In haste for post.

Yours George.

[ALS]   THE ATHENÆUM, | PALL MALL, S.W.1
                                        Thursday [28 Oct. 1937]

My dear Dobbs

I dont think you should meet me with that cold upon you. Heaven knows
what the weather will be like. I shall manage all right. I am much stronger
now.¹

I have just come from BBC rehersal & think I shall be good to morrow
night.²

Last night Dulac & Helen dined with me at the Ivy. He mentioned that
3 days ago he had had a letter from Madam Rixens saying that she had
not yet heard from you. Helen had had a letter from you saying you had
written. I wonder what has happened. Fearing you may have put a wrong
address I enclose the true address.³

                                                    Yours affecly
                                                    WB Yeats

[TLS]   RIVERSDALE, | WILLBROOK, |
                                   RATHFARNHAM, | DUBLIN.
                                            November 20 1937

My dear Anne

Very many thanks for letter about Baty (and Bertin). Better write to the
O.C. at Abbey Theatre.... more official.¹ I did not write to you about the
Sara Payne Ballet because the news came in about Tanya and my mind was
full of that.² I am sending under separate cover Abbey Programme, Payne
Programme, and one or two Press cuttings. All the costumes looked very
well except that those damned bitches of witches had cut their dresses far
too short and looked like bloody English Spinsters (which they all were...)
And I DID NOT like Maeve. For one thing she had put a belt round her
waist which made her look as if she was wearing an old fashioned dinner frock, and My God she is bunchy! How many woollies and petticoats
had she on? Wish you had been there to tear them off her. The scene was

    ¹ GY did, however, meet him at Holyhead as usual.
    ² 'My Own Poetry Again', 'A programme introduced and read by W. B. Yeats assisted by
Margot Ruddock', was broadcast on 29 Oct. 1937.
    ³ AY's lodgings were with Madame Rixens, who lived at 18 Rue du Moulin de Beurre,
Paris XIV; see note to 11 Oct. 1937.

    ¹ Frank O'Connor; see letter of 4 Oct. 1937.
    ² Tanya Moiseiwitsch was ill in England; ABY had designed the costumes for Sara Payne's
new ballet on Cuchullain (see letter 7 July 1937).

really rather impressive, the monolith most admirable and the lighting good. The papers make too little of Cuchullain. True, he did not 'dance' but I confess I thought his poses and movements far better than the leaps and bounds into the air which people always expect from male dancers. Lily Hannigan as the Banshee was completely and perfectly enchanting. Maeve I thought danced badly. AND—JesusMaryand-Joseph how frightful all the shows before it were....I do not like poems spoken to dancing! Especially badly spoken to poses. We did all that sort of thing fifty years ago, only then we did it with one mouth, two arms and two legs.. Now it is done with one or more mouth, and other peoples arms and legs. Both have comic value.[3]

I don't know what was in Lennox's introduction to Granville Barker because it came sealed.[4] It is the first introduction I have ever seen 'sealed.' In fact since Hamlet steamed open the letter to the King of England it has been accepted by everyone that such letters are left open. I must spank Lennox next time I see him. Did you get Edmund Dulac's letter of introduction?? He was asked to send it to you in Paris.

A new Play by Vincent Carroll (one act) comes on at the Abbey next week. I hear Tanya had already done the design, and ninetofive is carrying it out.[5] Hope she will not forget to put size in the paint. It would be sad if the draught from the back of the stage slowly blew off the paint—though possibly the audience would think it was the very latest in decor...like the falling of leaves in the autumn.

I am just dragging out your father for a drive, so unless I have any further bright ideas about all I have forgotten to say 'I will now close. Hope this finds you in the pink as it leaves me'. (This was the invariable end to the Tommies letters during the war)

Yours affly George Y.

xx oooo xx ooooxx

[3] The ballet *Doomed Cuchulain* tells of the last hours of the Celtic hero's life, danced by D. B. 'Des' Dalton, who later moved to South Africa. He meets three Women of the Sidhe and the Washer at the Ford, the Banshee, danced by Elizabeth 'Lily' Hannigan, later Mrs Patrick Collins (1918–92), who as a governess in France worked in the Resistance in the Second World War. Also on the programme were various short dances of which one was done to a recitation of WBY's poem 'The Stolen Child'. Maeve was danced by Sara Payne.

[4] The playwright, actor, and director Harley Granville Barker (1877–1946) was director of the British Institute in Paris (1937–9).

[5] *Coggerers* by Paul Vincent Carroll opened on 22 Nov. 1937; ABY and Tanya had nicknamed Tanya's temporary assistant 'ninetofive' because of her insistence on sticking to a schedule.

[ALS] RIVERSDALE, | WILLBROOK, |
RATHFARNHAM, | DUBLIN.
December 21 1937

Dearest Anne

Your wire arrived this morning—Glad you are alive & have not suddenly left Paris for an unknown destination!! Blast you for costing me seven shillings for reply paid Telegram....—

I enclose cover of book sent by <u>Una</u>.[1] I don't send book which is 'Vincent van Gogh' by Walter Pach,[2] '30 reproductions 6 plates in full color' published by Artbook Museum, New York, 1936.

I suggest you write to her c/o Abbey Theatre, Dublin, 'please forward'—I don't know where the company will be next. They are due to go to Boston. God knows what address....—

I need hardly tell you that having 'prised open' the parcel, yr father has been reading the book & has found several re-productions of pictures he had not seen before!! There is an enchanting 'Vegetable Garden' (No. 22, in colour) in which there are no vegetables portrayed in the unpleasant way that one sees them growing in one's own veg: garden!! And a photograph of 'At the Loom' & so on. In fact a niceness book.

We have now a white persian kitten, most excellent kitten, well-mannered, but somewhat too active.

The O.C. was here yesterday. He insists that you stay in Paris for the appointed time & don't get side-tracked by any theories of yr father's. Will type letter later about this.[3]

Damn & blast you for not writing—<u>Have you heard from Tanya</u>? She sent me a card of wishes for Xmas; but put no address. I have written her a card—c/o Abbey—but God knows if it will be sent on to her—...

Yours affly, indignantly & so on—

George Yeats
('Your loving Mother')

---

[1] Una 'Aideen' O'Connor, who was on tour in the United States with the Abbey company.

[2] Walter Pach (1883–1958), American artist, critic, and art historian who had advised John Quinn on his art collection, had been instrumental in the organization of the 1913 New York Armory Show ('The International Exhibition of Modern Art'), and through his writings championed the artists of the modernist movement.

[3] GY's letter to ABY of 27 Dec. 1937 elaborates on the argument between Frank O'Connor and WBY: 'I was relieved to get your no I letter because owing to no letter from you for some time your father got very worked up, decided you were wasting your time, wrote to O'C about it, saw him twice, wanted you re-called to Dublin, wrote to Ninette de Valois (Sadler Wells) to know if you could be taken on there, got answers suggesting you went for three months from January 1st; the O'C obviously wanting you to stay in Paris I was called in and agreed with the O'C. Your father was rather disgruntled because I had not backed him up'.

1938

RIVERSDALE, | WILLBROOK, |
RATHFARNHAM, | DUBLIN.
January 11 1938

My dear Willy

Glad to hear that you arrived safely with good weather.[1] I enclose some letters...one from 'Moya'[2], or at least I think it is her writing!!

Got back to Dublin yesterday morning; no news of any sort except that Lady Yarrow[3] wrote a long rambling letter, addressed to us both, from the Shelbourne Hotel, complaining about the 'torture on the Abbey stage of a little helpless kitten' in Sean O'Faolain's play.[4] Two sheets. I have made telephone enquiries from various people and no one seems to think the cat made any objections; apparently on one night at least during the fortnight it made its exit left, as it had been instructed, after both its appearances on the stage. I havent thought out a response to her yet.. She and her friend left the theatre (as a protest) and 'sent for the producer'. The 'producer' told her that he did not himself like the episode of the cat on the stage and he would do his best to persuade the author to cut it. Hunt had the devil of a time teaching the cat its part, in fact Anne told me that he was keeping a regular cattery at the Abbey in order to select a biddable beast. Most of the cat-actors leaped across the footlights on to the heads of the orchestra, or skidded on the top of the piano and crashed on to the notes. Not so good.

---

[1] As soon as he and Edith Shackleton arrived in Monte Carlo on 9 Jan. 1938 WBY sent a wire to GY, who with MBY had accompanied him as far as London on 5 January.

[2] Moya Llewelyn Davies (1881–1943), committed nationalist, daughter of the Fenian MP James O'Connor, and co-translator of Maurice O'Sullivan's *Twenty Years a Growing*; she claimed to have served as one of Michael Collins's spies by providing a 'safe house' for Collins, and her arrest in March 1921 as responsible for hiring a building for the propaganda department led to her imprisonment in Mountjoy and the dismissal of her husband Compton Llewelyn-Davies (1868–1935) from his position as Solicitor General of the British Post Office and ally of Lloyd George in land reform. Since late 1936, on behalf of the Academy and with the collaboration of Higgins, she had hosted a number of readings by Irish poets in her home; WBY was also advising her on a novel she was writing.

[3] Eleanor, Lady Yarrow, née Barnes (1870–1953), suffragist, pianist, and author of *As the Water Flows: A Record of Adventures in a Canoe on the Rivers and Trout Streams of Southern England* (1927) and the biography of her husband, the philanthropic wealthy engineer and shipbuilder Sir Alfred Yarrow (1842–1932); in 1935 she arranged to have thirty copies of nine of WBY's poems privately printed by the Cuala Press with frontispiece by Victor Brown.

[4] *She Had to Do Something* by Seán Ó'Faoláin, which required a live cat on stage, was produced by Hugh Hunt and opened at the Abbey 27 Dec. 1937.

I now understand why Bryan Guiness⁵ once asked me 'Have you heard lately from our mad friend Lady Yarrow?'

Tanya is back—so much for the O'C's ferocity of statement!

Hope you are sunning yourself well.

Yours affly
George.

[ALS + Encl]   Hotel Terminus | Monte Carlo | France
Jan 11 (1938)

My dear Dobbs

My window or windows—there are 3 in my room—look on to blue sea & bright sun light & the shore & mountain side you remember,¹ much such a view as we had at Rapallo. About ¾ of an hour before we reached Monte Carlo there was snow on the ground but here flowers. At the moment I am just about to begin my days work, sitting up at the desk in my room & Edith Shackleton has gone off to the Casino. They discovered her yesterday & there has been work on the phone—an article probably under weigh. I am very well, no sign of breathing trouble & I sleep only too much

I send the enclosed for Anne fearing she may have heard I passed through Paris and think I should have seen her²

Yrs affectionly
WB Yeats

I am writing at my essay. General aproval by Dulac etc makes me return to 'On the Old boiler'—each number to contain two or three lines of explanation perhaps in verse

Please read my letter to Anne & put spelling right & make it legible.

[Encl¹]   Hotel Terminus | Monte Carlo | France
Jan 11 [1938]

My dear Anne

I passed through Paris on Saturday evening, & wanted to ask you to come & see me in the train. But I did not know the date or route until it was too

---

⁵ Bryan Walter Guinness (1905–92), poet and novelist whose first wife (div. 1933) was the celebrated Nancy Mitford; he and GY were very distant cousins, as both mothers were descendants of the Earl of Buchan (*BG*, xxii).

¹ They had visited Monte Carlo occasionally when living in Rapallo.

² See next letter, forwarded by GY to Paris, apparently without alterations.

¹ See previous letter to GY.

late to give you proper notice. I was afraid of upsetting some arrangement of yours

You are a good letter writer, & all you tell us is good so you need have no fear of my 'side tracking you' but you can always go to the 'Old Vic' any time if you want to & work under a lot of different producers.[2] But tell your French instructors or any others that their ladders & stairs & platforms will soon be as dead as crinolenes or glass cases full of wax flowers. Hamlet must act not pose.

Though I did not see you in Paris I am still your affectionate father

WBYeats

Here all is blue sea & bright sun light

[ALS]   Hotel Terminus | Monte Carlo
                                              Sunday [16 Jan. 1938[1]]

My dear Dobbs

Various events have made me put off writing & now the post goes out in a few minuites. I will write to-morrow

Devine[2] has retired—a paraletic stroke which leaves him as good a doctor as ever prevents him from calling on a patient. His wife came to recommend me Dutch doctor. He has sold his practice but new man cannot move in 'until the Prince returns'. Devine probably goes to London to act as a consultant.

Much news to-morrow

Yrs affectly
W.B.Y.

[ALS]   Hotel Terminus | Monte Carlo | France
                                              Monday [17 Jan. 1938]

My dear Dobbs

When I wrote yesterday I said stirring events had kept me from writing. The events were all one. On Tuesday some sort of foliage, red-cabbage or the like disagreed with me & I got a violent digestive upset. When it

---

[2] See note to GY's letter of 21 Dec. 1937.

[1] From now on all WBY's letters are dated by GY.

[2] Dr James Arthur Devine (1869–1939), the local doctor who had attended WBY the year before, was a Canadian who after a notable career in the Boer War eventually retired to Monte Carlo, where he became the doctor to the British community.

continued in violence I sent for the Dutch doctor. At first could not write, then I would not write till I could say I was well again. Yesterday when I wrote you that short note I was almost well, to day I am quite well. Presenly I shall get up & go out. The weather is as it has been evry day bright & sunny. We are still as you may notice in the same expensive hotel, very comfortable & well cared for & may stay for a week or so. Edith Shackleton should join her sister in Paris on

P.T.O

Feb 5. Could you be here by then? You will find I hope that I have finished the pamphet 'On the Old Boiler'.

I am writing in bed the window nearest to the bed wide open, a gentle warm wind flowing in from to time but generally the air quite still. My breathing is perfectly normal & but for that red cabbage I think I should be better than I have been for a long time.

The Athenaeum servants stole those shirrts. Beyond question I left them in the locker. I am having two made here. Edith Shackleton can take me into the fashionable gambling rooms where the general public is not admitted & that needs a dress shirrt. The one I brought was greatly admired by the best shirrt shop here

Yrs affecly
WB Yeats

P.S

What do you think of taking a flat for two months or are you tired of house keeping. It would be cheaper than a hotel. If you would like this Edith Shackleton & I could probably find one. We could take it for two months. I saw an advertisemen of one which was offered for three.

Sir John Keane has written in the name of the Kildare St Club asking me to stay on for another year at any rate. The want me as bait for other Irish writers. Who among the writers we know can afford that club?[1]

[TLS & MS]

RIVERSDALE, | WILLBROOK, |
RATHFARNHAM, | DUBLIN.
Jan 20 1938

My dear Willy

I am very sorry about that upset; and hope you are really over it by now. Red cabbage is peculiarly indigestible even when very well cooked! By the

---

[1] Lt.-Col. Sir John Keane, 5th Baronet (1873–1956), barrister, Senator, and governor of the Bank of Ireland. WBY had resigned from the conservative Kildare Street Club because he could no longer afford the fees; he himself narrowly avoided being black-balled, having been elected by 22 votes with three members voting against him (McDowell, *Land & Learning*, 101).

way you should probably avoid <u>endive</u> in salads. It is a thing one gets a great deal of in France as a rule.

Shall I arrive on the 5th, or do you want me to over-lap? Unless I hear to the contrary I shall arrive on <u>Saturday fifth evening</u>. That is to say I shall go straight from Dublin to Paris and stay Friday night in Paris to see Anne and travel to Monte Carlo (or wherever you are then) by the day train leaving Paris nine am. If I am to arrive on the fourth I shall arrive Friday evening by same train. By doing this I shall avoid sleeper on train and have Anne to dinner on the Thursday or Friday as the case may be.

I would on the whole rather not have to cope with a flat and servant, for the two months; but if you are very anxious to get out of hotels you might find something. We might find a flat that we could take <u>next year</u> for three months. So often one finds that there are not enough bedclothes pillows and things to eat off etc!

The Dermod O'Briens are going to Cap D'Ail, so that is rather a place to be avoided! Neither of us would like a great deal of Mrs O'Brien's company I think.[1]

I wrote a long letter yesterday but will send it later[2] as I am in a hurry to get this to the post.

Do look after yourself.

G.

[MS] Of course if it were <u>necessary</u> I could now come out <u>any time</u>, as Michael has gone back to school.

[TLS & MS Dict]

Monte Carlo.
January 21.1938.

My dear Anne,

Forgive my dictating but when I have done my morning's work with the pen I am tired and will probably go on procrastinating rather than writing. Besides, I have had the devil of an upset in my inside. I am very much better now. Tomorrow I move to the Hotel Carlton, Menton.

You no doubt know that those Javanese puppets are meant to cast shadows on walls or great sheets. Do you remember the shadows at the end of the second act of that bad play of Cocteau's done by the Gate theatre?[1] They were, I think, thrown from Javanese puppets. Dulac has two or three.

---

[1] Thomas MacGreevy's notebook with quotations from WBY includes 'Mrs Dermod O'Brien is a bundle of exasperated commonplaces' (TCD MS 8061).

[2] This letter is missing.

[1] *The Infernal Machine,* Jean Cocteau's four-act reworking of the Oedipus myth translated by Carl Wildman, was produced by MacLiammóir and Edwards at the Gate Theatre in August 1937.

I remember one letter from you about Ezra Pound's translation. He is, of course, not an Oriental scholar like Waley but he has a much finer feeling for English.

I am delighted that you should be seeing George Pitoeff's work for though I do not know it I know he has a high reputation. The Theatre Maturin is probably named from an early Victorian Irish writer, one of whose novels made a great impression on Balzac.[2] He hated people talking to him when he was writing a book so he used to put a wafer on his forehead.

We did 'Dr. Knock' in Dublin. That was ten years ago, before you began to take any notice of the world.[3]

You write a good, lively letter. Thank you.

[MS]

Your affectionately
WB Yeats

Beautiful warm weather here & I enjoy life.

[TLS]
RIVERSDALE, | WILLBROOK, |
RATHFARNHAM, | DUBLIN.
Saturday Jan 22 1938

My dear Willy

I was delighted to get your telegram[1] this evening because it showed me that you must be well. You would not, I think, have got my air mail letter saying that I was not enthusiastic about the idea of a flat in Monte Carlo. (That letter was only posted on Thursday)

I find that if I leave Paris by a day train I cannot arrive until after 11 pm. I therefore change all my arrangements and must travel by night. That means that I arrive in Mentone either at 11 am or 12 midday. on the <u>fourth or the fifth</u>. Please let me know at once which day I should arrive.

Frank O'Connor wants Anne to stay in Paris for a further month; I have agreed. He seems to think from her letters to him that she is learning a vast amount etc. I had a talk with Hunt and Tanya before O'Connor burst this bombshell. They both said that Anne was, from her letters, 'getting every ounce' out of her time there, and when I told them both that O'Connor had said she should stay another month they unanimously agreed. Tanya's present assistant is booked now for another month. I think it is really right that Anne should have

---

[2] Charles Robert Maturin (1780–1824), Irish clergyman and writer of Gothic plays and novels; both Balzac and Baudelaire praised his novel *Melmoth the Wanderer* (1820).

[3] *Knock, ou le triomphe de la médecine* (1923), the satire by the French playwright Jules Romains (1885–1972), was produced as *Dr Knock* by the DDL on 24–5 Jan. 1926.

[1] This telegram is missing.

stayed in Paris. I did not like disagreeing with you about her going to Sadler-Wells-Old-Vic. but I thought that if she were re-called to a new position she might lose her independence and so lose also the conviction that she is making her own career.² I think I told you when we were both in London circa January 6th–8th, that Ninette de Valois had said to me that Anne could go there at any time. Sadler Wells is re-building, they have bought two blocks of houses, and one of there new schemes is to have a 'paint room' of their own.

Yours affly
George.

[ALS]   Carlton Hotel, Mentone.¹
Jan 23 [1938]

My dear Dobbs

This a charming hotel with the sea in front & my window wide open, & cheap (12/- including food) & I am content with life. I am well again. I am working well.² What ailed me was something the doctor calls 'Hotel Infection'—the unexpected encounter with red-cabbage or the like, aparantly the hale & hearty are liable to it.

I have had a pleasant lively letter from Anne all about the things she bought with my present.

Nothing happens except in my head—so what can I write

Yours affectionly
W B Y.

[ALS]   HOTEL CARLTON | SUR LA MER | MENTON
Jan 24 [1938]

My dear Dobbs: Your letter & the proofs came to day.¹ I write shortly to catch the 5 o clock post. I have been sitting out in the sun & time slipped past

Come as much earlier as you like but not later than Feb 4 as Edith Shackleton must go on Feb 5.

I look forward greatly to your coming & to your being here with me in this beatiful weather

---

² Cf. Richard Ellmann's notes of interview with Frank O'Connor: 'Yeats didn't want Anne—then 18—to go to Paris to study stage design—was going to send her to London. O'Connor said it was a waste of money to send her to London and at length persuaded him to let her go to Paris. George saw him to the door and smiled broadly, "I'm glad you told him that; he's had this coming for a long while."' (University of Tulsa, 1947 notebook).

¹ The hotel address is now 6 Ave General de Gaulle.
² By the end of February he had written seven poems during his stay in France.

¹ Proofs for *New Poems*, published by the Cuala Press on 18 May 1938.

I will send proofs to-morrow

Sir John Keane, damn his eyes, has written in the name of the Club Committee asking me to stay another year, as they are using me as a bate for other writers[2]

Yrs affecly
WB Yeats

[ALS] HOTEL CARLTON | SUR LA MER | MENTON
[26] Jan [1938]

My dear Dobbs

I send you the remainder of the proofs under another cover. The weather is still beatiful—I am writing by an open window, the [sea] keeping up its loud murmur some fifty yards away. Since I have conquered the red cabbage (& that took about eight days) I am better than I have been for years & working more steadily in a beautiful bright dream. Even Lolly & her affairs far off.

I have it clearly in my head that Lolly must pay my royalties & evrybody elses, & pay so much per cent on her debts for only then is she solvent. If I live a few years she can do it from this year on, & she & her girls feel & work the better for it.[1]

I am fixing my London broad cast for the second week in April & have written to Starkie on the subject.

I have had no letters from anybody except you & the BBC & I have not had that 'long letter' you spoke of.

I think with pleasure of spending what will be left of spring & then summer & autumn in Dublin working with Higgins & then returning here to this bright dream.

Yrs ev
WB Yeats

[TLS & MS] RIVERSDALE, | WILLBROOK, |
RATHFARNHAM, | DUBLIN.
January 27 1938

My dear Willy

I wired to you this morning that I will arrive on Friday February 4th by BLUE TRAIN (so if your hotel has a bus tell it to meet me!)

---

[2] See note to 17 Jan. 1938.

[1] WBY spent the last few years of his life attempting to set the affairs of the Cuala Press in order; see 1 Nov. 1938.

I shall be most annoyed if you get up and meet me, so dont think of doing so!

I am bringing the THREE CANDLES booklets and the first eight years of your letters to Lady G. which I can type while on holiday...¹ To say nothing of various other things such as the two photographs of Sally Purser's portraits of Maud Gonne. (Impossible to trace the sculptor of bust in Municipal)²

[MS] In haste for post.

Yours

George Y.

[ALS]   HOTEL CARLTON | SUR LA MER | MENTON
Saturday [29 Jan. 1938]

My dear Dobbs

Your train arrives about 11, I think, at any rate Edith Shackleton will meet it. A taki will bring you here in a few minuites You will find me working in bed as usual. Your room will be ready, & the weather in all probability clear and sunny

Yrs affecly

WB Yeats

Am reading Jack's book,¹ so far with joy.

[TLS]   RIVERSDALE, | WILLBROOK, |
RATHFARNHAM, | DUBLIN.
Jan 30 1938

Dear Willy

You complain in your letter dated 'Jan' (postmark Jan 26 1938) that you have had no letters 'from anybody except you and the BBC'. If I may say so, that is just nonsense, because I have forwarded to you a number of letters including two or three from Swami. I have kept a 'postbook' in which I have written down letters forwarded to you. I wrote to you a few days ago saying

---

¹ A two-volume edition of WBY's letters to AG was planned for the Cuala Press but never materialized.

² The bronze painted plaster bust of Maud Gonne in the gallery, now called the Hugh Lane Municipal Gallery of Modern Art, was by the Irish sculptor Laurence Campbell (1911–64); Sarah Purser's oil painting of Gonne, also in the Gallery, is frequently reproduced.

¹ *The Charmed Life* (1938), JackBY's fantasy novel, was described by WBY as 'my brother's extreme book..., his *Faust*, his pursuit of all that through its unpredictable, unarrangeable reality, least resembles knowledge. His style fits his purpose, for every sentence has its own taste, tint and smell' (*On the Boiler* (Cuala, 1939), 36).

that Dorothy Wellesley had wired to me asking for your address. I sent her the Mentone address. Of course if you would like to see all the American letters full of nonsense, you can have 'em—they're a gift Did you expect me to forward 'for your consideration' the letters from Scott-James etc re serial publication:???? No, I am sure you did not, because you would know that that would delay serial publication which is now continuing quite nicely.

What is now nice to report is that on Tuesday morning February 1st, I go with 'our Mr Sparkes' of the College Street Studios to the Municipal Gallery to superintend with the Curator, Mr John F. Kelly,[1] the photographing at different angles of the Laurence Campbell bust of Maud Gonne, I wrote to you that Laurence Campbell had not replied to any letters. Or perhaps I told you this before you left? He is in Sweden. Anyway, the arrangement now is with his brother[2] that Mr Sparkes meets myself and Mr Kelly at Charlemont House and we get a variety of photographs taken which will be sent to France for you to choose from. You will also have photographs of the two Sally Purser pictures which she says on a postcard 'will not photograph well'.

I am also getting from the Municipal photographs of your father's portraits of Standish O'Grady and Douglas Hyde.

I think that Mr John F Kelly must be sent one of your three candle press privately printed 'Speech and Two Poems' as a tribute to his activities (I bring out his correspondance).

I am giving everyone the address 'C/O Thomas Cook and Sons Mentone, France', because after a month more in Mentone we might like to wander somewhere else. In any case it will prevent Lolly discovering ancient butties and planting them on us. She is very anxious to do this; 'Violet[3] has friends in Mentone if you feel lonely'. NO, NO, NO! !

If we find a flat or villa we like I think we must still keep ourselves free of an address except to friends outside Dublin?

George—

Lost my pen!

[ALS]	Carlton Hotel, Menton, France
Feb 10 [1938]

My dear Anne: It was good of you to send those crystalise fruit. And I like the box. Now that the fruit are eaten it serves as a tray for small oranges

---

[1] The College Studios, 31 Westmoreland Street, were the photographers of choice by the National Gallery of Ireland also; John F. Kelly (d. 1995), also known as O'Kelly, was a portrait painter.

[2] Christopher Campbell (1908–72), painter and stained glass artist.

[3] WBY's cousin Violet Montgomery Gordon.

which I eat in considerable numbers. & I like your letters to your mother & my self—so full of animation. At your age I think I was meloncholy, weighed down by the troubles of the world, but you are gay & that is much better. But then you have not my difficulty in spelling, or if you have you don't care, & that is a great help in letter writing.

You would like this bright, serene, artificial place where the sun & the sea always shine.[1] Your mother has hired a wheeled-chair & pushes me along by the sea. In the morning I write poetry & after lunch she pushes, then I sleep & write letters & read Jacks new book '<u>A Charmed Life</u>' which is as delightful and inconsequent as the <Old Testament> Bible. You can begin it any where as you can the Bible & it is almost as improving. Now I am going to lie down to go to sleap, as your mother has very properly told me to do

Your affection father

W.B.Yeats

(Getting on in years but amiable)

[TLS]

RIVERSDALE, | WILLBROOK, |
RATHFARNHAM, | DUBLIN.
Wednesday March 30 1938

My dear Willy

Had hoped for a note to say you were well or some remark of the sort. If you arent, ask Edith to say so! Michael very much better today.[1] He had three days of temperature between 100 and 104 and I was alarmed, but on the fourth day he dropped to 95.6 and has remained there, and the leg now seems very comfortable. It is to be 'unwrapped' on Friday. Michael of course <u>looks</u> horrible. I dont suppose you remember Anne aetat 1¾ weeping when she first saw her face in a mirror after chicken pox! Hers was nothing

---

[1] GY's letter to ABY of 9 Feb. 1938 offers a slightly different view of the hotel and WBY's creative process: 'This is a rather fearful place—full of retired English army people and the like; they talk of nothing but politics in loud and piercing voices. Your father only penetrates to that part of the world between one and three, and at dinner in the evening. He sang all through lunch yesterday to the frank astonishment of a few foreigners and disguised horror of the British!! The British look like people who had to learn some poetry by heart at school some forty or fifty years ago but who have never thought of it as emanating from an individual; I am sure they think "it" grows like a cabbage or a fish by some peculiar dispensation of providence.'

[1] In mid-February 1938 GY learned that MBY had been rushed to the hospital with a septic leg, but was soon recovering in the College infirmary. After arriving in London on 23 March GY hurried directly home to Dublin, having learned that he had also contracted chicken pox. ABY returned from Paris in early March. WBY went to Penns in the Rocks, then on the 29th to Steyning, not returning to Dublin until 13 May.

compared with Michael's, but Michael has had constant applications of a lotion which poor Anne's doc didnt give her.

The Company is not expected from USA for another month, or so Anne tells me, and their letters 'home' are all full of affection for 'Fred', instead of dislike of 'Mr Higgins'!! Another triumph for Higgins.

Brenda Gogarty[2] has just rung me up to ask if Anne would dine tomorrow at eight. I accepted for Anne, I rang up Anne at Abbey, to ask if she could go to a hairdresser and get her fur trimmed—at present it looks like the Wild Man from Borneo—but she says calmly 'We are painting until 7 pm and the hairdressers will be shut and I cant possibly go out tomorrow before six when the hairdressers will be shut, please ask John to buy a shampoo powder and you and Mary can do something tonight.' She spilt almost a whole pot of water paint on her head yesterday, and it was cleaned off in a hurry—hence my anxiety! Otherwise all is well.

Frank O'Connor seems to be living happily with his lady, and has sent Lolly the manuscript of his book of poems with one or two minor corrections.[3]

Anne says that the Abbey 'hopes you will not be in Dublin for their production of "Baile's Strand".' I dont know whether that means that she would like you to see her costumes etc, or whether she would prefer you not to see them until she has had a chance of making alterations in view of a further production. I asked her to use her own design for one cloak instead of using the Ricketts cloak (Cuchullain).[4] She felt timid about the cloak of Cuchulain because he says 'Nine Queens out of the Country under Wave have woven it with the fleeces under sea and they were <u>long embroidering at it</u> ...'[5] My own feeling is that those few words would not make the audience wait for a heavily worked coat. She made a design which seemed to me to fit so much better with all her other things that I regret the importation of Ricketts..

Do please let me know how you are and that you have not lost all the sunshine and olive trees of our hotel.

Yours
George Yeats

---

[2] Oliver St John Gogarty's daughter Brenda Marjorie (1911–86), later Mrs Desmond J. Williams.

[3] *Lords and Commons*, translations from the Irish by Frank O'Connor, was published by Cuala, 25 Oct. 1938. The Welsh actress Evelyn Bowen (1911–94), recently separated from the actor Robert Speaight, had appeared as guest actress in the Abbey production of *She Had to do Something* by Sean ÓFaoláin in December 1937; her divorce and subsequent marriage to O'Connor were not acknowledged in Ireland, which caused great difficulty with de Valera's government. After she and O'Connor were divorced she married Dr Abraham Garbary and continued to act, teach, and direct in Canada until her death.

[4] The theatre had for many years continued to use the costumes designed by Charles Ricketts when *On Baile's Strand* was revived in 1915.

[5] GY has marked this typed passage with an asterisk.

[ALS]   THE CHANTRY HOUSE, | STEYNING | SUSSEX.
                                    Thursday, March 31 [1938]

My dear Dobbs

I am quite well. At Penns I found Dorothy & read out my poems & my essay,[1] next day Turner & Hylda arrived. Turner read the essay & says he accepts it all & says it is coming at the right moment. Dorothy excited by the poems, especially 'Apperitions'. On Monday Edith came & motored me here next day. On the day we left I got your letter & as I had proofs yesterday to correct for Faber & Faber[2] I have not left your letter long unanswered. I have just come in from the garden where I have sat for the last hour working on a new poem.

I think I shall be in England till after May 2. Dorothy is not going away, but Hilda is & Dorothy wants me at Pens from April 23 to May 2 that Hilda, who will have returned by then, may help to get down some people I want to meet.

I am delighted that Anne should do <u>On Baile's Strand</u>. But I cannot understand from your letter quite what she is doing. Is she doing all the costumes or using Ricketts in part?

Michael is having a bad time & I am very sorry for him —two such ailments togeather.

Gerald Heard has gone—I think to Arizona—& says he will not return 'until wars & rumours of wars have passed away.'

                                        Yours affly
                                        WB Yeats

When I was at Penns last Autumn & alarmed about Dorothy I meditated by myself & got the impression first of a garden & then of green trees & I told Hilda & said that I thought green trees were the best surrounding for Dorothy & suggested motor rides among trees she not to know why. At dinner the other night she began talking of her dreams & described a constant dream of a garden followed by green trees. Hilda gave a surprised look.

[ALS]   THE CHANTRY HOUSE, | STEYNING | SUSSEX.
                                            April 6 [1938]

My dear Dobbs

No news except that I am well & in the middle of my one act play which will be something for Anne to do a setting for.[1]

---

[1] His essay was *On the Boiler*, while with DW he was revising 'Long-Legged Fly'.

[2] *Aphorisms of Yoga* was published by Faber and Faber in June 1938.

[1] *Purgatory*, which ABY designed for its first production; see letters of 26 July 1938.

Lennox & Miss Somerville have conspired to propose for election to the Academy Miss Cummins whose sole fame depends on her real or alleged Automatic writings about the Apostles.[2]

He has announced a performance at the Festival[3] of my <u>Player Queen</u> without asking leave & has asked me to choose been Shelah Richards & Ria Mooney.[4] I have refused both. It is my one potentially popular play & dont want it killed

Yrs affly

WB Yeats

I have written a fine lyric. I will send you the hole bunch corrected in a few days.

I imagine that Lennox support of Miss Cummins is politeness to Miss Sumerville. He no doubt counts on her rejection

[ALS] THE CHANTRY HOUSE, | STEYNING | SUSSEX.

April 6 [1938]

My dear Anne

I think it is to day <u>Bailes Strand</u> with your setting comes on?[1] Please send me cuttings etc. I get no Abbey news I do not even know the cast.

Please tell me when Higgins & the company come back. You must know all the gossip.

Your affectate father

WB Yeats

---

[2] WBY seems to have forgotten that Geraldine Dorothy Cummins (1890–1969) co-authored with Susanne Rouviere Day, also from Cork, two plays produced by the Abbey, *Broken Faith* (1913) and *Fox and Geese* (1917). Originally trained in automatic writing by Hester Dowden, she produced material for two books purporting to be communicated by F. W. H. Myers (1843–1901) who helped found the Psychical Research Society, and many other works including *Scriptures of Cleophas* (1930, 1933), *The Childhood of Jesus* (1937); she also published two novels, a biography of fellow suffragist Edith Somerville (1952), and an autobiography, *Unseen Adventures* (1951), which documented thirty-four years of psychical research; see note to 8 Apr. 1938.

[3] Plans were being made for an Abbey Theatre Festival of plays and lectures to be held 6–20 Aug. 1938.

[4] After LR saw her performance in the DDL, Ria Mooney (1904–73) was invited to join the Abbey Theatre in 1924, achieving notoriety by playing the role of the prostitute Rosie Redmond in O'Casey's *The Plough and the Stars*; from 1926 she toured England and the United States with the Irish Players, remaining in New York (1928–30) as assistant director with the Civic Repertory Theatre established by the English actor and director Eva Le Gallienne (1899–1991). On her return to Dublin in the 1930s she performed with the Gate Theatre, from 1934 returned to the Abbey to perform and teach acting in the Abbey Theatre programme, produced verse plays for Austin Clarke's Lyric Theatre Company, and in 1944 became director of the Gaiety Theatre School of Acting, finally returning to the Abbey Theatre as its first woman artistic director (1948–63).

[1] WBY was two days late; *On Baile's Strand* was revived with ABY's designs on 4 Apr. 1938.

[TLS]   RIVERSDALE, | WILLBROOK, |
                                             RATHFARNHAM, | DUBLIN.
                                                            April 8 1938

My dear Willy

Thank you for two letters, the second arrived this morning. Glad to hear
you are well. Lennox rang me up a couple of days ago to ask if you were
going to the Academy dinner in London tomorrow. I told him I thought
it most unlikely that you would be in London and that it was even more
unlikely that you would go to London for the dinner!! By the way, Miss
Cummins has produced at least one novel (Cork country life, I read one
which Tom sent me, but am no judge of novels..)[1]

Regarding 'Player Queen', I heard it was being proposed for the Festival
and at once sent Hunt a message that you must be asked for permission, and
also told Lennox the same thing. I think I suggested a year or more ago to
you that you ought to write a note to the Abbey Board that no play of yours
was to be put on unless your permission was given before rehearsals were
started. As a matter of fact 'Baile's Strand' was rather better done, I thought,
than any play for a long time.[2] I liked Cuchullain; but I am told (on the telephone) that Cuchullain (Liam Redmond) had 'left out all the poetry'. I was
in the Gallery because I could not leave Michael for very long and I did not
want to have to explain to Ganly and his vast O'Brien clan why I was not
staying for <u>his</u> play.[3] I heard every word of Cuchullain's without the slightest
strain, and that at the Abbey is pretty good!!, and was immensely excited by
his (Redmond's) general performance. Stephenson (Conchubar) really bad;
the women not good but tolerable; Fool (Cusack) good.[4]

Michael's leg was taken out of plaster four days ago. No improvement
whatever. It is very decidedly better today. He has gone 'septic' everywhere

[1] GY could always count on Tom MacGreevy, like Geraldine Cummins an occasional
lodger in Hester Dowden's London home, to keep her *au courant* with books and gossip; Cummins had by now published two novels, *The Land they Loved* (1919) and *Fires of Beltaine* (1936),
both rooted in her experiences in Cork.

[2] In a letter to Hunt of 26 July 1938 praising the production, GY did make one objection,
that there should not be keening offstage when the Fool and Blind Man reveal that Cuchulain
has killed his own son (*InteLex*, acc.7281).

[3] *The Dear Queen* by Andrew Ganly (1908–82) a dentist, playwright, and novelist, later best
known for his novel *The Desert Sky* (1966), was first produced at the Abbey on 4 Apr. 1938;
his wife was the artist Rose Brigid Ganly (1909–2002), one of Dermod and Mabel O'Brien's
five children.

[4] William Gerard 'Liam' Redmond (1913–89) joined the company in 1935, making his debut
in O'Casey's *The Silver Tassie*, and later became a regular actor in film and British television;
Cyril James Cusack (1910–93) joined the Abbey in 1931 and performed many major roles during the next thirteen years, as well as directing the Gaelic Players (1935–6). Other roles were
taken by W. O'Gorman as the Blind Man, and Wilfrid Brambell (1912–85), later to achieve
fame as a TV actor, as the Young Man.

he can, assisted or perhaps instigated by chickenpox, and my entire time is taken in putting on and taking off dressings. As soon as one section clears another one breaks out. However there is a very marked improvement in the last two days so I hope he may start healing up from now on.

I havent seen anyone except doctors…but have heard a vast amount of gossip from people on the telephone! Frank O'Connor's departure with Mrs Spaight seems to have put ideas into the heads of quite a number of people, who are either upping and doing likewise, or contemplating the divorce of spouse or spouses after years of—shall we call it 'toleration'?

Yours G.

[APS¹]   [The Chantry House, Steyning]
[12 Apr. 1938]

How about date of company return. I am staying at house <marked with an arrow> on left of picture.

WBY.

[ALS]   c/o Miss Heald, The Chantry House, Sussex
April 17 [1938]

My dear Dobbs: I went to London on Tuesday & stayed two days. George Barnes had asked me to come. He & I talked broad-casts for an hour & I heard 'Poets Pub' on the gramaphone with amused disgust.¹ That evening I dined with Dulacs & read them my poems about which he & she are enthusiastic. Next day I lunched with Elizabeth Pelham & her sister.² I read them my essay & was told as Turner had told me before that this was the moment for it which makes me fear that I shall be forestalled. Stayed five & a half hours talking. Next day I returned here—tired but well. Since then I have somewhat re-written the poems & the essay, & now must start work on my play again. Dulacs admiration for the plot which I told him, has encouged. At the end of next week I go to Dorothys. I think my play will be in verse but I am not sure. This morning I have had a letter from Lolly—'Somebody who would put a little money' etc but amiable & much

---

¹ This post card addressed to ABY at Riversdale is a photograph of Chantry Green, Steyning. The 'first company' returned from their American tour at the end of May.

¹ 'In the Poet's Pub' was broadcast 2 Apr. 1937 (see 3 Apr. 1937).

² Lady Prudence Mary Pelham, later Mrs Guy Rawston Branch, then Buhler (1910–52), Elizabeth's younger sister, a sculptor and the only woman apprentice of Eric Gill.

praise, intelligent praise of Annes staging of 'On Bailes Strand'. She praises Cuchulain bare smooth head & says that the costumes made the characters look heroic. Anne has not answered a note & a card of mine asking when the players return from America.

Yrs affecly
WB Yeats

Give me news of Michael..

[TLS]
RIVERSDALE, | WILLBROOK, |
RATHFARNHAM, | DUBLIN.
April 20 1938

My dear Willy

Many thanks for letter... Of course I had rather expected that you would re-write that essay again!!

On Friday, 22nd, I am taking Michael to the Claremont Hotel, Howth for a week. He needs a change very badly. He cant go far from Dublin owing to his infernal leg. He looks allright when you see him on profile from the left side, but the right side of his face is horribly scarred. Some of this will tone down with time! Anyway he is no longer infectious. He has not been able to wear spectacles very much so I have had to keep him amused as he cant read much without them. In fact I am rather tired!!

In one letter you talk of returning on May 2nd. That is a Monday, so if you can delay till Tuesday 3rd, please do. Monday is a bad day as trains and boats are always full—Any day except Monday or Friday.

I gave Anne your message about her not replying to your 'note and card'. As far as I know the Company are not returning until the end of May, perhaps early June. I asked Anne to enquire from Gorman—she was probably waiting until Lent was over because Gorman is always 'very cross with the Protestants during Lent'. (Incidentally Anne admitted that she had not written, but had 'meant to'.) She has been pretty busy with the new production of 'Plough'[1]—all the sets had to be renewed and all the props bought afresh as the old ones had all gone to America.

The family hedgehog drowned itself in the Lily pond—after hinting to John for two weeks that it must be removed, I was obliged today to say that it must be removed at once! I found that he was under the impression that it would finally sink to the bottom and make good manure for the lilies.

Anne has adopted a new fashion of hairdressing which I privately think most unbecoming, but have not said so!

---

[1] Sean O'Casey's *The Plough and the Stars* was revived at the Abbey on 18 Apr. 1938.

Tell Dorothy Wellesley that the two roses which did *not* flower last year are now in full bud, they are 'Austrian Copper' and 'Austrian Yellow'.

Yours
George.

[ALS] THE CHANTRY HOUSE, | STEYNING | SUSSEX.

April 21 [1938]

My dear Dobbs: I go to London (Athenaeum) this afternoon on Saturday I go to Penns in the Rocks, Withyham, Sussex on Monday May 2 I go to London. Stay two days to see Cecil Harmsworth[1] if I can, on Thursday go to Oxford—see May Morris next day (embroidery) on Saturday I give lunch to Bowra & others & blot out a cause of moral discomfort. I can return to Dublin on Monday May 9 or any day that week. When does Higgins return? I should prefer not to have to go into explanations with Lolly before he arrives.[2] How is Michael? Will I be in the way.

I am working hard & in good health

Yrs affecly
WB Yeats

I tried to phone you one night about Michael but could not get in. Then came your satisfactory letter.

[ALS] THE ATHENÆUM, | PALL MALL, S.W.1

April 23 [1938]

My dear Dobbs

I am just off to Penns in the Rocks where I shall stay until May 2.

D. S. MacColl[1] was our chief enemy in the matter of the Lane pictures. He has now changed over to our side and I think the next <u>Mercury</u>

---

[1] Cecil Harmsworth made a loan to Cuala of £150 towards the establishment of the limited company.

[2] In an effort to counteract ECY's increasing debts and put the press on a more stable footing, on 12 Oct. 1938 the Cuala Press was reorganized as a limited company with four members of the Board: WBY, ECY, Higgins, and GY, who was to act as chair when WBY was away.

[1] Dugald Sutherland MacColl (1859–1948), influential art critic and founder of the National Arts Collection Fund, had been keeper of the Tate Gallery (1906–11) and the Wallace Collection (1911–24), and was for long vehemently opposed to the Hugh Lane collection returning to Dublin. 'A Last Word on the Hugh Lane Affair' appeared in the London *Mercury and Bookman*, 21 May 1938, and WBY published a response in the June issue of the magazine, concluding, 'Though Dr. MacColl's account of Sir Hugh Lane's character is neither generous nor true, I thank him for his article. He was our chief opponent for many years and I am glad that feud is finished.'

will contain an article by him urging the return of the pictures. This should win our case if De Velera has not forgotten his promise to push the matter.

I want you to get Lolly to send a bound volume of Broadsides to Scott James (Review copy). He has promised a review. I think it would be wise too if Lolly would insert an advertisement of The Broadsides into evry copy of my poems sent out. (You might inspect advertisment)

I shall I hope see Cecil Harmsworth when I return to London.

I am beginning to long for home. But there are things to do here & I am spending almost nothing & doing much work.

Scott James wants the new poems. He heard them read out on Sunday last.

Turner comes in a few minutes to take me to Penns

Yrs ev
WB Yeats

You no doubt say in the papers that Ottoline has died. I have written to Philip Morrell[2]

[ALS]   PENNS IN THE ROCKS, | WITHYHAM, | SUSSEX.
April 25 [1938]

My dear Dobbs

Lolly writes 'We have now 173 subscribers for your New Poems & the edition is 450'.

I cannot allow her to send copies for review. Nor can we afford to delay my Macmillan book of verse beyond this autumn or next spring. As it is there will be a drop in our income this year because MacMillan will have nothing new except Hernes Egg. Lolly will have a large number of unsold copies of new poems.

I suggest destruction of 100 copies of new poems & a new circular stating either that the first circular stated the number wrongly, or, & this I would prefer lie & all a new circular stating a mistake had been made as to the number of copies Cuala was entitled to print, and that they have now destroyed 100 copies (or I might, even invent a truthful statement). An edition of 350 is much more likely to sell to collectors than a larger edition. The value of the 100 copies (to be arrived at subtracting the expense of printing 350 copies of a book of verse from the total expenses), even if bound, should be under £50. If I paid half Lolly might be redie for the sacrifice

---

[2] Ottoline Morell died on 21 Apr. 1938; see below, 21 July 1938, for details of her death.

If the edition is reduced to 350 Lolly will close the year with a sale of say 250 & even if I publish my own book then the rest will sell off

Lolly only wants to do two books this year but that means bankruptcy. She would hardly get her expenses much less do anything to pay off debt. Besides I count on a rumpus over 'On the Boiler' to advertise Cuala. I brought all this on my self by asking when the Press would be free

I am working at my play—it is in verse & will be strange & powerful but very short. It will make part of my next book of verse.

Yours affly

WB Yeats

Sorry to write all this business

[ALS]   PENNS IN THE ROCKS, | WITHYHAM, | SUSSEX.

[26 Apr. 1938[1]]

My dear Dobbs

Lolly complains about having a lot of unsold books at the end of the year. I do not think that matters if these books will sell—but I think the large edition of my book will not sell. If 100 copies were destroyed it would be sufficient to announce that only 350 copies have been published not 450 as oreginally intended. If all the copies are not yet bound the loss may be slight.

All my immediate plans for Cuala depend upon 'On the Boiler' It can be sent for review & I am preparing publicity for it but it should come out as soon as can be managed.

Turner has come & gone—Jeanes the astronomer[2] was here for tea, and consider a vain person & a bore. He has a pretty wife, who if the general hope is fulfilled will run away. She is at present devoted. Dorothy distaste may be intensefied by the fact that Jeanes had tried to marry Hilda. Hilda is here of course, self less & able. Others are coming connected with our conspiracy 'Modernity' in literature.

Yrs affly

WB Yeats

I have asked Lolly to write by return, or if possible wire, the number of unbound copies if any of New Poems

---

[1] Dated by GY.

[2] James Hopwood Jeans (1877–1946), English astronomer, physicist, and mathematician who after retiring from Cambridge wrote a number of popular books on science; his second wife, whom he married in 1935, was the Austrian organist and musicologist Susi Jeans, née Suzanne Hock (1911–93), who remained with her husband until his death, producing three children.

[ALS]   PENNS IN THE ROCKS, | WITHYHAM, | SUSSEX.
                                                        April 27 [1938]

My dear Dobbs

I gathered from Lolly letters that she disliked the idea of many books left
over at end of year and so made my suggestion. <On second thoughts I wrote
to Lolly to allow> I pointed out that I must publish a book of poems (containing <u>New Poems</u>) with Macmillan, next winter or your income would fall too
much. I said that an edition of 350 would would almost sell out before winter
but that 450 would not. She says now that my book is selling well but she had
complained to me of having 'only 173 subscribers'. I have no objection to her
printing the large edition now that she knows I will not delay my own book.

Lolly said she cannot do a third book till October. I think it will be best to
get 'On the Boiler' printed by some commercial printer & made to look as like
the old 'Samhain'[1] as possible & put something of this sort upon the cover.
                         'On the Boiler
   An occasional publication, written by WB Yeats, printed by (say) Peter
   Piper of Pepper Hill & sold by Elizabeth Yeats at the Cuala Industries 132
   Lower Baggot Street, price 2/6 edition limited to 500 copies.
I would pay the printer, & Lolly would make as much by selling it as if she
had herself printed it, or almost. She could then have for October book
O'Connors 'Art O Leary' poem—14 pages—illustrated by Jack. A good
Xmas book. O Connor & Jack have agreed.[2]

This has been a very good week—the conversation has been better than
on any previous visit. There are the right guests & the house is becoming a
centre of activity at last.

I am keep well & working hard

                                                        Yours affly
                                                        WB Yeats

[TLS]   RIVERSDALE, | WILLBROOK, |
                                   RATHFARNHAM, | DUBLIN.
                                                        April 29 1938[1]

My dear Willy

I hope you are not giving too much thought to Lolly's complaints!! You
know what she is. If she does not like her new hat she immediately thinks

---

[1] Three issues of *Beltaine* (1899–1900), an occasional magazine edited by WBY, were published by the Irish Literary Theatre; these were followed by seven issues of *Samhain* (1901–8),
enlarged and including play texts as well as theoretical essays and announcements.
   [2] *A Lament of Art O'Leary*, with six illustrations by JackBY, was not published by Cuala until
June 1940.
   [1] GY has also typed in 'Tel—95758'.

up every grievance she ever had and pours it all out. I have been watching her weekly accounts very carefully and I do not think she has anything to complain of.[2] The new pact[3] removes duties from all the things she sends to England (also on Lily's embroideries!) and this must within a year make a very considerable difference in both their sales.

I have three letters from you regarding the new Cuala Book. I dont know a. what Lolly wrote to you. b. what you have written to Lolly. I do not agree at all with your idea of scrapping 100 copies of 'New Poems' published by Cuala. Your last book of poems published by them was in an edition of 450 followed by a book of Frank O'Connor's poems 250 copies, and that year was the best they have ever had. I have no belief in the 'Collectors' desire for small edition only, because your poems have always sold from Cuala in the larger editions and as far as I know no complaint has ever been made by any 'collector' about the number of volumes issued. Nor do I think that the printing etc of the Cuala books is so good as to induce any 'collector' to buy them for any reason except desire to read the contents in a 'first edition', which desire would be as completely satisfied by a first edition published by Macmillan and Co.

You may remember that you and I went very thoroughly into the question of the number to be published by Cuala, with especial reference to that good year when your last volume of poems was published by them, and that we were in complete agreement about numbers.

I am sorry if I seem to oppose you; I only do so because I think Lolly has probably been Lollyish. It is nonsense for her to say that she has 'a lot of unsold books at the end of the year'. What she is at is that you are away and she thinks she can work you up when you are alone.

If she cannot—as you tell me she says—print 'On the Old Boiler', I suggest it should be printed (not by the Candle Press!!) by a commercial press in Dublin at your expense and sold by Cuala on a profit sharing basis. This could be easily managed. The Richview Press are doing quite good stuff.[4]

Michael and I arrived home this morning. He has a nice tale of a football match between St Columba's and Belvedere College (R.C. run by Priests). One of the Belvedere Priests was walking up and down the touch line and was overhead muttering 'Hail Mary, Mother of God, don't let the heretics win.'

Yours
George Yeats

---

[2] Under a new arrangement in which WBY took over negotiations with the National Bank and guaranteed Cuala's debt until April 1938, ECY was to send weekly accounts to WBY.

[3] On 25 Apr. 1938 the Anglo-Irish Trade Agreement was signed, abolishing the 20% tariffs Ireland and the United Kingdom had placed on imported goods in an effort to end the economic war of the previous five years.

[4] The Richview Press was owned by the venerable Dublin publishers and booksellers Browne & Nolan.

[ALS]   THE CHANTRY HOUSE, | STEYNING | SUSSEX.
                                                      May 3 [1938]

My dear Dobbs

I want if possible three or four more days to finish my play & three short
new sections for <u>On</u> the <u>Boiler</u>. Will it suit you if I return on Friday morning
May 13? I am a little anxious about putting my return off so long as I told
Lennox I would return this week. You might ring Lennox on the phone.
I am most anxious to have no decision come to about my plays for the Festival. If there is need I can return on Monday. I may have a compromise
of an acceptable nature to propose about <u>Player Queen</u>. There will be too
my new play.

One reason for delay is that I want to rest my visit to Oxford on May 7.
I have a lunch & dinner there & there will be a long motor journey. I tired
myself out by a meroculos week at Penns in the Rocks which seems at last
to have become the Centre of intellect I have longed for.

I want to write a long letter but there is the play. I must begin that toil.
I wish I knew when Higgins gets back to Dublin.

                                                    Yours affecly
                                                    WB Yeats

It is most kind of you to promise to meet me at Holihead.

[ALS]   THE ATHENÆUM, | PALL MALL, S.W.1
                                                      May 5 [1938]

My dear Dobbs

I finished my play this morning but it needs a couple of days to copy out
and revise. To morrow I go to Oxford & on Saturday give that lunch & dine
in the evening with a John Sparrow of All Souls to meet a Eugenic expert.[1]
I came up yesterday from Steyning saw Harmsworth in the afternoon about
Cuala affairs & Dulac in the evening. Too day a little tired but well. On
Sunday Monday & Tuesday I shall be at Steyning & resting. On Wednesday
I return to London that I may meet Toynbee[2] ('Study of History') and on

---

[1] Sparrow's guests were the economist Roy F. Harrod (1900–78) and the left-wing philosopher Stuart Newton Hampshire (1914–2004), neither of them in sympathy with eugenics,
although Harrod's theory of evolution in entrepreneurial behaviour may have misled his host
(see Foster ii. 721 and note).

[2] WBY had long wanted to meet the prolific author Arnold Joseph Toynbee (1889–1975),
director of studies at the Royal Institute of International Affairs (1925–55); WBY owned the
first three of twelve volumes of *A Study of History* (2nd edn. 1935), where his philosophy of history as the rise and fall of civilizations appealed to WBY.

Friday I return to Dublin. This is all supposing you dont fetch me home next Monday by letter or wire.

I am suffering from an entire lack of base fiction, may have to take Taxi some where to get some

Anne has not replied to my question about Companys return—however she no doubt thinks I have heard from some body else which I have not, except that you think it will be end of month. I have nothing from the horse's mouth

Yrs ev
WB Yeats

[TLS]   RIVERSDALE, | WILLBROOK, |
                                           RATHFARNHAM, | DUBLIN.
                                           May 6 1938

My dear Willy

You will have got my letter[1] saying that I telephoned to Lennox and that he said there was no reason for your returning earlier than you wished because it would now be impossible to put on 'Player Queen'. I would wire to you but I have no idea what your Oxford address will be.

I am asking Edith to see that you get your digitalin mixture made up and take it twice a day!![2] You will, as usual, be doing too much at the end of your English visit. Please dont forget to ask for the chemist's bill.

I have repeatedly reminded Anne to write. She wrote, and I see her letter still on the mantelpiece in her bedroom! I enclose it. She will probably be annoyed. <u>NO</u>. I have just been up to collect it and I find that it has gone—

Paddy Carolan is dying. He came back from USA about three weeks ago and has been in a nursing home. He has T.B. One lung was 'deflated' but the other lung, I am told, is almost hopeless. Gorman tells me that he may 'linger on for some weeks', but that the case is regarded as hopeless. There is to be a 'Benefit performance', on the 29th of this month, to raise funds for him. Do you think that you should perhaps send a cheque—£5 minimum— to add to the 'benefit'? We can talk about it when you return. I think, in any case that you should attend the performance. It would probably please him

---

[1] This letter is missing.

[2] 'Dear Miss Shackelton [sic] A letter of WBY's dated May 5th suggests that his next week is going to be very full. Do, please, extract from him his prescription for the digitalis mixture and make him take it twice a day while he is still with you! <u>You</u> know his habit of packing in to the last week all the people he wants to see, and <u>I</u> know his habit of arriving home very exhausted. If he seems tired, <u>three</u> times a day. That journey from London to Dublin is most fatiguing. Yours affly George Y' (Houghton bMS Eng 338.12 (2)).

very much to know that you had done so. He collapsed when the players were in California and Barry Fitzgerald[3] took all his parts.

I enclose a letter from Frank O'Connor. I do not send the play because I know you will not have time to read it. Do please keep his letter.[4]

Yours G.Y.

[ALS]   THE CHANTRY HOUSE, | STEYNING | SUSSEX.

Wednesday [13 July 1938]

My dear Dobbs: I finished my journey without fateague & was motored on here yesterday.[1] On Monaday (18) I go to Penns in the Rocks. I have been sitting in the garden in the sun & warm breaze & I have motored through the country. And this morning came a new poetical theme & material for a new crazy Jane poem—I had almost forgotten that poor lady.[2] I saw Turner at the club & shall meet him again at Dorothy's. I am little pleasantly tired & will lie down before dinner

Yours affly
WB Yeats

[TLS]   RIVERSDALE, | WILLBROOK, |
RATHFARNHAM, | DUBLIN.

July 14 [1938]

My dear Willy

I only arrived home this morning having decided to prance round and about Liverpool, my decision being partly influenced because I could not get a berth on Liverpool–Dublin boat Monday night, and the Tuesday boat was

---

[3] Barry Fitzgerald (1888–1961) was the stage name of William Joseph Shields who, although acting at the Abbey from 1915, worked as a civil servant 1909–29; after making his film debut in 1936 in Sean O'Casey's *The Plough and the Stars* he remained in the United States, performing on stage, radio, and film until retiring to Dublin in 1959. While touring with the Abbey in 1934 he was voted best character of the year by the New York theatre critics for his role as Fluther Good in *The Plough and the Stars* and he received an Academy Award Oscar for his role in *Going my Way* (1944). One of the dependable Paddy Carolan's chief parts was as Captain Boyle in Juno and the Paycock.

[4] Enclosure missing. The reference is probably to *Time's Pocket*, a play in five acts by O'Connor which received its first production at the Abbey on 26 Dec. 1938 and which WBY found 'very moving'; see letter of 4 Jan. 1939.

[1] He had arrived at the Athenaeum on 8 July.

[2] Six 'Crazy Jane' poems were written during 1929–30 and published in *Words for Music Perhaps and Other Poems* (1932); her last appearance, 'Crazy Jane on the Mountain', first appeared without a title in *On the Boiler* (1939) and was reprinted in *Last Poems and Plays* (1940).

an old boat. I had forgotten that Tuesday was July 12th.[1] I got involved in a colossal crowd about 9.pm on emerging from a cinema, in Lime Street. About fifteen thousand 'Liverpool Irish' were waiting for the Orange procession. As I had never seen an Orange procession I decided to wait. The crowd got thicker and thicker; it started more or less with elderly 'shawlies' and their men, and then 'shawlies' with infants of all ages,[2] and finally youth and youth entirely intoxicated male and female. The females all wore little orange paper caps like the caps the American navy wear, but instead of patriotic emblems on the caps they had such remarks printed on them as 'Squeeze me' 'I'm no angel', 'Atta Boy'. I thought of getting out of it, but the crowd was too thick, and I finally managed to get against a wall with a stout American sightseer in front of me. Two nuns idiotically appeared in the middle of Lime St. and a man jumped out at them and they were surrounded by men booing. Police on horseback rushed the crowd, foot police finally surrounded the two nuns and got them into a car and a little later a black Maria arrived and departed with a few men. My stout American just went on saying 'Oh My! Oh MY!! OOHH MMYY! OH MY!' in crescendo, until the procession itself arrived about 10.15 pm and the crowd unlocked itself and I got away from him. The procession most orderly; banners, uniforms, females in white with sashes etc, and drums and drums and drums. The nastiest crowd I've ever been in, and I've been in a lot! When I told Mary,[3] she said 'Liverpool Irish are funny People. I was in Liverpool once when a new piece of land was to be blessed for the building of a new chapel. The streets were lined with Catholics from all the Sodalities and there was a lovely procession with all the representatives of the Sodalities in uniform carrying candles and they all went to the place where the Bishop was blessing the land and the candles were all lit and the moment the land was blessed they all came away and they went wild and murdered everybody and Dora said "that's nothing" & took me down some side streets which were beautifully decorated with banners and streamers across the street and figures of the Blessed Virgin in every window and everybody was drinking pots and jugs of beer and dancing in the streets and you wouldnt think they were Catholics at all'.

Hope you arrived as little tired as possible?

Yours affly

George.

Liverpool crowds smell horrible!

[1] The holiday celebrating the 1690 Battle of the Boyne, which resulted in the defeat of the Irish Catholic Jacobite army by the forces of William III, was annually marked with marches by the Orange Order in all areas where there is a large Irish population.

[2] Working class women who wrapped themselves and their babies in a heavy woollen rug, usually of plaid; also used in Ireland to describe female travellers or tinkers.

[3] Mary Martin, GY's housekeeper.

[ALS]   PENNS IN THE ROCKS, | WITHYHAM, | SUSSEX.
                                              July 21 [1938]

My dear Dobbs
   I came here two days ago & shall be here until next Monday when I go
back to Steyning. There is no one here but Dorothy. Some body or other
having failed to turn up. She is outside on the lawn reading <u>On</u> <u>the</u> <u>Boiler</u>.
She have just told me the strange tale of Ottolines death. She was at a Nursing Home near Tunbridge Wells kept by a Dr Cameron.[1] Phillip was there
too for his heart. One day Dr Cameron brought a heart specialist to tell
Ottoline that Phillip had only a year to live. The shock killed Ottoline who
died in a few days. The day after her death Dr Cameron died. Dorothy says
'was it suiside. It was the only thing he could do. Everybody knew the story.
The nursing home was finished'. Phillip is of course a live & in fair vigour
so far as one knows.
   You wrote me a most vivid & vital letter about your Liverpool experience.
   I have begun a second poem & am well. Cornish[2] it seems told Dorothy
that she gave me too much to eat. So my diet is all right
                                              Yours affectionly
                                              WB Yeats

[on back of envelope]
You forgot to pack up that powder puff

[ALS]   PENNS IN THE ROCKS, | WITHYHAM, | SUSSEX.
                                              Friday [22 July 1938]

My dear Dobbs
   You did not pack that powder puff. The last time I saw it it was in the
study. If you have it you might send it me to Steyning.
   I did not not report that Ottoline story right. She was not staying at Dr
Camerons home (but had done so). She went there to see Phillip. The shock

---

   [1] In poor health much of her life, Ottoline Morrell had recently spent several months in
the International Clinic at Sherwood Park in Tunbridge Wells, run by Dr Alexander John
Douglas Cameron (1887–1938); when Philip Morrell became ill while they were on holiday at
Cap Martin, they returned to her trusted doctor, whose diagnosis of Philip's enlarged heart
caused Ottoline to suffer a relapse. She was treated with injections of the experimental drug
Prontasil, a powerful antibiotic, but at twice the recommended dosage and for longer than recommended. When the medical authorities initiated an investigation of Dr Cameron's misuse
of the drug, he committed suicide. Undaunted, Ottoline returned to the clinic but died while
Cameron's assistant was giving her a further injection of Prontasil. None of the numerous
obituaries mentioned that 'heart failure' was given as the official cause of death.
   [2] Wellesley's butler.

was so great that she had to be given a bed & died almost immediately. Her temepereture, when she heard the news, went up to 105.[1]

Yrs ev
WB Yeats

[ALS]   PENNS IN THE ROCKS, | WITHYHAM, | SUSSEX.
July 22 [1938]

My dear Dobbs

I enclose a silly letter from Lolly.[1] I replied 'The money is entered in the audit as a debt nor could George & I consider it other wise. I told Cecil Harmsworth that I would let him know later what percentage we would pay him. It is however much better to pay him off'

I wrote but that sentence—I do not feal I can be stern with Lolly until she has signed her letter to the bank.

Yrs ev
WB Yeats

I have finished my second poem.[2]

[TLS]   RIVERSDALE, | WILLBROOK, |
RATHFARNHAM, | DUBLIN.
Saturday July 23rd [1938]

My dear Willy

Glad to get your letter dated 'July 21' & so beautifully spelt and written that I think you must be feeling very well! That is rather a tragic story about Ottoline. I wonder if the doctor thought she was mainly suffering from nerves and that a shock would be good for her? I remember your cousin Hilda Gordon being ill for a long time and a consultant saying that 'it was largely a case of nerves', that she must not be allowed to relapse into neurasthenia, must be allowed to sleep alone etc, etc, and in a few weeks she died in a nursing home. I have never known what she died of

---

[1] See note to 21 July 1938 for the most accurate version; Philip Morrell lived for another five years.

[1] Enclosure missing, but suggesting that the money from Cecil Harmsworth was a gift and that it would be insulting to return it.

[2] Probably 'Crazy Jane on the Mountain'. On the back of the envelope GY has written '30 Strand Road/Harold's Cross'.

because the Gordons have always been so distressed about it that they could not talk.[1]

Glad also that Cornish is limiting your diet. I saw the Hunt–Tanya production of Blanco Posnet.[2] I liked Tanya's settings, hated her costumes, and returned home on the last bus trying to remember Stephens poem 'the noise of silence'[3] and failing to remember it, cursing and swearing all the way about noisy productions, noisy to the eye and to the ear, screaming yelling howling shouting gesturing—booo. But I suppose the only alternative is contained in that horrible word 'restrained'. Certainly when the stage yells and shouts the audience takes its cue. Now do please not repeat my violent remarks to 'your Board'....

I find that I can get to Chester very comfortably from Glasgow and arrive at 4.5 pm. There is an excellent train from Euston at <u>1.35 pm</u> arriving Chester 5.5 pm. So unless I hear to the contrary I shall meet you at Chester on <u>Monday August 8th at 5.5 pm</u>. However there is a lot of time before then, and I shall have to make some arrangement about letting you know some Scotch addresses. My plan is that Michael and I sail from Dublin to Glasgow on Monday August 1st, arriving on Tuesday at 10 am. I think one day will do me for the 'Exhibition'[4] (Michael can return later if he wants to) and then we proceed with our minimum hand luggage around Loch Lomond etc stopping when we see places we like.

Anne and Hunt had a long session regarding setting for 'Purgatory', and Sean Barlow[5] was given design. To Anne's amazement two morning later she found Sean had not only built the tree (which is to be solid) but also made the back-cloth.... She has evidently got on Sean's right side.

Yours affly
George

---

[1] Hilda Gordon died about 1919.

[2] *The Shewing-up of Blanco Posnet* by Bernard Shaw was revived at the Abbey Theatre the week of 18 July 1938 in a double bill with *Maurice Harte* by T. C. Murray.

[3] 'In the Night' by James Stephens, published in *Songs from the Clay* (1915), begins 'There always is a noise when it is dark; | It is the noise of silence and the noise | Of blindness.'

[4] The Empire Exhibition in Glasgow was an international exposition held in Bellahouston Park, Glasgow, 3 May–28 Oct. 1938, featuring national pavilions from the members of the British Empire, the most notable structures being the Palace of Engineering and the Palace of Industry and the 300-foot high Tower of Empire.

[5] Seaghan ('Sean') Barlow (1880–1972), who joined the theatre company in 1902 before the Abbey itself was built, was not only responsible for making (and often designing) sets and property, but frequently was also called upon to play minor roles; he stayed with the theatre for more than sixty years (see *Ireland's Abbey Theatre: A History, 1899–1951*, 69–76).

[ALCS]   PENNS IN THE ROCKS, | WITHYHAM, | SUSSEX.
Saturday [23] July [1938]

My dear Dobbs

I have just had a note from Elizabeth Pelham to say that Swami MSS has never reached her.¹ About a month ago we sent her a letter & I think a wire asking if it had done so. Instead of answering she made enquiries herself.

You might look if you the registration docket. If not it may not have been sent at all.

Yrs ev
WB Yeats

[TLS]   RIVERSDALE, | WILLBROOK, |
RATHFARNHAM, | DUBLIN.
July 26. 1938

My dear Willy

I will go down to the post office this morning to inquire about the parcel which did not reach Elizabeth Pelham. I have the receipt.¹ I am longing to have a real row with the Rathfarnham postoffice. While I was in Liverpool I sent Mary a reply-paid telegram and got no reply for 36 hours so wired again. The first wire had been left at Riversdale <u>Templeogue</u> as 'there was no one of the name of Martin at Riversdale Rathfarnham'!!!!! Mary has been here for over five years and has had letters of course sent here from the postoffice.

The P.O. did the same thing last year to Frank Craig who was staying with his sister, Mrs Farren; Olive wired to say that she had safely arrived at Killybegs (Donegal). As she was motoring all the way alone with the two small children Frank was nearly mad with anxiety at not hearing.² The telegram was returned to Killybegs Post Office <u>by post</u> marked 'no one of that name at…' I forget the name of the house. They never even took the trouble to send the wire up to the house!

---

¹ Pelham had agreed, at WBY's request, to read Swami's translation of the *Avadhuta Gita* and correct the English.

¹ The package containing Swami's MS was eventually delivered.

² Francis Brownrigg Craig (1881–1943), whose wife Olive Craig was a close friend of GY's; the Craigs had two children, Diana (later Mrs Andreas Briner) and David (later Wing Commander).

Abbey packed last night for 'Moon in the Yellow River'.[3] Front stalls almost entirely American.

I got a lot of stories about Fred in America from Aideen O'Connor[4] who stayed here Sunday night. When they were in danger of having to return to Ireland from Chicago owing to collapse of first agents (Shubert) Fred went by plane from Chicago to New York 'in very bad weather and he had never flown before';[5] the players heard nothing for two days, and then Boss[6] got a wire saying they were to open in San Francisco the next week with such and such a play. The Players were so relieved (they didnt want to go home) that they celebrated all night. Aideen said very solemnly 'Mr Higgins has a very good business head'. He seems to have won their respect, and even Eileen Crowe has come to like him!! He never missed a performance or dress rehearsal of Playboy the whole eight months, and descended on them with threats of suspension if anyone made the least slip.. At present the company is longing for him to come back to Dublin to make further changes in the productions of the Synge and other plays!

McCormack is to play the Priest in 'Well of the Saints'.[7] Apparently Tanya went to him about his costume 'as the wig worn by Stephenson would not fit him'. He said 'O, I remember exactly the costume I wore before'...and Tanya had to give up.

Hunt is threatening to have a <u>MOON</u> in the backcloth of 'Purgatory'. Anne is refusing. If she does not win, she is going to say that she does not wish to have her name on the programme as designer of the setting. He talks of having a round hole (stage left) covered with gauze and lit from the back. I told Anne to say that you did not want a moon, only moonlight. I shall probably hear from her tonight the latest developments.

Sorry about the powder puff, which I send under separate cover. I send also Dorothy Sayers books.[8] Long-winded. I thought you had repudiated the powder puff as too large; that is why I did not pack it.

Yours affly
George.

---

[3] *The Moon in the Yellow River* by Denis Johnston was produced at the Abbey during the week of 25 July 1938.

[4] Una 'Aideen' O'Connor; see letter of 16 Mar. 1937.

[5] The Shubert organization was established by the Shubert brothers in 1892 and by the mid-1930s controlled a network of more than 1,000 theatres from New York City to Portland, Oregon, operating, managing, and booking shows; by 1931, badly affected by the depression, they had filed for bankruptcy, re-forming the company in 1933 as Select Theatres Corporation, producing a number of musicals and revues. 'Fred' is F. R. Higgins.

[6] Arthur 'Boss' Shields was manager on the American tour.

[7] *The Well of the Saints* and *Riders to the Sea* by J. M. Synge were performed on 9 Aug. 1938 as part of the Abbey Theatre festival.

[8] The most recent detective novels by Dorothy L. Sayers were *Gaudy Night* (1935) and *Busman's Honeymoon* (1937).

[TLS]   RIVERSDALE, | WILLBROOK, |
                         RATHFARNHAM, | DUBLIN.
                                      July 26 1938

Second letter <u>Urgent</u>
My dear Willy

Hunt has just rung me up with various questions. He asks if, as 'Purgatory' comes between three other plays, it should be introduced by music, or
'percussion' or drums. I said that as far as I knew you did not want any of
these things; that you wanted a bald production, no noises off, the whole
to be concentrated on the two characters OLD MAN and BOY, and the
appearance of the woman at the lit window of the burnt out house.

I told him that Anne had told me that he had an idea of a moon in the
backcloth, lit; and that I thought you wanted an indication of moonlight but
NO MOON.

He asked if he could cut the line about 'I will cut a stick out of that tree'
and if you would give him a line instead, as the OLD MAN would probably
have a stick in his hand.[1] I agreed, but gave him your address at Steyning so
that he could write about this. Please reply to him by return!!!

                                                            G.Y.

[ALS]   THE CHANTRY HOUSE, | STEYNING | SUSSEX.
                                      Wednesday [3 Aug. 1938]

My dear Dobbs

Yesterday I drove over to Elizabeth Pelham's for tea. When I got back
I found your wire. It was then too late for the post. This however should
reach you.[1]

I am still extremely well, owing perhaps to my eating little & that mainly
fruit & salad, between breakfast & dinner, & doing a half hours exercise
each day. I am finishing my fourth poem.

Two or three days ago I went over Shelley's old house 'Field Place', an
exciting old house. A rich brewer[2] with excellent taste has bought it.

---

[1] The Old Man's speech originally read 'Sit down upon this stone, or I | Will cut a stick
out of that tree'; WBY changed the text to 'Stop! Sit there upon that stone' (Sandra F. Siegel,
Purgatory Manuscript Materials Including the Author's Final Text by W. B. Yeats (Ithaca, NY, 1986)).
In a letter to Hunt he confirmed this change and also suggested that there be two gauze
windows so that the window in which the wife/mother is seen alone would be different from
that of the bridal chamber.

[1] His letter is addressed to 'Mrs Yeats | 18 Lynedeh Crescent | Charing Cross | Glasgow'.

[2] 'Field Place' near Warnham in Sussex, the birthplace of Percy Bysshe Shelley, was purchased by the brewery owner Guy Nicholas Charrington (1889–1958) in 1929; still retaining
some of the Tudor timber-framed structure, it was restored by Charrington and furnished
with his collection of antiques and paintings.

I shall be at Chester at the hour you said—& at I suppose the Rail way Hotel. I dont think you mentioned any particular hotel.

The Mercury wants more poetry. The editor has I think written you on the subject. With my four new poems you will have about a dozen—of which about ten might suit him.[3]

Yours affecly
WB Yeats

[ALS]   THE CHANTRY HOUSE, | STEYNING | SUSSEX.
Thursday [4 Aug. 1938]

My dear Dobbs

I wrote to you by return to that Glasgow address. You will probably have had letters sent on[1], so I will not repeat what I said except to say that I am well, better than I have been for a long while & that I will get to Chester by the train that arrives there at 5.5. (I suppose we go to the Railway Hotel,) & that to morrow morning I shall finish my fourth poem.

This village takes me very seriously. The woman opposite told her next door neighbour that she could not understand why a man of my importance visited at so small a house & the Head Master of the Grammar School (A Tudor building a hundred yards up the street) asked the English Master if 'Mr Yeats has a police guard' as he had 'noticed some unusual movements among the police' & the English Master came over to enquire.

Yours affly
WB Yeats

My present plan is to motor up to London on Monday & catch the train which reaches Chester at 1.5. There is nobody I want to see in London & the motor journey will not tire me as much as being on a loose end in London. I rather want to avoid Dulac until 'The Boiler' is out

---

[3] The December issue of *The London Mercury* published 'Hound Voice', 'High Talk', 'John Kinsella's Lament for Mrs. Mary Moore', 'The Apparitions', and 'A Nativity'. The January issue included 'Man and the Echo', 'The Circus Animal's Desertion', and 'Politics'. These were followed in March 1939 after WBY's death by 'News for the Delphic Oracle', 'A Bronze Head', 'The Statues', and 'Long Legged Fly'.

[1] He has addressed this letter to Tarbet Hotel Loch Lomond; it was sent on to Inversnaid Hotel. WBY and GY met in Chester on 8 July, travelling back to Dublin together. On a postcard to ABY showing the interior of Robert Burns's cottage, GY asks her to wear her 'new frock' on her father's return.

[ALS]   THE CHANTRY HOUSE, | STEYNING | SUSSEX.
                                        [27 Oct. 1938[1]]

My dear Dobbs
    All well—no symptoms. Did some good work yesterday. Bright cold air.
    Great indignation in Steyning over the mismangement of billetting the
refugees—working woman who had to go to work evry day ordered to take
charge of two children each, day boy from Grammer School sent home that
class rooms might be used as bed rooms, boarders left without class rooms,
no food supply etc, no medical supervision to ensure that infected children
were not planted on healthy families. Indignation increased by fact that
though gass-masks were served out the village has now declared for billet-
ting purposes 'safe'.[2]
    Read much of Mauds book[3] last night—sufficiently upset by it to have a
not very good night. Very much herself always—remarkable intellect at the
service of the will, no will at the service of the intellect.
    I wonder how you got on at Longford & how the Cuala meeting went
off.[4]
    Edith Shackleton tells me she has written to you[5]

                                                    Yrs always
                                                    WB Yeats

[TLS & MS]   RIVERSDALE, | WILLBROOK, |
                                 RATHFARNHAM, | DUBLIN.
                                           November 1 1938

My dear Willy
    Many thanks for letter. Yes, I went down to Longford and pages proofs are
promised 'immediately'. They have no <u>Italics</u> so I arranged for the stage directions to be printed in brackets and smaller type. I did not think the 'Manager'

---

    [1] Dated by GY; on 25 October WBY left Dublin for what would be the last time.
    [2] In 1938 and 1939 nearly 10,000 children were brought to England from Europe to live in
hostels or with families.
    [3] On 16 July WBY had given Maud Gonne permission to 'say what you like about me'
when she published her autobiography, *A Servant of the Queen* (London, 1938) (*G–YL*, 451, mis-
dated June).
    [4] On Higgins's advice *On the Boiler* was sent to the Longford Printing Press in Longford,
about 75 miles from Dublin, but unfamiliarity with the material which included poetry, a play,
and prose had led to many delays; when completed there were so many errors that this first
edition was destroyed, the printing handed over to Alex. Thom & Co. of Dublin, and finally
published by Cuala Press after WBY's death. In WBY's absence GY was also chairing the
regular Cuala Board meeting (see letter of 1 Nov. 1938).
    [5] The letter is not extant.

very brilliant! He is an uncouth lad called 'Dan' who looks like Tony Quinn in 'A MINUTE'S WAIT'; I dont know if you ever saw Tony Quinn in that play.[1]

The Cuala meeting went off amicably except that Lolly's Minutes were rather a joke. The arrangement now is that Higgins keeps rough minutes and Lolly is to copy them into the book. There was a slight contretemps over the Minutes as Lolly had written them out like an essay—no paragraphing—and all out of sequence. As Chairman I pointed out that the various matters which came under finance were not kept together, upon which she declared that the agenda from which she had written up the minutes had no 'finance' written on it. She had lost the agenda and an undercurrent of argument was kept up all the meeting (suppressed by me frequently) and at the last moment she remembered the agenda was in the printing room!! She fetched it in triumph and said 'I was right, the word finance was <u>not</u> on the agenda'. The word was 'accounts'. Fred and I nearly got the giggles, but he apologised nobly for having written accounts instead of finance. As she seemed ruffled I took her firmly out and gave her a pale sherry and sandwiches at the Shelbourne and she became most amiable. I have suggested to her that she should have the cup of tea at four which she is accustomed to. She says she gets too exhausted to think if she misses it.

The Abbey party[2] went off satisfactorily; Hunt's mother was there (to add to respectability ...) and Higgins brought Anne home safely and determinedly. Anne said that there was drink off-stage—corks were heard popping and people slank away in twos and threes and returned looking a little brighter; Lennox and Fred Johnson[3] both absolutely sober.

I will write to Edith later in the day; in a hurry to get this to the morning post.

Yours
G.

[MS] Michael has been in the Sanitorium[4]—Nothing much wrong—High temperature for 2 days for no apparent reason. He looked rather pale yesterday but will be allowed up today. He slept for almost 48 hours & Collis[5] thinks he was just overtired. He has been working very hard & is of course growing fast.

---

[1] *A Minute's Wait* was first produced at the Abbey Theatre on 27 Aug. 1914, followed by two more brief farces, *The Philosopher* (1915) and *Tommy Tom Tom* (1917), before journalist and short story writer Martin J. McHugh (1870–1951) left Dublin for England; GY may be thinking of Quinn's performance in *A Minute's Wait* which was included, along with AG's *The Rising of the Moon* and the dramatization of a short story by Frank O'Connor, in John Ford's film *The Rising of the Moon* (1957). Tony Quinn (1899–1967) joined the company in 1919 before moving in 1927 to London and New York, where he performed in a number of O'Casey's plays.

[2] The Abbey directors gave a farewell party for Hugh Hunt, whose position as managing director ended in October 1938.

[3] By now LR's relationship with the Yeatses had deteriorated through his alcoholism, despite GY's own periodic drinking bouts (see *BG*, 24–5, 474, 514, 597).

[4] The College infirmary.

[5] Robert Collis was a specialist in rheumatic fever; see note to 30 Sept. 1936.

[ALS] THE CHANTRY HOUSE, | STEYNING | SUSSEX.
Nov 5 [1938]

My dear Dobbs

I got a letter from Hilda Matheson some days ago postponing our visit to the villa until early Jan¹ as the doctor 'has at last taken Dorothys state seriously' & told her to have a month in the villa in the charge of a nurse before visitors come. I did not write at once because in your last letter you spoke of writing later that day to Edith & thought our letters might cross. (no letter has come) Now please go on with our plans exactly as arranged. Michael can stay at the hotel—I of course will pay—until we go to Dorothy, buy new clothes change nothing.

I go to Penns for a few days, I think on Friday next, & will arrange about <u>Broadsides</u> on which subject Dorothy is greatly excited. She insists on doing all correspondence with the English poets (unless the doctor has intervened).²

I have just come in from the garden where neighbours & their children are letting off fire works, and according to the directions of the BBC the two cats have been shut up in a room where they cannot see the alarming sight—they have escaped once.

The Duke of Leinster is next door or will be to-morrow & I have made it plain that I am not open to any invitations.³ One of Gogortys sons—there are two are there not?⁴ comes in a few days to the same house.

The prose draft of my play seems finished except for a kind of prologue.⁵

Yrs ev
WB Yeats

[TLS & MS] RIVERSDALE, | WILLBROOK, |
RATHFARNHAM, | DUBLIN.¹
Sunday [6 Nov. 1938]

My dear Willy

No newses; Higgins has written to you he tells me about various things. He may have told you that Anne sprained her foot at the Abbey; it is improving

¹ Wellesley had taken a villa near Menton and invited the Yeatses to join her there.
² They were contemplating a new series of *Broadsides*, which did not materialize.
³ The Marquess of Kildare Gerald FitzGerald, 8th Duke of Leinster (1914–2004).
⁴ The Gogartys had one daughter, Brenda (1911–86), and two sons, Oliver 'Noll' (1908–99) and Dermot (1908–86).
⁵ *The Death of Cuchulain.*

¹ Original in Houghton Library, Harvard.

daily, and the weather being hot and sunny she sits out in your chair with her foot up on your rest! She may be able to go back to Abbey the end of next week, but Dr Shaw² says if she starts using foot too soon it will only swell up again. Michael is up again. Lordy what a household we are.

I imagine you and I start for the S. of France the end of this month; anyway I am making arrangements for departure then. I shall want cheques to buy tickets and Cooks cheques about ten days in advance.

Tanya is here for the week-end.³

[MS] Hope you are well—

Yours
George.

[ALS]   RIVERSDALE, | WILLBROOK, |
                                         RATHFARNHAM, | DUBLIN.
November 8. 1938

My dear Willy

I wrote to Dorothy abt Portière etc but I heard a couple of days ago from her that she is not coming to London & has sent my letter to Ezra.¹ He suggests sending your letters in a sealed packet 'to Lennox or whoever will ultimately be editing 'em'. I have written <u>not</u> to do this!! asked him to send them to Athenaeum addressed to you. You can bring them back on your return from S. of France.² If posted to Dublin they will be opened (& I am sure greatly enjoyed) by the Customs!

We are having a tram & bus strike. Damn nuisance. Hope you are well

Yours affly
G.

[ALS]   THE CHANTRY HOUSE, | STEYNING | SUSSEX.
Nov 9 [1938]

My dear Dobbs

I suggest that we go to France on the 25th or 26th at latest (This climate now that it has got damp does not suit me.) That you come to London

---

² Probably Dr Dick Shaw (see 6 Nov. 1935).

³ ABY and Tanya Moiseiwitsch, who would soon be leaving the Abbey also, were by now close friends.

¹ OS had died on 3 Oct. 1938; DP being ill, EP had gone to London to deal with the estate. From there he wrote asking whether WBY still wanted an embroidered portière, a hanging to be placed over a door, that he had once admired.

² When his letters to OS arrived WBY went through them, destroying many.

some days before we start (say on Monday Nov 21). If this suits you I will postpone the few things I have to do in London until you come. I will be there when you arrive.

Please wire when you get this. I go to Penns in the Rocks on Friday Nov 11 & stay till Monday Nov 14 & then return here. Unless you decide not to stay in London in which case I may do my London business next week.

This is a hurried note to catch post.

Yrs ev
WB Yeats

[ALS]   THE CHANTRY HOUSE, | STEYNING | SUSSEX.
Nov 10 [1938]

My dear Dobbs

I enclose a checque for £150. I will send more if you need it. I have still travellers checques for £35. Buy what ever clothes you need as well as the tickets, & travellers checques

I go to Dorothy to-morrow. I go to London Monday. I have asked Ezra, who is rather urgent to dine on Tuesday night will ask somebody or other to meet him. I can get him apart to arrange business. I return here on Wednesday & shall stay here until I go up to meet you.

Yrs ev
WB Yeats

[ALS]   RIVERSDALE, | WILLBROOK, |
RATHFARNHAM, | DUBLIN.
November 11 1938

My dear Willy

I wired to you that I would make all arrangements for leaving London on Nov. 26th. I cant very well go before because it was arranged that the invitations to the Cuala Sale (Nov.24 & 25) should be sent out in my name as well as Lolly's, so I shall have to be there all the afternoon both days. I will cross by Liverpool night of 25th. Sorry the damp weather is upsetting you: dont forget to take your mixture if breathing bad.

In haste for post

Yours affly
G.

[ALS¹]   PENNS IN THE ROCKS, | WITHYHAM, | SUSSEX.
Nov 13 [1938]

My dear Dobbs

That all sounds very crowded. There is no reason why we should go to France on Nov 26 if two or three or more days later were more convenient to you.

I go to London (Savile—Athenaeum full) on Monday & on Tuesday have a number of people to dinner at Carleton Gardens (Athenaeum Annex).

On Tuesday, Hilda Matheson tells me, Dorothy goes to London 'to buy clothes that she may be able to entertain Mrs Yeats properly —she has only a tweed & a black velvet left'

Dorothy patriotic fervour seems much abated owing I think to the fact that the man in charge of billeting of children etc in this neighbourhood was 'the German jew' who built a house on her horizon, in spite of her opposition.

I go back to Steyning on Wednesday

If you see Higgins say that Dorothy is hard at work selecting poems for the next <u>Broadside</u>.

Ezra, who comes to dinner on Tuesday writes that my recent poems are 'rather good' which for him is rapturous aproval.

Yrs ev
WB Yeats

[ALS]   SAVILE CLUB, / 69, BROOK STREET. W.1.
Monday [14 Nov. 1938]

My dear Dobbs

I am here as the Athenaeum is packed with bishops.¹ I go back to Steyning on Wednesday. To morrow night I have a number of people including Ezra Pound to dinner at the Athanaeum Annexe.

Four or five days ago I sent you a checque for £150. Please let me know if it arrived. Write to Steyning

Yrs ev
WB Yeats²

---

¹ GY has written 'Personal' on the envelope.

¹ The Autumn Session of the Church Assembly opened 14 Nov. 1938 in the Central Hall, Westminster, presided over by the Archbishop of Canterbury; many of the bishops attending were members of the Athenaeum.

² GY has written 'Personal' on the envelope.

[TLS] RIVERSDALE, | WILLBROOK, |
RATHFARNHAM, | DUBLIN.
November 15 1938

My dear Willy

I wired to you yesterday that cheque had arrived. Please sign enclosed form and send it back to me by return. You will see that I am getting you £100 in Cooks Travellers cheques. I shall go to London via Liverpool on the night of Thursday Nov. 24th and we shall leave London either 25th or 26th.

I wrote to you that I had to stay for the two day Cuala sale as my name had been printed on the invitation (enclosed)[1] as I am obliged to be present on both days. Also I am anxious to placate Lolly as far as possible...

I shall bring of course the books we made a list of, and if you want any others let me know at once.

I have got 'cartes de Tourisme' from the French Legation which will save the nuisance of getting Cartes d'identité in France (compulsory for a stay of more than two months.)

Did I tell you that the Gogartys are going to live in London? Mrs Gogarty will spend her usual six months of the year in Galway.. I think he hated the idea of living in a flat in Dublin after that big house; and anyway he can carry on his journalistic work better from London.[2]

Yours
G.

[ALS] THE CHANTRY HOUSE, | STEYNING | SUSSEX.
Nov 17 [1938]

My dear Dobbs

Letter just come. I return form signed.

All goes well. Got back here last night.

Had people to dinner at club without ill effects on leggs.

Have gone down in weight.

Pleasant at Dorothy's. An indignant dispute between Dorothy & Hilda.

Dorothy: 'It was all nonsense, digging that trench in the middle of a field.'

---

[1] Enclosure missing.

[2] Having sold their house in Ely Place, Mrs Gogarty remained in Ireland when Gogarty took consulting rooms in London; in September 1939 he went without her to the United States on a lecture tour and, apart from a few return visits to see his family and friends in Ireland, lived in New York until his death, becoming an American citizen and earning his living by writing.

Hilda: It may be nonsense but the government are not to blame. How can they consider special circumstances. Everybody with more than a certain number of employees had to dig a trench.'

Dorothy: 'Well I have just filled it up.'

Hilda: 'You did that because I had gone to London for the day. The goverment says trenches are not to be filled up but used to store wood supports & wire netting & then grassed over.'

Dorothy

'Under no circumstances will I sit in a dug-out with my employees listening to the gramaphone.'

Yrs ev
WB Yeats

Please bring in addition to the books I named Lady Gregory 'Cuchulain of Muirthemne'. I want it for place names in my play. Bring also Milton.

[ALS]   THE CHANTRY HOUSE, | STEYNING | SUSSEX.
Nov 18 [1938]

My dear Dobbs

Dorothy asked if we three could meet before you & I go to Italy. I have written to say that there seems only the evening of Nov 25 at the club. I imagine you have made all arrangements now—tickets, places etc.

Have I sent you enough money? I doubt if you have left your self any thing for clothes. Would you like £50

I am very well & seem to have gone down a couple of pounds in weight in the last ten days.

Yrs ev
WB Yeats

Of course if you cared to stay till Monday or Tuesday that would be very pleasant & we could get dates out of Dorothy

[TLS]   RIVERSDALE, | WILLBROOK, |
RATHFARNHAM, | DUBLIN.
November 20 1938

My dear Willy

I return the form for the Cooks Travellers Cheques because you only signed it in one place; I marked the two places with an 'X'. Please sign again in the space for <u>specimen signature</u> and return form with letter enclosed, which you must sign, in stamped envelope. It will save time if it goes direct to Cooks. I only received your letter last night....

Will you spend Friday night at the club and meet me at Victoria station in time for train ferry, or will you stay night of Friday November 25 at Grosvenor Hotel with me?[1] You might let me know. <u>If you stay at Club</u> I shall go to a small hotel near Victoria Station. I bring all the books you want, etc, we leave Victoria station on train ferry train at 9.30 for 10 pm on Saturday night.

I arrive in London circa 1 pm on Friday.

G.

IF LETTER COULD BE POSTED IN THE MORNING IT WOULD PROBABLY GET TO LONDON IN TIME FOR IRISH MAIL

[ALS[1]]   THE CHANTRY HOUSE, | STEYNING | SUSSEX.
                                                    Nov 21 [1938]

My dear Dobbs

I have sent note with signature to Cooks (your letter has just come). I shall go to London on Thursday & stay at Club. I do not yet know if Dorothy can dine with us on Friday night. It is perhaps unlikely. Please send me a note or wire to Club (Athenaeum) to say when & where we meet on Friday. Can we lunch at Grosvener or will you lunch with me?

I must go to club at first at any rate as I have things to take out of, & put into locker

                                                    Yrs affly
                                                    WB Yeats

I am longing to be off.

[TLS]   RIVERSDALE, | WILLBROOK, |
                          RATHFARNHAM, | DUBLIN.
                          Monday Nov 21 [1938]

My dear Willy

All our reservations have been made so impossible to change date of departure. We leave London on Saturday Nov. 26th at ten pm (train ferry). I have a lunch engagement on Saturday, but tea would be possible. On the whole I would rather not.. But leave it to you!!

---

[1] Grosvenor House Hotel, 86–90 Park Lane, was a luxury hotel opened in 1929.

[1] GY has written 'Personal' on the envelope.

I am not sure if I shall go to London on Thursday night or on Friday morning, will wire to you as soon as I know. Dont post any letters here later than Tuesday (except the letter to Cooks) as our posts are so uncertain. I shall stay at Grosvenor on Friday night; so write there and arrange what time I can get you on the telephone, also which club you are staying at. Please ask the valet to pack in Duchess¹ all your night things. If you have not room for everything in your luggage I can leave a suitcase for you at the club.

If you dont get this letter until Wednesday and have posted a letter 'later than Tuesday' you might wire; I can then ring up the Rathfarnham postoffice to say I am expecting an important letter and will they be sure and send it up at once!

Yours
G.

[TLS]
RIVERSDALE, | WILLBROOK, |
RATHFARNHAM, | DUBLIN.
Tuesday [22 Nov. 1938]

My dear Willy

I will come to lunch at the club (Carlton Gdns) at 1.30 on Friday unless I find a letter at the Grosvenor Hotel saying I am not to.¹

I dont at all want to dine on Friday as I said in a previous letter!! But if you have made the arrangement I suppose I must.... What a very obstinate person you are!

I shall be glad to get away for a time, freedom from the telephone will be a rest. I am rather dreading the two long afternoons at Cuala; Lolly seems to expect me to stay from 3. to 6.30 each day... bloody. I shall have to make appropriate remarks to all the people I have known and avoided for the last twenty years.

Fearful gale here today.

Yours
G.

¹ A small overnight case.

¹ GY arrived in time to lunch with DW at 6 Carlton Gardens, the ladies' annexe to the Athenaeum. In the afternoon they attended a production of Shaw's *Geneva*, which had opened in August, and which WBY considered 'most moving' and 'topical' and a possible production for the Abbey Theatre; GY liked the acting, and to ABY reported in detail on the costumes and scenery.

1939

HOTEL IDÉAL-SÉJOUR | CAP-MARTIN |
FRANCE (A..M.)
January 4 1939

My dear Anne

I thank you for your present. It would be no compliment to you to say that I have some of it still; I have not. At this moment I am eating a bit of somebody else's chocolate.

You have told me quite a lot of things, but not what look there is on Higgins. Can you judge by a drop in his eye, or the shape of his waist or his walk, that he is thinking about the 'Boiler'; that the proofs have been seen through the press. Or perhaps you might get at it by palmistry, if he is too busy to speak [MS]——no ask him to tea & find out by his tea leaves.

[TS] I approve of your jars and bottles, but I think you should look at the da Vinci note-books before spending a lot of money on them. I dipped into them a good deal in a five guinea edition Edward Martyn had; it was published at the end of last century and is no doubt in the College Library. My memory is that I got a few fine things but there was very little there for a man of my trade. I imagine that the Dublin critics were very mischievious over O'Connor's play. All sound criticism everywhere should go on the principle that until his qualities are known you must not attack a man's faults. Coleridge lays the principle down in so many words, but the Dublin critics are cruel because ignorant men. I am disturbed by the thought of what effect all this may have on O'Connor.

Yours affly
WB Yeats

[MS] I am glad you are our designer now. It sets my imagination off—damn dark scenes.²

---

¹ ABY has sketched a stage design on the back of the envelope. This letter and the three following have all been typed on GY's machine and addressed to ABY at the Abbey Theatre, but ABY's replies, if there were any, are missing.

² *Time's Pocket*, produced after the Yeatses left for France, caused several weeks of controversy. The manager replacing Hunt, Frank Dermody (1910–78), who had produced O'Connor's play, was criticized for the amateurishness of movement and 'atrocious' lighting, although Tanya Moiseiwitsch's costume designs were praised, as was the acting. In spite of this unfortunate beginning, Dermody became one of the chief producers 1939–47 and 1956–73, directing all the plays in Irish, and was also in charge of the Abbey School of Acting.

[TLS Dict]   HOTEL IDÉAL-SÉJOUR | CAP-MARTIN |
                               FRANCE (A..M.)
                               January 10 1939

My dear Anne
    Will you please ask Higgins if he received the corrected page proofs of
'On the Boiler' which I sent him. If he has received them but has not sent
them on to the Longford Printing Press, Longford, please get them back
from him and send them off by registered post with the enclosed letter.[1]
Please let me have a reply by return of post.

                                            Yrs ever
                                            WB Yeats

[TLS Dict]   HOTEL IDÉAL-SÉJOUR | CAP-MARTIN |
                               FRANCE (A..M.)
                               January 12 1939

My dear Anne
    Here is something I forgot to put into my recent letter. Can you find out
for me any address through which I can find Liam Redmond. If you cant
hear where he is you might look up for me the address of his brother in law
Donagh McDonagh.[1] You would find it in Thoms Directory.

[TLS Dict]   HOTEL IDÉAL-SÉJOUR | CAP-MARTIN |
                               FRANCE (A..M.)
                               January 15 1938 [1939]

Dear Anne
    Have the proofs been sent back to the Longford Printing Press yet? If
not, please alter the date of my PREFACE from July to <u>October</u>. This is
important. If the proofs have been returned, please telephone to Longford
and ask for the manager and ask him if this can be done.

                                            Yours ev
                                            WB Yeats

[1] The letter is missing, but asks for a revise of the corrected page proofs WBY had previously sent to Higgins (*CL InteLex*, acc. 7367).

[1] Donagh MacDonagh (1912–68), lawyer, playwright, and poet, interested in the ballad
form, was the son of Thomas MacDonagh who had been executed in 1916; his sister Barbara
was married to Liam Redmond.

[ALS] HOTEL IDÉAL-SÉJOUR | CAP-MARTIN | FRANCE (A..M.)
                                                    January 28.1939

Dearest Anne.

I wired to you today. Until last night there was a faint hope, but about 3 this morning the doctor told me it would be a matter of a day or perhaps of hours. I have wired Lennox asking if you could stay there for a few days.[1] I will wire you there. I am so glad he had the news that you were to be designer at the Abbey while he was still able to be very pleased about that.

                                                    Much love
                                                    Mother.

[1] MBY was told the news of WBY's death by the headmaster at St Columba's and chose to stay in the college. WBY's brother and sisters were not informed until Sunday 29 January. An Anglican burial service took place in Roquebrune on Monday (*BG*, 561–5).

POST-SCRIPT

WBY died at 2.30 p.m. on 28 January 1939, with George at his side. Dorothy Wellesley was staying nearby and Edith Heald arrived after he had sunk into a coma. Following her husband's wishes George arranged for burial at Roquebrune cemetery above their hotel in Cap-Martin; she hoped a re-burial in Drumcliff could take place a year later, fulfilling the instructions in 'Under Ben Bulben', the last poem Yeats dictated to her. But the war intervened, and it was not until September 1948 that he was taken to his last resting place.

Widowed when only 46, George was left to care for two teenaged children. She would always miss 'the strange, chaotic, varied and completely unified personality' with whom she had shared so much and could 'talk about everybody & everything'. But her responsibilities towards WBY's work remained hers for almost thirty years. She moved to a house in Palmerston Road, Rathmines, and died alone there on 23 August 1968.

Anne moved on in 1941 from stage design to a successful career as a full-time painter. In 1947 she was elected to the committee of the Irish Exhibition of Living Art and had many solo exhibitions in Ireland and abroad. She never married and died on 4 July 2001 in Dalkey, where she had a home close by her brother's.

Michael attended TCD, became a barrister, and then pursued his interest in politics, like his father serving in the Seanad (1951–4 and 1961–81), from 1969 to 1973 as Cathaoirleach (chairman). In 1973 he became a Vice-President of the European Union, and from 1980 until his retirement in 1986 was a member of the Secretariat of the Council of Ministers in Brussels. He married the Irish harpist Gráinne Ni hEigeartargh in 1949 and they had four children. He died on 3 January 2007.

George, Anne, and Michael all bequeathed WBY's manuscripts, paintings, and library to the nation. Thoor Ballylee has been a National Monument since 1960.

INDEX OF NAMES

GENERAL INDEX